INTRODUCTION TO COUNSELING

Perspectives for the 1990s

DAVE CAPUZZI and
Portland State University

DOUGLAS R. GROSS, Editors
Arizona State University

ALLYN AND BACON
Boston   London   Toronto   Sydney   Tokyo   Singapore

DEDICATION

To Celia Capuzzi, who encourages me in all that I want to be and accomplish.

To Lola Gross, who provides the support necessary in all my endeavors.

Series Editorial Assistant: Carol Craig
Production Coordinator: Lisa Feder
Editorial-Production Service: York Production Services
Cover Administrator: Linda Dickinson
Cover Designer: Suzanne Harbison
Manufacturing Buyer: Megan Cochran

Copyright © 1991 by Allyn and Bacon
A Division of Simon & Schuster, Inc.
160 Gould Street
Needham Heights, Massachusetts 02194

Library of Congress Cataloging-in-Publication Data

Introduction to counseling : perspectives for the 1990s / Dave Capuzzi and Douglas R. Gross, editors.
   p.   cm.
Includes index.
ISBN 0-205-12821-1
1. Counseling. I. Capuzzi, Dave. II. Gross, Douglas R.
BF637.C6I535   1991
158'.3--dc20   90-47721
                                                          CIP

Printed in the United States of America
10 9 8 7 6 5 4 3 2 1   95 94 93 92 91 90

Contents ■

and *Nicholas A. Vacc, Ed.D., N.C.C.*
Professor, Counselor Education
University of North Carolina
Greensboro, North Carolina

Linda Seligman, Ph.D., L.P.C.
Professor, Department of Educational Leadership and Human
Development
Director of Center for Counseling and Consultation
George Mason University
Fairfax, Virginia

Ann Vernon, Ph.D.
Associate Professor
University of Northern Iowa
Cedar Falls, Iowa

Claire G. Cole, Ed.D.
Executive Assistant to the Superintendent
Montgomery County Schools
Blacksburg, Virginia

David K. Brooks, Jr., Ph.D., C.C.M.H.C.
Assistant Professor, Counselor Education
Kent State University
Kent, Ohio

Larry B. Golden, Ph.D.
Associate Professor, Counseling and Guidance
University of Texas at San Antonio
San Antonio, Texas
and *Ardis Sherwood, Graduate Assistant*

Preface

THE PROFESSION OF counseling is best described as a process through which counselors interact with clients to assist these individuals in learning about and dealing with themselves and their environment and the roles and responsibilities inherent in this interactive process. Individuals exploring counseling as a career choice need to be aware of the personal, professional, and societal demands that are placed on the professional counselor. The role of the professional counselor calls for individuals who are skilled and knowledgeable in the process and theory that undergird the profession, who are able and willing to reach deeper levels of self-understanding, and who are able to integrate this skill, knowledge, and self-understanding to provide the effective counseling interaction to which clients are entitled. Individuals attempting to decide whether this is the right career choice for them will find the information contained in this text helpful in the decision-making process.

The book is unique both in its format and in its content. The contributed-authors format provides state-of-the-art information by experts in their respective fields. The content provides readers with areas not often addressed in introductory texts. Examples of these include a chapter devoted to what it means to be psychologically healthy, a chapter devoted to counseling from a rehabilitative perspective, a chapter devoted to client diagnosis and assessment and the inclusion of the DSM-III-R, a chapter that takes a comprehensive look at the mental health counseling profession, and a chapter that explains nontraditional approaches to counseling. Both format and content enhance the readability of the book and should increase student interest in the material.

The book is designed for students who are taking a preliminary course in the counseling field and who are trying to determine if they are well matched to the profession of counseling. The book presents a comprehensive overview of the major aspects of counseling as a profession and provides its reader with insight into the myriad of issues that

viii

surround not only the process of counseling and its many populations but also the personal dynamics of the counselor that have an impact upon this process. We know that one text cannot adequately address all the factors that make up this complex profession. We have, however, attempted to provide our readers with a broad perspective on the profession of counseling. The following overview highlights the major features of the text.

OVERVIEW

The format for this coedited text is based upon the contributions of 25 authors selected for their expertise in various areas of counseling. With few exceptions, each chapter contains information specific to a topic and uses case examples to demonstrate the various concepts within the chapter. The text is divided into the following four sections: (I) Counseling Foundations; (II) Counseling in Specific Settings; (III) Counseling Specialized Populations; and (IV) Counseling Perspectives.

Part One—Counseling Foundations (Chapters 1 through 10)—begins with information dealing with the philosophical and historical perspectives that serve as the foundation of the counseling profession. Building upon this foundation, chapters dealing with "What Does It Mean to Be Psychologically Healthy?," "The Helping Relationship," "A Framework for Theories in Counseling," "Individual Counseling," "Group Counseling," "Career Counseling," "Testing and Counseling," "Diagnosis in Counseling," and "Nontraditional Approaches to Counseling" are included.

Part Two—Counseling in Specific Settings (Chapters 11 and 12)—presents information relative to counseling in not only educational settings but also the areas of mental health and private practice. These chapters, "School Counseling" and "Mental Health Counseling," highlight specific processes and procedures that have applications to these diverse settings.

Part Three—Counseling Specialized Populations (Chapters 13 through 18)—covers the wide spectrum of clients who present for the services of the counselor. Included in this section are special approaches for dealing with children and adolescents, the elderly, couples and families, gay and lesbian clients, minorities, and disabled clients. Each chapter includes not only a discussion of the special needs of these populations but also specialized approaches and techniques that have been found to be effective with these groups.

Part Four—Counseling Perspectives (Chapters 19 and 20)—presents information dealing with both the ethical and legal directives that have application to both the counselor and the client and to the process of counseling itself. Several case examples are given to illustrate the major issues. This section also contains our concluding chapter entitled, "Counseling in the Twenty-first Century," which addresses counseling as the profession moves into the next century.

Every attempt has been made by the editors and contributors to provide the reader with current information in each of the 20 areas of focus. It is our hope that *Introduction to Counseling: Perspectives for the 1990s* will provide the neophyte with the foundation needed to make a decision regarding future study in the professional area of counseling.

ACKNOWLEDGMENTS

We would like to thank the 25 authors who contributed their time, expertise, and experience to the development of this textbook for the beginning professional. We would also like to thank our families, who provided the support to make our writing and editing efforts possible, as well as the counselor education facilities at Portland State and Arizona State universities. Our thanks are also directed to Ray Short and other staff of Allyn and Bacon for their encouragement and editing skills. Special recognition is given to Susan Friel, graduate assistant at Portland State University, who worked so diligently and so competently to make this task less difficult.

Special acknowledgment must be given to the Office of Academic Affairs of Portland State University. A special faculty development grant to the senior author/editor facilitated the employment of Susan Friel to assist with the development of *Introduction to Counseling: Perspectives for the 1990s.*

ABOUT THE EDITORS

Dave Capuzzi, Ph.D., N.C.C., is past president of the American Association for Counseling and Development, assistant dean for academic development for the School of Education, and professor of counselor education at Portland State University in Portland, Oregon. Prior to affiliating with Portland State University in 1978, he served in faculty positions at Florida State University, Our Lady of the Lake University of San Antonio, and the University of Wyoming.

Dr. Capuzzi's writings have appeared in journals such as *Counselor Education and Supervision, Counseling and Values, Humanistic Education and Development,* and the *Journal for Specialists in Group Work.* From 1980 to 1984, he served as editor of *The School Counselor.* Dr. Capuzzi has authored a number of textbook chapters and monographs on the topic of preventing adolescent suicide and is co-editor and author, with Dr. Larry Golden, of *Helping Families Help Children: Family Interventions with School Related Problems* (1986) and *Preventing Adolescent Suicide* (1988). In 1989 he co-authored and edited with Douglas R. Gross *Youth At Risk: A Resource for Counselors, Teachers and Parents.*

Dr. Capuzzi has won a number of awards for his contributions of service and expertise to professional groups. Among these awards are the Kitty Cole Human Rights Award of the American Association for Counseling and Development, the Leona Tyler Award of the Oregon Counseling Association, the Outstanding Service Award of the Western Region of the American Association for Counseling and Development, and the Silver Award for Editorial Excellence of the Society of National Association Publications.

A frequent speaker at professional conferences and institutes, Dr. Capuzzi also has consulted with a variety of school districts and community agencies interested in initiating counseling and intervention strategies for adolescents at risk for suicide. He has facilitated the development of suicide prevention, crisis management, and postvention programs in communities in 23 states.

Douglas R. Gross, Ph.D., is currently program coordinator of the counseling program at Arizona State University. Dr. Gross has a professional work history that includes public school teaching, counseling, and administration. For the past 21 years, he has served as a faculty member in the counseling program at Arizona State University.

Dr. Gross has been president of the Arizona Counselors Association, president of the Western Association for Counselor Education and Supervision, chairperson of the Western Regional Branch Assembly of the American Association for Counseling and Development (AACD), president of the Association for Humanistic Education and Development, treasurer of the AACD, and parliamentarian of the AACD. He currently is serving as the immediate past president of the Association for Humanistic Education and Development. Dr. Gross has contributed chapters to four books: *Youth at Risk: A Resource for Counselors, Teachers and Parents* (1989), *Foundations of Mental Health Counseling* (1986), *Counseling: Theory, Process and Practice* (1977), and *The Counselor's Handbook* (1974). His research has appeared in the *Journal of Counseling Psychology,* the *Journal of Counseling and Development,* the *Association for Counselor Education and Supervision Journal,* the *Journal of Educational Research, Counseling and Human Development, Arizona Counselors Journal,* the *Texas Counseling Journal,* and the *AMHCA Journal.*

Dr. Gross has received several awards, including the 1981 Distinguished Professional Service Award from the American Association for Counseling and Development, the 1987 Teacher of the Year Award from the College of Education at Arizona State University, and, most recently, the 1989 Leadership Award from the Association for Counselor Education and Supervision.

Dr. Gross also serves as a consultant to several alcohol and drug programs in the state of Arizona.

CONTRIBUTORS

Part One: Counseling Foundations

Chapter One: The Counseling Profession:
A Historical Perspective
Perry J. Rockwell, Jr., Ph.D., is professor emeritus of counselor education at the University of Wisconsin at Platteville. He received his B.S., M.S. (history), and Ph.D. degrees from the University of Wisconsin at Madison.

Dr. Rockwell has both taught and counseled in a variety of schools and colleges in several states. He has a continuing interest in the social effects of guidance and counseling on society and of social pressures on the profession. He has been active in AACD at local, state, and national levels since 1958.

*Chapter Two: What Does It Mean to Be
Psychologically Healthy?*
Richard T. Kinnier, Ph.D., is an associate professor in the counseling
psychology program at Arizona State University. He received his Bachelor of Arts in psychology from Boston College in 1971, his Masters Degree in Counseling from Teachers College, Columbia University, in 1973,
and his Ph.D. from Stanford University in 1982.

Dr. Kinnier has worked as a counselor in a variety of settings including a state hospital, psychiatric outpatient program, and university
counseling center, and presently teaches courses in both introductory
and advanced counseling. His current research interests are in the
areas of values and decision making.

Chapter Three: The Helping Relationship
Art Terry, Ph.D., is an assistant professor in counselor education and
has developed and teaches the interpersonal (helping) relationship
course at Portland State University. This course is a three-credit class
introducing beginning counseling students to microcounseling skills and
interview techniques.

Dr. Terry also is a university supervisor in the practicum/internship component of the professional sequence for the counseling major.

In addition to his work in communication skill-building, Dr. Terry
has made significant contributions to the counseling profession in the
study of stress-coping mechanisms, client-assessment techniques, career and lifestyle counseling, transitions, and relationship counseling.

Carol A. Burden, Ed.D., now a counselor educator at Portland
State University, received her doctorate from the University of Illinois,
Champaign–Urbana. Her interest areas have focused on women's issues, specifically career counseling, eating disorders, and assertiveness
training.

Margaret M. Pedersen, M.B.A., is finishing her M.S. degree in
counselor education at Portland State University. She received her
M.B.A. degree with a specialization in organizational behavior from the
University of Michigan in 1984 and holds a B.A. degree from U.C.L.A.
She works with university faculty and medical, graduate, and undergraduate students as an education coordinator and counselor. Ms. Pedersen is currently doing an internship at a hospital-based employee assistance program in the Portland area.

*Chapter Four: A Framework for Theories in Counseling,
and Chapter Five: Individual Counseling*
J. Jeffries McWhirter, Ph.D., A.B.P.B., is a professor in the
counseling psychology program in the Division of Psychology in Education at Arizona State University. He is the author of 16 books, mono-

graphs, and training manuals, and of over 70 chapters and articles that have been published in professional journals. He has been a visiting (summer) professor to 18 universities, including a Senior Fulbright-Hays lectureship to Hacettepe University, Ankara, Turkey. In 1984–1985 he was a Fulbright Senior Scholar to Catholic College of Education–Sydney and the Western Australia College of Advanced Education.

In addition to his work in counseling theories, Dr. McWhirter's areas of special interest include small group research, family counseling and parent education, learning disabilities, and the international aspects of counseling.

Benedict Thomas McWhirter, M.C., is currently a doctoral student in the Program of Counseling Psychology at Arizona State University. He received his Master of Counseling degree from Arizona State University and his Bachelor of Arts from the University of Notre Dame. He holds student affiliate memberships with the American Psychological Association, the American Psychological Society, and the American Association for Counseling and Development, and has published chapters as well as articles in journals such as the *Journal for Specialists in Group Work* and the *Journal of Counseling and Development*.

Mr. McWhirter has worked as an academic program specialist for learning-disabled college students and currently teaches study skills and university survival strategies at Arizona State University. His areas of research interest include loneliness and depression, learning disabilities, multicultural issues in counseling, and cognitive-behavioral intervention strategies.

Chapter Six: Group Counseling
Dave Capuzzi, Ph.D., N.C.C., and **Douglas R. Gross, Ph.D.**; See "About the Editors," above.

Chapter Seven: Career Counseling: An Introduction
Ellen Hawley McWhirter, M.C., is a doctoral student in the Program of Counseling Psychology at Arizona State University. She received her Bachelor of Arts degree from the University of Notre Dame and her Master of Counseling degree from Arizona State University. She holds student affiliate memberships with the American Psychological Association, the American Psychological Society, and the American Association for Counseling and Development. She has published articles in journals such as *Psychology of Women Quarterly* and the *Journal of Career Development*.

Ms. McWhirter has worked as an instructor for the Head Start program and as a home educator for families with developmentally disabled infants. She currently teaches study skills and university survival strategies to undergraduates at Arizona State University. Her research interests include career education, minority career development, and multicultural counseling.

Chapter Eight: Testing and Counseling

Larry C. Loesch, Ph.D., N.C.C., professor and graduate coordinator in the Department of Counselor Education at the University of Florida, received his doctorate in counselor education from Kent State University in 1973. He is a National Certified Counselor and serves as the Examinations Coordinator for the National Board for Certified Counselors.

Dr. Loesch is a corecipient of the 1983 AACD Research Award, a former president of AMEG and of FACD, a past editor of *Measurement and Evaluation in Guidance,* and a recipient of the 1986 AMECD Exemplary Practices Award. He has authored or coauthored more than 80 professional publications, and is the 1990–1991 President of Chi Sigma Iota, Counseling Academic and Professional Honor Society International.

Nicholas A. Vacc, Ed.D., is professor and chairperson of the Department of Counseling and Specialized Educational Development at the University of North Carolina at Greensboro. He received his doctorate in counseling from the State University of New York at Albany. He is a National Certified Counselor and serves as Examination Consultant for the National Board for Certified Counselors. He is a member of the American Association for Counseling and Development and the American Psychological Association, a Fellow in the American Orthopsychiatric Association, and treasurer of Chi Sigma Iota.

Dr. Vacc recently taught courses and consulted in New Zealand and regularly conducts in-service training and supervision workshops for counselors and other mental health professionals. His prior employment experience includes work in residence life, counseling with veterans and their dependents, and directing a university counseling center. Nicholas is former editor of *Measurement and Evaluation in Counseling and Development* (formerly known as *Measurement and Evaluation in Guidance*), past chairperson of the AACD Council of Journal Editors, and former president of the North Carolina Association of Measurement and Evaluation in Counseling and Development.

Chapter Nine: Diagnosis in Counseling

Linda Seligman, Ph.D., L.P.C., is professor of counseling and development in the Department of Educational Leadership and Human Development at George Mason University in Fairfax, Virginia, where she has taught for the past 12 years. She is also the director of the Center for Counseling and Consultation in Springfield, Virginia, and Bethesda, Maryland, which she founded in 1986. She received an A.B. degree in English and American Literature from Brandeis University, an M.A. in

Guidance and Counseling, and a Ph.D. in Counseling Psychology from Columbia University and is a licensed psychologist and counselor.

Dr. Seligman's multifaceted professional life includes teaching, supervision, counseling, writing, and research. In addition to teaching and counseling, Dr. Seligman has served as a consultant for many government, professional, and human service agencies and has presented workshops throughout the country on diagnosis and treatment planning. Dr. Seligman is also the past editor of the *Journal of Mental Health Counseling*. She is the author of three books (*Diagnosis and Treatment Planning in Counseling, Assessment in Developmental Career Counseling,* and *Selective Effective Treatment: A Comprehensive and Systematic Guide to Treating Adult Mental Disorders*) and over 30 professional articles.

Chapter Ten: Nontraditional Approaches to Counseling

Ann Vernon, Ph.D., is an associate professor and coordinator of counseling at the University of Northern Iowa, Cedar Falls. Dr. Vernon is a former elementary school counselor and currently has a private practice, where she works primarily with children and adolescents. As an approved supervisor of rational-emotive therapy, Dr. Vernon is the director of the Midwest Center for Rational-Emotive Therapy and has just authored *Thinking, Feeling, Behaving: An Emotional Educational Program for Children and Adolescents.*

Dr. Vernon is a consultant and workshop leader in the areas of communication, stress, parenting, counseling techniques, and relationships.

Part Two: Counseling In Specific Settings

Chapter Eleven: School Counseling

Claire G. Cole, Ed.D., serves as director of the Principals' Assessment Center, Virginia Tech, in Blacksburg, Virginia, and teaches courses in counseling for Virginia Tech and for the University of Virginia. Dr. Cole holds an Ed.D. degree in counseling from Virginia Tech and Masters of Science and Bachelor of Science degrees from Radford University in Radford, Virginia.

Dr. Cole is the author of numerous articles on middle school counseling and is currently the editor of *The School Counselor*. She is coauthor of the book *Helping Relationships and Strategies* and of monographs for the National Middle School Association.

Chapter Twelve: Mental Health Counseling

David K. Brooks, Jr., Ph.D., C.C.M.H.C., is a member of the Counseling and Human Development Services Department at the College of Education, Kent State University. He received his doctorate in counseling from the University of Georgia in 1984. He has served as president of the American Mental Health Counselors Association and as a member of both the Governing Council and the Executive Committee of the American Association for Counseling and Development. He is a member of the board of the Council for Accreditation of Counseling and Related Educational Programs.

Dr. Brooks received the Carl D. Perkins Government Relations Award from AACD in 1989 in recognition of his contributions to the counselor licensure movement. His professional interests include counselor identity, role, and function; life-skills training; and counseling supervision.

Part Three: Counseling Specialized Populations

Chapter Thirteen: Counseling Children and Adolescents
Larry B. Golden, Ph.D., is an associate professor of counseling and guidance at the University of Texas at San Antonio. Dr. Golden is also a psychologist and specializes in counseling children and families. He received a Ph.D. in counseling psychology from Arizona State University, an M.S. in child counseling form the City University of New York, and a B.Ed. in elementary education from the University of Miami. His published books are *AACD Ethical Standards Casebook*, 4th Ed. (1989), *Preventing Adolescent Suicide* (1988), *Helping Families Help Children: Family Interventions with School-Related Problems* (1986), and *Psychotherapeutic Techniques in School Psychology* (1984).

Ardis Sherwood is the graduate assistant for the Rehabilitation Counseling program at Portland State University, and is a graduate student in the Community Counseling Specialization program at Portland State University. After she receives her master's degree, she plans to obtain her doctoral degree in counseling psychology and establish a private practice that will focus on marriage counseling and family therapy. Ms. Sherwood recently coauthored a chapter on adolescent unwed mothers in Dave Capuzzi and Douglas R. Gross' book *Youth at Risk: A Resource for Counselors, Teachers and Parents* (1989).

Chapter Fourteen: Counseling the Older Adult
Douglas R. Gross, Ph.D., and **Dave Capuzzi, Ph.D., N.C.C.**; see "About the Editors," above.

Chapter Fifteen: Counseling Couples and Families
Frank C. Noble, Ed.D., is currently a professor of the Division of Psychology in Education at Arizona State University and coordinator, of the

Family Therapy Program, for the Milton H. Erickson Center for Hypnosis and Psychotherapy in Phoenix, Arizona. He received his bachelor's degree from Northern Illinois University, and his master's and doctorate from the University of Illinois. Dr. Noble has taught counseling at the University of Illinois, Rutgers University, George Peabody College of Vanderbilt University, and Arizona State University.

Chapter Sixteen: Counseling Gay and Lesbian Clients

Reese M. House, Ed.D., N.C.C., is professor of counseling and guidance at Oregon State University. He has worked as a counselor educator since 1969. In addition to working with gay and lesbian clients, his areas of interest include death, dying, and loss issues; AIDS education and counseling; and group work in counseling and gerontology.

Dr. House has a doctorate in counseling from Oregon State University and a Master of Arts degree from Ball State University.

Chapter Seventeen: Counseling Visible Racial/Ethnic Group (VREG) Men and Women

Chalmer E. Thompson, Ph.D., is currently an assistant professor in the graduate school of education, counseling psychology program at the University of California, Santa Barbara. Dr. Thompson received her doctorate in 1988 from the University of Maryland, College Park, in counseling psychology. Her research interests include counseling process and outcome in cross-race and same-race dyads, the adjustment and retention of black students at predominantly white institutions, and the integration of racial identity development theory in multicultural counseling. She was awarded a fellowship from the American Psychological Association Minority Fellowship Program during her graduate study.

Donald R. Atkinson, Ph.D., is professor of education in the Counseling Psychology Program at the University of California, Santa Barbara. He is a coauthor of two books, *Counseling American Minorities: A Cross-Cultural Perspective* and *Counseling Non-Ethnic American Minorities,* as well as numerous journal articles on cross-cultural counseling. His current research efforts are focused on identifying ways in which counselors and clients can overcome cultural barriers to the counseling process.

Chapter Eighteen: Counseling Clients with Disabilities

Hanoch Livneh, Ph.D., is associate professor for counselor education and coordinator of Rehabilitation Counseling Specialization, Department of Counselor Education, at Portland State University. He received his B.A. from the Hebrew University, Jerusalem, Israel (1971), and his M.A. (1973) and Ph.D. (1976) degrees in rehabilitation counseling psychology from the University of Wisconsin, Madison.

Prior to joining Portland State University in 1988, Dr. Livneh served as the director of the rehabilitation counseling program and as professor of counseling and educational psychology at Rhode Island College. He is a coauthor of the book *The Measurement of Attitudes Toward People with Disabilities: Methods, Psychometrics and Scales* and has published over 40 professional articles and book chapters. He is a Certified Rehabilitation Counselor and a National Certified Counselor.

Part Four: Counseling Perspectives

Chapter Nineteen: Ethical and Legal Issues Related to Counseling

Sharon Robinson, Ph.D., N.C.C., is professor of counseling psychology in the Division of Psychology in Education, at Arizona State University in Tempe, Arizona. She has been teaching and lecturing on mental health ethics for ten years.

Dr. Robinson has coauthored one of the few empirical studies of applied ethics of mental health counselors. In addition to teaching and researching professional ethics, Dr. Robinson often serves as an expert witness on professional behavior.

Chapter Twenty: Counseling in the Twenty-first Century

Brook B. Collison, Ph.D., is associate professor of counseling and guidance at Oregon State University. Dr. Collison received a Ph.D. in Counseling Psychology from the University of Missouri, Columbia.

Dr. Collison was formerly a counselor educator at The Wichita State University and has experience as a school counselor at both the junior high and senior high school levels. He is a member of the American Association for Counseling and Development and served as its president from 1987 to 1988.

INTRODUCTION TO COUNSELING: PERSPECTIVES FOR THE 1990S

Dave Capuzzi, Ph.D., N.C.C.
Portland State University
Portland, Oregon

Douglas R. Gross, Ph.D.
Arizona State University
Tempe, Arizona

PART ONE ■

Counseling Foundations

Counseling as a profession encompasses a number of core modalities in which the counselor needs to be proficient. This section provides the beginning counseling student with an overview of both the historical context of counseling and the basic skill areas in which the counselor operates.

The development of counseling as a distinct profession is outlined in Chapter One: "The Counseling Profession: A Historical Perspective." The roots of counseling are traced to the vocational guidance movement at the beginning of this century and the progression and expansion of the counselor's role in our society.

The context and assumptions within which counselors and mental health professionals operate are examined in Chapter Two: "What Does It Mean to Be Psychologically Healthy?" The author discusses how cultural values have influenced the "standard" criteria for mental health in our society. A possible model for viewing positive mental health is described in which self-acceptance, self-awareness, and a clear sense of reality are basic components. The chapter discusses the need for individuals to experience a sense of balance and a feeling of purpose in their lives, whatever their cultural context.

Chapter Three—"The Helping Relationship"—presents to students the characteristics and qualities that distinguish helping professionals. Personal qualities that effective helpers possess are described, as well as such basic skills as the counselor's reflecting and listening skills, attention to nonverbal cues, and the ability to observe and follow perceptively a client's patterns of speech and behavior. These core skills provide a foundation for the beginning counselor to both understand the counseling process and become more self-aware about his or her own interpersonal interactions.

Theory provides a framework to understand human behavior and assists the counselor in making decisions regarding the course of therapy. In its essence, theory is highly practical, since it enables the counselor to maintain a consistent and conscious therapeutic relationship with the client and to use interventions that are solidly anchored to the particular client's goals. Chapter 4—"A Framework for Theories in Counseling"—outlines the importance of theory in counseling and gives an overview of the major schools of counseling and psychotherapy. The authors discuss the value of an informed, eclectic approach in which the counselor consciously and carefully selects an approach that is most likely to be effective and constructive with a particular client or situation. The responsibility of counselors today to integrate and synthesize counseling theories into their own personalized approach is stressed.

Chapter Five—"Individual Counseling"—provides information on approaches to working therapeutically with individual clients, including more in-depth descriptions of differing approaches such as Freudian, cognitive-emotional therapy, and Rogers' client-centered approach. Mechanisms of change within the individual are discussed, as well as rationales for understanding how individual problems develop. Chapter Six—"Group Counseling"—presents the basic components of group counseling, including a discussion of the history of group counseling, types of group work, qualities of the effective group leader, and common myths that beginning counselors and therapists often hold about the nature of group work.

Counseling as a profession had its roots in the vocational guidance movement of the early part of this century, and working with career and vocational issues remains a significant part of many counselor's roles today. Chapter Seven—"Career Counseling: An Introduction"—provides an introduction to the different theories and styles of career counseling. It also outlines the stages of career exploration and tools and interventions that the career counselor can use to assist the client in such a search. The author describes the major vocational tests that a counselor might use to gain more information about a client's career and vocational needs.

The role of testing and use of assessment instruments within the counseling profession are described in more depth in Chapter Eight, "Testing and Counseling." The authors present a number of key terms and concepts and describe various categories of tests that a counselor might have occasion to use with a client.

Chapter Nine—"Diagnosis in Counseling"—provides a comprehensive outline of the major categories currently used by the therapeutic community in providing accurate diagnosis and assessment. The importance of diagnosis within the overall counseling process is described, as well as the benefits and risks inherent in the process of diagnosis.

Counselors need to remain open to new innovative methods and theories that may increase their professional effectiveness. Section I concludes with Chapter Ten—"Nontraditional Approaches to Counseling"—which describes a number of alternative approaches to working with clients. Many of these approaches are becoming more and more well known as their effectiveness has been demonstrated. Such alternative therapies include music and art therapy, movement therapy, and the creative use of guided imagery. Such interventions are exciting in the possibilities they present for the counselor wishing to assist his or her client in self-expression and personal growth; such approaches may become more widely used in the future.

1.

The Counseling Profession: A Historical Perspective

PERRY J. ROCKWELL, JR., PH.D.
Professor Emeritus, Counselor Education
University of Wisconsin
Platteville, Wisconsin

EARLY HISTORICAL BACKGROUND

Historical and Social Factors

If one assumes that counseling is advising, counselors have existed since people have appeared on earth. Mothers, fathers, friends, lovers, and social leaders all provide such counsel whether sought after or not. The idea of a professional person educated for counseling is relatively new. The confluence of social and economic factors leading to such a concept and its implementation could only have occurred in the United States.

A representative democracy demands an educated citizenry taking responsibility for the government itself. As the new democracy developed, so did the ideal of education for all citizens. Toward the end of the nineteenth century, the curriculum of schools began to change and choices among school subjects became available. Help with such choices was necessary. Jessie Davis, one of the pioneers in counseling, declared in his autobiography that he had graduated from school "fairly well prepared to live in the Middle Ages" (Davis, 1956, p. 57). His experiences led directly to the establishment of guidance and counseling services in schools.

Other factors were providing pressures that made the development of professionals to help people make choices inevitable. The industrial revolution and its attendant job specialization and technologic advances were some of those pressures. There was also an increase in democracy after the Civil War ended in 1865. If the United States had continued to exist as a slave society or a closed class society, there would have been little need for the development of counseling services.

The population of the country was on the increase and the census of 1890 revealed that the frontier was essentially closed. Larger cities were growing increasingly more crowded, and immigrants to the United States and other citizens could no longer move westward or eastward without regard for others. "Free" land was all but gone. It became necessary to remain near the cities to work, to live, and to get along with one's neighbors. Providing assistance in the choices necessary to life in large industrially based cities became permanent.

At the same time, the new science of psychology was studying the differences among individuals. Instruments for appraisal of persons were in their infancy but were known to the pioneers who noted the need for counseling services. As these tools developed more sophistication, they were adapted and/or adopted by counselors.

Pressures from various socioeconomic factors also led to the kaleidoscope we know as counseling today. The history of counseling has continued the thread of individual choice in a society that prizes freedom to choose as an ideal. Like a kaleidoscope, the form, emphasis, and brightness of various aspects of counseling have changed as society changes. The profession still holds the value of the person in society as the highest good.

Perhaps the earliest notion of professional counseling in response to these pressures was that of Lysander S. Richards. In 1881 Richards published a slim volume titled *Vocophy*. This was "The New Profession, A system enabling a person to name the calling or vocation one is best suited to follow" (Richards, 1881). His work has been dismissed because there is no documented proof that he actually established the services he advocated. Nevertheless, his ideas foreshadowed what was to come.

He called his counselors "vocophers" and urged that they study occupations and the persons they counseled. Richards urged that every community of 10,000 people have at lease six such counselors. While he believed that phrenology was the most developed science upon which to base the vocopher's advice, he advocated caution in using the results of phrenologic examinations. He was aware of the new science of psychology developing in departments of philosophy. He thought that psychology held much promise but needed to be developed. Richards urged vocophers to continue to study it (Richards, 1881).

Richards also included letters from various famous people of the day in his volume, *Vocophy*. He believed that aspirants to particular occupations should consider what successful people had to say about the qualifications for success in that field. Letters from Grant, Longfellow, Westinghouse, and others, which described the ingredients for success in their occupations, were included in his volume.

Later, a series of pamphlets published by the Metropolitan Life Insurance Company in the 1960s and used widely by school counselors asked the question, "Should your child be a ____?" A famous person in a field would describe what was necessary for success in that field. The use of successful people to provide career information is used by counselors today.

Richards also seemed advanced for his time regarding his view of women and work. He said that if a woman could do the work "though at present solely followed by man, there can be no objection, whether normally or religiously considered, to her following it" (Richards, 1881, preface). He deplored the drifting of youth from job to job without consideration of what would be best for them and for society. He was cautious in his approach to the sciences (especially phrenology) of his day.

Whether Richards influenced those who followed is speculative. Influence is the quicksilver of history. He was active in the literary societies in the Boston area, as was Frank Parsons. Did they meet? Debate? Richards' *Vocophy* was in the Harvard Library in the 1890s. Parsons (1894) expressed ideas similar to those of Richards in an article published in the late 1890s. Brewer (1942) noted that Meyer Bloomfield, a colleague of Parsons at the Breadwinners Institute, mentioned Richards in his Harvard courses, as did Henry C. Metcalf of Tufts and Frank Locke of the YMCA in Boston.

Frank Parsons and the "Boston Example"

There is no question of the credit given to Frank Parsons for leading the way to vocational guidance. Parsons had a long history of concern for economic and political reforms that would benefit people. Other pioneers in the field credited him with being the first counselor (Davis, 1914; Reed, 1944), and he has often been referred to as the "father of guidance."

Parsons alone, of those persons who had some direct connection with the organization and extension of guidance services, had a definite, well thought out, and organized social philosophy, which he articulated often and at length (Rockwell, 1958). Parsons' writings ranged from a lengthy (836 pages) tome about the history and political development of New Zealand to brief paragraphs in magazines commenting on various incidents of the day that, to him, seemed of some social significance.

Parsons was one of the many persons in the late nineteenth and early twentieth centuries who was striving to make the world a better place in which to live. These people saw in the growth of large private fortunes based upon industrial might and the resultant political power a clear danger to the realization of a more perfect society based upon the brotherhood of all men. They were humanitarians all; each seeking the good things in life for the individual within society. Parsons found himself in the company of such notables of this movement as Henry D. Lloyd, Edward Bellamy, Phillip Brooks, and Benjamin O. Flower (Rockwell, 1958).

Parsons believed it was better to select a vocation scientifically than to drift through a variety of vocations, perhaps never finding one that would be best for the person and thus make society a better place in which to live. Meyer Bloomfield, director of the Civic Service House in Boston, asked Parsons to establish such a service within the Civic Service House. Thus, Parsons became director of what was called the Breadwinners' Institute from 1905 through 1907 (Brewer, 1942).

Parsons developed a plan for individualized counseling and opened the Vocational Bureau of Boston in January of 1908. Parsons was the director and vocational counselor.

Although Parsons was but one of many who were seeking social reforms in that day, he was able to secure the support of the leaders of powerful groups in business, labor, education, and politics. His report to the members of the board controlling the Vocational Bureau was the first recorded instance of the use of the term "vocational guidance." (Brewer [1942] published the report as an appendix to his *History*.) Parsons' report emphasized that counseling was not designed to make decisions for counselees. "No attempt is made, of course, to decide FOR (sic) the applicant what his calling should be; but the Bureau tries to help him arrive at a wise, well-founded conclusion for himself" (Brewer, 1942, p. 304).

Parsons did plan for the education of counselors. His plan was outlined in his book, *Choosing a Vocation*, published posthumously.

Parsons' prescriptions about how counselees should examine themselves and their lives reflected his political and social philosophy (Rockwell, 1958, pp. 74–130).

Other Early Influences

The need for counseling about vocational choice seems to have permeated American society of the late nineteenth and early twentieth centuries. Jessie B. Davis, the son of a Baptist minister, had been unsure of what he wanted to do with his life throughout his educational career. He was questioned thoroughly by Charles Thurber, one of his professors at Cornell University, and that left a lasting impression on him. He began to use the professor's methods in his work with students at the Central High School in Detroit. In 1907, he became principal of the Grand Rapids Central School and was able to implement his ideas of self-study, occupational study, and examination of self in relation to the chosen occupation throughout the seventh through twelfth grades (Brewer, 1942, p. 51). This was done primarily through essays written in English classes. Essay topics varied from self-examination of values and ideals to the selection of a vocation by the twelfth grade. Throughout the topics, social and civic ethics were emphasized (Davis, 1914). Davis' religious background was reflected in topics such as "Am I my brother's keeper?" "The Y.M.C.A.," "The Big Brother Movement," "The men and religion forward movement and the unemployed" and "Resolved: That a man who has gone into bankruptcy is still under moral obligation to pay his debts." Davis has been identified as bringing the concept of social gospelism to the guidance movement (Rockwell, 1958, pp. 131–147).

Anna Y. Reed in Seattle and Eli Weaver in New York established counseling services based on Social Darwinian concepts (Rockwell, 1958). Social Darwinism is the theory that the most powerful groups in a society have become that way because they have adapted best to that society. It is an application of Darwin's biologic theory of evolution to social organization. Reed came to the need for counseling services through her study of newsboys, penal institutions, and charity schools. In making pleas for such assistance she emphasized that business people were the most successful and that counseling should be designed to help youth emulate them. She equated morality and business ideals and was much concerned that whatever course of action was taken on any social question it be taken on the basis of social research, economy, and how it would be accepted by the business world. Reed urged that schools use the example of business and keep before children the dollar sign, which she believed every pupil understood (Reed, 1916).

The guidance services that Reed developed were in the nature of placement agencies in which an individual's worth was judged by his acceptability to employers. Other programs, she said, "savored too much of a philanthropic or social service proposition and too little of a practical commercial venture" (Reed, 1920, p. 62).

Eli Weaver also believed in working within the framework of the existing society and looked upon counseling as a means of keeping the wheels of the machinery well oiled. He was chairman of the Students' Aid Committee of the High School Teachers' Association of New York in 1905. In developing the work of his committee, Weaver concluded that the students were in need of advice and counsel before their entrance into the work-a-day world. He had no funds or active help from school authorities, but was able to secure the volunteer services of teachers to work with young people in New York. By 1910, he was able to report that every high school in the city of New York had a committee of teachers actively attempting to aid boys and girls discover what they could do best and how to secure a job in which their abilities could be used to the fullest advantage (Brewer, 1942; Rockwell, 1958).

BEGINNINGS OF PROFESSIONAL ORGANIZATIONS AND PROFESSIONAL IDENTITY

The early pioneers in counseling reflected society's need for workers who were skilled and happy in what they did. A distinct influence in early counseling was the vocational education movement. In 1906 the National Society for the Promotion of Industrial Education (NSPIE) was formed. People who were advocates of vocational counseling served on its board and later on the board of the Vocation Bureau established by Parsons. Ralph Albertson, an employment supervisor at William Filene's Sons Company and confidant of Frank Parsons, became secretary of the Board of Trustees of the Vocation Bureau (Stephens, 1970). Frank Snedden, a vocational educator from Massachusetts, is given credit for suggesting that a vocational guidance conference separate from the NSPIE be held (Brewer, 1942). Such conferences were held in 1911 and 1912.

At a third national conference in 1913, the National Vocational Guidance Association (NVGA) was formed (Norris, 1954). Frank Leavitt became the first president and noted the economic, educational, and social demands for guidance (and the counseling it entailed) and that it was necessary "for the very preservation of society itself" (Norris, 1954, p. 17). Counseling in regard to career choice remained an integral part of the movement. In 1985 the NVGA became the National Career Development Association (NCDA).

Beginnings of Mental Health Counseling

The economic, educational, and social reform forces that led to the organization of the NCDA led also to other movements, which were later incorporated into the kaleidoscope we call counseling today. Clifford Beers, who had suffered harsh treatment for mental illness in several institutions for the disturbed, published a book about his experience (Beers, 1908). The publication sparked the development of the mental hygiene movement, which stimulated studies of persons with behavior problems. The results of studies of children with problems supported the concept of providing counseling for all children in schools. Beginning at about the same time as vocational guidance but with a parallel development, mental health counselors have become a part of the mainstream of professional counseling.

A scientific approach to social problems had become popular in the late nineteenth and early twentieth centuries. G. Stanley Hall had founded Clark University in 1888 with an emphasis on graduate study and research. His efforts led to the study of the development of children's mental and physical abilities. The scientific approach to social problems was based on the assumption that the answer to a social problem could be discovered through objective research. Such an approach was influential in the establishment of counseling services in New Orleans.

Emphasis on Vocational Youth Guidance

David Spence Hill, who organized the first guidance and counseling services in New Orleans, was a graduate of Clark University during the presidency of G. Stanley Hall. As Director of Research for the New Orleans schools, he discovered a need for guidance while researching whether there was a need for a vocational school in his district (Rockwell, 1958). While he concluded that there was a need for such a high school, he believed it necessary to assist youth in assessing their abilities and in learning about the opportunities that would best help them use those abilities. He was aware of the appraisal work being done by Binet and attempted to use the Binet tasks in helping the students in the New Orleans schools. He realized the need for counseling because of his belief that the education of an individual must be of the highest order. Counseling based on scientific research would help secure the best education for each pupil.

If counselors were to help youth to know themselves and to match their characteristics with qualifications for jobs, it was necessary to have some means of measuring individual characteristics. Counselors relied a great deal on questioning youth about their abilities and their desires. There was the implicit assumption that counselees knew themselves and could reason about their reported skills and their qualifications for jobs. A counselor's task was to help them in this process through the use of greater maturity and objective judgment. The development of tests and appraisal instruments lent a scientific air to the process.

Influences of World War I and the Development of Testing

The army had enlisted the aid of psychologists to classify men during World War I. The Army Alpha and Army Beta tests of intelligence were developed to screen and classify army personnel. In the period following World War I, the number and variety of such instruments proliferated, and even though counselors were not the major creators of the instruments, they became users. To quantify a person's intelligence, aptitude, achievement, interests, and personality gave a great deal of credence to a counselor's judgment about that person. "It is not surprising that vocational guidance became first attracted to and then addicted to testing" (Ginzberg, 1971, p. 30).

Psychological testing became ubiquitous in industrial personnel classification, in education, and in counseling offices. Knowledge about and skill in using standardized tests became part of the education of a counselor. Data derived from appraisal instruments were used to make better judgements about counselees and to advise them about what was the wisest decision to make. Large commercial producers of psychometric devices had developed. The process of developing and marketing tests to industry, education, government, and counselors in private practice became quite sophisticated. Counselors were expected to be experts in selecting and using appropriate instruments from a myriad of those offered. Their use in the counseling process became such that testing and counseling were often considered synonymous.

The practice of using tests in counseling was not without controversy. Criteria for psychometric instruments used in decision-making were not published until the American Psychological Association's *Technical Recommendations for Psychological Tests and Diagnostic Techniques* in 1954. Publications such as *Testing, Testing, Testing* (Joint Committee, 1962), *The Educational Decision-Makers*

(Cicourel & Kitsuse, 1963), and *The Brain Watchers* (Gross, 1962) are examples of many voices questioning the reliance on test data by counselors and others.

The idea of matching persons with jobs continued throughout the history of counseling. It was formalized in the directive theory of counseling advocated by Williamson (Williamson, 1939); a trait-factor approach to counseling that, with modifications, exists today as clinical counseling. The malleability of both individuals and jobs was emphasized in the use of test data by Rothney and Roens (1949) and the critical analysis of tests before use by Rothney, Danielson, and Heiman (1959).

The Depression Era and Government Involvement

The Great Depression, with its loss of employment for millions of people, saw the development of governmentally sponsored programs that included a counseling component with an emphasis on classification. Both the Civilian Conservation Corps (CCC) and the National Youth Administration (NYA) attempted to help youth find themselves in the occupational scene of the 1930s (Miller, 1971). In 1938 the George–Dean Act had appropriated $14 million for vocational education, and by 1938 the Occupational Information and Guidance Service was established (Picchioni & Bonk, 1983). The *Dictionary of Occupational Titles* began publication in 1939 and became a basic resource for counselors matching persons with jobs (Picchioni & Bonk, 1983). Society would be better if persons and their occupations were matched for greater efficiency and satisfaction. The federal government became influential in the field of counseling and remains so today.

The following list shows governmental action and legislation that have had an impact on the development of the counseling profession (Baruth & Robinson, 1987):

1944   The Veterans Administration established a nationwide network of guidance services to assist veterans. The services included vocational rehabilitation, counseling, training, and advisement.

1944   The United State Employment Service was begun under the influence of the War Manpower Commission. Fifteen hundred offices were established and employment "counselors" were used.

1946   The George–Barden Act provided government support for establishing training programs for counselors. The emphasis was on vocational guidance and established a precedent for funding of training for counselors.

1958   The National Defense and Education Act (NDEA) was passed in response to Sputnick and the view that the United States was lagging behind the Soviet Union in technologic expertise. The emphasis of the act was on improving math and science performance in our public schools; counseling in the schools was seen as an important function in helping students explore their abilities, options, and interests in relation to career development. Title V of this act specifically addressed counseling through grants to schools to carry out counseling activities. Title V–D authorized contracts to institutions of higher education to improve the training of counselors in the schools.

1963   The Community Mental Health Centers Act created over 2000 mental health centers that provided direct counseling services to people in the community as well as providing outreach and coordination of other services.

1964   The NDEA Amendment continued to impact counseling through the addition of counselors in the public schools aimed at reducing the counselor:student ratio.

1960s   The Elementary and Secondary Education Act (ESEA) did much to develop and expand the role of the elementary school counseling program and the services provided by the elementary school counselor.

The entrance of the government into counseling reflected what had been an increasing concern throughout society for the betterment of all persons. There was a belief in the betterment of persons for the person's sake alone, the reform of society, and the need for business and industry to achieve their objectives better. There was a plethora of organizations dedicated to these ends. In 1934 a number of them met to form the American Council of Guidance and Personnel Associations (ACGPA) (Brewer, 1942, p. 152):

American College Personnel Association
National Association of Deans of Women
National Federation of Bureau of Occupations
National Vocational Guidance Association
Personnel Research Foundation
Teachers' College Personnel Association

By 1939 others were added, and the name was changed to the Council of Guidance and Personnel Associations (CGPA):

Alliance for the Guidance of Rural Youth
International Association of Altrusa Clubs
National Federation of Business and Professional
    Women's Clubs
Western Personnel Service
American Association of Collegiate Registrars
    (withdrew in 1941)
Institute of Women's Professional Relations

Kiwanis International and the Association of YMCA Secretaries met with the group from time to time.

Brewer (1942) stated that the October, 1938, issue of *Occupations,* the publication of the NVGA, listed 96 organizations interested in furthering vocational guidance among the young people of the nation. Counseling, per se, was coming to the forefront of concerns within the vocational guidance movement. All groups seemed dedicated to placing "square pegs in square holes" through the use of tests.

Influence of World War II

With the breakdown of international relationships and the need for increase preparedness for war, the Army developed a needed classification tool, the Army General Classification Test (AGCT). Prior to and during World War II millions of men and women were tested and assigned to particular duties according to their test scores and their requests. The armed forces stationed counselors and psychologists at many induction and separation centers. Picchioni and Bonk quote Mitchell Dreese of the Adjutant General's Office as saying that counseling "is essentially the same whether it be in the home, the church, the school, industry, business, or the Army" (Picchioni & Bonk, 1983, p. 54). The process was certainly an extensive use of the scientific approach to counseling. Society, through its representatives in government, had become embroiled in what counseling should be and what it should become. It has not relinquished that interest through all the forms, shapes, and colors of the kaleidoscope counseling has become.

CARL ROGERS AND THE CLIENT-CENTERED MOVEMENT

In reviewing a history of what has happened, it is often difficult to know whether events have shaped a leader of an era or whether a person has influenced events. There seems little doubt that Carl R. Rogers, his ideas, and his disciples affected counseling from its core outward. Rogers' idea was that individuals had the capacity to explore themselves and to make decisions without an authoritative judgment from a counselor. He became interested in the process of counseling and pioneered the electronic recording and filming of counseling sessions, an unheard-of idea at that time. Working in the academic environment of Ohio State University and the University of Chicago, Rogers published his ideas in *Counseling and Psychotherapy: Newer Concepts in Practice* in 1942 and *Client-Centered Therapy* in 1951.

Rogers saw little need to make diagnoses of client problems or to provide information or direction to those he called clients. He emphasized the importance of the relationship between the counselor and client. In his system the client rather than the counselor was the most important factor. Since there was no advice given or persuasion used to follow a particular course, Rogers' system became known as nondirective counseling. It is not the purpose of this chapter to delineate all of the postulates of what became known as client-centered counseling, and, later, person-centered counseling. It can be noted, however, that the impact that approach had on counseling has continued to the present day.

Rogers' ideas were extremely popular. It seemed that counselors could be trained to provide warmth and empathy relatively easily. There was no need to know lists of symptomatic behaviors that could be placed into a diagnostic construct. Counselors would have no need to learn the statistical concepts necessary to understand psychometric devices to use with counselees. Counselors would not need to feel responsible for counselees who followed alternatives suggested by the counselor. Client-centered ideas of respect for the person and the right to choose and determine one's destiny fit snugly into the American ideal of freedom for individual development. It seemed the essence of democracy.

Client-centeredness was applied to a wide range of human relationships other than counseling. Teachers were to facilitate learning by providing an atmosphere of unconditional positive regard in which students would find whatever information they desired to learn. Husbands and wives would relate to each other and their children in like manner. Employers and employees would relate well and work toward their common good through the use of what has now become known as relationship therapy. Many programs at counseling conventions debated the issue of client-centered vs. trait-factored counseling. The 1950s and 1960s was an exciting time in the counseling profession.

Rogers, himself, remained within the scientific approach to counseling. He continued to use tests and appraisal devices, albeit not within a counseling relationship. Perhaps others administered the devised needed tests and did preliminary interviewing and follow-up procedures, but they were done. His concern was to learn what went on in the counseling process, to learn what worked (for him) and what did not. His was a search for necessary and sufficient conditions under which effective counseling could take place.

Whenever research about client-centered counseling was reported by Rogers, it was supported by psychometric data. Certainly one of the effects of Rogers on the profession was to emphasize the process of counseling and research about counseling. The ensuing debates about the primacy of feeling or rationality as a proper basis of counseling stimulated professional counselors to research their processes and techniques. Theories were refined and new instruments for determining their efficacy were developed. Counselors-in-training became as familiar with recording devices as they were with textbooks.

CONTINUING DEVELOPMENT OF PROFESSIONAL IDENTITY

The ferment about counseling was of long standing. At least four times the NVGA had considered a name change to better reflect the concern members had about the total adjustment of their clients: 1922, 1929, 1941, 1944, and 1948 (Norris, 1954). For a variety of reasons the NVGA continued its separate identity within the federation of guidance and personnel associations.

Members of the associations belonging to the federation were also considering whether it was wise or efficient to attempt to belong to several organizations doing essentially the same thing. Groups belonging to the federation had the practice of meeting in conventions at the same time and place. By the late 1940s groups had established their identities in work settings and members had begun to see commonalities of purpose and function. The name of the federation had changed from the American Council of Guidance and Personnel Associations (ACGPA) to the Council of Guidance and Personnel Associations (CGPA) in 1939 so there was precedence for a name change.

In 1948 Daniel Feder, as chair of CGPA and president of NVGA, urged consideration of forming a national organization to include individuals as well as associations. A Committee on Unification was appointed to develop a plan for such an organization. Its plan was presented at the 1950 convention and forwarded to the organizations concerned (McDaniels, 1964). Both the National Vocational Guidance Association and the American College Personnel Association approved the plan and arranged their constitutions to join the new organization as divisions in 1951. The National Association of Women Deans (NAWD) declined to participate. At this time the Personnel and Guidance Association (PGA) was born.

When the new PGA met in Los Angeles in 1952 there were four divisions: American College Personnel Association (ACPA), National Association of Guidance Supervisors and College Trainers (NAGSCT),

National Vocational Guidance Association (NVGA), and Student Personnel Association for Teacher Education (SPATE) (Picchioni & Bonk, 1983). Again, NAWD chose not to become a part of the new organization. Because the initials PGA could become confused with the Professional Golfers Association, delegates to the convention voted to add American to the title, thus APGA.

Beginnings of National Divisions to Reflect Counseling Specializations

Before the convention was over, the first division using the term *counseling* was accepted: the American School Counselors Association (ASCA). The acceptance was tentative because of some formalities but was accomplished (McDaniels, 1964). Unification had been achieved. The basic format of autonomous divisions working within an umbrella organization has continued to the present time. Divisions have been added as members' interests or counselor work settings changed due to changes in socioeconomic milieu.

In 1957 the effects of the Veterans Administration's attempts to meet the needs of returning (from World War II) servicemen and women resulted in the organization of the American Rehabilitation Counseling Association (ARCA). Soon the model of training counselors for rehabilitation settings had become the model for training all counselors in those institutions receiving money from the Veterans Administration. Rehabilitation services soon spread to service all persons needing help with a disability—not just those with a service-connected problem. In 1961 the NAGSCT changed the name of their association to the Association for Counselor Educators and Supervisors (ACES). The acronym not only sounded better when spoken but also better reflected the concept of education rather than a Pavlovian training.

Two divisions joined in 1965. Professionals who used psychometric instruments in their settings needed an organization to help them improve the use of such instruments and to communicate among themselves. The Association for Measurement and Evaluation in Guidance (AMEG) became a division. Nineteen years later, in 1984, the division's name was changed to the Association for Measurement and Evaluation in Counseling and Development (AMECD) to reflect the changing nature of its work and to be consistent with the name change that had occurred in APGA. The second division joining APGA in 1965 was the National Employment Counselors Association (NECA).

The number of divisions in APGA remained static for seven years, but the 1970s saw the formation and acceptance of several divisions. There was increasing concern about minority representation within the structure of APGA. That concern developed into an interest-based division, the Association for Non-White Concerns in Personnel and Guidance (ANWIC), was added in 1972. The Association changed its name to the Association for Multicultural Counseling and Development (AMCD) to reflect the broadening and increasingly pluralistic nature of counselor work settings and to be consistent with the name change of APGA.

The National Catholic Guidance Conference was accepted as a division in 1974, but by 1977 had changed its name to the Association for Religious and Value Issues in Counseling (ARVIC). Another interest-based association attained division status in 1973 with the acceptance of the Association for Specialists in Group Work (ASGW). Group work has had a history alongside counseling on an individual basis. Parsons, Bloomfield, Davis, and other pioneers in the field used groups in their work. The impetus of the group dynamics field of study, T-groups, and the client-centered groups of Rogers and his disciples brought group work to the fore as a specialty.

Counseling had originated out of social needs in the late nineteenth and early twentieth centuries. As the twenty-first century approaches, the profession through its organizations continues to be responsive to social needs. When the United States felt it needed help in meeting manpower needs for defense and passed the National Defense Act in 1958, counselor education institutions responded by developing short- and long-term institutes to educate school counselors. Under this act high schools were able to secure the services of counselors and higher educational institutions were stimulated to inaugurate or to expand their counselor education programs. Thousands of school counselors became available.

As the demand for school counselors diminished, a need for counselors in a variety of community agencies developed. The profession responded, and in 1978 the American Mental Health Counselors Association (AMHCA) became a division of APGA. It soon became the fastest growing and, for a time, largest of the divisions within APGA. In 1986, as a reflection of the aging of the population and the problems attendant on growing old in a youth-oriented society, an Association for Adult Development and Aging (AADA) was organized within what had become the American Association for Counseling and Development (AACD). In 1990, the latest division, the International Association of Marriage and Family Counselers became a part of AACD.

Prior to 1983 the APGA began to feel pressures from the membership for a name change that would accurately reflect the purposes and work activities of the members. The terms "guidance" and "personnel" were onerous to some members. Comments such as "Guidance is for missiles" and "Personnel says we select and classify people into pigeon holes!" were heard at APGA conventions and regional meetings. In addition to describing the profession better, the term "counseling" was more prestigious and understood by the public. Several divisions already recognized counseling in their titles (ASCA, ARCA, ARVIC, NECA, and AMCHA) and two affiliate organizations, the Public Offender's Counselor Association (POCA) which had been a division from 1974 to 1984; and which changed its name in 1990 to the International Association for Addictions and Offender Counselors (IAAOC) and the Military Educators and Counselors Association (MECA), 1984 also recognized counseling in their titles.

In order to have a clearer identity in society and to attract new members in a changing society, the APGA became the American Association for Counseling and Development in 1983. Names changed in divisions to reflect the new emphasis. NVGA became the National Career Development Association (NCDA) in 1984. AMEG became the Association for Measurement and Evaluation Counseling and Development (AMECD), also in 1984. The Association for Non-White Concerns recognized the changing nature of the population in its new title, Association for Multicultural Counseling and Development (AMCD). In July of 1989, the AACD had over 56,000 members working in a wide variety of work settings with a multitude of interests aimed at helping people in a changing, dynamic, and complex society.

Not all of the organizational problems have been solved. Within the structure of AACD there are state branches (e.g., Wisconsin Association for Counseling and Development). Within each state there are local area organizations. There is no unified membership or dues structure of support for AACD, although officers of each branch must belong to the AACD. In the future, AACD will need the financial as well as the psychological support of all who call themselves counselors. Nevertheless, AACD remains the strongest organization representing counselors on the national scene.

CURRENT TRENDS WITHIN THE PROFESSION OF COUNSELING

As social pressures turned the kaleidoscope that is counseling, counselors have responded with new forms and modifications of techniques. Guidance services have been extended throughout school systems. In the mid-1960s the NDEA of 1958 was expanded to support the education of counselors to serve in grades kindergarten through fourteen. Since then, a number of states have mandated the provision of guidance services (including counselors) at the elementary level. The assumption is that the provision of such services will encourage normal development and hence fewer problems at the secondary level. In the education of elementary counselors emphasis was placed on the use of groups and play techniques such as the use of puppets. The profession attempted to respond to the needs of the population.

Within the profession there were several developments to ensure that persons being trained to perform counseling functions were receiving an adequate education and, once educated, were performing their tasks well. In 1960 ACES and ASCA had begun a study that led to the development of standards that were to be followed by institutions purporting to prepare counselors. Between the years 1964 and 1969 standards for graduate programs preparing counselors from elementary school through college level were developed. By 1977, the standards were adopted by APGA. The Council for Accreditation of Counseling and Related Educational Programs (CACREP) became the official accrediting body for AACD in 1981 (Altekruse, 1989). The second move was to license counselors in private practice.

The licensure move came about because of the numbers of AACD members who were entering private practice and work settings other than schools and coming into conflict with psychological licensing laws that restricted their activities and made it difficult to receive third-party payments from insurance companies. Licensing was perceived as a sign of professional status and as a protection of the public from persons who operated as counselors without the knowledge or skills of a counselor. Virginia was the first state to pass such a licensure law in 1976 (Picchioni & Bonk, 1983). In 1989, AACD headquarters listed 32 states that had passed counselor licensure laws. It is expected that eventually all states will have such laws.

In addition to the efforts that have led to accreditation of counselor education programs and licensure for counselors, two other certification efforts should be noted. The National Board of Certified Counselors (NBCC) was initiated by AACD in 1982 to establish and monitor a national certification system for counselors. It has since become an independently incorporated nonprofit organization that has certified more than 18,000 professional counselors. NBCC compliments the specialty certification currently available to mental health, rehabilitation, and career counselors. Counselors wishing certification by NBCC as a National Certified Counselor (NCC) must pass the NBCC examination given in a variety of sites each year. Founded in 1979 through the efforts of the American Mental Health Counselors Association, the National Academy of Certified Clinical Mental Health Counselors maintains and monitors a national certification process that recognizes mental health counselors through educational and competency-based criteria for their clinical skills in the delivery of clinical mental health counseling services.

Several organizations that have also contributed to recent trends and accomplishments within the counseling and human development profession should be noted. In 1979, the AACD Foundation was established and incorporated as a separate, not-for-profit group. The Foundation, now known as the Counseling and Human Development Foundation (CHDF), was designed to help improve counseling, guidance, and human development and to assist and support AACD by holding, managing, and purchasing property as well as funding special activities of significance to the profession. The foundation sponsors an annual Professional Enhancement Grants and Awards Program for Scholarly Research Projects. Seven special AACD awards are made each year from memorial funds initiated by the Foundation, and fund-raising efforts are periodically coordinated by the Foundation. Chi Sigma Iota, a national honorary for Counselor Education, was founded in 1985. Its purpose is to recognize and promote excellence in counseling. Membership is comprised of students, faculty, and practitioners who share a common interest in promoting quality in research and practices in counseling. Chapters of Chi Sigma Iota emphasize continuing education, professional development, networking, and leadership development. (As this textbook went to press there were approximately 90 chapters with a little more than 3000 members.) Chi Sigma Iota funds graduate students to attend the national convention of AACD and has identified a network of distinguished scholars who serve as resources to chapters.

The International Association of Counseling Services (IACS), an affiliate of the American Association for Counseling and Development, offers program evaluation, accredits qualified centers and agencies, publishes an annual Directory of Counselor Services in the public interest, and sponsors a variety of activities and programs to help counseling centers and agencies take cooperative action on professional matters.

Counselors in the United States, regardless of work setting or theoretical orientation, are linked by the common belief that a person has the capacity and right to choose directions and activities that are most personally satisfying. Choices must be made within the bounds of social and moral value systems that will not bring harm to self or to others. The counselors who were the pioneers and the counselors who work now are dedicated to helping individuals find their way in an increasingly complex society.

Counselors are active in dealing with a great number of social problems that affect the population with whom they work. Society seems in turmoil in trying to deal with the use of illegal drugs, changing family structures, the effect of technology on occupations and employment, and complex pluralism leading to the development of special persons at risk of being inundated by the majority. There is not space here to discuss each issue and the role of a counselor in dealing with these and future issues. The reader is referred to an excellent discussion of these and other issues as they relate to counselors, Herr's *Counseling in a Dynamic Society: Opportunities and Challenges,* a 1989 publication of AACD. Counselors must have faith that through their systematic, scientific, and professional efforts individuals and groups will be served well.

REFERENCES

Altekruse, M. (1989). *History of standards development.* (Unpublished data presented at a meeting of the North Central Association for Counseling and Development, Milwaukee, WI.)

Baruth, L. G., & Robinson, E. H., III (1987). *An introduction to the counseling profession.* New Jersey: Prentice-Hall, Inc.

Beers, C. W. (1908). *A mind that found itself.* New York: Doubleday.

Brewer, J. M. (1942). *History of vocational guidance.* New York: Harper.

Cicourel, A. V., & Kitsuse, J. I. (1963). *The educational decision-makers.* Indianapolis, IN: Bobbs-Merrill.

Davis, H. V. (1955). *Frank Parsons and vocational guidance.* Unpublished doctoral dissertation. St. Louis, MO: Washington University.

Davis, J. B. (1914). *Moral and vocational guidance.* Boston: Ginn & Co.

Davis, J. B. (1956). *Saga of a schoolmaster:* An autobiography. Boston: Boston University Press.

Ginzberg, E. (1971). *Career guidance.* New York: McGraw-Hill.

Gross, M. L. (1962). *The brain watchers.* New York: Random House.

Herr, E. L. (1989). *Counseling in a dynamic society: Opportunities and challenges.* Washington, DC: AACD.

Joint Committee on Testing (1962). *Testing, testing, testing.* Washington, D.C.: American Association of School Administrators.

McDaniels, C. O. (1964). *The history and development of the American Personnel and Guidance Association, 1952–1963.* Unpublished doctoral dissertation, Charlottesville, VA: University of Virginia.

Miller, C. H. (1971). *Foundations of guidance* (2nd ed.). New York: Harper & Row.

Norris, W. (1954). *The history and development of the National Vocational Guidance Association.* Unpublished doctoral dissertation. Washington, DC: George Washington University.

Parsons, F. (1894). The philosophy of mutualism. *The Arena, 9,* 738–815.

Parsons, F. (1909). *Choosing a vocation.* Boston: Houghton-Mifflin.

Picchioni, A. P., & Bonk, E. C. (1983). *A comprehensive history of guidance in the United States.* Austin, TX: Texas Personnel and Guidance Association.

Reed, A. Y. (1913). *Seattle children in school and industry.* Seattle, WA: Board of School Directors.

Reed, A. Y. (1916). *Vocational guidance report 1913–1916.* Seattle, WA: Board of School Directors.

Reed, A. Y. (1920). *Junior wage earners.* New York: Macmillan.

Reed, A. Y. (1944). *Guidance and personnel services in education.* Ithaca, NY: Cornell University Press.

Richards, L. S. (1881). *Vocophy.* Marlboro, MA: Pratt Brothers.

Rockwell, P. J., Jr. (1958). *Social concepts in the published writings of some pioneers in guidance.* Unpublished doctoral dissertation. Madison, WI: University of Wisconsin.

Rogers, C. R. (1942). *Counseling and psychotherapy.* Boston: Houghton-Mifflin.

Rogers, C. R. (1951). *Client-centered therapy.* Boston: Houghton-Mifflin.

Rothney, J. W. M., & Roens, B. A. (1949). *Counseling the individual student.* New York: William Sloane Associates.

Rothney, J. W. M., Daniels, P. J., & Heiman, R. A. (1959). *Measurement for guidance.* New York: Harper & Row.

Stephens, W. R. (1970). *Social reform and the origins of vocational guidance.* New York: Harper & Row.

Stephens, W. R. (1954). *Technical recommendations for psychological tests and diagnostic techniques.* Washington, DC: American Psychological Association.

Williamson, E. G. (1939). *How to counsel students.* New York: McGraw-Hill.

2.

What Does It Mean To ■ Be Psychologically Healthy?

RICHARD T. KINNIER
Arizona State University
Tempe, Arizona

IMAGINE A PSYCHOLOGICAL HEALTH contest between the John Wayne persona of the 1950s silver screen and the Leo Buscalia persona of the 1980s lecture circuit. Which persona would win? Among John Wayne's celluloid traits were his stoicism and his readiness to fight. He rarely displayed any weaknesses or "shared his feelings" with anyone. In contrast, Leo Buscalia's most salient public traits have been his readiness to cry and "share his feelings" with everyone. Is "strong and silent" healthier than "vulnerable and expressive?" For males? For females? Does the answer depend entirely upon the biases of the judges and the context of a specific time and place?

In this chapter I will attempt to identify the main components of psychological health. Since a major goal of most counseling is to reduce psychological distress and increase psychological well-being or health, then it is important to ask the question, "What does it actually mean to be psychologically healthy?" The question is not an easy one to answer, however. Before I attempt to answer it, let us first consider some of the reasons that it is such a difficult question.

WHY IT IS A DIFFICULT QUESTION

Traditionally, mental health theoreticians and practitioners have avoided trying to establish the criteria of psychological health. Rather, their focus has been more on identifying symptoms of psychological pathology. It has seemed easier for professionals and laypersons alike to agree about the undesirability of certain behaviors and emotions than it has been for them to agree about which behaviors and emotions are most indicative of psychological health. For example, virtually everyone would agree that the self-mutilating behaviors of some autistic chidren (e.g., head banging, eye gouging) are pathological behaviors that should be eliminated. In contrast, fewer people would agree that altruistic behavior is usually indicative of a high level of psychological health. In fact, a popular psychodynamic suspicion about altruistic behavior is that it may often serve as a cover for personal insecurities or feelings of guilt experienced by the altruistic person. Unfortunately, there are no psychological health referees or judges out there who can make final authoritative calls on conflicting interpretations.

It may seem tempting, therefore, to define psychological health simply as the absence of agreed-upon pathological symptoms and leave it at that. Thirty years ago Jahoda (1958) rejected that idea. Consider that just because a cigarette smoker has not yet experienced negative consequences from smoking does not mean that the smoker or the behavior of smoking is healthy. And because a person is not currently depressed does not necessarily mean that he or she is happy or psychologically healthy. So the state of psychological health must be something more than just being asymptomatic. But what?

Unfortunately, the establishment of clear universal criteria for psychological health is impeded by the reality that any conception is inextricably woven into a particular cultural and temporal background (Jahoda, 1958). Imagine the John Wayne and Leo Buscalia psychological health contest alluded to at the beginning of this chapter. In the context of the 1950s America, John Wayne might win, as some of the 1950s judges would probably rate Leo Buscalia low for what they perceive as his overemotional and rather effeminate characteristics. However, in a 1980s contest, Leo would probably gain points for those traits of sensivity and openness while John would lose points for his perceived emotional rigidity. Some of the 1980s judges might even suspect John

Wayne of being homophobic. We can only guess who would win (and why he would win) in a twenty-first century contest. Undoubtedly, the outcome would be affected by *where* the contest was held: John Wayne's fans might be wise to call for the contest to be held within a homophobic culture.

In a more serious vein, there are very real examples of how culture has influenced the presumed criteria of psychological health. Prior to 1973, homosexuality was classified as a psychological disorder or "deviancy" by the American Psychiatric Association. In 1973, the Board of Trustees of the American Psychiatric Association decided to transform homosexuality into a "preference" (Stoller, Marmor, & Biever, 1973). In America during the 1970s assertive behavior came to be viewed by many as indicative of psychological health. During the 1950s similar behavior would more likely have been regarded as antisocial or selfish, as it would be in Japan, then and now. Perhaps the biggest change in perceptions about what is considered healthy or "normal" during the past few decades has occurred in the area of "gender-appropriate" behavior. A case study is illustrative. Osipow (1983) described a case analysis that occurred during the 1950s in which a woman told her therapist that she wanted to be a mathematician. The therapist interpreted her interest and career plan as an unhealthy rejection of her femininity and an escape from the emotional demands of her life as a woman. The therapist believed that the client had made progress when she finally relinquished her career aspirations and accepted her primary role as a mother. Imagine how a contemporary audience would respond to that case analysis if it was presented today.

That example raises other questions relevant to what it means to be psychologically healthy: Is it healthier for individuals to conform to societal expectations or to rebel against them? Are rebels and heretics who live in "sick" societies extraordinarily healthy? Is any individual or group really capable of objectively determining the health of a particular society or individual? Given these perhaps unresolvable issues it is understandable that few theoreticians have attempted to establish universal criteria of psychological health.

Jahoda (1958) was aware of these issues but nevertheless made the attempt over 30 years ago. She developed a list of six criteria for what she called "positive mental health." According to her, the healthy individual (1) has a positive attitude toward him- or herself (i.e., self-acceptance), (2) is continually growing or moving toward self-actualization, (3) has a sense of purpose or meaning in his or her life, (4) can function independently or autonomously in the world, (5) perceives reality (without significant distortion), and (6) has attained mastery in the environment (i.e., adequate in love and competent in work).

I will attempt to build upon, extend, and update Jahoda's list of criteria. My goal is to construct a list that is relevant to North Americans living in the late twentieth century. Clearly such a list would need at least modification (perhaps even significant revision) for other times and places. Also, the list is not exhaustive, and I expect that some people will disagree with some criteria that I have included or failed to include. Finally, although it is artificial to dichotomize or separate the mind and the body, I will limit my focus to psychological criteria, as did Jahoda.

The methodology that I have used to construct the list is fairly informal. Over the course of several years I have surveyed the relevant psychological literature looking for what various theoreticians and researchers have stated or implied were criteria of psychological health. As certain themes emerged repeatedly, I added them to the list. Criteria that appeared infrequently (e.g., staying active, living in the present) were not included. I encourage the reader to evaluate the list critically. Does each criterion seem reasonable? Is the supporting evidence for its inclusion compelling? From your knowledge and experience, should any of the criteia be modified or deleted? Do you think any other criteria should be added to the list?

CRITERIA OF PSYCHOLOGICAL HEALTH

What are the "ingredients" of psychological health? My list consists of nine (Table 2–1). Let us consider each.

Self-Love (but Not Self-Infatuation)

Psychologically healthy individuals feel a strong sense of self-acceptance and self-love (i.e., self-esteem) but are not self-obsessed.

There seems to be a consensus among mental health theoreticians that basic self-esteem is an essential component of psychological health (see, for example, Allport, 1961; Baumeister, 1988; Erikson, 1968; Jahoda, 1958; Jung, 1954; Maslow, 1970; Rogers, 1961; Sullivan, 1953). Low self-esteem has been implicated in numerous psychopathologies such as depression (e.g., Beck, 1976), interpersonal problems (e.g., Sullivan, 1953), and substance abuse (e.g., Newcomb & Bentler, 1989)—to name just a few. Conversely, the variable that correlates highest and most consistently with subjective well-being is self-esteem (see Diener, 1984).

TABLE 2–1 Criteria of Psychological Health.

1. Self-love (but not self-infatuation)
2. Self-knowledge
3. Self-confidence and self-control
4. A clear (though slightly optimistic) perception of reality
5. Courage and resilience
6. Balance and moderation
7. Love of others
8. Love of life
9. Purpose in life

Basic self-esteem also seems to be a prerequisite for attaining other important ingredients of psychological health. As pointed out by Erikson (1968) and Sullivan (1953), individuals must love and respect themselves before they can truly love others. And, according to Maslow (1970), a strong foundation of self-esteem is a prerequisite for becoming self-actualized.

Basic self-esteem should not be confused with unconditional self-esteem, self-infatuation, or extreme self-centeredness, however. Self-infatuation has been identified popularly as the sociopathy of the "me decades" (i.e., the 1970s and 1980s). Seligman (cited in Buie, 1988) has observed an increase in the incidence of depression over these past two decades and suggested that the depression may have been caused partly by the "waxing of the individual and waning of the commons" (p. 18). In other words, the glorification or "cult" of the individual may be hazardous to psychological health. Seligman suggested that this may be so because the self ultimately "is a very small unit" and "is a very poor site for meaning" (p. 18).

The "worship" of self is not only a rather meaningless endeavor, but also it is usually a lonely one. Extreme self lovers make poor friends and lovers. Consider the following example of a self-centered therapy junkie I knew during the 1970s. He was the father of two children (ages 7 and 4) but he rarely spent any time with them because of all the "self-growth" workshops and groups he attended. One Saturday morning he got up, quickly fed himself, and was about to leave for yet another group grope for self. His children (who had to find their own breakfast) reminded their father of his promise to take them to the park that morning. The father angrily snapped that he was going to his workshop and then responded to their confused and disappointed pleas with the explanation, "I go to these workshops for you—they will help me become a better father." Perhaps this self-infatuated father was actually more interested in his image as a father than in his children's needs.

In summary, psychologically healthy individuals are self-accepting. They love and respect themselves but are not self-infatuated.

Self-Knowledge

Psychologically healthy individuals know themselves well. They are aware of their true feelings and motives. They are regularly (though not obsessively) introspective.

Of all the goals of psychotherapy and counseling, the goal of self-knowledge is probably the most central and universal. Consistent with Socrates' famous dictum to "know thyself" and the idea that the "truth will set you free," Freud and his revisionists (e.g., Adler, Erikson, Fromm, Horney, Jung) believed that the uncovering and understanding of one's unconscious needs, fears, and conflicts was a prerequisite for psychological health (Hall & Lindzey, 1985). Theoreticians from other major orientations clearly agree about the importance of self-exploration and self-knowledge. For example, from the humanistic camp, Rogers (1961) described the healthy or "congruent" person as one who is clearly aware and accepting of his or her true or "organismic" feelings. The cognitive behaviorists similarly emphasize the importance of self-knowledge even though they use a different language. For example, Mahoney and Thoresen (1974) entitled a section of their book "Know Thy Controlling Variables" (p. 22).

In summary, psychologically healthy individuals are committed to understanding themselves. They regularly (but not obsessively) attempt to become aware of and to understand their unconscious motives, true feelings, and/or "controlling variables."

Self-Confidence and Self-Control

Psychologically healthy individuals have confidence in themselves. They can function independently when they need to and be assertive when they want to be assertive. They believe that they are basically in control of their lives (i.e., internal locus of control) and feel capable of accomplishing their goals.

The importance of the individual having a basic sense of personal autonomy and competence has been emphasized by numerous theoreticians, including Erikson (1963), Fromm (1955), Horney (1950), Jahoda (1958), Maslow (1970), and Rogers (1961). Adler (cited in Hall & Lindzey, 1985) believed that the primary challenge for all individuals is for them to overcome their feelings of inferiority. Failure to do so can result in "learned helplessness" and an external locus-of-control perspective, both of which are correlates of depression (see Peterson & Seligman, 1984).

Bandura's (1977, 1989) model of self-efficacy predicts that people who believe they are capable of attaining a specific goal are more likely to persist in efforts to attain that goal. And while persistence is no guarantee of success, persistence usually increases the chances of success. Successful attainment then reinforces self-efficacy. Thus, people who are generally confident or specifically self-efficacious tend to get more of what they want in life than those who are not. Consequently, the variables of self-efficacy, internal locus of control, and subjective well-being are positively intercorrelated (Diener, 1984).

Assertiveness is generally regarded as "healthy" behavior. Being assertive allows individuals to get more of what they want and to avoid what they don't want. Assertiveness is an important tool for helping adolescents resist peer pressure to abuse drugs (see Newcomb & Bentler, 1989). However, extreme assertiveness, like self-infatuation, can be unhealthy. The behavior of constantly asserting one's rights, always refusing to yield to others, and never compromising is often seen as obnoxious and selfish. People who exhibit those behaviors risk alienating others and losing friends.

In summary, psychologically healthy individuals are self-confident (though not grandiose). They are able to function autonomously and believe that they are largely in control of their own lives. They can be assertive when they need to be but are not obnoxiously assertive.

A Clear (Though Slightly Optimistic) Perception of Reality

Psychologically healthy individuals basically have a clear perception of reality. Occasional minor distortions of reality are typically on the optimistic side.

Our perceptions of the world are always subjective, but fortunately some societal consensus exists about what comprises reality. Significant departures from that consensus (i.e., products of serious illusions) are considered psychotic—and obviously unhealthy. Minor distortions of reality (e.g., defense mechanisms) have traditionally been considered neurotic (Taylor & Brown, 1988). One traditional goal of psychotherapy for the defense-generated neuroses has been to expose and dismantle individuals' defensive perceptions. Consider an example of rationalization—a person wants a particular job, does not get it, and then tells him- or herself that the job was inferior anyway. It used to be considered a healthy goal to help such a person to acknowledge his or her repressed feelings of disappointment and hurt from the rejection rather than cover them up.

Recently there has been among many professional therapists a subtle shift in attitudes about defense mechanisms and illusions (see Snyder, 1988; Taylor & Brown, 1988). The new thinking is that the *moderate* and *temporary* use of defense mechanisms and illusions often can be psychologically beneficial and, therefore, "healthy" for many individuals. Adaptive illusions, according to Taylor and Brown (1988), include overly positive self perceptions and exaggerated perceptions of personal control over situations.

To some extent the intervention of cognitive restructuring can be viewed as "training" in how to use defense mechanisms and illusions effectively or to reinterpret events or experiences more positively (e.g., Beck, 1976). In the rationalization example above, if the person was depressed about the job rejection, a cognitive therapist might likely try to help him or her "reframe" the experience so that it becomes a less disappointing, even a positive one. The chosen reinterpretation may be something like, "There will be other jobs and I can learn from this experience." Whether this is considered rationalization or adaptive cognitive restructuring, this kind of reinterpretation is generally regarded as healthy these days.

The defense mechanism of denial (as long as it is not in extreme or long-term form) can also serve as a health-preserving buffer. When many people receive news of a serious medical diagnosis for themselves, their first reaction is often numbness or an inability to fully grasp the implications of the diagnosis. This is a mild form of denial and it can protect the individual from reacting in an impulsive and possibly dangerous way (e.g., suicide). Psychologically healthy individuals may first use this type of mild denial and then gradually emerge from the denial as they properly adjust and adapt to the new situation.

An optimistic viewpoint correlates with positive mood and subjective well-being (see Bandura, 1986; Diener, 1984). From a sociobiological perspective, Tiger (1979) has argued that survival favors the optimist. In primitive times the optimistic hunter was more likely than the pessimistic hunter to continue the hunt. And long hunts tend to yield more success than short hunts. Thus, optimism, like positive self-efficacy, tends to result in better outcomes for the individual.

In summary, psychologically healthy individuals usually perceive reality clearly, but with a slight bias toward optimism. They view themselves, their potentials, and their futures in a positive light. Occasionally they will use defense mechanisms to cope with acute crisis situations. Their defensive responses will be mild and short-lived, however.

Courage and Resilience

Psychologically healthy individuals find the courage to confront their own fears, accept responsibility (or lack of it) for their behavior, and are prepared to take risks when it is reasonable to do so. They adapt to new situations and "bounce back" after crises and setbacks.

Franklin Roosevelt once said that all we have to fear is fear itself. This idea sums up an underlying principle found within all of the major psychotherapeutic theories about fear and fear reduction—fear is finally overcome only after it is confronted directly. From the psychodynamic perspective, the goal is to uncover and confront the psychic source(s) of one's fears (Hall & Lindsey, 1985). When the sources of the anxieties are re-experienced and examined in the "light of consciousness," they tend to lose their power to paralyze or imprison the person. The cognitive–behavioral interventions for overcoming fears and phobias (e.g., systematic desensitization, flooding, participant modeling) all involve helping the person eventually to confront the feared stimulus. If the feared stimulus is confronted repeatedly and no aversive consequences occur, then the fear is reduced or extinguished. So the key to overcoming fear starts with the person finding the courage and determination to confront his or her fears.

Among the greatest of human fears, according to existentialist and humanistic psychologists (see Hall & Lindzey, 1985), is the fear of responsibility. We are responsible for much of what happens to us—responsible for our successes and failures, and our actions and our choices not to act. The fear is rooted in the possibility that we may fail to live up to our potential and "waste" our opportunity. Being healthy may involve accepting that responsibility. Maslow's paragon of psychological health—the self-actualized person—does accept the personal responsibility and guilt (when it is deserved), admits mistakes, and learns from those mistakes.

Living is a risky business. Psychologically healthy individuals understand and accept that reality. They are also prepared to take additional risks on occasion. Kinnier and Metha (1989) found that the life regret of "I should have taken more risks in my life" was quite common and discriminated between those who were most and least satisfied with how they had lived their lives—more of the least satisfied cited that regret. And 44 percent of the 11,000 women that Kagan (1985) interviewed said that "taking risks" was very important for their own career success.

In a life where danger and risk abound, failures, crises, and setbacks are inevitable. Psychologically healthy individuals accept this reality. They have become adept at adapting to new challenging situations and have learned how to "bounce back" from setbacks (Bandura, 1989). Kobasa, Maddi, and Kahn (1982) identified the constellation trait of "hardiness" that seems to be associated with survival, adjustment, and adaptation. The "hardy" individual, according to Kobasa et al. (1982), typically is optimistic, self-confident, purposeful, and tends to reframe crises as challenges to be overcome.

In summary, psychologically healthy individuals courageously confront their fears and accept their responsibility. They are prepared to take risks when appropriate. They accept setbacks and failures as part of life and, as the popular song says, after a fall they "pick themselves up, dust themselves off, and start all over again."

Balance and Moderation

Psychologically healthy individuals live "balanced" lives—they work *and* play, laugh *and* cry; they are selfish *and* altruistic, logical *and* intuitive. They are rarely extremists, fanatics, or gluttons. They don't "put all their eggs in one basket" and they rarely do anything in excess (e.g., work, eat, sleep, etc.)

This theme of "balance and moderation" emerged within the criteria discussed earlier: The healthy person loves him- or herself—but not too much; is self-knowledgeable—but not self-obsessed; is autonomous—but not a loner; is assertive—but not obnoxious.

The ancient Greek philosophers extolled the virtues of balance and moderation. For example, Aristotle believed that the wisest choice was often located somewhere near the mean of the two opposing options or positions. In this century, Maslow (1971) prescribed that individuals should seek to integrate their opposing needs (i.e., compromise rather than choose an extreme). Aristotle and Maslow implied that the wisest and healthiest among us would, as a rule, seek resolutions or life policies that balance the pull of our opposing values or needs. Kinnier (1984) found some support for this notion—individuals who resolved their conflicts by seeking a "middle course" were more satisfied with their choices than those who chose one extreme of their "splits."

Balance is a recurring theme in the literature. Freud (cited in Hall & Lindzey, 1985) recognized that individuals seek a balance between satisfying their instinctual desires and societal demands. He also advocated the reduction, not elimination, of tension within individuals. Jung's writings are replete with the theme of balance. He advocated that the individual seek balance and integration—between the physical and spiritual realms, between the conscious and unconscious levels, and between male and female traits (i.e., anima and animus). Gilligan (1982) prescribed that both men and women should attempt to balance their affiliative and achievement needs.

Extremism or immoderation is generally considered a symptom of pathology. Immoderation in activities like eating, drinking, gambling, or working is often referred to as an unhealthy addiction. Even the behaviors that are normally seen as health promoting (such as physical exercise) can become dangerous activities when done in excess.

In summary, psychologically healthy individuals are balanced, grounded, and exercise moderation in most endeavors. They are not one-sided, extremist, or gluttonous.

Love of Others

Psychologically healthy individuals love at least one person besides themselves. They have the capacity and desire to care deeply about the welfare of another person, persons, and/or humanity in general. Or to paraphrase Barbra Streisand, people who need people are the psychologically healthiest people in the world.

It is widely believed by mental health professionals across different theoretical orientations (and apparently by Barbra Streisand also) that the need to belong to a group or family, the capacity to love, and the desire to become close to another person or persons are prerequisites for psychological health (e.g., see Adler, 1978; Allport, 1961; Erikson, 1968; Freud, 1930; Fromm, 1955; Jahoda, 1958; Maslow, 1970).

Sullivan (1953) believed that individuals could only be understood as social creatures, and Erikson's (1968) psychosocial stages of development similarly emphasize the importance of social relationships for all individuals. Within Erikson's framework, the child first judges whether others can be trusted. As a young adult, the person searches for an intimate relationship. As an older adult, the primary social roles are usually parent, grandparent, and/or mentor. Maslow's (1970) description of the self-actualized person and Adler's (cited in Hall & Lindzey, 1985) construct of "social interest" emphasize that caring about others is one of the most important and fulfilling aspects of life.

One of the greatest fears that people have is the fear of being alone (see Holmes & Rahe, 1967). And in surveys that ask individuals to list the most important things in their lives, "love," "romance," "family," and "friends" consistently are at the top of those lists (e.g., Campbell, 1981; Cantril, 1965; Flanagan, 1978; Klinger, 1977). These are not only considered important, but are also clearly linked to subjective well-being (see Diener, 1984).

In summary, psychologically healthy individuals can and do want to love and care about others. They need others and are intimate with at least one other person.

Love of Life

Psychologically healthy individuals truly appreciate and enjoy various aspects of life. They are generally active, curious, and enthusiastic. They don't take themselves too seriously and appreciate the humorous view of life. They are open to new experiences, are often spontaneous, and do take time to "smell the roses." They tend to view life as an opportunity—an opportunity to learn, to grow, and to share with others.

Much of the above is a paraphrase of Maslow's (1967; 1970) description of the self-actualized person. Maslow and others (e.g., Allport, 1961; Fromm, 1955; Jung, 1954) have promoted the psychological benefits of humor, spontaneity, and openness. These traits have also been associated with the more frequent occurrence of peak experiences (see Maslow, 1967; Noble, 1987). Peak experiences are often joyful, inspiring, and typically spiritual in nature. Such experiences are not uncommon for those who have been close to death. In interviewing hundreds of people who had experienced "near death" (i.e., were clinically dead for a short period), Ring (1984) discovered recurrent themes: Most of those who had "died" described the experience as exhilarating and clarifying. They became more appreciative of life, more spontaneous, relaxed, and compassionate toward others. Perhaps their dramatic experiences should be instructive to the rest of us about what may matter most in life.

In summary, psychologically healthy individuals are openminded, somewhat adventurous (though not reckless), and curious. They usually feel relaxed and don't take themselves too seriously. They like to laugh. They are continually growing, learning, and appreciating others and the mysteries in life.

Purpose in Life

Psychologically healthy individuals have found meaning and purpose in their lives. They are committed to something outside of themselves.

I have saved this criterion for last because I believe it is the *crème de la crème* of the criteria. Many writers have emphasized the importance of individuals attaining a sense of meaning and purpose in their lives (e.g., Adler, 1930; Allport, 1961; Erikson, 1959; Frankl, 1959; Fromm, 1955; Klinger, 1977; Maslow, 1959; Rogers, 1961). The humanistic psychologists have paid particular attention to this issue. While they acknowledge the importance of the individual's basic psychological needs of safety, self-esteem, and connectedness with others, they view the individual's quest for meaning or purpose in life as a universal need and the crowning prerequisite for self-actualization.

A lack of meaning in an individual's life has often been implicated in psychological dysfunction (Maslow, 1959) and even in the tragic act of suicide (Lifton, 1979). Conversely, Frankl's (1959) accounts of concentration camp survivors suggest that human beings can endure the most horrible conditions if they possess a clear sense of meaning or purpose in their lives. Frankl (1959) was fond of paraphrasing Nietzsche's belief that, "he who has a *why* to live can bear with almost any *how*" (p. xi).

What is meaningful? The humanistic psychologists are quick to stress that each individual must search for and discover that for him- or herself. The humanistic writers also warn that the search for meaning can be frustrating and depressing at times, but as Frankl (1959) consoled, the need to find meaning and the (sometime) agony of the search are not symptoms of illness but of the human condition.

Among the most meaningful aspects of life for many people are work or career, love, family, and a spiritual perspective (see Kinnier & Freitag, 1990). While variation exists between individuals, the important thing, according to Seligman (cited in Buie, 1988), is that individuals find something that is outside of themselves to invest with meaning or purpose—be it a cause, a set of principles, other people, or God. As George Bernard Shaw (1903) so eloquently exclaimed,

> This is the true joy in life, the being used for a purpose, recognized by yourself as a mighty one; the being thoroughly worn out before you are thrown on the scrap heap; the being a force of Nature instead of a feverish selfish little clod of ailments and grievances complaining that the world will not devote itself to making you happy (p. xxxi).

THE MISGUIDED PURSUIT OF HAPPINESS

Being happy is *not* one of the criteria of psychological health. And, as has been reiterated by countless therapists over the decades, the goal of therapy is health, not happiness. But because the general public often tends to equate psychological health with happiness, in this section I would like to examine what the literature says about the nature of happiness.

In a review on happiness written over 20 years ago, Wilson (1967) formulated a general profile of the "happy" person. Such a person, according to Wilson, is most likely young, physically healthy, self-confident, well-educated, well-paid, extroverted, worry-free, religious, married, satisfied at work, and would have modest aspirations. Diener's updated review (1984) suggests that these variables correlate (but only moderately) with subjective well-being. For example, on average, wealthy persons tend to be slightly happier than poor persons, but many wealthy people describe themselves as unhappy and many poor people consider themselves to be happy (Campbell, 1981).

In general, much of the research on subjective well-being seems to support the popular idea that happiness is elusive. For example, Diener (1984) pointed out that while involuntary unemployment is clearly associated with unhappiness, satisfaction with one's work correlates only moderately. While marital and family satisfaction are strong predictors of subjective well-being, children often have a negative effect on marital satisfaction. And although many couples believe that having children is a prerequisite for fulfillment, voluntarily childless couples do not appear to be less happy than couples with children (see Veevers, 1980). Good health, though a strong predictor of life satisfaction for the elderly (Larson, 1978), is a weak predictor for younger persons (Diener, 1984).

The empirical research suggests that individuals who believe, "If only I get 'X', I will be happy," are usually wrong. The great theoreticians of human behavior, including Freud (1930), Frankl (1959), and Maslow (1962), believed that human beings were destined to disappointment if they ever hoped to attain a state of permanent contentment during their lives. According to them, fulfilled needs and accomplishments are inevitably replaced by new needs and goals. In Maslovian terms, human beings are perpetually "becoming" or striving.

Several theories are useful for explaining how happiness typically eludes those who pursue it. Perhaps the best known is adaptation-level theory (see Brickman, Coates, & Janoff-Bulman, 1978; Helson, 1964). This theory predicts that the effects of positive and negative events and situations such as poverty, wealth, sickness, and health "wear off" over time. As Klinger (1977) described it,

> Romantic love notoriously cools if it ripens into a close open relationship. Prestige, power, and fame pall with time. People envied because they lead 'the sweet life' or because they are celebrities nevertheless become bored (p. 116).

In support of this phenomenon, Brickman et al. (1978) found that state lottery winners were not happier than others after a period of time. Individuals habituate to their changing situations and eventually tend to "regress" to their previous levels of happiness.

Social comparison also is a dynamic that moderates the individual's perception of being happy or unhappy (see Diener, 1984). Individuals tend to judge their situations regarding wealth, health, prestige, and the like with their peers—and individuals' peer groups change as their environments change. For example, Cantril (1965) found that while disease and premature death are more prevalent in India than in America, more Americans than Indians expressed concern or worry about their health. Similarly, relatively wealthier Americans were just as concerned about their economic situations as were Indians. It was in this sense that Tiger (1979) referred to prosperity as meaning, not "enough," but "more."

Perhaps a lesson to be learned from the research and theories on subjective well-being or happiness is that the search for happiness "out there" (e.g., money, career success, the perfect mate, family, etc.) is misguided because expectations usually exceed reality. The achievement of goals can potentially become a series of disappointments. This is what Oscar Wilde (1908) was referring to when he suggested that there were two tragedies in life—not getting what one wanted and getting it. He felt that getting what one wanted was the real tragedy. While Oscar Wilde may have overstated the case for poetic impact, the psychological literature suggests that individuals would be wise to have modest expectations and not pursue happiness as a goal in life. As Frankl (1967) warned,

> ...'pursuit of happiness' amounts to a self contradiction: the more we strive for happiness the less we attain it. Peace of mind also must content itself with being a side effect, for it is self-destroying as an intention (p. 41).

CONCLUSION

In summary, psychologically healthy individuals tend not to pursue happiness actively. They know themselves well, love (but are not infatuated with) themselves, and are reasonably self-confident. They are autonomous and self-sufficient but also love and care about others. They confront their fears directly and accept reality as it is (with perhaps a slight bias toward being optimistic). They accept responsibility for their actions, take reasonable risks on occasion, adapt to new situations fairly quickly, and "bounce back" after crises or setbacks. They truly appreciate and enjoy various aspects of life and often act spontaneously. They seek balance (e.g., some work, some play) and typically maintain a lifestyle of moderation. Finally, they honestly seek and find at least some meaning or purpose in their existence that extends beyond self-preservation and self-gratification—they believe in something greater than themselves.

It is clear that these criteria are interdependent. According to Horney (1950), many psychological problems consist of "vicious circles" whereby interdependency if the key dynamic. An example that Horney used was that if people are not loved, they often will experience low self-esteem, which often leads to "acting-out" or antisocial behavior. Those who are antisocial are rarely loved . . . and so on.

One can think of numerous interdependency dynamics of the criteria described in this chapter. The following are a few. Those who are self-confident and optimistic are more likely to persist in their efforts to achieve their goals. Persistence, more often than the lack of persistence, results in success. The experience of success reinforces self-confidence and optimism, which reinforces persistence. . . . Those who love themselves too little or too much are less likely to establish quality relationships. For those who love themselves too little, the absence of a good relationship can confirm their low self-esteem, i.e., "Nobody loves me, therefore I am probably worthless." For those who love themselves too much, they may need to distort reality significantly in order to explain their social isolation while "saving face," e.g., tell themselves, "People are intimidated by my incredible intellect." Their distorted (and perhaps repugnant) perceptions of themselves and the world may well further alienate others.

The relationship between the criteria is synergistic. For full psychological health, all must operate "in sync" within the "system" of criteria. A similar situation appears to exist between the physical and psychological spheres within individuals. The body and the mind (or the physical and psychological) are not separate realms or entities; rather, they function synergistically within the individual. A biologic event like the flu affects the person's emotional state, and a primarily psychosocial event like being rejected can cause a somatic reaction (e.g., indigestion). In this chapter I chose to focus exclusively on criteria of psychological health. This was done because of space constraints and was not meant to imply that the mind and body are dichotomous entities. For a recent discussion on the broader psycho-physio-sociologic aspects of health, see Seeman (1989).

As I indicated in the introduction, the nine criteria I listed are far from "universal," complete, or perhaps even valid. Basically, this list represents my inevitably biased review of the literature and informal extraction of criteria that seem relevant to North American culture during the late twentieth century. I would hope that this chapter might prompt other researchers to undertake a more formal project for identifying the central criteria for psychological/physical health. Such a project should employ more formal research methods, such as using expert judge ratings for selecting, clarifying, and perhaps weighting the criteria. It would be especially useful and interesting if the same project was undertaken within different cultures and repeated over time. That would allow us to discover how relative or universal health criteria are.

I would like to conclude by presenting one more rationale for the endeavor of identifying the criteria of psychological health. In contemporary society, the medical and allied professions have established criteria or prescriptions for physical health (as opposed to treatments for illness). For example, the suggestions to exercise regularly and to eat more fiber are commonly heard prescriptions for promoting physical health. Perhaps mental health professionals could make a more powerful impact on problem prevention if they too began publicly advocating specific psychologically healthy attitudes and goals rather than primarily focusing on the elimination of negative attitudes and behaviors.

REFERENCES

Adler, A. (1930). Individual psychology. In C. Murchison (Ed.), *Psychologies of 1930*. Worcester, MA: Clark University Press.

Adler, A. (1978). Cooperation between the sexes. In H. L. Ansbacher & R. R. Ansbacher (Eds.), *Writings on women, love, and marriage, sexuality and its disorders*. Garden City, NY: Doubleday.

Allport, G. W. (1961). *Pattern and growth in personality*. New York: Holt, Rinehart & Winston.

Bandura, A. (1977). *Social learning theory*. Englewood Cliffs, NJ: Prentice-Hall.

Bandura, A. (1986). *Social foundations of thought and action: A social cognitive theory*. Englewood Cliffs, NJ: Prentice-Hall.

Bandura, A. (1989). Human agency in social cognitive theory. *American Psychologist, 44*, 1175–1184.

Baumeister, R. F. (1988, August). *The problem of life's meaning*. Paper presented at the annual convention of the American Psychological Association.

Beck, A. (1976). *Cognitive therapy and emotional disorders*. New York: International Universities Press.

Brickman, P., Coates, D., & Janoff-Bulman, R. (1978). Lottery winners and accident victims: Is happiness relative? *Journal of Personality and Social Psychology, 36*, 917–927.

Buie, J. (1988, October). "Me" decades generate depression. *APA Monitor*, p. 18.

Campbell, A. (1981). *The sense of well-being in America.* New York: McGraw-Hill.

Cantril, H. (1965). *The patterns of human concerns.* New Brunswick, NJ: Rutgers University Press.

Diener, E. (1984). Subjective well-being. *Psychological Bulletin, 95,* 542–575.

Erikson, E. H. (1959). *Identity and the life cycle. Psychological Issues, 1,* 18–164.

Erikson, E. H. (1963). *Childhood and society* (2nd ed.). New York: W. W. Norton

Erikson, E. H. (1968). *Identity: Youth and crisis.* New York: W. W. Norton.

Flanagan, J. C. (1978). A research approach for improving our quality of life. *American Psychologist, 33,* 138–147.

Frankl, V. E. (1959). *Man's search for meaning: An introduction to logotherapy.* New York: Simon & Schuster.

Frankl, V. E. (1967). *Psychotherapy and existentialism.* New York: Simon & Schuster.

Freud, S. (1930). *Civilization and its discontents.* (J. Strachey, trans. & Ed.). New York: W. W. Norton.

Fromm, E. (1955). *The sane society.* New York: Rinehart.

Gilligan, C. (1982). *In a different voice.* Cambridge, MA: Harvard University Press.

Hall, C. S., & Lindzey, G. (1985). *Introduction to theories of personality.* New York: John Wiley.

Helson, H. (1964). *Adaptation-level theory.* New York: Harper & Row.

Holmes, T. H., & Rahe, R. H. (1967). The Social Readjustment Rating Scale. *Journal of Psychosomatic Research, 11,* 213–218.

Horney, K. (1950). *Neurosis and human growth.* New York: W. W. Norton

Jahoda, M. (1958). *Current concepts of positive mental health.* New York: Basic Books

Jung, C. G. (1954). *The development of personality.* Princeton, NJ: Princeton University Press.

Kagan, J. (1985, October). Who succeeds, who doesn't?: Results of a major survey. *Working Woman,* pp. 113–117, 154–156.

Kinnier, R. T. (1984). Choosing the mean versus an extreme resolution for intrapersonal values conflicts: Is the mean usually more golden? *Counseling and Values, 28,* 207–212.

Kinnier, R. T., & Freitag, E. T. (1990). The best things in life. *Guidance and Counselling.*

Kinnier, R. T., & Metha, A. T. (1989). Regrets and priorities at three stages of life. *Counseling and Values, 33,* 182–193.

Klinger, E. (1977). *Meaning and void.* Minneapolis, MN: University of Minnesota Press.

Kobasa, S. C., Maddi, S. R., & Kahn, S. (1982). Hardiness and health: A prospective study. *Journal of Personality and Social Psychology, 42,* 168–177.

Larson, R. (1978). Thirty years of research on the subjective well-being of older Americans. *Journal of Gerontology, 33,* 109–125.

Lifton, R. J. (1979). *The broken connection.* New York: Simon & Schuster.

Mahoney, M. J. & Thoresen, C. E. (1974). *Self-control: Power to the person.* Monterey, CA: Brooks/Cole.

Maslow, A. H. (Ed.). (1959). *New knowledge in human values.* New York: Harper & Brothers.

Maslow, A. H. (Ed.) (1962). *Toward a psychology of being.* Princeton, NJ: Van Nostrand

Maslow, A. H. (1967). Neurosis as a failure of personal growth. *Humanitas, 3,* 153–170.

Maslow, A. H. (1970). *Motivation and personality* (2nd ed.). New York: Harper & Brothers.

Maslow, A. N. (1971). *The farther reaches of human nature.* New York: The Viking Press.

Newcomb, M. D., & Bentler, P. M. (1989). Substance use and abuse among children and teenagers. *American Psychologist, 44,* 242–248.

Noble, K. D. (1987). Psychological health and the experience of transcendence. *The Counseling Psychologist,* 15, 601–614.

Osipow, S. H. (1983). *Theories of career development* (3rd ed.). Englewood Cliffs, NJ: Prentice-Hall.

Peterson, C., & Seligman, M. E. P. (1984). Causal explanations as a risk factor for depression: Theory and evidence. *Psychological Review, 91,* 347–374.

Ring, K. (1984). *Heading toward Omega: In search of the meaning of the near-death experience.* New York: Quill.

Rogers, C. R. (1961). *On becoming a person.* Boston: Houghton-Mifflin.

Seeman, J. (1989). Toward a model of positive mental health. *American Psychologist, 44,* 1099–1109.

Shaw, G. B. (1903). *Man and superman.* London: Constable & Company, Ltd.

Snyder, C. R. (1988, August). *Self-illusions: When are they adaptive?* Symposium conducted at the 96th annual meeting of the American Psychological Association, Atlanta, GA.

Stoller, R. J., Marmor, J., & Bieber, R. (1973). A symposium: Should homosexuality be in the APA nomenclature? *American Journal of Psychiatry, 130,* 1207–1216.

Sullivan, H. S. (1953). *The interpersonal theory of psychiatry.* New York: W. W. Norton.

Taylor, S. E., & Brown, J. D. (1988). Illusion and well-being: A social psychological perspective on mental health. *Psychological Bulletin, 103,* 193–210.

Tiger, L. (1979). *Optimism: The biology of hope.* New York: Simon & Schuster.

Veevers, J. E. (1980). *Childless by choice.* Toronto: Butterworths.

Wilde, O. (1908). *Lady Windermere's fan.* London: Methuen.

Wilson, W. (1967). Correlates of avowed happiness. *Psychological Bulletin, 67,* 294–306.

3.

The Helping Relationship

ART TERRY, PH.D.
CAROL A. BURDEN, ED.D.
MARGARET M. PEDERSEN, M.B.A., M.S.
Portland State University
Portland, Oregon

MOST PEOPLE FIND THEMSELVES engaged in some type of helping relationship nearly every day. Some helping occurs informally while other helping happens in a more formal way. Friends and family usually help one another in a reciprocal, informal way while helping professionals such as counselors, psychologists, or social workers help their clients within a formal, unidirectional relationship. In a friendship, people share concerns and give each other information and advice. Professional helping, on the other hand, places much more responsibility on the helper, who must strive to be objective and helpful in more directed, purposeful ways. The professional helping relationship is unique in that an independent, mature, more fully functioning individual emerges from a dependent, interactive helping relationship.

This chapter focuses on the characteristics, knowledge, and skills needed by the counselor to build effective counselor–client helping relationships. The first section describes the helping relationship and the following section reviews what research has shown to be the characteristics of effective counselors. The skills needed to be a good helper or counselor are discussed in the rest of the chapter. Throughout the skills sections, you will find examples taken from conversations between a counselor and client; we have added these examples to demonstrate more clearly specific techniques you might use when working with clients. A description of the case from which these excerpts were drawn can be found on page 47.

As you read through this chapter, try to look at yourself and see how closely you fit the description of an effective counselor.

WHAT IS THE HELPING RELATIONSHIP?

In the helping relationship, individuals work together to resolve a concern or difficulty and/or foster the personal growth and development of one of the two people. Rogers (1961) defined a helping relationship as one "in which at least one of the parties has the intent of promoting the growth, development, maturity, improved functioning and improved coping with life of the other [party]" (p. 39). The goals of any counselor–client relationship, whether in educational, career, or personal counseling, can be put into four basic goal areas: changes in behavior and lifestyle, increased awareness or insight and understanding, relief from suffering, or changes in thoughts and self-perceptions (Brammer, 1988).

An important aspect of the helping relationship is that it is a process that enables a person to grow in directions chosen by that person. It is the counselor's job to make the client aware of possible alternatives and encourage client acceptance of responsibility for taking action on one or more of these alternatives.

The helping relationship minimally can be broken down into two phases—that of relationship building and that of facilitating positive action. In the first phase, the goal is to build a foundation of mutual trust. Once that trust is established, the helper, in the second phase, facilitates client actions that will lead toward client growth and development.

Most helping occurs on a one-to-one basis, and studies of quality one-to-one relationships have shown that it is the attitudes and feelings of the counselor, rather than the theoretical orientation, that are important. Procedures and techniques are much less important than the counselor's attitudes and beliefs. It is important to understand that it is the way in which the counselor's attitudes and procedures are perceived that makes a difference to the client, and it is the client's perception that is crucial to a good helping relationship (Rogers, 1961).

The ultimate goal of a professional helping relationship should be to promote the development of and more appropriate behavior from the client. The specific goals for a given client are determined collaboratively by the counselor and the client as they interact in the helping relationship. In the next section we will examine the characteristics of individuals who serve as these effective competent counselors.

WHAT ARE THE CHARACTERISTICS OF EFFECTIVE COUNSELORS?

Effective counselors have specific personal qualities and are able to convey those qualities to the people they help. There is an increasing amount of evidence supporting the concept that helpers are only as effective as they are self-aware and able to use themselves as vehicles of change (Okun, 1987). As you read through this section, you might think about each quality or trait and see how it fits for you.

Combs (1986) summarized 13 studies that looked at helpers in a variety of settings. These studies supported the view that there are differences in the beliefs of effective and ineffective person-centered helpers. Effective counselors are interested in and committed to an understanding of the specialized knowledge of the field and find it personally meaningful. They also believe that the people they help are capable, adequate, trustworthy, dependable, and friendly. Effective counselors focus on positive self-beliefs and have confidence in themselves, their abilities, and their worth. They like people and have a feeling of oneness with others. Effective counselors use interventions that focus on the individual's perception of self and expand the individual's view of life rather than narrowing it. They are committed to freeing rather than controlling the client and are able to be objectively involved with, rather than alienated from, their clients.

The term "self-actualized" has been used by Patterson (1974) to describe a constellation of characteristics that effective counselors possess. Aware and accepting of self, they are individuals who are likewise aware of their environment and interact with it in a reality oriented way. In living, they are open to a full range of experiences and feelings, are spontaneous, and have a sense of humor. When interacting with others, they are able to be involved, yet remain somewhat detached (Cormier & Cormier, 1985). They are empathic, compassionate, and believing of the client's world. In the process of dealing with problems and issues, they are able to help clients clearly see their own worlds while adding a fresh perspective to the issues. Trusted by others, these individuals are authentic (Pietrofesa et al., 1978), trustworthy (Strong, 1968), and ethical individuals.

Counseling is demanding work, and effective counselors have high energy levels (Carkhuff, 1986). Intense focusing with another individual, trying to hear clearly, often needing to tolerate ambiguity (Piertrofesa et al., 1978), and taking appropriate risks can put heavy demands on the counselor's energy.

Rogers (1958) identified four conditions that he believed all counselors should possess. These necessary, but not necessarily sufficient, core conditions were (1) unconditional positive regard for the individual, (2) genuineness, (3) congruence, and (4) empathy. Later, Carkhuff and Berenson (1967) added two additional traits or skills to the list: respect and concreteness. Thirteen years later, Ivey and Simek-Downing (1980) labeled these traits communications skills, and added warmth, immediacy, and confrontation to the list.

The following sections on helping skills are intended to help you gain a better understanding of the traits and skills needed to be an effective counselor.

CASE STUDY

On the intake form, Lisa described herself as 33 and married with three children. She came to counseling because she was feeling desperate and needed to talk her problem over with someone. She'd lived a lie for many years and now she was certain she would get caught. Her husband, Peter, was to come to counseling with her, but backed out at the last minute, hoping that she wouldn't go either.

Peter and Lisa first met when they lived in California; she worked as a waitress in a restaurant where he often came to eat. They started dating, and it wasn't long until they were serious about each other. In Lisa's view, the only obstacle to their marriage was that he was not yet divorced. Peter told her that it would take time but there was no question that he would get a divorce.

They talked about what it would be like to be together. She was such a contrast to his former wife, who he said was really crazy. One day he happened to mention that he had two kids—a boy and a girl. They were with his wife, but he'd like to get them before they became crazy too. Soon they were talking about all living together; she would take care of the kids until the divorce was final. This sounded wonderful to Lisa, since she didn't want to be a waitress all her life.

Peter, Lisa, and the children had been living together for 3 years when they moved to the Chicago area. Peter was tired of his current job and had heard that there were great opportunities there. When they got there, the only work he found that paid a decent wage was that of night watchman at a big plant. He liked the title of "security officer" but really didn't like working nights. This turned out to be a very difficult time for Lisa because she found out that she was pregnant and she had to keep the kids quiet during the day while Peter slept.

When she came to counseling, Lisa's most immediate concern was that they had just purchased a house, representing themselves as husband and wife. At the time she wasn't worried because she knew that they would soon be married. But several weeks later, she proposed to Peter that they now should legalize their relationship, especially since they had a two-year-old daughter. Lisa was absolutely appalled when he told her that he had never initiated any divorce action.

As time went on, Lisa became more aware of problems in their relationship. Peter drank too much and became more demanding and threatening. He had hit her only once, but his attitude and the gun he carried made her feel very intimidated and threatened. She didn't want to stay with him, but she had no place else to go.

She was concerned about leaving him because of the children. If she took only their daughter, what might happen to the other two children? She'd grown to love them, but didn't want to be accused of kidnapping. She also wasn't certain that she could support herself, let alone three more!

The intimidation and verbal abuse by her husband escalated, as did the drinking. He forbid her to go to counseling. She knew she must leave him, but didn't know where to go.

EPILOGUE

With the counselor's help, Lisa explored the alternatives available to her. She called legal aid for advice about the children. One evening, he became extremely physically abusive with her and she had to call the police to restrain him. The next day Lisa took the children and moved into a "safe house."

BASIC SKILLS

According to Ivey (1988), the aim of counseling is personal and social development. He has described a hierarchy of microcounseling skills that define what the counselor does in an interview to achieve specific results. Ivey's hierarchy rests on a foundation of attending behavior and basic listening skills. Our list of skills is based on Ivey's model with additional information taken from Ivey, Ivey, and Simek-Downing (1987), Cormier and Cormier (1985), and Pietrofesa, Hoffman, and Splete (1984).

Attending Skills

Attending behavior, including eye contact, body language, vocal quality, and verbal tracking, is one of the most powerful communication skills. In the counseling relationship, counselors communicate through body language and words that their complete attention is on the client's nonverbal and verbal behaviors. Eye contact, facial expressions, and body posture are the physical fundamentals that indicate to others that you are either carefully attending or not attending to them.

Eye Contact
Good eye contact is not an unwavering stare, but a gaze that is maintained with attention to cultural differences. It tells the other person that you are interested in them and what they have to say. Effective mutual gazing occurs more frequently when there is greater physical distance between counselor and client, when comfortable, less personal topics are being discussed, when neither person is trying to hide something, when there is adequate rapport between counselor and client, when one is listening rather than talking, and when both people are from cultures that emphasize rather than sanction visual contacts in interaction.

Attentive Body Language
Body orientation can encourage or discourage interpersonal interactions. In our culture, a slight forward body lean and a relaxed, comfortable posture are usually received favorably and indicate interest in the client. This relaxed posture should be active enough to let the other person know that the counselor is listening with interest. Egan (1982) uses the acronym *SOLER* to describe this attentive body posture. The letters stand for *S*quarely—face the client, *O*pen—body posture, *L*ean—forward slightly, *E*ye—contact, and *R*elaxed—manner.

Distance

The distance between counselor and client also affects communication. There is an optimal "comfort zone" for conversing that is largely controlled by cultural influences. It is about an arm's length in American culture. It is imperative that the counselor be aware of the level of comfort or discomfort that the client is experiencing with the distance and adjust it if necessary.

The distance between counselor and client may become so close that it involves *touch*. Humanistic models suggest that touch that is genuinely felt may help create within the client a willingness to be open and share. Recently, Driscoll, Newman, and Seals (1988) found that college students observing videotapes felt that counselors who touched their college-age clients were more caring than counselors who did not. Suiter and Goodyear (1985) found that counselors who used a semi-embrace with clients were seen as less trustworthy than counselors who either did not touch, or only touched their clients' hands or shoulders. There was also greater acceptability of touch when it was initiated by female counselors. It must be emphasized, though, that touch without genuine feeling behind it may be more harmful than helpful. The type of touch that is generally considered acceptable is one that is long enough (1–3 seconds) to make contact yet does not create uncomfortable feelings. Most professionals who do touch believe that appropriate touching is contact of the counselor's hand or forearm with the client's hand, arm, shoulder, or upper back.

While there are many things counselors can do to convey an interest in their clients, there are certain mannerisms that are distracting. Behaviors such as gum chewing, cigarette smoking, or continual change of body position may seriously affect any interpersonal interaction and convey a sense of disinterest.

Vocal Tone

Another aspect of attending behavior is voice tone. A warm, pleasant, caring voice strongly indicates an interest and willingness to listen to the client. The pitch, volume, and rate of speech can convey much of the feeling that one has toward another person or situation. Scherer (1986) has shown that the use of specific paralinguistic cues can convey either high or low levels of self-confidence. A stiff, loud voice with a quick rhythm conveys self-confidence, while a soft, quiet voice with lower tone, slow rhythm, and some hesitations conveys a lower level of self-confidence. These cues of self-confidence can affect client perceptions of counselor expertness, attractiveness, trustworthiness, and associated satisfaction with the counseling relationship (Barak, Shapira, & Fisher, 1988).

Verbal Tracking

Even when the client engages in long irrelevant discourses, the counselor needs to remain relaxed and follow the client's topic and logic. The counselor can choose to either attend or ignore certain portions of client statements—this is termed **selective attention**. The portions of the client statements to which a counselor attends depends upon the counselor's professional orientation and beliefs. It is imperative that counselors be aware of their own patterns of selective attention, for the topics their clients discuss will tend to be partially determined by the topics to which they unconsciously attend.

Silence is another important part of verbal attending behavior. The counselor's ability to remain silent while clients are silent forces clients to listen to themselves and/or the counselor more carefully. Remaining silent is often an excellent tactic to start a reluctant client talking because silence is perceived by nearly everyone as a demanding condition that must be filled with a response. The challenge for beginning counselors is learning to be comfortable enough with silence to use it effectively.

The Basic Listening Skills

The basic listening skills include client observation; the use of open and closed questions; the use of encouraging, paraphrasing, and summarization statements; and reflection of client feelings.

Client Observation

Simply observing the client provides the counselor with a rich source of "silent information." Noticing and paying attention to the **physiological cues** expressed in another person's appearance and physique provides a way to identify the internal emotional responses of the other person. Bandler and Grinder (1979) have identified four cues—changes in skin color, lip size, muscle tone, and/or breathing—that reflect the internal emotional processes and the physiologic changes occurring within the client. These physiologic messages are difficult to hide because they are generally involuntary reactions of the autonomic nervous system. Observing subtle changes in these areas can silently reveal the moments of emotional change for a client.

The points during the interview at which eye contact is broken, the voice changes, skin color changes, shifts in body posture occur, or changes in muscle tension or facial expression take place may indicate the time at which important information is being revealed. Observations of discrepancies between nonverbal behavior and what is being said should be checked out with the client by the use of such questions as "Are you aware that you are smiling as you talk about the sadness you feel?"

In smoothly flowing interactions, **movement synchrony** and **movement complementarity** often occur between counselor and client. Movement symmetry occurs when the two unconsciously assume the same physical posture—somewhat like dancing with one another. Movement complementarity is the passing of movement back and forth in rhythm such as when one person speaks and the other nods in agreement before the first person finishes the sentence. The lack of symmetry and complementarity is often a sign that the interview is on the wrong track.

Sometimes as a counselor you might find yourself feeling awkward and distant from clients, not understanding their nonverbal behavior. One route to understanding the other person is to consciously imitate or mirror their behavior for a short time. According to Ivey, Ivey, and Simek-Downing (1987), if you attend carefully to your own body once you start mirroring, you will find that changes in the client's movements actually stimulate your own body to move. Once you assume the same posture as the client, you will find yourself in better synchrony and harmony with that client.

Verbal Behavior
In addition to client nonverbal behavior, one can also learn a great deal from the verbal behavior. At the most basic level, the counselor should note **topic changes** or **topic exclusions** and any **key words** that appear again and again. For example, when the client continues to use "should" or "ought" statements, it may indicate a lack of control in those areas and should be explored further.

Sentence structure is an important clue to how the clients view the world. Are clients the subject or the object of the sentence? (Do they feel that they do the acting or are acted upon?) Are things always in the past, the present, or the future? Are there key words and descriptions that give a clue to clients' world view? Hearing certain patterns of words and ideas gives clues to clients' typical thought processes.

Incongruities, discrepancies, and **double messages** are heard constantly in counseling interviews. They are often at the root of a client's immobility and inability to respond creatively. The "Freudian slip" is an example of such an incongruity. When counselors notice such incongruities, they may either choose to hold back and say nothing or try to bring the discrepancy into the client's awareness immediately. The emotional state of the client and the impact upon the relationship should be the main consideration when making this decision. In time-limited or certain theoretical frameworks such as Gestalt, immediate confrontation may be essential.

Listening is an extremely important dimension of counselors' work. They need to be sure that they are hearing their clients accurately and clients must know that the counselor has heard them accurately, seen their point of view, and felt the world as they experience it. One way to improve communication and let clients know that they have been heard is by understanding and using the neurolinguistic approach to communication. Briefly, Neurolinguistic Programming (NLP) is a systematic approach to improving communication by identifying how people structure their language (Bandler & Grinder, 1979). One area of focus is on an individual's representational system—his or her preferred use of sensory modalities (visual, auditory, or kinesthetic). People who favor the visual modality express themselves more often with words such as "see," "perspective," "visualize," and "bright." Those who prefer the auditory mode express themselves more frequently through words such as "hear," "sound," "noise," "loud," and "resonate." Finally, persons who prefer the kinesthetic mode use words such as "feel," "grasp," "handle," "tough," and "soft." When the listener matches the words with the speaker in responding to the speaker, improved communication should occur (Haynie, 1982).

Questions

The use of questions can open communication. In the helping relationship, effective, open communication is especially necessary from the counselor. It facilitates moving the client from self-exploration through increased understanding and finally commitment to appropriate action. By using specific verbal leads, the counselor is able to bring out the major facts, feelings, and constructs that a client brings to the session. Effective use of open and closed questions can encourage the client to talk more freely and openly.

Open questions are considered by some to be the most valuable of the attending skills. Open questions usually begin with "what," "how," "why," "could," or "would" and require the client to provide a longer, more open response. These questions are not easily answered with a "yes" or "no" and convey an invitation to talk. Open questions are used to begin interviews; to encourage clients to express more information; to elicit examples of particular behaviors, thoughts, or feelings; and to increase the client's commitment to communicate.

COUNSELOR   What would you like to discuss today?

or

How did that make you feel?

or

Why do you think he acted that way?

Sometimes a client will be very talkative and ramble or jump from topic to topic. In such a case, **closed questions** can be used to gather information, give clarity, gain focus, and narrow the area of discussion. These closed questions usually begin with the word "is," "are," "do," or "did." One must use caution though, because extensive use of closed questions can deter conversation. A questioning counselor can appear to have all the power in the relationship and this inequality can destroy the counselor–client relationship, especially in their initial encounters.

Clients from some cultures are rapidly turned off by counselor questions, as are those clients who have not developed trust in their counselors. Frequently the same information can be obtained by asking the clients what goals they have, how they feel about those goals, and how they plan to attain them. Asking too many questions at once can confuse the client. "Why" questions are especially troublesome because they may put clients on the defensive and cause them discomfort.

Since questions may cause resistance with some clients, the skills of encouraging, paraphrasing, summarization, and reflection of feeling may be used to obtain similar information yet seem less intrusive to the client.

Encouraging, Paraphrasing, and Summarizing

The skill of **encouraging** includes the use of both "encouragers" and "restatements," which punctuate the interview and provide a smooth flow. Using encouragers such as head nods, a positive facial expression, or verbal utterances such as "umm" or "uh-huh" is an active way to let clients know that they have been heard and understood. Encouragers can be used to influence the direction taken by the client and are part of selective attention as described above.

One powerful type of encourager is for the counselor to respond with a restatement of a "key word" or a short phrase from the client's statement, often in a questioning tone of voice.

LISA I often feel afraid around him.

COUNSELOR Afraid of him?

The **paraphrase** uses some of these same key words from the client's statement, but adds some counselor observations. It is an encapsulated rephrase of the content of the client's message in the counselor's words. The strength of the paraphrase is that the counselor is giving of self, yet is paying primary attention to the client's frame of reference. This skill is frequently very helpful in letting clients clarify issues that may have been cloudy as well as letting them know that they have been heard accurately.

A good paraphrase has four main parts, including

1. some aspect of the client's mode of receiving information (visual, auditory, kinesthetic);
2. key words and constructs used by the client;
3. a summary of the essence of what the client has said; and
4. a check-out of the counselor's accuracy in hearing, i.e., "Is that right?" or "Is that close?"

Paraphrasing frequently leads to an excited "That's right, exactly right!" from the client. Such exclamations can lead to better understanding of the problem on the part of both client and counselor.

LISA   I'd like to run away and never come back, but what would happen to the kids?

COUNSELOR   It sounds like you're feeling trapped and confused. If you only had yourself to think about, you'd know what to do, but you really care about the children.

LISA   You're right! I do feel trapped and confused!

Summarizations are similar to paraphrasing, except that they "paraphrase" a longer period of conversation. It is the gathering together of a client's verbalizations, facts, feelings, and meanings and restating them for the client as accurately as possible. This summarization frequently gives the client a feeling of movement as ideas and feelings are explored (Brammer, 1988).

Summarizations may be useful in the beginning of a session to warm up a client or at other times to bring closure to discussion on a theme. They can be used to add direction and coherence to a session that seems to be going nowhere (Egan, 1982). Summarizations are also valuable to counselors as a check-out of the accuracy of their understanding of the information that has just been gathered.

The following is an example of a summarization in an interview with Lisa.

COUNSELOR You're feeling overwhelmed because so many things seem wrong—you're feeling the need to be protective of the kids and yourself. You're less certain you'll ever be married or even want to be married to Peter.

Reflection of Feelings

Besides hearing the words of the client accurately, the counselor must uncover and recognize the emotions underlying those words. Reflecting client feelings is very similar to paraphrasing except that the paraphrase is associated with facts while reflection of feelings is associated with the emotions related to those facts. This skill is used to discover and sort out positive and negative client feelings and can be done using either open or closed questions or inference. It is important for the counselor to have learned how to label accurately emotions such as angry, glad, sad, fearful, or scared before trying to reflect the emotions of others.

A reflection of feelings consists of five basic parts:

1. a sentence stem using the clients' method of receiving information (auditory, visual, kinesthetic);
2. use of the pronoun "you";
3. a feeling label or emotion stem;
4. a context or setting for the emotion; and
5. the correct tense of the reflection (frequently it is the present tense, e.g., "Right now, you are angry.")

A check-out may also be added to see that the reflection is accurate.

LISA I just don't know what to do.

COUNSELOR It sounds like right now with all these responsibilities, you're feeling trapped, confused, and immobilized. You're not certain which way to turn. Is that how you feel?

Self-Attending Skills

Individuals who are aware of their own values, beliefs, and assets are much more likely to find it easier to "be with" clients, help clients explore personal issues, and facilitate client action. Therefore, the self-attending skills are extremely important for each person who wishes to be an effective counselor. There are several components to the self-attending process. Shulman (1979) referred to these counselor components as "tuning-in." The first component in the "tuning-in" process is self-awareness.

Self-Awareness

The knowledge and understanding that the counselor has of the counseling setting and self is extremely important to the self-attending process. Practically speaking, the counselor should not attempt to consciously rehearse how counselors are "supposed" to be. The effective counselor acts professionally, but does not put on a professional front, play acting some imaginary expert counselor. Effective counselors know their strengths as well as their weaknesses and by understanding themselves are able to overcome self-consciousness and devote complete attention to what the client is trying to share.

Centering and Relaxing

Development of centering skills assumes that the helper regards the human personality as something beyond a collection of its components. Centering is a process of getting "in-touch" and then "in-tune" with one's person, or total self. Centering results in awareness of peace, harmony, unity, and strength (Brammer, 1988) and allows the counselor to be there in the here and now for each client.

One of the best ways to relax in the counseling setting is to focus on breathing, counting slowly while inhaling and exhaling. There are also a number of ways to induce relaxation through direct suggestion. Systematic relaxation of large muscle groups can be done by alternately tensing and releasing these muscles. Relaxation skills can be used by counselors to reduce anxiety and physical tension in both themselves and their clients.

Humor

The counselor who can enjoy and use **humor** effectively has an invaluable asset. The healing power of humor has long been valued, but its place in therapy is only slowly gaining respect (Keller, 1984). Although counseling is serious business, there are many truly humorous dimensions to the human condition and when humor appears as a natural outgrowth of the counselor–client relationship it should be attended to. Humor can provide a means of connecting with clients, and counselors need to affirm any humor presented by their clients. Laughter and joking can release built-up tensions and laughing at one's self can be extremely therapeutic—since it requires seeing one's problems in a whole new perspective.

Nonjudgmental Attitude Toward Self

Counselors need to have a broad awareness of their own value positions. They must be able to answer very clearly the questions, "Who am I?" "What is important to me?" "Am I nonjudgmental?" (Brammer, 1988).

This awareness aids counselors in being honest with themselves and their clients and in being free from judgments about themselves. In addition it helps the counselor avoid unwarranted or unethical use of clients to satisfy personal needs. While counselors may have opinions about traits of people they like and want to associate with, one characteristic of effective counselors is that they try to suspend judgment of clients.

Nonjudgmental Attitude Toward Others
This attitude is one of respect for a client's individuality and worth as a person and is very similar to Rogers' (1961) concept of "unconditional positive regard." It allows clients to be open and to be themselves because they know that the person they are in a relationship with (the counselor) will not be judging them or what they say. The counselor conveys this nonjudgmental attitude by being warm, accepting, and respectful toward the client; this is especially important in the early phases of the relationship.

Respect describes the helping skill that communicates this acceptance of the client as a person of worth and dignity (Rogers, 1957). In utilizing this skill, the counselor demonstrates a belief in clients' abilities to deal with their own problems in the presence of a facilitative person. Often counselors express this respect by what they do not do rather than what they do—such as not giving advice. Respectful counselors use communication skills to actualize the power, ability, and skills already possessed by the client. In other words, the counselor believes in the problem-solving ability of the client. This skill is very important in facilitating an effective helping relationship. It communicates a willingness to work with the client, and an interest and belief in the client as a person of worth (Cormier & Cormier, 1985).

The way you nonverbally attend to the client is one way you express respect (Egan, 1982). Respectful behavior conveys the message "I'm glad I'm here. I'm glad you're here." Respect is also expressed through appropriate warmth, understanding, and caring.

The use of respect entails suspending judgment of the client (Cormier & Cormier, 1985; Egan, 1982). Rogers (1967) has effectively described this kind of respect as the ability of the counselor to "communicate to his client a deep and genuine caring for him as a person with potentialities, a caring uncontaminated by evaluations of his thought, feelings or behaviors" (p. 102).

LISA   I am really feeling very helpless. I like staying home and taking care of the kids. Going back to work isn't something I want to do.

COUNSELOR   The dilemma you face is complicated by something that you like to do and something you don't really want to do.

Respect is rarely found alone in communication. It usually occurs in combination with empathy and genuineness.

Genuineness
When counselors relate to clients naturally and openly, they are being genuine. Being a counselor is not a role played by the individual, in-

stead, it is the appropriate revelation of one's own feelings and thoughts. Egan (1975) cautions "being role free is not license; freedom from role means that the counselor should not use the role or facade of counselor to protect himself, to substitute for effectiveness, or to fool the client" (p. 92).

The effective use of genuineness reduces the emotional distance between the counselor and client (Cormier & Cormier, 1985). It breaks down the role distance and links them together, allowing clients to see the counselor as a person similar to them.

The genuine counselor is spontaneous, nondefensive, and consistent in relationships.

LISA   Do you think I'm as crazy and mixed up as I feel?

COUNSELOR   Your confusion and indecisiveness makes you wonder if you're crazy. You don't appear that way to me.

Concreteness

In the process of exploring problems or issues, a client often presents an incomplete representation of what has happened. The goal of concreteness is to make the data gained through self-exploration more specific and concrete. It is the task of the counselor to help the client clarify the pieces of the puzzle and fit them together so that the whole makes sense to the client. This clarification increases the likelihood that an organized, specific, workable action plan can be implemented and accepted by the client. When encouraging concreteness, one attempts to focus the situation, to make clear all facets of the issue, including the accompanying behaviors and feelings.

There are several ways to help clients become more concrete and focused. when a client makes a vague statement, the counselor can reflect in a more concrete way. At times, a rambling client may need to be focused. The effective use of concreteness in such situations may feel like interrupting, but should lead to increased counselor–client interaction. When counselor invitations to be more concrete or specific are necessary, leads such as "what" and "how" rather than "why" will usually produce more relevant and specific information (Egan, 1982).

LISA   I'm really confused about what to do.

COUNSELOR   You're feeling stuck and confused because you always thought you'd be married and now you're not so certain he wants that to happen.

or

COUNSELOR   I'm unclear as to what has specifically happened that has led to the confusion.

or

COUNSELOR   Help me to understand what events are most closely related to this confusion you're feeling.

Effective use of concreteness keeps the counseling session productively focused and aims at making vague experiences, behaviors, and feelings more specific. The more specific the information, the better the understanding and the more effective future actions will be.

ADVANCED SKILLS AND CONCEPTS

The first goal of helping is the facilitation of client self-exploration. This exploration helps both the counselor and client understand the client's problem. The client begins to focus and see more clearly the puzzles of life and is led skillfully to identify the missing pieces and blocks. This exploration involves a look at the real self, and related issues. The process leads to insightful self-understanding that invites the client to change or take action.

Once the beginning counselor is adept at using the basic counseling skills, advanced skills and concepts can be added to the repertoire. These skills and concepts are more action-oriented and allow the counselor to facilitate client self-understanding, change, and eventual termination of the helping relationship. The advanced understanding skills include advanced accurate empathy, self-disclosure, confrontation, and immediacy.

Understanding Skills

Advanced Accurate Empathy
Empathy forms the foundation and atmospheric core of the helping relationship. It involves listening for basic or surface messages with frequent, but brief, responses to those messages. The counselor sees the world from the client's frame of reference and communicates that it has been understood. The goal is to move the client toward identification and exploration of critical topics and feelings. During this early self-exploration phase, the counselor must be sensitive to signs of client stress or resistance and try to judge whether these arise from lack of accurate response or from being too accurate too quickly. As the counselor moves the client beyond exploration to self-understanding and action, advanced skills and concepts become more important.

While primary level empathy gets at relevant feelings and mean-•
ings that are near the surface, the skill of advanced accurate empathy
gets at feelings and meanings that are somehow buried, hidden, or beyond the immediate reach of the client (Egan, 1982). The most basic
form of advanced accurate empathy is to give expression and understanding to what the client only implies. It forces the client to take a
deeper look at self.

Advanced accurate empathy includes the identification of themes
presented by the client. Feeling, behavioral, experiential, or combined
themes may occur. Once the counselor recognizes the themes, the task
is to communicate the relevant ones to the client in a way that will be
heard and understood. The themes must be based solidly on an accurate
understanding of the client's feelings, experiences, and behaviors and
communicated as concretely as possible using the client's experiences
and communication style.

The act of bringing together in a summary way relevant core materials that the client has presented in a fragmented way is part of advanced accurate empathy. The counselor helps the client fill in the missing links in the information. When it becomes apparent that two
aspects of client information are closely linked, this information should
be shared, but the counselor must guard against premature speculation
or unfounded linkages.

As the counselor explores the deeper, underlying meaning of an experience of the client, the skill of reflection of meaning can be used. It
provides a way for the client to develop a new world view and interpret
old situations or information in new ways. Because information is always subject to individual interpretation (Gelatt, 1989), the counselor
needs to reframe the situation, belief, or experience to help the client
view it from a different perspective and also check out that the interpretation is correct.

Advanced accurate empathy gets at more critical, deeper, and delicate issues and, therefore, puts the client under additional stress. To
avoid overwhelming the client and building resistances, the counselor's
empathetic responses should be tentative and cautious. Leads such as
"From what you have said . . . ," "Could it be that . . . ," or "It seems like
. . ." may be most helpful.

Counselors may find it helpful to reflect back to clients what they
see as the meaning of an experience.

LISA Finding out about his kids was somewhat of a surprise.

COUNSELOR It seems like finding out about the children didn't
matter as long as the two of you could be together.

Self-Disclosure

Hendrick (1988) and Peca-Baker and Friedlander (1987) have both recently found that clients want to have information about their counselors. Sharing oneself can be a powerful intervention for making contact with clients, but it should not be an indiscriminate sharing of personal problems with clients.

Self-disclosure is defined as any information counselors convey about themselves to clients (Cormier & Cormier, 1985; Cozby, 1973). It can generate a more open, facilitative counseling atmosphere, encourage client talk and additional trust, and create a more equal relationship. In some instances, a self-disclosing counselor may be perceived as more caring than one who does not disclose. At times counselor self-disclosure can present a model for clients to increase their own levels of disclosure about events and feelings (McCarthy, 1982).

The use of self-disclosure as a skill involves consideration of timing, goals, genuineness, and appropriateness. Effective self-disclosure does not add another burden to an already burdened client (Egan, 1982), and it should not distract the client from his or her own problems. The counselor must consider how the client will use and benefit from the information shared.

Perhaps the most important type of self-disclosure is that which focuses on the relationship between you and your client. If you are having a difficult time listening to a client, for example, it could be useful to let them know that it is difficult. However, it helps to only describe your own feelings and reactions and not judge the client. It may be fairly easy for the counselor to self-disclose, but making the disclosure relevant to the client is the important and more complex task (Ivey, 1988). The counselor's self-disclosure should be genuine and fairly close in mood and content to the client's experience. As a counselor, you must remember that self-disclosure is appropriate only when it is genuine, benefits the client, and adds to client movement or understanding, and when it does not interfere with the counseling process or contribute to raised levels of client anxiety (Cormier & Cormier, 1985).

LISA   I can't believe I was so dumb and gullible.

COUNSELOR   It seems like you shouldn't have been so trusting. I've found when I get in these situations that it helps to be good to myself.

How willing are you to engage in appropriate and relevant self-disclosure? You become vulnerable when you share your own experiences, feelings, and reactions, yet can you expect your clients to become vulnerable in front of you if you rarely show them anything of yourself?

Good self-disclosure is a kind of sharing that clients can use to grow, and it lets them know how you're perceiving and experiencing them.

Most evidence indicates that a moderate amount of self-disclosure has more impact than too little or too much. Counselors who disclose very little risk being seen as aloof, weak, and role-conscious (Egan, 1982), while the counselor who discloses too much may be seen as lacking in discretion, being untrustworthy (Levin & Gergen, 1969), seeming preoccupied (Cozby, 1973), or needing assistance.

Confrontation
Confrontation is a skill that is used when there are discrepancies, conflicts, or mixed messages being sent by the client. The mixed messages may occur between the verbal and nonverbal messages sent by the client or between two contradictory verbal messages. Egan (1975) describes confrontation as "the responsible unmasking of the discrepancies, distortions, games, and smoke screens the client uses to hide both from self-understanding and from constructive behavioral change" (p. 158).

When confronting a client, the counselor must always exercise concern for the client's understanding of the challenge so that there will be client progress, not denial and flight. To do this effectively, the counselor must accurately reflect the situation. Using a tentative reflection is important, especially if it is early in the relationship. Consideration should also be given to the state of the client; an already distressed, confused, or disorganized client will not benefit from a confrontation. In fact, confrontation with such a client may add to the distress or confusion.

LISA I was really hurt when he told me that he hadn't filed for a divorce at all. All along I thought it had been done 3 years ago. . . . I just can't leave him.

COUNSELOR You're feeling really torn. You're not legally married to him, so why can't you just walk away from him?

Confrontation should be done with care and may be more effective if done gradually. A gradual confrontation will give the client time to assimilate information. Good counselor practice demands a careful balance of confrontation with supporting qualities of warmth, positive regard, and respect (Ivey, Ivey, & Simek-Downing, 1987).

Immediacy
The phenomenon of immediacy involves the counselor's sensitivity to the immediate situation and an understanding of what is occurring at the

moment with clients (Pietrofesa, Hoffman, & Splete, 1984). It involves the ability to discuss directly and openly with another person what is happening in the "here and now" of an interpersonal relationship (Egan, 1975). This is sometimes referred to as "you–me" talk.

The use of immediacy combines the skills of confrontation and self-disclosure and requires that the counselor reveal feelings and/or challenge to the client to deal openly with feelings. The purpose of immediacy responses is to help clients understand themselves more clearly, especially what is happening and how they are relating at that moment in the counseling session. As interviews move more to the present tense, the counselor's presence in the interview becomes more powerful and important (Ivey, 1988), and the counselor is modeling a kind of behavior that clients can use to become more effective in all their relationships.

Counselors usually know what is happening in a session, but do not always act upon it. Acting on what is happening at the moment is part of the phenomenon of immediacy. When either counselor or client has unverbalized thoughts or feelings that seem to be getting in the way of progress, the counselor should bring it up for discussion.

LISA   I'm not exactly certain how to tell you about all the other messes in my life.

COUNSELOR   It sounds like something is getting in the way of your trusting me to understand everything that's happened in your life.

There are many areas or issues in which the skill of immediacy might be used: trust, differences in style, directionless sessions, dependency, counterdependency, and attraction are areas where "you–me" talk might pay off (Egan, 1982). Other areas might include concern for the client's welfare, lack of follow-through on homework, and the client questioning the value of counseling.

Carkhuff (1969) suggests that the counselor ask, during the course of the interview, "What is the client trying to tell me that he can't tell me directly?" The answer lies buried in the verbal and nonverbal behavior of the client. The skilled helper can dig it out and make it an "immediacy" topic.

In considering whether to use immediacy, the counselor should decide whether it is appropriate to focus the relationship on here-and-now concerns at this specific time. If so, then counselor-initiated leads will focus on the identification and communication of feelings. The counselor must seriously consider word choice; as in many other cases, a tentative statement may be more inviting of a client response.

Action

The goal of counseling is to have a client come away form the process changed. This growth or change often entails the counselor and client working together in some kind of action plan appropriate to the client's stated goals. These action plans should grow out of the theoretical orientation of the counselor. For instance, a behaviorally oriented counselor will be more inclined to use behavioral contracts and/or systematic desensitization. A transactional analysis therapist, on the other hand, will focus on ego states, game playing, or life scripts.

It is important for the counselor to remember that the theoretical orientation is secondary to the development of effective core skills. These skills seem to be shared by all effective helpers and really address the quality of the interaction between the counselor and the client.

Termination

The ending of a helping relationship can be either one of the most gratifying or one of the most difficult and frustrating aspects of the relationship. Termination may occur either by mutual agreement or prematurely. When counselor and client agree that the goals of counseling have been accomplished, they may mutually agree that it is time to terminate. Sadness about parting and some client anxiety may be expected, but by exploring and sharing feelings, each person is more likely to leave feeling a sense of growth and accomplishment because goals have been achieved. It is important to leave time to discuss these feelings and, for a smooth termination, it is important for both individuals to know when the last session will occur.

Premature termination may be initiated by either the counselor or the client. When counselor-initiated termination occurs, the client needs to be informed as early as possible or reminded that only a limited number of sessions are available. Premature termination occurs most frequently in schools and agencies with session limits. On rare occasions, it may occur because of irreconcilable differences or perceived lack of commitment by the client. When the counselor does terminate the sessions, the reasons must be specified to the client. Most counselors agree that early termination by the counselor violates the premise that clients are in charge of solving their own problems, and early termination may lead to feelings of personal rejection in the client. These feelings should be dealt with before termination is complete. Referring the individual to another agency and/or keeping the door open for future sessions are sometimes helpful.

When the sessions are prematurely terminated by the client, the counselor should try to explore with the client the reasons for termination. Letting clients know that they are in charge of the decision to return in the future can be beneficial, as is the exploration of possible referral resources.

When termination is mutual or initiated by the counselor, several steps can benefit the outcome of the relationship (Ward, 1984). There should be discussion and evaluation of the goals that have already been reached. Closure issues and feelings need to be discussed and clients need to be prepared for similar happenings in the future. Clients should be prepared for self-reliance and continued self-help. Finally, in the last session, discussion should be lighter and more social; Okun (1987) often shares a poster with the client that symbolizes the significance of the client's journey. The termination process should not focus on the generation of new problems or issues but should bring appreciation of the growth that has already occurred.

CONCLUSION

Combs' (1986) research summary suggests that individuals seeking to become counselors must examine their beliefs about themselves; about their abilities regarding others; about how people grow, change, and obtain power and control in a relationship; and about whose world view is most important. It necessitates self-exploration, self-knowledge, and positive self-acceptance.

This awareness of yourself and your beliefs and values should lead to an examination of such key questions as:

- Who am I?
- What is important to me?
- Why do I want to be a helper?
- Am I a person who believes in myself, acknowledging and understanding my strengths and weaknesses?
- Am I excited and committed to continuing my own growth, self-understanding, and self-knowledge?
- Do I see other people as competent and powerful or do most people need *my* help?
- Who makes the decisions in my relationships?
- Am I willing to let another person be in charge of his or her own decisions, especially if they are different choices than I would make?
- Am I able to experience and feel what others tell me or do I tend to dwell on the facts, remaining objective and uninvolved?

- Do I enjoy learning about human behavior and see its relevance to myself and others or is it something that takes too much time and energy?

REFERENCES

Bandler, R., & Grinder, J. (1979). *Frogs into princes.* Moab, UT: Real Peoples Press.

Barak, A., Shapira, G., & Fisher, W. A. (1988). Effects of verbal and vocal cues of counselor self-confidence on clients' perceptions. *Counselor Education and Supervision, 27,* 355–367.

Brammer, L. M. (1988). *The helping relationship: Process and skills.* Englewood Cliffs, NJ: Prentice-Hall.

Carkhuff, R. (1969). *Helping and human relations.* Vol. I and II. New York: Holt, Rinehart & Winston.

Carkhuff, R. R. (1986). *The art of helping* (5th ed.). Amherst, MA: Human Resource Development Press.

Carkhuff, R., & Berenson, B. (1967). *Beyond counseling and therapy.* New York: Holt, Rinehart & Winston.

Combs, A. W. (1986). What makes a good helper? A person-centered approach. *Person-centered Review, 1*(1), 51–61.

Cormier, W. H., & Cormier, L. S. (1985). *Interviewing strategies for helpers.* Monterey, CA: Brooks/Cole.

Cozby, P. C. (1973). Self-disclosure: A literature review. *Psychological Bulletin, 79,* 73–91.

Driscoli, M. S., Newman, D. L., & Seals, J. M. (1988). The effect of touch on perception of counselors. *Counselor Education and Supervision, 27,* 344–354.

Egan, G. (1975). *The skilled helper.* Monterey, CA: Brooks/Cole.

Egan, G. (1982). *The skilled helper* (2nd ed.). Monterey, CA: Brooks/Cole.

Gelatt, H. B. (1989). Positive uncertainty: A new decision-making framework for counseling. *Journal of Counseling Psychology, 36*(2), 252–256.

Haynie, N. A. (1982). Learning how to learn. In Gazda, G. M., W. C. Childers, & R. P. Walters, *Interpersonal communication: A handbook for health professionals,* pp. 21–39. Rockville, MD: Aspen Systems.

Hendrick, S. S. (1988). Counselor self-disclosure. *Journal of Counseling and Development, 66*(9), 419–424.

Ivey, A. E. (1988). *Intentional interviewing and counseling: Facilitating client development.* Monterey, CA: Brooks/Cole.

Ivey, A. E., Ivey, M. B., & Simek-Downing, L. (1987). *Counseling and psychotherapy: Integrating skills, theory and practice.* Englewood Cliffs, NJ: Prentice-Hall.

Ivey, A. E., & Simek-Downing, L. (1980). *Counseling and psychotherapy.* Englewood Cliffs, NJ: Prentice-Hall.

Keller, D. (1984). *Humor as therapy.* Wauwatosa, WI: Med-Psych Publications.

Levin, F. M., & Gergen, K. J. (1969). Revealingness, ingratiation, and the disclosure of self. *Proceedings of the 77th Annual Convention of the American Psychological Association, 4*(1) 447–448.

McCarthy, P. (1982). Differential effects of counselor self-referrent responses and counselor status. *Journal of Counseling Psychology, 29,* 125–311.

Okun, B. F. (1987). *Effective helping: Interviewing and counseling techniques* (3rd ed.). Monterey, CA: Brooks/Cole Publishing.

Patterson, C. H. (1974). *Relationship counseling and psychotherapy.* New York: Harper & Row.

Peca-Baker, T. A., & Friedlander, M. L. (1987). Effects on role expectations on clients' perceptions of disclosing and nondisclosing counselors. *Journal of Counseling and Development, 66*(2), 78–81.

Pietrofesa, J. J., Hoffman, A. & Splete, H. H. (1984). *Counseling: An introduction.* Boston: Houghton-Mifflin.

Pietrofesa, J. J., Hoffman, A., Splete, H. H., & Pinto, D. V. (1978). *Counseling: Theory, research & practice.* Chicago: Rand McNally.

Rogers, C. R. (1957). The necessary and sufficient conditions of therapeutic personality change. *Journal of Consulting Psychology, 21,* 95–103.

Rogers, C. R. (1958). The characteristics of a helping relationship. *Personnel and Guidance Journal, 37,* 6–16

Rogers, C. R. (1961). *On becoming a person.* Boston: Houghton-Mifflin.

Rogers, C. R. (1967). *The therapeutic relationship and its impact.* Madison, WI: The University of Wisconsin Press.

Scherer, K. R. (1986). Vocal affect expression: A review and a model for future research. *Psychological Bulletin, 99,* 143–165.

Shulman, L. (1979). *The skills of helping individuals and groups.* Itasca, IL: F. E. Peacock Publishers.

Strong, S. R. (1968). Counseling: An interpersonal influence process. *Journal of Counseling Psychology, 15,* 215–224.

Suiter, R. L., & Goodyear, R. K. (1985). Male and female counselor and client perceptions of four levels of counselor touch. *Journal of Counseling Psychology, 32*(4), 645–648.

Ward, D. E. (1984). Termination of individual counseling: Concepts and strategies. *Journal of Counseling and Development, 63*(1), 21–26.

4.

A Framework for Theories in Counseling

■

J. JEFFRIES MCWHIRTER, PH.D, ABPP
BENEDICT T. MCWHIRTER, M.C.
Arizona State University
Tempe, Arizona

THE NEED FOR THEORY

Why does a counselor focus on certain events in an interview and ignore others? How does a counselor know what data are important in trying to understand clients? What is involved in the counselor's decision to reflect affect with one client and discuss ideas with another? What method and what criteria does the counselor use to evaluate success or failure as a helper? To answer the above questions one needs to focus on the theoretical foundations that underlie the counselor's behavior. This theoretical foundation is the vehicle by which a person can organize observations into a pattern that will assist in understanding what has been observed. The above questions focus on helper behavior, which is based upon assumptions regarding behavior. To make these assumptions explicit encourages greater precision in answering the questions.

Unfortunately, practitioners often become frustrated with the amount of literature that focuses on theoretical issues. Underlying this frustration seems to be the belief that theory and practice are dichotomized into two distinct and separate categories. A frequent complaint of practitioners-in-training is directed toward professors and instructors who are too theoretical in their orientations and toward courses that are too theoretical in their content. Students often complain: "All this talk about theory doesn't help me in my situation. Why don't we discuss the practical aspects of helping?" In reality, however, a good theory is highly practical. Theory and practice cannot be dichotomized into two separate camps. Practitioners do operate from a counseling theory. Although they may not have it well defined or be able to verbalize it, some sort of theory is implied by the counselor's beliefs and behaviors.

Individuals who feel they can operate entirely without a theory, even those who assume an antitheoretical position, are basing their behavior on implicit theory even though vaguely defined. There is no other way they can decide what to do. Intuition, sometimes proposed as a substitute for theory, is itself but a crude type of hypothesizing.

Not infrequently, then, practitioners make only implicit assumptions about their world. They "fly by the seat of their pants." Their decision to behave in a certain way, to focus on certain information, is based on poorly formulated or unconsciously held theoretical formulations. In this situation, therapists' working behaviors are influenced by a tool over which they have little or no control. The explanatory and predicative aspects of theory are greatly limited by its implicitness. The abstractions and inferences derived from observed events have no consistency or pattern.

Human beings, however, abhor isolated events. People must fit events together into a pattern to understand and control them. Theory is necessary to organize the isolated events confronting the counselor. Because the helper's behavior and practice are inextricably intertwined to theory and because the helper's behavior and practice are so critical to success or failure with the client, counselors have an obligation to develop a systematic theoretical rationale for their work. Counselors do not have the luxury of artists in achieving their aims. The license that artists use in the practice of their art is denied counselors in their practice. Counselors must be precise where artists may be vague; explicit where artists are implicit; use logic and reason when artists may use emotion and connotation. Without a systematic theoretical base, helpers lack the breadth, depth, and consistency that are so important to their work. They lack a unifying theme to give their interactions support and focus. Unexamined and implicit theories contain incongruities that may result in unpredictable and inconsistent counselor behavior. Theories, then, grow out of the need to make sense out of life and provide consistency and unity, which allow for greater focus.

Counseling theories are systematic ways of viewing the helping process. Counselors' behaviors are influenced by the frame of reference with which they view counseling. Theories are tools; abstractions created by psychologists and counselors to guide them as they explore the intricacies of the client's world. And, ultimately, theories have a single purpose: the organization of information and data into more usable, more communicable, and more practical forms.

Essentially, a theory is a hypothetical explanation for observed events. It is a framework that imposes some sort of order on these events and initially is a guess that seems to make sense. Theory is a possible world that can be checked against the real world.

A useful theory goes beyond an explanation of events that have already taken place. It should lead to the prediction of future events that involve the same sort of behaviors. Thus, a theory of change must conform to events that have previously been observed and should lead the observer to predict the effects of various elements in the counseling process. If the prediction proves accurate, then the validity of the theory is enhanced and the helper has gained greater control of the problem-solving situation.

To summarize, there are three ways in which counseling theories can help counselors in their quest to help others. First, the theory contributes to a greater understanding of an individual's behavior. It provides a way of organizing relevant, available, and observable data about a client into a framework that allows greater unity and greater predictability. Second, the theory suggests guidelines that provide signs of success or failure of counseling activities. Essentially, the theory becomes a "working model" to explain what clients *may* be like and what *may* be helpful to them. Built into the "working model" is an appreciation of what constitutes success or failure. The end result is twofold: helpers reach a deeper and richer understanding of what their client *is* like, and their theory is enriched in ways that make it more useful in working with future clients. Finally, and perhaps most important for the practitioner, the theory directly influences the strategy of change that counselors select to use with their client as well as the counseling procedures that are most applicable with a given client or with a particular presenting problem.

To make the theory more useful and more practical, counselors must do two things. First, insofar as they are able, they must make explicit—through conscious evaluation and examination—the informal theory that they hold. Second, they must become aware of the more formalized statements of various theoretical positions. These two tasks should not be undertaken in isolation; indeed, they cannot be.

Over 30 years ago, Leona Tyler (1980) suggested that counselors need many different varieties of theoretical concepts with some degree of organization to provide confidence and peace of mind. By examining approaches to counseling that have been expounded by theorists and by increased awareness of the interpersonal hypotheses by which they are operating, counselors can develop a theoretical rationale for their work. The intent of this chapter and the next is to provide the counseling practitioner and the counselor-in-training with working models within major theoretical points of view.

Practitioners must develop their own personal theory of change. This can be done by drawing upon the appealing ideas of other persons who have been particularly adept at developing theoretical formulations of change. It is possible for practitioners to consider a relatively few but central persons who have presented systematic and comprehensive theoretical approaches to counseling. Essentially, knowledge of existing theories will help therapists expand on their own perceived theory of change so that their efforts toward helping the client create positive change are enhanced.

"SCHOOLS" OF COUNSELING

The existence of a variety of theoretical approaches within counseling and psychology has created problems. One of the striking characteristics of the field has been the prolific growth of "schools" of counseling and therapy. Each of the schools has introduced its own innovations in procedures, techniques, and theories, which result in a bewildering diversity of opinion. Much of the problem exists around the fact that many of the disagreements are statements of opinion and not statements of fact. Most schools were founded by a charismatic leader who attracted loyal disciples. Since there has been very little scientific basis for many approaches, disagreement and hostility based on poorly defined concepts and armchair theories have frequently existed between the various schools. Essentially, schools are the inevitable consequence of theories based on intuition, faith, and tenacity. A partial advantage of the almost semireligious nature of schools is that followers of a particular approach have worked hard to define and elaborate their positions. In attempting to validate the value of their orientation, the writing and research that followed led many schools to develop a somewhat formal theoretical position.

The existence of these formal theoretical positions is vital to the helping process. They provide counselors with a basis from which to operate with their clients. They provide a way of explaining and predicting client behavior as well as suggesting procedures for altering that behavior. Effective, professional counselors must be aware of the basic concepts supporting the major approaches. Counselors who are unaware of formal theories are locked into a world of their own.

Most counseling approaches have reported some success; it seems unlikely that any open current position is entirely correct. The dogmatic schools of counseling and psychotherapy were perhaps necessary for desirable changes of professional and public climate. However, increasing the effectiveness of counselors in dealing with a broad range of client problems will probably demand new integrations of ideas from various approaches (Howard, Nance, & Myers, 1986). At this point, there is no single theoretical formulation existing to explain all facets of human behavior. No single approach to counseling—whether it is a theory of personality or a set of techniques for modifying personality—has been found that can completely explain the behavior of all individuals (Goldfried, 1980, 1982; Ivey, 1980; Tyler, 1980). Consequently, it is our belief that a major pitfall for counselors is to assume that a single theoretical approach is pertinent to all individuals.

Closely related to the above argument is the potential failure of a single theory to be helpful with a specific client's problem. Certain kinds of client problems lend themselves much more directly to certain theoretical explanations and treatments than do other problems (Howard, Nance, & Myers, 1986). In other words, some theoretical approaches are much more pertinent and are more directly applicable for certain presenting problems than are other approaches (cf. Beutler, 1983). In addition, during the course of the helping relationship clients' needs change in terms of the shifting orientation to their problems. New goals emerge as earlier ones are accomplished; new targets present themselves as old ones are influenced to change. Counselors' ability to shift their orientation to meet client needs and goals will potentially improve the chances of effectiveness in positive client outcome.

One response to limit the above problems is to integrate several existing theoretical approaches to counseling in the hope that the helper will be able to apply theory and methods more effectively. In certain areas this integration has taken place (Beutler, 1983; Howard, Nance, & Myers, 1986; Lazarus, 1976). Some 30 years ago, for example, theoretical models in counseling emphasized the difference between the nondirective and the directive stance in the counseling interview. Resulting arguments tended to emphasize a single dimension of the counseling process, and it is not presently adequate to illustrate the various positions now held by many counselors. What was formerly called nondirective counseling—frequently seen as passivity on the part of the counselor, engaging in the reflection of feeling, clarification of content, and so forth—is used by most helpers at least a portion of the time. In a similar way, what was formerly called directive counseling—often including activity on the part of the counselor, the use of objective data, and diagnosis of problem behavior—is now used by most counselors to some degree in the counseling process. The primary point of this discussion, and the primary proposal here, is that counselors can have greater impact, can become more effective in their work, and can make a greater contribution to their clientele if they purposefully maintain an eclectic position in the selection of a theoretical model and the use of this model in the counseling relationship.

The brand of eclecticism proposed here assumes that counselors are highly trained and have some experience in a number of counseling approaches. Indeed, it is negligent for counselors to call themselves eclectic unless they are well versed in a variety of specific theories that support their eclectic position. A thorough knowledge of several counseling theories will broaden helpers' capacity to organize their observations and to plan appropriate interventions. In the working situation, counselors should be at home with a variety of theoretical approaches and should be able to select an approach to counseling that is most likely to meet the specific needs of clients. Since the concept of eclecticism within counseling is of great importance, it will serve us well to discuss some alternatives to the eclectic approach as well as various aspects of eclecticism.

ECLECTIC COUNSELING

Eclecticism means to select methods or doctrines from various sources or systems. Eclectic counseling is based on concepts taken deliberately from a variety of theoretical positions rather than concepts based exclusively on one orientation. The eclectic individual believes that a single viewpoint and theoretical position is limiting and that concepts, procedures, and techniques from many sources must be used to best serve the needs of the person(s) seeking help. When counselors deliberately attempt to incorporate into their practice the terminology, techniques, concepts, and procedures of more than one unified theory, the result is eclecticism. The key word is *deliberately*. True eclectic counselors have a consistent purpose and philosophy in their practice and deliberately use techniques and procedures from various schools that they believe are most appropriate to use in order to help each client. From knowledge of cognition, affect, and behavior, and from understanding of environment and systems issues, eclectic helpers develop a repertoire of problem-solving methods. They then select the most appropriate method for the particular client and the specific problem.

Eclecticism is frequently misunderstood to mean an indiscriminate and arbitrary collection of theoretical scraps and pieces. When individuals do this and do not make a sincere and serious attempt to understand

and include various viewpoints into their counseling practice, they are following a procedure based on the idea that "there's much good to be said on all sides." Eclecticism used in this way is vague, superficial, non-descriptive and contributes to the legitimate charge of "fuzzy-headed wishy-washiness." The use of eclecticism in this sense reinforces the belief that eclecticism is popular because it removes the necessity to "take sides" and enables counselors to do what they "want" in counseling.

There are, then, three positions that a counselor may adopt in regard to the selection of a theoretical rational. These positions are formalism,[1] syncretism, and eclecticism.

Formalism

Because they have to believe in something, formalist counselors accept an "all-or-nothing" attitude toward the strongest, most meaningful theory that presents itself to them. If they happen to have selected an adequate theory, they are provided a high degree of consistency and a rational order upon which to base their practice. They are able to operate within a circumscribed and formalized theoretical framework. Usually, however, a single theory does not adequately explain or predict the variety of client issues, concerns, and problems that confront counselors. The dilemma that faces the purist counselor is that all aspects of the theory are seen as equally acceptable, useful, and truthful. Figure 4-1 provides a graphic illustration of the formalist position.[2]

EXAMPLE Carl Rogers has completely explained the most effective and appropriate ingredients in counseling process and outcome. Consequently, Rogerian Person-Centered counseling is the all-inclusive, perfect theory of counseling.

ANALOGY Prunes are the only kind of fruit worth eating. They taste the best and are the best for you at all times. If you eat prunes you will need no other fruit.

PROBLEMS The purist approach implies that all parts of the concept are equally strong and defensible. In addition, dogmatic and emotional involvement with the theory are increased and maximized.

---

[1]. Another term that conveys the same notion is the term "purism." These terms—purist and formalist—are used interchangeably here.

[2]. For this section, we have utilized and paraphrased the schema that Bischof (1964) in his first edition developed to explain the purist, the synthesist, and the eclecticist positions in theories of personality.

FIGURE 4–1 Formalist/Purist

The square represents the complete frame
of reference for the counselor. It is pure,
unblemished, and uncontaminated. It
includes nothing else.

Syncretism

Helping is an applied science. Counselors are concerned with positive outcomes and with effectiveness. The majority tend to be pragmatists, discarding that which does not work and retaining that which does. Not infrequently a pragmatic attitude leads to the unsystematic and uncritical combination of many threads, scraps, and pieces of various theories. The origin and intent of many of the ideas are obscured in the general melee of the system. The relationship between the concepts are loosely formed. The syncretistic position is practical until the time comes for practitioners to review and challenge one of the threads of their system. As with a ball of tangled yarn, they cannot do this without pulling apart most of the structure. The unraveling may lead to so much confusion that they become thoroughly lost within their own system. The syncretist position is summarized in Figure 4–2.

EXAMPLE Rogers, Ellis, Perls, and Wolpe have developed theories that make sense. All of them have been of help to their clients. There is much good to be said about all of them. No one of them provides the best answer about any facet of helping, but taking the best of them will be most useful.

ANALOGY The juice from many fruits (prune, orange, plum, pineapple) is blended and served as one liquid: the perfect drink. It contains a mixture of the best fruit juices combined into one grand and delicious drink.

PROBLEM The syncretist system does not permit analysis. To examine is to destroy. If one of the components of the approach is called into

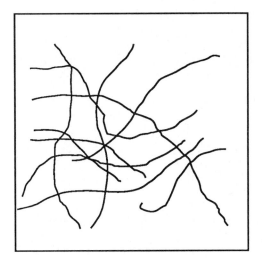

FIGURE 4–2 Syncretist

The square represents the conceptual framework of the helper. The interwoven and interconnecting lines are separate ideas and concepts that overlap and intermingle with each other into a unified mass.

question, the entire structure is threatened. In addition there is no rationale or central theme to the mix.

Eclecticism

Eclecticism in counseling is the selection by the helper of an approach that meets the needs of the client and that is particularly adaptable to a problem or situation. Helpers have selected and put into their conceptual framework both theoretical principles and practical procedures that have been examined for their worth. They know where they got a concept; they can locate it in the structure; they can remove it for examination without disordering the system. The pieces of the theory and the practice can receive more, or less, emphasis as seems appropriate. The diagram in Figure 4–3 further explains the eclectic position.

EXAMPLE Rogers' concepts of accurate empathy, positive regard, and genuineness seem highly important and help form the basic relationship that most counseling approaches use. Wolpe's reciprocal inhibition appears very useful, particularly with anxious and fearful clients. Ellis' illogical sentences and their use in the thought process seem particularly suitable for some clients.

ANALOGY A fruit salad combining several fruits (prunes, plums, oranges, pineapples) is served as a single dish with a bonding agent such as a dressing, which serves as a unifying factor.

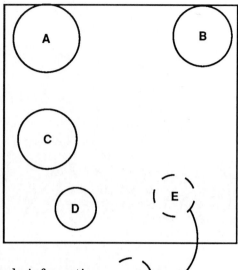

FIGURE 4–3 Eclecticist

Again, the square represents the helper's frame of reference. The lettered circles represent the various components of the system. The distance between the circles and their varying sizes are important. One component, E, has been removed for examination.

PROBLEMS AND SOLUTIONS   One needs information, understanding, and exposure to several counseling approaches. The model suggests and allows for continuous evaluation of the distinct components without the destruction of the total structure. Let us assume that E represents Wolpe's reciprocal inhibition theory and practice. As counselors continue to see a particular client, they become aware that their client's need is often related to interpersonal anxiety. Counselors' desire to be increasingly effective "helpers" to their clients leads them to examine in greater detail the theoretical approaches that may provide their clients with additional aid. Having used relaxation training and hierarchy construction to help test anxiety problems in previous clients, counselors' further reading, study, and thinking leads them into their eclectic position and to apply that approach to their clients' interpersonal anxiety concerns. The theory is evaluated in the context of the client population and in light of a particular client problem.

Figure 4–3 schematically represents several different and important aspects of the eclectic position. The varying sizes of the circles represent the relative importance accorded to the various components. Concepts in A have more weight and carry more value than concepts in B. This is easily seen by the differences in the size of the circles. The distance between A and C and between A and B suggests that there is more similarity between the concepts in A and the concepts in C than there are between A and B.

The figure also demonstrates the allowance for continuous evaluation of the distinct components without the destruction of the total structure. E has been pulled out for examination and the decision to eliminate or reinsert it may be carried out. The opportunity for continuous evaluation of distinct parts is not possible for the formalist or the syncretist without the destruction of the whole.

Finally, and perhaps most importantly, the model assumes that the eclectic position identifies the sources of the ideas included with the framework. Individuals adopting this position are provided with the ability and security to live with their present theory and return to the original source or to new research findings to compare, evaluate, and extend their ideas.

The bonding agent in the eclectic position is the personness of therapists. Counselors need a variety of theoretical concepts that become understood and organized around and within themselves. Counselors' own personality, philosophy, knowledge, and skills are the principal determinants as to how they choose to interact in a problem-solving situation. Dealing with the client system directly as the change agent or initiating an action system to relieve the problem are strategies determined by the helper. Essentially, this eclectic model provides an organization that is a dynamic, growing process with a consistent unity that maintains itself in spite of constant modification and extension. The importance of the personality of the helper to eclecticism is critical and is considered next.

THE PERSONNESS OF THE COUNSELOR

Utilizing the eclectic position, ultimately individual practitioners must adopt their own approaches. Not all helpers can be expected to be comfortable with a given problem-solving method. Since counselors differ in value systems, need systems, and personality structure, there must also be differences in the application of the counseling approaches used. Just as a counseling technique must be suited to the needs of the client, it must also be suited to the needs of the helper. Essentially, counselors draw to themselves approaches that are most congenial. Ideally, these approaches should also provide strong evidence of effectiveness and validity. Counselors integrate these approaches into a conceptualization and a style they are able to use effectively. Of course, the helper's selection of various theories is not entirely objective. Counselors' philosophy of life and their own personality influence the data to which they are sensitive. Their philosophy and personality contribute to their counseling repertoire. Essentially, it is romantic to assume that counselors can accept and internalize that which is foreign and repulsive to their own personal makeup and experience. Counselors cannot operate maturely and professionally in borrowed clothes. Preferably their suit is tailor made with the cloth and style selected upon the basis of their own individual tastes.

Theory follows personality. Therefore, adequate consideration must be given to the personal characteristics of the counselor, and clear self-exploration on the part of the counselor is essential. Indeed, the helper's needs, values, defenses, and perceptions are critical to the helping process.

Since the "counselor as a person" is a basic element in the counseling relationship, counselors' behavior cannot be contrived, mechanical, and forced if they are to establish an effective working relationship with their client. The theoretical position counselors choose will ultimately lead them to emphasize certain aspects of their personality in the helping role. The theoretical position should not force the counselor to try to become a radically different person.

An important function of a counselor education program is to provide an opportunity for prospective counselors to learn to develop, test, and modify their own personal theory of counseling. This personal theory is obtained through interpersonal experiences. These experiences are obtained in group and individual counseling sessions in which the student participates as client, in human relations laboratory experiences, in group dynamics, and in the counseling practicum. The major objectives of these kinds of experiences are increased awareness of self in interpersonal relationships and increased sensitivity to feedback from others in such relationships. Counselors also develop their personal theory by increased exposure to rich sources of theoretical frames of reference.

Increasing counselor knowledge and understanding, especially *self*-knowledge and *self*-understanding, creates shifts in the counselor's adaptation of theory. Beginning helpers, as they become aware of various approaches, are likely to develop a loose affinity for certain approaches in contrast to other approaches. Indeed, beginning helpers, when they discover a theoretical approach that has high appeal for them, sometimes resemble the proverbial "kid with a new toy." Hopefully, as they learn more about these approaches, as they experience the application of these in simulation, role-played, or "real" situations, they will continue to learn more about themselves and about the components of their eclectic theory. Initially, helpers in training should examine the aspects of their personality that create an attraction for a particular theory. Equally important, they should examine the neutral or negative responses toward other theories. This active examination of self and of theories is a continual process whereby counselors increase in both self-knowledge and self-development as well as in an understanding and application of theory. In short, as they continue to develop self-knowledge, the theoretical views tend to become more useful and applicable. Essentially, the various theories become integrated within the context of the individual helper's style.

Consideration must also be given to the influence that personality and helper/client interaction have on the counseling process and outcome. The idiosyncratic characteristics and personal qualities of the individual helper must be capitalized for promoting greater therapeutic benefits for the client. Keeping this consideration in mind, helpers need to develop a conceptual framework that may in part help them to consolidate and define the theories they choose to utilize.

PSYCHOLOGICAL FUNCTIONING: A CONCEPTUAL FRAMEWORK

One way of conceptualizing how individuals function is in terms of three processes that, on the surface, appear to be quite distinct and separate: behavior, affect, and cognition. In working with a client, we can usually identify problems, such as deficiencies or excesses of some behaviors, inappropriate or extreme emotions, and faulty, illogical thinking. Often a client's particular problem seems to fall into one of the three categories. The difficulty that a client experiences may manifest itself primarily in one form or another, but in actuality these three processes are always overlapping, interdependent, and mutually reinforcing. Problem behavior may stem from or result in unrealistic thinking and inappropriate emotions, and disturbing feelings may cause or be caused by certain dysfunctional behaviors and unwarranted thoughts. Consequently, a change in one facet will bring about simultaneous modification in the others.

Figure 4–4 illustrates this tripartite model of psychological functioning. The circle represents the total organism, integrating cognitive, effective, and behavioral responses and acting as a whole. The divisions between the components delineate the three types of responses, but do not imply static and indivisible processes. The arrows demonstrate the interrelationship, the blending and mingling of the three functions.

It is important to realize that the interactive relationship depicted in Figure 4–4 exists in *any* problem with which a person might struggle. For the purpose of therapeutic intervention, however, it is often useful to separate the problem into its components and examine each aspect individually. This makes it easier to apply specific corrective measures. It also helps clients become aware of the various aspects of their experience and understand better how these aspects influence each other. Since these three components and their interaction are essential to understanding clients and the role of the counselor in the therapeutic process, it is pertinent to discuss each of the components at this time.

Affect

Individuals have an emotional component to their personality. Feelings are extremely important aspects of the inner life of the individual. Feeling, emotion, affect are all descriptive of a mental state with particular physiologic responses and motor expression and are usually related to some external situation or object.

People do not always distinguish clearly between thoughts and feelings, and our language reflects this confusion. For example, "I feel he doesn't love me anymore" does not express a feeling, but rather a thought. "I feel hurt," on the other hand, does express a feeling. When dealing with clients, counselors may have to pay particular attention to eliciting genuine feelings as opposed to cognitive statements couched in "feeling" language.

Behavior

Behavior is viewed as a pattern of responses learned by the person through interaction with the environment. Generally, this aspect of individuals refers to their objective, observable behavior, which includes motor responses.

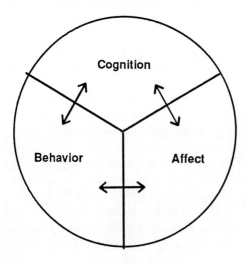

FIGURE 4–4 A model of psychological functioning

Here again, as part of dealing with behavior, the worker may have to help clients and their significant others to distinguish between behavior and inferences about behavior. "He's lazy" is not a description of behavior, it is an inference. "He does not do his homework and his chores around the house" is a description of behavior.

Cognition

People have an innate capacity for cognition, and thought is one of the most important characteristics of human beings. Thinking and cognition refer to the meanings and symbols that people attach to transactions in the world, and the associations they make between events. Among the many cognitive processes with which a counselor will be concerned are interpretation, evaluation, explanation, and inference. We want to examine the assumptions, judgments, and assessments clients make; the expectations, beliefs, opinions, and convictions they hold; the premises and hypotheses under which they operate; and the conclusions they draw about their experience. All these concepts involve reasoning and thinking and are important contributors to a client's internal and interpersonal dynamics.

Since these processes often occur at a low level of awareness, it is sometimes necessary for counselors to bring the client's thinking out in the open before change can take place. In a similar way, as counselors help the individual identify and clarify affect as well as specify problematic behavior, the stage is set to ameliorate dysfunctional interactions with others. These cognitive processes are especially important in problem solving with families because of the frequency, repetitiveness, and mutual reinforcement of interactions that occurs in families (see Chapter 15).

Most theories of individual counseling tend to focus on a singular facet of the client. For example, reality therapy and behavior modification strategies such as operant conditioning and contingency management deal with the person's behavior. Rational-emotive therapy, transactional analysis, and cognitive restructuring approaches as well as individual psychology from the Adlerian and Dreikurs framework tend to highlight the individual's thinking process. Person-centered and Gestalt techniques as well as relationship and communication skills-building techniques tend to have an impact on the feelings of the client. When deciding on specific intervention techniques, it becomes important to select from those approaches that are especially suited to the particular process—behavioral, affective, cognitive—to be changed. In reality each of the theories, while approaching change from a primary perspective, is not unmindful of the other areas. To a greater or lesser extent, each expects and obtains change in the other areas.

It is impossible for counselors to deal with all facets of their client in their entirety at the same time. They must focus on only a portion of a client's concerns and, therefore, be concerned with particular feelings, thoughts, and actions only at a particular point in time in the counseling process. The fragments the counselor chooses to focus on are of prime importance. Although, again, movement in one area stimulates movement in the others.

PROBLEM-SOLVING APPROACHES

As mentioned earlier in this chapter, the present eclectic position does not represent a new theory of counseling, but rather a pragmatic device for applying counseling approaches. One of the implicit assumptions of this position is that a variety of theoretical approaches have the potential for beneficial application to client problems. More effective helping can be achieved by accepting an eclectic theoretical-technical position. The current eclectic approach offers a frame of reference for the application of counseling theories and approaches and may provide the groundwork for future integration of a variety of theories.

The eclectic helper selects an approach that is most likely to produce client growth and improvement. In order to accomplish this, the practitioner must be thoroughly schooled in various theoretical models; must understand the application of varying approaches that arise out of different theoretical bases; and must have some experience in the practice of that approach.

PHILOSOPHICAL POSITIONS

There are almost as many approaches to the counseling process as there are counselors. However, most counselors owe some allegiance to three major theoretical, philosophical influences—psychodynamic, behavioral (or cognitive-behavioral), and humanistic. Generally, counseling theories have emerged from one or the other of these three basic positions. These positions represent a basic philosophical stance that one might take regarding one's perception of the world and of human beings. Historically, these three viewpoints were considered forces that at various points in the development of psychology and counseling became a major focus for the development of personality and counseling theories. Essentially, the philosophy of these theories provides a backdrop to more specific theories of counseling. In the following chapter we will identify and apply to a client case study three specific counseling theories that have their roots in these three positions. Here, we wish to consider the basic philosophy that undergirds the three forces.

Psychoanalytic Theory

This force, originated by Sigmund Freud, has the longest history of any of the presently used theories (Gladding, 1988). Freud was the first to discover that human behavior followed certain lawful patterns and, thus, was the first to bring order out of chaos. In addition to orthodox psychoanalytic therapy, psychoanalytic theory includes the neo-Freudians such as Alfred Adler, Eric Erickson, Eric Fromm, Karen Horney, Carl Jung, Wilhelm Reich, and Harry Stack Sullivan. Similarly, currently popular Eric Berne (Transactional Analysis), Alexander Lowen (Bio-energetics), and even Fritz Perls (Gestalt therapy) all have their roots in traditional Freudian thought.

The basic philosophical underpinnings of psychoanalytic theory suggest that human beings are greatly influenced by unconscious dynamic forces and by early experiences. Unconscious motives and conflicts are central in current behavior and irrational forces are quite strong. Individuals are driven by sexual (libido) and aggressive impulses. It is posited that repressed childhood conflicts create current pathology in human interactions.

Traditional psychoanalytic thought holds to a generally negative and deterministic view of humans (Corey, 1986). That is, human beings are selfish, impulsive, and irrational beings whose behavior is predetermined by biologic variables. Sexual and aggressive forces dynamically interact to create conflicts for the individual. Individuals repress painful childhood experiences so that some thoughts are more accessible to conscious awareness than others. According to Freud, human beings are determined by irrational forces, biologic and instinctual needs and drives, unconscious motivations, and psychosexual events that occurred during the first five years of life.

Behavioral and Cognitive-Behavioral Theory

Behavioral theory was developed out of laboratory research done in the 1920s and 1930s principally as a reaction to the inability of scientists to measure and evaluate the outcomes of psychoanalytic approaches to helping. Behavioral therapy placed psychological change and intervention into the context of education (learning) rather than medicine and emphasized the need to predict and measure outcome based on observable, objective, and measurable variables. Behavioral theory can be separated into two basic approaches. These include the radical behavioralism of B. F. Skinner (1971) and the more recent cognitive-behavioral approaches. A number of tenets form the basic philosophy of radical behaviorism. Behavior is learned from situational and environmental factors and not from within the organism. Because all behavior is learned, it can be unlearned. Since people have no control over their behavior from within, there is no self-determinism and human beings are able to be manipulated. Values, feelings, and thoughts are ignored because only concrete observable behavior is considered. In short, situational cues create specific behavior and that behavior's consequences shape and control it further. Behavior is cued by stimuli that precede it and is shaped and controlled by reinforcing stimuli that follow it. In radical behaviorism there is no emphasis on internal factors.

Although behavioral approaches are currently very diverse, some commonalities do exist between most. All of them

1. Focus on current influences rather than on historical determinates of behavior.
2. Emphasize the observation of overt behavioral change as the main criteria by which treatment is evaluated.
3. Specify treatment goals in concrete, objective terms that help in replication.
4. Rely on basic research as a source of hypotheses about treatment and specific therapy techniques.
5. Define problems in therapy specifically so treatment and measurement are possible.

A major development in the past several years is the cognitive-behavioral perspective (Mahoney & Lyddon, 1988). Utilizing many of the principles of radical behaviorism, cognitive-behavioral approaches expand and apply behavioral principles to various mediating variables. That is, cognitive-behavioral approaches deal with irrationality and thinking processes as mediators of behavior. Cognitive-behavioral approaches tend to be instructive, directive, and verbally oriented. The individual client's thoughts and feelings are assumed to function in the same way that overt behavior functions. In other words, thoughts and feelings, in the cognitive-behavioral approach, can be considered either stimuli and/or reinforcement properties (Bandura, 1969; 1977).

Humanistic Theory

Freudian psychology is concerned with the unconscious and with hidden meanings. Behaviorism provides a polar position with emphasis on observed behavior, stimulus response patterns, and concrete action. Both approaches have tended to represent mechanistic and predetermined views of human beings, although in more modern usage of these theories an underlying humanism and optimism have developed. This increasingly hopeful and optimistic view of humankind is at least partially due to the major "third force" in psychology—the humanistic tradition.

The humanistic and existential theories of helping focus on the uniqueness of each person's internal perspective, which determines one's reality. This approach emphasizes the here and now, rather than the what was or what will be. How people perceive the world and feel about themselves and their environment are also emphasized rather than focusing on their adjustment to prevailing societal norms. Humanistic approaches also emphasize affective rather than cognitive or behavioral domains within the individual.

The term "humanistic counseling" does not so much imply a systematic psychology or a collection of techniques, but rather alludes to a therapeutic attitude based on a philosophy of life and an existence. This humanistic attitude governs the counselor's interactions with the client.

Humanistic counseling evolved both in Europe and in the United States as a reaction to the determinism of Freudian psychoanalysis and to the mechanism of the behavioral psychologists. Its major proponents in the United States are Carl Rogers, Rollo May, Victor Frankel, Fritz Perls, Eric Fromm, Abraham Maslow, and Gordon Alport. The humanistic perspective emphasizes the subjective, personal, experiential aspects of human existence. This approach reflects the idea that objective interpretations and analysis of behavior are more accurate than subjective, personal analyses.

CONCLUSION

What we have tried to do in this chapter is to discuss the place of theory in counseling, emphasize eclecticism as an appropriate stance for counseling practice, highlight the personal characteristics of the helper in selecting from theories, provide a framework to apply those strategies, and emphasize the philosophical backdrop for theory development and adaptation. In the next chapter, using a case study methodology, we focus on three specific theories that represent distinct ways in which counselors go about the business of helping clients.

Even though we distinguish separate theories in the following chapter, the principles that we outline in the current chapter were combined in helping a specific client. Hopefully, the reader will be able to discern how elements in this chapter are actualized.

REFERENCES

Bandura, A. (1969). *Principles of behavior modification.* New York: Holt, Rinehart & Winston.

Bandura, A. (1977). Self-efficacy: Toward a unifying theory of behavioral change. *Psychological Review, 84,* 191–215.

Beutler, L. E. (1983). *Eclectic psychotherapy: A systematic approach.* New York: Pergamon Press.

Bischof, L. J. (1964). *Interpreting personality theories.* New York: Harper and Row.

Corey, G. (1986). *Theory and practice of counseling and psychotherapy* (3rd ed.). Monterey, CA: Brooks/Cole.

Gladding, S. T. (1988). *Counseling: A comprehensive profession.* Columbus OH: Merrill.

Goldfried, M. R. (1980). Toward the delineation of therapeutic change principles. *American Psychologist, 35,* 991–999.

Goldfried, M. R. (Ed.). (1982). *Converging themes in psychotherapy.* New York: Springer.

Howard, G. S., Nance, D. W., & Myers, P. (1986). Adaptive counseling and therapy: An integrative, eclectic model. *The Counseling Psychologist, 14*(3), 363–442.

Ivey, A. E. (1980). Counseling 2000: Time to take charge. *The Counseling Psychologist, 8,* 12–16.

Lazarus, A. A. (1976). *Multimodal behavior therapy.* New York: Springer.

Mahoney, M. J., & Lyddon, W. J. (1988). Recent developments in cognitive approaches to counseling and psychotherapy. *The Counseling Psychologist, 16*(2), 190–234.

Skinner, B. F. (1971). *Beyond freedom and dignity.* New York: Knopf.

Tyler, L. E. (1980). The next twenty years. In J. M. Whiteley & B. R. Fretz (Eds.), *The present and future of counseling psychology.* Monterey, CA: Brooks/Cole.

5.

Individual Counseling ■

BENEDICT T. MCWHIRTER, M.C.
J. JEFFRIES MCWHIRTER, PH.D., ABPP
Arizona State University
Tempe, Arizona

IN THE LAST CHAPTER we identified three philosophical positions
that counselors might adopt as they go about the business of developing
a system of helping that is most appropriate for them. In this chapter we
intend to present a specific counseling theory approach for each of the
philosophical positions that illustrates and illuminates that framework.
The three theories that we will consider are Carl Rogers' person-centered theory reflecting the humanistic tradition, Albert Ellis' rational
emotive therapy representing the behavioral/cognitive-behavioral focus,
and current psychoanalytic perspectives that have recently been articulated by Robbins (1989). For each of the theories we will discuss the theoretical rationale for problem development and the mechanisms of
change proposed by the theory that augments change and facilitates
client growth. This second component will also include the techniques,
processes, and/or attributes that are important in implementing the theories. Given the space limitations the reader needs to be aware that our
discussion is greatly restricted. Consequently, we have provided at the
end of this chapter additional readings for students who want to do further in-depth study of the theories.

In addition to an abbreviated discussion of the theoretical constructs of each theory, we will apply each of the approaches to a single

case study. Our intent is to provide the reader with specific issues that an individual theory will bring to bear in helping clients deal with their concerns. The following case study, the story of "Sally," is based on the case records of one of the authors, modified to ensure anonymity. Interventions from each of the theoretical perspectives were used with Sally. As discussed in the previous chapter, this eclectic approach to counseling has great therapeutic benefits and is effective for explaining what are often very complex client concerns. As the reader will see, an eclectic approach proved to be very effective for helping Sally deal with a variety of issues that she wanted to work on in counseling.

THE STORY OF SALLY

Sally was a 36-year-old Caucasian woman who entered counseling hoping to deal with a variety of issues and concerns that had been bothering her and getting in the way of her leading a fulfilling life. She expressed the desire to improve her interaction with significant others, coworkers and acquaintances. She reported being troubled by intense feelings of depression and loneliness, as well as feelings of anger and resentment that she fosters toward people in her past and present. Sally hoped to decrease what she referred to as her "bitchy" behavior, to stop interpreting messages and situations in a consistently self-critical way, and to put closure on a two-year dating relationship.

Sally described a very difficult childhood in which her father's family continuously criticized and ridiculed her. She pointed out that her parents never defended her and even restricted her from protesting against her relatives' verbal onslaught. She felt that from a very early age she experienced rejection and loneliness. Sally reported that her intimate relationships as an adult have mirrored her relationships with her relatives as a child. In other words, Sally believed that she has always sought out and involved herself with people who are similar to those family members who have caused her so much pain in the past. She had been married and divorced three times, and described each of these relationships as being very destructive: her first husband "beat her," her second husband was a "drug addict," and her last husband "wanted a mother." She explained that her marriage relationships reflected her need to win people over and gain their approval, especially people who remind her of past relatives who never approved of her and were so "emotionally abusive" toward her.

Sally expressed concern that she now gives herself the same negative messages that she has heard all her life. She reported that she does not understand why she continues to "kick herself" in spite of the fact that she is now 1000 miles away from her family. She stated that at times she really hates herself. She expressed strong fears of being mistreated and rejected in the future as she has been in the past. She expressed frustration with her behavior, but tended to avoid in-depth discussion of her feelings and had to be prompted by the counselor to do so. It was surmised that her feelings were very intense and difficult for her to manage. Sally began counseling with an expressed desire to change or better manage these complex issues in her life.

Let us turn now to our theories and discover how each would identify the development of Sally's problem and then go about helping her to modify her affect, cognition, and behavior so that she can lead a more productive and satisfying life.

A PSYCHODYNAMICALLY ORIENTED APPROACH

The central purpose of this section is to consider the broad aspects of Freudian thought and practical constructs that may be useful to beginning therapists. The psychodynamic approach being presented here is *not* pure Freudian psychotherapy. While based on traditional theory, the presentation here is only one adaptation of psychodynamic thought (see Robbins [1989] for an excellent discussion of contemporary psychoanalysis in counseling).

Rationale: How Problems Evolve

The psychoanalytic approach stresses the influence of genetic impulses (instincts), the concept of life energy (libido), the importance of the client's life history (psychosexual and/or psychosocial development), the influence of early experiences on the later personality of the individual, and the irrationality and unconscious sources of human behavior (Robbins, 1989). Freud viewed people as inherently instinctual creatures, driven by their strivings for infantile gratification. Throughout life, the individual is strongly motivated to seek out satisfaction of one of two primitive instinctual drives: aggression and sex. The resulting conflict obscures the process of one's emotional awareness and perception of self and others. Thus, we distort the reality of the world around us by using defense mechanisms which protect our ego by allowing us to block out important information and to subjectively redefine that which we do not accept.

The psychoanalytic concepts of levels of awareness are significant contributions. Freud held that three different levels of awareness influence personality development: the conscious, the preconscious, and the unconscious. At any one time an individual can be aware or conscious of only a very limited number of things. The conscious level consists of those thoughts of which the individual is aware at the moment. The preconscious includes information that can be brought to the conscious level relatively easily. The third level of awareness is the unconscious. In the analytic tradition this is the most important portion of the mind because it largely determines human behavior. Certain information cannot readily be brought to the conscious level. In fact, one resists awareness of it. The traditional example is the person who hates his or her father, yet is unaware that these feelings exist. In psychoanalytic theory, the importance of these unconscious feelings is that they constantly strive to become conscious and the individual then expends considerable energy to keep them in the unconscious. Thus, people are in a constant state of internal conflict of which they are not aware.

This concept of the unconscious, and the resulting internal conflict, is further complicated by a series of structural elements known as the *id,* the *ego,* and the *superego.* These elements are also a source of internal conflict. The largest element is the id, which has the characteristics of being irrational, unorganized, primitive, pleasure-oriented, and unconscious. The id is the source of the libido or energy-in-life-force and serves as the source of drives and basic wishes for death and life.

The second element of the structure is the ego, which functions as a controlling reality-oriented, mastery mechanism. The ego serves as a mediator between the superego and the id. In traditional Freudian theory, the ego is sometimes seen as being at the mercy of the other two competing forces. In more modern theory, however, the task of the therapist is seen as helping the ego decide and balance id and superego (Kohut, 1971).

The third aspect of the structure is the superego, which functions as a controlling agent in the personality. In many ways the concept is similar to the popular term "conscience." Social mores and parental moral attitudes are internalized by the individual and become an important functional and instructional part of the personality in later years.

Depression and anxiety frequently result from the conflicts between the id, ego, and superego. Thus, negative emotions develop from unconscious memories of past childhood experiences, from frightening impulses from the id (such as aggressive desires that may be forbidden), from guilt derived from an overdeveloped superego, or from the inadequacies of the ego to resolve this internal conflict.

This anxiety is threatening to the individual and may be repressed by the ego defense mechanisms, which serve to protect the personality from itself. Unfortunately, ego defense mechanisms also tend to deny, falsify, or otherwise destroy reality (Freud, 1936). Thus, the individual's personality development is impeded and realistic problem-solving procedures are limited.

The complex task of the counselor is to help the client uncover the structure of anxiety so that personal reconstruction can begin. In the case of Sally, the psychodynamically-oriented counselor believes that the origin and solution to her problems lie deep within her personality. For example, her excessive anxiety and depression might well be explained by the conflict between her angry, hostile feelings toward her parents and her superego, which continues to insist that parents are to be loved. Her ego defense mechanism of turning against self and identification with the aggressor force her to expend considerable energy hiding the conflicts from herself and contribute to her self-derogatory behavior. One of the therapeutic tasks is to help her become more aware of her style of handling her unconscious thoughts and anxieties and to find more personally satisfying and socially approved ways of resolving tensions. Thus, the goal becomes making the unconscious more conscious—that is, helping Sally know and use more mature ways to use her psychic energies and to become more aware of distorted behaviors that result from threatening unconscious impulses. This awareness of her unconscious feelings will result in more rationality, spontaneity, and other values implicit in a more mature personality.

Mechanisms of Change

The purpose of psychodynamic counseling with Sally is to make her conscious of unconscious material. The two means by which this is done is through *transference* and a *therapeutic alliance*. Gelso and Carter (1985) provide an excellent discussion of these techniques with the counselor-client relation. Transference occurs when the client reexperiences emotions and attitudes originally present in earlier relationships, often the parent–child relationship, but others as well, and directs them toward the counselor. In the case of Sally, transference expressed itself in Sally's negativistic and "whiney" attitude about the perceived lack of help she was receiving from the counselor. In discussions with her about her early childhood experiences, it became clear that this aspect of her personality was developed in her relationship with her cousins. Eventually she was able to work through her unresolved conflicts with her cousins by means of the transference relationship. In a careful and gentle way the counselor analyzed her transference relationship in order to help her understand how she was misperceiving, misinterpreting, and misresponding to the counselor and to other people outside the counseling relationship because of experiences in those earlier relationships.

That is, the transference relationship and its interpretation to the client helped her achieve insight and a corrective emotional experience by means of *abreaction,* or the expression and discharge of repressed emotions by catharsis.

The interpretation of the transference information and Sally's acceptance of it was based on the therapeutic alliance developed between the counselor and Sally. This therapeutic alliance, or the working alliance, is the alignment that occurs between the counselor and the client. More precisely, this alliance occurs between the reasonable side of the client (that is, the observing and reasonable ego in analytic terms) and the counselor's therapizing or working side. The working alliance consists of three parts. The first component is an emotional bond between the counselor and the client. The second component is a conceptual agreement between the two about the goals of counseling. The third component is a mutual acceptance of the tasks involved in the work of therapy. Thus, there is a positive attachment between the counselor and the client and an acceptance of desired goals by both participants. Also, the counselor and the client agree on which in-therapy and extra-therapy tasks will be helpful in obtaining the goals. In the case of Sally these three factors were carefully nourished by the counselor to lead to a positive outcome.

Summary of the Psychodynamic Approach

Counselors using a psychodynamic approach in order to be effective with their clients need to recognize that there are motivating forces within people that are not entirely conscious. They must understand the significance of childhood experiences and use the concept of transference in the counseling relationship. They need to know how people defend themselves from external and internal threats with ego defense mechanisms and other methods of resistance. Finally, they need to use effectively the counseling process of a working therapeutic alliance to analyze the transference of the client so that clients can achieve a successful outcome of self-understanding of their internal conflicts.

A COGNITIVE-BEHAVIORAL APPROACH

Behavior therapy comprises various approaches in the helping relationship, such as applied behavioral analysis, behavior modification, and stimulus response approaches. Social learning theory (Bandura, 1969, 1977) is particularly important. From the behavioral perspective, human actions are determined by their immediate consequences in the environment. With Bandura's (1969) discussion of mediating variables, the door was open to consider a person's thoughts, feelings, hopes, and dreams as an internal environment that operates on behavior just as the external environment does. This emphasis on the cognitive aspects of behavior has been particularly helpful to counselors because it has stimulated cognitive-behavioral approaches to helping. Thus, the cognitive-behavioral approach allows the counselor to focus on the helper attributions, appraisals, expectancies, and belief systems. These internal mediating variables and their effects are then related to the cognitive processes on emotions and behaviors. Currently, there are over 20 major cognitive interventions used in counseling (Mahoney & Lyddon, 1988).

Predating the paradigm shift from radical behaviorism to cognitive-behaviorism are the tenants of rational emotive therapy (RET). Rational emotive therapy, developed by Albert Ellis (1962), is based on the belief that people need to change their way of thinking (cognitive restructuring) to correct faulty and irrational thinking. Since Ellis is considered by practitioners to be one of the two most influential theorists in this century, it is appropriate to use his approach to illustrate one application of cognitive-behavioral counseling.

Rationale: How Problems Evolve

Essentially, Ellis (1962) suggests that emotional disturbance is the result of irrational and illogical thinking that occurs in the form of internalized sentences or verbal symbols that compromise an irrational system of beliefs. Thus, according to RET, emotional disturbances arise to a large degree from thinking or cognitive processes. Ellis recognizes, however, that emotion is a complex mode of behavior that is intricately tied to a variety of sensing and response processes and states.

The major assumptions of rational emotive therapy is that thoughts cause feelings. In other words, it is not other people or events that makes one feel upset or bad, but one's belief or view about these persons or events that creates emotional distress. Ellis proposes an A–B–C–D–E model as a cognitive intervention strategy (Ellis, 1985). In the A–B–C–D–E model, the client learns to recognize activating events (A), corresponding *beliefs* about the events (B), and behavioral and emotional *consequences* (C). The counselor then helps the client to *dispute* (D) the old belief system and to attend to the new behavioral and emotional *effects* (E) of increased rational thinking. Let us consider each of these components separately and in relationship to Sally's problems.

Activating Event
Maladaptive thoughts are often activated by an unfortunate or obnoxious person or situation in the client's life. Usually the presence of

person or situation is partly what prompts the client to enter counseling. In the case of Sally, for example, her recent volatile breakup with a man she had been dating for 2 years brought on a great deal of stress and depression. The relationship, and the manner in which it ended, led Sally to begin to recognize her pattern of entering into destructive relationships. These events also led her to begin to believe that her own thoughts, behaviors, and messages within the relationship contributed to its termination as well as to other problems in her life. Sally's failure to understand the causes of her own behavior, thoughts, and feelings, however, is what prompted her to begin counseling.

Consequences

The emotional consequences of the activating event are the C in Ellis' formula. In the case of many clients the negative emotions of guilt, anger, depression, and anxiety are emotional consequences that for naive clients appear to be directly caused by the activating event. In Sally's case she strongly believed that her feelings of rejection, sadness, and depression were directly related to the emotional turmoil in her relationship with her father and his family and not simply in her current relationship. Sally felt that she was repeatedly rejected and indirectly told that she was a terrible person. She illustrated this by reporting her feelings when her parents would not allow her to "fight back" when her relatives criticized and "verbally abused" her. These past events, like similar current events, are what Sally perceived to be the causes of her anger, depression, and self-hate. These perceptions appear to be at the root of her own belief system about herself and about the world around her.

Mechanisms of Change

Belief System

Identifying the client's belief system is a major focus of RET and is the beginning step in the mechanism of change. Ellis emphasizes that this belief system is an intermediate variable between the activating event and the negative consequence of the emotion. Ellis (1962) also states that a client's belief system is heavily contaminated by irrational beliefs. Since the client is likely to make the connection between A and C, a good bit of the work of the RET counselor is to help the client identify certain irrational beliefs that are really the underlying cause of the negative feelings. Ellis (1962) has identified 11 irrational ideas that would seem inevitably to lead to widespread neurosis. These illogical ideas are adhered to in an absolutistic and dogmatic way and become a part of the individual's internal dialogue of "self-talk." The 11 irrational beliefs are

1. It is essential that one be loved or approved of by virtually everyone in his community for whatever he does.

2. One must be perfectly confident, adequate, and achieving to consider one self worthwhile.

3. Some people are wicked, bad, or villainous and therefore deserve to be punished.

4. When things are not as one wants them to be it is a terrible catastrophe.

5. Unhappiness is caused by outside circumstances and the individual has no control over them.

6. Fearsome and dangerous things are causes for great concern and the possibility must continuously be dwelt upon.

7. It is easier to avoid certain difficulties and self-responsibilities than to face up to them.

8. One should be dependent on others and must have someone stronger on whom to rely.

9. Past events and experiences are the determiners of present behavior; the influences of the past cannot be eradicated.

10. One must be quite upset over other people's disturbances and problems.

11. There is always a perfect or correct solution to every problem and it must be found or the results will be catastrophic (p. 61).

Two main tenets of RET counseling are to (1) demonstrate to the client that his or her self-talk is the source of the disturbance, and (2) help the client to reevaluate this self-talk in order to eliminate it and the underlying illogical ideas. Sally, for example, felt that she had always been the butt of jokes, criticized incessantly, and told in different ways that she was a worthless and unlikable person. She also made statements within her counseling sessions, such as "I need to prove to myself that I'm acceptable," and "The most I could hope for is to be stuck with losers and to be victimized," and "I guess I need to be lectured to; I don't like yelling at myself, but that's what I end up doing." The counselor helped Sally clarify how she perceived events and interpreted messages from others as well as from herself. This clarification process was important to ascertain her belief system about herself and about significant situations. As these perceptions and interpretations became clear, the counselor helped Sally to realize her self-talk and the messages she had been giving herself that included irrational statements such as those illustrated by Ellis.

Dispute

The real work of rational emotive counseling takes place at this stage. The counselor actively challenges the client's existing belief system with the intent of eliminating the irrational beliefs and helping the client to acquire and internalize a new and more rational philosophy. The process of clarifying interpretations and uncovering the illogical, irrational nature of Sally's messages was argued with Sally. The counselor provided new, more supportive and logical self-statements such as "I can be disliked by certain people and still be a good and worthwhile person." Homework was suggested for her. Whenever she remembered being disliked by another, she was instructed to repeat three times to herself the sentence "But I still am a good and worthwhile person." In counseling sessions, the illogicalness of needing to be loved by everyone was consistently disputed. These strategies were positively effective for her. She began to realize that her self-critical, irrational belief system augmented her depression and anger and contributed to problems in her relationships. By changing her belief system, she began to recognize more effective and positive ways of seeing herself and of relating with others.

New Effects

In Ellis' approach, the work that the counselor does within the dispute (D) stage helps to modify the beliefs (B). Emphasis is then placed on the resulting new effects (E). New effects typically include changes in behavior and diminished emotional distress. The client is encouraged to notice these changes and to rejoice in them. Thus, in working with Sally the RET counselor would proceed through several steps. The counselor shows Sally that she is being illogical. She is helped to understand how and why she became so. The counselor would demonstrate the relationship between her irrational ideas and her unhappiness. The counselor unmasks Sally's past and present illogical thinking or self-defeating verbalizations by (1) bringing them forcefully to her attention; (2) showing her how they are causing and maintaining her unhappiness and disturbance; (3) demonstrating exactly what the illogical links and internalized thoughts and sentences are; and (4) teaching her how to rethink these sentences so that her internalized thoughts become more efficient and logical. Sally is shown that she is maintaining her disturbance by continuing to think illogically. She is encouraged to change by abandoning her illogical thinking and developing more realistic and rational explanations and expectations of herself, of others, and of her environment.

Summary of Rational Emotive Therapy

The basic assumption of the RET approach to counseling is that most people in our society develop many irrational ways of thinking. These irrational thoughts lead to inappropriate and/or irrational behavior. Thus, counseling must be designed to help people to recognize and change these irrational beliefs into more rational ones. The accomplishment of this goal requires a confrontive and supportive counselor who has the capacity to actively engage the client.

In this section we discuss person-centered counseling, one of the major

PERSON-CENTERED APPROACH

theories in the humanistic framework. This theory, developed by Carl Rogers, has evolved during the past 50 years and has been known during various times of its evolution as nondirective, client-centered, and Rogerian counseling. The present use of the term "person-centered" reflects the current expansion of this theory.

Rationale: How Problems Evolve

A central issue in person-centered theory lies in how the individual perceives the world. What the individual perceives in his or her phenomenological field is more important than the actual reality. Said in another way, what the individual *perceives* to be ocurring *is* the reality. Thus, a consistent effort to understand and experience as far as possible the uniqueness that underlies each person is basic to person-centered counseling. Person-centered theory is not concerned primarily with causes of behavior or with changing behavior directly. Rather, it focuses on the current experiences, feelings, and interactions of the individual.

Person-centered counseling is also a self-theory, based on a belief that people act in accordance with their self-concept. One's self-concept is heavily influenced by experiences with others. As a person interacts with the environment in his or her perceptual field, the self-concept begins to develop. For a healthy self to emerge, a person needs *positive regard,* such as love, warmth, respect, acceptance, and care.

Often in childhood, as well as later in life, a person is given *conditional regard* by parents and others. These messages from parents and others to the child indicate what the child must do or how the child must be in order to receive acceptance. Feelings of worth develop if the person behaves in certain ways because conditional acceptance teaches the person to feel valued only when conforming to others' wishes. Sometimes, however, a person may have to deny or distort a perception when someone upon whom the person depends for approval sees the situation differently. The individual is thus caught in a dilemma because of the incongruity between self-perception and experience. If a person does not do as others wish, he or she is not valued and accepted. Yet if a person conforms, he or she opens up a gap between the *real self* that the person is and the *ideal self* the person is striving to become. The further the real self is from the ideal self, the more alienated and maladjusted a person becomes. In other words, conflict arises when individuals must choose between the need for positive regard and other personal needs that are not in accord with significant others' conditions of worth. This concept of the self is a learned attribute, a progressive concept starting from birth and developing steadily through childhood, adolescence, and adulthood like an unfolding spiral.

In Sally's case, she has experienced a contradiction between the conditions of worth that were placed on her as a child and her own needs and self-perceptions. For example, she received direct or indirect messages from her parents that she should not "fight back" or confront her cousins and other relatives for being verbally abusive toward her. They stated to her, "You're better than they are, you don't need to fight back." Even though Sally sensed the contradiction in this situation, she has incorporated the conflict into her self-system. Further, much of her present negative interaction with others reflects a self-concept that has tried to incorporate these two competing and contradictory messages. Thus, Sally harbors a great deal of anger and resentment toward her family and toward others who remind her of her family. She fairly frequently lashes out in self-defeating ways toward people in current relationships because they "remind" her of family members against whom she was never able to "fight back."

From the person-centered perspective, Sally's poor self-concept is not only the result of a long history of negative messages from others, which Sally now believes, but also from the contradiction between the conditions of how she should be and act in order to be a good, acceptable person and how she, in fact, behaves toward and thinks about others.

For a long period of time Sally has given herself the message that she is an undesirable, unacceptable person. Unfortunately, Sally's self-concept seems to have been formed on this premise, so that she now finds it difficult to respond to others and to herself in a caring and accepting way. Her marriage relationships further enhance her negative self-image because they have reinforced her feeling that she is a "failure" and a "victim" and will "always be stuck with losers."

The person-centered counselor would attempt to clarify the complexity of Sally's self-concept in order to begin efforts toward ameliorating much of her pain and frustration that is related to it.

Mechanisms of Change

Self-Actualization

Within the humanistic framework, the self-actualizing tendency is the primary motivating force of the human organism. Self-actualization is an inherent tendency of people to move in directions that can be described as growth, adjustment, socialization, health, independence, self-realization, and autonomy. Thus, in the person-centered approach, an essential characteristic of humans is that they have an innate capacity to interact with their environment in ways designed to maintain and enhance the self. Rogers (1951) emphasized that the client's natural capacity for growth and development is an important human characteristic upon which counseling should rely. Even with her pain, frustration, and self-defeating behaviors, Sally has a basic tendency toward self-enhancement and is compelled toward constructive, positive outcomes, given the right conditions.

The Core Conditions

In his historically important article, Rogers (1957) identified those conditions that characterize an effective client–counselor relationship. They are

1. The two persons are in psychological contact.

2. The first person (i.e., the client) is in a state of incongruence, being vulnerable or anxious.

3. The second person (i.e., the counselor) is congruent and integrated in the relationship.

4. The counselor experiences unconditional positive regard for the client.

5. The counselor experiences an empathic understanding of the client's internal frame of reference and works to communicate this experience to the client.

6. The communcication to the client of the counselor's empathic understanding and unconditional positive regard is achieved at least to a minimal degree.

This article stimulated an enormous amount of research (Carkhuff, 1969a, 1969b; Rogers, 1967) that defined the necessary core conditions as "geniuneness, accurate empathy, and nonpossessive warmth (or respect)." These terms parallel Rogers' congruency, empathic understanding, and unconditional positive regard. These core conditions offered by the counselor to the client result in a therapeutic relationship that allows the client's self-actualizing tendency to emerge. Because of their importance to the person-centered theory we will discuss each of the core conditions below.

UNCONDITIONAL POSITIVE REGARD   This condition or counselor attitude has also been referred to as "nonpossessive warmth," "warmth," and "regard" and is equivalent to respect, appreciation, and acceptance of another person. It can be described as the counselor's ability to experience a warm acceptance of every aspect of the client's personality. "Nonpossessive" or "unconditionally" implies that the counselor does not qualify his or her acceptance of the client but accepts the client fully as a separate person with a right to his or her own thoughts, words, actions, and feelings.

Unconditional positive regard from the counselor to Sally was crucial to the helping relationship, especially in view of the fact that Sally's feelings of worth and her negative self-concept were based on certain conditions. The counselor offered positive regard with no conditional clauses and no strings attached. This caring, accepting attitude of Sally's individuality comes from the belief that she could discover within herself the necessary resources for her own growth. Eventually, she will come to the understanding that she is capable of taking charge of her own life.

CONGRUENCE   Congruence, or genuineness, refers to the counselor's capacity to be "real" in the relationship. Thus, genuineness is used to denote honesty, directness, and sincerity, and an absence of a professional facade. Rogers (1961) defines congruences as follows:

> By this we mean that the feelings that the counselor is experiencing are available to his awareness, that he is able to live with these feelings, be

them in the relationship, and able to communicate them if appropriate....It means that he is being himself, not denying himself. (p. 417).

Genuineness, then, is the counselor's ability to be psychologically open and transparent to the client in therapy. The counselor is real and genuine in the relationship, demonstrating a consistency between his own feeling and experiencing at the moment and his verbalizations to the client.

In Sally's case, the counselor's consistency and willingness to be real in the relationship with her provided Sally with a reality base that could be trusted and that took away some of the risk of sharing herself with another person. It was the counselor's realness—the openness to his experience with Sally—that was a critical element for her change. it allowed her to be real and to come into touch with and express her own immediate feelings.

EMPATHY   Empathic understanding, or empathy, may be defined as one's ability to perceive and understand another's feelings, their intensity, and their meaning. The main work of a counselor is to understand accurately and sensitively the client's feelings and experiences as these are revealed during moment-by-moment interaction of the counseling session. The counselor strives to sense fully and accurately the inner world of the client's subjective experience. By the counselor's empathic understanding, he or she hopes to help clients get closer to themselves and to experience more of their deeper feelings.

The concept of accurate empathy, like the other core conditions, has evolved over the years in the direction of freeing the counselor to be a more active participant in the therapeutic encounter. High levels of accurate empathy go beyond recognition of obvious feelings to a sensing of the less obvious and less clearly experienced feelings of the client. The client's obvious feelings are, of course, understood and recognized, but the counselor also strives to understand those aspects of feeling that are present within the client but less clearly perceived and communicated.

In one interview, Sally expressed that her depression and feelings of resentment typically drove her to do things to others that pushed them away or kept them from getting close to her. Sally expressed how she behaved, but failed to indicate her feelings about the consequences of her behavior. The counselor focused on these unspoken feelings in order to help Sally come more into touch with them and, ultimately, with herself. When the counselor asked Sally to describe her loneliness, she began to cry. Since loneliness was the result of her behaviors toward others, helping her to recognize and deal with it was a major factor in her continuing growth.

Summary of the Person-Centered Approach

A major component of person-centered theory is the belief in an innate positive growth potential for the self-actualizing power of the individual. This is coupled with the postulation of a self-concept. The main intent in counseling is to develop a relationship between the counselor and the client. Crucial to this relationship are the counselor's attitude of genuine concern, regard, and acceptance of the client and an ability to experience and communicate accurate empathy to the other person. Thus, the effort and ability to build and maintain an anxiety-reducing and nonthreatening relationship in which growth can take place is an essential component of person-centered therapy.

CONCLUSION

In this chapter we have attempted to highlight some of the theoretical and therapeutic contributions of three counseling theories within the psychoanalytic, cognitive-behavioral, and humanistic traditions in psychology. We have discussed aspects of a psychoanalytic model, Ellis' rational emotive therapy, and Rogers' person-centered approach and attempted to demonstrate each of their contributions to the process of counseling individuals toward achieving positive change and growth. The case of Sally provided a means for demonstrating these contributions.

Hopefully, these two chapters overviewing theoretical issues in counseling and the application of three specific theories within the counseling process will both help you understand your own theoretical framework and heighten your interest in understanding more about the theories themselves. Unfortunately, the attempt to synthesize these positions into two short chapters must inevitably lead to some distortion. Since it has not been possible in the available space to deal with all the nuances necessary for a clear explanation of the points of view, readers are encouraged to further their understanding of these approaches through additional reading. The reading list, given at the end of the chapter will help you get started in further exploration of these views and approaches.

REFERENCES

Bandura, A. (1969). *Principles of behavior modification.* New York: Holt, Rinehart & Winston.

Bandura, A. (1977). Self-efficacy: Toward a unifying theory of behavioral change. *Psychological Review, 84,* 191–215.

Carkhuff, R. R. (1969a, 1969b). *Helping and human relations.* (Vol. 1, Vol. 2). New York: Holt, Rinehart & Winston.

Carkhuff, R. R. (1969b). *Helping and human relations.* (Vol. 2). New York: Holt, Rinehart & Winston.

Ellis, A. (1962). *Reason and emotion in psychotherapy.* New York: Lyle Stuart.

Ellis, A. (1985). Expanding the ABC's of rational-emotive therapy. In M. J. Mahoney & A. Freeman (Eds.). *Cognition and psychotherapy* (pp. 313–323). New York: Plenum.

Freud, A. (1936). *The writings of Anna Freud: Vol. 2. The ego and the mechanisms of defense.* New York: International Universities Press.

Gelso, C. J., & Carter, J. A. (1985). The relationship in counseling and psychotherapy: Components, consequences, and theoretical antecedents. *The Counseling Psychologist, 13,* 155–243.

Kohut, H. (1971). *Analysis of the self.* New York: International Universities Press.

Mahoney, M. J., & Lyddon, W. J. (1988). Recent developments in cognitive approaches to counseling psychology. *The Counseling Psychologist, 16*(2), 190–234.

Robbins, S. B. (1989). Role of contemporary psychoanalysis in counseling psychology. *Journal of Counseling Psychology, 36*(3), 267–278.

Rogers, C. R. (1951). *Client-centered therapy.* Boston: Houghton-Mifflin.

Rogers, C. R. (1957). The necessary and sufficient conditions of therapeutic personality change. *Journal of Consulting Psychology, 21,* 95–103.

Rogers, C. R. (1961). *On becoming a person.* Boston: Houghton-Mifflin.

Rogers, C. R. (1967). The conditions of change from a client-centered viewpoint. In B. Berenson & R. Carkhuff (Eds.), *Sources of gain in counseling and psychotherapy.* New York: Holt, Rinehart & Winston.

ADDITIONAL READING

Psychodynamic Theory

Alexander, F. (1963). *Fundamentals of psychoanalysis.* New York: W. W. Norton.

Freud, A. (1946). *The ego and the mechanisms of defense.* New York: International Universities Press.

Freud, S. (1943). *A general introduction to psychoanalysis.* Garden City, NY: Doubleday.

Guntrip, H. (1979). *Psychoanalytic theory, therapy, and the self.* New York: Guilford.

Kohut, H. (1971). *The analysis of self.* New York: International Universities Press.

Cognitive-Behavioral Theory

Beck, A. T. (1976). *Cognitive therapy and the emotional disorders.* New York: International Universities Press.

Ellis, A. (1962). *Reasons and emotion in psychotherapy.* New York: Lyle Stuart.

Ellis, A., & Harper, R. (1972). *A new guide to rational living.* Englewood Cliffs, NJ: Prentice-Hall.

Person-Centered Theory

Carkhuff, R., & Berenson, B. (1967). *Beyond counseling and therapy.* New York: Holt, Rinehart & Winston.

Rogers, C. (1951). *Client-centered therapy.* Boston: Houghton-Mifflin.

Rogers, C. (1961). *On becoming a person.* Boston: Houghton-Mifflin.

Rogers, C. (1980). *A way of being.* Boston: Houghton-Mifflin.

6.

Group Counseling ▪

DAVE CAPUZZI, PH.D, N.C.C.
Portland State University,
Portland, Oregon
DOUGLAS R. GROSS, PH.D.
Arizona State University,
Tempe, Arizona

THE LAST DECADE OF the twentieth century poses problems and possibilities that should be of high interest to the beginning counselor enrolled in a counselor education program and considering becoming a group work specialist. If we believe that the 1950s may have symbolized "the individual in society," the 1960s "the individual against society," the 1970s "the individual's conflict with self," and the 1980s "the individual's integration into the family," the society of the 1990s and beyond may clearly be characterized as "the individual's integration with the machine" (Shapiro & Bernadett-Shapiro, 1985). Much of the work in educational, employment, and day-to-day living situations will be done by computers; connections between colleagues, friends, and family members will be maintained by telephone lines, word processors, and modems. The replacement of consistent social contact with friends and coworkers by the video display terminal will create a much greater need for interpersonal communication on a person-to-person basis. Groups will provide an antidote to human isolation, and more and more counselors and other human development specialists will be called upon to serve as group facilitators. The beginning counseling and human development specialist will experience crescendoing opportunities and escalating concomitant responsibilities as a group work specialist.

The purpose of this chapter is to provide an introduction to group work for those interested in pursuing follow-up education and supervision in the context of masters and doctoral preparation experiences. The history of group work, types of groups, myths connected with group work, stages of group life, characteristics of group facilitators, group facilitation: responsibilities and interventions, and the issues and ethics of group work will all be overviewed.

THE HISTORY OF GROUP WORK

Beginnings

As noted by Vriend (1985), the first half of the twentieth century was characterized by lively interest, experimentation, and research in the promising new field of group dynamics. Behavior in small groups, leadership styles, membership roles, communication variables, and so on were all examined and studied for their application to groups in a variety of settings (Hare, Borgatta, & Bales, 1967).

In 1947, a history-making conference in Bethel, Maine, was attended by a multidisciplinary group of researchers and practitioners from university and community settings throughout North America. The National Training Laboratory (NTL) in Group Development of the National Education Association held its first "laboratory session" and T-groups (the "T" is for training) and the laboratory method were born (Bradford, Gibb, & Benne, 1964). First, using themselves as experimental subjects, participants at the conference created a laboratory situation in which the behavior of the participants was more important than any effort or technique employed. The situation created a safe place for group members to explore their own behavior, feelings and the responses of others to them as people separate from social, work, and family roles. Under the direction of the NTL, such conferences continued each summer and the T-group movement grew and achieved national visibility.

As time passed, T-groups appeared on university campuses and in other settings. The T-group provided a fresh concept with tremendous appeal as opportunity was provided for group members to become more "sensitive," to "grow emotionally," and to "realize their human potential." The country began hearing about the "human potential movement" and of exciting developments in California, particularly at the Esalen Institute at Big Sur and at the Center for the Studies of the Person founded by Carl R. Rogers and his colleagues. Soon there were a variety of marathon and encounter groups; it was an era of openness, self-awareness, and getting in touch with feelings.

The 1960s and 1970s

The 1960s were a time of social upheaval and questioning. There were riots on campuses and in cities as civil rights groups struggled to raise the consciousness of the nation relative to years of unfair discrimination and prejudice. Leaders such as John F. Kennedy and Martin Luther King, Jr., became the idolized champions and international symbols of a people's determination to change a society and to promote social responsibility. The nation united in grief-stricken disbelief as its heroes were martyred, and determination to counter the human rights violations of the decades escalated. As the 1960s ended, the encounter group movement, emphasizing personal consciousness and connection with others, reached its zenith, then gradually waned as events such as the Watergate scandal, the first presidential resignation in the history of the United States, the Charles Manson killings, the group killings at the Munich Olympics, and the rise of fanatic cults made people in all parts of the country question the extent to which permissiveness and "human potential" should be allowed to develop (Janis 1972; Rowe & Winborn, 1973).

For professionals in education and mental health, however, the 1960s and 1970s were decades of maintained interest in group work despite the highs and lows of societal fervor and dismay. Mental health centers conducted more and more group sessions for clients, and counselor education, counseling psychology, psychology, and social work departments on university campuses instituted more and more course work and supervised experiences in aspects of group work. In 1973, the Association for Specialists in Group Work (ASGW) was formed and by 1974 it had become a division of the American Association for Counseling and Development (at that time named the American Personnel and Guidance Association). Similar developments took place in the context of other large professional groups such as the American Psychological Association and the National Association of Social Workers.

The 1980s

The 1980s witnessed increasing interest in group work and in working with specialized populations. There are groups for alcoholics, adult children of alcoholics, incest victims, adults molested as children, persons who are overweight, underassertive persons, and those who have been victims of violent crimes. There are groups for the elderly, for those dealing with death and other losses, for the eating-disordered, the smoker, and the victims of the holocaust (Shapiro & Bernadett-Shapiro, 1985). This increasing specialization has brought with it an increasing need for higher standards for preparation of the group work specialist as evidenced by the development of ethical standards for group work specialists (ASGW, 1983) and the inclusion in the standards of the Council for Accreditation of Counseling and Related Educational Programs (CACREP, 1988) of specific group work specialist preparation guidelines for the graduate-level university educator to follow. At the same time, this increasing specialization has brought with it a reliance on what has become known as the self-help group composed of individuals who share a specific affliction. Usually, such groups are not facilitated by a professional, and this set of circumstances can be in conflict with the values and standards of professional group work.

Although the future of group work will be discussed at the end of this chapter, it should be noted that the practice of the group work professional will require increasing levels of expertise and an enhanced ability to participate in and apply the results of needed research. The history-making national conference for group work specialists, conceptualized and sponsored by ASGW in early 1990 in Florida, symbolizes the importance of group work to the clients served by the counseling and human development professional.

TYPES OF GROUPS

Most textbooks for introduction to counseling courses begin the discussion of group work by attempting to make distinctions among group therapy, group counseling, and group guidance. In general, *group therapy* is described as being longer-term, more remedially and therapeutically focused, and more likely to be facilitated by a facilitator with doctoral-level preparation and a more "clinical" orientation. *Group counseling* may be differentiated from group therapy by its focus on conscious problems, by the fact that it is not aimed at major personality changes, by an orientation toward short-term issues, and by the fact that it is not as concerned with the treatment of the more severe psychological and behavioral disorders (Corey & Corey, 1987). *Group guidance* usually is descriptive of a classroom group in a K through 12 setting in which the leader presents information or conducts mental health education. In contrast to a group therapy or group counseling situation involving no more than eight to ten group participants, a group guidance experience could involve 20 to 40 group participants, lessening opportunities for individual participation and facilitator observation and intervention.

For the purposes of this chapter the four-part paradigm suggested below (Scheidlinger, 1985) is presented as a point of departure for classifying groups. The reader may wish to do additional reading relative to group "types" from sources such as Corey (1985), Dinkmeyer and Muro (1979), Gazda (1984), or Ohlsen (1977).

Category I—Group Psychotherapy

Group psychotherapy refers to a psychosocial process in which a mental health professional, trained in psychology or counseling psychology as well as in psychopathology, uses emotional interactions in small, carefully constructed groups to assist individuals in the process of overcoming personality and interpersonal dysfunctions. A clinical orientation, which includes assessment of each potential group member's strengths and weaknesses as well as suitability for group membership, is generally assumed. Group psychotherapy practitioners require extensive educational and supervisory experience prior to independent practice because of the long-term nature of the group psychotherapy process and the chronic nature of the problems of group members.

Category II—Therapeutic Groups

"Therapeutic" groups include all the group approaches (other than group psychotherapy) that are used by counseling and human development professionals in in-patient, out-patient, or private practice settings. These groups are usually used as an auxiliary or conjoint experience in addition to the primary mode of treatment (which could be either individual, group, or family focused). Often, such groups are directed toward remediation or achievement of optimal functioning. Art therapy, movement therapy, socialization, and behavior therapy groups are a few examples of the types of groups that might be classified in this category.

Category III—Human Development and Training Groups

Human development and training groups could perhaps be described as being more closely allied to affective and cognitive mental health education than to therapeutic groups. This does not mean that participation in such a group precludes personal growth and an enhanced sense of well-being. The personal expressive, consciousness-raising, and sensitivity groups that can be classified in this category may have purposes such as decreasing social isolation; making relationships more genuine; coping with divorce, death, or other losses; dealing with life transitions, or understanding sexuality.

Category IV—Self-help Groups

Self-help groups are usually voluntary group experiences for participants who share a common problem or need. Many self-help groups are conducted without the presence of a professional facilitator. Alcoholics Anonymous, Al-Anon, Parents Without Partners, and Overeaters Anonymous are examples of self-help groups that are relatively well known and established in most communities.

MYTHS CONNECTED WITH GROUP WORK

Counselors who are group work specialists are usually quite enthusiastic about the benefits for clients of participation in a small group. Indeed, the outcomes of a competently facilitated group experience can be such that personal growth occurs. Often the memory of such an experience has an impact on clients well into the future. On the other hand, group work, as with other forms of therapeutic assistance (e.g., individual or family), can be for better or for worse (Carkhuff, 1969). Many group workers follow a belief system that can be challenged by empirical facts.

Beginning counselors are well advised to be aware of a number of myths connected with group work so they don't base their "practices" on a belief system not supported by research (Anderson, 1985).

Myth #1: Everyone Benefits from Group Experience

Groups do provide benefits. The research on the psychosocial outcomes demonstrate that groups are a powerful modality for learning, which can be used outside the group experience itself (Bednar & Lawlis, 1971; Gazda & Peters, 1975; Parloff & Dies, 1978). There are times, however, when membership in a group can be harmful. Some research shows that one of every ten group members can be hurt (Lieberman, Yalom, & Miles, 1973). The research findings that seem to relate most to individuals who get injured in groups suggest some important principles for the beginning counselor to understand: (1) those who join groups and who have the potential to be hurt by the experience have unrealistic expectations, and (2) these expectations seem to be reinforced by the facilitator who coerces the member to meet them (DeJulio, Bentley, & Cockayne, 1979; Lieberman, Yalom, & Miles, 1973; Stava & Bednar, 1979). Prevention of harm requires that the expectations members have for the group are realistic and that the facilitator maintains a reasonable perspective.

Myth #2: Groups Can Be Composed to Ensure Effective Outcomes

The fact is that we do not know enough about how to compose groups using the pregroup screening interview. In general, objective criteria (e.g., age, sex, socioeconomic status, presenting problem, etc.) can be used to keep groups homogeneous in some respects, but behavioral characteristics should be selected for on a heterogeneous basis (Bertcher & Maple, 1977). The most consistent finding is that it is a good idea to compose a group in such a manner that each member is compatible with at least one other member (Stava & Bednar, 1979). This practice seems to prevent the evolution of neglected isolates or scapegoats in a group.

The essence of group process in terms of benefit to members and effective outcomes is perceived mutual aid (e.g., helping others, a feeling of belonging, interpersonal learning, instillation of hope, etc.) (Butler & Fuhriman, 1980; Long & Cope, 1980; Yalom, 1975).

Myth #3: The Group Revolves Around the Charisma of the Leader

It is true that leaders influence groups tremendously, but there are two general findings in the research on groups that should be noted. First, the group, independent of the leader, has an impact on outcomes. Second, the most effective group leaders are those who help the group develop so that members are primary sources of help to one another (Ashkenas & Tandon, 1979; Lungren, 1971).

As noted by Anderson (1985), research on leadership styles has identified four particular leader functions that facilitate the group's functioning:

1. *Providing:* This is the provider role of relationships and climate-setting through such skills as support, affection, praise, protection, warmth, acceptance, genuineness, and concern.
2. *Processing:* This is the processor role of illuminating the meaning of the process through such skills as explaining, clarifying, interpreting, and

providing a cognitive framework for change or translating feelings and experiences into ideas.

3. *Catalyzing:* This is the catalyst role of stimulating interaction and emotional expression through such skills as reaching for feelings, challenging, confronting, and suggesting; using program activities such as structured experiences; and modeling.

4. *Directing:* This is the director role through such skills as setting limits, roles, norms and goals; managing time; pacing; stopping; interceding; and suggesting procedures. (p. 272)

Providing and processing seem to have a linear relationship to outcomes: the higher the providing (or caring) and the higher the processing (or clarifying), the higher the positive outcomes. Catalyzing and directing have a curvilinear relationship to outcomes. Too much or too little catalyzing or directing results in lower positive outcomes (Lieberman, Yalom, & Miles, 1973).

Myth #4: Leaders Can Direct Through the Use of Structured Exercises or Experiences

Structured exercises create early cohesion (Levin & Kurtz, 1974; Lieberman, Yalom, & Miles, 1973); they help create early expression of positive and negative feelings. However, they restrict members from dealing with such group themes as affection, closeness, distance, trust, mistrust, genuineness, and lack of genuineness. All these areas form the very basis for group process and should be dealt with in a way that is not hampered by a large amount of structure. The best principle around which to plan and use structured exercises to get groups started and to keep them going can best be stated as "to overplan and to underuse."

Myth #5: Therapeutic Change in Groups Comes About Through a Focus on Here-and-Now Experiences

Much of the research on groups indicates that corrective emotional experiences in the here-and-now of the group increase the intensity of the experience for members (Levine, 1971; Lieberman, Yalom, & Miles, 1973; Snortum & Myers, 1971; Zimpfer, 1967). The intensity of emotional experiences does not, however, appear to be related to outcomes. Higher-level outcomes in groups are achieved by members who develop "insight" or cognitive understanding of emotional experiences in the group and can transfer that understanding into their lives outside the group. The Gestaltists' influence on groups in the 1960s and 1970s (Perls, 1969) suggested that members should "lose your mind and come to your senses" and "stay with the here-and-now." Research suggests that members "use your mind and your senses" and "focus on the there-and-then as well as on the here-and now."

Myth #6: Major Member Learning in Groups Is Derived from Self-Disclosure and Feedback

There is an assumption that most of the learning of members in a group comes from self-disclosure in exchange for feedback (Jacobs, 1974). To a large extent, this statement is a myth. Self-disclosure and feedback per se make little difference in terms of outcomes (Anchor, 1979; Bean & Houston, 1978). It is the use of self-disclosure and feedback that appears to make the difference (Martin & Jacobs, 1980). Self-disclosure and feedback appear useful only when deeply personal sharing is understood and appreciated and the feedback is accurate (Berzon, Pious, and Farson, 1963; Goldstein, Bednar, & Yanell, 1979; Frank & Ascher, 1951). The actual benefit of self-disclosure and feedback is connected with how these processes facilitate empathy among members. It is empathy, or the actual experience of being understood by other members, that catalyzes personal growth and understanding in the context of a group.

Myth #7: The Group Facilitator Can Work Effectively with A Group Without Understanding Group Process and Group Dynamics

Groups experience a natural evolution and unfolding of processes and dynamics. Anderson (1979) labeled these stages as those of trust, autonomy, closeness, interdependence, and termination (TACIT). Tuckman (1965) suggested a more dramatic labeling of forming, storming, norming, performing, and adjourning. Two reviews, which include over 200 studies of group dynamics and group process (Cohen & Smith, 1976; La Coursiere, 1980), revealed remarkably similar patterns (despite differences in the labels chosen as descriptors) in the evolution of group processes as a group evolves through stages. It is extremely important for group facilitators to understand group processes and dynamics to do a competent job of enhancing membership benefits derived from participation.

Myth #8: Change Experienced by Group Participation Is Not Maintained over Time

Groups are powerful! Changes can be maintained by group members as much as six months to a year later even when groups meet for only three or four months (Lieberman, Yalom, & Miles, 1973).

STAGES OF GROUP LIFE

In an outstanding article, David G. Zimpfer (1986) pointed out that since the 1940s much has been written about the developmental phases or stages through which a small group progresses over time (Braaten, 1975; Bales, 1950; Hare, 1973; Golembiewski, 1962; Hill & Gruner, 1973; Thelen & Dickerman, 1949; Tuckman, 1965). He also noted that recent contributions to this topic range from descriptive, classificatory schemes (e.g., the initial, transitional, working, and final stages presented by Corey in 1985) to detailed analyses of a single phase of group development (e.g., the 1965 exploration of authority relations in T-groups presented by Reid). Zimpfer's recommendation to the group work specialist is to select the theory or model of small group development that applies to the kind of group to be conducted. Zimpfer's (1986) suggestion was to view stages of group life in terms of the following classifications: (1) counseling and psychotherapy groups, (2) encounter and personal growth groups, and (3) training and self-analytic groups. A summary of the Zimpfer paradigm follows.

Counseling and Psychotherapy Groups

Martin and Hill (1957) presented a theory of group life that described six stages. Each of the six stages was described in terms of a major therapeutic problem confronting the group; each stage identified characteristic member behaviors. The first stage is one of unshared behavior. In this stage members feel isolated and unsure of the group even though they hope that group participation will prove helpful. As members begin to react to each other, the second stage, socialization, begins. This stage is characterized by stereotypical, cautious, and superficial discussion. The third stage begins as members explore interpersonal potential and the here-and-now of group life. There is an active exchange of emotions and the focus of exploring the problems and personalities of group members is important. The fourth stage begins as members begin to understand the meanings of relationships that have developed within the group, the effect that meeting each other's emotional needs has on their behavior, and the application of these insights to relationships outside the group. Stage five occurs when members become aware of the totality of the group experience and individual problems become group problems. The final stage, if reached, occurs when the role of the facilitator is diminished because the group develops the ability to diagnose and cope with its problems, similar to what can occur in a well-functioning society.

Encounter and Personal Growth Groups

One of the best known descriptions of the stages experienced by encounter and personal growth groups was posited by Carl R. Rogers in 1967. He described the evolution of groups of intermediate duration (20 to 60 hours of group sessions) via a series of observations and noted that groups often experience some of these patterns simultaneously.

- Milling around: In this stage members feel a lack of direction or structure from the facilitator.
- Resistance to personal expression or exploration: Only the "public" self is revealed. Emphasis is on making an impression and private, more personal data, if shared, are viewed with lack of confidence relative to appropriateness.
- Description of past feelings: Members find it safe to share past feelings because such sharing seems less threatening than sharing present feelings.
- Expression of negative feelings: These are usually the first "here-and-now" disclosures and usually relate to negative feelings about other group members or the leader.
- Expression and exploration of personally meaningful material: As this stage takes place, members trust that personal information can be shared in an atmosphere of acceptance.
- Expression of immediate interpersonal feelings: Both positive and negative feelings experienced at the moment are shared by one member with another.
- Development of a healing capacity in the group: Members begin showing a genuine and spontaneous ability to help one another.
- Cracking of facades: Members begin valuing genuine behavior and become impatient with others' defenses.
- Individuals receive feedback: Members provide each other with data about how they appear to others.
- Confrontation: Members directly communicate their positive and negative reactions to each other.
- Helping relationships outside group sessions: Members help each other through offering support, empathy, etc.
- Basic encounter: Members "connect" with one another in a more direct way than in day-to-day living. This is an intense, growth-enhancing aspect of group experience.
- Expression of positive feelings and closeness: These are derived from increasing trust and intense, genuine levels of self-revelation.
- Behavior changes in the group: Individuals become more spontaneous, creative, and thoughtful of one another.

Training and Self-Analytic Groups

Bennis and Shephard's (1956) conceptualization of stages of group life was psychodynamic in nature. They proposed that some group members are conflicted (i.e., compulsive in adapting certain roles) and others are unconflicted. The members who are unconflicted with respect to authority and personal relationships are responsible for the major movements of the group toward acceptable communication.

Bennis and Shephard's conceptual model depicts training and self-analytic groups as progressing through two major phases, each with three subphases. In the first phase, the authority phase, members are concerned with issues of dependence and power. Initially, the members behave as if they are part of an ordinary conversation group and they are dependent upon the leader for direction. Then, the most assertive counterdependent members attack the leader and search for new ways of organizing the group. In the final aspect of the authority phase, members assert their independence, become involved in the group, and assume leadership formerly perceived as being in the exclusive purview of the leader.

In the intimacy phase, the members cope with the problems of interdependence and personal relationships. The first subphase is one of enchantment, high morale, and self-satisfaction. Little need for further development is perceived. Later, members begin to realize new possibilities for personal relationships; they wonder how close or how distant they should be; they reevaluate the purpose of the group. Some disenchantment occurs accompanied by ambivalence, tardiness, absenteeism, and disparaging remarks. Finally, members "regroup" and treat each other with renewed acceptance and genuineness. As the training ends, they gradually withdraw their involvement and summarize their progress.

Mann (1967) more recently articulated a theory of group development emphasizing four themes: nurturance, control, sexuality, and competence.

Before proceeding to the next major topical area of this chapter, we wish to make several points as noted by Zimpfer (1986) about the applications of "stage theory" to facilitating groups:

1. It is important to choose an appropriate developmental theory for the group you wish to conduct. Doing so will enhance both the insight and competence of the facilitator.

2. "Stage theory" provides a basis for diagnosing the group with respect to its pacing. Facilitators can assess whether a group is dealing sufficiently with issues connected with a particular stage.

3. Stage theory can also be used to assess individual progress in relation to other members in the group.

4. Facilitators can use their knowledge of how groups progress to assist in the process of moving a group from one stage to another.

5. Understanding group stages can assist the leader in sensing the approaching termination of a group and assisting in the process of closure and integration and application of group-based learning.

CHARACTERISTICS OF GROUP LEADERS

Many writers who are expert in group counseling have described the personal traits and characteristics of effective group counselors (Dinkmeyer & Muro, 1979; Kottler, 1983; Corey & Corey, 1987). As expressed by Gerald Corey in 1985:

> It is my belief that group leaders can acquire extensive theoretical and practical knowledge of group dynamics and be skilled in diagnostic and technical procedures yet be ineffective in stimulating growth and change in the members of their groups. Leaders bring to every group their personal qualities, values, and life experiences. In order to promote growth in the members' lives, leaders need to live growth-oriented lives themselves. In order to foster honest self-investigation in others, leaders need to have the courage to engage in self-appraisal themselves. In order to inspire others to break away from deadening ways of being, leaders need to be willing to seek new experiences themselves. In short, the most effective group direction is found in the kind of life the group members see the leader demonstrating and not in the words they hear the leader saying. (p. 39)

We believe that there are characteristics that the effective group leader must possess in order to do an effective job of facilitating group process. The reader is directed to sources such as Arbuckle (1975), Carkhuff and Berenson (1977), Jourard (1971), Truax and Carkhuff (1967), and Yalom (1975) for other readings on this topic. Corey's 1985 presentation is summarized below as a constructive point of departure for the beginning counselor.

PRESENCE   The leader's ability to be emotionally present as group members share their experience is important. Leaders who are in touch with their own life experiences and associated emotions are usually better able to communicate empathy and understanding because of being able to relate to similar circumstances or emotions.

PERSONAL POWER   Personal power comes from a sense of self-confidence and a realization of the influence the leader has on a group. Personal power that is channeled in a way that enhances the ability of each group member to identify and build upon strengths, overcome problems, and cope more effectively with stressors is both essential and "curative."

COURAGE   Group facilitators must be courageous. They must take risks by expressing their reactions to aspects of group process, confronting, sharing a few life experiences, acting on a combination of intuition and observation, and directing the appropriate portion of the group movement and discussion.

WILLINGNESS TO CONFRONT ONESELF   It takes courage to deal with group members; it is not easy to role model, confront, convey empathy, and achieve a good balance between catalyzing interaction and allowing the group to "unfold." It also takes courage on the part of the group leader to confront self. As Corey (1985) so aptly stated:

> Self-confrontation can take the form of posing and answering questions such as the following:
> • Why am I leading groups? What am I getting from this activity?
> • Why do I behave as I do in a group? What impact do my attitudes, values, biases, feelings, and behavior have on the people in the group?
> • What needs of mine are served by being a group leader? And to what degree?
> • Do I ever use the groups I lead to satisfy my personal needs at the expense of the members' needs? (p. 40)

Self-confrontation must be an ongoing process for the leader since the leader facilitates the capacity of members in a group to ask related questions about themselves.

SELF-AWARENESS   It is difficult to serve in any kind of a counseling role without a highly developed sense of self-awareness. Needs, defenses, apprehensions, relationship conflicts, and unresolved personal issues of any kind all come into play in the process of facilitating a group. They can enhance or detract from the leader's ability to lead the group depending upon the level of awareness of the group leader and the degree to which they make the leader's role more difficult. Many counselor education departments require graduate students to obtain counseling outside the department, for the purpose of resolving "unfinished business" so personal issues do not impede their ability to serve constructively in a counseling role.

SINCERITY   Sincerity on the part of a group counselor is usually considered to be related to the leader's genuine interest in the welfare of the group and the individual group member. Sincerity also relates to the leader's ability to be direct and to encourage each member to explore aspects of self that could easily be distorted or denied completely.

AUTHENTICITY   Effective leaders are able to be real, congruent, honest, and open as they respond to the interactions in a group. Authenticity means that the leader knows who he or she really is and has a sense of comfort and acceptance about self that results in an ability to be honest about feelings and reactions to the group in a way that is constructive to individuals as well as the group as a whole.

SENSE OF IDENTITY   Group leaders often assist members of a group in the process of clarifying values and becoming "inner" rather than "outer" directed. If the leader of a group has not clarified personal values, meanings, goals, and expectations, it may be difficult to help others with the same process.

BELIEF IN GROUP PROCESS   Leaders must be positive about the healing capacity of groups and their belief in the benefits of a group experience. If they are unsure, tentative, or unenthusiastic, the same "tenor" will develop among members of the group. As noted in the earlier discussion of myths, the outcome of a group experience is not totally dependent on the leader; however, the leader does convey messages, nonverbally as well as verbally, that do have an impact on the overall benefit of the experience.

CREATIVITY   Leaders who can be spontaneous in their approach to a group can often facilitate better communication, insight, and personal growth than those who become dependent on structured interventions and techniques. Creative facilitators are usually accepting of members who are different from themselves and flexible about approaching members and groups in ways that seem congruent with the particular group. In addition, a certain amount of creativity and spontaneity is necessary to cope with the "unexpected"; in a group situation the leader will continuously be presented with comments, problems, and reactions that could not have been anticipated prior to a given session.

STAMINA AND ENERGY   Unlike an individual counseling session during which the facilitator listens to and interacts with one client, group facilitation requires "tracking," remembering, diagnosing, etc. several clients simultaneously. Such a set of circumstances requires additional alertness, observation, responsiveness, and proactivity and energy. It is not a good idea for a counselor to overschedule the timing and number of groups for which he or she is responsible. Many counselors prefer the cofacilitation model so that the cofacilitator can assume part of the responsibility for group process and observation.

GROUP FACILITATION: RESPONSIBILITIES AND INTERVENTIONS

Responsibilities

One of the most important responsibilities of counselors interested in becoming group work specialists is to have a thorough understanding of what elements or factors are important in making groups effective in helping those who participate. Even though the group approach is a well-established mode of "treatment," the question of what it is about groups that makes them effective must be asked and understood by anyone interested in facilitating a group. One difficulty in answering such a question is that the therapeutic change that results from group participation is a result of a complex set of variables including leadership style, membership roles, and aspects of group process.

In a fascinating discussion of this topic, George and Dustin (1988) promote Bloch's (1986) definition of a therapeutic factor as "an element occurring in group therapy that contributes to improvement in a patient's condition and is a function of the actions of the group therapist, the patient, or fellow group members" (p. 679). Although this definition sounds somewhat "clinical," its application to all types of groups is apparent because it helps distinguish among therapeutic elements, conditions for change, and techniques. Conditions for change are necessary for the operation of therapeutic elements but do not, in and of themselves, have therapeutic force. An example of this is the fact that a sense of belonging and acceptance—a therapeutic element that enhances personal growth in groups—cannot emerge unless the "condition" of the actual presence of several good listeners in the group exists. Likewise, a technique, such as asking members to talk about a self-esteem inventory they have filled out, does not have a direct therapeutic effect but may be used to enhance a sense of belonging and acceptance (George & Dustin, 1988).

Group work specialists have a responsibility to understand the research that has been done on therapeutic elements of groups so they can develop the skills to create a group climate that enhances personal growth. Corsini and Rosenburg (1955) published one of the earlier efforts to produce a classification of therapeutic elements in groups. They abstracted therapeutic factors published in 300 pre-1955 articles on group counseling and clustered them into nine major categories:

1. Acceptance: A sense of belonging.
2. Altruism: A sense of being helpful to others.
3. Universalization: The realization that group members are not alone in the experiencing of their problems.
4. Intellectualization: The process of acquiring self-knowledge.
5. Reality testing: Recognition of the reality of issues such as defenses and family conflicts.
6. Transference: Strong attachment to either the therapist or other group members.
7. Interaction: The process of relating to other group members that results in personal growth.
8. Spectator therapy: Growth that occurs through listening to other group members.
9. Ventilation: The release of feelings that had previously been repressed.

In 1957, Hill interviewed 19 group therapists in an attempt to take the classification of therapeutic elements in groups further. He proposed the six elements of catharsis, feelings of belongingness, spectator therapy, insights, peer agency (universality), and socialization. Berzon, Pious, and Farson (1963) used group members rather than leaders as the source of information about therapeutic elements. Their classification included

1. Increased awareness of emotional dynamics.
2. Recognizing similarity to others.
3. Feeling positive regard, acceptance, and sympathy for others.
4. Seeing self as seen by others.
5. Expressing self congruently, articulately, or assertively in the group.
6. Witnessing honesty, courage, openness, or expressions of emotionality in others.
7. Feeling warmth and closeness in the group.
8. Feeling responded to by others.
9. Feeling warmth and closeness generally in the group.
10. Ventilating emotions.

A very different set of therapeutic elements connected with group experience was proposed by Ohlsen in 1977. His list differs from earlier proposals in that it emphasizes client attitudes about the group experience. Ohlsen's paradigm included 14 elements that he labeled as "therapeutic forces":

1. Attractiveness of the group.
2. Acceptance by the group.

3. Expectations.
4. Belonging.
5. Security within the group.
6. Client readiness.
7. Client commitment.
8. Client participation.
9. Client acceptance of responsibility.
10. Congruence.
11. Feedback.
12. Openness.
13. Therapeutic tension.
14. Therapeutic norms.

In what is now considered a landmark classification of "curative factors," Yalom (1970, 1975) proposed a list of therapeutic elements based on research he and his colleagues conducted:

1. Installation of hope.
2. Universality.
3. Imparting of information.
4. Altruism.
5. The corrective recapitulation of the primary family group.
6. Development of socializing techniques.
7. Imitative behavior.
8. Interpersonal learning.
9. Group cohesiveness.
10. Catharsis.
11. Existential factors.

It is not possible to present all the possibilities for viewing the therapeutic elements of a positive group experience. It is possible, however, to encourage the beginning counselor to study the research relating to these elements prior to facilitating or cofacilitating groups under close supervision. The leadership style of each group facilitator needs to be understood and analyzed with respect to the contribution that style makes toward creating a therapeutic milieu. Likewise, the interventions or techniques used by a facilitator need to be evaluated on the basis of whether they are enhancing or detracting from the development of the elements of a group experience which benefit clients.

Interventions

Numerous approaches to the topic of intervention strategies for groups can be found in the literature on groups. Corey (1985) approached the topic by discussing active listening, restating, clarifying, summarizing, questioning, interpreting, confronting, reflecting feelings, supporting, empathizing, facilitating, initiating, goal setting, evaluating, giving feedback, suggesting, protecting, disclosing oneself, modeling, dealing with silence, blocking, and terminating. Dinkmeyer and Muro (1971) discussed the topic by focusing upon promoting cohesiveness, summarizing, promoting interaction, resolving conflicts, tone setting, structuring and limit setting, blocking, linking, providing support, reflecting, protecting, questioning, and regulating. Bates, Johnson, and Blaker (1982) emphasized confrontation, attending behavior, feedback, use of questions, levels of interaction, and opening and closing a session. They also presented the four major functions of group leaders as traffic director, model, interaction catalyst, and communication facilitator.

Individuals new to the profession of counseling may better relate to the topic of intervention strategies by becoming familiar with circumstances during which the group leader must take responsibility for intervening in the group's "process." A helpful model (and a favorite of ours) is that presented by Dyer and Vriend in 1973 in terms of 10 occasions when intervention is required:

1. A group member speaks for everyone. It is not unusual for a member of a group to say something like, "We think we should...," "This is how we all feel," or "We were wondering why..." This happens when an individual does not feel comfortable making a statement such as "I think we should..." or "I am wondering why...." or when an individual group member is hoping to engender support for a point of view. The problem with allowing the "we" syndrome to operate in a group is that it inhibits individual members from expressing individual feelings and thoughts. Appropriate interventions on the part of the group facilitator might be, "You mentioned 'we' a number of times. Are you speaking for yourself or for everyone?" or "What do each of you think about the statement that was just made?"

2. An individual speaks for another individual in the group. "I think I know what he means" or "She is not really saying how she feels; I can explain it for her" are statements that one group member may make for another. When one person in the group speaks for another it often means that a judgment has been made about the capacity of the other person to communicate or that the other person is about to self-disclose "uncomfortable" information. Regardless of the motivation behind such a circumstance, the person who is allowing another group member to do the "talking" needs to evaluate why this is happening and whether the same thing occurs outside the group. In addition, the "talker" needs to evaluate the inclination to make decisions and/or rescue others.

Appropriate interventions include: "Did Jim state your feelings more clearly than you can?" or "How does it feel to have someone rescue you?" Statements such as "Did you feel that June needed your assistance?" or "Do you find it difficult to hold back when you think you know what someone else is going to say?" are possible interventions for the "talker."

3. A group member focuses on persons, conditions, or events outside the group. Often group counseling sessions can turn into "gripe sessions." Complaining about a colleague, friend, or a partner can be enjoyable for group members if they are allowed to reinforce each other. The problem with allowing such emphasis to occur is that such a process erroneously substantiates that others are at fault and that group members do not have to take responsibility for aspects of their behavior.

Possible interventions for the group work specialist include: "You keep talking about your wife as the cause of your unhappiness. Isn't it more important to ask yourself what contributions you can make to improve your relationship?" or "Does complaining about someone else really mean you think you would be happier if they could change?"

4. Someone seeks the approval of the facilitator or a group member before or after speaking. Some group members seek nonverbal acceptance from the leader or another group member (e.g., a nod, a glance, a smile). Such individuals may be intimidated by authority figures or personal strength or have low self-esteem and seek sources of support and acceptance outside themselves. One possible intervention is for the counselor to look at another member, forcing the speaker to change the direction of his or her delivery. Another possibility is to say something like, "You always look at me as you speak, almost as if you are asking permission."

5. Someone says, "I don't want to hurt her feelings so I won't say what I'd like to say." It is not unusual for such a sentiment to be expressed in a group, particularly in the early stages. Sometimes this happens when a member thinks another member of the group is too fragile for feedback; other times such reluctance is because the provider of the potential feedback is concerned about being "liked" by other group members. The group facilitator should explore reasons for apprehension about providing feedback, which can include asking the group member to check with the person to whom feedback may be directed to determine whether such fears are totally valid.

6. A group member suggests that his problems are due to someone else. Although this item overlaps with No. 3, this situation represents a different problem than a "group gripe" session. A single group member may periodically attribute difficulties and unhappiness to someone else. Interventions such as "Who is really the only person who can be in charge of you?" or "How can other people determine your mood so much of the time?" are called for in such a case. We are not suggesting a stance that would be perceived as lacking empathy and acceptance. It is, however, important to facilitate responsibility for self on the part of each group member.

7. An individual suggests that "I've always been that way." Such a suggestion is indicative of irrational thinking and lack of motivation to change. Believing that the past determines all of one's future is something that a group member can believe to such an extent that his or her future growth is inhibited. The group facilitator must assist such a member to identify thinking errors that lead to lack of effectiveness in specific areas. Such a member needs to learn that he or she is not doomed to repeat the mistakes of the past. "You're suggesting that your past has such a hold over you that you will never be any different" or "Do you feel that everyone has certain parts of his life over which he has no control?" are possible statements that will stimulate examination of faulty thinking and assumptions.

8. Someone in the group suggests, "I'll wait, and it will change." Often, group members are willing to talk about their self-defeating behavior during a group session but aren't willing to make an effort outside the group to behave differently. At times, they take the position that they can postpone action and things will correct themselves. A competent group leader will help members develop strategies for doing something about their problems outside the group and will develop a method of "tracking" or "checking in" with members to evaluate progress.

9. Discrepant behavior appears. Group leader intervention is essential when discrepancies occur in a member's behavior in the group. Examples of such discrepancies include a difference in what a member is currently saying and what he or she said earlier, a lack of congruence between what a member is saying and what he or she is doing in the group, a difference between how a member sees himself or herself and how others in the group see him or her, or a difference between how a member reports feelings and how nonverbal cues communicate what is going on inside. Interventions used to identify discrepancies may be confrontational in nature because the leader usually needs to describe the discrepancies noted so the group member can begin to identify, evaluate, and change aspects of such behavior.

10. A member bores the group by rambling. Sometimes members use talking as a way of seeking approval. At times such talking becomes "overtalk." The counselor can ask other members to react to the "intellectualizer" and let such a person know how such rambling affects others. If such behavior is not addressed, other members may develop a sense of anger and hostility toward the "offender."

ISSUES AND ETHICS: SOME CONCLUDING REMARKS

Although a thorough discussion of issues and ethics in group counseling is beyond the scope of this chapter, it is important for the beginning counselor to be introduced to this topic. The "Ethical Guidelines for Group Leaders," published in 1980 by the Association for Specialists in Group Work (ASGW), as well as the "Professional Standards for Training of Group Counselors" (ASGW, 1983) are both excellent points of departure for the counselor interested in groups. In addition, both of these sets of guidelines serve as useful adjuncts to the "Ethical Standards" of the American Association for Counseling and Development (1988).

ASGW (1983) recommends that the group work specialist acquire *knowledge competencies* (e.g., understanding principles of group dynamics, the roles of members in groups, the contributions of research in group work, etc.), *skill competencies* (e.g., diagnosing self-defeating behavior in groups, intervening at critical times in group process, using assessment procedures to evaluate the outcomes of a group, etc.), and *supervised clinical experience* (e.g., observing group counseling, coleading groups with supervision, participating as a member in a group). Interestingly, these very training standards have become an issue with some counselor preparation programs as they struggle to obtain a balance between the didactic and clinical components of the set of educational and supervisory experiences required to prepare an individual to do a competent job of group counseling. The clinical supervisory aspects of preparing the group work specialist are costly for universities, and often counselor educators are encouraged to abandon such efforts in favor of classroom didactics.

Another example of some of the issues connected with group counseling has to do with continuing education after the completion of masters and/or doctoral degree programs. Although the National Board for Certified Counselors (NBCC) requires those who achieve the National Certified Counselor (N.C.C.) credential to obtain 100 hours of continuing education every five years, there is no specification of how much of this professional enhancement activity should be focused on aspects of group work, if group work is the declared area of specialization of an N.C.C. In time, there may be a specific continuing education requirement for the group work specialist.

The "Ethical Guidelines for Group Leaders" help clarify the nature of ethical responsibility of the counselor in a group setting. These guidelines present standards in three areas: (1) the leader's responsibility for providing information about group work to clients; (2) the leader's responsibility for providing group counseling services to clients; and (3) the leader's responsibility for safeguarding the standards of ethical practice. One of the greatest single sources of ethical dilemma in group counseling situations has to do with confidentiality. Counselors have an obligation not to disclose information about the client without the client's consent unless the client is dangerous to self or others. Yet, the very nature of a group counseling situation makes it difficult to ensure that each member of a group will respect the other's right to privacy.

Other issues such as recruitment and informed consent, screening and selection of group members, voluntary and involuntary participation, psychological risks, uses and abuses of group techniques, therapist competence, interpersonal relationships in groups, and follow-up all form the basis for considerable discussion and evaluation. In addition, these issues emphasize the necessity of adequate education, supervision, and advance time to consider the ramifications and responsibilities connected with becoming a group specialist.

Group experiences can be powerful growth-enhancing opportunities for clients, or they can be pressured, stifling encounters to be avoided. Each of us has a professional obligation to assess our readiness to facilitate or cofacilitate a group. Our clients deserve the best experience we can provide.

REFERENCES

American Association for Counseling and Development (1988). *Ethical standards* (rev. ed.). Alexandria, VA: AACD.

Anchor, K. N. (1979). High- and low-risk self-disclosure in group psychotherapy. *Small Group Behavior, 10*, 279–283.

Anderson, J. D. (1979). Social work with groups in the generic base of social work practice. *Social Work With Groups, 2*, 281–293.

Anderson, J. D. (1985). Working with groups: Little-known facts that challenge well-known myths. *Small Group Behavior, 16*(3), 267–283.

Arbuckle, D. (1975). *Counseling and psychotherapy: An existential-humanistic view.* Boston: Allyn & Bacon.

Ashkenas, R., & Tandon, R. (1979). Eclectic approach to small group facilitation. *Small Group Behavior, 10,* 224–241.

Association for Specialists in Group Work (1980). *Ethical guidelines for group leaders.* Alexandria, VA: ASGW.

Association for Specialists in Group Work (1983). *Professional standards for training of group counselors.* Alexandria, VA: ASGW.

Bales, R. F. (1950). *Interaction process analysis: A method for study of small groups.* Reading, MA: Addison-Wesley.

Bates, M., Johnson, C. D., & Blaker, K. E. (1982). *Group leadership: A manual for group counseling leaders* (2nd ed.). Denver, CO: Love Publishing.

Bean, B. W., & Houston, B. K. (1978). Self-concept and self-disclosure in encounter groups. *Small Group Behavior, 9,* 549–554.

Bednar, R., & Lawlis, G. (1971). Empirical research in group psychotherapy. In S. L. Garfield and A. E. Bergin (Eds.), *Handbook of psychotherapy and behavior change.* (2nd ed.), (pp. 420–439). New York: John Wiley.

Bennis, W. G., & Shephard, H. A. (1956). A theory of group development. *Human Relations, 4,* 415–437.

Bertcher, H. J., & Maple, F. F. (1977). *Creating Groups.* Beverly Hills, CA: Sage.

Berzon, B., Pious, C., & Farson, R. (1963). The therapeutic event in group psychotherapy: A study of subjective reports by group members. *Journal of Individual Psychology, 19,* 204–212.

Bloch, S. (1986). Therapeutic factors in group psychotherapy. In A. J. Frances & R. E. Hales (Eds.), *Annual Review,* Vol. 5 (pp. 678–698). Washington, DC: American Psychiatric Press.

Braaten, L. J. (1975). Developmental phases of encounter groups and related intensive groups. *Interpersonal Development, 5,* 112–129.

Bradford, L. P., Gibb, J. R., & Benne, K. D. (Eds.). (1964). *T-group theory and laboratory method: Innovation in re-education.* New York: John Wiley.

Butler, T., & Fuhriman, A. (1980). Patient perspective on the curative process: A comparison of day treatment and outpatient psychotherapy groups. *Small Group Behavior, 11,* 371–388.

Carkhuff, R. R. (1969). *Helping and human relations: A primer for lay and professional helpers.* Vol. II: *Practice and research.* New York: Holt, Rinehart & Winston.

Carkhuff, R. R., & Berenson, B. G. (1977). *Beyond counseling and therapy* (2nd ed.). New York: Holt, Rinehart & Winston.

Cohen, A. M., & Smith, D. R. (1976). *The critical incident in growth groups: Theory and techniques.* La Jolla, CA: University Associates.

Corey, G. (1985). *Theory and practice of group counseling* (2nd ed.). Monterey, CA: Brooks/Cole.

Corey, G., & Corey, M. S. (1987). *Groups: Process and practice* (3rd ed.). Monterey, CA: Brooks/Cole.

Corsini, R., & Rosenberg, B. (1955). Mechanisms of group psychotherapy: Processes and dynamics. *Journal of Abnormal and Social Psychology, 51,* 406–411.

Council for Accreditation of Counseling and Related Educational Programs (1988). *Accreditation procedures manual and application.* Alexandria, VA: CACREP.

De Julio, S. J., Bentley, J., & Cockayne, T. (1979). Pregroup norm setting: Effects on encounter group interaction. *Small Group Behavior, 10,* 368–388.

Dinkmeyer, D. C., & Muro, J. J. (1971). *Group counseling: Theory and practice.* Ithaca, IL: F. E. Peacock Publishers.

Dinkmeyer, D. C., & Muro, J. J. (1979). *Group counseling: Theory and practice* (2nd ed.). Ithaca, IL: F. E. Peacock Publishers.

Dyer, W. W., & Vriend, J. (1973). Effective group counseling process interventions. *Educational Technology, 13*(1), 61–67.

Frank, J., & Ascher, E. (1951). The corrective emotional experience in group therapy. *American Journal of Psychiatry, 108,* 126–131.

Gazda, G. (1984). *Group counseling* (3rd ed.). Dubuque, IA: William C. Brown.

Gazda, G. M., & Peters, R. W. (1975). An analysis of human research in group psychotherapy, group counseling and human relations training. In G. M. Gazda (Ed.), *Basic approaches to group psychotherapy and group counseling* (pp. 38–54). Springfield, IL: Charles C Thomas.

George, R. L., & Dustin, D. (1988). *Group counseling: Theory and practice.* Englewood Cliffs, NJ: Prentice-Hall.

Goldstein, M. J., Bednar, R. L., & Yanell, B. (1979). Personal risk associated with self-disclosure, interpersonal feedback, and group confrontation in group psychotherapy. *Small Group Behavior, 9,* 579–587.

Golembiewski, R. T. (1962). *The small group: An analysis of research concepts and operations.* Chicago: University of Chicago Press.

Hare, A. P., Borgatta, E. F., & Bales, R. F. (Eds.). (1967). *Small groups: Studies in social interaction* (rev. ed.). New York: Knopf.

Hare, A. P. (1973). Theories of group development and categories for interaction analysis. *Small Group Behavior, 4,* 259–304.

Hill, W. F. (1957). Analysis of interviews of group therapists' papers. *Provo Papers, 1,* 1.

Hill, W. F., & Gruner, L. (1973). A study of development in open and closed groups. *Small Group Behavior, 4,* 355–381.

Jacobs, A. (1974). The use of feedback in groups. In A. Jacobs & W. W Spradline (Eds.), *The group as an agent of change* (pp. 31–49). New York: Behavioral Publications.

Janis, I. L. (1972). *Victims of groupthink: A psychological study of foreign-policy decisions and fiascos.* Boston: Houghton-Mifflin.

Jourard, S. (1971). *The transparent self* (rev. ed.). New York: Van Nostrand Reinhold.

Kottler, J. A. (1983). *Pragmatic group leadership.* Monterey, CA: Brooks/Cole.

La Coursiere, R. (1980). *The life-cycle of groups: Group development stage theory.* New York: Human Sciences.

Levin, E. M., & Kurtz, R. P. (1974). Participant perceptions following structured and nonstructured human relations training. *Journal of Counseling Psychology, 21,* 514–532.

Levine, N. (1971). Emotional factors in group development. *Human Relations, 24,* 65–89.

Lieberman, M. A., Yalom, I. D., & Miles, M. B. (1973). *Encounter groups: First facts.* New York: Basic Books.

Long, L. D., & Cope, C. S. (1980). Curative factors in a male felony offender group. *Small Group Behavior, 11,* 389–398.

Lungren, D. C. (1971). Trainer style and patterns of group development. *Journal of Applied Behavioral Science,* 689–709.

Mann, R. D. (1967). *Interpersonal styles and group development.* New York: John Wiley.

Martin, E. A., & Hill, W. F. (1957). Toward a theory of group development: Six phases of therapy group development. *International Journal of Group Psychotherapy, 7,* 20–30.

Martin, L., & Jacobs, M. (1980). Structured feedback delivered in small groups. *Small Group Behavior, 1,* 88–107.

Ohlsen, M. M. (1977). *Group counseling* (2nd ed.). New York: Holt, Rinehart & Winston.

Parloff, M. B., & Dies, R. R. (1978). Group therapy outcome instrument: Guidelines for conducting research. *Small Group Behavior, 9,* 243–286.

Perls, F. (1969). *Gestalt therapy verbatim.* New York: Bantam.

Reid., C. H. (1965). The authority cycle in small group development. *Adult Leadership, 1,* 308–310.

Rogers, C. R. (1967). The process of the basic encounter group. In J. F. T. Bugental (Ed.), *Challenges of humanistic psychology* (pp. 261–278). New York: McGraw-Hill.

Rowe, W., & Winborn, B. B. (1973). What people fear about group work: An analysis of 36 selected critical articles. *Educational Technology, 13*(1), 53–57.

Scheidlinger, S. (1985). Group treatment of adolescents: An overview. *American Journal of Orthopsychiatry, 55*(1), 102–111.

Shapiro, J. L., & Bernadett-Shapiro, S. (1985). Group work to 2001: Hal or haven (from isolation)? *Journal for Specialists in Group Work, 10*(2), 83–87.

Snortum, J. R., & Myers, H. F. (1971). Intensity of T-group relations as function of interaction. *International Journal of Group Psychotherapy, 21,* 190–201.

Stava, L. J., & Bednar, R. L. (1979). Process and outcome in encounter groups: The effect of group composition. *Small Group Behavior, 10,* 200–213.

Thelen, H., & Dickerman, W. (1949). Stereotypes and the growth of groups. *Educational Leadership, 6,* 309–316.

Truax, C. B., & Carkhuff, R. R. (1967). *Toward effective counseling and psychotherapy: Training and practice.* Chicago: Aldine.

Tuckman, B. W. (1965). Developmental sequences in small groups. *Psychological Bulletin, 63,* 384–389.

Vriend, J. (1985). We've come a long way, group. *Journal for Specialists in Group Work, 10*(2), 63–67.

Yalom, I. D. (1970). *The theory and practice of group psychotherapy.* New York: Basic Books.

Yalom, I. D. (1975). *The theory and practice of group psychotherapy* (2nd ed.). New York: Basic Books.

Zimpfer, D. G. (1967). Expression of feelings in group counseling. *Personnel and Guidance Journal, 45,* 703–708.

Zimpfer, D. G. (1986). Planning for groups based on their developmental phases. *Journal for Specialists in Group Work, 11*(3), 180–187.

7.

Career Counseling: An Introduction

ELLEN HAWLEY MCWHIRTER, M. C.
Arizona State University
Tempe, Arizona

Trying to eliminate her nervous fidgeting by clasping her hands under the table, the novice counselor watches as the cards are handed out. Who will this first client be? Am I going to know what to say? The anticipation builds as each member of the group is provided with demographics and a single phrase describing the client's main concern. She releases a hand to reach for the blue index card and quickly skims its contents. Female, OK, age 23, great, concern.... The counselor stifles a sigh of disappointment. No thrill, no challenge here. "Seeking career counseling."

A recent study by Pinkney and Jacobs (1985) suggests that beginning counselors may have negative attitudes about career counseling and are disinterested in spending counseling time engaged in career counseling activities. Perhaps these negative attitudes are based on the impression that career counseling is no more than a process of going through endless inventories and reference material to find the right job for a rather dull, helpless person. Contrary to these impressions, however, career counseling is an intriguing and complex area of counseling that requires an in-depth knowledge of human nature and involves an active, collaborative relationship between the counselor and the client. It is hoped that the information provided in this chapter will diminish any unfounded negative impressions the reader may have and illustrate the variety and challenge inherent in the tasks of career counselors.

Condensing the theory and practice of contemporary career counseling into a single chapter is a formidable task, and requires the elimination or scant coverage of many important aspects of career counseling. The purpose of this chapter is to introduce the beginning counselor to a developmental perspective of career counseling, and to introduce the basic components and activities that are considered the territory of the career counselor. In order to accommodate this purpose within space limitations, evaluation and critique of current theories and interventions will be minimized. Emphasis will be placed on description, with references provided for more detailed analysis of the history, theory, and research related to career counseling. The beginning counselor is urged to consult contemporary career textbooks such as those by Isaacson (1985), Osipow (1983), and Zunker (1986), and career journals such as *Career Development Quarterly, Journal of Counseling and Development,* and *Journal of Vocational Behavior.*

Before proceeding with a discussion of career development theories, two definitions are in order. Recent recognition of the pervasive nature of work in human lives has led to broader and more developmental definitions of career. "Career" will be defined in this chapter as not just people's jobs and job-related behaviors but the sum total of their attitudes, roles, relationships, and endeavors related to the world of work. Referring to the changing views of work, Super (1984) writes:

> With this recognition, and with the development of suitable methods and materials, counseling's concern for human development can manifest itself in career counseling that takes into account the changing life-career roles of developing people, can help them prepare better for their diverse roles and for their role changes, and can thus help them find more nearly complete self-realization as they go through life (p. 34).

While acknowledging the potential negative effects of losing the distinction between career and life patterns, Rounds and Tinsley (1984) note that the expanded definition of career has placed the study of careers within the less restrictive context of life-span developmental psychology. Currently, most approaches to career counseling acknowledge some aspect of the developmental nature of careers.

Keeping in mind this definition of career, "career counseling" may be simply described as the process of assisting clients in the assessment and resolution of their career-related problems. Thus the focus of career counseling could be any of the following: improvement of parenting and communication skills; development of strategies to increase marital satisfaction in a dual-career situation; exploration of decision-making techniques and enhancement of decision-making skills; the search for leisure activities consistent with physical and financial limitations; exploration of roles and role conflicts accompanied by stress management training; or any of the more traditional activities of career counseling such as choosing an occupation to pursue, developing better interview skills, compiling a resume, and teaching strategies for gathering occupational information.

It should be clear by now that career counseling is not a dusty corner of the field of counseling; nor is it a dry, technical endeavor. Career counseling is a vital, interesting, and complex area within counseling that may involve working with individuals and groups of all backgrounds and ages. Indeed, it is also an area of counseling thoroughly grounded in history. Although beyond the scope of this chapter, the reader is encouraged to learn how the field of career counseling has developed in the twentieth century.

THEORIES OF CAREER COUNSELING

Krumboltz recently argued that while the purpose, emphasis, and vocabulary of the major theories of career counseling may differ, there are no fundamental disagreements between them (Krumboltz, 1989). Comparing theories to maps, Krumboltz points out how they are similar: both represent an oversimplification of reality; both distort certain features; both employ symbols to depict reality and are intended to provide a big picture; and, finally, the usefulness of both maps and theories is dependent on the purpose for which they are used. The various career counseling theories represent different aspects of the same territory; no one theory covers the entire area, and the theories overlap. Although further development is needed in career theory, the ultimate goal is not to develop a "perfect" theory but theories that are "perfect" for given purposes.

Among the implications that might be drawn from Krumboltz' analogy is one very pertinent to the beginning career counselor. Theoretical viewpoints cannot be adopted or rejected on the basis of their "goodness" or "badness" without specifically attending to their intended scope, emphasis, and purpose. A theory useful for understanding one aspect of the career development process may shed little light on another. Rigid adherence to one particular theory may, therefore, be detrimental to understanding the career process in its entirety. This is not to say that one should carry about a hodgepodge of unrelated concepts and explanations, but that theories should be used according to their intended purposes.

Some of the major theories of career development will be briefly described below. Although only the most central concepts of each have been presented, more detailed reviews of each theory and critiques of the related research are available in the texts mentioned above or in Gottfredson (1981).

Psychodynamic Theories

One approach to understanding career behavior is represented in psychodynamic theories. Psychodynamic explanations focus on work as a means of need satisfaction and an outlet for sublimated wishes (Osipow, 1983). For example a psychodynamically oriented counselor might analyze the client interested in becoming a surgeon or a butcher in terms of oral aggressive needs. The counselor would be interested in how the client's impulses and needs are translated into work interests.

Watkins (1989) discusses psychodynamic applications to career counseling in terms of three different frameworks: classical, Ericksonian, and Adlerian. Each of those three frameworks shares a common impediment: they lack meaningful applications to practical, concrete techniques of career counseling. The client interested in surgery might be provided with traditional psychoanalysis, but no specific career interventions exist within the psychoanalytic theoretical framework. Reliance on the unconscious and other difficult-to-quantify concepts has resulted in a weak research basis and a lack of empirical support for occupational choices. Largely for these reasons, psychoanalytic approaches to career counseling have not gained prominence. Nevertheless, one important contribution made by psychoanalytic approaches is the important role that early developmental processes and parent–child relationships play in career development (Zunker, 1986).

Trait-and-Factor Theory

The trait-and-factor approach to career counseling was established in the work of Parsons (1909) and has been modified and extended since that time. Most authors credit the origin of vocational counseling to Frank Parsons. Although the turn of the century was witness to a variety of innovative guidance programs, Parsons conceptualized a plan for career guidance that is still viable in contemporary formulations of career guidance. Parsons proposed a three step model for helping individuals choose a vocation, summarized as follows: (1) develop knowledge about self, including aptitudes, interests, and resources; (2) develop knowledge about the world of work, including the advantages, disadvantages, opportunities, and requirements associated with different occupations; and (3) find a suitable match between the individual and the world of work (Parsons, 1909). His work stimulated increased interest in vocational guidance nationwide (Zunker, 1986).

The trait-and-factor approach to career counseling was virtually the only widely practiced approach until the 1950s (Isaacson, 1985). Today, there is some argument as to whether the trait-and-factor approach has been absorbed into other theories or whether it still exists as a separate and viable theory (Rounds, 1989). Regardless of one's conclusion, it is clear that the elements of trait-and-factor theory have informed most contemporary theories of career development (Isaacson, 1985).

A career counselor ascribing to the trait-and-factor approach would structure the counseling experience according to the three steps outlined by Parsons (1909). First, the counselor would generate information about the client's aptitudes, interests, goals, resources, and so on. Next, the counselor would use his or her knowledge of occupations to assist the client's exploration of possible career alternatives. After a sufficient amount of self and occupational knowledge has been accrued by the client, the counselor would facilitate the client's choice of an occupation that is consistent with the identified personal qualities and interests.

The work of John Holland has been classified under both trait approaches to career development (Osipow, 1983) and personality-based theories of career development (Isaacson, 1985). Holland assumes that people develop relatively permanent sets of behaviors or personalities that they seek to express through occupational choices. In addition, he asserts that people project their views of themselves and of the work-world onto occupational titles. Assessment of these projections serves to identify information about the occupational areas that might be most satisfying for an individual, as well as to illuminate relevant aspects of the individual's personality.

Holland (1973) proposes that there are six basic types of work environments in American society, and six corresponding modal personal orientations. Modal personal orientations are the way the person typically responds to environmental demands. People achieve the most work satisfaction when their work environment matches their modal personal orientation. For example, positions in education or social welfare are considered "social" occupational environments and would be most suited to "social" personal orientations, that is, people who perceive themselves to be sociable, skilled at dealing with others, and concerned with helping others and solving human problems. Some people are dominant in one particular orientation, while others exhibit a combination of orientations in their interactions with the environment.

The five orientations in addition to the "social" orientation are "realistic," "investigative," "conventional," "enterprising," and "artistic." Each will be briefly presented.

"Realistic" persons are described as aggressive, concrete, and masculine, as interested in activities requiring physical strength, and as less likely to be sensitive and socially skilled. Corresponding work environments are found in the skilled trades such as plumbing or machine operation, and in the technical trades such as mechanics and photography.

"Investigative" persons are described as preferring to think rather than act, as intellectual, abstract, and analytical. Work environments most suited to the investigative orientation are scientific, such as those of the chemist or mathematician, as well as the technical environments of the computer programmer and the electronics worker.

"Conventional" persons are practical, well-controlled, conservative, and prefer structure and conformity to the abstract and the unique. Conventional environments are typified in those of the office worker, the bookkeeper, and the credit manager.

An "enterprising" individual is likely to prefer leadership roles, and to be aggressive, extroverted, persuasive, and dominant. Managerial positions in personnel and production, and positions in real estate, life insurance, and other sales areas correspond most closely to the "enterprising" work environment.

Holland's final personality orientation, "artistic," corresponds to persons who are imaginative, independent, emotionally expressive, introspective, and feminine; their preferred work environments include those of the artist, the musician, and the writer. Holland (1973) provides a much more detailed description of the modal orientations, which may be helpful for the counselor interested in further exploration of these concepts.

Counselors grounded in Holland's approach will generally attempt to determine the client's modal personal orientation and then explore corresponding work orientations. In this sense, the trait-and-factor approach is represented. Several instruments are available for assessing modal orientations, the most common of which are probably the Strong Campbell Interest Inventory and Holland's Self-Directed Search. The work of Lofquist and Dawis is another variation or extension of trait-and-factor approaches to career counseling (Lofquist and Dawis, 1969, 1984).

Social Learning Theory

Perhaps the foremost proponent of the social learning approach to career counseling is Krumboltz (Krumboltz, Mitchell, & Jones, 1976; Kinnier &

Krumboltz, 1984). Krumboltz et al. identify four types of factors that influence career decision-making: (1) genetic endowment and special abilities; (2) environmental conditions and events; (3) learning experiences; and (4) task-approach skills. They define task-approach skills as the skills an individual applies to new tasks and problems, including cognitive processes, work habits, and values. Every individual is born into specific environmental conditions with certain genetic characteristics; these interact to influence the life experiences, opportunities, and learning of the individual. Learning experiences are followed by rewards or punishments that also influence the individual's development. According to Krumboltz et al., career choice is influenced by individuals' unique learning experiences in the course of their lifetimes.

Task-approach skills, self-observation generalizations, and actions are the result of an individual's learning experiences. Self-observation generalizations are the self statements made by individuals after assessing their performance or potential performance against learned standards. They are expressed in the form of interests. Actions are decision-related behaviors that emerge from the individual's task-approach skills and self-observation generalizations.

A counselor approaching career clients from a social learning perspective would be interested in the learning experiences that have influenced the client's career choices. Often a client's inaccurate self-observations, maladaptive beliefs (Mitchell & Krumboltz, 1984b), or deficient task-approach skills are a barrier to exploration of potential career choices. The counselor's role is to assess each of these possibilities and others in the process of facilitating the client's career choices. Kinnier and Krumboltz (1984) present a helpful discussion of major obstacles in career counseling and techniques for overcoming them consistent with a social learning perspective.

Another variable that has received increasing attention in relation to social learning approaches to career choice is self-efficacy (Bandura, 1982). Self-efficacy expectations, or beliefs about one's performance abilities in relation to specific tasks, appear to be a moderating variable in the career decision-making process (Betz & Hackett, 1981; Hackett & Betz, 1981; Rotberg, Brown, & Ware, 1987). Several recent reviews have considered the relationship between self-efficacy and career-related behaviors (Borders & Archadel, 1987; Lent & Hackett, 1987).

Developmental Theories

Developmental career theories view the selection and implementation of careers as part of a long-term developmental process that begins early in life and ends with death. Developmental theorists recognize the contributions of early experiences, life events and opportunities, and the maturation process on the development of interests, the exploration process, and career outcomes. Most contemporary theories of career choice incorporate elements of the developmental perspective (Jepsen, 1984). In this chapter, "career" has been defined from a developmental perspective in recognition of the widespread acceptance of career as an ongoing, lifelong process.

Ginzberg, Ginsburg, Axelrad, and Herma (1951) were among the first theorists to link the developmental theory with occupational choice. Their work, along with the work of Teideman and O'Hara (1963) and others, has been valuable in shaping developmental theories. Two developmental approaches will be discussed in this section. First, in recognition of his extensive and continuing influence on career development theory, the work of Donald Super will be considered. This will be followed by a discussion of Linda Gottfredson's (1981) theory of circumscription and compromise.

Super's Developmental Theory

Super (1957, 1963) contends that individuals select occupations consistent with their self-concept. Research generated by Super's theory of self-concept has indicated

> ...vocational self-concept develops through physical and mental growth, observations of work, identification with working adults, general environment, and general experiences (Zunker, 1986, p. 23).

Super argues that the manner in which people implement their self-concepts into occupational choices is a function of their developmental life stage. It therefore follows that vocational behaviors should be examined in the context of the particular demands of a person's developmental life stage.

The vocational developmental stages formulated by Super are as follows: (1) growth (ages 0–14) is characterized by the development of interests, aptitudes, and needs in conjunction with the self concept; (2) exploration (ages 15–24) consists of a tentative phase of narrowing down options; (3) establishment (ages 25–44) is characterized by choosing and implementing a career and stabilization within that career; (4) maintenance (ages 45–64) involves the continued efforts to improve work position; and (5) decline (ages 65 and above) is characterized by preparation for retirement and retirement itself. Five primary developmental vocational tasks have also been described by Super.

Throughout the lifespan, individuals are called upon to fulfill the demands of a variety of roles, such as student, sibling, spouse, parent, worker, and citizen. One focus of career counselors ascribing to Super's theory is the interaction of these life roles with vocational development and behaviors. Career maturity is another important concept proposed by Super (1974). The articulation of career maturity in terms of specific, stage-related attitudes and competencies has been a significant contribution to career counseling and career education programming (Zunker, 1986). Assessment of the client's career maturity often helps to set the stage for appropriate interventions.

Circumscription and Compromise

Gottfredson's (1981) theory of circumscription and compromise is the newest contribution to career theories. This theory, which incorporates elements of a social systems approach into a developmental perspective, focuses on the influence of gender, social class, and intelligence upon career aspirations and choices. Gottfredson contends that the importance of these variables has been overlooked by other theorists. According to her theory, all people have a unique "zone of acceptable alternatives," which consists of the range of occupations acceptable for consideration and which reflects their view of where they fit in society. This zone is bounded by the greatest and least amount of effort individuals are willing to expend in order to attain that career, as well as by their willingness to pursue careers nontraditional for their gender. For example, an individual might consider a range of occupations perceived to be more prestigious than secretarial work, such as nursing or management, but not as demanding as becoming a lawyer or a doctor. If the individual is male, he might automatically rule out nursing because it is a traditionally female profession and inconsistent with his perceived sex role.

Gottfredson postulates that as the self-concept develops, people become oriented to the implications of size and power (ages 3–5), sex roles (ages 6–8), social evaluation (ages 9–13), and finally, as their interests emerge, they become oriented to or aware of their internal unique self (ages 14 and older). The zone of acceptable alternatives is narrowed or circumscribed as age increases; occupations perceived as incongruent with sex roles are the first occupations to be eliminated. Next, those occupations perceived as too low in prestige for people's respective social classes will be dropped from consideration. Occupations demanding what they perceive as too much effort will also be eliminated. When compromise in occupational choices is required, Gottfredson argues that people will first sacrifice their interests related to work, i.e., their internal unique self. Next they will compromise on their ideas of prestige or settle for an occupation with a less positive social evaluation. Only as a last resort will people compromise on their perception of sex roles and choose an occupation that they believe is suited for the opposite sex.

These and other elements of Gottfredson's theory will certainly be challenged and modified as a result of empirical research accumulate.

Career counselors ascribing to this theory will be interested in the client's process of circumscription and compromise. As the circumscription of aspirations is thought to occur by early adolescence, early intervention may be optimal. Counselors may assess vocational priorities with respect to prestige and sex. Use of instruments that assess interests and abilities as well as vocational decision-making skills may reveal skill deficits and provide potential directions to explore.

A FRAMEWORK FOR CAREER COUNSELING

The remainder of this chapter is devoted to presenting a simple schema for conceptualizing the career counseling process, with specific recommendations for counselors identified along the way. Horan (1979) has described counseling in terms of three phases: assessment, intervention, and evaluation. This model provides a simple organizational framework for career counseling (Kinnier & Krumboltz, 1984) that can incorporate the wide range of activities that constitute career counseling.

Salomone (1988) contends that many career counselors operate under the assumption that there are three stages to career counseling: self-exploration, exploration of the world of work, and creating a satisfying match between self and work. Recall that these steps are rooted in the work of Parsons. What is missing from this model, argues Salomone, are two additional stages: implementation of educational and vocational decisions, and assisting clients to adjust to the new environment resulting from their career decision. It is often assumed that once a career choice has been made and steps toward achieving this goal identified, the counseling process is finished. However, for many clients, implementation of these steps represents a barrier equal to the original problem of making a career decision. Additionally, beginning a new job or an educational program may involve a variety of income, relationship, and general lifestyle adjustments. Consideration of these factors will enable the counselor to be responsive to the various developmental needs of their clients during different points in the counseling process. Each of Salomone's (1988) five stages will be incorporated into Horan's (1979) model within the second phase of counseling, the intervention phase.

Assessment

The assessment phase of career counseling begins when the client walks through the door. As with personal counseling, the counselor should immediately begin gathering information through both nonverbal and verbal behaviors. The client's eye contact, posture, self-presentation, and manner of dress may all provide pieces of information that enhance the counseling process. For example, feedback about a client's tendency to mumble and avoid eye contact may prove extremely useful to the client with a string of unsuccessful interviews. Well-developed and acute powers of observation lead to feedback that is more concrete and potentially useful to the client.

Verbal assessment procedures must incorporate the basic listening skills described elsewhere in this book. Consistent use of these listening skills will facilitate an atmosphere in which the client feels safe, understood, and accepted. The counselor should identify early in the session what the client is seeking in career counseling. As we have defined career from a developmental perspective, a wide array of problems and concerns fall under the rubric of "career," and an even wider range of goals may unfold in the assessment process. Counselors should view client goals as a function of the client's developmental stage and tailor interventions accordingly. By carefully establishing what the client hopes to get out of career counseling, the counselor can address misconceptions and unrealistic expectations right from the start. Direct and open-ended questioning, paraphrasing, and perception-checking will facilitate this process.

Another component of the assessment phase is clarification of the counselor's style and approach to counseling and of the client's role. Unfortunately, many clients perceive counseling as a set of dictates or answers to be passively swallowed without any effort on their part. Allowing clients to participate in this fashion not only puts a great burden on the counselor but also is a great disservice to the client. An active and collaborative role in which clients take full responsibility for their actions and choices is optimal (Kinnier & Krumboltz, 1984). This active role facilitates the empowerment of clients and leaves them better prepared to deal with future problems and concerns (Gannon, 1982, McWhirler, in press).

Before moving to the intervention phase of counseling, it is important to establish the results of the client's previous efforts to resolve his or her career dilemma, or to estimate a baseline of the behavior the client wishes to change or develop. For example, if the client is interested in developing job search skills, the counselor should establish which skills the client possesses at the outset of counseling. Knowing the client's initial state is an extremely important, and often neglected, prerequisite to evaluation of counseling interventions (Horan, 1979).

Intervention

Once the nature of counseling has been clarified and a specific goal or goals have been established, the intervention phase of career counseling may begin. Interventions will vary depending upon the specific needs of the client, the theoretical framework of the counselor, and the counselor's knowledge of available resources. The number of assessment instruments, references, and resources related to career development has expanded so rapidly in recent years (Rounds & Tinsley, 1984) that the beginning counselor may find the prospect of intervention a bit overwhelming. In this section, some of the most common intervention approaches and instruments will be presented.

Because most career interventions are useful across several theoretical frameworks, they will not be discussed in reference to specific theoretical orientations. This section will be divided according to Salomone's five stages. This arrangement is more applicable to clients interested in career exploration and selection than those with concerns related to dual careers and other issues; however, it provides an efficient way to present, in a limited space, the information most central to career counseling. Readers should note that interventions discussed with respect to one stage will not always be associated with that stage of counseling in actual practice; individual client needs rather than adherence to a formula should influence the type and order of the interventions employed.

Stage 1: Knowledge About Self

INTERESTS   Because of the important relationship between interests and occupations, many career interventions incorporate a process of identifying and exploring the client's interests. A variety of approaches to interest measurement exist; some of the most common will be described here. Some of the informal approaches will be presented first, followed by descriptions of several popular interest inventories. More detailed information about such inventories and the other tests discussed in this chapter is available in Buros' *Mental Measurements Yearbook* (1986), Isaacson's *Basics of Career Counseling* (1985), and Kapes' and Mastie's *A Counselor's Guide to Career Assessment Instruments* (1988). Finally, several microcomputer programs with an interest-assessment component will be described.

The structured interview is one vehicle for learning about the work-related interests of the client (Amundsen & Cochran, 1984). One example of the structured interview is the life career assessment, or the LCA, discussed in detail by Gysbers and Moore (1987). Career genograms, the detailed analysis of a family's work-related history, may help the client to identify concrete areas of interest and how they developed (Gysbers & Moore, 1987; Okiishi, 1987). Review of the client's previous jobs, activities, and accomplishments may provide another starting point for discussion of interests. The counselor must be sure to break down each experience into its component parts to avoid erroneous conclusions. For example, the client who volunteers at a nursing home may enjoy interacting with the elderly; on the other hand, attractive features of the job could be related to autonomy, being in charge of other volunteers, working in the kitchen, or a host of other possibilities. The counselor and client should attempt to draw up a highly specific list of interests, as this will facilitate the task of identifying potential options.

These informal means of interest assessment may be used alone or in conjunction with formal or published inventories. The counselor should provide the client with information concerning the use of assessment instruments so that they can determine together if this is a desirable option. As there may be differences between the interests assessed by formal means and those verbally expressed by the client (Slaney, 1978), several means of interest assessment should be employed. The self-administered Vocational Card Sort (Slaney, 1978) elicits expressed vocational interests in a manner comparable to other inventories.

The decision to use any assessment instrument should be carefully considered. While time-saving merits may be unquestionable, sole reliance on such instruments may indirectly communicate to clients that they are not capable of identifying their own interests. In addition, indiscriminate reliance on instruments can lead to a "gas station" style of counseling: drive in, take test, explain, drive out, "thank you for shopping at the counseling center." The counselor should employ a system of self-checks to assess continuously whether the client is receiving optimal service with the use of a formal instrument.

Strong Campbell Interest Inventory. The Strong Campbell Interest Inventory (SCII) is among the most widely used interest inventories. It was created by Strong in 1927, revised by David Campbell in the 1960s and 1970s, and most recently revised by Jo-Ida Hansen in 1981 (Isaacson, 1985).

The results of the SCII permit clients to contrast their interests with those of people in over 100 different occupations. Separate scales exist for males and females to reduce bias related to gender differences. Contrary to many a client's hopes, the SCII does not provide information concerning how successful a person might be in a chosen field, nor does it indicate areas that a client should or should not pursue. What it does provide is a launching point for exploration of career options that have never been considered, and a point of departure for discussing why certain career interests are congruent or incongruent with those of persons employed in that field. The SCII is organized according to Holland's (1973) typology of modal orientations, so the client can easily determine the orientations with which his or her interests most closely coincide. This may help the client to focus in upon a particular group of careers to explore more thoroughly.

Self-Directed Search. The Self-Directed Search (SDS) was developed by John Holland and published in 1977, and may be considered a "blue collar" counterpart to the SCII. The SDS is a self-administered inventory that assesses an individual's activities, competencies, and career interests, and translates this information into matching career options. The results of the inventory correspond with Holland's occupational typology and are also cross-referenced with the *Dictionary of Occupational Titles* (DOT). The SDS is thorough and relatively easy to administer; caution should be exercised when interpreting the results of this instrument for female clients, however, due to sex-role stereotyping in some of the items (Isaacson, 1985).

Kuder Occupational Interest Survey. The Kuder Occupational Interest Survey (KOIS) is available in several forms. It was first published by G. Frederick Kuder in 1966 and was revised in 1979. Form DD provides interest comparisons to persons in a variety of occupations and college majors, making the inventory useful for high school and college students and out-of-school adults (Isaacson, 1985). There are fewer data available on the validity and reliability of this instrument because it is relatively new. Form E, published in 1963, focuses on the initial stages of self- and occupational exploration, and is most useful to students in grades eight through ten.

OVIS II. The Ohio Vocational Interest Survey (OVIS) was developed by Ayres D'Costa, David Winefordner, John Odgers, and Paul Koons in 1970, and the OVIS II was developed in 1981. The OVIS II focuses on individual characteristics and relates them to occupational requirements. This interest inventory is based on the same classification system as the DOT and the *Occupational Outlook Handbook* (OOH) and facilitates the client's use of these additional references to investigate specific occupations. A microcomputer version of the OVIS II is currently available (Hoyt, 1986).

In addition to the OVIS II, there are several other interactive microcomputer programs that can facilitate a client's self-exploration through assessment of interests. Each program also contains other components, such as values assessment, occupational information, and skills assessment. A brief review of three such programs follows. Before utilizing microcomputer systems, the counselor may wish to consult Krumboltz' (1985) discussion of the presuppositions underlying computer use in career counseling.

SIGI+. SIGI+ is a new extension of SIGI, the System of Interactive Guidance and Information, which is described in a later section of this chapter. SIGI+ contains nine components, beginning with a system overview followed by a self-assessment section. In this section, users are guided through an inventory of their interests, values, and skills. Other sections of SIGI+ allow users to learn about careers that correspond to the results of their inventory, as well as providing advice on financial assistance, suggestions for decision-making, training requirements for specific occupations, and a large quantity of additional occupational information.

Discover. The Discover program, like SIGI+, contains interest, ability, and values inventories to facilitate the user's self-assessment. Strategies for identifying occupations, occupational information, and information about educational institutions are available with the Discover program. In addition, Discover contains a section that incorporates Holland's Self-Directed Search. A newer version of Discover, called Discover for Adult Learners, was developed for unemployed adults or those in the process of school or job market re-entry or career changes. Among other developments, Discover for Adult Learners contains a skills inventory that incorporates the user's previous work experiences.

Eureka's Micro SKILLS. Eureka's Micro SKILLS (Maze & Mayall, 1983) is a computer program that begins with a skills inventory similar to the process described in Bolles' *What Color Is Your Parachute?* (1985). This inventory is especially useful for adults re-entering the workforce or changing careers, owing to its focus on experience as well as interests.

APTITUDES Gathering knowledge about the self should also include assessment of the client's aptitudes and skills. Knowing what the client does well facilitates the identification of career-related skills or careers at which the client may succeed. One common informal way to assess aptitudes is by reviewing grades in various subject areas. However, this presents only a limited amount of information. Clients should be encouraged to identify the specific types of class activities in which they were successful: oral presentations, group projects, detailed notetaking, debates, etc. Work-related successes should also be noted: was the client ever complimented for achievements in productivity, facility cleanliness, or record-keeping? Clients might be encouraged to interview others for additional information about their special talents or skills. Be wary of the client who claims a general lack of proficiency; such a claim is usually more reflective of a low self-concept than of actual performance. The counselor should be prepared to dig deeply and specifically to obtain information about aptitudes, since obvious signs of success such as grades and awards are often the only signs to which people attend. In addition to the informal information gathering, some circumstances may warrant the use of an aptitude test.

Differential Aptitude Test. The Differential Aptitude Test (DAT) was developed by Bennet, Seashore, and Westman and first published in 1947. Since that time several forms have been developed and revised. The DAT is widely used across the country by schools and counseling services and has proven extremely useful to high school students trying to determine how they might fare in future educational endeavors.

Counselors should be aware that while this instrument is useful in the prediction of general academic success, it is not useful for the prediction of success in specific academic areas, nor does prediction extend to the area of occupational success.

General Aptitude Test Battery. The General Aptitude Test Battery (GATB) was developed by the U.S. Employment Service and published in 1947, with periodic revisions since that time. A unique advantage of the GATB is that this test allows clients to compare themselves with actual workers in specific occupations. The GATB has often been used to assist in job placement, and can be used in conjunction with the new Employment Service Interest Inventory to facilitate the exploration of job possibilities in the DOT and the OOH (Isaacson, 1985).

Other aptitude tests in current use are the Flannigan Aptitude Classification Test and the Otis-Lennon Mental Ability Test. Isaacson (1985) and Buros (1986) provide information on these tests.

VALUES Values clarification is an important component of the career counseling process (Kinnier & Krumboltz, 1984). In order to make realistic decisions about future occupational pursuits, an individual should have a good idea about the relative importance of values such as family time, income, prestige, autonomy, and a wide variety of other values that are affected by the nature of an occupation. For example, an individual who highly values family time is not likely to be satisfied with a traveling sales position, nor would someone valuing autonomy fare well in a job that involves constant scrutiny by a supervisor. Often clients begin career counseling without ever having considered the relationship between occupational choices and value satisfaction. The counselor must be prepared to initiate and accompany the client's exploration of values, as well as anticipate the potential value conflicts and means of satisfaction in the occupations under consideration.

Changing values are not infrequently an impetus of the decision to seek career counseling. Loss due to death, divorce, or changes in health status may necessitate a re-prioritization of values. In such a case, income may replace helping others, or job security may supersede autonomy in an individual's values hierarchy. Counselors should be sensitive to the changing nature of values over an individual's lifespan and the implications of value changes for career choices.

Kinnier and Krumboltz (1984) have summarized the basic processes involved in many values clarification exercises. They find that most such exercises include one or a combination of the following: identification and analysis of the values issue; examination of past experiences, preferences, behaviors, and decisions that are related to the present issues; investigation of how others view the issue (by direct questioning or imagining what respected others would do in a similar situation); testing or self-confrontation about tentative choices, positions, or resolutions; finding personal environments that are conducive to clear thought about, or temporary escape from, the issue ("sleeping on it" or quiet meditation); and making the "best" tentative resolution and living in accordance with it, revising if needed. Counselors can use widely available strategies devised and published by others or create their own variations of values clarification techniques.

Some clarification exercises involve consideration of values in light of one's mortality. The "Lifeline" exercise requires the client to imagine having a terminal illness and to review priorities from this mindset; "Epitaph" and "Obituary" exercises require clients to write down their own version of how they want to be remembered after they have died (Kinnier & Krumboltz, 1984).

The Work Values Inventory developed by Super is one example of a paper-and-pencil instrument for assessing work-related values. Other available instruments include the Work Environment Preference Schedule, the Study of Values, and the Survey of Interpersonal Values. The latter two instruments are designed to explore both work-related and personal values.

SIGI. The System of Interactive Guidance and Information (SIGI) is a microcomputer program primarily geared toward helping users clarify their most important values and providing information about careers consistent with the values identified. There are 10 values that the user must evaluate in terms of importance: income, prestige, independence, helping others, security, variety, leadership, interest field, leisure, and early entry. In a review of research on computer-assisted counseling systems, Cairo (1983) reports that SIGI users better understood their values and career goals, had better knowledge about sources of job satisfaction, had more definite overall career plans, and felt more confident about their decision-making abilities after using the SIGI program.

Stage 2: Knowledge About World of Work

Career counselors are responsible for introducing clients to resources for occupational information. More specifically, part of the counselor's job is to ensure that clients are able to obtain career-related information independently in the future. Occupational information is vast and constantly changing, and keeping up to date can be a staggering task. Fortunately, many resources are available that significantly reduce the amount of time and research required of both the counselor and the client. In this section, informal, formal, and microcomputer sources or career information will be presented.

Informal processes of obtaining career information can be interesting and rewarding for the client. The most direct way to find out about a career of interest is to talk to someone already doing it! The client can locate potential interviewees from a variety of sources including friends, relatives, and classmates; local alumni associations, service and professional organizations; and even the local phone directory. The counselor may help the client formulate a set of questions that will maximize the amount and value of the information yielded by the subsequent interview. "Shadowing," or following individuals on the job, is an option that provides an even more concrete idea of what a particular career involves.

College and university campuses provide another rich source of occupational information. Clients may wish to seek out instructors in their field of interest for insights into the nature of specific occupations. Libraries offer journals and magazines serving professional audiences; these resources will provide information on current developments and the cutting edge of research in the field. Additionally, libraries contain reference materials such as labor market statistics, occupational forecasts, and descriptive information.

Three excellent reference materials that may be found in counseling centers, career development centers, and libraries are the *Dictionary of Occupational Titles* (DOT), the *Occupational Outlook Handbook* (OOH), and the *Guide for Occupational Exploration* (GOE). These periodically updated manuals provide detailed information in everyday language about hundreds of specific occupations. The GOE is useful in linking interest inventory results with the occupations listed in the DOT, and provides information such as the nature of specific jobs, the skills and abilities required, how to prepare for entry into the field, and how to determine whether such work might be of interest to an individual. Occupations discussed in the DOT and the GOE are classified according to a nine-digit coding system. Counselors should be familiar with the particular classification system in use before introducing references to clients, in order to maximize utility and minimize client confusion. Beale (1987) discusses ways to use the DOT with students that may be applied to the counseling setting.

Computerized guidance programs are another source of occupational information. The Guidance Information System (GIS) allows the user to access information in any of six files: occupations, four-year colleges, two-year colleges, graduate schools, financial-aid information, and armed services occupations (Isaacson, 1985). The user simply enters the characteristics of interest into the computer and is provided with a listing of corresponding schools, programs, or occupations. For example, a client may be interested in pursuing a liberal arts degree at a private institution in the East or the Midwest. Using GIS, the client can enter these characteristics and receive a list of private Eastern and Midwestern schools that provide degrees in liberal arts. SIGI and Discover also have large amounts of occupational information.

The relative ease with which computer files can be updated and accessed makes computers an invaluable source of current occupational information.

Stage 3: Creating a Match

For the client interested in choosing an occupation, this stage of career counseling refers to the process of deciding which occupations are consistent with the client's skills, interests, and values. Eventually, the client will have to pick one or a group of closely related occupations to pursue. The counselor can facilitate this process by assisting in the decision-making process.

Decision making is a part of life, but unfortunately many people lack the skills important for making effective decisions. Horan (1979) has devised a summary model of decision making that incorporates the basic structure of 22 decision-making models. This model has recently been applied to career counseling interventions (Olson, McWhirter, & Horan, 1989). The four components of this model are (1) conceptualization of the problem as one of choice; (2) enlargement of the response repertoire; (3) identification of discriminative stimuli; and (4) response selection. Enlargement of the response repertoire refers to the process of generating a large number of alternative actions. Identification of discriminative stimuli involves weighing the advantages and disadvantages of each potential course of action, as well as assessing the probable results of each. For example, while the advantages of writing a Pulitzer Prize-winning book are many, the probability of doing so is quite slim. Teaching clients this or other decision-making models provides them with a skill generalizable to a multitude of situations and helps ensure subsequent satisfaction with the decisions they make. The interested counselor may wish to consult Horan (1979) or Mitchell and Krumboltz (1984a) for additional information related to decision making in counseling.

Stage 4: Implementation of a Decision

Salomone (1988) raises the issue that once a decision has been made, the task of the career counselor is not over. The client may lack specific skills or information necessary for successful implementation of the decision. The counselor should be prepared to assist the client in developing these skills or obtaining the information in areas such as resume writing, interviewing, assertiveness, or communication. If part of the client's decision involves actions such as changing a behavior, developing a hobby, or participating in a new organization, the counselor can be a valuable source of support and encouragement. Oftentimes the simple scheduling of tasks will be enough motivation for the hesitant client to follow through on decisions.

Anxiety may interfere with the client's motivation to carry out a plan of action. Anxiety is often founded upon irrational beliefs or expectations. According to Kinnier and Krumboltz (1984), maladaptive or irrational beliefs are a common obstacle to career development, and they recommend cognitive restructuring as one means to address this problem. Cognitive restructuring involves identifying irrational beliefs and replacing them with rational and realistic thoughts. Nevo (1987) has identified a set of common irrational beliefs with respect to careers, including, "There's only one perfect job for me." The counselor's familiarity with the job world and with the client's skills and personality can be used to reduce anxiety and encourage action.

Stage 5: Adjustment to New Setting

Sometimes the goals established in career counseling will result in the client moving into a new environment. This may be the result of a job promotion, the start of a new job, enrollment in an academic program, a change of residence, or a combination of these and other changes. The client may be challenged to cope with a new set of demands and expectations, as well as to interact with unfamiliar groups and individuals. Issues formerly perceived as the substance of personal counseling are commonly a part of career counseling. Often clients are dealing with career concerns as a result of developmental issues such as divorce, children leaving home, and changing economic circumstances. Stress inoculation and relaxation training are two means of assisting clients to deal with the anxiety associated with these new situations.

Communication and human relations skills training may help the client interact in a healthy and productive way with new coworkers, supervisors, and acquaintances. Assertiveness training may help clients secure what they need from the environment without infringing upon the rights of others. Strategies for dealing with loneliness, frustration, and feelings of inadequacy may also serve an important function at this time.

At the close of this section, it is important to stress again that the arrangement of specific interventions with specific stages in career counseling is by no means set in stone. For example, cognitive restructuring may be called for as the client begins the self-assessment process and at a variety of other points in the career counseling process. In addition, career counseling interventions need not follow each and every one of the five steps identified by Salomone (1988). Rather, the process should be dictated by the nature of the client's concern and the plan that the counselor and client establish together.

Evaluation

The third phase of Horan's (1979) counseling model is evaluation. As indicated earlier, evaluation is a sorely neglected aspect of career counseling. While many career counselors are aware of the immediate effects of counseling, such as the choice of a college major, in general practice there is very little formal follow-up. It is good practice for counselors to end every counseling relationship with an evaluation of the process. Such an evaluation may be incorporated into one of the final sessions and is of benefit to both the counselor and the client. Potential closing topics to cover are similar to those of personal counseling: the relative helpfulness of the counselor's suggestions and interventions; the degree of comfort experienced by the client throughout the process; the extent to which the client felt like an active participant and collaborator; topics on which the client might have wanted to spend more or less time; and what the client might like to have done differently. Feedback for clients might include the counselor's perceptions of their relevant strengths and weaknesses, changes and progress noted by the counselor, and suggestions for future directions.

There is also a need in career counseling for more formal evaluations of the relative effectiveness of various interventions. Surprisingly little is known about how various career interventions affect the vocational development process. A thorough review of research on developmental aspects of vocational behavior is provided by Jepsen (1984), along with suggestions for future research. The vocational journals mentioned earlier in this chapter also provide an excellent source of research ideas.

Special Populations

One final topic offered for consideration is the differing needs of special populations. The vast majority of research in career development has been drawn from the behaviors of middle to upper class white male subjects. Career interventions suited for this population will not necessarily be appropriate for or meet the needs of individuals of differing social and cultural backgrounds. For example, career counselors working with women and ethnic minority clients may need to explore carefully the effects of stereotypes and discrimination on their career aspirations and behaviors. Considerations and recommendations for working with female career clients are provided in special issues of the *Journal of Career Development* (1988, Vol. 14, No. 4), and *Applied Psychology: An International Review* (1988, Vol. 37, No. 2). The growing body of literature on career self-efficacy has many practical implications for working with women clients. Chapters by Zunker (1986) and Osipow (1983), as well as a brief section by Isaacson (1985), may also prove helpful in identifying and addressing the specific needs of female career clients.

Resources for career counseling with ethnic minority clients are more difficult to locate. Books by Isaacson (1985), Osipow (1983), Yost and Corbishley (1987), and Zunker (1986) address this topic with varying amounts of detail. Articles addressing general cultural issues as they relate to career counseling include those by Pine and Innis (1987) and Sundal-Hansen (1985). Resources for personal counseling with women and ethnic minority clients may provide helpful insights for career counselors. Additionally, career counselors are urged to consult professional journals for information on considerations for working with specific ethnic minority populations.

CONCLUSION

Career counseling is a vital and dynamic area of counseling. While a variety of theoretical perspectives currently inform the career counselor, a developmental perspective has been emphasized in the definition and description of career counseling. The framework presented in this chapter may serve as an initial organizer for viewing the role and activities of the career counselor, while the references listed may guide future, more in-depth exploration of career development theories and career interventions. Hopefully, beginning counselors will continue to pursue the vast resources of available information in the area of career counseling. Further exploration and utilization of these resources can make the process of career counseling a productive, challenging, and enjoyable experience for both the counselor and the client.

REFERENCES

Amundson, N. E., and Cochran, L. (1984). Analyzing experiences using adaptation of a heuristic approach. *Canadian-Counsellor, 18*(4), 183–186.

Applied Psychology: An International Review (1988). Special issue: Women's occupational plans and decisions. *37*(2).

Bandura, A. (1982). Self-efficacy mechanism in human agency. *American Psychologist, 37*(2), 122–147.

Beale, A. V. (1987). Discovering the treasures of the D.O.T.: Activities that work. *School Counselor, 34*(4), 308–311.

Betz, N. and Hackett, G. (1981). The relationship of career related self-efficacy expectations to perceived career options. *Journal of Counseling Psychology, 28,* 399–410.

Bolles, R. N. (1985). *What Color Is Your Parachute?* Berkeley, CA: Ten Speed Press.

Borders, L., & Archadel, K. A. (1987). Self-beliefs and career counseling. *Journal of Career Development, 14*(2), 69–79.

Buros, O. K. (Ed.). (1986). *The Ninth Mental Measurement Yearbook.* Highland Park, NJ: Gryphon Press.

Cairo, P. C. (1983). Evaluating the effects of computer-assisted counseling systems: A selective review. *The Counseling Psychologist, 11*(4), 55–59.

Gannon, L. (1982). The role of power in psychotherapy. *Women & Therapy, 1*(2), 3–11.

Ginzberg, E., Ginsburg, S. W., Axelrad, S., & Herma, J. L. (1951). *Occupational choice: An approach to a general theory.* New York: Columbia University Press.

Gottfredson, L. S. (1981). Circumscription and compromise: A developmental theory of occupational aspirations. *Journal of Counseling Psychology, 28*(6), 545–579.

Gysbers, N. C., & Moore, E. J. (1987). *Career counseling: Skills and techniques for practitioners.* Englewood Cliffs, NJ: Prentice-Hall.

Hackett, G., & Betz, N. (1981). A self-efficacy approach to the career development of women. *Journal of Vocational Behavior, 3,* 326–339.

Holland, J. L. (1973). *Making vocational choices: A theory of careers.* Englewood Cliffs, NJ: Prentice-Hall.

Holland, J. L. (1985). *The self-directed search: Professional manual—1985 edition.* Odessa, FL: Psychological Assessment Resources.

Horan, J. J. (1979). *Counseling for effective decision making: A cognitive-behavioral perspective.* Monterey, CA: Wadsworth Publishing.

Hoyt, K. B. (1986). Ohio Vocational Interest Survey (OVIS II), Microcomputer Version. *Journal of Counseling and Development, 64,* 655–657.

Isaacson, L. E. (1985). *Basics of career counseling.* Boston: Allyn & Bacon.

Jepsen, D. A. (1984). The developmental perspective on vocational behavior: A review of theory and research. In S. Brown & R. Lent (Eds.), *Handbook of Counseling Psychology.* New York: John Wiley.

Journal of Rational Emotive and Cognitive Behavior Therapy (1988). Special issue: Cognitive-behavior therapy with women, *6*(1–2).

Kapes, J. T., & Mastie, M. M. (1988). *A counselor's guide to career assessment instruments.* Alexandria, VA: National Career Development Association.

Kinnier, R. T., & Krumboltz, J. D. (1984). Procedures for successful career counseling. In N. Gysbers (Ed.), *Designing careers: Counseling to enhance education, work and leisure.* San Francisco: Jossey-Bass.

Krumboltz, J. D., Mitchell, A. M., & Jones, G. B. (1976). A social learning theory of career selection. *The Counseling Psychologist, 6*(1), 71–81.

Krumboltz, J. D. (1985). Presuppositions underlying computer use in career counseling. *Journal of Career Development, 12*(2), 165–170.

Krumboltz, J. D. (1989, August). The social learning theory of career decision making. Paper presented at the annual convention of the American Psychological Assocation, New Orleans, LA.

Lent, R. W., and Hackett, G. (1987). Career self-efficacy: Empirical status and future directions. *Journal of Vocational Behavior, 30,* 347–382.

Lofquist, L. H., & Dawis, R. V. (1969). *Adjustment to work.* Englewood Cliffs, NJ: Prentice-Hall.

Lofquist, L. H., & Dawis, R. V. (1984). Research on work adjustment and satisfaction: Implications for career counseling. In S. Brown and R. Lent (Eds.), *Handbook of counseling psychology*. New York: John Wiley.

Maze, M., & Mayall, D. (1983). *Eureka Skills Inventory Counselor's Manual*. Richmond, CA: Eureka Corporation.

McWhirler, E. H. (in press). Empowerment in Counseling. *Journal of Counseling and Development*.

Mitchell, L. K., & Krumboltz, J. D. (1984a). Research on human decision making: Implications for career decision making and counseling. In S. Brown and R. Lent (Eds.), *Handbook of counseling psychology*. New York: John Wiley.

Mitchell, L. K., & Krumboltz, J. D. (1984b). Social learning approach to career decision making: Krumboltz's theory. In D. Brown & L. Brooks (Eds.), *Career choice and development*. San Francisco: Jossey-Bass.

Nevo, O. (1987). Irrational expectations in career counseling and their confronting arguments. *Career Development Quarterly, 35*(3), 239–250.

Okiishi, R. W. (1987). The genogram as a tool in career counseling. *Journal of Counseling and Development, 66*(3), 139–143.

Olson, C., McWhirter, E. H. and Horan, J. J. (1989). A decision making model applied to career counseling. *Journal of Career Development, 16*(2), 19–23.

Osipow, S. H. (1983). *Theories of career development* (3rd ed.). Englewood Cliffs, NJ: Prentice-Hall.

Parsons, F. (1909). *Choosing a vocation*. Boston: Houghton-Mifflin.

Pine, G. J., & Innis, G. (1987). Cultural and individual work values. *Career Development Quarterly, 35*(4) 279–287.

Pinkney, J. W., & Jacobs, D. (1985). New counselors and personal interest in the task of career counseling. *Journal of Counseling Psychology, 32*(3), 454–457.

Rotberg, H. L., Brown, D., & Ware, W. B. (1987). Career self-efficacy expectations and perceived range of career options in community college students. *Journal of Counseling Psychology, 34*(2), 164–170.

Rounds, J. B., Jr. (1989, August). Trait and factor career counseling. Paper presented at the annual convention of the American Psychological Association, New Orleans, LA.

Rounds, J. B., Jr., & Tinsley, H. E. A. (1984). Diagnosis and treatment of vocational problems. In S. Brown and R. Lent (Eds.), *Handbook of counseling psychology*. New York: John Wiley.

Salomone, P. R. (1988). Career counseling: Steps and stages beyond Parsons. *The Career Development Quarterly, 36*, 218–221.

Slaney, R. B. (1978). Expressed and inventoried vocational interests: A comparison of instruments. *Journal of Counseling Psychology, 25*, 520–529.

Sundal-Hansen, L. S. (1985). Work-family linkages: Neglected factors in career guidance across culture. *Vocational Guidance Quarterly, 33*(3), 202–212.

Super, D. E. (1957). *The psychology of careers*. New York: Harper & Brothers.

Super, D. E. (1963). Self-concepts in vocational development. In D. E. Super et al. (Eds.), *Career development: Self-concept theory*. New York: CEEB Research Monograph No. 4.

Super, D. E. (1974). *Measuring vocational maturity for counseling and evaluation*. Washington, D C: National Vocational Guidance Association.

Super, D. E. (1984). Perspectives on the meaning and value of work. In N. Gysbers (Ed.), *Designing careers: Counseling to enhance education, work, and leisure.* San Francisco: Jossey-Bass.

Teideman, D. V., & O'Hara, R. P. (1963). *Career development: Choice and adjustment.* Princeton, NJ: College Entrance Examination Board.

Watkins, C. E., Jr. (1989, August). Psychodynamic career counseling. Paper presented at the annual convention of the American Psychological Association, New Orleans, LA.

Yost, E. B., & Corbishley, M. A. (1987). *Career counseling.* San Francisco: Jossey-Bass.

Zunker, V. G. (1986). *Career counseling: Applied concepts of life planning.* Monterey, CA: Brooks/Cole.

8.

Testing and Counseling ■

LARRY C. LOESCH, PH.D., N.C.C.
University of Florida
Gainesville, Florida

NICHOLAS A. VACC, ED.D., N.C.C.
University of North Carolina
Greensboro, North Carolina

IN VIEW OF COUNSELORS' ever increasing needs for valid information about their clients, the importance of the relationship between counseling and testing continues to increase. In the introduction of his historically significant text, *Using Tests in Counseling*, Goldman (1971) proposed that testing and counseling are inextricably linked. He wrote:

> The types of tests used, and the ways in which testing is conducted, differ to some extent, but all have in common a relationship between counselor and counselee in which the latter's well-being, adjustment, and choices are paramount...." (p.1).

Unfortunately, some counselors have been reluctant to accept the proposal that appraisal is an integral part of counseling. Instead, they view appraisal as an "adjunct" to their counseling activities. This perspective ignores the reality that counselors quite routinely, but subjectively, gather and interpret information from and about their clients.

158

and interpretation are important parts of the counseling process. They also recognize that systematic appraisal procedures can facilitate and enhance achievement of counseling goals and subsequently the efficiency of their counseling efforts.

Some counselors' attitudes toward "testing," in part, reflect confusion about semantics. *Measurement* may be considered the assignment of numeric or categorical values to human attributes according to rules (Crocker & Algina, 1986). *Assessment* subsumes measurement and can be considered the data gathering process or method (Vacc & Loesch, 1987). *Evaluation* subsumes assessment and can be considered the interpretation and application of measurement data according to rules (Mehrens & Lehmann, 1984, 1987). *Appraisal* is sometimes considered synonymous with assessment (e.g., Litwack, 1986), but more frequently with evaluation. Unfortunately, *testing* has been used as a synonym for each and all of these terms!

Testing (particularly as a synonym to appraisal/evaluation) can involve value judgments being made about measurement results, and therefore about people. For this reason, testing has become equated with "labeling" people. Most counselors do not want to be viewed as "labeling" people because of the social implications and because it connotes being "nonhumanistic" or "uncaring." Thus, counselors often decry testing based on misapplied connotations. It is not the act of making judgments that must be avoided, for counseling processes are fraught with counselors' value judgments. Rather, it is making unfounded and/or invalid value judgments that must be avoided. Given the substantial evidence that clinicians' subjective judgments correlate poorly with more objective indices of human attributes (Crocker & Algina, 1986), counselors are well advised to seek the best assessment procedures available. Thus testing, when properly understood and used, is a significant aid, not a hindrance, to the counseling process.

USES OF TESTS IN COUNSELING

Anastasia (1982) and Cronbach (1984) have listed general uses for testing, while others (e.g. Litwack, 1986; Shertzer & Linden, 1979; Vacc & Loesch, 1987) have identified more specific counseling applications. The following is a summary of primary counseling-related uses of testing.

Preliminary (Problem) Exploration and/or Diagnosis

For counseling processes to be efficient, counselors must gain accurate information about clients as rapidly as possible. One means of gaining accurate information to improve counselors' efficiency is testing. Substantive information about clients' characteristics, problems, and behaviors can be gained expeditiously when testing is an integral part of initial counseling activities.

Testing in this context has several distinct advantages to counselors' interactions with clients. First, it enhances comprehensive and systematic inquiry. Second, testing enables (in most cases) normative comparison of a client's personal data with that of other, similar persons. Third, it typically results in a relatively concise summary of client characteristics. Finally, testing may "uncover" client characteristics about which even the client is unaware. Overall, testing facilitates counselors in obtaining essential information quickly.

Selection or Screening

Testing in this context usually involves evaluation of applicant attributes (e.g., level of aptitude or capability) for use in educational, institutional, admission, or business/industry employment decision-making. Test results often are used to supplement more subjectively obtained information (i.e., personal judgments) so that decision making is more precise, thereby benefiting both applicants and employers.

Testing for selection or screening purposes has advantages similar to those for preliminary exploration or diagnosis. Comprehensive information can be obtained systematically and rapidly. For example, it is common in employment screening for applicants to complete a "test battery" as part of the application process. The ability to make normative comparisons of test results is particularly important in selection or screening processes. Admissions officers and employment personnel often establish "statistical decision-making rules" based on numeric test-result criteria, to supplement personal-judgment criteria in decision-making processes.

Placement and/or Planning

Test results are often used by counselors to help them determine the most appropriate situations (e.g., educational programs or occupational categories) in which to place people. This use of testing is similar to the selection or screening use, except the focus of placement is typically narrower than that for the selection process. For example, determining assignment to a particular program of studies within an institution of higher learning is usually a narrower focus than determining eligibility for admission to the institution. Similarly, determining an applicant's appropriate job classification may be narrower in scope than determining the applicant's suitability for employment.

Testing for placement usually involves obtaining data about level of aptitude or competency. Tests used for such purposes may assess general attributes (e.g., when intelligence test scores are used as one of the criteria for placement in an academically gifted program) or relatively specific abilities (e.g., when work sample tests are used to determine the speed with which a person can perform a job-specific task).

Planning for the uses of tests usually involves the assessment of an ability level or competency. Often the processes are indistinguishable. In some instances, tests are used specifically to determine areas of functioning where increased competency is needed. Planning involves identifying the best ways to facilitate the necessary improvement.

Facilitation of Self-Understanding

A primary reason clients seek counseling services is for the facilitation of self-understanding. Counselors' effectiveness in facilitating clients self-understanding is largely contingent upon the clients' trust in the counselor. Clients must strongly "believe in" their counselor before they will accept exploration into areas of self-understanding. This trust is difficult to achieve in the early stages of the counseling process. Testing is one means by which counselors can obtain information that enhances feedback to clients. Use of "objective" test information may then serve to increase counselors' "credibility" with their clients.

The normative aspects of test results may also be useful in facilitating clients' self-understanding. Clients often wish to know how their characteristics, abilities, and behaviors compare with those of other people. Test results provided in normative contexts can be a basis for comparison. One possible use for clients would be to identify specific aspects of themselves that they may wish to change. Testing in the capacity of facilitating self-understanding serves to help clients identify counseling goals.

The testing process, when focusing on characteristic behaviors, may also facilitate clients' self-understanding. Many tests incorporate logical, systematic, and relatively "transparent" approaches to the analysis of human behavior. Thus, actually engaging in the testing process may enable clients to learn new ways of evaluating themselves.

Assessment of Individual Progress

Effective counseling is synonymous with client change, which is presumably perceived by the client as positive. However, demonstration of client change is often difficult, particularly if left to subjective interpretations by clients or counselors. Testing can be a more objective way of obtaining client change information. For example, pre- and post-counseling assessments of client attitudes, attributes, and/or behaviors can provide data for evaluating the degree of change.

One of the more difficult aspects of counseling is maintaining a high level of client motivation throughout the counseling process. This difficulty increases as the length of the counseling process increases. The counselor's provision of "encouraging" feedback, as well as the client's self-monitoring, helps to maintain client motivation. However, these are subjective processes. Periodic use of tests that yield "objective" indications of client change can be a powerful reinforcer of client motivation.

Licensure or Certification

Testing has recently become a significant factor in many professional counselors' personal careers. A greatly increased emphasis on counselor credentialing in the past decade has resulted in the development of several major, national counselor certifications and over 30 state-level counselor licensure procedures. With these procedures, counselors have to exceed a minimum criterion score on an examination in order to become certified. Thus, the counseling profession has embraced testing as an effective and efficient method for obtaining useful information.

BASIC CONCEPTS IN TESTING

Tests used for counseling and related purposes are usually evaluated by three major attributes: validity, reliability, and appropriateness.

Validity

Anastasia (1982) defined validity as the extent to which a test measures what it purports to measure. Messick (1989) provided clarification of that common definition when he wrote, "Validity is an integrated evaluative judgment of the degree to which empirical evidence and theoretical rationales support the *adequacy* and *appropriateness* of *inferences* and *actions* based on test scores or other modes of assessment" (p. 13). Messick's definition emphasizes that, ultimately, validity is based on judgment and is the most important in consideration of how test results are used. Validity is the primary criterion upon which any test should be evaluated (Gladding, 1988).

Three major types of validity are discussed in the professional literature. *Content validity* refers to the extent to which a test is an accurate representative sample of the domain to which inferences will be made (Mehrens & Lehmann, 1984). Domains of interest to counselors include human attributes, characteristics, behaviors, attitudes, and abilities. Content validity evaluation is usually associated with measures of cognitive abilities. *Construct validity* is the accuracy with which test scores reflect levels or degrees of psychological constructs (Cronbach, 1984). Construct validity is particularly important for evaluating measures of personality dynamics, attitudes, or interests. *Criterion-related validity* refers to the extent to which test scores are predictably associated with other, often behavioral, criteria (Anastasia, 1982). Performance and competency measures in particular must have criterion-related validity.

Reliability

The consistency of measurement results yielded by a test is known as reliability (Anastasia, 1982; Cronbach, 1984). Similar to validity, three types of reliability are usually described in the literature. *Stability,* sometimes called test–retest reliability, indicates the likelihood of a person achieving the same or a similar test score if the test is administered on two or more different occasions. *Equivalence,* sometimes called parallel forms reliability, indicates the extent to which two versions of a measure yield the same or essentially similar results. *Internal consistency* reliability indicates the extent to which each item within a test (or subscale) correlates with the total test (or subscale) score. The type of reliability deemed most important depends on the nature of the testing situation.

Appropriateness

A test is appropriate if factors extraneous to the purpose and nature of the test itself (e.g., size of print type used, testing conditions, or reading level of test content) have no influence on performance or response to the test.

Validity, reliability, and appropriateness are interrelated but not necessarily interdependent. A valid test is necessarily reliable and appropriate. However, a test can produce reliable (i.e., consistent) but invalid results. Similarly, an inappropriate test (e.g., one for which the content reading level is too high for respondents) can produce reliable but not valid results.

Norm-referenced and *criterion-referenced* are two terms commonly used to describe tests. The distinction between the two types of tests is usually made in regard to the interpretation of the results from each type (Mehrens & Lehmann, 1984). In norm-referenced testing, a respondent's test score is reported in comparison to performance on the same test by other persons. Percentiles, or "standardized," scores are commonly used to indicate *relative* performance. For example, a person whose score is at the eighty-fifth percentile is interpreted to have performed on the test at a level equal to or surpassing 85 percent of the persons in the "norm" group for the test. These persons presumably are similar to the respondent in important ways. Norm-referenced testing necessitates the establishment of normative data but not of specific behavioral criteria.

In criterion-referenced testing, a respondent's test score is interpreted in comparison to some specified behavioral domain or criterion of proficiency. A respondent's score indicates how many criterion-specific tasks (i.e., items) the respondent completed successfully. Criterion-referenced testing involves the development of specific behavioral criteria and the relationships of test items to those criteria.

Tests have been characterized and/or differentiated through the use of a wide variety of other terms. The following are brief descriptions of terms commonly used in the testing literature.

Standardized Tests

Mehrens and Lehmann (1987) wrote,

> "*Standardized tests*...are commercially prepared by experts in measurement and the subject matter. They provide methods for obtaining samples of behavior under uniform procedures—that is, the same fixed set of [items] is administered with the same set of directions and timing constraints, and the scoring procedure is carefully delineated and kept constant" (p. 7).

Conversely, so-called nonstandardized tests are frequently user-prepared, and administration procedures may vary depending on the situation.

Individual and Group Tests

Individual tests are designed to be administered to one person by a single administrator. These tests usually involve the administrator "tailoring" the testing procedure (e.g., determining the time allowed for responding) to a specific respondent and/or testing situation. A group test is one that can be administered to more than one person at a time.

Power and Speed Tests

In most types of testing, interest is in maximum and/or thorough respondent performance. Therefore, testing time allotments exceed time needed by respondents to complete the test. Such tests are called power tests. Intellectual ability, aptitude, and achievement tests are common examples of power tests. In contrast, speed tests involve speed of performance as dynamic in the assessment process. Task completion tests (e.g., typing or other manual dexterity skills tests) are common examples of speed tests.

Vertical and Horizontal Tests

Tests that have different but conceptually and structurally related forms based on some hierarchy (e.g., age category, developmental level, or grade) are known as vertical tests. Tests conceptually and structurally related that assess within a number of different domains simultaneously within a defined category (e.g., age group or grade level) are known as horizontal tests. Aptitude or achievement "test batteries," such as those commonly used in schools, are both vertical and horizontal tests.

Structured and Unstructured Tests

These tests differ by the response task. In a structured test, the respondent is presented with a clear stimulus (e.g., an item stem) and instructed to select the appropriate response from those presented (e.g., response choices). In an unstructured test the respondent is presented with a clear or an ambiguous stimulus and is instructed to construct a response. This differentiation is evident in different types of personality inventories.

Computerized Tests

Rapid technologic advancements are being made in the uses of computers, particularly microcomputers, for testing. In computerized testing, the respondent "interacts" with a computer by providing responses, usually through keyboard input, to stimuli (e.g., questions) presented on a computer monitor. Both the number and type of tests being transformed to computer application is increasing at an exponential rate.

The major advantages of computerized testing are that responses are made easily, respondents have considerable control over the rate of interaction (i.e., responding), test scoring and data analyses are rapidly completed, and local "data sets" (e.g., local normative data) are easily established. The major limitations of computerized testing concern the "security" of tests and testing procedures. Significant recent improvements in computerized testing have helped to minimize these concerns, however. Computerized testing holds promise to be the "method of choice" in the near future (APA, 1986).

Paper-and-Pencil Tests

A majority of tests are "paper-and-pencil" tests, where respondents provide responses directly on tests, test booklets, or accompanying answer or response sheets. However, the connotation of the term paper-and-pencil tests has been broadened beyond the restrictive (literal) definition to encompass almost all structured tests, including computerized versions of those tests.

Performance Tests

Tests that require respondents to complete physical tasks to allow evaluation of skill or competence levels are known as performance tests. They also are referred to as "work sample" tests. Performance or work sample tests are used most frequently in the context of vocational or vocational rehabilitation counseling.

The following are methods that may be thought of as tests because they yield data for evaluation purposes. However, they differ from the preceding tests in that data are not provided by the person to whom the data applies.

Structured and Open-Response Interviews

In a structured interview, the interviewer asks the interviewee a predetermined set of questions. Responses from the interviewee are classified (or coded) into predetermined potential response categories. Questions posed in an open-response interview are also predetermined, but categories of potential responses are not. Rather, post hoc analyses are made in an attempt to "sort out" respondent information.

Rating Scales

The use of rating scales involves a rater providing an indication of another person's level or degree of an attribute, attitude, or characteristic in terms of predetermined stimuli (i.e., items). Rating scales may be used to assess "live" behavior through media (e.g., audiotape, videotape, or photographic) that records the behavior.

Behavior Observations

In making behavior observations, an observer views (sometimes on videotape) a person in a situation and records frequencies with which predetermined behaviors occur. Behavior observation and rating techniques are often used in the same contexts. For example, counselor trainees' verbal responses in counseling sessions are typically counted by type and rated for level of effectiveness by supervisors.

Checklists

When used as assessment techniques, checklists contain either sets of behaviors or attributes. For behaviors, responses usually reflect perceived frequencies of occurrence. For attributes, responses usually reflect perceived presence or absence. Checklist responses can be self-reported, provided by another person (e.g., a counselor), or both.

DOCUMENTS PERTINENT TO TESTING

There are at least four types of documents pertinent to testing with which counselors should be familiar. In *ethical standards documents,* which are covered elsewhere in this book, counselors should be familiar with the sections pertaining to testing. *Guidelines for uses of tests* are covered later in this chapter. The third type is *test manuals.* A good test manual contains the theoretical bases of the test; evidence of validity, reliability, and appropriateness; normative or criterion data; and other information necessary for proper use of the test. Good tests have good test manuals, and good counselors make use of these manuals. Indeed, maximum benefit cannot be derived from a test unless the user is familiar with the material presented in the test manual.

The fourth type of testing documents is the single document, *Standards for Educational and Psychological Testing* (APA, 1985). The *Standards* were developed through collaborative effort of the American Psychological Association (APA), American Educational Research Association, and National Council on Measurement in Education, and are published by the APA. The *Standards* are the recognized criteria against which tests, testing procedures, test manuals, and other test information should be evaluated. Counselors should become thoroughly familiar with these Standards in order to critique, select, and use tests effectively for counseling purposes.

RECENT TRENDS IN TESTING

A relatively recent but highly significant trend in testing is the application of Item Response Theory (IRT) in test development practices. McKinley (1989) wrote:

> The attractiveness of IRT as both a research and measurement tool is derived primarily from its *parameter invariance* properties. The property of invariance means that the item statistics that are obtained from the application of the IRT model are independent of the sample of examinees to which a test (or other instrument) is administered. Likewise, the personal statistics obtained for examinees are independent of the items included in the test. This is in marked contrast to more traditional statistics, such as item and examinee proportion-correct or number-correct scores (p. 37).

In "traditional" item analyses, resultant statistics are, technically, applicable only to the norm (usually a group) from which the response data were derived; other groups would have other item statistics. Relatedly, item statistical data in traditional analyses are unique to the set of items included. Use of IRT models yields data that are, theoretically, invariant with regard to both the sample of examinees and the sample of items.

Thorough discussion of IRT models is beyond the scope of this chapter. However, interested readers are referred to McKinley (1989) for a good overview of IRT or to Hambleton (1989) or Crocker and Algina (1986) for complete discussions. The advent or IRT models has resulted in the development of far better tests, particularly in testing for achievement, aptitude, and licensure or certification.

Another recent trend in testing is the use of more theoretically sound and legally defensible methods for establishing minimum criterion scores. A minimum criterion score is the "cutoff point" in a test's score range. Persons who achieve a score above the minimum criterion score set for the test are distinguished from those who do not. For example, counselor licensure or certification examinations have minimum criterion scores. Counselors who obtain a score exceeding the minimum criterion score have fulfilled one of the licensure or certification ability criteria. Similarly, minimum criterion scores have been established for examinations used for academic admissions or for employment screening.

Minimum criterion scores have long been used, but traditionally they have been set capriciously. More recently, methods such as those conceived by Nedelsky, Ebel, and Anghoff have been used in a variety of circumstances (Livingston & Zieky, 1982). These methods result in more equitable decision making and thereby greatly improve the validity of test results for decision-making purposes. Counselors who are involved in using tests for decision-making (e.g., selection) purposes should become familiar with various "accepted" methods for establishing minimum criterion scores.

TEST BIAS

No discussion of basic concepts in testing would be complete without a discussion of test bias. It has been defined as "...differential validity of a given interpretation of a test score for any definable, relevant subgroup of test takers" (Cole & Moss, 1989, p. 205). Test bias becomes evident when at least two distinctly identifiable groups achieve different results on a test. These differences can be attributed to factors (e.g., gender or race) that, theoretically, should not be bases for the differences. It is important to note that while test bias is usually thought of as a characteristic of test items, its most significant (and usually detrimental) impact concerns interpretations of test data and the actions taken on the basis of these interpretations.

A variety of methods have been developed to alleviate test bias, including empirical means. Test developers are conscientiously striving to produce nonbiased tests. Nonetheless, there remains a considerable number of tests that are biased. Therefore, counselors must be sensitive to test results that may be biased. They should strive to ensure that their interpretations of test results are not flawed from being based on biased data.

MAJOR TYPES OF TESTS

Specific tests are usually described according to their respective individual characteristics, such as those described in the previous section. More commonly, tests are grouped according to the general human dynamic being assessed. Therefore, counselors typically use five major types of standardized tests; achievement, aptitude, intelligence, interest, and personality.

Achievement Tests

Achievement tests are developed to measure the effects of relatively specific programs of instruction or training (Anastasia, 1982). Accordingly, achievement tests are used widely in educational systems and institutions. However, achievement tests are also used in business and industry settings to determine the need for or effects of "on the job" or other specialized training. In either case, achievement tests are designed to provide information about how much has been learned up to the date of assessment as a result of educational experiences.

Structured or guided learning activities, such as school curricula, are intended to enable participants to learn the content of specific knowledge and skill domains. Achievement tests are developed to be related to those domains. Thus, content validity considerations are particularly important in evaluating achievement tests. As achievement tests are generally administered one time at the end of a course of study, internal consistency reliability is a primary consideration in their evaluation.

Achievement tests typically are subdivided into three types: single-subject-matter, survey batteries, and diagnostic. The purpose of *single-subject-matter* achievement tests is to assess the level of knowledge retention for a specifically defined content domain. This type of test is most commonly used in schools. However, they are sometimes used in other specialized training programs such as construction or trade apprenticeship programs. *Survey battery* achievement tests are collections of single-subject-matter tests. Achievement test batteries contain subtests, each of which is designed to measure achievement in a specific area. Achievement test batteries have several advantages over a collection of single-subject-matter tests. Administration procedures are simplified by the similarity in each subsection. Testing costs often are less for achievement test batteries because printing, test booklet binding, answer sheet printing, and processing costs are usually minimized. The greatest advantage of achievement test batteries, however, is that all subtests in the battery have the same norm group. This commonality facilitates comparisons among a respondent's relative levels of achievement across areas tested.

Diagnostic achievement tests are primarily concerned with measuring skills or abilities. For example, diagnostic tests can be used to determine which reading, writing, or mathematical skills students are able to perform. Diagnostic achievement tests are sometimes referred to as "deficit measurement" tests because they reveal skills that have not yet been mastered. Subsequent instruction can be focused specifically upon the development of these skills. It should be noted that although diagnostic tests identify skills that have not yet been achieved, they do not reveal *why* the skills have not been achieved. Achievement tests yield descriptive but not causal relationship results.

Clearly there is a trend toward the development of criterion-referenced achievement tests paralleling the trend toward the development of curricular competency objectives in schools. This latter trend should help clarify the objectives schools are trying to accomplish. However, it may result in greater tendencies to "teach to the test," particularly when curricular and test competencies are highly similar. Therefore, counselors using achievement tests should consider the instruction underlying test results.

Aptitude Tests

Traditionally, aptitude tests have been defined as tests intended for the prediction of an individual's future behavior. For example, aptitude tests have been used to predict future performance in an academic curriculum area or in a specialized vocational activity such as computer programming. The traditionally used definition has the advantage of implying how the tests are to be used (i.e., for prediction). However, the definition does not clarify why aptitude tests have greater predictive power than other types of tests, or how they differ from other types of tests.

The nature and purposes of aptitude testing are best conceived within the global context of evaluation of human abilities. Within that context, intelligence testing is considered to be the measurement and evaluation of potentially generalized human functioning. Aptitude testing within that context is conceived as the measurement and evaluation of potential functioning within more specific domains of human behavior. In general, the narrower the domain of human functioning into which prediction is to be made, the easier it is to develop effective predictive tests. Thus, aptitude tests have greater predictive power because they usually focus on specific areas of human functioning.

The physical formats of most aptitude tests are similar to other measures of cognitive functioning (e.g., intelligence or achievement tests). They frequently contain multiple-choice items, with a few tests containing manual or other dexterity tasks. The difference between aptitude and achievement tests lies in the criteria to which the items are theoretically related. Items in achievement tests are presumed to be related to academic and learning experiences to which respondents have been *previously* exposed. Items in aptitude tests are presumed to be related to learning or occupational tasks that respondents will be *expected* to master or accomplish in the future.

Although theoretical distinctions can be made between aptitude and achievement tests, practical distinctions are difficult to operationalize. All human performance on tests is contingent upon respondents' previous learning and life experiences. For example, there is considerable debate as to whether the Scholastic Aptitude Test (SAT) is an achievement or an aptitude test. Ostensibly, it is an aptitude test because it is used to predict secondary school students' performance in college curricula. Presumably, individual items are closely related to the types of mental functioning tasks that college students are required to master. However, SAT scores have high positive correlations with students' high school grade point averages (GPAs), which have high positive correlations with secondary school level achievement tests. Further, most students who complete the SAT have been enrolled in "college prep" curricula that focused upon mastery of academic skills (i.e., skills necessary for successful performance in college). School systems publicize increases in the average SAT scores for graduates (as if the SAT was an achievement test) while colleges extol the positive correlations between SAT scores and GPAs (as if the SAT were an aptitude test). The debate will not likely be ended soon.

Aptitude tests are usually categorized into either single-domain or multifactor batteries. The differentiation is the same as that for achievement tests. Single-domain aptitude tests focus upon a specific aspect of human performance such as a particular type of academic performance or job behavior. Aptitude (multifactor) test batteries are assemblies of single-domain tests, having a common format, administration procedure, and norm group. Regardless of type, criterion-related validity (specifically *predictive* validity) is most important for aptitude tests. Similar to achievement tests, internal consistency reliability is the most important type for aptitude tests. For large-scale testing programs equivalent-forms reliability also is important.

Counselors use aptitude test results primarily in academic and/or vocational counseling contexts. Because of the "faith" many people place in aptitude test results, it is imperative that counselors establish that aptitude tests have validity for the respective contexts in which predictions are made. Erroneous "predictions" of performance can have long-term detrimental effects for clients.

Intelligence Tests

No area in testing has created greater hatred or more heated debate than the nature and effective measurement of intelligence (Anastasia, 1982). Considerable interest exists among professionals in being able to evaluate an individual's "level of mental ability" because of the many significant implications that can be derived from such knowledge. However, while many of these implications serve the benefit of humankind, some can be construed as highly unethical. Therefore, it may be best that neither a definitive explanation nor a fully valid measurement of intelligence has yet been conceived.

The voluminous literature on intelligence testing prohibits more than a cursory coverage of the topic. Therefore, only a few of the major concepts are addressed here. At the core of intelligence testing is how intelligence is defined. Some, following the lead of Binet, conceive of intelligence as a *unitary* (also called unifactor) construct. In brief, they believe that intelligence is a single, generalized human ability that underlies all human functioning. In contrast, others, following the lead of Wechsler, believe that intelligence is the sum total of a large and diverse set of specific mental abilities. That is, they believe that intelligence is a *multifactor* construct. A variety of intelligence tests have been developed based on these definitions. The result is that different intelligence tests yield from one to twenty or more (subscale) scores depending on the definition used as the basis for the respective tests.

Intelligence tests are also classified as *group* or *individual* tests. Group intelligence tests are usually of the "paper-and-pencil" variety. They are heavily dependent on facility in the use of language and are designed to be administered to large groups of persons during a single administration. As the name implies, individual intelligence tests are designed to be administered to one person at a time. Individual intelligence tests place emphasis on the use of language (through inclusion of "paper-and-pencil" components), but also include "performance" tasks to be completed by respondents. The significant advantage of individual intelligence tests over group intelligence tests is that competent administrators can learn much about *how* a person responds to a testing task (i.e., method of problem solving and/or affective reactions) by careful observation during the testing session. The significant disadvantage of individual intelligence testing is the cost of administering tests on an individual basis.

Intelligence tests (or subsections of them) are also described as verbal or nonverbal. A "verbal" intelligence test employs the use of language, such as providing definitions of words in a "vocabulary" subtest. In a "nonverbal" intelligence test, persons can respond without having to interpret written or spoken language. Traditionally, such tests have been composed of a variety of tasks involving figures, diagrams, symbols, or drawings. However, the term has come to include "performance" tests (or subtests) in which the respondents physically manipulate objects. Most well-accepted individual intelligence tests include both verbal and nonverbal subtests. Most group intelligence tests are verbal, although a few nonverbal group intelligence tests ("culture-fair") have been developed.

The immense general interest in intelligence assessment has subjected intelligence testing to intense scrutiny, which has resulted in substantial criticism being aimed at intelligence tests. A common criticism is that intelligence tests are really "academic aptitude" tests; items in them seem closely related to the types of abilities needed to be successful in academic systems. Another criticism is that intelligence tests are biased; they favor persons from upper socioeconomic classifications because of the types of values reflected in the tests. However, the most significant criticism for counselors is that intelligence tests are culturally and/or racially biased. Arguments and counterarguments have emerged as to why and how intelligence tests are racially or culturally biased. At the very least, there is a basis for questioning possible bias in intelligence tests. Therefore, counselors who intend to use intelligence tests should spend considerable time studying available expository and empirical information about intelligence testing.

Interest Inventories

Interest inventories were developed as a means to assess a person's relative preferences for (i.e., feelings about) engaging in a variety of conceptually related activities (Mehrens & Lehmann, 1984). Although the vast majority of interest inventories focus upon assessment of vocational interest, avocational (or leisure) interest inventories are sometimes useful to counselors. However, the following discussion relates only to vocational interest inventories because of their predominance.

Vocational interest inventories are intended to provide information on a person's interests in various vocations or occupations. To achieve this goal respondents indicate their degree of preference on a scale with incremental values for each of a large set of activities. The activities that respondents prefer are obtained and related to types of work activities that are characteristic of various occupations. Noteworthy is that activities for which preference information is obtained may not be obviously related to particular occupations. That is, respondents typically do not know which activities are conceptually and/or empirically related to particular occupations.

Associations between activities and occupations are established by having persons who report being "satisfied" in an occupation indicate their preferences for a variety of activities. Activities that are most frequently preferred by "satisfied" workers become associated with the respective occupations. Thus, vocational interest assessment is a comparison of a respondent's pattern of activity preferences with those of persons reporting satisfaction in various occupations. Vocational interest assessment has reached a degree of sophistication such that interest levels in a variety of occupations are achieved through responses to a small number of items (i.e., activities).

For counseling purposes, the basic assumption underlying interest assessment is that people are prone to engage in activities they prefer. Thus, a *very* simplistic view of "vocational" counseling is that of "pairing" people's interests with activities inherent in occupations, with interest assessment as a major component of the process. However, such a simplistic view belies the limitations of vocational interest assessment.

Chief among the limitations of interest assessment is that "high interest" in an occupation is not necessarily synonymous with "aptitude for" an occupation. Unfortunately, clients who are poorly counseled often erroneously assume that interest and aptitude are equivalent, and may subsequently make misinformed decisions. Another limitation of interest assessment is susceptibility to response sets. For example, some people report high levels of interest in particular activities because they believe it is socially acceptable to do so. Perhaps this explains why many young people "overselect" the "higher" professions as occupational goals although they do not have the requisite aptitudes for those professions. A third limitation is reliability. Interests often fluctuate because of the influences of life experience, maturation, social context, and/or economic need. Thus, even the best of vocational interest inventories have low stability reliability coefficients. Finally, there is the potential for gender bias in interest assessment. Clearly gender roles and situations in the workplace are changing. These changes result in gender-specific or non-gender-specific normative data for interest inventories. Development costs restrict frequencies of instrument and/or normative refinements. Therefore, the continuing possibility exists that vocational interest inventory results can be misinterpreted because of gender bias.

These limitations notwithstanding, assessment of vocational interests is used frequently by counselors. Several reasons underlie this trend. One is that clients seek the most expedient means of finding satisfying and rewarding work. A second reason is that interest assessment is nonthreatening to clients; it is acceptable to have a lack of interest in an area. A third is that clients view interest assessment as a way to understand themselves without fear of disclosing their "deficiencies." In summary, counselors and clients favor interest assessment because it provides information that is easily obtained in counseling processes.

Personality Inventories

A definition of personality assessment is difficult because of its multifaceted nature. However, personality inventories are designed to yield information about a person's characteristics, traits, behaviors, attitudes, opinions, and/or emotions (Anastasia, 1982; Litwack, 1986; Mehrens & Lehmann, 1984). Personality assessment is particularly germane to the work of counselors, but it is the most complex type of assessment. Counselors should be knowledgeable in psychometric principles and personality theory. Additionally, they should have substantive supervised practice before using personality assessment instruments.

Personality inventories are classified as *structured* or *unstructured*. Structured personality inventories contain a set of items that are interpreted in the same way by all examinees (Mehrens & Lehmann, 1984). These inventories contain a set of potential item responses from among which a respondent selects one as most appropriate (i.e., pertinent to or characteristic of self). Structured personality inventories are sometimes referred to as self-report inventories (Anastasia, 1982). Responses are selected by respondents, not from the interpretations of administrators. Structured personality inventories yield the quantitative scores based on predetermined scoring criteria. They are intended to be interpreted in comparison to normative data.

Unstructured personality inventories contain stimuli that can be interpreted in different ways by different respondents. Unstructured personality inventories are sometimes referred to as "projective" tests because in many of them respondents are required to "project" thoughts or feelings onto the stimuli presented (Mehrens & Lehmann, 1984). Although "scoring" procedures have been developed for some unstructured personality inventories, results are more commonly "clinical interpretations" of responses made.

Personality inventories have a number of limitations, many of which are similar to those of interest inventories. For example, personality inventories are susceptible to "faking." In these instances, clients subvert the validity of the assessment by providing responses they believe will make them "look good" or "look bad." Personality inventories also are susceptible to invalidity through contextual bias. What is a "perfectly normal" response in one context may be evaluated as an exceptionally deviant response in another. Clients may also perceive the use of personality inventories as threatening. While clients may be intrigued about the nature of their personalities, fear of "negative" attributes often outweighs curiosity-based motivation to respond openly and honestly.

The use of personality inventories can be beneficial in helping clients gain insights into their functioning. Most counselors do not receive extensive training in personality assessment. Therefore, they should restrict the use of personality inventories to persons who are functioning normally but who have areas of concern they want to remediate. In general, counselors will derive the most benefit from the use of structured or self-report inventories.

RESPONSIBILITIES OF TEST USERS

Counselors' effective use of tests is directly related to the degree of responsibility they assume. Historically, guidelines for responsible uses of tests had to be extrapolated from statements of ethical standards. A vast majority of counselors have attempted to use tests ethically and, therefore, responsibly. However, their effort was limited by a lack of specificity in ethical standards statements. In response to this situation, the American Association for Counseling and Development (AACD), through its Association for Measurement and Evaluation in Counseling and Development (AMECD) division, developed the *Policy Statement on the Responsibilities of Test Users* (AACD/AMECD, 1989). The following are comments on major sections of that policy statement.

With regard to test decisions, counselors (as test users) are responsible for determination of information assessment needs and clarification of the objectives for and limitations of testing for each circumstance. Thus, counselors (not clients or others) have the final authority for decisions about test use in their profession. Qualifications of test users also are an important factor in the testing process. They should be considered with regard to the purposes of testing, characteristics of the tests, conditions of test use, and the roles of other professionals.

Emphasized in the test selection guidelines is that careful consideration should be given to each test's validity, reliability, appropriateness, and other technical characteristics. Also, respondent participation in the test selection process is desirable, if appropriate and/or possible.

Test administration procedures should be conducted by qualified administrators who give proper test orientation and directions in appropriate testing conditions. Test scoring should be conducted only by fully qualified persons to ensure accurate results.

Provided within the policy statement guidelines are test interpretations in the contexts of uses for placement, prediction, description, assessment of growth, and program evaluation. The importance of appropriate norms, technical factors, and the effects of variations in administration and scoring are emphasized. Guidelines for communicating test results in individual or group contexts are explained in the last section of the policy statement.

Unfortunately, only these brief comments on the policy statement can be provided here. Counselors who use tests should carefully read the entire statement.

TESTING IN PROGRAM EVALUATION

Counselors should be familiar with the "program evaluation literature." However, many counselors erroneously believe that generating and reporting test results is synonymous with program evaluation. Testing is an aspect of program evaluation, but a "testing program" does not replace program evaluation. Effective program evaluation involves gathering a wide variety of objective (empirical) and subjective information about program impacts. Test results are just one part of this process.

Formative and *summative* are the two major types of program evaluation processes. In formative program evaluation, data are gathered while the program is in progress so that process adjustments and modifications can be made to maximize the program's effectiveness. Summative program evaluation involves gathering data at the conclusion of a program in order to determine the extent of the program's impact. Carefully and effectively designed program evaluation processes usually encompass both types.

Testing and test results can be used in either type of program evaluation process. For example, test data derived while counseling and/or other programmatic activities are being conducted can be used to identify needed changes in those activities. Test data obtained after a program has been concluded can be used for analysis and evaluation of which activities were effective. In either case, if tests are used within appropriate guidelines they can be invaluable resources in program evaluation processes.

Just as program evaluation is not synonymous with testing, neither is it synonymous with research. However, research designs and principles often are incorporated into program evaluation processes. Specifically, summative program evaluation processes involve "pre-post" testing, which includes tests being administered before a program begins and the same (or equivalent forms) administered at the program's end. In addition to the concern about test validity, this type of procedure requires concern for the appropriateness and reliability of tests used. Thus, major concerns regarding test use for counseling purposes are at least equally important for program evaluation purposes.

The need for counselors to be accountable for their activities has been widely publicized. Program evaluation processes should be a part of counselors' accountability efforts because these processes reflect the full scope of services rendered by counselors. However, counselors need to be involved in program evaluation activities because competent counselors know about tests and testing, and therefore should serve as resources for the development of program evaluation procedures.

CONCLUSION

Testing is an integral and legitimate part of a counselor's professional functioning. However, counselors have a choice about the attitudes they adopt toward testing. They can view it as a "necessary evil" and employ minimal effort toward testing functions, or they can take the time and effort to gain understanding of psychometric principles, tests, and testing processes. Such efforts will reap the many benefits of the fully effective uses of tests in counseling. Counselors who adopt this latter perspective will find that testing is a valuable resource, and one that enhances many of their professional activities.

REFERENCES

American Association for Counseling and Development/Association for Measurement and Evaluation in Counseling and Development (1989). *Policy statement on the responsibilities of test users*. Washington, DC: AACD.

American Psychological Association, American Educational Research Association, & National Council on Measurement in Education (1985). *Standards for educational and psychological testing*. Washington, DC: APA.

American Psychological Association (1986). *Guidelines for computer-based tests and interpretations*. Washington, DC: APA.

Anastasia, A. (1982). *Psychological testing* (5th ed.). New York: Macmillan.

Cole, N. S., & Moss, P. A. (1989). Bias in test use. In R. L. Linn (Ed.)., *Educational measurement* (3rd ed.), (pp. 201–220). New York: American Council on Education & Macmillan.

Cronbach, L. J. (1984). *Essentials of psychological testing* (4th ed.). New York: Harper & Row.

Crocker, L., & Algina, J. (1986). *Introduction to classical and modern test theory.* New York: Holt, Rinehart, and Winston.

Gladding, S. T. (1988), *Counseling: a comprehensive profession.* Columbus, OH: Merrill.

Goldman, L. (1971). *Using tests in counseling* (2nd ed.). New York: Appleton-Century-Crofts.

Hambleton, R. K. (1989). Principles and selected applications of item response theory. In R. L. Linn (Ed.), *Educational measurement* (3rd ed.) (pp. 147–200). New York: American Council on Education & Macmillan.

Litwack, L. (1986). Appraisal of the individual. In M. D. Lewis, R. L. Hayes, & J. A. Lewis (Eds.), *An introduction to the counseling profession* (pp. 251–277). Itasca, IL: Peacock.

Livingston, S. A., & Zieky, M. J. (1982). *Passing scores: A manual for setting standards of performance on educational and psychological tests.* Princeton, NJ: Educational Testing Service.

McKinley, R. L. (1989). An introduction to item response theory. *Measurement and Evaluation in Counseling and Development, 22,* 37–57.

Mehrens, W. A., & Lehmann, I. J. (1984). *Measurement and evaluation in education and psychology* (3rd ed.). New York: Holt, Rinehart and Winston.

Mehrens, W. A., & Lehmann, I. J. (1987). *Using standardized tests in education* (4th ed.). New York: Longman.

Messick, S. (1989). Validity. In R. L. Linn (Ed.), *Educational measurement* (3rd ed.) (pp. 13–104). New York: American Council on Education & Macmillan.

Shertzer, B., & Linden, J. (1979). *Fundamentals of individual appraisal: Assessment techniques for counselors.* Boston: Houghton-Mifflin.

Vacc, N. A., & Loesch, L. C. (1987). *Counseling as a profession.* Muncie, IN: Accelerated Development, Inc.

9.

Diagnosis in Counseling

LINDA SELIGMAN, PH.D., L.P.C.
George Mason University
Fairfax, Virginia

IMPORTANCE OF DIAGNOSIS

Alice, age 20, consults a counselor at her college because of feelings of depression. She tells the counselor that she has barely been able to get out of bed for the past month. She has been eating little, has not attended most of her classes, and has thought about cutting her wrists to end it all. She can offer no explanation for her mood change and says she has never felt like this before.

Michael, age 28, sought help from a community mental health center for depression. Although he has been going to work and fulfilling his family obligations, he has felt very hopeless for over a month. Michael reports a 10-year history of unstable moods with long periods of depression as well as episodes of hyperactivity and high elation.

Susan, age 11, is brought to her pediatrician by her mother who states that Susan has been depressed and crying for the past month, since her parents separated. Although she does become much more cheerful when her father visits, she is moody and irritable much of the time and has been doing poorly in school.

Robert, age 45, seeks help from a psychiatrist for longstanding depression. He has a long history of alcohol and drug abuse, of multiple physical complaints, and of several alcohol-related accidents. He has begun several treatment programs but has not been able to remain drug- or alcohol-free for more than a few weeks.

Cheryl, too, seeks counseling for her depression. At 35, she has achieved a great deal. Married with two children, she is a successful writer and photographer. However, she has been troubled by feelings of sadness of at least several years' duration that she has been unable to ward off on her own. Although she has been able to function well and conceal those feelings from others, she has finally decided to seek help.

All five of these people sought help for depression. However, all of their depressions differ in several respects: presence of an apparent precipitant, duration, frequency, severity, and accompanying symptoms. Similarly, the diagnoses, the treatments, and the prognosis for each person's disorder differ.

Alice is probably experiencing a major depression, single episode, melancholic type. This form of depression tends to respond fairly quickly to several forms of counseling (e.g., cognitive, interpersonal), often in combination with antidepressant medication. Michael is suffering from a bipolar disorder, depressed type. This disorder is frequently chronic without treatment but is very amenable to treatment through a combination of counseling and medication. Susan has experienced a recent loss and is reacting to that loss with an adjustment disorder with depressed mood. Counseling has a high probability of alleviating Susan's discouragement fairly quickly. Robert, on the other hand, may well be suffering from an organic mental disorder, caused by some combination of his substance abuse and his illnesses and accidents. Prognosis here is far less favorable and treatment may entail hospitalization. Cheryl has probably been troubled by a form of depression called dysthymia. Medication and hospitalization are rarely necessary for treatment of dysthymia but its response to counseling varies and is difficult to predict.

The importance of diagnosis can be seen from these examples. Without an accurate diagnosis, it is difficult to determine the proper treatment for a disorder and to assess whether a client is likely to benefit from counseling. In the above examples, Susan, and probably Cheryl, are good candidates for counseling. Alice and Michael might also benefit from counseling, but probably only as part of a team effort, with counselors and psychiatrists working together to ameliorate the depression. Robert's case is too complicated by physiologic concerns for counseling to be a primary focus of treatment at present. Perhaps once he has been medically evaluated and detoxified, counseling can facilitate his adjustment to a healthier lifestyle and complement other forms of treatment, but Robert clearly needs intervention that cannot be provided by counseling.

Benefits of Diagnosis

The importance of diagnosis in determining the appropriate treatment for a mental disorder and in indicating when counseling is likely to be effective and when a referral is necessary are probably the major reasons why counselors should be able to make diagnoses. However, there are many other reasons why diagnosis is a fundamental skill in the counselor's repertoire (Hershenson, Power, & Seligman, 1989).

1. A diagnostic system provides a consistent framework as well as a set of criteria for naming and describing mental disorders.

2. Knowing the diagnosis for a client's concerns can help counselors to anticipate the typical course of the disorder and to develop a clearer understanding of the client's symptoms.

3. Use of a diagnostic system promotes accountability; it enables counselors to make use of the growing body of literature on treatment effectiveness (e.g., what types of interventions are most likely to ameliorate a given disorder) and to more easily assess and improve the quality of their counseling.

4. The process of diagnosis employs a common language, used by all other mental health disciplines, thereby facilitating parity, credibility, communication, and collaboration.

5. Diagnoses are linked to several standardized inventories (e.g., the Minnesota Multiphasic Personality Inventory, the Millon Clinical Multiaxial Inventory), enabling counselors to understand these inventories and use them as a source of information on their clients.

6. Counselors are on safer legal ground and are less vulnerable to malpractice if they have made a diagnosis and treatment plan according to an accepted system.

7. Using a standardized system of diagnosis facilitates counselors' eligibility for insurance reimbursement for their services, thereby making counseling affordable to many people who would not otherwise be able to afford help.

8. Sharing diagnoses with clients, when appropriate, can help clients to understand what is happening to them and to experience less guilt and self-blame over the problems they are presenting and their need for help. Knowing that others have experienced similar symptoms

and that information is available about their conditions can also reassure clients.

9. Explaining to clients that they have a diagnosable mental disorder can unbalance previously established views of their difficulties and can help them to take a fresh look at their issues and perhaps increase their openness to treatment.

10. Clients' awareness that they have a diagnosable mental disorder can reduce the likelihood that they will blame others for their problems and erroneously externalize their concerns.

Risks of Diagnosis

Although there are many arguments in favor of the use of a standard diagnostic system, there are some risks inherent in the use of such a system

1. Attaching a diagnostic label to someone can be stigmatizing if misused and can lead to negative perceptions of that person at school, at work, or in the family if the diagnosis becomes known.

2. In some cases, knowing the diagnostic term for a person's symptoms can be more discouraging and threatening than viewing the problem in lay terms. For example, parents may be more comfortable dealing with a child they view as behaving badly than with one who has a conduct disorder.

3. Diagnosis can lead to over-generalizing, to viewing clients as their mental disorders (i.e., a borderline, a depressive) rather than as a person with a particular set of concerns, and can promote a focus on pathology rather than on health.

4. Although the linear process of diagnosis can facilitate information and treatment planning, as mentioned above, it can make it more difficult to think about clients in developmental and systemic terms and to take a holistic view of clients and their environments.

5. Similarly, attaching a diagnostic label to one person puts the focus of treatment on the individual rather than on a family or social system. This can reinforce the family's perception of that person as its only problem and can make it more difficult for a family to work together on shared issues and concerns.

6. In addition, the widely accepted systems of diagnosis have all been developed out of a Western concept of mental illness and may have limited relevance to people from other cultures.

Although there are clearly some risks inherent in the process of diagnosis, most of the risks can be avoided by skillful counseling, judicious presentation of diagnostic information to avoid misunderstanding by clients and their families, and maintenance of the client's confidentiality whenever possible. It is up to the counselor, then, to maximize the benefits and minimize the risks of diagnosis.

GROWING IMPORTANCE OF DIAGNOSIS

Some counselors and counseling students may feel uncomfortable with the idea of making diagnoses, particularly counselors who are primarily interested in counseling in school or business settings. They may view their role as emphasizing support and information-giving and may refer clients who have mental disorders to other mental health practitioners. Consequently, they may feel little need to learn about diagnosis. Other counselors may have a strongly humanistic bent in their counseling orientation and may believe that the process of labeling clients is antithetical to their idea of the counselor's role.

However, changes in the field of counseling make it important for all counselors to be familiar with the process of diagnosis. Until the 1970s, "counselor" usually meant school counselor, typically someone working in a secondary school, whose primary tasks were administrative: testing, scheduling, and facilitating college admissions. In the past 15 years, however, the counselor's role has expanded greatly, with particular growth in mental health counseling. The American Mental Health Counselors Association, with over 12,000 members, is one of the largest divisions of the American Association for Counseling and Development. Over half the states have licensure or certification legislation for counselors and a growing number of states are passing so-called Freedom of Choice legislation that requires insurance companies to provide third-party payments for credentialed counselors. Mastery of diagnosis will not only improve the effectiveness of mental health counselors but also is commonly required by their places of employment where diagnoses are needed for accountability, determination of treatment effectiveness, record-keeping, and insurance reimbursement.

Counselors in schools and businesses should also be familiar with the process of diagnosis, although for somewhat different reasons. Being able to make a diagnosis of a client's concerns enables those counselors to determine whether they can provide services that will help the client or whether a referral is needed, it can help them to select the most appropriate referral, and it can help them anticipate the probable course of their client's condition and response to treatment. Making a diagnosis also can help counselors in schools and businesses to assess whether it is desirable for a client to remain in the school or business, possibly with some extra help, or whether the client needs an environment providing more support and assistance. Diagnosis, therefore, is an important skill for both mental health counselors and those working in other settings.

THE DSM-III-R AND OTHER DIAGNOSTIC SYSTEMS

The most widely used diagnostic system in the United States is the *Diagnostic and Statistical Manual of Mental Disorders* (third revision) (DSM-III-R), published in 1987 by the American Psychiatric Association. The first edition of the DSM appeared in 1952. It was developed primarily by and for psychiatrists and presented a psychobiological view of the nature of emotional disorders. It was replaced in 1958 by the DSM-II, a landmark publication in the field of mental health that looked at mental disorders primarily in terms of psychoses, neuroses, and personality disorders.

The DSM-II remained in use for 22 years. However, by the mid-1970s, it became evident that many of the concepts and terminology in that volume were outdated and imprecise. A joint committee of psychiatrists and psychologists was formed to revise the volume. The involvement of psychologists in the revision of the DSM was important for mental health counselors because it indicated that medical training was not needed for clinicians to use the DSM.

After extensive field trials involving over 500 clinicians, the DSM-III was published in 1980. The DSM-III was more comprehensive and more detailed than its predecessor and was designed to be more precise and less stigmatizing in its language. The DSM-III made some major changes in definition and terminology used for mental disorders. For example, the term "neurosis," which had become a pejorative and common term in the language, was no longer recommended; depressive neurosis, for example, was renamed dysthymic disorder. Schizophrenia was defined more narrowly and was used to describe only severe disorders involving evident loss of contact with reality.

Despite the monumental effort that went into the preparation of the DSM-III, its revision was begun as soon as it was published, culminating in the 1987 publication of the *Diagnostic and Statistical Manual of Mental Disorders* (third edition, revised) (DSM-III-R). This volume reflected changes arising from increased knowledge of mental disorders as well as from changes in attitudes and perceptions. For example, in the 1952 edition of the DSM, homosexuality was viewed as a mental disorder. By the late 1970s, this diagnosis had become controversial, with some continuing to view homosexuality as a mental disorder and others opposing that position. The DSM-III reflected a compromise, with a diagnosis of ego-dystonic homosexuality. That diagnosis described people who were not only homosexual but also were unhappy with their sexual orientation and identification; only under those circumstances was homosexuality viewed as a mental disorder. However, by the mid-1980s, even that diagnosis seemed biased since there was no diagnosis for ego-dystonic heterosexuality. Consequently, the DSM-III-R does not have a diagnosis relating specifically to homosexuality.

It can be seen from the frequent revisions of the DSM that knowledge of mental disorders is a vital and changing body of information. New material is constantly being discovered about the brain, the emotions, and their interaction and impact. In many ways, we are still novices in our understanding of the psychology of people. As a result, our current information is often inadequate and imprecise. Although the DSM makes an important contribution to clarifying and organizing mental disorders, it is a complex publication whose skillful use requires sound clinical judgment as well as experience. A subsequent section of this chapter provides an introduction to the major types of mental disorders and will provide readers some familiarity with the DSM-III-R. Browsing through the volume and using it as one might use a dictionary, looking up diagnoses of interest, making tentative diagnoses of case studies, will increase comfort and familiarity with that sometimes intimidating volume. However, true ease of use of the DSM rarely comes without considerable clinical experience.

Although the DSM-III-R seems to be the standard for diagnostic nomenclature in the United States, another system of diagnosis is also used, particularly in medically oriented settings. The *Manual of the International Statistical Classification of Diseases, Injuries, and Causes of Death* (1978), known in the United States as the ICD-9-CM, is an international publication sponsored by the World Health Organization. The ICD-9 delineates diagnoses for both physical and mental disorders, with Volume 1 of that publication providing extensive information on mental disorders. Although there are many similarities between the DSM-III-R and the ICD-9, the DSM has the benefit of nearly 10 years of additional knowledge in the field and, consequently, is nearly always more useful to the clinician. Consequently, little further attention will be devoted in this chapter to the ICD-9. However, the ICD may become a more important publication for counselors in a few years. Presently, coordinated revision of both publications is planned for 1993, when we will have the DSM-IV and the ICD-10.

DEFINITION OF A MENTAL DISORDER

In DSM-III-R each of the mental disorders is conceptualized as a clinically significant behavioral or psychological syndrome or pattern that occurs in a person and that is associated with present distress [a painful symptom] or disability [impairment in one or more important areas of functioning] or with significantly increased risk of suffering death, pain, disability, or an important loss of freedom. In addition, this syndrome or pattern must not be merely an expectable response to a particular event...(DMS-III-R, 1987, p. xxii).

According to the DSM-III-R, then, a mental disorder is characterized by distress, disability, and/or risk. At least one of these features must be present in order for a client to be diagnosed as having a mental disorder. Although these features are often present in combination, illustrations are provided of the features in isolation to clarify their nature.

Beth sought counseling after her fiance broke their engagement for the third time. She was an attractive, successful lawyer who had continued to perform well at her job despite her personal turmoil. A very private person, Beth continued to see her friends and family and go to work every day showing little or no evidence of her distress. However, every night she cried herself to sleep and even had some fleeting suicidal thoughts. Although Beth manifested no disability nor was she really at risk, she was certainly experiencing distress and had a diagnosable mental disorder, adjustment disorder with depressed mood.

Frank, on the other hand, a 14-year-old who was brought to counseling by his parents, reported that his life was great; he saw his only problem as his parents' nagging. Frank cut classes at whim and spent at least several days each week hanging out at the neighborhood shopping center with his friends. When he needed money, he took it from his mother's purse or from younger children. Frank had little distress about his situation and was not yet at risk, although his use of alcohol and his illegal behavior were potential risk factors. Frank's disorder, a conduct disorder, group type, was characterized primarily by disability. His functioning was extremely poor, both at home and at school.

Hilda reported neither distress nor disability when she consulted a counselor at the suggestion of her family physician. At 5'6" tall, Hilda weighed 100 lbs. and was quite pleased with her figure, estimating that she had only another 5 to 10 pounds to lose. Hilda had anorexia nervosa and had dieted herself into a life-threatening physical condition.

As the DSM definition cited previously indicates, a mental disorder must not only entail distress, disability, or risk, it must be internal and must not be only an expectable response to an event. The DSM does not provide a framework for diagnosing families; it focuses on individuals. This may present a shortcoming to counselors who emphasize the family context in treating clients, although the DSM can help them to understand family differences, patterns, and dynamics through diagnosis of individuals.

Some symptoms are really expectable responses rather than mental disorders. For example, Jessica consulted a counselor after the birth of her third child within the past five years. Although she was a caring and knowledgeable parent, she felt overwhelmed and had difficulty getting the help she needed and managing her time. Counseling could certainly help Jessica handle the many demands on her and the stress she and her husband were feeling, but Jessica did not have a mental disorder. Her reactions caused no risk to herself or the children, did not reflect disability, and were characterized by appropriate, understandable, and manageable distress. Jessica would be diagnosed as experiencing a life circumstance problem rather than a mental disorder.

DESCRIPTION OF THE DSM-III-R

Multiaxial Diagnosis

Whether or not clients who present for counseling have mental disorders, a multiaxial diagnosis offers counselors a way to organize the information they have on clients' symptoms, their physical conditions, their levels of coping, and the stressers they are experiencing. A full or multiaxial diagnosis involves assessing the client according to five axes.

Axis I includes a list of what the DSM calls Clinical Syndromes and V codes (conditions not attributable to a mental disorder). According to the DSM-III-R, *Axis II* includes Developmental Disorders and Personality Disorders, disorders that "...generally begin in childhood or adolescence and persist in a stable form (without periods of remission or exacerbation) into adult life" (p. 16). Understanding the difference between Axis I and Axis II can be difficult but may be facilitated through the use of a medical model. If these axes were listing physical rather than emotional disorders, Axis I would include such conditions as strep throat, cancer, and insect bites. While these conditions vary enormously in terms of severity, treatment, and prognosis, what they have in common is that they are not lifelong, they develop in a person who may have been free of the condition for many years, and they are potentially curable. Axis II conditions, viewed from a medical framework, would include lifelong ailments such as an immune system deficiency or a curvature of the spine. These disorders may present less severe symptoms than some of those on Axis I but they are always present in one form or another and have a pervasive and enduring impact on a person's life. Axis II includes a small percentage of the diagnoses in the DSM-III-R: developmental disorders such as mental retardation; pervasive developmental disorders; academic, language, or motor skills disorders; and personality disorders are listed on Axis II. All other disorders are included on Axis I.

Clients may have one diagnosis on an axis, more than one diagnosis on an axis, or no diagnosis at all on one or both axes. Each diagnosis is associated with a five-digit code number, provided in the DSM-III-R. When the diagnosis is listed, both name and number are specified (e.g., 313.81 oppositional defiant disorder). DSM numbers and terminology are also used when there are no diagnoses (e.g., V71.09 No diagnosis or condition on Axis II). When more than one diagnosis is listed on an axis, the diagnoses are listed in order of treatment priority.

Axis III, Physical Disorders and Conditions, is the most straightforward of the five. On this axis, the clinician lists any physical disorders or conditions that might be relevant to understanding the client's emotional condition. This would include such conditions as migraine headaches that might be related to stress as well a conditions such as cancer or diabetes that might have an impact on the client's emotional adjustment.

Axis IV, Severity of Psychosocial Stressers, enables the clinician to evaluate the recent stressers in clients' lives. Stressers occurring during the past year would be listed and their severity rated on a 1 to 6 scale, based on how the stressers would affect the average person (not on the particular impact they are having on a given client). Lower numbers reflect lower stress. This axis includes positive stressers (e.g., marriage, promotion) as well as negative stressers (e.g., death in family, academic failure).

Axis V, Global Assessment of Functioning, is a measure of the client's overall level of performance; psychological, social, and occupational. The client is rated twice on this 1 to 90 scale, once for current functioning and once for highest functioning in the past year, with higher numbers indicating higher functioning. A comparison of these two ratings indicates whether the client's functioning has declined over the past year.

Axes IV and V are particularly useful in treatment planning. Clients with high ratings on Axis IV and low ratings on Axis V are experiencing considerable stress and have poor levels of functioning. They may require a multifaceted treatment plan, including counseling, medication, and possibly hospitalization. On the other hand, clients with an opposite profile, low ratings on Axis IV and high ratings on Axis V, are experiencing more manageable stress and have good coping mechanisms. Such clients are likely to make good use of counseling.

The following example of a multiaxial diagnosis illustrates how such a diagnosis can quickly provide a broad and rich picture of a client:

Axis I: 296.23 Major depression, single episode, severe, without psychotic features.
           300.23 Social phobia.
Axis II: 301.60 Dependent personality disorder (provisional).
Axis III: Headaches.
Axis IV: Psychosocial stresser: Marital separation, change in residence. Severity: 3—Moderate (predominantly acute circumstances).
Axis V: Current global assessment of functioning (GAF): 45. Highest GAF in the past year: 65.

The above diagnosis was made on a 52-year-old woman, Karen M., who sought counseling after she separated from her husband and she and her 17-year-old son moved into an apartment. Karen presented symptoms of severe depression, including insomnia, feelings of worthlessness and guilt, suicidal ideation, and weight loss, that had been present for two months. She blamed herself for her husband's infidelity and subsequent decision to divorce her and stated that she could not imagine life without her husband. From the multiaxial diagnosis, it can be seen that although this was the client's first episode of depression (single episode), she had some preexisting emotional difficulties. She was extremely uncomfortable in social situations and avoided any public situations that might expose her to embarrassment (social phobia). Although she had a part-time job as a bookkeeper, Karen reported that she was most comfortable at home with her family and only worked because her husband insisted they needed a greater income. Karen also probably had a dependent personality disorder, although that was difficult to ascertain because her depression colored the way she presented herself. However, it sounded as though Karen had a longstanding and deeply ingrained pattern of depending on others to make decisions for her, putting her own needs second to those of others, being easily hurt by any slight or criticism, and having little initiative. Karen had sought medical treatment for her headaches (listed on Axis III) and had been given analgesic medication, but the physician suggested the headaches were probably stress-related. Axis IV indicates that the average person would experience marital separation and moving as moderately stressful, although Karen experienced these events as even more stressful. Finally, Axis V reflects a large decline (20 points) in Karen's functioning over the past year. Her highest level of functioning, 65, was not very good to begin with and reflected moderate impairment in social and occupational functioning. However, with the onset of her severe depression, Karen's functioning declined to the point that she was unable to go to work, she neglected herself and her child, and refused social contact. From this picture of Karen, a treatment plan could readily be developed that would help Karen recover from her depression and possibly also ameliorate her longstanding disorders.

REVIEW OF THE DSM-III-R

The DMS-III-R is divided into 18 broad categories of mental disorder. Although it is beyond the scope of this chapter to teach or interpret the DSM, a brief review of each of the 18 sections is provided here to give readers some general familiarity with the major types of mental disorder. There are many specific types of mental disorder included in each broad category that may not even be cited here. Readers planning to use the DSM with their clients will need to study that book and probably take additional coursework or training in the use of the DSM.

Disorders Usually First Evident in Infancy, Childhood, or Adolescence

This is the largest and most comprehensive category in the DSM and includes disorders that typically begin during the early years, although some may persist into adulthood. Many of the other diagnoses in the manual can be applied to children and adolescents but most of the disorders they experience will be included in this first category. Types of disorders in this group include mental retardation; pervasive developmental disorder, commonly known as autism; specific developmental disorders or what are usually called learning disabilities; disruptive behavior disorders (i.e., attention-deficit hyperactivity disorder, conduct disorder, and oppositional defiant disorder); anxiety disorders of childhood or adolescence (i.e., separation anxiety disorder, avoidant disorder, and overanxious disorder), eating disorders, (e.g., anorexia nervosa, bulimia nervosa, and rumination disorder of infancy); gender identity disorders; tic disorders; elimination disorders; speech disorders; and other disorders (e.g., identity disorder, reactive attachment disorder).

Of these, specific developmental disorders, attention-deficit hyperactivity disorder, conduct disorder, and separation anxiety disorder are particularly important to school counselors and others working with children of elementary school age. Children with *specific developmental disorders* typically have both social and academic impairment; although they are usually of normal intelligence, they have inordinate difficulty mastering a particular area of learning and, consequently, may experience criticism, teasing, and frustration before their difficulties are properly diagnosed and help is provided through both counseling and academic programs. Hyperactive children, diagnosed as having *attention-defict hyperactivity disorder*, also tend to have both academic and social problems as well as family difficulties; their distractibility and high level of motor activity make it hard for them to concentrate on schoolwork and engage in rewarding activities with friends and family. *Conduct disorder,* involving repeated violations of laws and rules (e.g., stealing, vandalism, truancy) is sometimes the precursor of adult antisocial or criminal behavior. Consequently, treatment of this disorder is important although client resistance and mistrust may be high. *Separation anxiety disorder* has been known as school phobia and typically involves difficulty separating from parents, accompanied by an avoidance of school. Early intervention is critical here, too, because the longer this disorder persists, the more difficult it usually is for the child to return to school.

Counselors working with older adolescents, perhaps in a college counseling center, should be familiar with the eating disorders of anorexia nervosa and bulimia nervosa. These are prevalent among adolescent females and, if left untreated, can be severely self-damaging and even fatal. Anorexia involves reduced eating, leading to a low body weight, while bulimia entails episodes of binge eating, typically accompanied by self-induced vomiting or excessive use of laxatives or diuretics to avoid weight gain.

Organic Mental Syndromes and Disorders

These disorders all involve some type of transient or permanent damage to the brain. Causes can include a blow to the head, drug or alcohol abuse, exposure to a toxic chemical or other substance, disease, or an abnormal aging process (e.g., Alzheimer's disease). These disorders are difficult to diagnose because their symptoms may mimic those of many other disorders. A careful history-taking, with questions designed to elicit any possible causes of organic damage, is often the best initial approach to diagnosis.

Counselors are rarely qualified to diagnose or treat organic mental syndromes or disorders. However, they should be familiar with the nature and typical symptoms of these disorders so that they may refer the clients whom they suspect of having organic damage to a psychiatrist or neurologist for a conclusive diagnosis. Counselors may become involved with clients with organic disorders as part of a treatment team; the counselor may be helpful to the family of the affected person or may work with the client to facilitate social and occupational adjustment in light of any limitations that may be imposed by the disorder.

Psychoactive Substance Use Disorders

Psychoactive substance use disorders are divided into two categories, psychoactive substance abuse and the more severe psychoactive substance dependence. These diagnoses describe people who use alcohol and other substances (e.g., amphetamines, cannabis, inhalants, nicotine, opioids, sedatives) in a self-damaging way, usually with the knowledge that they are being harmed by their substance abuse. Although these people may continue to maintain employment and may present a benign facade to friends and family, their performance and relationships are usually adversely affected by their substance abuse, and they may be endangering their lives by their dysfunctional behavior. Counselors in nearly all settings should be familiar with the diagnosis and treatment of this prevalent disorder, particularly counselors working in employee-assistance programs. Treatment for substance use disorders typically involves a multifaceted approach including group, individual, and family counseling as well as participation in a peer support group (e.g., Alcoholics Anonymous, Narcotics Anonymous).

Schizophrenia

Schizophrenia is a severe disorder characterized by psychotic symptoms such as delusions, hallucinations, and incoherence. Signs of the disorder, by definition, have been present for at least six months, and the client's overall functioning will have been impaired by this pervasive disorder. Schizophrenia is another disorder that is usually not treated primarily through counseling, since medication and at least a brief period of hospitalization are often needed to reduce symptoms. However, counselors may, once again, be part of a treatment team, focusing on improving family relationships or readjustment once the most severe symptoms of the disorder have subsided.

Delusional (Paranoid) Disorder

Delusional disorders are sometimes confused with schizophrenia because they present similar symptoms such as delusions or hallucinations.

However, a delusional disorder typically involves only limited impairment, with symptoms being circumscribed and focused on one stressful area. For example, a woman with marital difficulties may have a jealous type of delusional disorder, believing that her faithful husband is having multiple affairs with all of her friends. At the same time, she may function well in her work because that is not the site of the stresser.

Delusional disorders typically have a better prognosis than schizophrenia. Counselors may play a more prominent role in treating these disorders since they are less likely to require hospitalization or medication.

Psychotic Disorders Not Elsewhere Classified

Included in this section are two disorders that manifest with symptoms similar to that of schizophrenia. However, these disorders are of shorter duration; *brief reactive psychosis* lasts no more than one month and *schizophreniform disorder* no more than six months. These disorders are more likely than schizophrenia to have an apparent precipitant and to begin abruptly. When psychotic symptoms seem to have a precipitant, for example a traumatic bereavement such as the loss of one's family in an accident, and when the symptoms begin suddenly rather than gradually, the prognosis for recovery is improved.

Schizoaffective disorder, involving prominent schizophrenic symptoms as well as an affective syndrome (i.e., depression or mania), is also included in this section. A controversial disorder, some believe that it is really two coexisting disorders.

Mood Disorders

This section of the DSM includes disorders characterized primarily by manic or depressive features. Manic features are less commonly presented by clients. They are typified by an elevated and expansive mood, feelings of great power and worth, hyperactivity, and excessive pleasure-seeking. One client, a man in his mid-20s, employed as a teacher and planning to get married, reported during a manic episode, that he had decided he was destined to be a Hollywood movie star. In order to develop what he believed was an appropriate image, he resigned from his job, bought an expensive sports car, enrolled in three acting classes, and prepared to move to California. Clearly, manic features can be very disruptive and self-destructive.

Clients experiencing depression present quite different symptoms. They feel helpless and discouraged, have little self-esteem, and may have suicidal ideation. Physical symptoms of sleeping and eating problems as well as fatigue are also common.

Disorders in this section may be characterized by both manic and depressive syndromes (*bipolar disorder* and *cyclothymia*) or by depression alone (*major depression, dysthymia*). Depression is probably the most common symptom presented by people seeking counseling (Seligman, in press) and counselors should be well versed in the types of depressive disorders and the latest research on treating these disorders.

Anxiety Disorders

Anxiety is another symptom that is frequently presented to counselors. Several of the anxiety disorders involve a phobia, a persistent and exaggerated fear of an object or situation, leading to impairment through avoidance of the feared stimulus. Examples of phobias include fear of social embarrassment (*social phobia*), fear of places from which escape is difficult, such as crowds or public transportation (*agoraphobia*), and fear of snakes (*simple phobia*). *Panic disorder,* characterized by unexpected feelings of physical and emotional panic; *obsessive compulsive disorder,* characterized by recurrent unwanted thoughts or impulses; *posttraumatic stress disorder,* and *generalized anxiety disorder* also are included in this section. Posttraumatic stress disorder is frequently encountered by counselors on hot-lines or in crisis centers; it involves a cluster of symptoms (e.g., withdrawal, reexperiencing, anxiety) following a traumatic event (e.g., rape, accident).

Anxiety symptoms sometimes mimic those of physical conditions, and thorough diagnostic evaluation is important. Properly diagnosed, most anxiety symptoms respond well to a multifaceted treatment plan including improving coping mechanisms, desensitization, relaxation, and, in some cases, medication (Seligman, in press).

Somatoform Disorder

Probably the most familiar disorder in this section is *hypochondriasis,* but others (e.g., *conversion disorder, somatoform pain disorder*) are included as well. Clients with somatoform disorders are often referred for counseling by their physicians. These clients strongly believe they are experiencing some physical ailment; however, medical examinations fail to find any physical cause for their complaints. These clients typically have difficulty managing stress and expressing themselves verbally; their physical complaints characteristically are a way of expressing their negative feelings.

Dissociative Disorders

The best known of these disorders is *multiple personality disorder,* with television and film having familiarized us with the cases of Eve and Sybil. *Psychogenic fugue, psychogenic amnesia,* and *depersonalization disorder* are also included in this section. All of these disorders involve an alteration in consciousness (e.g., amnesia, alternate personality) that is neither organic nor psychotic. Until recently, these disorders were believed to be rare. However, new information on their prevalence is providing a different picture. We are still in the early stages of understanding the dynamics and treatment of these disorders.

Sexual Disorders

The DSM divides the sexual disorders into two groups, *paraphilias* and *sexual dysfunctions.* The two are very different in terms of their nature and treatment. Paraphilias involve sexual urges or behaviors that interfere with social adjustment and relationships. Examples are exhibitionism, sexual sadism, and pedophilia (sexual activity with children). Clients with these disorders commonly are resistant to change but may seek treatment because of a court mandate or at the insistence of an unhappy partner. On the other hand, clients with sexual dysfunction (e.g., sexual arousal disorder, premature ejaculation, inhibited orgasm) are usually eager for help, although they, too, may have been urged into treatment by an unhappy partner. Prognosis for treatment of sexual disorders seems strongly related to motivation.

Sleep Disorders

Those with sleep disorders include people who sleep too little (*insomnia disorders*), people who sleep too much (*hypersomnia disorders*), people with disturbing sleep patterns (*sleep–wake schedule disorder*), and people troubled by nightmares or sleepwalking. Emotions, environment, and physiology all can be causative factors in these disorders. A limited but growing body of information is available for counselors working with clients experiencing these newly defined emotional disorders.

Factitious Disorders

People with factitious disorders rarely present themselves for counseling in a straightforward fashion (Seligman, in press). These people enjoy the role of patient and deliberately feign physical or psychological symptoms so that they can assume a sick role. Often, their histories involve experiencing illness as rewarding, and they learn this dysfunctional way of getting attention. Little is known about treatment of this disorder because it is not often seen for treatment.

Impulse Control Disorders Not Elsewhere Classified

Disorders in this section typically involve a repetitive vicious cycle in which clients have a build-up of tension and anxiety. They release the tension in some dysfunctional and destructive way, they are then apologetic and promise change, but this resolve is short-lived when tension builds again. Disorders described in this section of the DSM include *intermittent explosive disorder* (e.g., spouse abusers), *kleptomania, pathological gambling*, and *pyromania*. Treatment typically involves behavior modification as well as help with stress management and social skills.

Adjustment Disorder

People who respond to a stresser (or multiple stressers) with relatively mild impairment or dysfunction beyond the expectable within three months of the stresser are characterized as having an adjustment disorder. These disorders, the mildest of the mental disorders described in the DSM-III-R, are common in people going through either negative life changes (e.g., a divorce, a bereavement, being fired from a job) or positive life changes (e.g., marriage, the birth of a child, graduation). These disorders are, by definition, time-limited and typically respond very well to counseling. If the disorder persists beyond six months, however, it is no longer viewed as an adjustment disorder and the diagnosis must be revised.

Psychological Factors Affecting Physical Condition

This disorder differs from somatization disorder and factitious disorder in that, although these clients, too, present with prominent concerns about physical complaints, their complaints do have a medical basis. However, their physical disorder is part of a cycle in which that disorder is exacerbating their emotional difficulties that, in turn, are contributing to a worsening of their physical complaints. Physical conditions often presented by clients with this disorder include migraine headaches, ulcers, eczema, and high blood pressure. Treatment of psychological factors affecting physical condition will almost always entail a team effort with counselor and physician working in collaboration.

Personality Disorders

Personality disorders, listed on Axis II of a multiaxial diagnosis, are longstanding, deeply ingrained disorders, typically evident by adolescence or early adulthood. Although these disorders are not as severe as some others in terms of the impairment they cause (e.g., schizophrenia, bipolar disorder), they are among the most treatment-resistant of the disorders. Personality disorders usually are manifested by pervasive patterns of dysfunction that show up in all areas of a person's life. Although people with these disorders may experience considerable unhappiness and seek help, they rarely have a good sense of themselves, a set of effective coping mechanisms, or an array of healthy peer relationships to fall back on. Consequently, therapy for clients experiencing personality disorders is often a lengthy and challenging process.

Personality disorders can take many forms. They can be characterized by patterns of suspiciousness, isolation, antisocial behavior, mood instability, grandiosity, dependence, or perfectionism. For example, many people with histories of criminal and irresponsible behavior, dating back to childhood, are diagnosed as having antisocial personality disorder, a disorder often seen by counselors working in corrections or substance abuse settings. For more information on personality disorders, readers are referred to Millon (1981).

V Codes for Conditions Not Attributable to a Mental Disorder That Are a Focus of Attention or Treatment

V code conditions, the last category described in the DSM-III-R, are not viewed as mental disorders. Rather, they are commonly experienced problems in living that are neither caused by nor related to a mental disorder and do not cause significant impairment or dysfunction. Examples of V code conditions include academic problems, marital problems, occupational problems, parent–child problems, and phase of life problems (e.g., graduation from school, retirement). Although people with these disorders may seek counseling and may derive considerable benefit from that process, they typically are emotionally healthy people with good resources who have just encountered a difficult period in their lives. Often people with these disorders, like people with adjustment disorders, learn and grow considerably from the counseling process and emerge from counseling healthier than they were when they began counseling.

DIAGNOSIS IN CONTEXT

This chapter has focused primarily on diagnosis. However, diagnosis is only one of three steps counselors should take before they begin working with a client. The other two steps, intake interviews and treatment planning, will be discussed briefly here.

Intake Interviews

Intake interviews precede diagnosis and provide the information upon which a diagnosis is made. Some agencies have a formal intake process that may entail a prospective client's being asked a series of predetermined questions, completing some forms and inventories, and possibly even meeting with more than one clinician (e.g., a counselor and a psychiatrist). In other settings, such as private practices and college counseling settings, the first counseling session serves as an intake interview. In a less structured way, the counselor gathers sufficient information about the client to enable the counselor to assess the urgency of the client's situation, to orient the client to the counseling process, to determine the client's suitability for continued counseling in that setting (or to make a referral), and to formulate a diagnosis.

Intake interviews vary widely in terms of their duration and thoroughness. They may be as brief as 15 minutes, focusing on presenting concerns and their development, or they may extend over several sessions of an hour or more in length, seeking to elicit a comprehensive picture of the client. Topics typically included in an intake interview include identifying information (e.g., client's age, occupation, marital status), presenting concerns, previous emotional difficulties, treatment history, present life situation, family of origin and present family, developmental history, social activities and relationships, career, and medical history (Seligman, 1980). While conducting an intake interview, counselors should gather information not only from the clients' words but also from their appearance, their behavior during the interview, their interaction with the counselor, their mood and display of emotion, their positive and negative reactions to the topics that are discussed, their contact with reality, and their thinking process. That information, too, is important in helping the counselor make an accurate diagnosis.

Treatment Planning

Treatment planning is the third step in the process that begins with the intake interview, proceeds through the diagnosis, and culminates in the treatment plan. This three-step process has been compared to the shape of an hourglass (Hershenson, Power, & Seligman, 1989). The data-collection process of the intake interview expands and provides breadth to the counselor's picture of the client. This information is processed and condensed into a diagnosis, analogous to the waist or narrow part of the hourglass. The focus is then expanded once again with treatment planning. Beginning with the establishment of mutually agreed upon goals, the treatment plan provides counselors with a map to guide their work with their clients.

Many models have been developed for treatment plans. One developed by the author will be presented here (Hershenson, Power, & Seligman, 1989; Seligman, 1980; Seligman, in press). In planning the treatment according to this model, the counselor makes the following choices or decisions in light of both the diagnosis and the goals that have been established:

1. Approximate duration of counseling (e.g., 12 weeks, 6 months).
2. Frequency of counseling (e.g., 1 session per week).
3. Level of counselor directiveness.
4. Level of exploration.
5. Balance of focus (cognitive, affective, or behavioral).
6. Theoretical counseling model and techniques.
7. Modality of counseling (e.g., individual, family, group).
8. Pacing.
9. Relevant counselor variables.
10. Assessments needed (e.g., Strong Campbell Interest Inventory, Myers-Briggs Type Indicator).
11. Adjunct services (e.g., Alcoholics Anonymous, Parents Without Partners).
12. Sequencing of parts of the treatment plan.
13. Prognosis.

By responding to each item in the outline of a treatment plan, counselors can develop a comprehensive and useful guide for working with a client.

ILLUSTRATION OF THE THREE-STEP PROCESS

The following case provides an abbreviated version of the three-step process of intake interview, diagnosis, and treatment plan. The case begins with a short summary of information obtained from the intake interview with the client, continues with a multiaxial diagnosis, and finishes with a brief treatment plan.

THE CASE OF AMBER

INTAKE INFORMATION

Amber, a 15-year-old black female, requested some help from her school counselor, who referred her and her family to the community mental health center. Amber was living with her mother, her 12-year-old brother, and her stepfather of two months. Amber's father had died three years ago in an automobile accident. Amber stated that she was very angry at her mother for remarrying and could not understand what she saw in her new husband, Jeff. Amber reported that her mother expected her to call Jeff "Dad" and to participate in family outings. Amber spent as much time away from home as she could and reported sadness and some loss of interest in academic and social activities since the marriage.

Prior to the marriage, Amber had been a quiet and capable student, earning satisfactory grades and participating in several school clubs. She had a small circle of girlfriends and had recently begun to date. Other than some grief and withdrawal around the time of her father's death, Amber was well-adjusted, and no history of problem behavior was reported. She seemed to be in good health and rarely missed school. She was attractive, of above-average intelligence, and well-oriented to reality.

DIAGNOSIS

Axis I: 309.00 Adjustment disorder with depressed mood, moderate.
Axis II: V71.09 No diagnosis or condition on Axis II.
Axis III: No physical disorders or conditions.
Axis IV: Psychosocial stressers: mother's remarriage. Severity: 3—Moderate.
Axis V: Current GAF: 65. Highest GAF past year: 80.

TREATMENT PLAN

Goals:
1. Reduce Amber's level of sadness.
2. Improve her relationships with her mother and stepfather.
3. Increase her interest in academic and social activities.

Summary of treatment plan: Amber is not in crisis and seems to have had a positive level of adjustment prior to her mother's remarriage. Consequently, Amber will be seen for counseling once a week. It is anticipated that the counseling will be relatively short-term (3 to 4 months). Amber is verbal and motivated; directiveness will, therefore, be fairly low as long as sessions do not become complaint sessions. She will need support and acceptance from the counselor since she is feeling rejected at home but also needs to be encouraged to deal further with her grief over her father's death and to communicate more with her mother and stepfather. Cognitive orientation will be emphasized; Amber is telling herself that she must not allow anyone to usurp her father's position in the family, and this is causing dysfunction. However, affect (sadness, anger) and behavior (avoidance of family, destructive patterns of communication) also need to be addressed. Such techniques as cognitive restructuring, practicing improved communicating skills, monitoring mood levels, and planning activities would be used in individual counseling. Family counseling, with the whole family as well as with Amber and her mother, Amber and her stepfather, and Amber and both parents will also be done. Focus will be on improved communication, helping Amber's parents to allow a more gradual development of the stepfather/stepdaughter relationship, and helping Amber to reestablish her close tie to her mother and understand her mother's decision to remarry. Counseling should move along fairly rapidly. Counselor variables do not seem important here; arguments could be made for assigning Amber to either a male or a female counselor. Her preference will be considered. The Beck Depression Inventory will be used to monitor Amber's level of depression. No adjunct programs seem indicated at present but Amber might benefit from learning more about her biologic father and his family, once her depression has lifted and she has reestablished ties with her present family. The prognosis for improvement is excellent, based on Amber's diagnosis, her motivation, and the support she is receiving from her family.

THE FUTURE FOR COUNSELING AND DIAGNOSIS

Most signs suggest that diagnosis will become an increasingly important skill for counselors. Presently, more than one half of the states have licensure or certification for counselors and that number continues to grow. In addition, several states have passed what has been called Freedom of Choice legislation that requires insurance companies doing business in that state and providing third-party payments for outpatient mental health services to provide such payments for counselors with appropriate state credentials. These legislative changes reflect the increasing number of counselors in private practice and mental health settings where diagnosis and third-party payments are important.

In addition, workshops and courses on diagnosis and treatment planning presented by this author have been attended by more and more counselors in school and college settings. They recognize that even if they do not treat clients with significant mental disorders, diagnosis can probably help them to identify clients they probably can work with effectively and to provide informed referrals to clients who should be treated in another setting.

Accountability has received increasing attention in the professional literature. It is difficult to assess the effectiveness of the counseling process, to determine the relationship between counseling interventions and client disorders, and to plan sound and thoughtful treatments without diagnoses and treatment plans. The emphasis on accountability contributes to the growing emphasis on diagnosis and treatment planning.

However, although counselors themselves seem to be recognizing the importance of diagnosis in their work, some others do not share that viewpoint. A lawsuit has been filed by a group of psychiatrists in Florida, alleging that nonmedical mental health practitioners do not have the training and expertise necessary to diagnose mental disorders. At this writing, that case had not yet been resolved and the Florida Mental Health Counselors Association was developing a strong defense. This case represents a threat to counselors throughout the country. Counselors should become informed about this and related developments and should protect their right to make diagnoses by becoming careful and well-informed diagnosticians who use diagnoses to facilitate treatment and to ensure that their clients obtain the help they need.

REFERENCES

Diagnostic and statistical manual of mental disorders (3rd ed., revised). 1987. Washington, DC: American Psychiatric Association.

Hershenson, D. B., Power, P. W., and Seligman, L. (1989). Mental health counseling theory: Present status and future prospects. *Journal of Mental Health Counseling, 11,* 44–69.

Manual of the international statistical classification of diseases, injuries, and causes of death, Vol. 1. (1978). Geneva: WHO.

Millon, T. (1981). *Disorders of personality: DSM-III, axis II.* New York: John Wiley.

Seligman, L. (1980). *Diagnosis and treatment planning in counseling.* New York: Human Sciences Press.

Seligman, L. (in press). *Selecting effective treatments for adult mental disorders: A comprehensive, systematic guide.* San Francisco: Jossey-Bass.

10

Nontraditional Approaches To Counseling

ANN VERNON, PH.D.
University of Northern Iowa
Cedar Falls, Iowa

EFFECTIVE COUNSELING ESTABLISHES A therapeutic relationship to help clients think, feel, and behave in more self-enhancing ways. As Caple (1985) noted, "Clients come to counseling seeking a different potentiality, a way to find something better than they presently know" (p. 173). In effect, the counselor makes a commitment to help clients become more aware, to conceptualize their experiences differently, and to see themselves and their ways of being more constructively. According to Hutchins and Cole (1986), in this process the client actively helps resolve specific personal issues. This implies that the counselor won't "fix it" so that the client will feel and act better, but rather that a mutual "working together" process can help the client overcome the dysfunctional aspects that interfere with her or his life.

However, counseling has basically been a mental arena, characterized by a predominantly verbal orientation, according to Nickerson and O'Laughlin (1982). In their opinion, this verbal orientation is very limiting. These authors advocate action therapies that use nonverbal relationship modes as an alternative to the traditional verbal approaches. They stress the importance of developing "a more relevant and effective means of helping people cope with psychological problems and life stresses" (p. 5). Allan and Clark (1984) concurred with this viewpoint, stating that verbal techniques alone are not sufficient for reluctant or nonverbal clients. Lawson (1987) noted that for many clients who seem relatively unaffected by the counseling process, standard techniques alone are inadequate.

Recently, information about counseling for individual learning styles has appeared in the literature and seems to support Nickerson and O'Laughlin's (1982) contention that verbal approaches to counseling are often ineffective (Griggs, 1983; Griggs et al., 1984; Griggs, 1985). Learning style refers to the way a person perceives and responds to the learning environment. Griggs (1983) cited the following learning-style elements: environmental stimuli such as light, sound, and temperature; emotional stimuli such as structure, persistence, motivation, and responsibility; sociologic stimuli such as peers, adults, self, and group; physical stimuli such as auditory, visual, tactual, kinesthetic, and time of day; and psychological stimuli such as global, analytic, impulsive, reflective, and cerebral dominance.

The learning-style approach assumes that individuals have unique learning patterns that should be accommodated in the counseling process. If this is not done, the client may resist (Griggs, 1985). Although Griggs noted that further research is needed to determine whether counseling outcomes improve if learning-style preferences complement counseling approaches, she did identify counseling techniques in addition to verbal interaction that are compatible with different learning styles: art therapy, imagery, bibliotherapy, psychodrama, and mime. Nickerson and O'Laughlin (1982) cited all of these as effective, action-oriented, nontraditional therapies.

This chapter will describe a variety of nontraditional counseling approaches that may be used either as a complement to a predominantly verbal orientation with a client, or as the primary therapeutic method. These approaches may be used with clients of all ages and in a variety of settings such as schools, hospitals, or mental health centers. As Nickerson and O'Laughlin (1982) noted, these therapies are relevant for nonverbal clients, and for anyone who "needs to explore and to integrate their behavior in a comprehensive and effective fashion" (p. 7).

ART

In the past several years, the use of art therapy appears to be increasing, particularly in work with children (Allan & Clark, 1984; Pinholster,

1983; Allan & Crandall, 1986). Rubin (1988) noted that "art, like talk, is simply a way of getting to know each other, another mode of communication" (p. 181). Cited as being particularly effective with reluctant, nonverbal clients, Allan and Clark (1984) stated that painting and drawing can facilitate growth and change as the counselor helps the client focus on symbolic areas of pain and growth in an accepting, understanding manner. Eydenberg (1986) indicated that art provides an emotional outlet for people who have difficulty communicating their needs, feelings, and desires, and is an effective way to help them begin to understand their confusion. Now art therapy is not only being used to work with people who have problems, but also its use is more prevalent in helping "normal" clients, where the emphasis is on growth and self-development (Wadeson, 1982).

The Process

Many art forms can be used to help clients gain self-awareness and work through emotional conflicts: painting, sculpting, modeling with clay, photography, drawing, printing/designing, or graphic art. According to Kenny (1987), the goal is communication between the helper and the client rather than mastery of art form or content. In the process, the client is encouraged to express feelings symbolically through an art form. As Allan (1982) noted, the counselor's role is basically that of a listener who responds to the client and allows him or her time and space to initiate interaction. After a given interval, the counselor might invite the client to share by issuing a simple invitation such as, "Would you like to tell me what's happening in your picture?" If working with a more seriously disturbed client with whom art media is used in each session, Allan indicated that the counselor's role may change. After several sessions, the counselor might become more active by relating the art to what is occurring in real life as well as emphasizing positive aspects that indicate growth.

Art media is an effective means of initiating contact with a client as illustrated in the following example.

Amanda, a third grader, was referred by her teacher because she seemed preoccupied and unhappy. In the initial setting, the counselor noted that Amanda seemed quite anxious and hesitant. To establish rapport and facilitate expression, the counselor put some modeling clay on the table and invited Amanda to play with it. At first, Amanda just rolled the clay around without molding it. The counselor made no comment, but simply communicated an attitude of acceptance. Presently Amanda began to shape the clay into a bridge. Next, she made a car and attached small clay dots to the car. As she placed the car on the bridge, the bridge collapsed. At this point the counselor asked Amanda if she would like to tell her about what was happening. Amanda explained that the dots were people...her family. The counselor reflected that something must have happened to the family in the car, and Amanda began to talk about how her family had had an accident because her Dad and Mom were drunk. She shared her feelings of fright and how she took care of her brothers and sister after the accident. As she talked she began to roll the clay and pound it, tears streaming down her cheeks. As the counselor supported her, it became apparent that the feelings Amanda needed to express would be more readily verbalized in future sessions as the counselor began to help Amanda deal with her painful situation.

Art media can be used in the manner previously illustrated, or in a more directed manner to facilitate a process. For example, clients could be instructed to draw their family, paint their life story, or illustrate a book that describes a situation with which they are dealing. They could be asked to sketch and color themselves in moods that they experienced recently, or be invited to draw a picture representing something that they need in their lives. Designing a T-shirt, a banner, or a bumper sticker with a motto they feel describes them is a good way to encourage personal growth and sharing, particularly with resistant adolescent clients.

Photography can also be used effectively to elicit feelings and create awareness. Amerikaner, Schauble, and Ziller (1982) outlined a method of using 12 client-created photographs describing how the client sees self to stimulate self-awareness. Photographs can also help clients assess what is blocking their personal effectiveness, as in the case of Tim.

Tim, a 35-year-old male, referred himself for counseling because he felt overwhelmed at work and under extreme stress. In the initial session Tim described feeling overwhelmed by his obligations and commitments at work, at home, and in the community. In the next session, the counselor handed Tim a Polaroid camera and asked him to take pictures of things, people, and places that were important to him and that he, perhaps at one time, had enjoyed. She also asked him to take pictures of things, places, or people that he thought were contributing to the stress and the feeling of being overwhelmed. He was instructed to put these pictures into two separate envelopes—one for the things that were important to him, and the other for the factors that he thought were contributing to the stress.

The following week, Tim returned with his pictures, which served as a springboard for a discussion about the events in his life that were taking precedence over the things that were important to him and his feelings of "have to" vs. "want to." Tim was asked to go through his envelope of pictures that created stress and select some that he could eliminate from his life. By actually being able to "see" what his stressers were, it was easier for Tim to identify what he could more readily eliminate. Then he and the counselor worked on strategies for dealing with the other sources of stress.

Implementation Considerations

In employing art, Rubin (1988) cautioned that experience and skill are necessary if working at a sophisticated level, but that specific training in art is not essential with simple expressive work and minimal interpretation. *Child Art Therapy* (Rubin, 1978), *The Art of Art Therapy* (Rubin, 1984), and *Window to Our Children* (Oaklander, 1978) are excellent resources for the professional interested in learning more about using art in a counseling relationship.

Rubin (1988) noted that therapeutic work through art may be one way for clients to feel in charge when other parts of their lives are overwhelming. As a trusting relationship is established, the counselor invites the client to share the meaning from his or her perspective. In essence, the counselor observes the client's work as it develops, attends to the nonverbal and verbal communication offered, and responds to clarify (Protinsky, 1978).

Kenny (1987) and Protinsky (1978) identified the following factors that may help the counselor understand clients' art work by considering the larger context of their world.

1. Dark colors or heavy shading generally indicate sadness, depression, or anger; excessive use of white may indicate emotional rigidity.

2. Small figures, particularly of self, may indicate insecurity, anxiety, or low self-esteem.

3. Sadness, violence, aggression, or other emotional disturbance are often represented with dark images, storms, accidents, fighting, or murder.

4. Texture of materials can provide insight: aggressive, angry clients might select bold or tough materials, whereas a nonassertive client might choose watercolors or something softer.

5. Clients with emotional disturbances tend to depict figures more grotesquely, stiff and rigid, or unintegrated, with some body parts being exaggerated. Excessive shading may indicate high anxiety.

The basic function of art therapy is to facilitate emotional expression from clients who do not communicate well verbally, and to execute the counseling process more effectively through visual representation. Art therapy can be used to put the client at ease during an initial session, can be used strategically in later sessions to help the client clarify and gain awareness, or can be used over a period of several sessions as the main vehicle to work through painful issues. As Kenny (1987) noted, "Although art itself does not resolve conflict or eliminate sources of anxiety, it does provide space in which awareness, acceptance, and growth can occur" (p. 33).

IMAGERY

The use of mental imagery has increased in recent years, especially in career counseling, life planning, and personal counseling (Skovolt, Morgan, & Negron-Cunningham, 1989). According to Skovolt et al. (1989), imagery "allows the client and counselor to bring into awareness unconscious material that is already influencing choices...and allow the client to try on alternative roles" (p. 287).

While free daydreams are often cited as one form of imagery, this section will describe the use of guided imagery and concrete images to help a client reconceptualize events and change behavior

Guided Imagery

Guided imagery is a structured, directed activity in which the counselor orchestrates a scenario for the client. Sometimes called guided fantasy, the process involves inducing relaxation, the actual fantasy, and processing the fantasy (Skovolt, Morgan, & Negron-Cunningham, 1989). The use of relaxation is important because it helps bridge the gap between prior activities and the imagery experience to move the client's focus from external to internal. In inducing relaxation, the client is instructed to close his or her eyes, get comfortable, focus on breathing, and relax (Thorne, 1985).

The following script was used with a middle-aged woman who suffered from anxiety and procrastinated about completing her housework and other chores. After being instructed to relax, Jana was invited to involve herself in this imagery experience.

> *Setting:* Imagine that it is next Monday. (pause) You are waking up in the morning. What time is it? (pause) You get up and eat breakfast. Who is there? (pause) You finish breakfast. You don't have to leave for work until noon. What needs to be done? What do you do first? (pause) How do you see yourself doing this task and how long does it take? Is anyone helping you? If not, how are you feeling about that? (pause) You finish this activity. What do you do now? (pause) It is now time to get ready to leave for work. (pause)

Work: You are now at work. Are you working alone or are you interacting with others? What tasks are you doing? Are you enjoying them? (pause)

Home: You have left work and are home again. Are you alone? (pause) If not, who is there? Do you interact with them? (pause) It is time to get dinner. Do you do this alone or does anyone help you? (pause) Now it is after dinner. What do you do? Who is with you? (pause) Now it is time for bed. Tomorrow you will not work and will be at home all day. What will you do? (pause)

End: You may open your eyes and we will discuss your experience.

In processing the imagery exercise, Jana said that it was not difficult to see what needed to be done, but it was hard to visualize what she would do first. Once she did select a task, it wasn't too difficult to see herself taking the necessary steps to complete it. She saw herself alone in doing the housework and resented that. She described the work portion of her day as basically enjoyable, where she had no trouble completing necessary tasks.

In reflecting on the exercise, it seemed helpful for Jana to list the chores that needed to be done each day so she wouldn't become anxious about deciding what to do. It was also appropriate to begin teaching her some assertiveness skills so that she could ask for help with the housework. The guided imagery effectively helped the counselor and client clarify issues and pinpoint target areas for goal setting and skill development.

Guided imagery has also been used successfully in career counseling where clients are asked to image "A Day in the Future"; "The Opposite Sex," growing up as the opposite sex and holding a job usually held by the opposite sex; or "Mid-Career Change or Retirement," focusing on shifting from the present career focus (Skovolt, Morgan, & Negron-Cunningham, 1989).

Use of Concrete Images

Images can also be used therapeutically in isolation to help stimulate thinking that can lead to more productive behavior. When using images this way, the counselor tries to relate the image to something familiar to the client or something that conveys a type of metaphor, as in the following example.

Eighteen-year-old Nat was in counseling for depression. Irrational beliefs in the form of exaggerations, overgeneralizations, and awfulizations contributed to his depression. In the session when the image was introduced, Nat was discussing an incident with his girlfriend. He assumed that because she didn't call him every day, she didn't care about him. He said he couldn't stand it if she found someone else.

In previous sessions the counselor had helped Nat dispute these irrational beliefs, but they continued to be quite prevalent. As Nat and the counselor were working on these irrational beliefs in the present session, the counselor glanced out the window and noticed a bug zapper. She called it to Nat's attention and asked him to watch the zapper and describe how it operated. The counselor explained to Nat that he could image that his head was a zapper, too—when he started to think irrationally, he should just visualize these irrational thoughts being deflected, just like the bugs were when they hit the zapper. While this may seem simplistic, it helped Nat stop his irrational thinking more effectively because he could quickly recall the bug zapper image and use this to trigger his disputations before he felt the negative effects of the irrational beliefs.

By listening carefully to the client's problem, it is not difficult to think of helpful images. Children who have difficulty controlling impulsive behavior might be asked to visualize a stop sign when they start to feel out of control. Pairing the visualization with self-statements such as "I don't have to hit; I can walk away" increases the effectiveness of the image. A child who is reluctant to go to bed because he is afraid of monsters can visualize himself in a scary Halloween costume, frightening away any monsters that might come into the room.

Thorne (1985) pointed out these benefits of imagery: it can be performed anywhere; it is nonthreatening and safe; and it strengthens problem-solving abilities, encourages creative thinking, helps in integrating internal and external data, and helps clients learn about themselves. While imagery might not work for everyone, for many clients it is an extremely effective method to access information and resolve problems.

MUSIC

Music is another effective counseling approach to use with a variety of populations to increase self-esteem and assertiveness (Maas, 1982), motivate slow learners (Yarbrough, Charboneau, & Wapnick, 1977), develop interpersonal relationships and a sense of purpose (Maas, 1982), and reduce disruptive behavior (McCarty et al., 1978). Music has also been used successfully with the mentally retarded, institutionalized elderly, emotionally disturbed, and sensory impaired clients (Maas, 1982) and with depressed clients in a hospital setting (Wadeson, 1982).

Bowman (1987) noted that music is a versatile tool that can reduce anxiety, elicit memories, communicate feelings, develop rapport, and intensify or create moods. Music is energizing, and also has a calming effect.

While music can be used as the primary method of treatment, it can also be incorporated into the therapy experience to facilitate the process more effectively. Or, music may be used to introduce or convey messages in classroom guidance sessions, and to clarify issues as a "homework" assignment. Song lyrics or tapes are perhaps the most accessible form of music, but for improvisation purposes, a guitar, drum, shaker, xylophone, or keyboard are useful.

Applications

Music can effectively establish rapport, particularly with teenagers who are often not self-referred. Having the radio softly tuned in to a popular rock station when the client walks into the office can help facilitate communication and relaxation. Generally it is best left to the client to initiate conversation about the music, but if he or she doesn't, the counselor might comment on the song, inquire whether or not the client likes to listen to music, and then ease into the traditional get-acquainted phase of the session. After a first session, one teenager commented to this author that he was surprised to hear the music and that it didn't make it seem like he was "going to a shrink." This helped establish trust by communicating to the client that the counselor had some understanding of where he was coming from.

To help clients get more in touch with what they are thinking and feeling, music can be a useful homework assignment. The client is invited to bring in tapes or record songs that illustrate how he or she is thinking or feeling that week. Clients can also find songs that express who they are, their conflicts, or their hopes. This is effective especially for teenagers, since music is such an important part of their life experience.

This approach was used with 14-year-old Annette, a depressed, nonverbal client who asked to see a counselor because of home conflicts. Despite the fact that she had initiated the counseling, it was difficult for Annette to express what was happening at home and why she was so upset. Annette was very willing to do the music assignment, and came back the following week with several tapes. The counselor invited her to play the tapes, briefly reflected on what she thought was expressed through the music, and then encouraged Annette to share how the songs related to her experiences. Annette opened up some, which facilitated verbal exchange about the problems.

After several sessions of discussing and working through some of her difficulties, Annette was again asked to bring in songs that told more about her current feelings. This time the songs were less conflictual and more hopeful. The use of music homework had helped the counselor understand Annette's pain and confusion so they could begin dealing with it. The music also provided a useful way to determine therapy progress.

Songs can also be used in classroom guidance lessons (Bowman, 1987). Depending on the particular theme of the lesson, the songs selected could be hard rock lyrics that communicate useful messages, or songs from albums that contain guidance oriented material, such as *Free To Be...You And Me* by Marlo Thomas or *Imagination and Me* by Joe Wayman. For example, with primary children, the song "It's All Right to Cry" from the Marlo Thomas album introduced a lesson on how everyone feels sad from time to time and that crying is a natural way to help deal with sad feelings. After playing the recording, children can be invited to sing the song. A discussion can follow about the main points in the song. Follow-up activities include making paper-plate faces to portray feelings such as happy, sad, mad, or disappointed, and inviting children to describe situations in which they have felt these emotions.

Advantages

Because music is a popular medium and readily available, counselors are only limited by their creativity to specific applications. Music can easily be integrated into therapy sessions to help clients clarify issues, communicate problems, or monitor progress. It can also be used improvisationally to encourage risk taking, spontaneity, and creative expression. Clients might be invited to experiment with various musical instruments to create a piece of music that is meaningful to them. Putting words to music adds yet another dimension. Improvisations can also be applied effectively in a group setting to encourage cooperation and cohesiveness.

If clients respond to the use of music, it provides a pleasurable way to connect with them to stimulate personal awareness and growth.

WRITING

Writing offers a powerful way for clients to clarify feelings and events, and gain a perspective on their problems. Brand (1987) noted that writing contributes to personal integration and provides a cathartic experience. For many clients, seeing something in writing has more impact than hearing it.

Writing as a therapeutic experience can take numerous forms, and the reader is encouraged to experiment with the variations later described to meet a client's needs most effectively. Obviously, for very young children, writing must be more simplistic, or the counselor may choose to serve as the recorder. In addition, some clients don't find certain forms of writing helpful and, therefore, it is important to gear the assignment to what the counselor deems will be most useful for achieving the therapeutic goals.

Therapeutic writing approaches range from structured to more open-ended. Examples of each are described in the following sections.

Autobiographies

Autobiographies are generally written one of two ways—describing a particular segment or aspect of one's life, or writing a chronicle that covers all of one's life history (Hutchins & Cole, 1986). How the autobiography is used depends on which approach most effectively assists the client to clarify concerns, express feelings, and work toward resolution. In either case, once the client provides the written material, the counselor helps the client clarify the issues by asking questions, probing for feelings, confronting discrepancies in the writing, identifying specific concerns, and setting goals for change.

In one case in which this approach was used, the counselor determined that because the client was struggling with a relationship with her spouse, it would help her to chronicle all past significant relationships and indicate how these relationships were established, what was meaningful about them, how they were terminated, and how the client felt. Having done this assignment, the client and counselor identified some patterns in the way that the client reacted to significant others.

In other instances, it might benefit the client to write a more detailed account of his or her life to see how perceptions and values change over time, and to develop some perspective about the future.

Correspondence

We typically think of correspondence as appropriate when face-to-face contact isn't possible. However, correspondence can also help clarify concerns and expression in other ways.

1. Clients can be encouraged to write letters to themselves to give themselves positive feedback about an accomplishment, or some advice about how to handle a particular problem.

2. Clients might find it useful to write a letter (probably unsent) to a person with whom they are in conflict to help them express thoughts

and clarify issues. This approach was used with an elderly client who was angry with his sister. To help him diffuse the anger and develop some perspective about the problem, he first put his thoughts on paper and then discussed his feelings with the counselor. The counselor helped him identify the behaviors that upset him and speculate on alternative viewpoints. As a homework assignment, the client rewrote the letter. When he brought it in the following week, the concerns were more succinctly expressed and the anger was more focused. The counselor showed the client ways to express the anger more assertively and how to dispute overgeneralizations and exaggerated thinking.

In this example, the client sent his letter, and it did not affect the relationship negatively, as the first letter might have. Instead, the first letter served as a valuable catharsis and a tool for the counselor to help the client clarify the problem and develop skills to address it more effectively.

In other cases, clients may not use the counselor as "editor," but may simply write a letter as a way of dealing with feelings. After they have written the letter they may keep it, give it to the person with whom they are in conflict, or tear it up. It is important for clients to realize that an unedited letter, which generally contains a lot of anger, may create more problems when received. On the other hand, such a letter can serve as a springboard for getting problems out in the open.

Journaling

Journaling is another form of expressive writing that some clients find useful. When unstructured journaling is used, the client is invited to write down thoughts and feelings about events each day. The journal can then be used as catharsis. During each session, the counselor can invite clients to share anything from the journal they felt was significant, anything they would like help with, or items they want to talk more about. With clients who are not very verbal, the journal can illuminate issues to encourage discussion. By recording thoughts and feelings, both client and counselor are better able to understand the dimensions of the problem, and the client can become more aware of and monitor his or her behavior (Hutchins & Cole, 1986).

Journaling can be, however, more structured, and the counselor presents the client with a list of suggestions to guide the writing. These suggestions may include identifying events that were pleasurable or upsetting, goals that were accomplished, people whom they enjoyed or did not enjoy being with, and feelings about each of these. Often clients initially need these guidelines but don't generally rely on the structure for long.

Structured Writing

Structured writing can be open-ended sentences, questionnaires, or writing in session. Hutchins and Cole (1986) cautioned that writing does not replace counselor–client interaction, but rather serves as a starting point for discussion as well as a way to help the client generate and synthesize data.

Open-ended Sentences

Open-ended sentences may be used to establish rapport to determine areas of concern to address during the counseling sessions. Children or adolescents, who are often more nonverbal, may readily respond to open-ended sentences. These can provide a valuable source of information and set the client at ease with a structure to which he or she can respond. With very young children, the counselor can serve as the recorder so the child doesn't have to labor over writing.

Open-ended sentences can be general starters such as these:

> I get upset when...
> If I could change something about me, it would be...
> I am happy when...
> In my free time I like to...

Or, the starters may be geared more specifically to an area of concern the client previously expressed, such as:

> I wish my friends would...
> Three things I consider important in a friend are...
> I think friends should...

Both of these strategies effectively collect information about thoughts and feelings that can be used as the counselor helps the client sort through concerns. In employing open-ended sentences, it is important to gear the starters to client's age level. It is not necessary to have a long list of starters...the real purpose is to elicit information that can be used in the counseling session, not simply the collection of data.

Questionnaires

Questionnaires generally elicit more information than open-ended sentences, but the reader is cautioned not to overwhelm the client with excessive amounts of paper-and-pencil data collection. This approach can stimulate the client to reflect on aspects of his or her life, but is not intended to replace completely verbal exchanges between counselor and client.

Questionnaires can elicit information on specific events, activities, or feelings, such as:

What three major decisions have had the most impact on your life?
What aspects of your relationship with your parents have had the most impact on your life?
How do you feel about the relationship you had with your siblings as you were growing up?

Writing in Session

For many clients, seeing things in print has more impact than hearing them. For this reason, clients might be encouraged to take notes during the counseling session and refer to these notes during the interim to work on aspects of the problem. In working with young children or clients who labor over writing, the counselor may opt to record key ideas that might be useful to the client.

PLAY

"The natural medium of communication for children is play and activity" (Landreth, 1987, p. 253). Because children's experiences are often communicated through play, it becomes an important vehicle to help them know and accept themselves. Through play, children are able to act out confusing or conflicting situations. Although the use of play in therapy was originally used with children, family therapists also use play therapy techniques (Ariel, Carel, & Tyano, 1985).

Play Therapy Approaches

Schaefer (1985) described three major approaches to play therapy: psychoanalytic, structured, and relationship. In the *psychoanalytic* approach, an interpretation of the child's action and words, as well as an analysis of the transference relationship, provides the child with insight into unconscious conflicts. A wide variety of toys is available for this play therapy and the child is free to select toys as he or she wises.

In the *structured*, more controlled approach, the counselor selects the appropriate toys that facilitate working on a particular problem. By structuring the play so that the child experiences the stressful situation, the counselor can reflect feelings to help release the emotional problem. If, for example, a child was having night terrors, the counselor might provide toy monsters who talked to each other during the play.

This helps to release the fears. The counselor may also play with the child to elicit other emotions (Schaefer, 1985).

The *relationship* approach is nondirective and stresses the importance of the counselor–child relationship. The counselor creates an atmosphere where the child feels accepted and understood so that the child can experience inner conflicts and work toward resolution. The assumption is that the child has the ability to solve problems and grow once he or she experiences this accepting relationship. In this approach, the child is free to select toys from a wide variety of materials provided. The counselor actively observes and reflects the child's thoughts and feelings.

Uses of Play

Ginott (1982) noted that "the child's play is his talk and the toys are his words" (p. 145). Play can be used in several different ways to meet the developmental needs of all children. Amster (1982) identified the following uses of play:

1. For diagnostic understanding. The counselor notes the child's interactions, inhibitions, preoccupations, perceptions, and expressions of feelings and ideas.

2. To establish a working relationship. For children who may be fearful, nonverbal, or resistant, the use of play can help establish an accepting relationship, as in the case of Ryan.

Ryan, age 6, was referred for an inability to relate effectively to others. In the initial interview he sat as far away from the counselor as possible and only shook his head in response to questions. Instead of continuing to talk, the counselor got out a can of shaving cream and squirted some onto a large tray. Then she started playing with it, shaping it into different forms. Ryan watched for a few minutes and then hesitantly approached the table and began to play. The counselor added more shaving cream and some food coloring. Ryan's eyes got big and he began making pictures out of the cream and chatting about what he was creating. By initiating the play that stimulated Ryan to interact, the counselor was able to establish a working relationship.

3. To facilitate verbalization. Frequently children will not or are not able to verbalize feelings about events. Play can be used to facilitate verbalization as well as provide a means of dealing with the issue. In the following situation, the counselor used a dart game to elicit angry feelings.

Dan was a third grade, behaviorally disordered student who was hostile and aggressive with other children and adults. After an angry confrontation with the principal, the teacher requested that the counselor work with Dan. Knowing that he would be defensive, the counselor set up a dart board equipped with rubber-tipped darts. When Dan entered the office, the counselor simply invited him to play darts. After several minutes of play, the counselor commented to Dan that he was really throwing the darts as if he were angry. Dan didn't comment, but simply continued to play. After awhile he stopped and sat down. The counselor asked if there was anything he'd like to talk about, and he began to share situations in which other kids picked on him, he'd call them names, and then got in trouble for name-calling. After discussing this for a while, the counselor asked Dan if he'd like to come back again to talk more about his anger and what he could do about it. He agreed to come, but expressed a desire to play darts again. Using the dart board initiated verbalization and let Dan express his hostile, angry feelings.

4. To teach new ways of playing and behaving in daily life. Many children simply lack social skills or are anxious about their performance. Play is a good vehicle for teaching alternative behaviors.

For example, 6-year-old Amy was the youngest in her family. The teacher reported that several children had complained that every time Amy played a game, she had to win. If she wasn't winning, she changed the rules. The counselor invited Amy to play a board game, and when she tried to change the rules, the counselor commented on this and they discussed Amy's need to win and what it said about her if she didn't win. After several sessions of this nature, the counselor invited several of Amy's friends in to play. Amy played the game without changing the rules. This experience seemed to be successful in teaching her alternative behaviors to help her interact more appropriately.

5. To help a child act out unconscious issues and relieve tension. Play is used as a catharsis and a way to act out fear and anxiety.

Regardless of how play is used, the therapeutic relationship is extremely important. Showing interest in what the child chooses to do and being patient and understanding are critical.

Selection of Materials

Materials for play therapy should be selected to facilitate contact with the child, encourage catharsis and expression of feelings, aid in developing insight, and provide opportunities for reality testing (Ginott, 1982). Landreth (1987) suggested the following materials: (a) real-life toys such as dolls, doll houses and furniture, play dishes, telephone, toy trucks, cars, and airplanes; (b) acting-out toys such as dart guns, toy soldiers, rubber knife, Bobo clown, dart board, pounding bench; and (c) toys for creative expression such as crayons, clay, paints, puppets, Nerf ball, pipe cleaners, and newsprint.

Toys selected should be in good condition. It is also important not to have too many toys so that the room is cluttered and junky. The specific use of the toys depends on whether the approach is structured, in which the counselor selects the toys to fit the child's problem, or nondirective, in which the child has more freedom to choose materials.

Games

Board games provide another way to establish rapport, facilitate verbalization, release feelings, and teach new behaviors. For preadolescents and adolescents in particular, board games can make counseling more enjoyable, and, thus, more productive.

Games such as checkers or chess generally work well in establishing rapport, as do other commercial board games. Once rapport has been established, the counselor may want to develop some games that specifically address the concerns with which the child is working. The case of Stephanie illustrates this point.

Stephanie, a fourth grader, was frequently upset because she overgeneralized about what her peers were thinking and, therefore, assumed that they didn't like her, were upset with her, or didn't ever want to be her friend. To help her recognize how she upset herself by mistaking what she thought for factual information, the counselor and Stephanie played a game called "Facts and Beliefs" (Vernon, 1989). They took turns drawing statements, identifying whether they were facts or beliefs, and putting an F or B on the gameboard. Examples of statements included "girls are smarter than boys," "kickball is a game," and "kids who go to this school are wonderful."

After the game was completed, the counselor asked Stephanie to identify the difference between a fact and a belief, and then had her make up some of her own fact and belief cards based on her encounters with friends. They were able to discuss Stephanie's tendency to mistake a fact—"my friend didn't sit by me in the lunchroom"—from a belief—"because she didn't sit by me there must be something wrong with me and she must not like me anymore." The game was a concrete way of helping this fourth grader work through her problem.

The actual process of play therapy is complex and needs more explanation than this brief overview. The value of play therapy is undisputed, and the reader is encouraged to read *Play Therapy: Dynamics of the Process of Counseling With Children* (Landreth, 1982) or *Handbook of Play Therapy* (Shaefer & O'Conner, 1983).

MORE CREATIVE APPROACHES

The number of creative approaches used in a counseling session is endless. The only limiting factors are the counselor's own creative abilities to develop effective methods of helping the client resolve issues. I have found the following approaches helpful in the process of working with clients.

Props

Using props during a session can stimulate thinking or elicit emotion about a problem. Props are a way, other than words, to reach the client. For example, a woman who was constantly pessimistic was given a set of old glasses and four round circles of paper—two black and two pink. She was instructed to tape the black paper on the glasses and talk about her day from a "doom and gloom" perspective. Next, she was asked to substitute the pink paper and describe her day as if she was looking through "rose-colored glasses." She and the counselor then discussed the difference in the two perspectives and set some goals for developing a more optimistic perception of events.

In working with a five-year-old on her anxieties about entering first grade, the counselor brought in a shoe box and some construction paper. Together they decorated it and labeled it the "worry box." Next, the counselor served as a recorder and wrote down each of Leslie's concerns about first grade on a separate card. After Leslie identified all of her concerns, and all of them had to do with school, the counselor suggested that the worries could stay in the box since school didn't start for two months. She suggested they put the box on a shelf in the closet, and concentrate instead on ways to be happy during the summer. Leslie liked this idea. When school was ready to start in the fall, she had forgotten all about the problems.

With another young client, using a tape recorder helped him become less dependent on the counselor and more skilled at solving his own problems. Adam had lots of worries, such as what he should do if someone teased him, what he should do if his mother wasn't home after school, and what he should do if he didn't understand how to do his schoolwork.

Because Adam's father was concerned that Adam might be "inventing" some problems because he really liked coming to counseling, the counselor decided to teach Adam how to be his own counselor. When he arrived for his session, she asked Adam what was bothering him that week. He shared a situation about his friend teasing him, and the counselor helped Adam develop some tease tolerance techniques. Adam was to ask himself if he was what his friend said he was, if names could hurt him, and how he could handle the situation if he couldn't control what came out of the other person's mouth. Next, the counselor said that she would pretend to be Adam and that Adam could be the counselor. As the counselor, Adam was asked to help solve a problem similar to his real one. After role playing this, Adam was given a tape recorder and a blank tape. During the week, whenever he had a problem, he could use the tape recorder and first be the person who has the problem and then switch roles and pretend to be the counselor who helps him solve the problem

When Adam returned for his next session, he played the tape for the counselor. He had recorded several problems and had done a good job of helping himself deal with his problems.

Props were useful in a marriage counseling session when a rope helped a couple see the "tug of war" state of their marriage and to understand how they each felt controlled. Each person held one end of the rope, pulled on it, and verbalized one of the ways he or she felt controlled by the partner. The counselor wrote down each of the statements so the couple could also see what each other said. This simple activity was a good stimulus for mobilizing some energy and illuminating some of the issues that needed to be solved.

Homework Suggestions

To facilitate self-reliance, homework assignments can effectively extend the concepts dealt with during the counseling session. The following ideas can be adapted and expanded upon, depending on the clients' age.

1. Have clients make a "mad pillow," which they decorate with pictures of things or people with whom they feel angry. When they experience anger, they can pound the pillow rather than act aggressively toward another person.

2. Suggest that when clients worry excessively about minor, as opposed to major, problems, they can buy a bubble pipe. As they use it, they can visualize the minor problems "blowing away."

3. Have persons dealing with a lot of anger write down, on separate pieces of paper, situations in which they have been angry. They should then collect as many rocks as they have slips of paper, and go to a river or open field. As they throw the rock away with force, they can yell out the anger-provoking situation.

4. If clients have difficulty accomplishing tasks because they're overwhelmed with the amount of work to be done, invite them to buy a timer, and set it for a given amount of time to work and a given amount of time to relax.

5. Recommend that clients make books out of written text and/or illustrations to express their perceptions about a problem and their methods of solving it.

GROUP APPLICATIONS

The nontraditional individual counseling approaches previously described can usually be applied in a group context. Each of the approaches is discussed with a brief explanation of group applicability.

Art

To facilitate group cohesiveness, participants can make a collage to represent their group, using finger paint and scraps of fabric and paper. In a self-awareness group, members could tear a shape out of construction paper that tells something about themselves as a way to introduce themselves to the group. To teach cooperation, group participants could be given paper, tape, and magazines and instructions to design an object of beauty. Roles that members play in developing this project could then be discussed. In a group setting, members might take turns drawing symbols that they feel represent other group members as a way to provide feedback on how they come across to others.

Imagery

Guided imagery can be readily applied to a group setting. In a classroom or small group, students could be led in a guided imagery relative to test taking, task completion, stress management, or cooperative behavior with classmates.

Guided imagery has also been used extensively in career development (Skovolt et al., 1989). Sarnoff and Remer's (1982) use of guided imagery in a group setting effectively helped participants generate career alternatives.

Music

Musical activities facilitate self-awareness and interpersonal relationships. In a classroom setting, students can compose and perform their own compositions related to guidance topics: feelings, self-concept, decision making, friendship, or values. Movement can also be incorporated into this experience.

Bowman (1987) described the "feelings ensemble." A class is divided into groups of five or six and each group is given a feeling word, which becomes the title of their composition. They are instructed to make up and perform a song in front of the class that describes their feeling word. They may use sound makers such as pencils or rulers or other classroom items, or the counselor can provide them with whistles, horns, harmonicas, or kazoos. After several minutes of planning, each group performs while other members of the class attempt to guess what feeling they are expressing.

Music is also a good way to build group identity and cohesiveness. Group members can compose a song or select a recording that expresses who they are. An alternative activity is the musical collage. Each individual group member selects short segments of songs that have meaning and tapes each of these segments to create a collage. After listening to each person's collage, group members discuss how the music represents that individual (Bowman, 1987).

Writing

Various forms of writing can be adapted for group use. Open-ended sentences can become a get-acquainted activity or prompt discussion and sharing. Questionnaires are also used this way, or they can be adapted to the specific focus of the group. For example, members of a stress-management group might be given a questionnaire about the ways they deal with stress. As responses are shared, members will benefit from hearing others' ideas.

In a classroom setting, students can be given journal topics related to self-awareness, clarification of values, or feelings about various issues. Examples of topics include:

Something I like best about myself is ...
Something I feel strongly about is ...
Something I'm good at doing is ...
Something that I value highly is ...

Topics of this nature encourage self-exploration. Journal writing can be further shared in student dyads or triads to clarify responses. In such a situation, participants must feel comfortable with the sharing and have the option to pass if they wish.

Play

For younger children, particularly in a school setting, play can be highly effective in a small group of four or five children to improve socialization skills. One or two children in the group are selected as good models, while the targeted individuals may need to develop cooperative vs. competitive behavior, learn to control aggression, become more comfortable with group interaction, or learn to share.

In the group setting, the play is generally more structured and the toys used are selected to help children work on the desirable behaviors. For instance, if two of the children in the group have difficulty sharing, the counselor may have only a can of blocks for all group members to use. As the children play with the blocks, the counselor reflects on the interaction and involves the children in discussing how it feels when friends share or don't share, thus attempting to develop behaviors that will transfer to other situations.

Board games can also be developed for group use. For an activity on feelings, for example, a game called "Feel Wheel" (Vernon, 1989) helps children develop a feeling vocabulary. Tic-Tac-Toe can be adapted to teach positive and negative behaviors in interpersonal relationships (Vernon, 1989).

CONCLUSION

Nontraditional approaches to counseling offer ways to supplement or give an alternative to the traditional verbal approaches. For counseling to be meaningful and effective, it is necessary to engage the client, and nontraditional approaches can do this in an enjoyable, self-motivating way. While best suited to clients who are not verbally oriented, these approaches can be effective with almost any client population (Nickerson & O'Laughlin, 1982).

The nontraditional approaches are not limited to those described in this chapter. Movement, dance, drama, and puppetry are other approaches that can meet client needs. No "universal" format exists for application; creativity of the counselor and assessment of what would most effectively engage the client guide the implementation. The training needed to use these nontraditional approaches depends on whether the nontraditional approaches are used to supplement a verbal approach or constitute the major aspect of the counseling. As Nickerson and O'Laughlin (1982) noted, the issue is perhaps one of degree. In other words, a counselor does not have to be an artist to use some art with clients who are not able to express themselves verbally, but if art were the primary modality, further training would be needed.

Nontraditional approaches have been used successfully with children and adolescents (Rubin, 1988), the mentally retarded (Roth & Barrett, 1982), chronic hospital populations (Lieff, 1982), learning-disabled clients (Landreth, Jacquot, & Allen, 1982), and child-abuse victims (In & McDermott, 1982). They can be used to treat specific problems or can be applied preventively, particularly in school settings.

The diversity of nontraditional counseling approaches can help effectively address a wide range of client needs. These methods will move counseling beyond the mental arena, which relies on verbal techniques, to a more comprehensive orientation using a multitude of approaches.

REFERENCES

Allan, J. (1982). Social drawing: A therapeutic approach with young children. In E. T. Nickerson and K. O'Laughlin (Eds.), *Helping through action: Action oriented therapies* (pp. 25–32). Amherst, MA: Human Resource Development Press.

Allan, J., & Clark, M. (1984). Directed art counseling. *Elementary School Guidance and Counseling, 19*, 116–124.

Allan, J., & Crandall, J. (1986). The rosebush: A visualization strategy. *Elementary School Guidance and Counseling, 21*, 44–51.

Amerikaner, M., Schauble, P., & Ziller, R. (1982). Images: The use of photographs in personal counseling. In E. T. Nickerson and K. O'Laughlin (Eds.), *Helping through action: Action oriented therapies* (pp. 33–41). Amherst, MA: Human Resource Development Press.

Amster, F. (1982). Differential uses of play in treatment of young children. In G. L. Landreth, (Ed.), *Play therapy: Dynamics of the process of counseling with children* (pp. 33–42). Springfield, IL: Charles C Thomas.

Ariel, S., Carel, C. A., & Tyano, S. (1985). Uses of children's make-believe play in family therapy: Theory and clinical examples. *Journal of Marital and Family Therapy, 11*, 47–60.

Bowman, R. P. (1987). Approaches for counseling children through music. *Elementary School Guidance and Counseling, 21,* 284–291.

Brand, A. G. (1987). Writing as counseling. *Elementary School Guidance and Counseling, 21,* 266–275.

Caple, R. (1985). Counseling and the self-organization paradigm. *Journal of Counseling and Development, 64,* 173–178.

Eydenberg, M. G. (1986). Art therapy for the severe and profound. *Child and Family Behavior Therapy, 8,* 1–3.

Ginott, H. G. (1982). A rationale for selecting toys in play therapy. In G. L. Landreth (Ed.), *Play therapy: Dynamics of the process of counseling with children* (pp. 145–152). Springfield, IL: Charles C Thomas.

Griggs, S. A. (1983). Counseling high school students for their individual learning styles. *Clearing House, 56,* 293–296.

Griggs, S. A. (1985). Counseling for individual learning styles. *Journal of Counseling and Development, 64,* 202–205.

Griggs, S. A., Price, G. E., Kopel, S., & Swine, W. (1984). The effects of group counseling on sixth grade students with different learning styles. *California Journal of Counseling and Development, 5,* 28–35.

Hutchins, D. E., & Cole, C. G. (1986). *Helping relationships and strategies.* Monterey, CA: Brooks/Cole.

In, P. A., & McDermott, J. F. (1982). Play therapy in the treatment of child abuse. In G. L. Landreth (Ed.), *Play therapy: Dynamics of the process of counseling with children,* (pp. 284–293). Springfield, IL: Charles C Thomas.

Kenny, A. (1987). An art activities approach: Counseling the gifted, creative, and talented. *Gifted Child Today, 10,* 33–37.

Landreth, G. L. (1982). *Play therapy: Dynamics of the process of counseling with children.* Springfield, IL: Charles . Thomas.

Landreth, G. L. (1987). Play therapy: Facilitative use of child's play in elementary school counseling. *Elementary School Guidance and Counseling, 21,* 253–261.

Landreth, G. L., Jacquot, W. S., & Allen, L. (1982). Using play therapy in a team approach to learning disabilities. In G. L. Landreth (Ed.), *Play therapy: Dynamics of the process of counseling with children* (pp. 284–293). Springfield, IL: Charles C Thomas.

Lawson, D. M. (1987). Using therapeutic stories in the counseling process. *Elementary School Guidance and Counseling, 22,* 134–142.

Lieff, J. (1982) Music as healer: Therapy with a chronic hospital population. In E. T. Nickerson & K. O'Laughlin (Eds.), *Helping through action: Action oriented therapies* (pp. 258–261). Amherst, MA: Human Resource Development Press.

Maas, J. (1982). Introduction to music therapy. In E. T. Nickerson & K. O'Laughlin (Eds.), *Helping through action: Action oriented therapies* (pp. 87–100). Amherst, MA: Human Resource Development Press.

McCarty, B. C., McElfresh, C. T., Rice, S. V., & Wilson, S. J. (1978). The effect of contingent background music on inappropriate bus behavior. *Journal of Music Therapy, 15,* 150–156.

Nickerson, E. T., & O'Laughlin, K. (Eds.) (1982). *Helping through action: Action oriented therapies.* Amherst, MA: Human Resource Development Press.

Oaklander, V. (1978). *Window to our children.* Moub, UT: Real People Press.

Pinholster, R. (1983). From dark to light: The use of drawing to counsel nonverbal children. *Elementary School Guidance and Counseling, 17,* 268–273.

Protinsky, H. (1978). Children's drawings as emotional indicators. *Elementary School Guidance and Counseling, 13,* 249–255.

Roth, E. A., & Barrett, R. P. (1982). Parallels in art and play therapy with a disturbed retarded child. In E. T. Nickerson & K. O'Laughlin (Eds.), *Helping through action: Action oriented therapies* (pp. 180–188). Amherst, MA: Human Resource Development Press.

Rubin, J. A. (1978). *Child art therapy.* New York: Van Nostrand Reinhold.

Rubin, J. A. (1984). *The art of art therapy.* New York: Brunner/Mazel.

Rubin, J. A. (1988). Art counseling: An alternative. *Elementary School Guidance and Counseling, 22,* 180–185.

Sarnoff, D., and Remer, P. (1982). The effects of guided imagery on the generation of career alternatives. *Journal of Vocational Behavior, 21,* 299–308.

Schaefer, C. E. (1985). Play therapy. *Early Child Development and Care, 19,* 95–108.

Schaefer, C. E., & O'Conner, K. L. (1983). *Handbook of play therapy.* New York: John Wiley.

Skovolt, T. M., Morgan, J. I., & Negron-Cunningham, H. (1989). Mental imagery in career counseling and life planning: A review of research and intervention methods. *Journal of Counseling and Development, 67,* 287–292.

Thomas, M. (1979). *Free to be…You and me.* (Record album). Carthage, IL: Good Apple.

Thorne, C. R. (1985) Guided imagery and fantasy in career counseling. Unpublished master's thesis, New Mexico State University, Las Cruces.

Vernon, A. (1989). *Thinking, feeling, behaving: An emotional education curriculum for children.* Champaign, IL: Research Press.

Wadeson, H. (1982). History and application of art therapy. In E. T. Nickerson & K. O'Laughlin (Eds.), *Helping through action: Action oriented therapies* (pp. 16–24). Amherst, MA: Human Resource Development Press.

Wayman, J. (1974). *Imagination and me.* Carthage, IL: Good Apple.

Yarbrough, C, Charboneau, M., & Wapnick, J. (1977). Music as reinforcement for current math and attending in ability assigned math classes. *Journal of Music Therapy, 14,* 77–78.

PART TWO ■

Counseling in
Specific Settings

This section describes the basic environments in which counselors today are most likely to work. Chapter Eleven, "School Counseling," provides a comprehensive overview of the many roles and professional activities that school counseling today may involve. The repertoire of skills that a school counselor may be required to draw upon are outlined: personal, individual, or group counseling; consultation; group guidance; and testing and other appraisal activities. The range of settings for educational counseling, from elementary through university and community college counseling, are outlined with attention to the special responsibilities and talents required for each particular environment. The chapter points out the importance for school counselors to act as generalists, being able to perform a number of services and roles and to refer students to other specialized services when necessary.

Chapter Twelve, "Mental Health Counseling," describes the other major settings in which the counselor may practice. The history of mental health counseling as a distinct profession is outlined, and the process of how counseling expanded from its early vocational focus to encompass therapeutic, mental health activities is described. Major events that have influenced this process, such as the Community Mental Health Act of 1963, which provided federal funding for community mental health agencies and programs, are presented, and the possibilities for the future of mental health counseling in the 1990s are considered. Mental health counselors have been engaged in a continuing process to earn recognition as mental health professionals similar to social workers, psychologists, and psychiatrists, and this process has supported the movement toward counselor licensure. As more and more states pass legislation enabling counselors, both in mental health and other specializations, to be recognized as practicing professionals, more and more counselors may choose to go into private practice, either as a full-time career option or as an adjunct to their other work. Both the positive aspects and the negative aspects of starting a private practice are outlined for the counselor.

As these chapters indicate, the role of counselors has continuously expanded and will inevitably continue to do so. As the opportunities for therapeutic mental health professions increase in our society, so will the settings and environments in which counselors may choose to practice.

11·

School Counseling ■

CLAIRE G. COLE, ED.D.
Montgomery County Schools
Blacksburg, Virginia

TRIVIA QUIZ

1. What professional group must understand developmental stages of clients from infancy through geriatric years?

2. Which person on the school's instructional staff generally has the highest professional training requirement?

3. Which professional group reaps much criticism for spending too much time doing what its members were historically employed to do?

4. Which is the only professional group in the American Association for Counseling and Development (AACD) to produce two different journals, as well as other publications for its members?

5. Which professional group in the schools has about the least organizational power, but frequently exercises a great deal of influence over what happens in students' lives?

ANSWERS TO TRIVIA QUIZ

1. *School counselors.* Counselors in educational settings span the range from preschool programs for handicapped infants to community college programs for senior citizens. Counselors working in schools deal with arguably the most diverse population in the mental health field.

2. *School counselors.* In most states, school counselors are credentialed only after they have been teachers, usually requiring at least master's level training, which is rarely a requirement for other nonadministrative positions in schools. Almost always a practicum is part of that degree program. At the university counseling level, a clinical psychologist frequently has the academic credentials similar to doctoral level faculty, plus extensive internship experience.

3. *School counselors.* Much of the impetus for public school counseling as it occurs today came from the advent of Sputnik and the push to get more students into college, particularly into mathematics and science. Counselors brought special knowledge of college admissions requirements and procedures to the teaching staff in the early 1960s. Now one of the most common criticisms of high school counselors is that they spend too much time helping college-bound students, to the neglect of other segments of the secondary school population.

4. *School counselors.* The American School Counselor Association (ASCA) is the only AACD division to publish two journals: *The School Counselor* for the general school counseling population and *Elementary School Guidance and Counseling* for persons particularly interested in elementary and middle level counseling. ASCA also publishes books and monographs on topics of interest to school counselors.

5. *School counselors.* Although having little authority through position—counselors rarely supervise anyone else and have no direct authority in the chain of command in a school—counselors often play a key role in the school through their ability to persuade others to act in the best interests of students. Counselors also probably receive more information about the school than anyone else—from parents, students, and teachers—and therefore may have more knowledge than just about anyone else about what is really going on in the school. Lacking the formal authority of the administrators and the professional numbers of the teachers, counselors usually rely on their communication skills to exert a great deal of influence to help a school become a healthy place for students.

OVERVIEW OF SCHOOL COUNSELING

The counseling profession in school settings is alive, expanding, and, with a few exceptions, thriving and healthy. As the educational mission in this country has expanded to include previously unserved student populations, so has the clientele of the school counselor increased. Student-clients range from infants with handicapping conditions in public schools to senior citizens in community college programs, defining school counseling as virtually a cradle-to-grave range of services. From the inception of counseling in schools as a narrow vocational focus for a small number of secondary students, the current menu of services offered in educational settings includes:

- educational and career information and counseling from preschool through retirement;
- parent and family counseling from infancy through college years;
- personal counseling from learning to get along and express feelings in primary grades through marital counseling at university counseling centers;
- confronting social issues from child abuse and neglect of tots through alcohol counseling and learning to cope with AIDS at the university setting;
- coordinating services for clients ranging from feeding and clothing neglected primary school children to abortion counseling for high school and university students.

Professionals involved in providing counseling to students in educational settings include:

- school counselors
- school psychologists and social workers
- clinical psychologists, counseling psychologists, licensed professional counselors, and psychiatrists, often on a consultation basis
- substance abuse counselors
- family planning counselors, often nurses or nurse-practitioners
- teachers, administrators, and others in teacher-advisory or home-based guidance programs, often at the elementary and middle-school levels.

These professionals are supported by such persons as clerical and data-processing assistants, peer helpers, residence hall advisors, and paraprofessionals who may assist in such places as career centers.

SERVICES

A wide range of activities occurs in the counseling offices from elementary through university levels, but counselors provide some basic services at most educational counseling settings. These include counseling, consultation and coordination of services, evaluation and testing, and group guidance and information.

Counseling is the common denominator of service offered at virtually all educational settings. Defined as "... a process in which a trained helper is asked to intervene in the life of a client to assist the client to engage in more effective behavior (how the client thinks, feels, and/or acts)" (Hutchins & Cole, 1986, p. 2), the counselor helps students to

1. define a concern or problem;
2. set realistic goals to change behavior related to that concern;
3. design procedures to meet those goals; and
4. evaluate progress toward meeting the goals, redefining procedures as necessary.

In most programs, counseling is considered the basic service and requires the greatest amount of the counselor's time. In some settings, counselors may be required or advised to spend a designated portion of their day in direct counseling service, such as in Virginia, where school counselors must, by state regulation, document that at least 60 percent of their time is spent in counseling.

Counseling in an educational setting nearly always includes personal counseling for the student's developmental level. Some counseling will be related to solving personal problems specific for the student; other counseling will be developmental in nature and not geared toward a specific problem. At the elementary level crisis counseling may include overcoming school phobia, while a developmental concern might be appropriate expression of feelings such as anger or fear. At the high school level, crisis counseling may include pregnancy counseling, while a developmental concern will be college selection. For students in middle level schools, crisis intervention will almost surely include learning how to get along with other group members, while a chief developmental concern will be changes occurring at puberty. For university students, developmental concerns may include learning how to separate from parents and live as an independent adult. Crisis counseling at the college level may include counseling drug users or date-rape victims.

Both group and individual counseling are important techniques in schools. Much individual counseling must be done, but group counseling is probably a much-underused technique. Most school counselors understand the value of group counseling, but many do not believe themselves sufficiently well trained to offer a comprehensive program of group counseling. Groups will vary in size and topic from level to level, with very small groups of very young children on the elementary level doing structured activities with the counselor, and larger, more "rap session" type groups in residence halls at the university level. The concerns presented by the student to the counselor will vary greatly: from the first grader's fear of coming to school, to the sixth grader's worry about why he is so much shorter than everyone else, to the high school couple's panic over pregnancy, to the community college student debating employment versus further schooling, requests for help will be very different at different levels of schooling. The counselor will select techniques and resources appropriate for the age level of the client, but the basic counseling process and the counselor–client relationship will be very similar.

Consultation is an indirect relationship in that the counselor works with someone else who then works directly with the client (Brown & Srebalus, 1988). A school counselor may consult with parents and teachers, helping them to learn strategies that will then enable them to work more effectively with the student. A counselor in an educational setting also typically works with other helping professionals for the benefit of the student. If the parents of a third grader believe they need counseling as an entire family, it is likely that the school counselor will choose to refer them to a family therapist outside the school setting. The school counselor, at the request of the parents, typically consults with the therapist to give a view of the child during school hours. The therapist will likely make suggestions to the school counselor about how school personnel can work more effectively with the third grader. The relationship between the school counselor and the family therapist is one of consultation.

As a part of the consultation process, the school counselor often becomes the coordinator of services given to a particular student (Cole, 1987). The counselor is often the contact person for helping professionals both within and outside the school setting, coordinating those professionals' efforts on behalf of the student. Often the school counselor is the contact person for educational specialists not within the school building, such as the speech therapist, occupational therapist, school psychologist, school social worker, and other itinerant specialists provided by the school department. If a helping service is not provided by the school or university, chances are that the counselor knows where to refer a client to that service. Most often the referral will be for therapeutic services beyond the school's capability, but there may be referrals for educational or career testing not done by the school or for other such services. A community college counselor, for example, can almost surely refer a veteran of the armed forces for services available through government facilities.

Testing and other forms of appraisal are often the domain of the school counselor (Seligman, 1987). Usually the counselor is responsible for whatever standardized tests are administered to the general population of students, such as ability, achievement, and interest testing. While the scheduling and administering of the tests can be done by others in the building, the counselor is probably the person best prepared to interpret test scores to students, parents, teachers, administrators, and the community at large. School counselors receive training in testing and other forms of evaluation, such as observation case study methods, as a part of their professional preparation. Often the counselor coordinates testing for special populations in the school, such as gifted students or those with learning problems. Results of the tests are very helpful to school counselors in advising students of their educational options and in helping them plan careers. Results on an entrance examination for law or medical school, for example, weigh heavily in career counseling for upper-level university students.

Group guidance and other information services are typically offered in schools (Brown & Srebalus, 1988). The content of the sessions may be very different from one level of schooling to the next, but in almost all educational settings, counselors from time to time serve in an instructional role to impart information to students. First graders learn about community helpers, while university seniors attend seminars on how to prepare a resume. Fifth graders learn what to expect at middle school, and community college students receive information on transferring to a university. Almost all counselors offer career and educational information through direct teaching, either in small groups in seminar-type settings or in classroom groups, such as elementary classroom guidance programs.

A VARIETY OF SETTINGS

Counseling occurs in many different educational settings, often distinguished by the school organizational pattern. Elementary, middle-level, high school, and higher-education counselors are usually seen as separate and distinct branches of school counseling, with different training available appropriate to the age and developmental level of the student-clients. There is much crossover: a middle-school counselor may change places with either an elementary or a high school professional, or a high school counselor may enter the ranks of community college student personnel workers. Occasionally, a student personnel worker in higher education will decide to become a public school counselor and apply knowledge about the college setting to students' counseling interests in high school. Each level can be clearly characterized, and persons receive training and develop skills for a specific level of educational setting. Increasingly, each level is seen as a distinct specialty with credentialing defined by the level of school being served.

Elementary school counseling is an area receiving much attention nationally at this time. Counselors have been in elementary schools for years in some areas of the country, but in others, the service is an unknown or relatively new educational endeavor. In recent years a number of states have mandated counseling for all elementary students, creating the fastest-growing population of new counselors currently in schools. Many states require a specific endorsement in elementary counseling, including course work in child development and elementary counseling techniques, as well as practicum experience at the elementary level. As at other levels, elementary counselors are often former elementary teachers seeking yet another way of working with students. Typically, higher ratios of counselors to students—perhaps one counselor to 500 students or more—exist in elementary schools than at the middle or high school level. Often the peripatetic elementary counselor serves students in several smaller elementary schools on an itinerant basis.

Individual and small group counseling combine with a classroom guidance program to enable an elementary counselor to have contact with such a large clientele. Elementary counselors spend much time in consultation with teachers and with parents who are very much involved with their children's education at the elementary level. Elementary counselors are likely to use puppets, songs, and games as a part of their classroom guidance presentation. As more attention is drawn toward early intervention with students who are potential school dropouts, the elementary counselor will likely assume a much more prominent position in early intervention with at-risk students.

A typical day for an elementary guidance counselor might look like this:

8:00 AM meet with new student and his mother; check completion of registration forms, immunizations, etc; review records from previous school, noting former special education placement, and confer with principal about which teacher he should be assigned to

8:30 introduce new student to teacher and confer with mother, explain new student's apparent eligibility for free lunch

8:40 check in with Cynthia, who is having a hard time overcoming school phobia; chat briefly with Cynthia and give her a hug

8:45 greet Andrew in his fourth grade classroom and give him much praise for getting to school on time, a problem discussed in his counseling group last week

8:50 organize calendar for the day, noting phone calls to make and letters to be written

8:55	make telephone calls to five parents: Randy's low achievement in reading, Arthur's teacher recommendation that he be tested for the gifted program, Cynthia's success so far in school today, Latanya's interest in geology and an upcoming Saturday program, and a request for a conference with Sandy's teacher and the principal
9:20	conduct classroom group guidance—kindergarten
9:50	same lesson, another kindergarten room
10:15	counsel four individuals referred by their teachers, for about 20 minutes per student, including collecting them from and returning them to their classrooms
11:35	eat lunch and travel to next school
12:30	confer with principal about upcoming orientation program for next year's kindergarten students
1:00	conduct classroom group guidance, third grade class
1:30	same lesson, another third grade class
2:00	counsel group of five boys who get in fights
2:45	confer with Sampson's teacher about his belligerent attitude toward authority
3:00	confer with Susan's parents, teacher, and the principal
3:30	attend committee meeting in central office to discuss need for transitional kindergarten classes

Middle-level school counseling is one of the more undefined parts of school counseling. Although almost one fourth of the public school students are in either middle or junior high schools, less literature is available to describe what the counselor does at this level, unlike elementary or high schools. Some states, aided by organizations such as the National Middle School Association, are beginning to define certification requirements and training programs for those working in middle-level schools, including counselors. Where a counselor to student ratio exists, it is likely to be lower than the elementary but higher than high schools—perhaps 400 students to one counselor, or higher. Many middle-level counselors are former high school counselors who chose middle-level students to work with, desiring an earlier intervention or a place where more counseling and less record-keeping and counting of credits occurs. Others, unfortunately, were relegated to the middle school because they had poor performance in high school settings. Few counselors in middle schools today were trained specifically for that level, although increasingly counselors in middle schools are seeking additional course work, conference presentations, state department assistance, publications, and resource materials designed specifically for that level. The National Middle Schools Association offers several publications dedicated to middle-level counseling problems and *The School Counselor* published a special issue in January 1986 on "Counseling Middle-Grade Students."

Counselors in middle schools work extensively with interdisciplinary teams of teachers, sometimes being assigned as a member of the team. Parents seek the assistance of middle-level counselors as their children move into adolescence, with the attendant frustrations and fears of parents. Group counseling is probably the most effective means of working with middle-level students, since their peer affiliations are so strong at this age. Career and educational counseling take on new interest and meaning for both students and parents as students make course choices that affect their future educational and occupational options. Feeling the conflicts and uncertainties of changing from children to adolescents, students want to know how to get along better with everyone: their peers, their boyfriend/girlfriend, parents, siblings, teachers, and others.

One organizational feature of many middle schools is the teacher-advisory program, in which teachers become first-line advisors to a small group of students. The intent of such a program is for each student to be known well by at least one adult in the building. Group guidance activities are usually a core part of the teacher-advisory program. The role of the counselor in such a program may be to plan the guidance portion of the program; to provide training for teachers and administrators who will serve as advisors; and to function as an advisor for a small group. Where there is a teacher-advisory program, there will likely be more referrals to the counselor as more teachers know their students well and refer them to counselors for more assistance than the teacher-advisor can provide.

A typical day for a middle school counselor might look like this:

8:00   chat briefly with three seventh grade girls before teacher advisory (TA) starts—no special topic, just friendly

8:05   attend parent conference with George, his parents, and the sixth grade Blue team about his unwillingness to do homework

8:30   meet with Mrs. Gray's teacher-advisory group, since her substitute feels uncomfortable carrying out the activity

9:00   organize day, check with secretary to see if letters of invitation to next week's guidance advisory committee went out, return parent phone calls

9:30   provide individual counseling for five students (four previously scheduled and one who dropped in): Carmen's dislike of participating in physical education class; Vincent's application for the summer gifted program; Tony's fear of being beaten up by the bigger guys; David's getting assigned to in-school suspension again; and Sally's possible participation in the group for students whose parents are divorcing

10:30   participate in weekly meeting with seventh grade Gold team to discuss students' progress

11:30   conduct Brown Bag Seminar in guidance office—counseling group for overweight students

12:15   Brown Bag Seminar—study skills group

1:00   counsel group of students having trouble getting along with peers

2:00   meet with high school counselors to discuss changes in course offerings

3:00   return parent phone calls
3:30   attend parent conference with eighth grade Blue team and Serona's mother about remedial summer school
7:30   host parent group—understanding the early adolescent

High school counseling is the most established group of school counselors. Some persons still in high school counseling were trained through the 1958 National Defense Education Act (NDEA), which funded institutes in the late 1950s and early 1960s. About 13,000 counselors received training in the first five years of that program (Borow & Humes, 1987). Usually mandated through state and regional accrediting standards, high school counselors enjoy the lowest—although usually still far too high—counselor to student ratios in the public schools, perhaps 350:1 or lower. High school counselors are also more likely to have clerical assistance, owing to the high volume of paper with which they must contend, especially college transcripts for students. Often they specialize in one grade level: the senior counselor works with seniors year after year, becoming an expert on college admissions procedures, how to enter the military, and other such topics. Sometimes a counselor begins work with a group of students entering as ninth graders and continues with that group through their senior year.

Educational and career counseling are important aspects of a high school counselor's job, since students must attain credits in certain subjects in order to graduate. It is traditionally the counselor's responsibility to maintain students' records and help them make wise selections for future education and work. Personal counseling becomes crucial as students make decisions about choosing colleges or applying for jobs, entering the military or evading registration for military service, and whether or not they will "just say no" or get involved with drugs, alcohol, sex, and a host of other adult decisions foisted upon many in early adolescence. While counselors at elementary and middle-school levels have earlier opportunities for intervention when perhaps the consequences for their students are not so grave, high school counselors too often find themselves presented with problems demanding immediate solutions that have long-range implications, such as whether or not to drop out of school or to continue a pregnancy. For too many counselors, trained to help students get into college or find a job, these kinds of problems are beyond the scope of their training—or even their imagination. Many high school students see their counselors as hopelessly out of sync with the times, unable to intervene or even to understand the pressures faced by today's teenagers. Polls of high school students rarely show the school counselor as the person to whom the student first turns for help.

A revitalization of the high school counselor's role has been envisioned by many as a needed improvement in school counseling. The March 1989 issue of *The School Counselor* contains a theme section on "The Role of the Secondary School Counselor."

A typical day for a high school counselor might look like this:

8:00   meet with teachers of Advanced Placement classes to discuss screening procedures

8:30   confer with secretary to check on progress of sending out transcripts and recommendations to colleges; write three recommendations

9:15   counsel individuals by appointment: Alfred's college options; Bobbi's ASVAB scores; Carla's selection as a peer counselor; Sid's decision to join the military; Thalia's worry about pregnancy; Neala's concern that she cannot afford graduation announcements and pictures; Chuck's fear that he doesn't have enough credits to graduate

11:00   meet with department heads to revise course selection guide

12:30   counsel group: planning for the future

1:30   visit Sharon's home, even though she's said she won't return to school

2:30   meet with homebound teacher to arrange instruction for Allen, who was injured in a car wreck

2:45   return phone calls

3:00   meet with college representative about being included in College Day

3:15   make presentation to faculty meeting on symptoms of depression in students and beginning crisis intervention team

College/university counseling is in many cases much more specialized than is public school counseling. While coordinated under the umbrella of student services, usually one department does admissions counseling; another, career counseling and job placement; another, residence hall advising; and yet another, personal counseling in a counseling center. In a smaller institution, one counselor may work in more than one of these areas.

Admissions officers are concerned with much more than simply processing student applications. Often their mission includes recruitment of various populations: minority students, outstanding high school students, transfers from community colleges, and other special groups. They probably have a great deal of contact with high school guidance counselors and often attend high school College Night programs with recruiters from other higher-education institutions. Often admissions personnel are also responsible for telling students what financial aid is available and for helping students through that maze. They give campus tours and orient students and their parents to the campus and the programs available there.

Career counselors and placement officers may or may not be a part of the counseling center that deals with personal problems on a university campus. Those responsible for career counseling and placement help students understand their options for jobs based on different major areas of study, often doing vocational interest testing. Students learn to prepare resumes and to search for jobs. Career Days, where prospective employers visit campus to explain future job options to students, are often a part of a comprehensive career planning program, and placement officers usually coordinate interviews for students with business and industry recruiters who visit campus. Sometimes placement services extend to alumni as well as students, greatly enlarging the scope of the placement officer's work beyond helping new graduates seek entry-level jobs.

Those responsible for student life on campus usually are a part of the student personnel team on a college or a university campus. Their duties range from arranging social activities at the beginning of the year to help new students meet others, to monitoring the activity of sororities and fraternities, to supervising student life in the residence halls. Often they plan preventive programs such as Alcohol Awareness Week or other such topics of concern to college-age students. Much of their work may be done in conjunction with the student health services, as well as with counseling center professionals. Likely they will train peer counselors who serve as residence-hall advisors to be first-line counselors for their fellow students.

Professionals employed in a university counseling center are likely to be clinical psychologists, counseling psychologists, or licensed professional counselors. These professionals operate much as they would at any other mental health center, on an appointment basis, dealing with a wide variety of mental health concerns: depression, sexuality, substance abuse, separation from parents, marital/relationship counseling, and other such topics. They provide group and individual counseling and often may do outreach by offering "rap groups" on topics of concern to students in the residence halls.

Community college counseling follows much the same model as does university, except for the absence of residence halls. Many community college students are part-time students, many of whom are returning to the work force or to education after a gap of several years. Thus, community college counselors work with a wider age span than do typical university or college student personnel workers. In a larger community college, there may be one counselor who works with veterans' affairs; another, with dropouts seeking further education; and another, with women returning to the workplace after several years' absence. Community college counselors must concern themselves with their students' placement in work, but also must be very knowledgeable about transfer possibilities to other colleges and universities. Often a community college counselor more closely resembles a high school counselor in the effort to help a student think through future plans for work and education.

In many states, the cost of community college courses makes an education available to many who could not attend other colleges and universities. Often, a community college counselor works with first-generation college students who do not have a family tradition of education beyond high school An important part of a community college counselor's job, as with any counselor, is to ensure that students see all possible options. Community college counselors often help students successfully bridge the gap between high school and college.

There is probably no typical day for a college or university counselor because of the diversity of the job of the counselor at that level. The counselor in a post-secondary institution is likely to be more specialized than is the elementary, middle-level, or high school generalist.

OTHER EDUCATIONAL SETTINGS

There are counselors who work in educational settings other than those described above who may have very specialized functions allied to the mission of their schools. A counselor in a very competitive private school, for example, may have as a prime task getting as many students as possible into prestigious colleges and universities. A counselor in a parochial school may add young people's spiritual welfare to the tasks already listed. Young people who are schooled in a prison system may have counselors who try to correct their antisocial behavior and help them understand the norms and requirements of society. The process used will be the same as for counselors in other educational settings: define the problem, set goals, design procedures, and evaluate effectiveness to bring about behavior changes.

DIFFERENCES AMONG SETTINGS

Counseling in an educational setting differs somewhat from similar work in an agency, private practice, or other setting.

1. The counselor in an educational setting usually has a fairly clearly defined mission: to help the student learn better. Many factors impinge on this learning, including family influences, peer influences, personal motivation, ability, degree of mental health of the student, and many, many more. Basically, though, the school counselor's mission is to help the student arrange the components of life so that learning can occur.

2. Students in an educational setting are usually readily available to the counselor. In an agency, a client may or may not keep an appointment. In a school, the counselor can usually meet the student-client readily. In fact, the counselor has the authority to command a student to the office—a practice one does not employ very often—which is absent in most other professional settings.

3. School counselors do not work in isolation. There are many other people in the building also interested in the same student: teachers, administrators, school psychologist, peers, and others. The counselor works in the school as a social setting, whereas a private practitioner may see the client only as an individual or as a part of a small family unit. The school counselor thus must understand the system and its foibles and must also be able to work in collaborative fashion with others surrounding the student.

4. School counselors work with a basically normal population. Most young people in schools are not "sick," although there are certainly some very unhealthy individuals. Most of the school counselor's efforts are directed toward a normal, healthy, reasonably well adjusted clientele.

5. The school counselor is accountable to someone, probably a school administrator, and ultimately to the public. There is likely to be more supervision of the work of the school counselor, with probably a formal evaluation every few years, than there is for a counselor in other settings.

6. The job of the school counselor is relatively protected. Mostly its continuation does not depend on someone's whim or the economy. In most states, school counseling positions are mandated by state education regulations. University and college counselors do not enjoy this degree of protection, but student personnel workers are recognized as a part of the higher education system.

7. School counselors work with large numbers of people, including some whom they would not choose. They rarely have the right of transferring a student-client to another counselor, or refusing to enter into a counseling relationship. Frequently someone else—a teacher, parent, or administrator—decides that the student needs counseling, placing student and counselor into a relationship that neither of them chose.

8. Much of the school counselor's work can be developmental and not focused on crisis. Too often, especially at the high school, the counselor becomes bogged down in paperwork and clerical tasks such as scheduling, or finds the greatest portion of time spent in crisis counseling. The role can be primarily working with students to enhance their career and educational development. Certainly elementary and middle-level counselors assist students with personal development.

9. The school counselor is a generalist. Counselors in schools do some work with careers, some with educational options, some with social problems, some with families, some with substance abuse, and some with a whole host of other areas. Counselors in agencies or private practice might specialize in any one of those areas. Rarely is a school counselor able to specialize, although counselors may have specialized knowledge for the students they work with, such as college admission procedures.

10. School counseling is a recognized branch of the profession. While the public may not be really clear on what a licensed professional counselor does, most people have at least a hazy—although too often negative—notion about what school counselors do. School counselors must work hard to make their publics view them in a positive manner, but they do not have to break new ground to identify themselves to people.

TRENDS AND FUTURE DIRECTIONS

Some issues are in the forefront of the counseling profession today. Many of these were identified by John Krumboltz, Dave Capuzzi, Norman Gysbers, and this author in a symposium called the "20/20 Conference" jointly sponsored by AACD and ERIC/CAPS in 1987 in Washington, DC, chronicled in *Building Strong School Counseling Programs* (Walz, 1988). Issues and areas of concern facing school counselors today include these:

1. How do counselors work with special populations, many of whom come from very different cultures than do most school counselors? What do counselors need to know about Asian-Americans, blacks, native Americans, Hispanics, and other American ethnic groups, not to mention non-English-speaking immigrants and political refugees? How does the counselor learn about the cultural values of those individuals and families; are there techniques more or less appropriate for individuals from different backgrounds?

2. How does the school counselor respond to an ever-growing diverse population in the schools? How does a university counselor help the learning disabled or severely orthopedically impaired young person? How will AIDS affect the public schools of our nation? How is career guidance different for the trainable mentally retarded student than for the intellectually gifted?

3. What is the school counselor's responsibility to the family? Who is the client, the student or the troubled family whose life is impairing the educational capacity of the student? Should school counselors be trained as family therapists?

4. How does the school counselor clearly define an appropriate role, in order to dump such tasks as routine clerical work, administrative duties, and enormous caseloads that preclude sufficient attention for anyone?

5. Are high school counselors sufficiently trained to do the job the public demands today? What changes need to be made in secondary counseling, and how can these best be accomplished?

6. How can counselors evaluate their work? To whom are they accountable and how is that accountability measured (Gysbers and Henderson, 1988)?

7. How can the public's often negative image of the school counselor be improved? How can school and university counselors demonstrate their worth to the students they serve and to those who make budgetary decisions?

Much work needs to be done yet to define the school counselor's role clearly and to ensure that all school counselors are well-trained, effective professionals. Counselors themselves, together with counselor educators and others interested in school counseling, working through such organizations as AACD and ASCA, must continue to work for a clear vision of the helping profession in schools.

REFERENCES

Borow, H., & Humes, C. (1987). Origins and growth of counseling. In C. Humes (Ed.), *Contemporary counseling*. Muncie, IN: Accelerated Development.

Brown, D., & Srebalus, D. (1988). *An introduction to the counseling profession*. Englewood Cliffs, NJ: Prentice-Hall.

Cole, C. (1987). Referral and collaborative working. In C. Humes (Ed.), *Contemporary counseling*. Muncie, IN: Accelerated Development.

Cole, C. (Ed.) (1989). The role of the secondary school Counselor (*Theme issue*). *The School Counselor, 36*(4), 249–280.

Dougherty, A. M. (Ed.) (1986). Counseling middle-grade students (Special issue). *The School Counselor, 33*(3).

Gysbers, N., & Henderson, P. (1988). *Developing and managing your school guidance program.* Alexandria, VA: AACD Press.

Hutchins, D., & Cole, C. (1986). *Helping relationships and strategies.* Monterey, CA: Brooks/Cole.

Seligman, L. (1987). Appraisal services. In C. Humes (Ed.), *Contemporary counseling*. Muncie, IN: Accelerated Development.

Walz, G. (Ed.) (1988). *Building strong school counseling programs.* Alexandria, VA: AACD Press.

12.

Mental Health Counseling

DAVID K. BROOKS, JR., PH.D., C.C.M.H.C.
Kent State University
Kent, Ohio

DURING THE LATE 1960s counselors began to diverge from the path that led from graduate school more or less directly to traditional positions in educational settings. The following two decades witnessed such an acceleration of this divergence that by the beginning of the 1990s the profession of counseling finds itself in a brave new world that bears little resemblance to the environment in which its practitioners applied their craft 25 years ago.

In 1965, certification had only one meaning. Now it has nearly half a dozen. Counselor education curricula 25 years ago were focused on the preparation of practitioners for secondary schools, graduating students after 30 semester hours, often without a practicum. Today, professionally accredited programs range in length from 48 to more than 60 semester hours and prepare students to practice as specialists in as many as six different program tracks. In 1965 any talk of diagnosis and treatment of mental and emotional disorders would have been viewed as heresy in counseling circles. In 1990 such issues are not only incorporated into the curricula of many counselor education programs, they are written into state law and federal regulations as competencies expected of professional counselors.

The diversification of counseling from its roots in educational and vocational guidance to the multiplicity of health care and community service settings in which the majority of its members now work is a fascinating story. It would be much less interesting if the leaders of the profession and its organizations had planned it this way. Fortunately for the telling of the story, they did not.

COUNSELORS: OUT OF SCHOOL AND OUT OF WORK

For most of the decade of the 1960s the job market for graduates of counselor education programs was a near cornucopia. Until late in the decade funding and programmatic support for school guidance positions were strong in virtually all areas of the United States. Beginning with the National Defense Education Act of 1958 and continuing with the Elementary and Secondary Education Act of 1965, federal funding for school guidance and counseling programs and parallel support at the state level set the kinds of expectations that counselor education programs took as a green light to produce as many graduates as possible.

Supply, Demand, and New Job Market Realities

As the decade neared an end, however, the budgetary demands of the war in Vietnam exerted a squeeze on federal dollars that was felt in many human services programs, including school counseling program funding. The reduction in federal support was soon followed by a corresponding decrease in state funding. School counseling positions were not on the endangered list, but they were not nearly as numerous as had formerly been the case. As frequently happens in situations such as this, there was a time lag during which the supply of graduates substantially outpaced the demand for positions. Before counselor education programs responded with enrollment policies that were more in keeping with the new realities of the school counseling market, several classes of graduates had experienced real hardship in finding the kinds of positions for which they had been trained.

A similarly adverse situation began to manifest itself for counselors trained at the doctoral level. Because counselor programs were shrinking in size, university positions for counselor educators were decreasing correspondingly. The other major career path for doctoral counselor education graduates, that of becoming licensed psychologists and pursuing positions either in university counseling centers or in the Veterans Administration, was increasingly blocked by new regulatory barriers erected by state psychology licensing boards (see below).

For newly graduated counselors at both master's and doctoral levels, therefore, the 1970s dawned with new realities and new uncertainties. Listings for practitioner positions in traditional educational and vocational settings were flooded with applicants. A de facto freeze was in effect for new hires in counselor education positions. It was clear that new options and new settings would have to be explored or a generation of counselor education graduates would be lost to the profession.

Mental Health, Agency, and Private Practice: Applying Counseling Skills in Different Settings

The Community Mental Health Centers Act of 1963 provided federal funding to establish community-based treatment centers as alternatives to the state hospital system that had been the cornerstone of public mental health services since the nineteenth century. Several significant federal studies (Brooks & Weikel, 1986) had suggested community mental health centers (CMHCs) as being both more humane and more effective than the mental health "warehouses" that many state hospitals had become.

The legislation anticipated that the CMHCs would be staffed by multidisciplinary treatment teams that included both the four "core provider" professions of psychiatry, psychology, social work, and nursing as well as paraprofessionals whose training background was unspecified. As the centers opened and as the staffing patterns began to emerge, the "paraprofessional" positions were often filled by master's level counselor education graduates.

Counselors trained at the doctoral level also found CMHCs to be receptive to their skills. Denied licensure as psychologists by state boards, they were often classified as psychologists by the centers, whose employees were frequently exempt from licensure requirements.

Community mental health centers were not the only noneducational settings in which counselor education graduates found employment in the late 1960s and early 1970s. Youth services bureaus, women's health centers, programs for displaced homemakers, cooperative employment training programs, parole programs, drug and alcohol rehabilitation programs, and community based veterans' centers were but a few of the nontraditional settings in which counselors worked.

Mental Health Counseling—The Identity Emerges

These kinds of postgraduate experiences had several effects on the profession. First of all, counselors discovered that they could be effective with client populations and issues very different from those for which many of them had been trained. In-service education programs, clinical supervision, and daily on-the-job training in CMHCs and other community-based settings, combined with their graduate training in individual and group counseling, appraisal, career development, and other basics of counselor education programs, fitted counselors to function in these environments with special combinations of skills and perspectives that were valued by supervisors, peers, and clients alike.

Another effect of the increasing number of counselors working in community settings, one that took a little longer to become apparent, was the reciprocal influence on graduate counselor education programs. In response to the needs of graduates in these different settings, institutions began to incorporate coursework in psychopathology and diagnosis and treatment planning. Perhaps more important was the changing nature of practicum and internship experiences. Once limited to school settings or to on-campus laboratories, practicum opportunities were increasingly available in the kinds of agency settings in which students were most likely to work after graduation. And some of the on-site supervision was beginning to be provided by the counselor education graduates who had broken the ground for counselors in these settings several years earlier.

A third effect of the emergence of counselors in CMHCs and other agency settings was the continuing awareness that they were different. They filled positions sometimes labeled as "psychologist" or "social worker," but more often classified as "psychiatric aide" or "mental health worker II." Despite the fact that they were rarely accorded identity in their work settings as counselors, they did not seek to attach themselves to their "core provider" colleagues. Reinforcing the sense of "differentness" was the reality of a status differential defined, among other criteria, by often significant differences in compensation between counselors and members of the core provider disciplines. Regardless of the level of clinical skill attained, counselors in CMHCs usually found it difficult to escape the most apparent vestiges of the "paraprofessional" stigma under which many of them were hired.

Closely related to these status and salary dimensions of identity was the lack of credentialing mechanisms that defined who counselors were, what their training was, and what their areas of clinical competency were. Prior to the late 1970s the only credentialing affecting counselors was the special case of teacher certification that endorsed counselors for practice in public schools. Not only was there substantial variability from state to state in the requirements for school counselor certification, the credential was in no way viewed as transferable to mental health or community agency settings. For all intents, therefore, counselors in these settings had no credentialing, either statutory or professional.

The other major area of shortcoming that such counselors experienced was the lack of a professional organization that represented their interests and responded to their needs. What was then the American Personnel and Guidance Association (APGA) had no division for counselors who worked in mental health agencies. Existing divisions for counselors in employment service, rehabilitation, and public offender settings met the needs of only a few. What was needed was a new association or a new division of APGA that was specifically aimed at counselors in mental health and other community agency settings.

In the mid-1970s forces were set in motion that were to address the difficulties that counselors were experiencing both in credentialing and in professional identity. Because these forces were soon to overlap and interact with each other, the formation and development of a new professional organization will be dealt with first, even though its inception was chronologically somewhat later than the beginnings of counselor licensure.

THE AMERICAN MENTAL HEALTH COUNSELORS ASSOCIATION

The incorporation of the American Mental Health Counselors Association (AMHCA) in Florida in November 1976 was the result of correspondence, organizational spadework, and, most important, an optimistic and idealistic vision of what the future of the mental health services delivery system ought to be about.

According to Weikel (1985), letters to the editor of the *APGA Guidepost* began appearing in 1975 that solicited interest in forming a new professional organization for counselors in mental health and other community agencies. After about a year of nonresponse, these petitions found a receptive audience in Nancy Spisso and James J. Messina of the Escambia County Mental Health Center in Pensacola, Florida. They responded to a letter from a group of counselors in Jamesville, Wisconsin, and at the same time began to stir up interest among friends and colleagues from the counselor education program at the University of Florida in Gainesville, of which Spisso was a recent graduate and where Messina had been an NIMH postdoctoral fellow. The so-called Gainesville-Jamesville axis was forged, which turned out to be only the beginning of a nationwide response to Spisso and Messina's idea.

Within weeks, several hundred persons had signed on and plans were in the works to petition APGA for division status. Unfortunately for this initial effort at affiliation, the APGA board of directors had just passed a moratorium on the establishment of new divisions. The core leadership of AMHCA decided to found an independent organization that would maintain close communication with APGA and perhaps seek division affiliation at a later time.

It was soon evident that "mental health counselor" was a professional identity with broad appeal and that there was a potentially sizable membership for the fledgling organization that was just waiting to be tapped. Growing to nearly 1500 members in less than a year and a half, AMHCA held its first national conference in March 1978 (Weikel, 1985). The leadership had decided to approach APGA once again about becoming a division. This time the APGA board was receptive, but the AMHCA membership on the ratification ballot nearly rejected affiliation. Even though some members resigned and some rather heated rhetoric was exchanged, AMHCA became APGA's thirteenth division on July 1, 1978. Membership continued to grow and soon the disaffected former members' negative effect on membership statistics was overcome.

AMHCA and APGA: An Uneasy Marriage

Almost from the beginning of its status as an APGA division, AMHCA challenged the parent organization on its priorities, its stewardship of fiscal resources, and its record of effective advocacy for counselors' interests.

Founded in 1952 as the result of a merger between four existing organizations, APGA was almost totally focused on educational issues in its legislative agenda at the state and federal levels because the majority of its members worked in educational settings, both in K–12 in public schools and in higher education institutions. Most of the individuals involved in APGA governance were practitioners in such settings or were counselor educators who trained school counselors and student personnel specialists. When AMHCA leaders began talking about mental health issues as association legislative priorities, their arguments did not always fall on deaf ears, but often on ears belonging to fellow counselors in need of time and reorientation to understand more fully what the arguments were about.

The AMHCA leaders even questioned the name of the parent organization, insisting that APGA change its name so that the word "counseling" was included. At first no one outside the AMHCA leadership took this argument seriously, but after several years of agitation and alliance building, mental health counselors were successful in accomplishing their objective. A coalition led by AMHCA and by the American College Personnel Association (ACPA), one of APGA's founding divisions, persuaded the APGA Senate in March 1983 to adopt "American Association for Counseling and Development" (AACD) as the parent organization's new name, effective July 1 of that year.

The AMHCA continued to grow, passing the American School Counselor Association (ASCA) as AACD's largest division in 1985 and reaching the 10,000-member milestone early in 1986. The division's leaders found that legislative and organizational priorities based on support for credentialing, on high standards for training, and on "bread-and-butter" issues such as third-party insurance reimbursement and advocacy for the right to practice had not only a sustained appeal for attracting new members, but that such priorities, if argued long and persuasively enough, tended to become AACD issues as well, within the limits that the following examples demonstrate.

In July 1987, the AACD Governing Council committed itself to a new task force on third-party reimbursement. This action was taken only after it was pointed out that private practitioners were the largest single group within the AACD membership, that there were more private practitioners within AACD than school counselors at the elementary, middle, and secondary levels, and that insurance reimbursement was not just an AMHCA issue, since the numbers of private practitioners within AACD exceeded AMHCA's total membership.

Similarly, in the following spring the Governing Council adopted criteria equivalent to those long advocated by AMHCA as the standard the association would recognize in its efforts aimed at reimbursement in both public and private sectors. This was probably a more radical step than the council otherwise would have taken, had AMHCA not been previously successful in achieving CHAMPUS recognition for mental health counselors (see the section on recognition and reimbursement below).

The AMHCA leadership thus found that the Governing Council was always more willing to embrace issues for which the statistics were unarguable or those that the federal government had already endorsed. Making AMHCA's case in the context of the logic of the situation, the social desirability of taking a proactive stance, and the wisdom of setting standards that did not regress toward the mean were always difficult.

Fiscal Management and Frustration

Among its other continuing issues with AACD leadership and management, AMHCA has insisted from the very beginning on getting its money's worth out of AACD affiliation. The AACD fiscal policies governing the ways in which division funds are handled, interest charges, investment options, and simple reporting of accounts are among the practices AMHCA has challenged. In most instances AMHCA has been successful in arguing for policy changes so that divisions' advantages are respected.

Even with these successes there remains a strong feeling, particularly among AMHCA's Council of Past Presidents, that the relationship with AACD has outlived its usefulness. The division's "dinosaurs" have no direct voice in policy, but their influence has been considerable during the decade of the 1980s, primarily because of the strong personal bonds among the past presidents and because they have actively sought to mentor new leaders.

Each presidency from 1980 on ended with a certain amount of frustration that the responsiveness of AACD's management to mental health counseling issues was always limited by the attitude of "we can only give you so much attention and support because we have to be attentive to the issues of the smaller divisions." This, when compared with the legislative success of sibling organizations such as the American Association for Marriage and Family Therapy, who benefit from a more single-minded agenda, has caused AMHCA's past leaders to weigh seriously the advantages of going it alone. Whether this secessionist sentiment becomes reality depends on the responsiveness of new AACD management to mental health counseling issues, on the relative influence AMHCA enjoys in restructured AACD governance, and on careful projections of the viability of an independent organization of mental health counselors.

Recognition and Reimbursement

Among AMHCA's goals from its founding had been the notion that mental health counselors should be recognized as service providers on an equal footing with the other nonmedical mental health disciplines, e.g., clinical psychology, social work, psychiatric nursing, and marriage and family therapy. Its professional certification standards (see the following section) had been designed with this goal in mind, the somewhat radical position being advanced that demonstrated competence rather than academic degree should be the criterion by which providers are recognized.

As early as 1981 AMHCA leaders were seeking recognition for mental health counselors as eligible providers under social security programs. The first breakthrough at the federal level came as the result not of a legislative success, but of a bureaucratic one. The Civilian Health and Medical Program of the Uniformed Services (CHAMPUS), after three years of lobbying by the AMHCA, in 1987 recognized certified or licensed mental health counselors as providers eligible for reimbursement under its programs with physician referral. Building on that victory, AMHCA next sought inclusion for mental health counselors as recognized providers under the Federal Employees Health Benefits Program (FEHBP). This is a legislative effort that, at the time this book went to press, has not achieved success.

Concurrent with these public sector initiatives has been substantial activity to achieve recognition by private insurance programs. The most direct route to such recognition is amendment of state insurance codes to permit "freedom of choice" statutes to extend to counselors as eligible providers. Such efforts have been successful in Virginia, Texas, Montana, and Vermont, with de facto recognition in Florida and Ohio.

The movement toward prepaid health plans, e.g., health maintenance organizations, has complicated mental health counselors' efforts in the recognition and reimbursement arena. Apparently operating beyond the reach of most freedom of choice statutes, such programs have as their primary objective the reduction of health care costs. All nonmedical providers, in both physical and mental health domains, tend to be viewed by the prepaid sector in the context of cost effectiveness rather than clinical effectiveness as caregivers. While mental health counselors could undercut other provider groups in terms of fees, such action would probably be counterproductive in the long run. Navigating these tricky and potentially treacherous waters is one of the major challenges currently facing the AMHCA membership.

MENTAL HEALTH COUNSELORS AND CREDENTIALING

A couple of years before AMHCA was organized, attention within the counseling community began to focus on the issue of credentialing. Initial concern surrounded the disenfranchisement of doctoral level counselor education graduates by state psychology licensing boards. The focus was soon broadened, however, to encompass master's level counselors as well. Mental health counselors were not involved in these early efforts because AMHCA had not yet been founded and because, when it was, the new organization directed its energies toward different credentialing objectives for the first several years.

Professional Certification

The critical element in AMHCA's strategy to achieve parity with the other nonmedical mental health providers was the structure it established in 1979 to administer a professional certification process for mental health counselors. The National Academy of Certified Clinical Mental Health Counselors administered its first examination to 50 "pioneer" certificants in February 1979 and was formally chartered as an independent, freestanding certification body in July of that year. It was closely allied to AMHCA, but in order to meet the standards recommended by a series of federal studies and embodied by the National Commission of Health Certifying Agencies (NCHCA), it was necessary for the Academy to be legally separate from the professional organization (Brooks & Weikel, 1986).

The Academy's certification process required applicants to submit an application form and nonrefundable fee, together with transcripts of graduate coursework, documentation of supervised experience, and recommendations from clinical supervisors. If those had been the only requirements for admission to the examination, thousands of counselors would doubtless have flocked to the Academy banner. Two additional requirements caused the expected flood of applicants to more nearly resemble a trickle. The first of these was the requirement that applicants submit a taped sample of clinical work accompanied by a critique. The second requirement, since dropped, was that recommendations from three present or former clients be submitted. While these criteria were not unreasonable by themselves, the combined effect presented a very discouraging prospect for large numbers of potential applicants, who were perhaps as influenced by the "hassle factor" of these latter requirements as they were by the sheer terror of peer review.

The NCHCA was founded with the intent that voluntary national certification would eventually replace state licensure as the credential of choice. The NCHCA standards were designed to become for all health-related professions the criteria by which eligibility for insurance reimbursement was determined. Thus the Academy's certification procedures, while setting what were viewed as extremely high professional standards, were also grounded in bread-and-butter pragmatism.

The CCMCH: A Rigorous Credential with Little Acceptance

Unfortunately for the Academy's founders, the rest of the health care community did not wholeheartedly buy into the NCHCA approach of voluntary national certification replacing state licensure as the predominant modality of professional credentialing. The mental health provider disciplines, especially psychology and social work, had been successful in their legislative efforts at achieving passage of state licensure laws and were not about to abandon the fruits of their labors. Furthermore, the insurance community proved itself less than enthusiastic about national voluntary certification. While individual certified clinical mental health counselors (CCMHCs) were reimbursed by health insurance plans in most states, the pattern of such recognition was far from uniform.

Confounding the acceptance of the CCMHC credential within the counseling profession was the establishment in 1982 of the National Board for Certified Counselors (NBCC). Created to develop a national generic certification, NBCC was funded at a much higher level than the Academy and, following an extensive publicity campaign, attracted within the profession broad interest for its embryonic credential. The resulting widespread awareness, coupled with an extremely liberal "grandfathering" policy led to numbers of applicants that exceeded even the most optimistic predictions. Nearly 14,000 individuals had been certified by NBCC by the time the "grandfathering" period expired.

With so few of their own demonstrating interest in the rigorous Academy certification process and with such widespread acceptance of a generic, nonclinical credential, AMHCA leaders found themselves literally in a situation of being all dressed up with no place to go—no place, that is, except to the counselor licensure movement that was experiencing such difficulty in the early 1980s.

Mental Health Counselors and Licensure

Because the AMHCA leadership was so committed to national certification as represented by the CCMHC, relatively little interest was devoted to the counselor licensure effort that had been underway since 1974 under the aegis of the APGA (later AACD) Licensure Committee. After nearly a decade's work, by 1983 counselor licensure laws had been passed in only seven states. Six of these states were in the South—Virginia, Arkansas, Alabama, Texas, Florida, and North Carolina—and the only one outside the region—Idaho—wasn't exactly a major population center. Clearly this was an area of professional endeavor that could benefit from the energy and commitment of mental health counselors.

At the time the first AMHCA Licensure Committee was appointed in 1979, the APGA Licensure Committee had been in operation for five years. Active licensure committees had been functioning for some time in ASCA and in the Association for Counselor Education and Supervision (ACES). As might be expected, the ASCA Licensure Committee was principally involved in educating school counselors about licensure and in encouraging them to become active in their state efforts. The ACES Licensure Committee had undertaken several research efforts, primarily membership surveys to determine the impact of exclusion by state psychology boards upon ACES members' professional interests and to ascertain how important the growing counselor licensure movement was to ACES members. The ACES committee disbanded around 1978, but the ASCA committee is still active.

The War Chest Grant Program

The AMHCA Licensure Committee set a somewhat different set of priorities for itself. Membership education was a small piece of the agenda, because while most mental health counselors knew the importance of licensure for their professional survival, not everyone was aware of the connections between licensure and Academy certification.

Making resources available to state licensure committees that had direct applicability to the legislative process was AMHCA's top priority. The "War Chest" grant was the vehicle developed for this purpose. Ignoring AACD's advice about making funds directly available for lobbying purposes, even to the point of grants being available to pay lobbyists, the AMHCA committee literally put its money where its mouth was. The grants program gave mental health counselors instant entrée and status in the operations of state licensure committees because the AMHCA committee demanded evidence of mental health counselor involvement before it released grant funds.

In 1981 Florida became the fifth state to pass a counselor licensure law and the first to use "licensed mental health counselor" rather than "licensed professional counselor" as the title protected by law. There was no substantive difference between the Florida law and the previous licensure statutes whose terminology sounded more "generic," in terms of definitions, academic and experience requirements, or examination requirements. The six states that have followed Florida in using this title (for a total of seven out of the 32 that had passed licensure laws as of December 1989) have included somewhat more clinical emphases in their legislative language or in their regulations. Some have also specified that the Academy examination be used, but regardless of the protected title most counselor licensure laws passed since mental health counselors began assuming leadership roles in state-level political activity in the early 1980s have tended not to be overly specialized in either language or intent.

Unfinished Business

As successful as the counselor licensure effort has been during the decade of the 1980s, there are still several pieces of unfinished business as far as mental health counselors are concerned. First, recognition by both third-party, i.e., traditional health insurance policies, and "fourth-party," i.e., prepaid health insurance plans, reimbursement programs remains to be accomplished. It seems desirable to attack both of these issues simultaneously, because if third-party payers are targeted first, the fourth-party segment of the industry may continue to grow so rapidly that it overtakes its more traditional cousin, rendering the "freedom of choice" issue moot.

The second piece of unfinished business has to do with translating the recognition resulting from successful licensure efforts to positions and descriptions in state personnel classification systems. No state, following the passage of a licensure law, has moved directly to ensure that mental health counselors are subsequently included by title in the personnel systems that dictate staffing patterns in community mental health centers and other wholly or partially publicly funded agencies. The effect is that while many mental health counselors enjoy the benefit of licensure in private practice, their colleagues in public agencies still suffer, in many instances, from the same status and salary inferiority that existed before the licensure law was passed.

A third area in need of resolution has to do with training standards and accreditation. The AMHCA had become a founding member of the Council for Accreditation of Counseling and Related Educational Programs (CACREP) when that body was established in 1981 as the counseling profession's accreditation agency. Through the first three sets of training standards, mental health counseling was not recognized as a program track on the same footing as school counseling or student affairs practice. The designation preferred by CACREP was Counseling in Community and Other Agency Settings. Finally, in the standards revision that became effective in 1988, mental health counseling was recognized as a separate program, but "community counseling" was retained as a category without specific content.

Mental health counseling apparently faces the same struggle for identity within the counseling profession as it does among peer professions outside of counseling. The issue to be resolved is whether in the next round of standards revision, to become effective in 1994, mental health counseling should back off from the stringency of its standards in the hope of incorporating "community counseling" or "agency counseling" under its rubric or should it hold to its standards and insist that these rather inoffensive, nondescript "programs" justify themselves in terms of a body of knowledge and standards for practice?

Fourth, mental health counseling needs to decide what to do about the CCMHC. The Academy's certificants still number fewer than 10 percent of those certified by NBCC. Is this elite credential, which seems so unattainable to so many mental health counselors, worth preserving, promoting, and financially supporting? Should the NBCC develop a specialty in clinical counseling, comparable to the specialty it presently administers in career counseling? Should the CCMHC standard be maintained in future government relations efforts, such as inclusion in the Federal Employees Health Benefits Program? These issues are so controversial within AMHCA leadership circles that to mention them in public, let alone take a position on them, requires a high level of both personal confidence and professional identity.

MENTAL HEALTH COUNSELING: IDENTITY, DEFINITIONS, AND TRAINING

A young, dynamic profession can be expected to undergo changes over time, especially in the way it sees itself. Mental health counseling has certainly exemplified this phenomenon. While there is no discernible movement toward orthodoxy in terms of identity or definition, it is interesting to compare two definitions that were formulated about seven years apart. This comparison is framed in Table 12–1.

Clearly, mental health counseling, at least in terms of the way its leaders see it, became more clinically oriented during the period of time from shortly after its founding to the mid-1980s. It is not too difficult to see that each definition was shaped to some extent by a political agenda. In 1978 the principal purpose was to define differences between mental health counseling and other specializations *within* professional counseling. By 1985 the aim had shifted toward defining mental health counseling so that it resembled the other mental health disciplines, especially those that were already receiving insurance reimbursement for their services.

Differences Within the Counseling Profession

What are the differences that these definitions reflect? How does mental health counseling differ from school counseling or from student affairs practice?

TABLE 12–1 Comparison of Definitions of Mental Health Counseling

Mental health counseling is:

the process of assisting individuals or groups, through a helping relationship, to achieve optimal mental health through personal and social development and adjustment to prevent the debilitating effects of certain somatic, emotional, and intra- and/or interpersonal disorders (AMHCA, 1978, p. 19).	the provision of professional counseling services, involving the principles of psychotherapy, human development, learning theory, group dynamics, and the etiology of mental illness and dysfunctional behavior to individuals, couples, families, and groups, for the purposes of treating psychopathology and promoting optimal mental health (NACCMHC Board, 1985).

First, mental health counseling differs from its sibling counseling specializations in the age of its clientele and in the probable type of presenting problem. Mental health counselors are more likely to deal with an adult client population, although some practitioners specialize in working with children and adolescents. Unlike school counselors and student affairs practitioners, therefore, mental health counselors deal with clients across the lifespan, even though most of the clients they see are likely to be adults past college age.

Most mental health counselors espouse a developmental perspective in terms of the way they view their clients. In this respect they are similar to school counselors and to student affairs practitioners. They are much more likely, however, to work with clients whose presenting problems extend beyond what would be considered as the normal range of functioning. As the 1985 definition from Table 12–1 indicates, mental health counselors deal with the diagnosis and treatment of mental and emotional disorders. Even so, most practitioners do not view their clients in the context of the medical or illness model. Rather, the treatment planning tends to focus on assessing client strengths and on psychoeducational approaches to helping clients overcome deficits.

Mental health counselors also differ from other counseling practitioners in the extent to which they work with couples and families. To be sure, school counselors are involved in parent conferences and work with children from dysfunctional families, and student affairs practitioners deal with couples issues in collegiate settings, but neither are as likely to be involved in treating couples or families over time as are mental health counselors.

Another difference between mental health counselors and other practitioners within the counseling "family" relates to the type and extent of interprofessional and interdisciplinary collaboration and consultation. Mental health counselors are much more likely to receive referrals from physicians and other health care providers than are counselors in educational settings. Similarly, physician consultation may also be necessary because the clients of mental health counselors sometimes need medication or even hospitalization in order for treatment gains to be maximized.

Finally, mental health counselors are more likely than their counseling colleagues to be in work settings where entrepreneurship is necessary for economic survival. School counselors and student affairs practitioners must promote their services, to be sure, but their survival in a position is not usually tied to the number of clients who come through the office door. With mental health counselors the situation is different, especially if they are in private practice. Accordingly, mental health counselors must constantly cultivate referral sources among fellow professionals as well as perform community service activities such as free speeches and workshops that keep their visibility high.

Similarities and Differences with Other Mental Health Professions

Mental health counseling is similar to all the other mental health provider disciplines in that all of them offer psychotherapy as a service to clients. From this point of commonality differences begin to emerge among the professions. Only psychiatrists, for example, can prescribe medication for their clients, but practitioners of each of the other disciplines must be knowledgeable about psychotropic medication because all of them, sooner or later, will have to refer a client to a psychiatrist for medication as an adjunct to psychotherapy.

Mental health counselors are like psychologists in that both professions tend to focus on individuals in their environments, both are skilled in psychometric instrumentation and its interpretation, and both are trained in individual, group, and often family intervention modalities. The professions differ in that psychology considers the doctorate to be the academic minimum for independent practice, while counseling takes the position that the master's degree with appropriate supervised experience is both the entry level and the terminal degree for practice. Another difference is that mental health counselors are trained in career development, while most psychologists (unless they are counseling psychologists) are not. Psychologists are, however, more likely to be trained in and to use projective measures of personality.

Counselors share with social workers their view of the master's degree as the standard for independent practice. In terms of their perspective on clients, social workers tend to see individuals in the context of communities and to view community resources as important adjuncts to psychotherapy. Counselors, on the other hand, while not denying the importance of such resources tend to put less emphasis on them as elements in a treatment plan. Social work training includes less training in psychological testing and in research than does that received by most counselors, and even with the new specialization of occupational social work, career development is not a curricular element in most social work training programs. Social workers usually have a broader range of opportunities for supervised field experience than do counselors, especially in hospital and other health care settings.

Mental health counselors and marriage and family therapists also have the terminal master's degree in common as the standard for independent practice. An important difference emerges in the area of theoretical orientation. While mental health counselors typically endorse a wide range of theoretical perspectives and most describe themselves as eclectic in both theory and practice, marriage and family therapists, with few exceptions, tend to embrace a family systems approach as the basis for interventions. Marriage and family therapy training requires extensive clinical experience working with couples and families under supervision, but like social work, little emphasis is placed on psychological assessment and career development.

Each of the nonmedical provider disciplines draws on important historical, theoretical, research, and practice backgrounds to inform its identity and to shape the interventions and perspectives of its practitioners. It should not be construed, however, that each profession's members are vastly different in performance from those of the other professions once the door to the consultation room is closed. Client experiences are likely to be very similar if they are working with practitioners, regardless of discipline, of more or less equivalent levels of expertise.

Training of Mental Health Counselors

As has already been mentioned, mental health counseling was recognized by CACREP in its 1988 standards revision as a separate program track for accreditation purposes. Mental health counseling had previously been lumped into an amorphous entity known as community or agency counseling. As of December 1989, no programs have been approved for accreditation under the 1988 standards as mental health counseling programs. Five programs approved under an earlier version of the standards are listed on the CACREP roster as mental health counseling programs. If there are no fully accredited programs, how are mental health counselors trained?

Most mental health counselors have master's degrees in counseling; academic credits well past the master's degree; extensive conference, seminar, and workshop training; independent reading and study; and several years of clinical experience under supervision. Some also have advanced institute training in particular approaches such as psychoanalysis, Gestalt, or rational emotive therapy. Most mental health counselors who have been in practice for a considerable period of time have learned what they know largely as the result of on-the-job training, usually with a hefty dose of supervision.

The CACREP standards for mental health counselor training are therefore an investment in the future of the profession. They do not reflect even remotely the level of formal graduate training received by most mental health counselors. This is not to imply that because formal graduate training may have been less than present training standards require that most mental health counselors are less than competent. On the contrary, the success and acceptance that mental health counselors have experienced in those states in which licensure has been a reality for eight to ten years argue rather convincingly that these most recent arrivals on the mental health practice scene are very competent indeed.

THE PRACTICE OF MENTAL HEALTH COUNSELING

When AMHCA was founded in 1976 it was expected that the majority of its members would work in community mental health centers. That may have been the pattern in the very early days, but by 1983 the largest single group within the membership (22 percent) was reported as private practitioners. Members reporting employment in community mental health centers represented only 11 percent, the fourth largest group within the association (AACD, 1983). By 1989 the private practice contingent had more than doubled in size, accounting for more than 46 percent of the AMHCA membership. Mental health counselors working in community health centers continued to decline proportionately, representing only 8 percent of AMHCA's membership by 1989, while counselors working in other types of community agencies accounted for less than 8% percent of the total. In terms of the overall AACD membership, in 1989 only 4.5 percent of the members reported working in community agencies, while 3.2 percent indicated employment in a community mental health center. In contrast, nearly 25 percent of AACD members reported their primary work setting as being private practice (AACD, 1989).

What does all this mean? Recent conversations with some of the founding members of AMHCA yielded two factors that could not have been foreseen at the time the association was organized that, in their eyes, account for the rapid growth of the private practitioner contingent and the rocket-like decline in the numbers of counselors working in community mental health centers and other community agencies.

The first of these factors was the phenomenal success of the counselor licensure movement during the decade of the 1980s. When AMHCA was founded, only Virginia had passed a counselor licensure law, and by the beginning of the new decade only Arkansas and Alabama had joined the ranks. The early AMHCA leadership can certainly be forgiven for all the energy they put into voluntary professional certification as a desirable alternative to licensure! As another new decade turns, 29 more states have counselor licensure laws on the books—an incredible record of legislative accomplishment.

The other major element accounting for the differences in the AMHCA membership profile can best be described in two words—Ronald Reagan. There is no evidence to support the contention that budget cuts suffered by community mental health centers were any more draconian than those borne by any other community agency, but the effect of the fiscal axe was more than sufficient to get the job done. Counselors in community mental health centers suffered a double blow. First, the CMHCs themselves were not nearly as bureaucratically entrenched as many agencies with longer histories and more stable sources of funding. Second, counselors had entered the CMHCs as paraprofessionals and, regardless of their level of clinical expertise, they did not hold the "power" positions enjoyed by members of more established professions. As has been noted, part of the unfinished business of the counselor licensure movement is to effect change in the state personnel classification systems that, in most instances, determine the status hierarchy in CMHCs.

The Lure of Private Practice

With counselor licensure laws passing at the rate of two or three each year and with the bleak prospects in agency settings showing no signs of alleviating, it is not surprising that mental health counselors saw opportunities for themselves in the entrepreneurial environment fostered by the Reagan administration. Some entered the private sector on a part-time basis, while others formed group practices to share the risk of setting up a new business. Regardless of how they got started, the important dimension is that they *did* get started—and in significant numbers. The more than 10,000 AACD members who report themselves as being in private practice is probably only a fraction of the total number, especially when one considers that there are nearly that many licensed professional counselors in the state of Texas alone!

Many counselors who have worked in agencies or schools have fantasies about private practice that collide with the realities of this new arena almost as soon as it is entered. The first fantasy usually has to do with being one's own boss. While true, most private practitioners view this in retrospect as a trade-off for a regular salary check and regular working hours. The reality is that if you don't work, you don't earn any money, and to have work, you frequently must see clients at their convenience, rather than your own. Being your own boss seems moot to most private practitioners most of the time.

Another fantasy is that you are able to put paperwork behind you and really deal with clients—really *be* a counselor. The reality here is that while the total impact of paperwork may be of lesser magnitude, there are limits to your effectiveness with clients past a certain point. Most mental health counselors in private practice limit themselves to around two dozen individual clients per week, at the most. Many practitioners find that the energy they have to give to the individual therapeutic relationship simply does not extend beyond this number. More than 25 individual client hours per week creates a real stresser and constitutes a block to therapeutic effectiveness.

The paperwork of private practice consists of such items as billing, filing insurance claims, promoting workshops, maintaining records of ongoing professional development for renewal of credentials, and keeping appropriate client records. Counseling, regardless of setting or specialization, is not a profession that can be practiced without paperwork of some kind. It's a matter of what kind of paper you prefer.

One of the private practice fantasies that for many practitioners has some base in reality is that there is a great deal of variety—or, at least, there is the potential for variety. If you spend approximately half your work hours (most private practitioners spend less) in individual therapy, what do you do with the rest of your time? Group counseling and psychotherapy is certainly one option, but most private practitioners engage in consultation, training, supervision, and sometimes part-time teaching to round out their schedules. Such activities not only provide variety, but many of them also nourish your referral base for the psychotherapy part of your practice. Remember, there is no such thing as a stable practice—it is either growing or declining. To be in a growing practice means constantly working on professional contacts and referral sources.

A hazard of private practice that receives little attention is the dimension of loneliness. This is particularly true if one is in solo practice. The most damaging result of such isolation is, of course, burnout. Private practitioners must attend to their needs for both personal and professional support systems if they are to continue to maintain their effectiveness as therapists and avoid the tragedy of burnout.

Mental health counseling, regardless of the setting, is a challenging, growing, dynamic professional specialization. Deciding to become a mental health counselor requires self-awareness, self-discipline, flexibility, creativity, and mental toughness to survive the hard times. It also requires compassion, sensitivity, and therapeutic competence. In all of these respects mental health counseling resembles counseling in other settings. What makes it different? Basically, it boils down to this: a clientele that extends across the lifespan, with particular attention to the adult years; dealing with client problems that are more debilitating than those usually encountered by school counselors or student affairs practitioners; a greater likelihood of dealing with couples and families than counselors of other specializations; diagnosis and treatment of mental and emotional disorders from a developmental perspective using psychoeducational interventions; collaboration and consultation with physicians and other health care providers; and the probability that supporting one's practice will require an entrepreneurial bent. Other than these differences, being a mental health counselor is not that different from being an elementary school counselor!

REFERENCES

American Association for Counseling and Development (1983). *AACD and division membership report*. Alexandria, VA: AACD.

American Association for Counseling and Development (1989). *AACD and division membership report*. Alexandria, VA: AACD.

American Mental Health Counselors Association (1978). *Report of AMHCA Certification Committee*. Unpublished report. Washington, DC: AMHCA.

Brooks, D. K., Jr., & Weikel, W. J. (1986). History and development of the mental health counseling movement. In: A. J. Palmo & W. J. Weikel (Eds.), *Foundations of mental health counseling* (pp. 5–28). Springfield, IL: Charles C Thomas.

National Academy of Certified Clinical Mental Health Counselors. (1985). *Definition of mental health counseling*. Alexandria, VA: NACCMHC.

Weikel, W. J. (1985). The American Mental Health Counselors Association. *Journal of Counseling and Development, 63*, 457–460.

PART THREE ■

Counseling Specialized Populations

In the previous two sections, the basic skills and theoretical bases for counseling were described. In Part Three, "Counseling Specialized Populations," these skills are applied to a number of specific groups with whom a counselor may work. Each of these special populations demands different combinations of skill, knowledge, and experience from the counselor.

Chapter Thirteen, "Counseling Children and Adolescents," provides a comprehensive overview of the current therapies and interventions that counselors are finding effective in working both with children and with adolescents, and summarizes the developmental and psychological concerns children and adolescents face. The authors describe a number of the major approaches used with such clients, including play therapy, individual counseling, family therapy, group work, and behavior modification. A case study is presented to examine a specific application of these interventions and programs.

Demographic statistics predict that the percentage of individuals over the age of 55 will be increasing in the coming decades. A knowledge of the specific counseling needs of older individuals will become increasingly more important as our society moves into the twenty-first century. Chapter Fourteen, "Counseling the Older Adult," presents a detailed description of the field of gerontologic counseling. The specialized needs and social realities of elderly individuals are presented. The importance of viewing older clients as individuals, and not from the basis of cultural stereotypes about aging and the elderly, is stressed. Specific developmental challenges that older individuals must cope with are also outlined. The current therapeutic approaches most widely used with older clients, such as reality orientation, reminiscing groups, and remotivation therapy, are described.

Family therapy assumes a systems approach to counseling, and stresses the overall interpersonal context in which the client's problems are occurring. Chapter Fifteen, "Counseling Couples and Families," provides a historical framework for viewing the development of marriage and family counseling and outlines the central concepts of family systems theory. The author presents an overview of the different schools of family therapy and stresses the importance of maintaining an integrative and eclectic approach to understanding and learning from these approaches. Core issues that often emerge in family counseling, such as boundary problems, low self-esteem, and inappropriate family hierarchies, are described. Stages in marriage and family counseling are outlined, with descriptions of appropriate interventions for each particular level.

Chapter Sixteen, "Counseling Gay and Lesbian Clients," surveys a field of growing importance to counselors. Issues involving gay individuals are becoming more visible in our society. While clients who happen to be gay should be viewed as individuals first and as gay persons second, the importance for the counselor of maintaining a sensitivity to the special concerns of gay clients is stressed. Self-identity, self-esteem, and relationship concerns may take on an enhanced intensity with gay clients, owing to the significant social, psychological, and interpersonal stresses they may experience. The author also provides an appendix of resources and organizations for gay individuals and for counselors wishing more information on gay-related issues.

Most counselors, regardless of their particular work setting or client population, will need to confront the issue of effective multicultural counseling. Chapter Seventeen, "Counseling Visible Racial/Ethnic Group Men and Women," addresses these concerns and provides a framework for understanding the economic and social environments in which many multicultural issues arise. Barriers to effective multicultural counseling are discussed within their historical context, and the current state of multicultural counseling within the United States is surveyed. The authors stress the importance of appropriate models of counselor education that provide training that is free from cultural stereotypes and biases. Guidelines for developing effective multicultural counseling skills are presented, including the necessity of each professional counselor's examining his or her own prejudices and assumptions about multicultural clients and about the counseling process itself.

Finally, this section continues with Chapter Eighteen, "Counseling Clients with Disabilities," in which an overview of both the goals and the major interventions for working with disabled clients is discussed. Physical and emotional factors in understanding disability are reviewed, with emphasis on helping clients to improve the overall quality of life and to come to terms with the conditions of their particular disability. The professional qualifications and necessary training for counselors wishing to pursue rehabilitation as a career choice are described.

13-

Counseling Children and Adolescents

LARRY GOLDEN, PH.D.
The University of Texas at San Antonio
San Antonio, Texas

ARDIS SHERWOOD, GRADUATE ASSISTANT
Portland State University
Portland, Oregon

COUNSELING APPROACHES AND THERAPEUTIC interventions for children and adolescents have historically been grounded on research findings that are developed with adult populations, and the adult counseling theories, procedures, and techniques that emanate from these studies are traditionally adapted and shaped to address childhood and adolescent mental health issues (Kazdin, 1989; Tuma, 1989). The instigation of theory and research on childhood dysfunction and the influence of developmental stages on the experience of childhood have been seriously neglected despite the fact that idiosyncratic issues surface in the treatment of children and adolescents owing to (1) the unique characteristics of their problems; (2) changes over the course of their development; (3) the mechanisms in which these problems are identified; and (4) the ways in which these problems are affected by home and school environments (Kazdin, 1988). The distinc-

275

tive themes that are associated with childhood and adolescent problem behaviors and mental health issues suggest that specific counseling strategies be developed for these populations.

CHILDHOOD AND ADOLESCENT COUNSELING CONSIDERATIONS

Developmental Concerns for Counselors

There is a fundamental difference in counseling strategies that are suitable for young children and adolescents and techniques that are appropriate for the adult population (Brandell, 1988; Saxe, Cross, & Silverman, 1988). The developmental processes of memory, language, conditional thinking, categorization abilities, and perception of rules determine the effectiveness, ineffectiveness, and even the harmful repercussions of certain counseling strategies. A thorough understanding of the developmental processes will facilitate anticipatory interventions and help the counselor predict the success of an intervention at a particular developmental stage. In addition, children are unique individuals who manifest a diversified range of dissimilar behavioral histories, temperamental traits, cognitive skills, and social and emotional capacities (Chess, 1988; Kendall, Lerner, & Craighead, 1984). The counselor should be aware of the individual child's developmental history, understand the child's personal capacity for development, be knowledgeable about the probability of future developmental events (Brandell, 1988; Kendall, Lerner, & Craighead, 1984), and thoroughly comprehend the child's cultural background.

Children process experiences dissimilarly at different points of their development because of the changes involved in the physical, cognitive, social, and emotional processes of normal development. For example, children in the preoperational stages of development will probably not be capable of using abstract rules for self-control (Kendall, Lerner, & Craighead, 1984), and when young children have not yet completely mastered language skills and have not acquired secondary thinking processes, an intervention based on verbalized communication is rarely successful (Brandell, 1988). Some appropriate therapeutic approaches for young children are relationship therapy (Kazdin et al., 1989; Moustakas, 1959), play therapy used alone or in combination with talking therapy, rewarding desirable behaviors, modeling, painting, drawing, therapeutic games, and rehearsing activities with children. Some therapeutic aids include dolls, puppets, stories, and fairy tales (Brandell, 1988; Kazdin, 1988; Lubetski, 1989).

Personality differentiation is less advanced in childhood than it is in adolescence and adulthood. Younger children have not yet developed an autonomous concept of self and lack an adequate frame of reference regarding reality, possibility, and value. They do not have the benefit of tempering the impact of current events with the moderating influence of past experiences, and tend to overexaggerate the importance of occurrences. Therefore, children can have more difficulty coping with stressful events than adolescents and adults. In addition, children's dependency on adults can make them highly vulnerable to experiences of rejection, disappointment, and failure (Coleman, Butcher, & Carson, 1984).

Identification of Problems and Referral to Counseling

The problem behaviors of childhood and adolescence can vary greatly over the typical course of development, and can emerge as part of the normal development process (e.g., the "terrible twos" or the "identity crisis" of adolescence). Children and adolescents commonly manifest behaviors that characterize maladjustment and emotional disturbance in adults, such as lying, destructiveness, excessive fears, hyperactivity, and fighting. Adults often find these behaviors disturbing, and may refer children for treatment because they do not realize that during the normal developmental cycle, these behaviors tend to disappear without any special intervention (Kazdin, 1988).

Children are referred to counseling for many diversified reasons. They may be victims of sexual or physical abuse, or may be manifesting dysfunctional reactions to stressful events in the home such as divorce and maladaptive parenting practices. Children often develop unwholesome adjustment behaviors in response to victimization, and parents may conceal factors that are related to abuse and neglect. Counselors should be aware that studies have shown that parental perception of dysfunctional behavior is significantly related to their own symptoms of psychopathology, and children are more frequently referred for treatment by parents who are experiencing marital dissension, low self-esteem, negative social contact, anxiety, depression, and excessive stress in the home or other environments (Kazdin, 1988, 1989).

Because children are generally referred to counseling by other persons, (e.g., parents and teachers), they usually do not see themselves as having a problem (Brandell, 1988). Children and young adolescents often perceive any problems as externally derived, and it is not until late adolescence that young people begin to understand that their own behavior might be a result of internal factors, such as their own thoughts and emotions (Kazdin, 1988). Adolescents may balk at the idea of counseling because they may not see any value or reason for this type of interaction.

The teenager's struggle for autonomy and ubiquitous "off my back" messages to adults have direct ramifications for counselors. Counselors (with the exception of peer helpers) may be seen by adolescents as their parents' "hired guns." Further, adolescents tend to be action oriented, and they may not readily respond to a "talking cure." Teens are responsive to interventions that recognize their overriding need for autonomy. It might be necessary for initial counseling strategies to focus on establishing a value for the counseling process, facilitating a motivation for the behavior change, and maintaining the adolescent in therapy. The active involvement of young people in treatment decisions can influence their motivation for treatment and increase their positive evaluation of the counseling process (Kazdin, 1988).

Focus of Treatment

Parent, family, and school factors all contribute to the functioning of children and adolescents, and childhood maladaptive behavior is not easily isolated from parental dysfunction and family action patterns (Kazdin, 1989). A fundamental counseling question involves the appropriate focus of diagnosis, assessment, and treatment. Should counseling interventions be directed solely toward the child or adolescent, the parents, the family, community influences, or should therapy incorporate all domains into the counseling process? This chapter will discuss individual counseling strategies that are especially useful with childhood and adolescent populations, considerations for adolescent group counseling, and a systems approach to counseling.

COUNSELING STRATEGIES FOR CHILDREN AND ADOLESCENTS

Individual Counseling Approaches for Children

Younger children experience more anxiety than older children (Kendall, Lerner, & Craighead, 1984). They are fundamentally dependent upon adults, and often undergo a sense of powerlessness when they are faced with new, unpredictable events (e.g., going to the hospital, starting school, birth of a sibling) and real or imaginary frightening experiences (e.g., fear of becoming lost or being abandoned by their parents, parental conflicts, divorce, abuse). Although their cognitive structures are not yet advanced enough to deal with the complex contingencies of life, children still seek to make sense of their worlds (Dibrell & Yamamoto, 1988).

Play therapy, nurture work, and behavior modification techniques are generally the best approaches for young children. Small children are "naturals" as clients. They tend to be more amenable to adult influences, they have an abiding faith that adults want to help them, and, consequently, they do not offer major resistance to counseling. Because of this intrinsic dependency of children on adults, the counselor should strive to develop an egalitarian counselor-to-child relationship. Counselors can convey their respect and acceptance of children by (1) attentively listening to the child's perspective of his or her world; (2) attributing importance to the child's viewpoint; (3) encouraging and rewarding his or her efforts; and (4) offering reassurance when the child experiences frustration or failure (Dibrell & Yamamoto, 1988).

Play Therapy

The healing power of play therapy resides in the relationship between child and counselor. According to Moustakas (1959), "The alive relationship between the therapist and the child is the essential dimension, perhaps the only significant reality, in the therapeutic process and in all interhuman growth" (p. xiii). Play therapy helps children express feelings and the content of their powerful imaginations through verbal and nonverbal means; it provides a language that serves as a springboard for communication.

Virginia Axline, a "founding mother" of play therapy, readily acknowledged Carl Rogers' contribution to play therapy. Axline's philosophy and methodology represent a translation of person-centered counseling into the language of childhood. Axline described the process as follows:

> The play-therapy room is good growing ground. In the security of this room where the **child** is the most important person, where he is in command of the situation and of himself, where no one tells him what to do, no one criticizes what he does, no one nags, or suggests, or goads him on, or pries into his private world, he suddenly feels that **here** he can unfold his wings; he can look squarely at himself, for he is accepted completely; he can test out his ideas; he can express himself fully, for this is his world, and he no longer has to compete with such other forces as adult authority or rival contemporaries or situations where he is a human pawn between bickering parents, or where he is the butt of someone else's frustrations and aggressions. He is an individual in his own right. He is treated with dignity and respect. He can say anything that he feels like saying—and he is accepted completely. He can hate and he can love and he can be as indifferent as the Great Stone Face and he is still accepted completely. He can be as fast as a whirlwind or as slow as molasses in January and he is neither restrained nor hurried. It is a unique experience for a child suddenly to find adult suggestions, mandates, rebukes, restraints, criticisms, disapprovals, support, intrusions gone. They are all replaced by complete acceptance and permissiveness to be himself. (Axline, 1947, pp. 16–17)

PROCEDURES Axline (1969) outlined the following basic principles of play therapy. The therapist:

1. Develops a warm relationship with the child.
2. Unconditionally accepts the child.
3. Establishes an atmosphere of permissiveness in which the child is completely free to express feelings.
4. Reflects the feelings the child is expressing.
5. Maintains respect for the child's ability to solve his or her own problems. The child is responsible for change.
6. Does not direct the child's actions or conversation. The child leads; the therapist follows.
7. Does not hurry the child. Therapy is a gradual process.
8. Initiates only those limits that are needed to anchor the therapy to reality. Limits help the child feel safe. The child realizes that if behavior or feelings get out of hand, the therapist will help the child reestablish control (Van Evra, 1983).

The playroom should be equipped with a variety of expressive materials: modeling clay and finger paints encourage creativity; dolls and puppets allow the child to set the stage for family interactions; and toy guns and knives enable the child to act out aggressive feelings. The child's play may emerge from actual situations or may represent a fantasy of the child.

INDICATIONS AND LIMITATIONS Play therapy is especially useful with withdrawn children who turn negative affect inward (as opposed to acting out). These children's unexpressed and unresolved feelings may be manifested as dysfunctional symptoms (e.g., bedwetting, nightmares, and school failure).

Play therapy is not without its "blind spots." In some cases, through a process called "triangulation," children misbehave in order to preserve a conflicted parental relationship. The child's symptoms enable the parents to avoid painful communication with each other. With its intense focus on the therapist–child relationship, such family dynamics may be ignored. Therefore, the play therapist must be alert to the signs of a troubled marriage. The effective counselor will use play therapy in tandem with family interventions and consultation with school personnel (Golden & Capuzzi, 1986; Keith, Westman, & Whitaker, 1989).

Behavior Modification
The basic assumptions of behavior modification are relatively simple (Rimm & Masters, 1979).

1. The behavioral counselor treats the behavioral manifestations of a psychological disorder. This is not to say that internal motives do not exist. Rather, the core of the psyche is a difficult, and in some cases forbidden, terrain, which may or may not yield, even after years of psychoanalysis. Behavioral counseling is more efficient.

2. "Here and now" behavior and situations that maintain problematic behaviors are the domain of the behavioral counselor. Historical information is useful only as it relates to the current problem behaviors. Further, changes in internal psychological states do not necessarily result in improved functioning.

3. Maladaptive behaviors are acquired through the same principles of learning as are normal behaviors. For example, research has shown that aggressive behaviors can be learned through observation of an adult model (Bandura, Ross, & Ross, 1963). Similarly, we know that more appropriate social behaviors (e.g., social skills) are also learned through modeling.

4. The goal of therapy is the achievement of measurable target behaviors. This permits an ongoing assessment of progress.

5. Behavior that is rewarded will be repeated. Therefore, it is important to find out what the child experiences as rewarding and whether the reward is readily available.

PROCEDURES Control of environmental contingencies is essential. It is not surprising, therefore, that behavior modification works best with "captive" populations (e.g., prison inmates, patients committed to psychiatric wards, and children in public schools). For example, a third-grader could be rewarded with a piece of sugarless candy for staying in his or her seat during a 30-minute reading group. This intervention would fail if the child (1) was free to quit coming to school; (2) was satiated with sugarless candy; (3) did not like sugarless candy. The ultimate goal, after gradually withdrawing the reward, is for the targeted or desired behavior to become habitual and environmentally reinforced.

INDICATIONS AND LIMITATIONS Behavior modification is especially effective with younger children, and can even be used with infants. Behavioral techniques have been used to reduce tantrums (Etzel & Gewirtz, 1967) and toilet train very young children (Foxx & Azrin, 1973). Behavior modification is more difficult with adolescents because reinforcers can get expensive. A six-year-old will behave to earn a "happy face" sticker; a sixteen-year-old may insist on a pickup truck with four-wheel drive! Moreover, teenagers are developmentally ready to benefit from a combination of cognitive and behavioral interventions.

Many people object to behavior modification because they view reinforcement of desirable behavior as nothing more than bribery. Parents do not want to "pay" their children to do their homework, brush their teeth, or use common courtesy. They want their children to be motivated by a sense of altruism, consideration, and responsibility. In reality, parents are almost always engaged in behavior modification. When parents yell at children or spank them, they are trying to convince them that a particular unwanted behavior has a high price. When parents ignore an "obnoxious" behavior, they are attempting to extinguish the recurrence of that activity. When parents praise, they are telling their children that they want them to maintain a certain behavior. Unfortunately, much of this behavior modification is unplanned and is not successful because the interventions are inconsistent. Worse yet, it can rely heavily on punishment strategies. Punishment is highly effective in changing behavior, but it has an unfortunate side effect. Punishment generates anger. Behavior modification is most appropriate when it is used as a positive method to systematically teach good habits to children who are not yet cognitively ready for internal forms of motivation.

Perhaps because it is so powerful, issue has been taken with the ethics of using behavior modification at all. What if the laws that govern human behavior were to fall into the hands of unscrupulous political leaders who would use them for social control? For what comfort it may be, human beings have proven themselves to be very, very difficult to control and George Orwell's *1984* has come and gone.

Individual Counseling Approaches for Adolescents

Adolescents experience profound physical changes, rapid growth in cognitive ability, a terrible hunger for peer approval, a bruising struggle for autonomy, and an onslaught of psychosocial stressers. Today's teenagers not only have to deal with the common developmental issues of adolescence (e.g., fear of negative evaluation, fights with friends, rejection by same-sex or opposite-sex friends, conflicts with adults, concerns about the future [Stark et al., 1989] and attachment and autonomy related issues, such as separation from family, leaving home, and getting a job [Moore, 1987]), but they also face many new and unprecedented issues of modern adolescence, such as family, national, and world instability and the threat of AIDS. In addition, our changing society has produced options for adolescents that perhaps give them choices that transcend their experiential capabilities. Contemporary adolescents must make decisions about sexual intercourse, contraception, abortion, family planning, and alcohol and drug use (Bauman & Riche, 1986). Furthermore, these developing individuals are subject to biological drives that have an impact on emotional, cognitive, and behavioral development (Moore, 1987). For example, girls who begin puberty early are more likely to become sexually active and use drugs (Magnusson, Stattin, & Allen, 1985), and late puberty for boys increases the likelihood of delinquency and school problems (Irwin & Millstein, 1986; Simmons, 1987).

Most teenagers are convinced that adults (especially parents) cannot comprehend their experiences, and they are afraid to expose their internal fears to people who are unable to understand their problems. Consequently, adolescents have a tendency to become (1) secretive because they fear ridicule; (2) irritable because they resent interference from adults who do not understand them; (3) boastful because they want to hide their insecurities; (4) depressed because nothing seems to work out according to their expectations; (5) rebellious because parents and schools seem to have interfering rules for everything; (6) defiant because this behavior makes their parents leave them alone (behavior modification); and (7) devious because direct confrontation can be too painful (Bauman & Riche, 1986).

Freud (1917) saw the struggle to establish independence from parents as central to the development of a strong ego. It was expected that in separating themselves, adolescents would resort to rebellion and outright hostility. Although teenagers may actively seek autonomy and independence, they can be ambivalent about leaving the safety of the nest for the wild world beyond, and may alternately express conflicting messages, "Let me go!" "Don't push me out!" Small wonder that parent eagles destroy the nest shortly after their fledglings take flight for the first time.

During adolescence, cognitive thinking processes become more flexible and abstract. Adolescents have the individual capacity to consider logically all the possibilities of a situation in order to solve a problem. They can immerse themselves "further and further into a topic, driven by the ability to generate the next hypothetical 'what if' " (Garbarino, 1985, p. 154). Commonly, this exhaustive exploration of a topic is self-directed; hence, the adolescent's typical self-consciousness and attention to personal appearance. David Elkind (1967) uses the term "imaginary audience" to portray teenagers as actors who believe they are constantly on stage. For the thirteen-year-old, leaving the classroom to go to the restroom can be a traumatic episode.

Cognitive Counseling

Albert Ellis is due credit for his ardent promotion of the cognitive approach that he dubbed rational emotive therapy (RET) (Beck &

Weishaar, 1989). Today, counselors have come to see the advantages of working with the conscious human mind, and cognitive psychology is a fertile field of scientific investigation.

The cognitive counselor assumes that feelings and behavior are mediated by thoughts (Brown & Prout, 1983). Unless an individual is actively psychotic (e.g., schizophrenic), conscious thoughts are accessible and malleable. Conversely, emotions may be buried and difficult to surface, and observable behaviors may be subject to forces in the environment that are beyond the control of the individual.

The cognitive counselor regards emotional disturbance and disordered behavior as the consequence of disturbed thinking. People who are psychologically disturbed will introduce a bias into the way they process information. According to Beck and Weishaar (1989), these cognitive distortions may take many forms.

1. *Arbitrary inference.* The individual develops and internalizes a belief lacking sufficient evidence to support his or her conclusion and will adhere to this belief, even when pragmatic data contradict the belief. Arbitrary interference is illustrated by the student who has previously experienced success in school, fails an exam, and concludes, "I am dumb. I'll never get anywhere."

2. *Selective abstraction.* A person uses a detail taken out of context to conceptualize an entire situation or relationship. For example, a young man feels devalued and becomes excessively jealous when he sees his girlfriend talking to another boy.

3. *Overgeneralization.* A person uses an isolated incident to develop a rule and then applies the rule to unrelated situations. An example is a youngster who enjoys an alcoholic drink at a party without ill effects, and then starts drinking immoderately in a variety of settings.

4. *Magnification and minimization.* The individual sees something as far more significant or insignificant than it actually is. An illustration of this phenomenon is a teenager who "catastrophizes", "I'll die if I don't get a date for the prom." Another example is an adolescent who dismisses the dangers of drunk driving as being greatly exaggerated. In fact, some adolescents act out of a false sense of indestructibility that leads to dangerous risk-taking behaviors (Elkind, 1979).

5. *Personalization.* Individuals attribute external events to themselves without evidence that logically supports a causal connection. For

example, a student waves to a friend in the hall, but her friend is lost in thought and does not respond. The student concludes, "I must have done something to make her mad at me."

6. *Dichotomous thinking.* A person polarizes experiences at one of two extreme positions. It's all or nothing! An example is a high school student who says, "If I don't get accepted at an Ivy League school, I would just as soon not go to college at all."

The cognitive counselor is interested in an "attitude shift," which changes the way the client thinks about a problem. As individuals move from the "concrete egocentrism" of middle childhood into adolescence, they are no longer restricted by the world of things (Russo, 1986). They can reflect on possibilities not yet experienced and project themselves into the future, and into the experience of other people. Behavior and emotion can be anticipated and controlled.

PROCEDURES   The counselor's job is to move the disturbed adolescent client from a self-defeating egocentric view of the world to an emphatic "sociocentric" viewpoint (Russo, 1986). Beck and Weishaar (1989) describe the therapeutic interventions that make this "attitude shift" possible.

1. *Collaborative empiricism.* The counselor and the client work as a team. They are coinvestigators, examining the evidence that would support or reject any assumption. For example, the counselor–client team might test the logic behind the assumption that, no matter how hard he or she tries, the client will not be able to improve his or her grades in algebra.

2. *Socratic dialogue.* This refers to a mode of inquiry. The counselor asks questions in order to help the client (a) clarify or define problems; (b) identify thoughts, images, and assumptions; (c) examine the meaning of events, and (d) assess the consequences of maintaining maladaptive thoughts and behaviors. The following are examples of appropriate questions. "How would you account for your father's anger with you?" "Describe exactly what happens when you ask a girl to go out with you." "Is your strategy for making friends working for you?"

3. *Guided discovery.* The counselor helps the client design new experiences or behavioral experiments that lead to new perspectives and skills. The counselor does not exhort or cajole the client to adopt a new set of beliefs. Rather, the counselor encourages the client in obtaining a more realistic perspective through the use of information. The counselor might invite the client to ask the algebra teacher for additional assistance outside the classroom. The client might also be asked to visualize this situation, and to imagine what the teacher might think or feel when the client asked for help.

There are other ways to engage adolescents at a cognitive level. For example, the adolescent's home and school environments should facilitate the opportunity to make choices in real life situations. Many adolescents have had very limited experience in problem solving, yet decision making is probably the most important cognitive task for adolescents (Schvaneveldt & Adams, 1983). Cognitive counselors can encourage youngsters to project themselves into the experience of others through psychodrama, storytelling, bibliotherapy, and videotaped scenarios (Russo, 1986).

Jay Haley describes a powerful cognitive-behavioral strategy in his book *Leaving Home: The Therapy of Disturbed Young People* (1980). Haley prompts teenage clients and their parents to redefine cognitively their perceptions of adolescent rebellion, and come to understand that the teenager is trying to become independent. Then Haley questions his teenage clients about their practical plans for leaving home, pointing out that many young people fail in the attempt because they are inadequately prepared.

For example, 15-year-old Cindy has tried to run away from home only to "crawl" back, unable to support herself.

COUNSELOR (to Cindy): "Cindy, the most important job you have to do is to realistically make plans for leaving home. What will you need to succeed? How can your parents help you get ready?"
The process of preparation for this crucial life task can be ego-enhancing for both parent and teenager (Haley, 1980).

INDICATIONS AND LIMITATIONS It is important to consider the child's level of cognitive development in order to select an appropriate intervention from the behavior to the cognitive approach continuum. Although there are cases in which cognitive counseling has been effective with small children, most young clients benefit from behavioral or affective approaches (Van Evra, 1983). Adolescents, on the other hand, simultaneously think and behave in a synthesized process, and cognitive and behavioral interventions are most effective when they are used at the same time. However, the cognitive organizational abilities of the adolescent client will quite likely determine how, if at all, new behavior will generalize beyond a specific treatment setting. As for affect, if teenagers can learn to think through a problem and then solve it successfully, they will feel better.

Group Counseling Approach for Adolescents

The group counseling approach is particularly suitable for adolescents because it provides a setting in which they can discover that their paradoxical involvements, emotions, and problems are not unique. The group experience provides a safe environment for adolescents to perceive and express their conflicting feelings; practice communication skills; safely experiment with reality; test their own limits; learn alternate appropriate behaviors and new skills by observational learning, modeling, behavior rehearsal, assertiveness training, and role playing; become more accepting of others; develop self-understanding and empathy toward others; reduce feelings of loneliness and isolation; and be instrumental in one another's growth (Corey & Corey, 1987; Thompson & Sherwood, 1989).

A major goal of group counseling is the development of a milieu of security and unconditional acceptance that will facilitate and support positive growth. Corey and Corey (1987) use these introductory words to convey this goal to adolescent group members.

> This is a place in which, we hope, you will come to feel free enough to say what you think and feel, without censoring or rehearsing. It is a place where you can reveal personal struggles, and find, with the help of others, a way of recognizing, understanding, and perhaps resolving certain problems. We hope a climate develops in which, because you feel that what you say is important and that you're respected for who you are, you will be able to discover the many selves within you. To a great degree, the value of the sessions depends on your level of commitment. If you merely show up and listen politely, you may leave disappointed. We hope that, as the sessions progress, you will think about what you want from this group and ask the group to help you get it. Our agenda will include anything you want to explore; there are no forbidden topics. We hope you will take risks here, saying and doing things you don't feel safe saying or doing in other social settings. In order to make many of the changes you wish to make, you'll have to take such risks. (pp. 287–288)

Although Corey and Corey (1987) give adolescent group members a great deal of freedom, they also advocate the formation of realistic limits and rules. They offer fundamental guidelines toward the establishment and orchestration of several types of adolescent groups. The following represent some essential counseling considerations for the leaders of a therapeutic adolescent group.

Sample Proposal for an Adolescent Group

GROUP TYPE The type and focus of the group should be clearly specified. For example, the therapeutic group for adolescents could be described as a personal-growth and self-exploration group for young people, ages 15 to 18. The counselor should inform potential participants that this group will not function as a therapy group designed to address the issues of young people who are severely disturbed, but will focus on the problems and concerns of the typical adolescent. The size of the group, duration, and meeting times should be determined prior to the formation of the group.

GOALS AND OBJECTIVES OF THE GROUP Group members will be invited to self-explore by examining their values, behaviors, and relationships with others; however, they will determine when and how much they will share. All participants will be expected to be active in the sessions, at least to the extent of sharing their reactions to the events within the group.

Each member will be assisted in developing specific, concrete personal goals. In addition, the following general goals will be promoted to provide direction for the group: (1) to develop an atmosphere of group trust that will facilitate honest sharing of feelings and attitudes, and to generalize this trust into everyday life; (2) to grow in self-acceptance and self-respect; (3) to clarify values and explore personal philosophies of life; (4) to become sensitive to the needs of others; (5) to become tolerant of others and accept and respect individual differences; (6) to learn to problem solve, make decisions, and accept the consequences of those decisions; (7) to increase the capacity to care for others; and (8) to learn specific ways of applying what is learned in the group to everyday experiences (Corey et al., 1988).

BASIC GROUND RULES FOR THE ADOLESCENT GROUP Members will be expected to attend all sessions, and to participate in these sessions by providing self-disclosure and feedback to other group members; maintain confidences of other group members; determine their own personal goals and the issues they are willing to explore; assist in the development of a group contract that states the changes desired by the group and the guidelines for the group process; not come to group meetings under the influence of drugs and/or alcohol; and obtain written permission from their parent(s) or guardian to participate in the group.

POSSIBLE TOPICS FOR GROUP EXPLORATION The topics explored in adolescent groups should be both structured and flexible. In the self-exploration group, the issues discussed by the group members should be limited to certain themes that are of concern to most young people. Group members will be allowed to choose which subjects are most meaningful to them. The format, however, should remain flexible because members may spontaneously introduce critical problems that are not related to the scheduled theme but are of immediate importance to the members of the group (e.g., suicide of a friend). Some suggested general themes for discussion are (1) how to cope with feelings of depression, guilt, anxiety, anger, rejection, loneliness, etc.; (2) how to manage conflicts related to school, parents, friends, etc.; (3) definitions of sex roles; (4) issues related to love, sex, and intimacy; (5) the development of a strong self-identity; and (6) the struggle toward autonomy.

Counselor Qualifications

According to Corey and Corey (1987), counselors who plan to do group work with adolescents and children not only should achieve the knowledge competencies, skill competencies, and suggested supervised experience for group leadership requirements that are outlined by the Association for Specialists in Group Work (ASGW), a division of the American Association for Counseling and Development, but also they should manifest the following important professional qualifications.

1. The counselor should have a thorough knowledge and understanding of the developmental tasks and stages of the targeted age group.

2. The counselor should be grounded in the application of counseling skills to group work.

3. The counselor should have obtained supervised training in working with minors in groups prior to leading a group alone.

4. The counselor should maintain a progressive knowledge of the contemporary literature and research that pertains to counseling children and adolescents.

A Systems Strategy

Experienced counselors are aware of the importance of working closely with the family when a child exhibits behavior problems. The family is in a powerful position to support or sabotage the best efforts of counselors and teachers who are attempting to help the child (Palmo et al., 1984). Family therapy is a method that focuses on the family in an attempt to help solve a child's behavior problems. (The reader is referred to another chapter in this book that is devoted to couples and family therapy.) Brief family consultation is still another way to incorporate the home and school milieu in the effort to help solve a child's behavior problems. Brief family consultation is a short-term strategy that is ideally suited to a school or agency setting where there are limitations on time. The skills involved draw upon those that are taught in most counselor education programs: active listening, behavior modification, and interpersonal communication.

Brief Family Consultation

Brief family consultation, in common with family therapy, is based on systems theory. Systems theorists assume that the presenting problem of the client is an interactive concern for all family members. Individual problems are seen as relationship problems. If a child is referred for counseling, it is assumed that he or she is the family symptom bearer, that all members of the family share some responsibility for maintaining psychopathology, and that the family must be the focus of treatment (Keith, Westman, & Whitaker, 1989). Families, like most systems, are organized along hierarchical lines and function according to definite rules. If one member of the family receives counseling, and changes, the delicate balance of roles and rules of the family may be upset. Other family members may become anxious and attempt to undermine the counseling. Thus, it is important to include the family in all therapy sessions.

PROCEDURES A functional family can make rapid gains in counseling, but a dysfunctional family may bog down in rigidly fixed patterns of communication and may resist the counselor's attempts at change. Therefore, a quick method of assessing the family is important to the success of a short-term strategy.

When evaluating the capacity of a particular family to respond to a brief intervention, the counselor can expect the functional family to achieve high scores on each of the following criteria: parental resources, absence of chronicity, communication between family members, parental authority, and rapport with professional helpers (Golden, 1988; Golden & Capuzzi, 1986).

1. *Parental resources.* Do these parents have the capability to provide for their child's basic need for food, shelter, and care? A stable marriage, an extended family, and gainful employment are resources that work in favor of the counselor's attempt to bring a child's misbehavior under control. On the other hand, immature, single parents have fewer resources at their disposal, and families that have a history of extreme poverty or alcoholism bring very limited resources to the task of managing childhood behavior problems.

2. *Absence of Chronicity.* An acute problem with an identifiable psychosocial stresser presents an opportunity for behavior management, but a chronic problem indicates that the family may need long-term therapy. A parent's response, "She's always been a difficult child," suggests a less favorable prognosis than, "His grades have gone downhill since October. That's when I lost my job."

3. *Communication between family members.* Can family members communicate well enough to solve problems? According to Satir (1972), there is a normal tendency to close down communication during periods of distress. In dysfunctional families, closed communication is the rule, not the exception. This closed system is maintained by yelling, blaming, sarcasm, or, more ominously, silence.

The following interaction illustrates a closed, defensive posture:

COUNSELOR (to Kristi): Tell your parents how much spelling homework you will be willing to do next week to earn television privileges.

FATHER: (Angrily interrupts) She would have to change her entire attitude, to say nothing of her personality.

MOTHER: It seems to me that the teacher is the one who needs a change of attitude. It is ridiculous to expect a child to do hours of homework after being in school all day.

With his sarcastic outburst, Father ensures that a meaningful dialogue with Kristi will be avoided. Mother reinforces her daughter's dependency by speaking on her behalf against the teacher. Her intervention also serves to deflect a discussion of Kristi's problems.

4. *Parental authority.* Are parents effective in asserting authority? Parents in functional families hold an "executive" position within the family organization. In dysfunctional families, parents surrender authority in the hope that conflict with a child can be avoided. Children from such families are often out of control.

5. *Rapport with professional helpers.* Can parents and professionals work together as a team? Are the child's teachers responsive to parents? Do parents return phone calls? Are they punctual for conferences? Central to the issue is a commitment to be persistent in the attempt to accomplish the goals of the treatment plan. The functional family does its "homework."

An accurate assessment of family functioning helps the counselor decide whether a short-term or a long-term intervention strategy is appropriate for a given family. A brief family consultation may be appropriate for a misbehaving child in a functional family, while a child from a dysfunctional family may benefit from a more family therapeutic approach. A family that exhibits seriously disordered behavior, such as alcoholism, child abuse, psychosis, or suicide, may require a crisis intervention and, perhaps, residential treatment for the disturbed family member.

Brief family consultation with a functional family is an intervention that is especially appropriate for the school counselor. The consultation process requires three to five face-to-face, 30 to 45 minute family conferences. This process is best described by an example of what the counselor might say to the parents in the initial interview. In this case, the child presents a problem of failing to complete homework assignments.

COUNSELOR: I am interested in working with you for a short period of time to help you get Mike to complete his homework every day. I think you can manage this situation with only a little help from me. There is cause for optimism. With the exception of homework, Mike earns average grades and is well behaved. As parents, you have shown that you want to cooperate with Mike's teachers to get this problem solved. For my part, I'll coordinate a team effort to include you, Mike's teachers, and Mike himself, if he is willing. If he is not, we are still going to try to change his behavior.

If the child's problems are school-related, teachers are included in the behavioral plan. Typically, the task of the teacher is to provide the parent with a daily report of the child's behavior.

The family (and, perhaps, the teacher) will want to know about time commitment. When a brief consultation exceeds five family conferences without a resolution of the problem, another option, such as referral for family therapy, is necessary. Note that the contacts with the family are called "conferences," not "sessions," because of the therapeutic associations of the latter term. Likewise, the term "consultation" serves to emphasize that the family does not need, nor will it receive, "therapy."

According to Haley (1980), parents must agree on three issues if they are to manage their child's behavior: (1) the specific behaviors that are desired from the child; (2) the mechanism by which the parents will know if their child has behaved in the desired way; and (3) the consequences for behavior or misbehavior. If marital discord surfaces, parents should be encouraged to work toward agreement for the good of the child, and deal with their marital problems at some later time.

Haley (1980) emphasizes the importance of putting parents in charge of managing the child's behavior problem. The distressed child is making a plea, albeit indirect, for parental control. The counselor should encourage the parents to take control of the resources that could serve as reinforcers. For example, an adolescent who is "independently wealthy," sporting a big allowance and a room full of electronic equipment, is in a position to ignore his or her parents' demand for behavior change. In this case, the child's allowance should be reduced to zero. He or she can earn money by behaving responsibly.

Family members may shut down communications in response to stressers, such as those caused by a child's misbehavior. Unfortunately, it is precisely during a stressful episode that open communication is most important. A gentle and respectful application of basic, active listening skills (e.g., paraphrasing, reflection) will usually facilitate communication among family members.

Many of the best-laid behavioral plans are defeated by ambivalence. In any brief strategy, the motto must be, "Go for it !" Continuation of problematic behavior, even in an otherwise competent child, may result in a negative and habitually dysfunctional style of coping with stress.

INDICATIONS AND LIMITATIONS A systems intervention can have great advantages over individual counseling. After all, children live with their families, not with their counselors. However, there are circumstances when an individual approach would be desirable. If the family system is highly maladaptive or destructive, the counselor may need to help the child develop sufficient self-worth and enough self-reliant behavior to function independently.

A weakness of the systems approach is that the process is crippled if a key family member refuses to participate. Another limitation is that an exclusive focus on family relationships may result in the neglect of the psychodynamics of individual family members.

THE CASE OF ANDREW

Andrew K., a third grader, was referred to the Parent Consultation Center[1] by his school guidance counselor. The center offers consultations on childhood behavior problems. Families are seen for a maximum of five conferences.

Andrew and his mother, a single parent, attended the first conference. The presenting problem was that Andrew was "hyper." His teachers complained that he would not remain seated in class, he

---

[1]The Parent Consultation Center is a collaborative project of the Northside Independent School District in San Antonio, Texas, and the University of Texas at San Antonio. The pilot project was founded by a grant from the American Association for Counseling and Development Foundation.

poked, tripped, and teased the other children, and he failed to complete assigned work. Mrs. K. also reported behavior problems at home. For example, Andrew had to be constantly "nagged" to finish the morning routine of getting dressed, brushing his teeth, eating breakfast, etc. If his mother pushed him too hard, Andrew would "throw a fit." Andrew spent every third weekend with his father, and Mrs. K. said that Andrew's behavioral problems were more extreme after these visitations. She also reported that Andrew wet the bed following his weekends with his father.

Prior to the divorce, which was finalized the summer before Andrew started third grade, there had only been occasional teacher complaints about behavior problems.

The consultant asked if there were any activities that held Andrew's attention for longer than 30 minutes. Mrs. K. said that Andrew could stay riveted on Nintendo games for hours, he was an alert soccer player, and he could concentrate for extended periods of time when he drew pictures of dinosaurs. Apparently, Andrew's hyperactivity was selective.

It was agreed that on-task, in-seat behavior during language arts would be targeted. By the second conference, Mrs. K. had asked for and was getting daily written reports from Andrew's language arts teacher. For each 15-minute period that Andrew stayed in his seat and remained on-task, the teacher affixed a star to a chart that Andrew kept at his desk. At home, the stars were redeemed for a variety of prizes chosen by Andrew—a trip to the zoo, pizza, Nintendo playing time, etc.

By the third conference, there had been a dramatic improvement. The fourth conference followed a weekend visitation with Mr. K., and the "hyper" behavior returned full force. Within a day, however, Andrew was back on track. At the fifth and final conference, Mrs. K. and Andrew proudly displayed a string of star-laden charts from the language arts teacher.

The bed wetting, however, was getting worse. Mrs. K. was convinced that the tension aroused by Andrew's visitations with Mr. K. was to blame. She said that Andrew's father wanted to punish her, and that he used Andrew as a tool for his revenge. She felt that Andrew might be better off if he didn't see his father at all.

In an individual interview, Andrew said that he felt that both parents said "mean" things about the other, and he felt "torn in two pieces." The consultant explained to Mrs. K. that her son was paying a very high price for this ongoing conflict, and made a referral for family counseling.

The family therapist saw the parents, both separately and together, for a total of 20 sessions. Occasionally, Andrew was included. The goals of family therapy were to (1) convince both parents that Andrew would suffer if they were unable to manage their mutual animosity; (2) create a path for direct communication, thereby preventing messages being sent through Andrew; and (3) encourage Andrew to accept the premise that he could love both his parents without being disloyal to either. As the parents were able to mediate their hostile impulses toward each other, the frequency of Andrew's bed wetting subsided.

The success of the brief consultation demonstrates the efficiency of behavioral techniques and a team approach. Parental sniping, however, threatened to sabotage the behavioral gains. The family therapist brought rationality to an otherwise chaotic family system, and the parents responded with alacrity to brief consultation and family therapy. Andrew was the direct beneficiary of this intervention because children require order and predictability in their lives.

With the benefit of hindsight, the K. family was evaluated on a scale of "1" (very weak) to "5" (very strong), using the criteria described in this chapter.

1. *Parental resources*. Although the parents were divorced, Mrs. K., the custodial parent, was financially secure. Mr. K.'s visitation rights were respected and he made regular child-support payments. However, the power of this family to resolve problems was diminished by the recent divorce. [Score = 3]
2. *Chronicity*. "Hyper" behavior and bed wetting were reported as only occasional problems prior to the third grade. [Score = 5]
3. *Communication between family members*. Andrew and his mother talked directly and honestly. Communication between the parents was "nonexistent." [Score = 2]
4. *Parental authority*. Mrs. K. was a decisive disciplinarian. Her fear that Andrew would someday choose his father over her, however, served to undermine her authority. [Score = 2]
5. *Rapport with professional helpers*. Mrs. K. was conscientious in follow-through on reports from Andrew's language arts teacher. Both parents were willing participants in family therapy. [Score = 5]

CONCLUSION

It is easier to list the problems that children do not have than it is to identify the myriad of emotional and behavioral maladies to which they are so vulnerable. Small children can be the victims of genetic and/or environmental deficits, and can learn to adapt to distressful experiences with dysfunctional behaviors. Unfortunately, the majority of emotionally and behaviorally disturbed children who need counseling interventions are unable to obtain assistance for themselves. Societal and parental attitudes and economic factors can, too often, determine which disturbed children receive help. When early problematic behaviors are untreated, the conduct that is difficult to tolerate in a child can become dangerous and uncontrollable in a teenager. The adolescent propensity for risk-taking, inability to delay gratification, hunger for and fear of autonomy, and need for peer approval can magnify and aggravate disordered behaviors.

A major concern for researchers and professionals who work with children is the identification of, and early intervention for, children who are at risk. Studies and counseling efforts are being directed toward identifying conditions in children's lives that elicit and/or maintain problem behaviors, and intervening before these children develop chronic and debilitating psychological problems.

Many of the potential dilemmas faced by modern young people are so serious that certain situations demand much more than personal counseling. For example, to prevent substance abuse or adolescent pregnancy, we must initiate massive educational programs. The counseling professional's role in these preventive approaches is to convey our knowledge about childhood and adolescent developmental processes and strategies for behavioral change to the educational effort.

In the final analysis, the counselor's major contribution, the *raison d'être* for the profession, is to enable personal growth in the context of a special relationship. It is a privilege to counsel with young people. Even when they are suffering from profound and dispiriting problems, they are far more amenable to change than are adults.

REFERENCES

Axline, V. (1947). *Play therapy.* Cambridge, MA: Houghton-Mifflin.

Axline, V. (1969). *Play therapy.* New York: Ballantine.

Bandura, A., Ross, D., & Ross, S. A. (1963). Vicarious reinforcement and imitative learning. *Journal of Abnormal and Social Psychology, 67,* 601–607.

Bauman, L., & Riche, R. (1986). *The nine most troublesome teenage problems and how to solve them.* New York: Ballantine.

Beck., A., & Weishaar, M. (1989). Cognitive therapy. In R. J. Corsini and D. Wedding (Eds.), *Current psychotherapies* (4th ed.). Itasca, IL: F. E. Peacock.

Brandell, J. (1988). Narrative and historical truth in child psychotherapy. *Psychoanalytic Psychology, 5*(3), 241–257.

Brown, D., & Prout, H. (1983). Behavioral approaches. In H. T. Prout and D. T. Brown (Eds.), *Counseling and psychotherapy with children and adolescents: Theory and practice for school and clinic settings.* Tampa, FL: Mariner.

Chess, S. (1988). Child and adolescent psychiatry come of age: A fifty year perspective. *Journal of the American Academy of Child and Adolescent Psychiatry, 27*(1), 1–7.

Coleman, J., Butcher, J., & Carson, R. (1984). *Abnormal psychology and modern life* (7th ed.). London: Scott, Foresman.

Corey, G., Corey, M., Callanan, P., & Russell, M. (1988). *Group techniques* (rev. ed.). Monterey, CA: Brooks/Cole.

Corey, M., & Corey, G. (1987). *Groups, process and practice* (3rd ed.). Monterey, CA: Brooks/Cole.

Dibrell, L., & Yamamoto, K. (1988). In their own words: Concerns of young children. *Child Psychiatry and Human Development, 19*(1), 14–25.

Elkind, D. (1967). Egocentricism in adolescence. *Child Development, 38,* 1025–1034.

Elkind, D. (1979). Imaginary audience behavior in children and adolescents. *Developmental Psychology, 15,* 38–44.

Etzel, B., & Gewirtz, J. (1967). Experimental modification of caretaker-maintained high rate operant crying 20-week-old infants: Extinction of crying with reinforcement of eye contact and smiling. *Journal of Experimental Child Psychology, 5,* 363–377.

Foxx, R. M., & Azrin, N. (1973). *Behavior research and therapy* (Vol. 2). New York: Pergamon.

Freud, S. (1917). Introductory lectures on psychoanalysis. In J. Strachey (Ed.), *The standard edition of the complete psychological works of Sigmund Freud* (Vol. 16). London: Hogarth.

Garbarino, J. (1985). *Adolescent development: An ecological perspective.* Columbus, OH: Merrill.

Golden, L. (1988). Quick assessment of family functioning. *The School Counselor, 3,* 179–184.

Golden, L., & Capuzzi, D. (1986). *Helping families help children: Family interventions with school-related problems.* Springfield, IL: Charles C Thomas.

Haley, J. (1980). *Leaving home: The therapy of disturbed young people.* New York: McGraw-Hill.

Irwin, C., & Millstein, S. (1986). Biopsychosocial correlates of risk-taking behaviors during adolescence. *Journal of Adolescent Health Care, 7,* 825–965.

Kazdin, A. (1988). *Child psychotherapy. Developing and identifying effective treatments.* New York: Pergamon.

Kazdin, A. (1989). Developmental psychopathology. Current research issues, and directions. *American Psychologist, 44*(2), 180–187.

Kazdin, A., Bass, D., Siegal, T., & Thomas, C. (1989). Cognitive-behavioral therapy and relationship therapy in the treatment of children referred for antisocial behavior. *Journal of Counseling and Clinical Psychology, 57*(4), 522–535.

Keith, D., Westman, J., & Whitaker, C. (1989). Contrasting child psychiatry and family therapy. *Child Psychiatry and Human Development, 19*(2), 87–97.

Kendall, P., Lerner, R., & Craighead, W. (1984). Human development and intervention in childhood psychopathology. *Child Development, 55*, 71–82.

Lubetski, M. (1989). The magic of fairy tales: Psychodrama and developmental perspectives. *Child Psychiatry and Human Development, 19*(4), 245–255.

Magnusson, D., Stattin, H., & Allen, V. (1985). Biological maturation and social development: A longitudinal study of some adjustment processes from mid-adolescence to adulthood. *Journal of Youth & Adolescence, 14,* 167–184.

Moore, D. (1987). Parent-adolescent separation: The construction of adulthood by late adolescents. *Developmental Psychology, 23*(2), 298–307.

Moustakas, C. (1959). *Psychotherapy with children.* New York: Harper Colophon.

Palmo, A., Lowry, L., Weldon, D., & Scioscia, T. (1984). Schools and family: Future perspectives for school counselors. *School Counselor, 31*, 272–278.

Rimm, D., & Masters, J. (1979). *Behavior therapy: Techniques and empirical findings* (2nd ed.). New York: Academic Press.

Russo, T. (1986). Cognitive counseling for adolescents. *Journal of Child and Adolescent Psychotherapy, 3,* 194–198.

Satir, V. (1972). *Peoplemaking.* Palo Alto, CA: Science and Behavior Books.

Saxe, L., Cross, T., & Silverman, N. (1988). Children's mental health: The gap between what we know and what we do. *American Psychologist, 43*(10), 800–812.

Schvaneveldt, J., & Adams, G. (1983). Adolescents and the decision-making process. *Theory into Practice, 22*, 98–104.

Simmons, R. (1987). Social transition and adolescent development. In C. E. Irwin (Ed.), *Adolescent health and social behavior: New directions in child development* (No. 37) (pp. 93–126). San Francisco: Jossey-Bass.

Stark, L., Spirito, A., Williams, C., & Guevremont, D. (1989). Common problems and coping strategies. I: Findings with normal adolescents. *Journal of Abnormal Child Psychology, 17*(2), 203–212.

Thompson, R., & Sherwood, A. (1989). Female, single and pregnant: Adolescent unwed mothers. In D. Capuzzi and D. Gross (Eds.), *Youth at risk: A resource for counselors, teachers, and parents.* Alexandria, VA: American Association for Counseling and Development.

Tuma, J. (1989). Mental health services for children. The state of the art. *American Psychologist, 44*(2), 188–199.

Van Evra, J. (1983). *Psychological disorders of children and adolescents.* Boston: Little, Brown.

14▪

Counseling the Older ▪ Adult

DOUGLAS R. GROSS, PH.D.
Arizona State University
Tempe, Arizona
DAVE CAPUZZI, PH.D., N.C.C.
Portland State University
Portland, Oregon

PAUL WAS IN THE final semester of his counseling program and was just beginning his internship. With the advice of his chairperson, Paul had purposely selected a clinic setting that served a population of people 65 years of age and older. He had been interested in working with older people and had taken two courses designed to provide him with information and experience in working with this population. His orientation to the setting had been completed two days ago; today he was to see his first client.

As he prepared for the session, Paul reviewed many of the things he had learned in his university course work. His office had been arranged so that the client would have both easy access and a comfortable chair. The time scheduled for the appointment had been arranged to accommodate both the client's concerns regarding transportation and an appointment with a physician in the same complex. An initial interview and an orientation meeting had been conducted by the intake person in the clinic and the schedule of fees had been explained and agreed upon by the client. Paul had reviewed the material collected during the intake interview and knew that the client was contemplating moving from her home into a residential setting. The case material revealed that the client did not accept this move. Paul's role was to explore with the client her feelings regarding the move and alternatives she might consider.

The client, a 72-year-old woman, arrived at the clinic a few minutes prior to the scheduled time. She was accompanied by her son and asked that he be allowed to join her in her session with Paul. Paul had not anticipated this but, wishing to make the client feel more comfortable, agreed. Paul's office was quickly rearranged to accommodate the son and the session began.

During the session, Paul discovered, based upon input from the son, that the client's health no longer allowed her to live alone. Arrangements were being made to move her to a full-care facility. The client was very disturbed about this move and insisted that the move was unnecessary. Further, she indicated that with more assistance from her son and his family she could remain in her home. Tears were obvious as she discussed how much she loved her home and its memories and her need to remain independent as long as possible. The session had reached a stalemate with both parties holding to their positions. Paul decided to talk with each of the parties separately, and the son said that he would wait outside.

In the sessions that followed, Paul discovered the fear and anger that the 72-year-old client was feeling. She was afraid that she was being placed in a facility to die and was angry that her son would do such a thing to her. She felt that she had always given him so much and cared for him when he needed her and now he was turning his back on her. She was determined to fight the move. During his session, the son explained that the move had been discussed at length, and he felt that his mother was accepting the fact that she could no longer remain alone. He was surprised by her current reaction and was at a loss as to what could be done to make the transition as positive as possible. He stated that he loved his mother and would do nothing to hurt her. The move was both supported and encouraged by her physician.

Paul brought the client and her son together and shared with them his perceptions of the situation. He encouraged them to talk with each other, as each had talked with him, and asked if they would be willing to return to the center to continue to discuss the situation. The client seemed somewhat hesitant but did agree to return the following Tuesday.

Paul sat for a short time after the client and her son left his office reviewing what had taken place. He decided that he needed to talk with his supervisor regarding the session and what he had done. He felt that perhaps he should have done more to bring resolution to the situation. He was able to see both sides of the issue, but his feelings were more strongly on the side of the client. He wanted her to be able to remain independent and felt that perhaps the son was not doing all he could to bring a more positive solution to the situation.

This scenario is one that is occurring more and more in various mental health settings. Counselors and mental health workers are being called upon to work with a clientele for which many are ill prepared. The clientele are the elderly who, owing to the lengthening of the life span, are increasing in numbers and will continue to have a profound impact on all areas of counseling and therapy. Today, there are more than 28 million people 65 years of age or older. Based on the projections of Siegel and Davidson (1984), this figure will climb to more than 35 million by the year 2000. This impact has been addressed by numerous authors (Sterns, Weis, & Perkins, 1984; Kart, Metress, & Metress, 1988; Gross, 1987, 1988; Myers & Shelton, 1987; Myers, 1988, 1989a; Gilkison & Drummond, 1988). According to Gross (1988), "The growing body of literature in the area of counseling and intervention strategies for the elderly addresses the emerging recognition that this population will continue to present itself in growing numbers to the counseling professional" (p. 3).

The purpose of this chapter is to present information relative to gerontologic counseling. This information will enable the reader to develop an understanding of the demographics of this population, the general and unique nature of the problems presented by this age group, research into counseling approaches that have proven to be effective in working with this population, and recommendations that should aid the counseling/mental health professional to serve this population more effectively.

DEMOGRAPHY OF AGING

To understand the demographics of the aging population in the United States, it is important for the reader to understand the numerical increase and its growing diversity in relation to age, sex, and marital status; geographic distribution; race and ethnicity; retirement, employment and income; and physical and mental health status. It is not the purpose of this chapter to present an in-depth analysis of these diverse factors. Each is presented to provide the reader with an overview, which should aid counselors and other mental health professionals to better understand this growing population that is and will continue to become an ongoing part of their caseloads.

The growing number of elderly people within the United States constitutes an escalating portion of our total population. According to Johnson and Stripling (1984), "Increasing longevity has raised the number of persons over age 65 from 3 million in 1900 to almost 23 million today" (p. 276). Projecting these figures into the twenty-first century, Atchley (1988) sees this population reaching 64.6 million by the year 2030. This number would represent approximately 21.2 percent of the total population and reflect a 9.1 percent increase over the 12.1 percent this population currently constitutes. Myers (1989a), in discussing these trends, states, "the proportion of older persons in the population was 1:25 in 1900, 1:9 in 1986, and is projected to be 1:5 in 2030" (p. 2).

A Composite Picture

Too often the aging population is viewed as a fairly homogeneous group of individuals. A closer look at variations in this population will prove this view to be far from the truth. The population is quite diverse and seems to parallel the diversity one would find in other segments of our population. The following discussion of these demographic variations highlights this diversity.

Age, Sex, and Marital Status

The elderly population itself is aging. According to the Special Committee on Aging (SCOA, 1983), one of the most rapidly growing age categories is that of people 85 years and older (the old-old). This population has increased 22 times between 1900 and the present and is expected to continue to be the fastest growing segment of this population. In comparison, persons 75 to 84 (the middle-old) have increased 11 percent, and persons 65 to 74 (the young-old) have increased 8 percent. According to Atchley (1988),

> ...by the year 2000 the young-old will have dropped to 50.5 percent of the older population. At the same time, the old-old will have increased from 6 percent of the older population in 1960 to 14.7 percent in 2000. In absolute numbers, the entire older population will more than double over the 40-year period, while the number of old-old will nearly quintuple! (pp. 25–26).

Variation is also noted in this population in the percentage of males to females. Of the approximately 28 million people 65 years of age and older, nearly two thirds are female. Approximately 50 percent of these older women are widows, whereas only 24 percent of older men are widowers. Only 17 percent of older men live alone or with nonrelatives, compared with 43 percent of older women (Myers, 1988).

These figures are probably not too surprising based on the data related to the greater life expectancy of women. What is surprising, however, is the fact that older men tend to remarry if they lose a spouse and women do not. The figures (SCOA, 1983) indicate that 83 percent of older men tend to live in newly constructed family environments as compared with 57 percent of the older women. Because women tend to marry older men and also to live longer, the American female can expect to be a widow for approximately 25 years.

Geographic Distribution

There is a degree of similarity between the distribution of the elderly and the distribution of the general population. States with the largest populations tend to have the largest population of elderly. According to the 1986 United States Senate Special Committee on Aging, in 1984 the following 10 states had the highest population of elderly people: California, New York, Florida, Pennsylvania, Texas, Illinois, Ohio, Michigan, New Jersey, and Massachusetts. Placing this in a different perspective, the states with the highest proportion of elderly, based upon their total population, are as follows: Florida, Arkansas, Rhode Island, Iowa, Pennsylvania, Missouri, South Dakota, Nebraska, Massachusetts, and Kansas.

The belief that a majority of elderly people uproot themselves and move is not true. The majority of older people continue to live in the same location. Of those who do move, approximately half move within the same community and the other half have tended to move to the following states: Florida, California, Arizona, Texas, and New Jersey (SCOA, 1983).

Race and Ethnicity

Racial and ethnic differences provide yet another variation within the elderly population. SCOA (1983) reported that in 1982 approximately 90 percent of people 65 years of age and older were white, with the remaining 10 percent composed of blacks (8 percent) and other races (2 percent). Comparing this to the total population within the United States, one finds these percentages to be in contrast to the general population breakdown in which 80 percent are white and 20 percent are nonwhite. From an ethnic perspective, the growing Hispanic-American population adds further evidence to these developing variations in the composition of the elderly population. In 1980, the Hispanic-American population accounted for 3 percent of the elderly. Due to birth rates, increased life expectancy, and immigration figures, it would seem safe to predict that by the twenty-first century racial and ethnic minorities will account for increasing percentages of the elderly population in the United States.

Retirement, Employment, and Income

Retirement, which at one point in our history was considered a luxury, is today the norm. According to SCOA (1983), 66 percent of older males were employed in the labor force in 1900. Today, less than 18 percent of this population is employed, and the projections are that this percentage will continue to decline as we move into the twenty-first century. The percentages for females for this same period show a much more stable pattern: 10 percent in the labor force in 1900 and a projection of 7 percent in the early part of the next century. The people who tend to remain in the labor force after the age of 70, the mandatory retirement age in many occupations, are those classified as professionals and those who are craftspersons. Both of these categories are descriptive of the self-employed, where no mandatory retirement age is specified.

Retirement brings with it a set of unique circumstances surrounding the elderly and is related to employment and income. A majority of those who retire do so with incomes stemming from pensions, Social Security, savings, and assistance from relatives. For the most part, this income is "fixed" and generally represents approximately 40 percent of the income the individual was receiving prior to retirement. With inflation generally on the rise in this country, the reduction, coupled with the "fixed" nature of the income, places the individual in a position of having to manage more carefully his or her income to meet not only the basic costs of living, but also the added costs, specifically those that deal with increasing taxes and expenses associated with health care, which come with retirement. Myers (1989a), in discussing income related to the elderly, indicated the following:

> In 1980, the median income for all persons aged 65+ was $6,593, compared with $12,387 for individuals aged 25 to 64. Older persons who live alone are further economically disadvantaged, as their median incomes are only $5,096 compared to $12,882 for families with a head of household over age 65. (p. 5)

Physical and Mental Health

One of the stereotypical pictures of the elderly is the view of individuals frail, weak, and suffering from a myriad of chronic disorders. As with all stereotypes, nothing could be further from the truth. According to Harris and Associates (1981), the overall self-reported health picture of the elderly is either "excellent" (42 percent) or "good" (38 percent). The remaining 20 percent reported either "only fair" (15 percent) or "poor" (5 percent). Based on these findings, 80 percent of the elderly are able to maintain the activities of daily living without the necessity of medical assistance. According to Myers (1989a), "Health status and independent daily functioning are not significantly reduced until at least age 75, but more likely reduced by age 85 or older" (p. 6).

Although the elderly account for nearly 25 percent of all prescription and over-the-counter drugs purchased in this country and are seen by physicians twice as often as their younger counterparts (Hicks et al., 1980), the overall health status of the majority of older persons is seen as excellent or good.

The mental health picture for the elderly, as described by Hicks et al. (1980), indicates that even though 60 percent of all residential patients in public mental hospitals are over 65, only 2 to 4 percent are represented in outpatient mental health treatment facilities. These percentages may reflect a variety of factors. It could be that the elderly, based upon values and attitudes, do not see the benefit in seeking such treatment. They may not understand the concepts that underlie counseling and therapy. It could be that the mental health facility, based upon personnel and facilities, is not prepared to work with this population. Regardless of the reasons, the elderly, as with their younger counterparts, can benefit from such assistance and need to receive information and encouragement from the mental health professional.

PROBLEMS AND CONCERNS OF THE ELDERLY

From a psychological viewpoint, the emotional and psychological problems of the elderly differ slightly from the emotional and psychological problems of their younger counterparts (Cavallaro & Ramsey, 1988; Gross, 1988). For example, feelings of anxiety, frustration, guilt, loneliness, despair, worthlessness, and fear are prevalent across all age levels. The young, as well as the old, must learn to cope daily with a multitude of life situations that test their emotional stability. The process of aging, however, brings with it a set of circumstances not only unique, but also telescoped into a brief period of years. These circumstances—physiologic, situational, and psychological in nature—force the elderly into changing patterns of behavior and lifestyles developed and ingrained over long periods of time. The following are but a sample of the changing life circumstances the elderly person is forced to confront.

Example 1: Loss of Work Role Identity, Increased Amount of Leisure Time, and Decreased Financial Support

For elderly people, the onset of retirement, either by choice or law, removes them from activities that for many years have been the focus of their self-identity. This work/career identity shaped not only their family life and their interactions with family members, but also their social life outside the family. What they did for a living was so much a part of who they were and how they were valued both by self and by others that this loss often creates an identity crisis. The degree of severity that surrounds this issue is related to the elderly person's ability to create a new identity.

With retirement comes increased amounts of leisure time. Time for which many elderly people are ill prepared. Leisure time, the dream of the full-time employee, often becomes the nightmare of elderly retirees. What will they do with this time? What will be done to replace the daily routines so much a part of their working years? How will they relate to significant others now that they are together for extended periods of time? These and other questions need to be addressed by the elderly, and education and planning are necessary if elderly people are to make a positive transition from work to leisure.

Retirement also brings a significant reduction in income. The majority of elderly enter this period of life on fixed incomes representing approximately 40 percent of their incomes prior to retirement. With increasing inflation, added expenses for health care, and rising taxes, the elderly often move from a financially independent state to a financially dependent state needing greater support from family, friends, and state and federal agencies. They may also find their lifestyles restricted to better conserve their fixed resources today to meet the continually escalating financial world of tomorrow.

Example 2: Loss of Significant Person(s) and Increased Loneliness and Separation

The aging process brings with it the reality of the terminal nature of relationships. Loss of significant people, due to geographical relocation or death, occurs often during this life period. Marital and social relationships that had existed and on which much of the significance of life centered end, and the elderly are called upon to cope and to find meaning in other aspects of their life. Sometimes this can be done with the support of family and friends. Sometimes it will require the intervention of helping professionals trained to work with this aspect of the aging process. In either case, the loss and its accompanying separation from the secure and familiar are issues all elderly people must confront.

Example 3: Geographic Relocation and Peer and Family Group Restructuring

Although the majority of elderly do not relocate during this life period, those who do by choice or by extenuating circumstances find themselves adjusting both to new environments and to the building of new family and social relationships. The reasons for such relocations vary with the individual. Often they represent movements to areas that are more conducive to leisure lifestyles, areas that are less demanding based on physical and physiologic disabilities, or areas that are closer to significant family members. Even when the relocation is by choice, the reconstruction process that follows is never easy and often brings with it stress, frustration, loneliness, separation, and regret.

Example 4: Increased Physiologic Disorders and Increasing Amounts of Dependence

Health often becomes a major issue for the elderly. Even though, as reported earlier, the majority of elderly people report their health as good to excellent, it is a period marked by physiologic decline. The body, like any complex machine, is beginning to wear down. The stress, anxiety, and frustration of this process takes a heavy toll on the elderly. They are often called upon to cope with health-related situations, both their own and those of loved ones, that demand both personal stamina and financial resources. Either or both of these may not be in great abundance during this period of life.

To compensate, the elderly are often forced to depend on others both for support and financial resources. Such dependence, following a life characterized by productivity and independence, is often difficult for the elderly to accept. The resulting anger, depression, and loss of self-esteem will need to be addressed if the individual is to cope effectively with the situation.

When these major life changes are viewed in terms of the rapidity of their onset, the lack of preparation for their encounter, and society's negative attitudes regarding the elderly, the prevalence of emotional and psychological problems is brought into clear focus. Any one of these changing life situations can produce emotional and psychological difficulties for the individual. In combination, they place the individual in a situation where the development of coping strategies is mandatory.

In attempting to deal with the myriad of physiologic, situational, and psychological changes that are part of the aging process, the elderly turn for assistance to family, friends, the church, physicians, counselors, and state and federal agencies. In doing so, they encounter both personal and societal barriers. These barriers include but are not limited to the following.

1. Lack of recognition of the need for help.
2. Personal values and fears regarding seeking assistance.
3. Ageism on the part of the helping professional.
4. Society's negative attitudes regarding the elderly.
5. Practical problems such as transportation and financial limitations.
6. Lack of awareness of existing support services.
7. Family pressure to keep problems within the family.
8. Separation from family members who could provide assistance.

The factors listed above place the elderly "at risk," at risk from both personal attitudes and values that keep them from seeking needed assistance and from lack of attention by the many professionals who could serve them. Counselors and mental health professionals are part of this professional service group. Based on demographic projections, they will see the elderly as clients in increasing numbers. It is, therefore, imperative that they be aware of what techniques and interventions are most appropriate and how to expand upon their existing skills to better serve this population. Furthermore, counselors working with elderly clients must take steps to explore their feelings regarding the aging process, examine personal and social values and attitudes about aging, and have foundational information regarding the physiologic, psychological, and sociologic aspects of aging.

COUNSELING PRINCIPLES

A basic premise of this chapter is that there is a common core of counseling approaches that are applicable across the life span. Skills in rapport building, active listening, ability to demonstrate caring, support, respect, and acceptance are as applicable to the client of eight as the client of eighty. According to Waters (1984):

> Regardless of the age of your client, you as a counselor need to communicate clearly, respond both to thoughts and feelings, ask effective questions, and confront when appropriate. It also is important to help people clarify their values and their goals in order to make decisions and develop action plans to implement these decisions. (p. 63)

Counseling is not age related. The goal of all counseling is to assist the individual in problem resolution and behavior change, regardless of age. When working with elderly clients, counselors need not put aside their basic skills and techniques and adopt a new set. What they need to do is to develop an awareness of the aging process and the factors within it that may necessitate adapting existing skills and techniques to meet more effectively the needs of the elderly.

Such adaptations are best understood in terms of a set of general counseling principles, which are more applicable to the elderly than perhaps the younger client. Such principles are directed at compensating for some of the "changing life situations" and "barriers" discussed earlier. These principles have general applicability to both individual and group counseling. Principle No. 1 is for counselors to expend more effort in enhancing the dignity and worth of the elderly client. Based upon ageist attitudes within society and often within the helping professions, the elderly clients are often led to believe that their value is less than that of their younger counterparts. Counselors will need to devote time and energy in restoring self-esteem and encouraging clients to review their successes, accomplishments, and positive aspects of their changing lifestyles. Further support for this principle can be found in Ganikos (1979).

Principle No. 2 requires counselors to expend more effort in "selling" the client on the positive benefits to be derived from counseling. Based upon long-established values and attitudes, the elderly client may well view counseling and the seeking of such assistance as a sign of weakness and place little value on the positive results of such a process. The counselor will need to reinforce the client's seeking assistance and demonstrate, through actions, the positive results that are possible through counseling. Further support for this principle can be found in Sargent (1980).

Principle No. 3 requires the counselor to attend more to the "physical environment" of counseling than might be necessary with a younger client. Based upon decreasing physical competencies, attention will need to involve factors such as noise distractions and counselor voice levels due to hearing loss, adequate lighting for those with visual impairments, furniture that will enhance the physical comfort of the client, thermostatic control to protect against extremes in temperatures, office accessibility, and the removal of items that impair ease of movement. Shorter sessions may also be appropriate owing to the difficulty the elderly may experience from sitting in one position for long periods of time. Further support for this principle can be found in Waters (1984).

Principle No. 4 addresses the issue of counselor–client involvement and the role of the counselor as advocate. The counselor in this situation needs to take a much more active/doing role to better serve the elderly client. This active/doing role may involve contacting agencies, family, attorneys, and other support personnel for the client. It may also entail serving as advocate for the client to represent effectively the needs and grievances of the older person. It might also entail transporting the client or taking the counseling services to the client, as would be the case with "shutins" or those who are incapacitated. Further support for this principle can be found in Wellman and McCormack (1984).

Principle No. 5 is the establishment of short-term goals that are clear cut and emphasize the present life situation for the client. Many of the problems the elderly client presents are those dealing with day-to-day living situations. The counselor, in aiding the client to find solutions to these problems, will not only reinforce the positive aspects of the counseling process, but also encourage the client to continue seeking assistance. Further support for this principle can be found in Myers (1989a).

Principle No. 6 demands attention to the dependence/independence issue characteristic of work with the elderly. Based upon changing life circumstances, the elderly are often forced into a more dependent lifestyle. The reasons vary from client to client but may be centered around health, finances, and family. The counselor needs to realize that a certain degree of dependence may well benefit the client and needs to be encouraged until the client is ready once again to assume an independent role. The majority of the elderly have functioned somewhat independently most of their adult lives. They often need assistance in seeing that it is still possible. Further support for this principle can be found in Waters (1984).

Principle No. 7 cautions the counselor to be sensitive to the possible age differential and the differing cultural, environmental, and value orientations that this difference in age may denote. With the exception of peer counseling, the counselor will generally be much younger than the client. This age difference could generate client resistance, anger, or resentment. It is important that the counselor be aware of this and learn to deal with it in an appropriate manner. The counselor, based upon his and her attitudes regarding aging, may experience some of the same reactions. Dealing with this at the beginning should enhance the probability of success.

It is also important that the counselor have some perspective on the clients' "place in history" and the significance this place holds in determining values and attitudes. Persons whose significant developmental period took place during the depression years of the 1930s or the war years of the 1940s may well be espousing values characteristic of that era. The counselor needs to accept this and not expect this person to incorporate easily values and attitudes descriptive of the 1980s. Further support for this principle can be found in Gross (1988).

Principle No. 8, the last of the general principles, cautions the counselor in the use of diagnostic tools (tests) with this population. Unlike their younger counterparts, the elderly have limited recent experience with such instruments, and their use may create undue anxiety. It is also important to keep in mind that many of the diagnostic instruments used in mental health do not have norm groups for this population and, therefore, the results obtained are questionable. It is important that the counselor, prior to using such tools, determine if tests are the best means of gaining the types of data needed. The numerous problems associated with this principle can be found in Gallagher, Thompson, and Levy (1980).

COUNSELING PROCEDURES

Based on the premise that counseling is not age related, it would appear that all theoretical systems, techniques, and intervention styles have applicability to the elderly population and are currently being used. Wellman and McCormack (1984), in a review of the outcome research in counseling older persons, reported the results of more than 90 studies. In this report, a myriad of approaches, including psychoanalytic (Brink, 1979); development (Kastenbaum, 1968); brief task-centered therapy (Saferstein, 1972); behavior management (Nigl & Jackson, 1981); peer counseling (Hayes & Burk, 1987); and cognitive behavioral (Meichenbaum, 1974) were cited. The results varied but all approaches appear to support the use of psychological intervention with this population. According to Wellman and McCormack (1984) much of the research reviewed suffered from methodologic weaknesses centering on controls, sampling, and sound theoretical rationales. They indicate, however, that procedures such as (1) regular continued contact; (2) brief psychotherapy approaches; (3) task-oriented and structured activities; (4) high levels of client involvement; (5) multidisciplinary team and peer counseling; and (6) group work seem to hold promise in working with the elderly. The authors further indicated that based upon their review the following goals for counseling with the elderly appear often:

1. to decrease anxiety and depression;
2. to reduce confusion and loss of contact with reality;
3. to increase socialization and improve interpersonal relationships;
4. to improve behavior within institutions;
5. to cope with crisis and transitional stress;
6. to become more accepting of self and the aging process (p. 82).

Both individual and group approaches to working with the elderly are supported in the literature (Myers & Shelton, 1987; Barry, 1984;

Glass & Grant, 1983; Pelsma & Flanagan, 1986; Allred & Dobson, 1987; Gross, 1988; Capuzzi & Gross, 1980; Kelly & Remley, 1987). Which is the most appropriate depends upon the client, the nature of the presenting problem, the resources available to both the client and the counselor, and the setting in which the counseling takes place. Along with the life circumstances identified earlier, it is important to keep in mind that treatment for the elderly presents the same variety of problems presented by younger clients. Issues dealing with alcohol and drug usage, abuse, loss, family, marriage, divorce, suicide, crime victimization, and career and avocational areas are often found to be continuing concerns among the elderly. Both individual and group approaches to this population are applicable.

Individual Approaches

In providing individual counseling or therapy to elderly clients, counselors have a variety of techniques, intervention strategies, and theoretical systems available to them. The only limitations seem to be those related to the skills and expertise of the counselor. Keeping in mind the eight principles mentioned previously, the following counseling skills are highly applicable to this population.

Active Listening Skills
The elderly, as with their younger counterparts, need to be heard. Use of such techniques as visual contact, encouragers, reflection of both content and feeling, paraphrasing, clarifying, questioning, and summarizing are all appropriate. Such techniques, when used appropriately, serve as encouragers, demonstrate caring, concern, and interest, and provide the client with an opportunity to share, vent feelings, to be understood, and gain self-respect.

Nonverbal Skills
Counseling with the elderly will be enhanced if the counselor is aware of and able to use effectively his or her knowledge of nonverbal communication patterns. Attention paid to body posture, eye contact, tone level, and rate of speech, although not the "royal road" to a person's inner self, is one road that aids the counselor in better understanding the client's communication more completely.

Relationship Variables
Relationship building with the elderly may demand more effort on the part of the counselor. The skills mentioned in this section should aid in facilitating this process but it is important to keep in mind that establishing trust with a much older person may require the counselor to give

consideration to his or her language, appearance, solicitous attitude, and values and attitudes related to aging and the elderly.

A second factor related to relationship building centers on the client's need for both support and challenge. Counselors working with this population need to understand that their view of the elderly as fragile may temper their ability to provide the challenge. If such is not part of the counseling process, the client may be denied the opportunity for change and growth.

Counseling Strategies

The following strategies are not presented in any priority listing. Each needs to be given careful consideration in working individually with this population.

1. Take into consideration the longevity of the client's life. In doing so, stress the positive accomplishments and encourage the client to use the many coping skills that he or she has demonstrated in reaching this stage of life.

2. Stress the benefits that counseling can provide. Often, the elderly view such assistance as a weakness on their part and believe counseling carries with it a stigma. Perhaps the words used to describe the service will need to be changed to attract this population. It might be more acceptable for the person to attend a discussion group rather than a therapy group.

3. Give attention to the physiologic needs of the client as these relate to mobility, hearing loss, visual acuity, and physical condition, e.g., sessions may need to be of shorter duration owing to the clients' inability to sit for extended periods of time.

4. Based upon the various professionals who may be working with the client, e.g., physician, social worker, agency personnel, establish more collaborative relationships than might be the case with the younger client.

5. Do not rule out problem areas that you believe are applicable only to a younger population. Drugs, alcohol, relationships are all viable issues in dealing with the elderly. Also, keep in mind that loss, and its impact, is more often experienced by the elderly.

6. In the selection of intervention techniques, use what is workable based upon the special needs and attitudinal set of the elderly client. Certain techniques, owing to their physical nature or affective emphasis, may not be appropriate for this population.

Group Approaches

Counselors selecting to use a group approach with the elderly client can gain a great deal of information and direction from reviewing such articles as Waters (1984); Capuzzi and Gross (1980); Burnside (1978); and Capuzzi et al. (1979). These authors offer not only special considerations that need to be made for working with elderly persons in groups such as time parameters, member selection, and group size, but also the types of groups that have proven to be particularly helpful with this population. Some of the advantages of the group approach mentioned by these authors include (1) discovering common bonds; (2) teaching social skills; (3) aiding in feelings of loneliness; (4) giving mutual assistance; (5) sharing feelings; and (6) providing shared purposes.

Whether selecting an individual or group modality for working with the elderly client, it is important to keep in mind that certain approaches to both individual and group work have been designed specifically to deal with the elderly from a rehabilitative perspective. The needs of the individual in a life-care facility may be quite different from the elderly person who maintains an independent lifestyle. In working with the individual in the life-care facility, the following selected approaches have proven to be helpful.

Reality Orientation Therapy
Reality orientation therapy, which combines both individual and group work, is directed at the individual who has experienced memory loss, confusion and time–place–person disorientation. The thrust of reality orientation therapy is the repetition and learning of basic personal information such as the individual's name, the place, the time of day, day of the week and date, the next meal, time of bath, and so on. If done on an informal basis within the care facility, it should be done on a 24-hour basis and it should be used by all persons who have contact with the elderly person. On a formal basis this is done in a class setting.

Milieu Therapy
Milieu therapy, which may make use of both individual and group work, is based on the concept that the social milieu of the care facility itself can be the instrument for treatment. The environment is organized to provide a more home-like atmosphere with the individual taking more responsibility, trying new skills, and being involved in decision making in a somewhat safe environment. Increased levels of activity, improvement in self-care, and increasing degrees of self-worth have resulted.

Reminiscing Groups
These groups are designed to encourage the sharing of memories with groups of six to eight members and are conducted in both institutional

and noninstitutional settings. This approach is similar to the "life review" process and in a group setting enhances a cohort effect, helping members identify and share accomplishments, tribulations, and viewpoints while at the same time increasing opportunities for socialization. Often music, visual aids, and memorabilia are used to aid in stimulating group discussion.

Remotivation Therapy

Remotivation therapy, which can be done in either a group or individual setting, seeks to encourage the moderately confused elderly patient to take a renewed interest in his or her surroundings by focusing attention on the simple, objective features of everyday life. Common topics are selected such as pets, gardening, and cooking, and people are encouraged to relate to these topics by drawing upon their own life experiences.

In working with the greater percentage of older people who continue to live independent lives, self-help groups, assertiveness training groups, growth groups, support groups, and the variety of special topic groups find equal applicability in work with the elderly as they do with a younger client population. Is counseling with the elderly different from work with the younger clients? The answer seems to be one of selective emphasis. In both individual and group work, all counseling interventions have applicability to the elderly. The counselor needs to adapt his or her approach to accommodate the unique factors that parallel the aging process.

CONCLUSION

As the number of elderly people increases, more will be seen in counseling. Counselors, whose preparation has primarily focused on working with a younger population, will need to adapt this preparation to work more effectively with the elderly client. Counselor educators will need to revise existing preparation programs to provide a curriculum that incorporates both didactic and experiential programming related to the elderly. In attempting to address this need, Myers (1989b), under a grant from the Administration on Aging, U.S. Department of Health and Human Services, has begun a national program for the development of a curriculum guide for the infusion of gerontologic counseling into counselor preparation programs. The program is still in the developmental stages but will address the growing need for updating current counselor preparation programs to better prepare counselors to work with the elderly.

As identified in this chapter, the counseling needs of the elderly are very similar to those of the younger client. When differences exist, they are best described in terms of a set of circumstances that are characteristic of the aging process. To aid the beginning counselor in better understanding what he or she needs to do to prepare for this clientele, the following recommendations are presented.

Recommendations

1. Counselors need to secure information regarding the aging process and physiologic, sociologic, and psychological factors that have an impact on this population.

2. Counselors need to clarify their values regarding aging from both a personal and other perspective. These values and attitudes will either enhance or impede their success with the elderly.

3. Counselors, in adopting current skills, will need to pay more attention to the physical setting in which counseling takes place. This environment needs to encourage, not discourage, the elderly client's participation.

4. Counselors will need to view their role with the elderly client more from an advocacy perspective. They need to be more actively involved with the day-to-day life of the client. As with any "at-risk" population, efforts to reduce this risk call for more active participation.

5. Counselors, trained and used to working with younger populations, need not fear or be apprehensive about involvement with the elderly. The elderly differ from their younger counterparts generally in increased life experiences and the rapidity of change descriptive of the aging process.

6. Counselors need to use the longevity and the developed coping strategies that accompany the aging process to enhance the clients' present life situation. The elderly have an advantage inasmuch as they have proven qualities of survival, which the counselor can use to improve self-esteem, interpersonal relations, family problems, loneliness, and a myriad of other concerns representative of this population.

The common theme of these recommendations is that counselors must pay more attention to and show more concern for the elderly. They must recognize their unique needs and, more importantly, treat them as fully deserving of the care counselors provide for younger people.

In the example that introduced this chapter, Paul did his best to apply what he had learned regarding working with an elderly client. He had paid attention to the physical environment and time considerations. He had studied the intake interview information and felt prepared to work with the client's concerns regarding her relocation. Paul had not anticipated the two clients who arrived but was flexible in attempting to deal with the situation. Both the individual sessions with the client and her son and the joint meetings left Paul questioning what he had done and feeling perhaps he should have done more. A meeting with his supervisor was scheduled to address some of these questions.

It is our hope that the information contained in this chapter will provide answers to some of these questions and that counselors such as Paul will enter the counseling relationship with more assurance that they have both the information and the skills necessary to deal with the elderly.

REFERENCES

Allred, G., & Dobson, J. (1987). Remotivation group interaction: Increasing children's contact with the elderly. *Elementary School Guidance and Counseling, 21*(3), 216–220.

Atchley, R. C. (1988). *Social forces and aging* (5th ed.). Belmont, CA: Wadsworth Publishing.

Barry, J. (1984). Responsibility-inducing interventions with older clients. *Journal of Counseling and Development, 63*(1), 51–52.

Brink, T. L. (1979). *Geriatric psychotherapy.* New York: Human Sciences.

Burnside, I. M. (1978). *Working with the elderly: Group process and technique.* North Scituate, MA: Duxbury Press.

Capuzzi, D., Gossman, L., Whiston, S., & Surdam, J. (1979). Group counseling for aged women. *The Personnel and Guidance Journal, 57*(6), 306–309.

Capuzzi, D., & Gross, D. (1980). Group work with the elderly: An overview for counselors. *The Personnel and Guidance Journal, 59*(4), 206–211.

Cavallaro, M., & Ramsey, M. (1988). Ethical issues in gerocounseling. *Counseling and Values, 32*(3), 221–227.

Gallagher, D., Thompson, L. W., & Levy, S. M. (1980). Clinical psychological assessment of older adults. In L. W. Poon (Ed.), *Aging in the 1980's* (pp. 120–138). Washington, DC: American Psychological Association.

Ganikos, M. L. (Ed.). (1979). *Counseling the aged.* Falls Church, VA: American Personnel and Guidance Association.

Gilkison, B., & Drummond, R. (1988). Academic self-concept of older adults in career transition. *Journal of Employment Counseling, 25*(1), 24–29.

Glass, J., & Grant, K. (1983). Counseling in the later years. *The Personnel and Guidance Journal, 62*(4), 210–218.

Gross, D. (1987). Aging and addiction: Perspective and recommendations. *Arizona Counseling Journal, 12*(1), 29–35.

Gross, D. (1988). Counseling and the elderly: Strategies, procedures and recommendations. *Counseling and Human Development.* Denver, CO: Love Publishing.

Harris, L., & Associates. (1981). *Aging in the eighties: America in transition.* Washington, DC: National Council on Aging.

Hayes, R. L., & Burk, M. J. (1987). Community-based prevention for elderly victims of crime and violence. *Journal of Mental Health Counseling, 9*(4), 210–219.

Hicks, R., Funkenstein, H., Drysken, M., & Davis, J. (1980). Geriatric psychopharmacology. In J. Birren, & B. Sloane (Eds.), *Handbook of mental health and aging.* Englewood Cliffs, NJ: Prentice-Hall.

Johnson, R. P., & Stripling, R. O. (1984). Bridging the gap between counselor educators and the administrators of programs for the elderly. *Counselor Education and Supervision, 23*(4), 276–289.

Kart, C., Metress, E., & Metress, S. (1988). *Aging health and society.* Boston/Portola Valley: Jones and Bartlett Publishers.

Kastenbaum, R. (1968). Perspectives on the development and modification of behavior in the aged: A developmental field perspective. *Gerontologist, 8,* 280–283.

Kelly, S., & Remley, T. (1987). Understanding and counseling elderly alcohol abusers. *AMHCA Journal, 9*(2), 105–113.

Meichenbaum, D. (1974). Self-instructional strategy training: A cognitive prosthesis for the aged. *Human Development, 17,* 273–280.

Myers, J. (1988). The mid/late life generation gap: Adult children with aging parents. *Journal of Counseling and Development, 66*(7), 331–335.

Myers, J. (1989a). *Adult children and aging parents.* Alexandria, VA: American Association For Counseling and Development.

Myers, J. (1989b). In fusing gerontological counseling into counselor preparation. Administration on Aging, U.S. Department of Health & Human Services (90AT0331). Alexandria, VA: American Association for Counseling and Development.

Myers, J., & Shelton, B. (1987). Abuse and older persons: Issues and implications for counselors. *Journal of Counseling and Development, 65*(7), 376–380.

Nigl, A. J., & Jackson, B. (1981). A behavior management program to increase social responses in psychogeriatric patients. *Journal of the Geriatrics Society, 29,* 92–95.

Pelsma, D., & Flanagan, M. (1986). Human relations training for the elderly. *Journal of Counseling and Development, 65*(1), 52–53.

Saferstein, S. (1972). Psychotherapy for geriatric patients. *New York State Journal of Medicine, 72,* 2743–2748.

Sargent, S. S. (Ed.). (1980). *Nontraditional therapy and counseling with the aging.* New York: Springer.

Siegel, J., & Davidson, M. (1984). *Demographic and socioeconomic aspects of aging in the United States.* Current Population Reports, special studies series (P-23 No. 138). Washington, DC: U.S. Department of Commerce, Bureau of the Census.

Special Committee on Aging (1983). *Developments in aging: 1983,* Vol. 1. Washington, DC: U.S. Government Printing Office.

Sterns, H., Weis, D., & Perkins, S. (1984). A conceptual approach to counseling older adults and their families. *The Counseling Psychologist, 12*(2), 55–61.

U.S. Senate Special Committee on Aging (1986). *Developments in aging: 1985,* Vol. 3. Washington, DC: U.S. Government Printing Office.

Waters, E. (1984). Building on what you know: Techniques for individual and group counseling with older people. *The Counseling Psychologist, 12*(2), 63–74.

Wellman, F., & McCormack, J. (1984). Counseling with older persons: A review of outcome research. *The Counseling Psychologist, 12*(2), 81–96.

15.

Counseling Couples and Families

FRANK C. NOBLE, ED.D.
Arizona State University
Tempe, Arizona

THE PLACEMENT OF THIS chapter in a section called "Counseling Specialized Populations" confirms Duncan Stanton's (1988) contention that, "Non-family therapists often view family therapy as (a) a modality, that (b) usually involves the nuclear family" (p. 8). He goes on to point out the inaccuracy of this conception, explaining that family therapy is based on a point of view that emphasizes the contextual nature of psychological problems.

> More fundamentally, it (family therapy) is a way of construing human problems that dictates certain actions for their alleviation. Its conceptual and data bases differ from most other (especially individually oriented) therapies in that the interpersonal context of a problem and the interplay between this context and the symptoms are of primary interest. An index patient is seen as responding to his or her social situation; those around the patient are noted to react to this response; the patient then reacts "back," and so on, in an on-going, give and take process. Interventions designed to alter this process derive from such interactional formulations. (p. 8)

It is, of course, possible for a counselor who is oriented to the treat-

320

ment of individuals to interview the members of a client's family in the course of treatment. However, this rarely occurs, since the individual orientation places the source of dysfunction within the client rather than focusing on the context in which the symptoms occur. Table 15–1 illustrates some of the other differences in perspective between a psychodynamic and a family therapy point of view. The psychodynamic approach is based in Freudian theory, and emphasizes internal constructs such as the id, ego, and superego; in contrast, family therapy is primarily based in systems theory and emphasizes interpersonal behavior. To further illuminate this paradigm shift, several concepts from systems theory will be illustrated within a human behavioral context.

Fundamental unity. The universe is one system with infinite levels of subsystems; analysis at any level needs to consider the levels above and below. To understand the individual, it is essential to analyze both the inter-individual context and the intra-individual subsystems. A person's strange behavior may be due to dysfunctional family interactions or may be due to a chemical imbalance in the individual's blood.

System change. Change in any part of a system will impact the whole system. If therapy with an individual is successful, the system of which the client is a part will be affected. Unfortunately, we will know of those changes only through the selective filter of our client, and that our chances of success are diminished by the homeostatic drag of the system.

TABLE 15–1   Two Contrasting Views of Therapy: Psychodynamic and Family Systems.

	Psychodynamic	*Family Systems*
Causality	linear	recursive
Time focus	past	present
Pathology	intrapsychic	interpersonal
Assessment	individual	systemic
Therapy	long-term catharsis transference abreaction insight	brief reframing restructuring problem-solving behavior change
Therapist	passive	active

Recursive causality. Inherent in the first two concepts is a nonlinear epistemology. Thus our observation that A causes B is due only to our punctuation of a behavioral sequence that fails to see what follows from B or what preceded A. Every act (or nonaction) provokes feedback, which alters the nature of the next act. In a family, "does he drink because she nags?" (his punctuation); or "does she nag because he drinks?" (her punctuation).

Homeostasis. Systems use negative feedback to maintain a steady state; positive feedback creates change in the system. If one member of a family begins to change, perhaps as the result of individual therapy, the usual routine interactions of the family will be disrupted, and the family will send messages designed to bring the person in therapy back into line.

Viability. The viability of a system is based on order and structure; entropy is disorder. In addition to structure, which is a static quality, the system must also be open to new input if it is to be capable of accommodating to its changing environment. A family with young children needs a generational hierarchy, but the hierarchy must also be open to modification as the children mature (Sieburg, 1985).

With this brief description of systems concepts, perhaps the following definition of family therapy, as stated by Wynne (1988), can be presented:

Family therapy is a psychotherapeutic approach that focuses on altering interactions between a couple, within a nuclear family or extended family, or between a family and other interpersonal systems, with the goal of alleviating problems initially presented by individual family members, family subsystems, the family as a whole, or other referral sources. (pp. 250–251)

THE HISTORY OF FAMILY THERAPY

The history of family therapy is relatively brief. It begins in the 1950s, with the seminal contributions of Nathan Ackerman, Theodore Lidz, Lyman Wynne, Murray Bowen, and Carl Whitaker. All of these psychiatrists, originally trained in the prevailing psychodynamic model, broke away from its restrictive influence and began to see that dysfunctional behavior was rooted in the individual's past and present family life. Each of these pioneers arrived at this insight relatively independently: Ackerman through his research on the mental health problems of the unemployed in Pennsylvania; Lidz studying the families of schizophrenics at Yale; Wynne treating patients with psychosis and ulcerative colitis in Massachusetts, and later doing research on the families of schizophrenics at the National Institute of Mental Health (NIMH); Bowen through his work with families at the Menninger Foundation and later with Wynne at NIMH; Whitaker through seeing families at Oak Ridge and his later work with families with a schizophrenic member at Emory. In his preface to *The Psychodynamics of Family Life* (1958), the first book-length treatment of this point-of-view, Ackerman said:

> This approach attempts to correlate the dynamic psychological processes of individual behavior with family behavior in order to be able to place individual clinical diagnosis and therapy within the broader frame of family diagnosis and therapy. It has been necessary, therefore, to explore a series of interrelated themes: the interdependence of individual and family stability at every stage of growth from infancy to old age; the role of family in the emotional development of the child; the family as stabilizer of the mental health of the adult; the family as conveyor belt for anxiety and conflict and as a carrier of the contagion of mental illness; the interplay of conflict between family and community, conflict in family relationships, and conflict within individual family members; and breakdown in adaptation and illness as symptoms of the group pathology of the family. (p. viii)

With this statement he did much to set the agenda for the next three decades.

During this same period, an unusual group of people assembled in Palo Alto to study the communication processes of schizophrenics. The project was headed by Gregory Bateson, an anthropologist, who hired Jay Haley, a recent graduate in communications theory, Don Jackson, a psychiatrist, and John Weakland, whose initial training was in chemical engineering. Early in the project, Haley began consulting with Milton Erickson who was known at that time primarily as a hypnotherapist. From this rich melange emerged the beginnings of strategic family therapy. In 1959, Jackson founded the Mental Research Institute (MRI) in Palo Alto and invited Virginia Satir to join him. When the Bateson project ended in 1961, Haley and Weakland also joined the staff at MRI.

Satir diverged from the pragmatic approach of strategic therapy when she left MRI to join the human potential movement at the Esalen Institute. With the publication of her book *Conjoint Family Therapy* in 1964, she established her own approach to family treatment, which incorporated elements of the thinking of the group at MRI within a framework of Gestalt and experiential therapy.

Structural family therapy emerged on the east coast in the work of Salvador Minuchin and his colleagues at Wyltwick School and later the Philadelphia Child Guidance Clinic (PCGC). At Wyltwick, Minuchin worked with the families of delinquent boys and at PCGC he did research on families with a member who was psychosomatic. Each of these projects resulted in a book that enriched our understanding of family functioning (Minuchin et al., 1967; Minuchin, Rosman, & Baker, 1978). He was joined by Haley in 1967, and they worked together for ten years. As might be expected, the concepts of strategic and structural therapy have much in common. Haley, who met his second wife, Cloe Madanes at the PCGC, left with her in 1977 to found the Family Therapy Institute of Washington, D.C.

Murray Bowen began his career at the Menninger Foundation and focused his research on families with a schizophrenic member. He continued this at the NIMH where, in 1954, he had the families of schizophrenic youngsters actually live in the hospital so that he could observe their interactions. In 1959, he moved to Georgetown University Medical Center where he has continued his development of transgenerational therapy.

Last, but not least, is Carl Whitaker, who is often referred to as the "clown prince of family therapy." Whitaker began his career as a gynecologist, but soon switched to psychiatry. He was chief psychiatrist at Oak Ridge, Tennessee, where he first began bringing the family into treatment with his patients. He moved from Oak Ridge to the chair of the Department of Psychiatry at Emory University in 1946. The publication of his first book, *The Roots of Psychotherapy* (1953), led to his dismissal, and he went into private practice for ten years. The book, which he co-authored with his colleague, Thomas Malone, challenged much of traditional psychodynamic thinking and was resoundingly condemned by the psychiatric establishment. In 1965, Whitaker began teaching at the University of Wisconsin where he is currently professor emeritus. He refers to his work as Symbolic-Experiential Family Therapy.

For a more complete treatment of the history of family therapy see the *Handbook of Family Therapy* (Gurman & Kniskern, 1981).

CHAPTER OVERVIEW

While it would be possible to follow this brief historical introduction with a detailed description of each of the major therapeutic approaches, I have elected to take a different approach. It is my contention that family therapy has moved beyond the "schools of therapy" orientation and that a systematic eclecticism is now possible. For the reader who is interested in a comparison of the various approaches, Table 15–2 presents a comparative assessment of some of the relevant aspects of family therapy.

The present attempt to reduce the emphasis on the differences between various approaches to family therapy has the support of at least one of the major figures in the field. Salvador Minuchin, writing as early as 1982, also decried the tendency to fragment the field into schools of therapy:

TABLE 15–2 A Comparison of Family Therapy Approaches

	Strategic (Haley)	Structural (Minuchin)	Transgenerational (Bowen)	Experiential (Whitaker)	Conjoint (Satir)
Who is included in therapy?	Everyone involved in the problem	Whoever is involved and accessible	The most motivated family member(s)	Who he decides should come	The pattern is flexible
What is the theory of dysfunction?	Confused hierarchy; communication; rigid behavioral sequences	Boundaries (enmeshed or disengaged); stable coalitions; power	Fusion (emotions control; symbiosis with family of origin); anxiety; triangulation	Rigidity of thought and behavior	Low self-esteem; poor communication; triangulation
What are the goals of therapy?	Solve the problem; restore hierarchy; introduce flexibility	Solve the problem; change the structure; increase flexibility	Greater differentiation of self; reduced anxiety	Increase family creativity; greater sense of belonging and individuation	Improved communication; personal growth
What is the method of assessment?	Structured initial interview; intervene and observe the reaction; focus on the present	Joining the family to experience its process; chart the family structure; focus on the present	Detailed family history over several generations using the genogram; focus on the past	Informal; not separated from treatment; focus on both past and present	Family life chronology is used to take history and assess present functioning

(continued)

TABLE 15-2 (continued)

	Strategic (Haley)	Structural (Minuchin)	Transgenerational (Bowen)	Experiential (Whitaker)	Conjoint (Satir)
What are the intervention procedures?	Directives are used to change behavior; they may be straightforward, paradoxical, or ordeals	Reframing is used to change the perception of the problem; structure is changed by unbalancing and increasing stress	Reducing anxiety by providing rational, untriangulated third party; coaching to aid in differentiation from family of origin	Increasing stress to force change; reframing symptoms as efforts at growth; affective confrontation	Modeling and coaching clear communication; family sculpting; guided interaction
What is the stance of the therapist?	Active, directive, but not self-revealing; planful, not spontaneous	Active, directive, personally involved; spontaneous; humorous	Interested but detached; reinforces calmness and rationality	Active, personally involved; encourages and models "craziness," co-therapy	Active, directive, matter-of-fact, nonjudgmental; models open communication

In early explorations of family therapy, the field increased its sophistication and expanded its territory. Naturally, the early explorers staked the unmarked corners with their trade names: strategic, systemic, structural, Bowenian, experiential, and so on. The old-timers knew that their private truths were only partial, and when they met around a cup of coffee, they gossiped about the beginnings and shared their uncertainties and hopes. But, lo and behold, their institutions grew, and they needed large buildings to accommodate all their students. Slowly, before anybody realized it, the buildings became castles, with turrets and drawbridges, and even watchmen in the towers. The castles were very expensive and they needed to justify their existence. Therefore, they demanded ownership of the total truth. . . . But the generation of elders is becoming older. The castles are becoming very expensive to run and, like the English aristocracy, the lords of the manor will soon be opening them only on Sunday for the new generation of tourists. Those who come to my castle will not find me there. (Minuchin, 1982, p. 662)

In what follows I have attempted to synthesize what I regard as some of the most useful of the ideas of the several therapists referred to above. We will begin first with a family systems perspective on the diagnosis of family dysfunction. This will be followed by sections on how to conduct the initial interview, family therapy techniques, legal and ethical questions, and research.

DIAGNOSIS OF FAMILY DYSFUNCTION

Tolstoy said in the opening line of *Anna Karenina*, "All happy families resemble one another, but each unhappy family is unhappy in its own way." Family therapists tend to reverse this position, believing that good family functioning is based in diversity, while family dysfunction is due to narrowness and rigidity. Haley (1967) goes so far as to argue that therapies that have a picture of "ideal" functioning are in fact limiting, in that they impose "a narrow ideology, thus preventing the diversity that human beings naturally display. To put the matter simply, if the goal of therapy is to introduce more complexity, then imposing on clients a psychological explanation of their own and other people's behavior is antitherapeutic" (p. 233).

When a systems orientation is applied to psychological problems, the diagnosis of the difficulty is very different from that presented in the DSM-III-R (1987). Rather than focusing on the internal state of the individual, the family systems approach looks for pathology in the interactions that occur between people who have significance for each other.

Rather than adopting a linear model of causality, the family systems approach perceives causality as circular or recursive. It's not that a child is rebellious because his or her father is too authoritarian, or that the father is authoritarian because the child is rebellious, but that both are caught up in a chronic repetitive sequence of behavior: the "game without end."

Rather than focusing on the way people think or feel, the family systems therapist tends to focus on what they do. The purpose of family therapy is not insight, but behavior change.

Within the broad commonality of the systems orientation, each of the major family therapists has emphasized different aspects of human functioning as the source of symptomatic behavior. The following sections provide a compilation of the thinking of a number of family therapists regarding symptomatic behavior.

FAMILY LIFE CYCLE Family dysfunction is often due to the failure to accomplish the developmental tasks demanded by the family life cycle (Table 15–3). The fullest conceptualization of a stage approach to family development is generally attributed to Carter and McGoldrick (1980), although the concept was already present in the thinking of Jay Haley in 1973. Since that time, most of the major family therapists have acknowledged the significance of family life cycle changes as a major source of stress and disequilibrium for the family. Inherent in the life cycle concept is the idea that there are certain developmental tasks that must be accomplished during periods of transition from one stage to another. Successful movement to the next development stage requires changes in the roles and structure of the family. If the family is unable to accommodate to the need for change, stress and symptomatology will occur.

It should be recognized that the demand for change is a normal part of family development. It is not these normal difficulties that create the problem, but rather the chronic mishandling of them. It is the attempted solution that is the problem. Denying the need for change, treating a normal developmental change as if it were a problem, and striving for perfection are all likely to result in family distress. In general, the reaction of a dysfunctional family to a demand for change is met by doing "more of the same." For example, an adolescent girl reaches puberty; parents become concerned for her safety and morality; they introduce or increase their control over her behavior; the girl resents their attempt to control her autonomy and begins to act out; the parents increase their control; etc. (Watzlawick, Weakland, & Fisch, 1974). In a family with young children, a problem might arise when the grandparents have difficulty in giving up their parental role with their own children, thus interfering with the discipline of their new grandchildren.

The problems associated with family life cycle changes are exacer-

TABLE 15–3 Stages of the Family Life Cycle.

Family Life Cycle Stage	Emotional Process of Transition: Key Principles	Second Order Changes in Family Status Required to Proceed Developmentally
1. Between Families: The Unattached Young Adult	Accepting parent–offspring separation	a. Differentiation of self in relation to family of origin b. Development of intimate peer relationships c. Establishment of self in work
2. The Joining of Families Through Marriage: The Newly Married Couple	Commitment to new system	a. Formation of marital system b. Realignment of relationships with extended families and friends to include spouse.
3. The Family with Young Children	Accepting new members into the system	a. Adjusting marital system to make space for child(ren) b. Taking on parenting roles c. Realignment of relationships with extended family to include parenting and grandparenting roles
4. The Family with Adolescents	Increasing flexibility of family boundaries to include children's independence	a. Shifting of parent–child relationship to permit adolescent to move in and out of system b. Refocus on mid-life marital and career issues c. Beginning shift toward concerns for older generation
5. Launching Children and Moving On	Accepting a multitude of exits from and entries into the family system	a. Renegotiation of marital system as a dyad b. Development of adult to adult relationships between grown children and their parents c. Realignment of relationships to include in-laws and grandchildren d. Dealing with disabilities and death of parents (grandparents)

(continued)

TABLE 15–3 (continued)

Family Life Cycle Stage	Emotional Process of Transition: Key Principles	Second Order Changes in Family Status Required to Proceed Developmentally
6. The Family in Later Life	Accepting the shifting of generational roles	a. Maintaining own and/or couple functioning and interests in face of physiologic decline; exploration of new familial and social role options b. Support for a more central role for middle generation c. Making room in the system for the wisdom and experience of the elderly; supporting the older generation without overfunctioning for them d. Dealing with loss of spouse, siblings and other peers and preparation for own death. Life review and integration.

Source: From *The Family Life Cycle: A Framework for Family Therapy* (p. 17) by E. A. Carter and M. McGoldrick, 1980. New York: Gardner Press. Copyright © 1980 by Gardner Press. Reprinted by permission.

bated in remarried families owing to the fact that, for most family members, individual development is out of synchronization with the developmental stage of the family (e.g., a newly remarried family is focused on issues of inclusion and forming of a viable entity; if that family contains an adolescent, he or she is focused on issues of separation and individuation).

FUSION IN THE NUCLEAR FAMILY AND/OR THE FAMILY OF ORIGIN Bowen (1978) conceived a scale of differentiation of self from 0 to 100. At the low end of the scale, people are fused or enmeshed with their families to the extent that they are unable to think or act independently. Their lives are ruled by emotional reactivity. According to Bowen, people diagnosed as schizophrenic would be extremely fused.

At the upper end of the scale, people have achieved emotional separation from their families, are able to act autonomously, and can choose to be rational in emotionally charged situations. The individual's level of differentiation is closely related to the differentiation of his or her parents, and the process is transgenerational in nature. People with low levels of differentiation (fusion) are particularly reactive to environmental stressors and when under stress are likely to resolve it by (1) withdrawal, (2) conflict, (3) dysfunction of one spouse, or (4) triangulation of a child that results in dysfunction. When the latter occurs, that child, who is caught in the tug of war between the parents, will be even less differentiated than the parents. This is the basis of the intergenerational transmission of dysfunction (Bowen, 1978; Kerr & Bowen, 1988).

BOUNDARY PROBLEMS According to Minuchin (1974) family boundaries are created by implicit rules that govern who talks to whom about what. When no rules exist, when everyone is privy to everyone else's thoughts and feelings, the boundary is said to diffuse and the individuals enmeshed (fused). When the rules are too strict and communication breaks down, the boundary is said to be rigid and the individuals disengaged. The preferred state is to have clear rules that allow both for individuation and togetherness. The similarity of this concept to Bowen's idea of differentiation of self is obvious, but Minuchin has developed it to refer to both extrafamilial boundaries and intrafamilial boundaries that separate subsystems (holons).

Family dysfunction can occur because the family is either disengaged from or enmeshed with the external environment. This is frequently a problem with remarried families where rules regarding contact with ex-spouses may be either rigid or lacking. Dysfunction can also occur when internal subsystems of the family are enmeshed or disengaged. The classic dysfunction in our culture is the mother who is enmeshed with a child (cross-generational coalition) and the father who is disengaged from both.

DYSFUNCTIONAL SEQUENCES Haley (1987) believes family dysfunction is often caused by behavioral sequences that are rigid, repetitive, and functionally autonomous. He describes such a sequence as follows:

1. One parent, usually the mother, is in an intense relationship with the child. By *intense* is meant a relationship that is both positive and negative and where the responses of each person are exaggeratedly important. The mother attempts to deal with the child with a mixture of affection and exasperation.
2. The child's symptomatic behavior becomes more extreme.
3. The mother, or the child, calls on the father for assistance in resolving their difficulty.

4. The father steps in to take charge and deal with the child.
5. Mother reacts against father, insisting that he is not dealing with the situation properly. Mother can react with an attack or with a threat to break off the relationship with father.
6. Father withdraws, giving up the attempt to disengage mother and child.
7. Mother and child deal with each other in a mixture of affection and exasperation until they reach a point where they are at an impasse (pp. 121–122).

Such patterns can repeat ad infinitum unless some new behavior is introduced into the sequence. It perhaps needs to be pointed out that the dysfunctional behavior should not be "blamed" on any of the individuals; all are equally involved and each could change the sequence by introducing a new incompatible element. Unfortunately, the family members are not usually aware of the complete sequence and in any case punctuate the sequence in such a way as to hold themselves blameless.

HIERARCHY PROBLEMS Haley (1987) and Minuchin (1974) both stress the importance of hierarchy problems in family dysfunction. Problems can occur when the hierarchy is either absent, ambiguous, or culturally inappropriate; that is, when no one is in charge, when it is unclear who is in charge, or when the person wielding the power is not sanctioned by cultural mores. Dysfunction may also be due to coalitions that cut across generational boundaries. An example of the latter would be when a father and child collude to avoid what they feel are the mother's overly rigid rules. Another common example would be in a family where there is marital conflict and both parents try to enlist the children on their side of the argument.

COMMUNICATION PROBLEMS Virginia Satir (1983) placed special emphasis on the way that people in a family communicate as a source of dysfunction. Communication may be inadequate owing to lack of clarity (e.g., information is deleted; "People get me down." Which people? How do they do that?). Communication can also be confusing because of a lack of topic continuity. This occurs when people are not really listening and their responses to the other become non sequiturs. When people are unwilling to reveal themselves or commit themselves to a statement or request, communication falters (e.g., "I don't suppose you would like to go to my mother's with me?" rather than "I would like you to go with me to my mother's.").

Sometimes communication is problematic because it is incongruent; either the nonverbal behavior or vocal tone communicates a message that contradicts the verbal content. Such incongruency is often the basis for irony and humor, but when it is unintentional and the message is not clarified, the receiver does not know how to respond. In the extreme case, this is the classic "double-bind," described by Bateson, Jackson, Haley, and Weakland (1956). Satir (1983) describes this, and the effect that such incongruent communication can have on a child:

> How do mates unconsciously induce a child to behave in such a way that he eventually gets identified as a "patient?" . . . What conditions must be present for a child to experience the pressures associated with a double bind?
> a. First, the child must be exposed to double-level messages repeatedly and over a long period of time.
> b. Second, these must come from persons who have survival significance for him....
> c. Third, perhaps most important of all, he must be conditioned from an early age not to ask, "Did you mean that or that?" but must accept his parents conflicting messages in all their impossibility. He must be faced with the hopeless task of translating them into a single way of behaving. (pp. 45–46)

LOW SELF-ESTEEM Satir (1983) also posits low self-esteem as the basis of much family difficulty and describes a process similar to Bowen's (1978) intergenerational transmission process to reveal how low self-esteem not only affects the individuals and couples, but also is "inherited" by their children. Description of the entire process is beyond the scope of this chapter. The essential elements include low self-esteem in both marital partners, intolerance of each other's differences, and seeking to improve their sense of self-esteem through their children. If the parents don't agree on how the children should behave, the children are confronted with the impossible task of pleasing both parents (another type of double-bind). Since they cannot please both parents, the children develop low self-esteem and may also become symptomatic.

CONFLICT OVER WHICH FAMILY OF ORIGIN TO MODEL Whitaker says:

> We assume that dysfunction is related to the struggle over whose family of origin this new family is going to model itself after. One way to view etiology asserts there is no such thing as a marriage; it is merely two scapegoats sent out by families to perpetrate themselves. (Whitaker & Keith, 1981, p. 196)

Young people who come from a common cultural background may be less likely to experience this problem, but in our polyglot society, the appropriate behaviors for "wife" or "husband" are often unclear, or represent role conflicts. When a child enters the picture before these roles

are synchronized, the new roles of "mother" and "father" further complicate the picture. Often the young couple find themselves acting just like
their parents, although they are reluctant to admit it.

NARROW AND RIGID BELIEFS AND SELF-PERCEPTS In a sense this brings us full
circle. To the extent that one's beliefs are narrow and unchanging,
adaptation to the demands of a changing environment or the
developmental demands of the family life cycle will be difficult. Milton
Erickson held ". . . that individuals with a symptom were constricted by
their own certainties, their own rules, whether these rules guided their
belief system, their perceptions of self, their patterns of physiological
response or relational habits, or their own ideas of contingency, (i.e., if A,
then B)" (Ritterman, 1986, p. 37). The symptom, per se, is not the
problem, but instead is "a metaphorical expression of a problem and
attempt at resolution . . . the underlying problem is understood to be
inflexibly patterned behavior resulting from internal and/or
interactional rules that proscribe available choices and prevent the
resolution of developmentally routine or unusual life dilemmas"
(Ritterman, 1986, p. 36).

When an individual or a family is unable to resolve a difficulty, it
is assumed that the conscious mind is imposing a narrow, restrictive
mind-set that does not allow the creative recovery of the resources necessary to solve the problem. From this point of view, the conscious, rational mind must be diverted to allow the creative potential of the unconscious to function. This is done through hypnosis or the use of
indirect methods such as metaphor.

THE INITIAL INTERVIEW

In order to gain a better understanding of how family therapists work,
let us take a look at how the initial interview is conducted. The following
description owes a great deal to Jay Haley (1987), but also incorporates
ideas from other therapists.

Presession Planning

Whenever possible, the therapist should determine in advance who will
attend the session, and have at least a general idea of the nature of the
presenting problems. Whitaker and Bumberry (1988) call this the "battle
for structure," and place great emphasis on the importance of the therapist determining who will attend the first session. It is their belief that if

the therapist does not have control at this stage, therapeutic leverage is lost and the family is less likely to be helped. This may entail a presession telephone call or the use of an intake form. On the basis of the data derived from this initial contact, a presession plan should be developed that will include the counselor's hypotheses about the underlying basis of the presenting problem, areas of inquiry that must be addressed to reject or confirm the hypotheses, and a general plan for the session.

The Joining Stage

The most important task of the initial interview is to join with the family, accommodating to their affective tone, tempo, language, and family structure. This is done through mimesis (Minuchin, 1974), sometimes referred to as pacing. Lankton (1980) advocates matching the family's style even to the extent of matching breathing, body movements, and representational system predicates (visual, auditory, kinesthetic). Care needs to be taken, however, that this does not become an offensive burlesque.

Tracking is another joining technique and consists of little more than Rogers-like "uh-huhs," reflection of content, and asking for clarification. During this time, the therapist should avoid comment or interpretation (Haley, 1987).

A third aspect of joining is maintenance (Minuchin, 1974), in which the therapist senses the family's structure and acts in such a way as to be included within it. If Dad acts as the "central switchboard" in this family, the therapist accommodates to that and contacts other members through him.

During the joining stage, the therapist should not allow the introduction of material related to the family problem. Only after some social contact has been made with every family member should the next stage begin (Haley, 1987). Joining, of course, is not finished at the end of this stage, but must be of concern throughout the therapy.

Virginia Satir provides a more structured approach to joining in her use of the "family life chronology" (1983); Bowen's (Kerr & Bowen, 1988) development of a family genogram is a similar approach. Both of these techniques, however, go beyond the joining stage and also gather data relevant to the problem.

The Problem Statement Stage

When significant contact has been made with all family members in the social or joining stage, the therapist introduces the problem stage. During the joining stage, the therapist has learned something of the family structure and hierarchy and uses this information to decide to whom the first question should be directed. Haley (1987) recommends that "the adult who seems less involved with the problem be spoken to first, and the person with the most power to bring the family back be treated with the most concern and respect" (p. 22). He also says that, in general, it is unwise to begin with the identified patient (IP).

Don't attempt to force a mute member to speak. This will often be the IP who has lots of practice in resisting adult coercion. Instead, ask another family member, "What would Johnny say if he chose to talk?" This can be repeated in a round robin if necessary, and in most instances, the mute member will feel the need to defend himself or clarify his real feelings.

The second decision the therapist must make is how the problem question should be framed. Obviously, the question can be as vague as, "What brings you here today?" or as specific as "What is the problem for which you are seeking help?" It can also be framed to elicit etiologic information or be future-focused on the kinds of changes that are desired. I generally prefer ambiguity and a focus on the future: "When this therapy is successful, how will your family be different?"

When everyone has had an opportunity to express what they see as the "pain in the family" (Satir, 1983), the therapist can begin to flesh out the details that will help to clarify the function that the problem serves in the family. The following series of questions may prove helpful.

1. Who has the problem?
2. Where else have you sought help and how did it work for you? What has been tried, by whom, and for how long? Is there anything you have tried that you feel could have been done more?
3. Why is the symptom a problem? Does anyone in the family not consider the symptom a problem? Who in the family is most upset by the problem?
4. How often does it occur? When? Where? Who reacts to it? In what way? What happens just before it occurs? What happens next?
5. When did the symptom begin? Why did you come in now?
6. How do you account for the problem?
7. Do the parents agree or disagree about the problem, its cause, and the best solution?
8. What would happen if the symptom got better or worse?
9. What do you hope will happen as the result of coming here? What is your ideal goal? What would you settle for? How optimistic are you about improvement? What do you want to

see the identified patient doing two weeks from now that would show progress? (Bergman, 1985).

The Interaction Stage

When the problem has been reasonably clarified or when it has become clear that the family is not in agreement regarding the nature of the problem, it is time for the therapist to introduce the interaction stage. During the earlier two stages, the therapist has maintained his or her centrality in the communication network, speaking in turn to each of the family members and blocking interruptions and attempts at dialogue between family members. This procedure tends to reduce tension and provide order and relatively clear communication, and also establishes the therapist's power and leadership in the therapeutic process. The focus in the problem phase has been on clarifying how the family views the problem. In the interaction stage, the therapist's focus will be on determining the patterns of interaction that sustain the problem. In order to get this information the therapist asks the family to "dance" in his or her presence (Minuchin, 1974).

This occurs most easily and naturally when the family is not in agreement regarding the problem. When this is true, the therapist can encourage them to discuss their differences and try to reach agreement. During this phase it is crucial that the therapist abdicate the center of the communication network. All attempts to communicate with the therapist should be referred back to a family member. The therapist does not, however, completely abandon the leadership position; instead the role changes to being the director of the family drama, introducing a third party when two seem to reach an impasse, or asking family members to change their seating patterns to facilitate new encounters (Minuchin, 1974; Haley, 1987).

On the other hand, if family members are in agreement regarding the problem that brings them to therapy (usually focusing on one person as the cause of the difficulty), they can be asked to perform the problem. "When Johnny doesn't take out the garbage, what happens? Who is first to notice? Show me how it works." In order to get the family to act, rather than talk about the problem, it will be necessary for the therapist to get to his or her feet, help the family to build an appropriate stage set (in fantasy), and set the scene into action.

Interactions that are developed from the idiosyncratic information presented by the family are most likely to reveal the information needed to understand the problem. Unfortunately, some families are so uncommunicative that the therapist is unable to elicit enough information to stage an appropriate interaction. When this occurs, it is well to have a few preplanned interaction situations available. One that is often useful, particularly in families with young children, is to ask the family to enact a day in their lives. Establish who sleeps where, move them into the appropriate places, and then have the alarm go off. If it is to be successful, the therapist will need to coach this interaction, slowing it down and focusing on the most simple, concrete details of family life. In a large family, who has access to the bathroom at what time is often a major source of conflict. Care must also be taken to ensure that all family members become involved. Other generic interactions might be to plan a family vacation together, or decide how to spend a free Saturday. Or, using building blocks or crayon and paper, have the family draw their living quarters and discuss who spends the most time with whom in what part of the house.

The purpose of the interaction stage is to determine the family hierarchy, to reveal any stable coalitions, to locate diffuse or rigid boundaries between family subsystems, and hopefully to reveal the chronically repeating interactional sequence that sustains the problem behavior. When this information has been obtained, the therapist is in a position to develop the interventions that will lead to beneficial change.

In-session Conference

When the therapist is working with an observing team, or even when working alone, it is useful at this point to leave the family and take a few minutes to think about what has been observed in order to abstract from the concrete interactions the patterns that need correction. When working with an observing team, it is often true that the observers are more able to perceive these patterns than the therapist who is immersed in the hypnotic pull of the family dance. It is for this reason that Carl Whitaker insists on working with a cotherapist (Whitaker & Bumberry, 1988). The purpose of the in-session conference is to assess the accuracy of the presession hypotheses and to reformulate them in light of the new data gathered during the session. When this has been done, it is possible to design directives (homework) that will begin to change the family's dysfunctional interactions. In some instances the appropriate homework is not clear, but it is my contention that some homework should still be assigned. Family therapy, or any kind of therapy for that matter, is unlikely to be successful if the therapy is encapsulated in the therapeutic hour. The therapist needs to make an assignment that will establish an on-going process that keeps the therapy salient throughout the week. When the therapist makes a homework assignment without being sure of its relevance, it is comforting to keep Jeff Zeig's dictum in mind. Zeig, who is an Ericksonian hypnotherapist, says his approach to therapy is "ready—shoot—aim" (1988). In other words, if you wait until you are absolutely sure of your interventions, therapy will be a long, drawn-out process. If you go with your hunches, and learn from the results, you will probably hit the bull's-eye much sooner.

Goal-setting Stage

As Haley (1987) has said, "If therapy is to end properly, it must begin properly—by negotiating a solvable problem and discovering the social situation that makes the problem necessary" (p. 8). The purpose of the goal-setting stage is to reach agreement with the family on a solvable problem and to initiate a process that will alter the social situation in such a way that the problem is no longer necessary. It is essential that the problem to be solved be stated in behavioral terms so that one will know when it has been solved. It is equally essential that the problem be one that the therapist believes is capable of solution. Often the process of operationalizing the complaint will be sufficient to produce a solvable problem. When a "rebellious child" problem is operationalized to "staying out after curfew," we have a target on which one can draw a bead. However, some problems, and this would include most of the categories of the DSM-III-R (1987), are not capable of solution. With ambiguous problems, the therapist must reframe the problem in such a way that it can be solved, and in such a way that the family will accept it. This is not an easy task and sometimes taxes the therapist's creative resources. A notable example would be a case in which Haley reframed a case of schizophrenia as "pseudo-schizophrenia" and then went on to help the family specify how the IP's behavior might be improved. It cannot be emphasized enough that the problem to be solved must be stated in behavioral terms; i.e., never negotiate to "improve communication," "raise self-esteem," or "make our family more cohesive."

When agreement has been reached regarding the problem, the therapist should assign homework that will have face validity with regard to the problem, but will also address the underlying structural or sequential changes that are necessary. In the case of "pseudo-schizophrenia" mentioned above, we might assume that the family is obsessively monitoring the patient, watching for abnormal behavior. An assignment that would utilize the obsessive nature of the family (pacing) and still institute a change would be to ask the family to keep an elaborate baseline measure of the "normal" behavior of the patient and bring it to the next session.

In a family with a daughter who is not keeping an assigned curfew, it might appear that the rebelliousness is being secretly (and perhaps unconsciously) reinforced by the father. An intervention might be to put dad in charge of the daughter's behavior for a week, asking him during the session to negotiate with his daughter the expectations and consequences of noncompliance.

Initial sessions, particularly with large families, often cannot be conducted within the usual 50-minute hour. If it is not possible to schedule a longer session, it is likely that it will take more than one session to establish the therapeutic contract. When this is true, one should still attempt to give some kind of homework assignment that will increase the power of the therapy. When in doubt, asking family members to each keep a baseline of the behavior that they see as problematic is a good first step.

Ending Stage

The therapist should end the session by setting a second appointment and specifying who should be present. The family should not be asked if they want to return; this should be assumed unless someone indicates otherwise.

Post-session

When working with a team, there should be a post-session debriefing to give an opportunity to share various perceptions of the family and the response to the interventions. When working alone, it is essential to record your impressions of the presenting problem, the family structure, hypotheses regarding needed changes and, most importantly, the homework that was assigned. The latter should be recorded verbatim, if possible, in order to check on the family compliance.

FAMILY THERAPY TECHNIQUES

In the preceding section the focus was on the process of conducting the initial interview. In this section, we will focus on the techniques utilized by the therapist throughout the therapy. The techniques offered here are derived from several therapeutic points of view.

Circular Questioning

Following Bateson's dictum that "information is a difference; difference is a relationship (or a change in the relationship)," the Milan group developed a technique they refer to as circular questioning (Selvini et al., 1980). The "circular" referred to here is epistemological; their questions are intended to uncover the complementarity of family relationships that make the presenting symptom necessary for family homeostasis. Every member of the family is invited to tell how he or she sees the relationship between two other family members; or between two different periods of time; or any other difference likely to be significant to the family. For example:

1. In terms of family relationships: "Tell us how you see the relationship between your sister and your mother."
2. In terms of specific interactive behaviors: "When your father gets mad at Bill, what does your mother do?"
3. In terms of differences in behavior: "Who gets most upset when Jimmy wets the bed, your father or your mother?"
4. In terms of ranking by various members of the family of a behavior or interaction: "Who is closest to your grandmother? Who is next, and next?"
5. In terms of change in the relationship before and after a precise event: "Did you and your sister fight more or less before your mother remarried?"
6. In terms of differences in respect to hypothetical circumstances: "If one of you kids should have to stay home, not get married, who would be best for your mother? Your father?" (Fleuridas, Nelson, & Rosenthal, 1986).

Perhaps it should be mentioned here, parenthetically, that this procedure would be anathemic to some other therapists, including Virginia Satir, who specifically proscribes "gossiping" and "mind-reading." However, the Milan group has demonstrated that often more can be obtained by asking a person what he or she thinks about others than by asking more personal questions. When this is done in the family context, where all can hear and respond, the result is quite different than it would be in an interview with an individual.

Reframing

Haley (1987) says, "It cannot be emphasized enough that the problem the therapist settles on must be a problem which the family wants changed but which is put in a form that makes it solvable" (p. 38). While some problems presented by families lend themselves readily to therapeutic intervention, frequently it is necessary for the therapist to reframe the problem. Reframing may include the following:

1. Operationalizing—casting the problem in observable, behavioral terms. The problem of "a child who is driving us crazy" is reframed by specifying the specific behaviors that are problematic and asking the parents to keep a record of their frequency of occurrence.
2. Emphasizing complementarity—describing the problem in an interactional context, rather than as the property of one member of the family. A father who is depressed is asked, "Who makes you depressed?"
3. Denominalizing—removing a reified diagnostic label and replacing it with a behavior that can be consciously controlled. Anorexia might be reframed as "a girl who refuses to eat."
4. Positive connotation—describing the symptomatic behavior as positively motivated in the service of the family system. A defiant, delinquent boy is described as particularly sensitive to family conflict and his behavior as a sacrificial act designed to keep the parents from divorce.

Giving Directives

Giving directives refers to creating or selecting an intervention that will attack the hypothesized basis of the presenting problem. According to Haley (1987), giving directives has several purposes:

> "...the main goal of therapy is to get people to behave differently and so to have different subjective experiences. Directives are a way of making those changes happen. . . . directives are used to intensify the relationship with the therapist. By telling people what to do the therapist gets involved in the action . . . directives are used to gather information. When a therapist tells people what to do, the ways they respond give information about them and about how they will respond to the changes wanted. Whether they do what the therapist asks, do not do it, forget to do it, or try and fail, the therapist has information she would not otherwise have. (p. 56)

Directives can be categorized as either compliance- or defiance-oriented. Compliance-oriented directives are offered to families who may be expected to carry out the assignment as given. When the therapist wants the family to carry out the directive, the following should be considered:

1. The directive should be framed in such a way as to use the language and imagery of the family and be focused on solving the problem presented by the family.
2. Don't ask the family *not* to do something; ask them to do something different.

3. Ask everyone to do something.
4. Be extremely concrete and repetitive (unless you have reason to be otherwise).
5. Arrange for concrete, specific feedback.
6. Practice the homework during the session, or at least ask the family to tell you in their own words what the assignment includes.
7. Use antisabotage techniques: brainstorm reasons why they might not be able to comply; suggest probable problems that might interfere with compliance; discuss how they can overcome the problems.

Compliance-oriented directives can be either straightforward or paradoxical; the main idea is that you want them to be carried out. An example of a straightforward directive would be to ask Dad to be in charge of the discipline, and ask Mom to keep a record of problem behaviors and report them for his consideration. An example of a compliance-oriented paradoxical directive would be to prescribe the symptom to occur at a special time and place.

The following are some examples of compliance-oriented directives:

1. Caring days: Ask a hostile couple to act as if they care for each other by daily performing five minor behaviors requested by his or her spouse (Stuart, 1980).
2. Role reversal: Ask a disengaged husband to give his enmeshed wife a vacation from responsibility for the children. He is to be totally responsible for the meting out of discipline; she may consult with him, but is not to be in charge.
3. Safe practice: Ask a man who is afraid of job interviews to apply for jobs that he would not take if they were offered.
4. Surprise: Ask a couple who are hostile and out of touch with each other to plan a surprise that will please the other, but would be so out of character that the other could never guess what it would be. Each should attempt to guess what the other will do, making a written record of his or her guesses.
5. Symptom prescription: Ask a single mother with two boys who are disrespectful to their mother and constantly fighting to hold a daily wrestling match where she is the referee and will enforce fair fighting; boys are to agree to reserve their fighting to these bouts. Mother is to insist on "the bouts" even if the boys are unwilling.

Defiance-oriented directives are offered to families whom one assumes to be resistant. The intention is to have the family defy the therapist in such a way as to eliminate the problem behavior. Defiance-oriented directives are always paradoxical. When the therapist wants the family to defy the directives the following should be considered:

1. Do this only with families that have demonstrated their resistance.
2. Use this only after you have joined the family sufficiently to make noncompliance a significant issue. Your relationship to the family should be clearly defined as one of bringing about change.
3. The problem to be solved should be clearly defined and agreed on.
4. The rationale for the directive must utilize the family language and imagery and provide an acceptable rationale for the directive. Haley (1987) says that designing paradoxical directives is easy; you simply observe how the family members are behaving and ask them to continue. How you make the directive appear reasonable and how you react to changes that occur are the hard parts.
5. Give the directive and ask for a report.
6. When the family reports that they did not carry out the homework, condemn the noncompliance and be puzzled and surprised by the symptom reduction. Don't take credit for the change!
7. Repeat the directive and warn against relapse.

The following are some examples of defiance-oriented directives:

1. Positive connotation. Reframe the problem behavior in positive terms and indicate that it would be dangerous for the family to change.
2. Symptom increase. Recommend that the problem behavior be increased in order to get a better understanding of it.
3. Restraining. Recommend that the family slow down in its attempts to solve the problem.
4. Symptom retention. Advise the family to retain a certain percent of the problem in order to remember how awful it was.
5. Predict relapse of a symptom that has been brought under control.

Ordeals

Ordeals are offered to families who are highly motivated to change but can't seem to accomplish their purpose. An ordeal is a behavior that is more obnoxious, frustrating, and time-consuming than the symptomatic behavior. The family must agree to perform the ordeal whenever the symptom occurs. In order to be successful, the ordeal should contain the following elements:

1. The problem must be clearly defined.
2. The person must be committed to getting over the problem.
3. An ordeal must be selected with the client's collaboration "...the ordeal should be voluntary by the person and good for the person experiencing it, but not necessarily for the person imposing it...to inadvertently cause a person to suffer is one thing; to arrange it deliberately is quite another" (Haley, 1984, p. 13).
4. The directive must be given with a rationale.
5. The ordeal must continue until the problem is solved.
6. The ordeal is in a social context. The therapist must be prepared to assist in the systemic reorganization that the elimination of the symptom will require (Haley, 1984).

An example of an ordeal might be a bulimic woman with a stingy husband. The woman has been binging and forcing herself to vomit for years. Her husband becomes aware of the symptom and they come to therapy. After establishing a relationship with them and ensuring the couple's commitment to solving the problem, the therapist might offer the following ordeal. When the wife feels she can no longer avoid a binge, she and her husband should go to the store and buy all the foods that the wife prefers to binge on, spending at least $25.00. They are then to return home and together they are to unwrap all of the food and stuff it down the garbage disposal. This is to continue until the wife no longer feels the need to binge.

Jay Haley developed the concept of ordeal therapy as the result of his experience with Milton Erickson. He presents some of Erickson's cases that use the ordeal in *Uncommon Therapy* (Haley, 1973); his further development of the concept is presented in his book *Ordeal Therapy* (Haley, 1984).

Rituals

Rituals can be used in therapy to help an individual or family move from one status or state to another. Rituals are particularly helpful in closing off past anger and guilt. The following examples illustrate their use:

1. Closing off the past. A couple who couldn't resist fighting over wrongs done by the other in the past were asked to write down

all their complaints, put them in a box, wrap them carefully, and bury them outside the therapist's window. They were told that the past was buried there and if they wanted to fight over it, they would have to come to the therapist's office. (Coppersmith, 1985).

2. "Rites of passage." A gentile couple were having difficulty dealing with their 13-year-old son. They were over involved and too restrictive; he was increasingly rebellious. They were asked to plan a "Christian bar mitzvah" to symbolize his coming of age.

Ambiguous Assignments

Assignments that are mysterious and apparently unrelated to the presenting problem can be helpful in encouraging a family to find its own solution to its problems. While what is to be done should be absolutely clear, the purpose for doing it should be completely obscure—at least to the clients. The purpose of the assignment is to depotentiate conscious, linear thinking about the problem and allow creativity in reframing to take place. Milton Erickson often asked people to climb Squaw Peak. The peak, located in north Phoenix near his home, offered a considerable, but not unreasonable, challenge and provided plenty of time to think about why the task was assigned (Lankton, 1988).

Another example would be a task we assigned to a 30-year-old son who was having trouble leaving home: "We'd like you to go to the store and buy a goldfish and everything you will need to take care of it." Interestingly, he defied the directive and instead bought a Christmas cactus because, "it will be easier to take with me when I leave after the holidays."

Assigning Directives

When a directive has been determined, the therapist must also decide how to present it to the family in a way that they will accept it (or in the case of paradox, reject it). It is important to allow plenty of time to seed the intervention, assign it, clarify it, and practice it. It is also important to couch the task in the family's language and to tie task completion to the presenting problem. Whenever possible, dramatize the assignment by delaying the actual presentation as you ruminate on whether the family is really ready for it. The extreme of this dramatization is the "devil's pact" where the assignment is delayed for several sessions and offered only after the family has agreed to comply without knowing what the assignment will be.

Haley (1987) decries the fact that most clinical training does not include the development of skill in the area of assigning directives and hence that most clinicians must learn it on their own. He indicates most of his own skill in this area was learned from Milton Erickson.

Collecting the Homework

A cardinal rule of this sort of therapy is to be sure to collect the homework, and to take either compliance or noncompliance very seriously. If the homework is ignored or not given sufficient attention, it signals very clearly to the family that compliance is not necessary. The reaction (or nonreaction) of the family to the assignment allows us to aim more carefully on our second attempt.

When the family has carried out the task, congratulate them and encourage them to process the experience. Do not explain why the assignment was given or interpret the outcome.

When the family has only partially complied or did not carry out the task, it is often best for the therapist to take the blame for the noncompliance, indicating either that perhaps the assignment was not sufficiently concrete and specific enough for this family to understand or that perhaps the therapist has miscalculated and the family was really not ready for such a task at this time. In either case, in order to demonstrate their capacity for understanding or their readiness for change, the family will be motivated to complete the next task that is assigned (Haley, 1987).

The techniques offered in the section above are, of course, only a brief introduction to the procedures used by various family therapists. Unfortunately, space does not allow a more complete discussion. I am particularly conscious of having omitted the in-session techniques of Virginia Satir (1983) and Carl Whitaker (1981) and the coaching techniques associated with the transgenerational work of Murray Bowen (Kerr & Bowen, 1988). Two very useful sources for family therapy techniques are the *Handbook of Structured Techniques in Marriage and Family Therapy* (Sherman & Fredman, 1986) and the *Family Therapy Source Book* (Piercy & Sprenkle, 1986).

LEGAL AND ETHICAL ISSUES

The ethical codes of the American Association for Counseling and Development (1981) and the American Psychological Association (1981) are applicable to the practice of family therapy, but the American Association of Marriage and Family Therapy code (1982) is perhaps more relevant. Elsewhere in this text (Chapter 19), Sharon Robinson has presented the legal and ethical issues related to counseling. However, when one assumes a family systems orientation, some special issues arise; some areas of practice that are especially problematic for the family therapist are as follows:

Responsibility—Who is the client? Is it possible to serve all members of a family even-handedly? Can you define the family system or the relationship as the client? Does insisting on seeing the whole family before treatment can begin deny treatment to those who are motivated? Is it ethical to coerce reluctant members into therapy?

Confidentiality—Is the promise of confidentiality given to the family as a unit, or does it apply to individual family members? What should be done about information obtained from an individual prior to the involvement of other family members? Can you offer confidentiality to children when seen in a family therapy context? If family members are seen separately during family therapy, should they be promised confidentiality? Does privileged communication exist for a family? Will a written agreement not to subpoena hold up legally? Can one member of the family waive privileged communication for all?

Therapist control—Is it appropriate for the therapist to increase the family stress in order to bring about change? Should the therapist use indirect (hypnotic, metaphoric) or paradoxical procedures that bypass conscious processes? Is the use of such techniques a violation of the concept of informed consent? In dealing with "inappropriate hierarchies" may the therapist impose his or her own values on the family? Is family therapy antithetical to the feminist perspective?

Informed consent—Who should consent to treatment? What needs to be disclosed? How can a therapist utilize defiance-oriented directives or paradox and also provide full disclosure? (Huber & Baruth, 1987; Margolin, 1982).

The current context does not allow space for resolution of these issues, and in fact, several of them cannot be readily resolved. The counselor who is interested in working within a family therapy perspective should, however, be aware of these issues and be prepared to grapple with them.

RESEARCH IN FAMILY THERAPY

Research into the efficacy of family therapy suffers from the same problems inherent in research into the efficacy of any form of therapy, or one might say, the problems inherent in most of social science research. In order to meet the demands of scientific rigor, the therapeutic process must be trivialized. When therapy is represented in all its complexity and interactive richness, experimental control is usually lost. Despite this quandary, research into the effectiveness of family therapy has grown exponentially. A summary of the published research in 1972 (Wells, Dilkes, & Trivelli) revealed only 13 studies; six years later that number had grown to over 200 studies (Gurman & Kniskern, 1978), and the beat goes on.

In a more recent summary of outcome research on family therapy, Gurman and Kniskern (1981) began with the following caveats:

> (a) In general, it is impossible to disentangle treatment effects from therapist effects in the studies done to date.
> (b) The treatments that have been studied have almost never followed "pure" applications of given treatment models.
> (c) With infrequent exceptions, it is impossible to be certain just what specific treatment interventions have actually been used, since treatment operations have almost never been described in detail. (p. 745)

In other words, one cannot be sure just what was done, nor do the studies adequately document to whom or by whom it was done; thus it is impossible to aggregate the results appropriately, and of course, it is even more impossible to make comparative statements of efficacy. Despite this lack of certainty, the authors were able to conclude that their analysis of the nonbehavioral family therapy research "suggests that such treatments are often effective beyond chance...(and that)...the effects of behavioral family therapies...is also quite positive" (Gurman & Kniskern, 1981, pp. 745–746). It seems possible that all of the man (or woman) hours involved in such research might have been better used.

Unless the reader should be left with the impression that only family therapy outcome research is of doubtful scientific value, let me cite the conclusions of what is considered to be one of the most extensive studies of the efficacy of therapy in general. This meta-analysis by Smith, Glass, and Miller (1980) included 475 studies of all kinds of psychotherapy.

> Psychotherapy is beneficial, consistently so and in many different ways. Its benefits are on a par with other expensive and ambitious interventions, such as schooling and medicine. The benefits of psychotherapy are not permanent, but then little is. (p. 183)
> Different types of psychotherapy (verbal or behavioral, psychodynamic, client-centered or systematic desensitization) do not produce different types or degrees of benefits. (p. 184)
> Differences in how psychotherapy is conducted (whether in groups or individually, by experienced or novice therapists, for long or short periods of time, and the like) make very little difference in how beneficial it is. (pp. 187–188)

Again, the elephant has labored and brought forth a gnat. It doesn't seem to matter what is done, to whom, or by whom; psychotherapy, like education, appears to have a salutary effect. One is left to wonder if given the same scientific scrutiny, the same might be said of religious experience, playing baseball, or watching television?

It is not my intention to denigrate psychotherapy. Rather, I am questioning the utility of research on the outcomes of psychotherapy. As suggested by Ryder (1988), attempts to prove the efficacy of family therapy are essentially politically motivated (in the sense of being self-serving), and morally questionable. In any case, such attempts are as likely to produce unequivocal results as the search for the Holy Grail. Given the paradigms that are currently acceptable to the scientific establishment, it is not possible to do an adequate research study on a phenomenon as complex as psychotherapy. Those who are motivated to deny the efficacy of family therapy "can be counted on to attribute apparently positive findings to poor statistics, inadequate randomization, evanescent enthusiasm (the old Hawthorne effect as applied to therapists), dropouts, trivial or fakeable measures and so on and on into the night" (Ryder, 1988, pp. 47–48). If this is the case (and I believe it is), it would seem that our time and effort might better be put into other endeavors—perhaps doing family therapy.

CONCLUSION

This chapter has attempted to introduce the reader to the contextual thinking that is the essence of family therapy. I have tried to illustrate this perspective through a description of the diagnostic system, the initial interview, and some of the techniques that are used. The efficacy of research in family therapy has been addressed, and some special legal and ethical issues that are of concern to family therapists have been raised. It is my hope that this brief introduction to the concepts and techniques of family therapy will whet the reader's appetite for further exploration. If that should prove to be the case, the items in the references which are starred* are good points of departure.

REFERENCES

Ackerman, N. (1958). *The psychodynamics of family life*. New York: Basic Books.

American Association for Counseling and Development. (1981). *Ethical standards*. Alexandria, VA: AACD.

American Association of Marriage and Family Therapists. (1982). *Code of professional ethics and standards for public information and advertising.* Upland, CA: AAMFT.

American Psychological Association. (1981). *Ethical principles of psychologists.* Washington, DC: APA.

American Psychiatric Association. (1987). *Diagnostic and statistical manual of mental disorders* (3rd ed., rev.). Washington, DC: APA.

Bateson, G., Jackson, D., Haley, J., & Weakland, J. (1956). Toward a theory of schizophrenia. *Behavioral Science, 1,* 251–264.

Bergman, J. (1985). *Fishing for barracuda.* New York: W. W. Norton.

Bowen, M. (1978). *Family therapy in clinical practice.* New York: Aronson.

Carter, E., & McGoldrick, M. (1980). *The family life cycle: A framework for family therapy.* New York: Gardner Press.

Coppersmith, E. (1985). We've got a secret. In A. Gurman (Ed.), *Casebook of family therapy.* New York: Guilford.

Fleuridas, C., Nelson, T., & Rosenthal, D. (1986). The evolution of circular questions: Training family therapists. *Journal of Marriage and Family Therapy, 12,* 113–127.

Gurman, A., & Kniskern, D. (1978). The outcomes of family therapy; implications for training and practice. In G. Berenson, H. White (Eds.), *Annual review of family therapy.* New York: Human Sciences Press.

Gurman, A., & Kniskern, D. (Eds.) (1981). *Handbook of family therapy.* New York: Brunner/Mazel.

Gurman, A., & Kniskern, D. (1981). Family therapy outcome research: Knowns and unknowns. In A. Gurman, & D. Kniskern (Eds.), *Handbook of family therapy.* New York: Brunner/Mazel.

Haley, J. (1973). *Uncommon therapy: The psychiatric techniques of Milton H. Erickson,* M.D. New York: W. W. Norton

Haley, J. (1984). *Ordeal therapy.* San Francisco: Jossey-Bass.

*Haley, J. (1987). *Problem solving therapy* (2nd ed.). San Francisco: Jossey-Bass.

Huber, C., & Baruth, L. (1987). *Ethical, legal and professional issues in the practice of marriage and family therapy.* Columbus OH: Merrill.

*Kerr, M., & Bowen, M. (1988). *Family evaluation.* New York: W. W. Norton.

Lankton, C. (1988). Task assignments: Logical and otherwise. In J. Zeig & S. Lankton (Eds.), *Developing Ericksonian therapy.* New York: Brunner/Mazel.

Lankton, S. (1980). *Practical magic.* Cupertino, CA: Meta Publications.

Margolin, G. (1982). Ethical and legal considerations in marital and family therapy. *American Psychologist, 37*(7), 788–801.

*Minuchin, S. (1974). *Families and family therapy.* Cambridge, MA: Harvard University Press.

Minuchin, S., Montalvo, B., Gurney, B., Rosman, B., & Schumer, F. (1967). *Families of the slums.* New York: Basic Books.

Minuchin, S., Rosman, B., & Baker, L. (1978). *Psychosomatic families.* Cambridge, MA: Harvard University Press.

Minuchin, S. (1982). Reflections on boundaries. *American Journal of Orthopsychiatry, 52,* 655–663.

Piercy, F., & Sprenkle, D. (1986). *Family therapy source book.* New York: Guilford.

Ritterman, M. (1986). Exploring relationships between Ericksonian hypnotherapy and family therapy. In S. de Shazer, & R. Kral (Eds.), *Indirect approaches in therapy*. Rockville, MD: Aspen Publications.

Ryder, R. (1988). The Holy Grail: Proven efficacy in family therapy. In L. Wynne (Ed.), *The state of the art in family therapy research: Controversies and recommendations*. New York: Family Process Press.

Satir, V. (1964). *Conjoint family therapy*. Palo Alto, CA: Science & Behavior Books.

*Satir, V. (1983). *Conjoint family therapy*, 3rd ed. Palo Alto, CA: Science & Behavior Books.

Selvini, M., Boscolo, L., Cecchin, G., & Prata, G. (1980). Hypothesizing-circularity-neutrality: Three guidelines for the conductor of the session. *Family Process, 19*(1), 3–12.

Sherman, R., & Fredman, N. (1986). *Handbook of structured techniques in marriage and family therapy*. New York: Brunner/Mazel.

Sieburg, E. (1985). *Family communication*. New York: Gardner Press.

Smith, M., Glass, G., & Miller, T. (1980). *The benefits of psychotherapy*. Baltimore: Johns Hopkins University Press.

Stanton, D. (1988). The lobster quadrille: Issues and dilemmas for family therapy research. In L. Wynne (Ed.), *The state of the art in family therapy research*. New York: Family Process Press.

Stuart, R. (1980). *Helping couples change*. New York: Guilford Press.

Watzlawick, P. (1966). Structured family interview. *Family Process, 5*, 256–271.

Watzlawick, P., Weakland, J., & Fisch, R. (1974). *Change: Principles of problem formation and problem resolution*. New York: W. W. Norton.

Wells, R., Dilkes, T., & Trivelli, N. (1972). The results of family therapy: A critical review of the literature. *Family Process, 7*, 189–207.

Whitaker, C., & Malone, T. (1953). *The roots of psychotherapy*. New York: Blakiston.

Whitaker, C., & Keith, D. (1981). Symbolic-experiential family therapy. In A. Gurman, & D. Kniskern (Eds.), *Handbook of family therapy*. New York: Brunner/Mazel.

*Whitaker, C., & Bumberry, W. (1988). *Dancing with the family: A symbolic-experiential approach*. New York: Brunner/Mazel.

Wynne, L. (1988). An overview of the state of the art. In L. Wynne, (Ed.), *The state of the art in family therapy research*. New York: Family Process Press.

Zeig, J. (1988). Personal communication.

16■

Counseling Gay and Lesbian Clients

REESE M. HOUSE, ED.D., N.C.C.
Oregon State University
Corvallis, Oregon

THERE ARE AT LEAST 20 to 25 million gay and lesbian[1] individuals in the United States, based on the conservative estimate that approximately 10 percent of the adult population is exclusively gay (Kinsey et al., 1953; Kinsey, Pomeroy, & Martin, 1948). These figures underestimate the true number of homoerotic people in society. Many individuals engage in homosexual activity from time to time, and many choose not to report such activity. As Kinsey and his colleagues wrote: "any question as to the number of persons in the world who are homosexual and the number who are heterosexual is unanswerable" (1948, p. 650).

Whatever the exact number of gays in the United States, they are becoming more visible. Before the 1970s, gays were a fairly invisible

---

[1]Gay is used as a general term for both men and women (Silberman & Hawkins, 1988). For the sake of linguistic simplicity the word gay will be used in this chapter to refer to both male and female homoerotic individuals, unless otherwise indicated in the text. Men who do identify themselves as being attracted to the same gender usually prefer to be called gay rather than homosexual, and most women who use an identifying term call themselves lesbian or gay women.

part of the American population. This invisibility was, to a large extent, by choice. The stigmatization of homosexuality in our society caused most gays to avoid the risks associated with disclosing their sexual orientation. "Hostility and discrimination at the hands of an unaccepting society created a climate of secrecy that did not permit challenges to the prevailing stereotypes" (Blumstein & Schwartz, 1983, p. 9). In the past 20 years, great numbers of gays have identified themselves and developed a community identity to counter negative reactions from society. As more and more people identify themselves as gay, all members of society, including counselors, are forced to address issues involving gay individuals.

All counselors have clients who are gay. Some of these clients will be self-identified as gay and some will hide their gay identity and pass as heterosexual. Some counselors may say, "I don't know anyone who is gay," or "No gay people will come to me as a high school counselor or pastoral counselor," or "I have no intention of having gay clients on my caseload." These perceptions are inaccurate. Whether a counselor has a private practice, works for an agency, school, church, or business, or is in the military, he or she will have clients who are homoerotic. This chapter provides an introduction to basic facts and issues about being gay that will help counselors become effective when working with gay clients and their families and friends.

Who Is Gay?

The initial challenge for counselors may be in determining that a client is gay. There is no typical gay or lesbian. Contrary to prevailing stereotypes, all gay males are not hairdressers with platform shoes and excessive jewelry. Neither do all lesbians wear flannel shirts and blue jeans. There is no description that is completely inclusive, and describing the "typical" gay male or lesbian is impossible. Homoerotic people come from a cross-section of races, nationalities, religions, socioeconomic levels, family backgrounds, geographic locations, and cultures. There are gay parents, spouses, children, teenagers, couples, grandparents, uncles, aunts, and cousins. Similarly, the sexual preference of an individual cannot be determined by occupation. Gays are business owners, ministers, teachers, lawyers, truck drivers, members of the armed services, and industrial workers. The following examples illustrate the diversity of gay clients. These illustrations show that gays face the same problems as other individuals, but that the special issue of sexual orientation requires counselors to adopt procedures that take this factor into consideration.

1. Sally and Jennifer are a lesbian couple who have been living as partners in the same small community for ten years. They are 31 and

34. Sally is a nurse and Jennifer works as a counselor in a drug treatment program. Sally and Jennifer decided they wanted to have a child together and Sally was artificially inseminated. Their son Kevin is now seven and attends public school. As co-parents, the two women attend school functions and work with Kevin's teachers on his academic and social progress. Sally and Jennifer face the same issues as any couple in raising a child. However, some teachers are uncomfortable working with Sally and Jennifer as co-parents and some children tease Kevin about having two mothers.

2. Chet is a 33-year-old male lawyer who has entered a 28-day treatment program for cocaine abuse. He is a successful attorney, practicing in a large law firm. He is gay and lives with his lover of three years. No one at work knows that he is gay. As a closeted individual, he is reluctant to discuss his sexual preference in the treatment program. However, the issue of being gay and closeted, which requires leading a "double" life, causes stress and exacerbates his abuse of cocaine. Chet must face his abuse issues in treatment and also needs to address the issues surrounding his gay life, or the treatment is not likely to be successful.

3. Joe is a 19-year-old freshman in college who was a star football player in high school. Joe confronts the usual stresses of all college freshmen. In addition, he has discovered that he is attracted to men. On a visit back home, he tries to discuss his feelings with his high school football coach, whom he trusts and respects. The football coach is unclear about how to respond to Joe and seeks the advice of the high school counselor.

These examples demonstrate that issues of sexual orientation arise in many contexts, with different degrees of significance, and can complicate day-to-day living problems. The causes of sexual orientation have not been determined. What is known "is that persons with diverse sexual orientations exist and that the existence of this diversity is not pathological" (Dworkin & Gutierrez, 1989, p. 7). The most recent studies suggest that sexual orientation results from neonatal hormonal activity and early childhood socialization (Money, 1987, 1988). Regardless of the cause of sexual orientation, the counselor needs to recognize and acknowledge issues facing gays in order to address them in a nonbiased and professional manner.

Definition of Gay and Lesbian

Stein & Cohen (1986) define homosexuality as "an attraction for a person of the same sex within one or more of the dimensions of affection, fantasy, or erotic desire" (p. 28). However, it is not always easy to define who is gay or lesbian. A significant number of people in society have same-sex relations. How do we know which of these individuals is lesbian or gay? What about the adolescent male who fantasizes about another boy in the classroom? Or the individual who has had a few same-sex experiences as a teenager? What about the husband of many years who occasionally has sex with a man? What about the woman who feels an occasional attraction to another woman? Or the person who has sexual desires for a person of the same gender but never acts upon the desire?

The answers to these and many other questions about sexual preferences are often confusing and unclear. And, as Krajeski (1986) noted, the terminology used in professional writing about homosexuality has often been imprecise. Part of the confusion results from the "popular misconception that homosexuality and sex are one and the same" (Blumenfeld & Raymond, 1988, p. 85). The fact that an individual engages in specific sexual conduct does not define that person as homosexual or heterosexual. Kinsey, Pomeroy, & Martin (1948) were the first to indicate that the labels "homosexuality" and "heterosexuality" do not describe most people. They concluded that people's preferences were not exclusive and that homosexuality and heterosexuality are poles on a continuum (Table 16–1). This continuum suggests that people engage in a range of sexual behavior. Some people always have sex with a person of the opposite gender. Others always have sex with a person of the same gender. However, many people act sexually with both genders. Most people cannot be clearly categorized at either affectional pole and cannot ac-

TABLE 16–1 The Kinsey Scale of the continuum of human sexual experience.

Kinsey Rating	Description
0	Exclusively heterosexual in psychological response and behavior
1	Predominantly heterosexual; incidental homosexual behavior
2	Predominantly heterosexual; more than incidental homosexual behavior
3	Equally heterosexual and homosexual in psychological response and behavior
4	Predominantly homosexual; more than incidental heterosexual behavior
5	Predominantly homosexual; incidental heterosexual behavior
6	Exclusively homosexual in psychological response and behavior

curately be identified as either "homosexual" or "heterosexual." The term "bisexual" emerged from the Kinsey continuum to describe those individuals who engage in sexual behavior with both sexes. Homoerotic people prefer intimate emotional and physical relationships with people of the same gender.

It is important to differentiate between "act" and "identity" when discussing sexual orientation. Individuals who focus only on the "act" believe that sexual acts or behaviors define the person. When using this concept, labels are given to the behaviors in question rather than to the person engaging in the behavior (Blumenfeld & Raymond, 1988). However, this behavior-based definition fails to recognize a holistic view of the person. For example, a teenager who experiments with same-sex behavior does not necessarily have a gay identity. The experimental behavior is just that, and to label someone as "homosexual" or "gay" because of such experimentation does not take into account the developmental nature of sexuality.

Those who ascribe to the "identity" theory assert that sexuality is "more than merely a behavior but is rather an aspect of personal identity which strongly influences the ways people live their lives and view the world at large" (Blumenfeld & Raymond, 1988, p. 77). Under this approach, being gay is associated with a lifestyle, not just sexual desires or behavior.

> Being gay is not merely the ability and willingness to engage in homosexual behavior. Indeed, being gay is being different, having a distinct identity, frequently in a way that is felt even before it is consciously or sexually expressed. Gayness is a special affinity and a special feeling toward people of the same gender; it is not the inability to love and to relate to others, nor is it a denial of the opposite sex. Rather it is a special capacity and need to love and to express one's love for people of the same gender in all the meanings of the term "love." (Woodman & Lenna, 1980, p. 11)

When members of society categorize any individual using only one dimension of humanness, a significant part of that person is omitted. This omission leads to stereotyping and labeling, which have a significant and detrimental impact on the individual. Examples of such stereotyping and labeling include "He is a dumb jock; what is he doing with a philosophy major?," "She's a woman; she shouldn't do that kind of work," "He's gay; he should not be allowed to work with children." All three of these statements focus on only one aspect of the individual. By focusing on an isolated aspect, the person in each of these three examples is unfairly judged to be unintelligent, physically weak, or morally deviant and not allowed the opportunity to demonstrate his or her own personal abilities. The more holistic approach to human behavior focuses on the integration of all aspects of the individual and includes the emotional, social, intellectual, spiritual, and physical dimensions of each person. This approach recognizes that individuals are unique and emphasizes the importance of looking at the whole person rather than determining someone's worth based on a single characteristic.

Counselors who work with gay individuals need to consider the more holistic view and realize that while sexual activity is a part of many relationships, it is frequently not the primary focus of relationships. Not all gay clients will come to counseling because they are gay or to address gay issues. Counselors need to address the issues that are presented and not make sexual orientation the problem. As counselors work with clients they need to be aware that clients may strongly object to being labeled based on their sexual orientation. Counselors would be wise to simply ask clients their terminology preference rather than use language that might offend clients.

HOMOPHOBIA

Cultural Homophobia

Gay people live in a homophobic culture. The term "homophobia" was first defined by Weinberg (1973) as a fear, dread, or loathing of individuals who define themselves as gay or lesbian. Perhaps it would be more accurate to describe homophobia as a fear of individuals who are "perceived" to be gay or lesbian. People who are homophobic rely upon their own preconceived ideas of sexuality. Silberman and Hawkins (1988) state "It is usually the larger society that defines homoerotic people as 'deviant' and therefore punishes them in a variety of ways" (p. 103). The entire society often makes a point of condemning, punishing, and outlawing the rights of gays to exist (Forstein, 1986). One recent study clearly demonstrates the pervasive nature of homophobia in our culture. Coles and Stokes (1985) surveyed the sexual attitudes of over 1000 American teenagers and found that 75 percent of those surveyed considered sex between two females to be disgusting and over 80 percent felt the same about sex between two males.

People who are homophobic downgrade, deny, stereotype, or ignore the existence of gays and lesbians. These phobic and negative responses range from individuals who tell "fag" jokes to the extreme example of violence such as hate crimes against gays. Hate crimes are popularly referred to as "fag" bashing. These homophobic reactions create a devalued minority in a hostile society. This hostility is reflected in the letters received by the *San Francisco Examiner* in response to its 16-part series on being "Gay in America." Letter writers said "It's not gay to be homosexual, it's disgusting, loathsome and perverted"; "You can print all the gay-lesbian articles you want, but those of us in mainstream

America who find the sordid sexual practices of gays and lesbians repugnant will never change our minds about these deviates."; and "Long live gay bashers!" (Rizzi, 1989; Warren, 1989; Wett, 1989).

Public figures have fueled the flames of bigotry through their public comments. Jerry Falwell, a fundamentalist Christian, stated that AIDS was "the judgment of God" on gays for "subanimal behavior." Morton Downey, a television talk show host, stated that he was "turned off by that type of sickness (homosexuality)." Anita Bryant, a singer turned political activist, asked "Why do you think homosexuals are called fruits? It's because they eat the forbidden fruit of the tree of life...which is male sperm." Jesse Helms, a Senator from North Carolina, said in testifying against a hate crimes bill "We have to call a spade a spade and a perverted human being a perverted human being." And Eddie Murphy, a comedian, includes stereotypical parodies in his routines, characterizing gays as limp-wristed and swishy ("A Special Report," 1989, p. 24). These examples of homophobia by public figures evince the general acceptance of homophobia in our culture. They also perpetuate homophobia, giving it the credibility of public statement without societal retribution. One need only imagine the response to similar statements about racial or religious minorities to see clearly the societal acceptance of public expressions of homophobia. Such comments create a polarization between gays and the members of society who purport and tolerate such homophobic comments.

Cultural homophobia is manifested in the widespread discrimination faced by gays. Gay individuals are discriminated against in employment and housing. Certain career positions such as teaching, the military, police, and public office are frequently available only to those who pass as heterosexual. Likewise, those who are known or perceived to be gay are frequently denied housing. Gays are even denied the sanctuary of many religious organizations on the basis of their sexual orientation. In a recent edict, Pope John Paul denounced homosexual activity as "an intrinsic moral evil" and called upon churches to dissociate themselves from gays. As a result many gay Catholic organizations have been evicted from church property and denied participation in church activities. Gays are also denied legal recognition as couples, leading to limitations on visitation rights in hospitals, lack of survivorship benefits, and the denial of the right to participate in a variety of other benefits available only to married couples.

Heterosexism

Cultural homophobia goes hand in hand with heterosexism, which is the assumption of normality and superiority by heterosexuals. Mollenkott (1985) defines heterosexism as a set of political assumptions that empower heterosexual persons, especially heterosexual white males, and excludes openly homosexual persons from social, religious, and political power. It is a system that demands heterosexuality in return for first-class citizenship. It is a system that forces homosexual persons into silence concerning the majority of their lives. (p. 14)

Heterosexism is the societal norm in the United States against which gays must struggle. It includes the subtle and indirect ways that the system reinforces heterosexuality as the only acceptable and viable life option. As Blumenfeld and Raymond (1988) state:

Very often heterosexism is quite subtle or indirect and may not even be apparent. When parents automatically expect that their children will marry a person of the other sex at some future date and will rear children within this union; when the only positive and satisfying relationships portrayed by the media are heterosexual; when teachers presume all of their students are straight and teach only about the contributions of heterosexuality these are examples of heterosexism. It also takes the form of pity—when the dominant group, looks upon sexual minorities as poor unfortunates who "can't help being the way they are." All this amounts to, in the words of author Christopher Isherwood, a "Heterosexual dictatorship." (p. 244)

Homophobia and heterosexism are the two faces of discrimination that gays confront in their daily lives. Heterosexism, the more insidious form of discrimination, occurs by neglect, omission, and/or distortion. Homophobia is discrimination by intent and design (Blumenfeld & Raymond, 1988).

Changing Attitudes

Despite the extent of homophobia and heterosexism in the United States, surveys indicate that the American public may be changing its attitudes toward gays and lesbians. In 1983, a survey by *Newsweek* magazine reported that 66 percent of the U.S. population felt that homosexuality was an unacceptable lifestyle (Blumenfeld & Raymond, 1988). In 1989, *The San Francisco Examiner,* which conducted the most extensive poll ever of attitudes toward gay people, concluded that Americans are becoming more accepting of gay people and gay rights ("A Special Report," 1989). In this national poll, the *Examiner* found that only 48 percent of the people surveyed believed that homosexuality was an unacceptable lifestyle. This change in attitude is also reflected in the belief of those surveyed that it is prejudicial to deny employment based on sexual orientation and that discrimination against homosexuals has diminished. Recent antidiscrimination law suits have been settled in favor of gays, which supports the changing attitudes of Americans. Although the most recent surveys are encouraging, they still show the continuing prevalence of homophobia in our society.

Internalized Homophobia

Homophobia is expressed by individuals in a number of ways. Perhaps the most devastating expression is internalized homophobia. Societal homophobia consists of the totality of negative attitudes concerning homosexuality, and internalized homophobia represents an internalization of these negative attitudes and assumptions by an individual (Sophie, 1987). The internalized homophobia results from the combination of negative attitudes apparent in cultural homophobia and an individual's own fear of being homosexual. Gay individuals learn to fear their sexual orientation from the negative attitudes expressed by others in society. "Bisexuals, lesbians, and gay males live in a world that teaches that same-sex activity is morally repulsive, psychologically damaging, or that it does not exist at all" (Blumenfeld & Raymond, 1988, p. 264). This negative information about their sexuality comes from credible sources such as friends, family, church, school, and mass media. When this information is internalized it creates substantial dissonance. This dissonance often results in low self-esteem, threatens the development of identity, and becomes a major source of distress for gay clients.

Homophobia in Counselors

Counselors are raised in the same homophobic culture as everyone else. Counselors may believe that they are not afflicted with homophobia and that they are immune to these negative responses toward gays. However, such immunity seems unlikely. Counselors who have not confronted their homophobic beliefs and behaviors provide inadequate, improper, and harmful services to gay clients and those related to or dependent on them (Moses & Hawkins, 1985). Table 16–2 poses personal homophobia assessment questions, developed by the National Association of Social Workers (NASW, 1985, pp. 153–154) to help counselors identify and address their own homophobia. The questions may also be used in counseling sessions with clients who are dealing with homophobia issues.

DEVELOPING AN IDENTITY: COMING OUT

Human development theories identify the development of a distinct identity and a positive construct of self-worth as primary tasks that are necessary for growth and a healthy mental and emotional state of being. People develop and define their identities and sense of self-worth through an interactive process between the individual and his or her environment. The ability to give and accept affirmation and love accompany this positive view of identity and self-worth. The interaction between self-affirming persons who trust one another and who are concerned with each other's welfare is intimacy.

This process of developing an identity as a gay person is called "coming out." Coming out is frequently a reason that homoerotic people find themselves in counseling. Coming out means to identify oneself as gay. There are many stages in the coming out process. The first step is for a homoerotic individual to acknowledge feelings for the same sex. Then, individuals will need to decide whether to share their sexual ori-

TABLE 16–2 Personal Homophobia Assessment.

1. Do you stop yourself from doing or saying certain things because someone might think you are gay or lesbian? If yes, what kinds of things?

2. Do you ever intentionally do or say things so that people will think you are nongay? If yes, what kinds of things?

3. Do you believe that gays or lesbians can influence others to become homoerotic? Do you think someone could influence you to change your sexual and affectional preference?

4. If you are a parent, how would you (or do you) feel about having a lesbian daughter or gay son?

5. How do you think you would feel if you discovered that one of your parents or parent figures, or a brother or sister, were gay or lesbian?

6. Are there any jobs, positions, or professions that you think lesbians and gays should be barred from holding or entering? If yes, why?

7. Would you go to a physician whom you knew or believed to be gay or lesbian if that person were of a different gender from you? If that person were of the same gender as you? If not, why not?

8. If someone you care about were to say to you, "I think I'm gay," would you suggest that the person see a therapist?

9. Have you ever been to a gay or lesbian bar, social club, party, or march? If not, why not?

10. Would you wear a button that says "How dare you assume that I'm heterosexual?" If not, why not?

11. Can you think of three positive aspects of a gay or lesbian lifestyle? Can you think of three negative aspects of a nongay lifestyle?

12. Have you ever laughed at a "queer" joke?

entation with others, such as parents, friends, children, employers, and coworkers. Clients need to understand why they wish to share information with others and the possible consequences.

Several "coming out" models provide a framework for understanding this process of identity development (Cass, 1984; Coleman, 1985; Falco, 1987; Lewis, 1984; Sophie, 1987). The author's model in Table 16–3 draws on each of these systems to identify the client's experiences and counselor's tasks for six coming out stages. It is important to remember that these stages will not necessarily occur in the order listed. Frequently individuals find themselves, after having gone through a stage, circling back to the same stage again when new thoughts, feelings, or actions occur.

The coming out process may occur at any age. Some individuals have indicated that they knew they were gay as early as age six or seven. If people come out during the teenage years, then development of sexual identity is congruent with adolescent development. However, coming out as a teenager can be particularly difficult because adolescents are generally financially and emotionally dependent on their parents. In addition, parental acceptance and approval are very important to young people and adolescents take the risk of being thrown out of their homes by parents if they identify themselves as gay (Silberman & Hawkins, 1988). Many individuals do not come out until later years and thus may need to resolve some adolescent issues long after their chronological adolescence has passed. Some individuals "come out" as senior citizens. Whenever gays come out they will be addressing an identity crisis and will need assistance in sorting through the coming out issues and developing a positive sense of self.

The task of coming out is made difficult because gays typically are not born into gay families. They suffer oppression alone, without benefit of advice or emotional support from relatives or friends. Most gays have few role models and no self-validating and visible culture on which to pattern themselves (Forstein, 1986). Since the development of a defined and positive identity by gays is frequently not encouraged or supported by friends and family or by society, it is essential for counselors to be positive and supportive as clients work through the coming out process.

There are a myriad of issues to be addressed in the development of identity and the coming out process. The alternatives open to the individual and the ramifications of the decision must be explored and clarified. It is important to be aware of the process and the interrelationship between developing an identity and coming out. Clients may need assistance in looking at both the positive and negative aspects of coming out. Counselors will need to use personal history assessment techniques to determine how to assist the client in the decision-making process about coming out. The client who is anticipating self-disclosure concerning sex-

Table 16–3 The Coming Out Stages.

PRE-DISCLOSURE (Pre-coming out [Coleman]; Being different [Lewis]; Identity confusion [Cass]; Recognizing and accepting lesbian feelings [Sophie]).

Client experience: Awareness of being different—may be vague. May not be able to talk about feelings. Confused, alienated, defensive, and beginning to wonder about the possibility of being gay. Probably has not disclosed feelings of being different to anyone.

Counselor task: Help client identify both internal and external conflicts. Assist client in talking about thoughts and feelings without judging or labeling. Help client understand that feelings and thoughts are acceptable. Help client look at consequences of acting on thoughts and feelings. Be open to the client's awareness.

DISCLOSURE (Coming out [Coleman]; Dissonance [Lewis]; Identity Comparison [Cass]; Coming out to self [Sophie]).

Client experience: Acknowledges homoerotic feelings and identifies self as possibly gay. Faces and copes with resultant conflict with heterosexual lifestyle including homophobia and heterosexism. Experiences confusion, questions values, roles, and self-concept. Is concerned about possible loss of friends and family. Expresses strong attraction to individuals of the same gender.

Counselor task: Accept client's acknowledged feelings and thoughts. Help client understand that homoerotic feelings and thoughts are acceptable. Help client through grieving process, work through denial, shame, anxiety, anger, alienation, and self-esteem issues. Encourage client to reevaluate expectations and goals. Help client develop positive image of gays and lesbians. Help client value their personhood. Help client sort through issues of sex role identification. Provide client with gay community resources, such as publications, support groups, and spiritual groups. Ask client questions about coming out, such as "How will people react to your coming out?" "Who in your life will be affected by your coming out?" "Have you acted on your sexual thoughts?"

EXPLORATION/EXPERIMENTATION (Exploration [Coleman], Relationships [Lewis], Identity tolerance [Cass], Coming out to others [Sophie]).

Client experience: Experiments with social and sexual relationships. Decides who to come out to, in what setting, to how many people, how much and what to say. Feels intense emotion and is uncertain of social skills. Needs to find supportive community and gain a positive self-concept.

Counselor task: Help client to decide about coming out. Help cope with the consequences of coming out. Help client establish support network while continuing to accept feelings and thoughts. Help client develop self-esteem and interpersonal skills. Assist client in understanding the intensity of feelings and the awkwardness in social relationships. Help client develop a model for pursuing relationships including dating, courtship, and sexual behavior.

IDENTITY DEVELOPMENT (First relationships [Coleman], Stable identity [Lewis], Identity acceptance [Cass]).

Client experience: Develops and learns to live in same-sex relationships. Begins to attribute value to being gay by taking part in gay subculture. Develops skill of "passing" as heterosexual and decides when it is appropriate to be "out." Feels more positive about being gay.

Counselor's task: Help client with continuing issues of self-esteem. Help client with frustration and pain of being rejected by some people. Be supportive of relationship issues. Help client with communication skills and role development in relationships. Help client understand that some relationships may not last and to learn from the loss.

IDENTITY PRIZING (Identity pride [Cass]).

Client experience: Values the homoerotic experience above the heterosexual. Accepts self as valuable and contributing member of society. Enjoys and values gay subculture and friends gained as a gay person. Comes out to more people. Experiences anger and rejection from members of society, yet maintains a positive sense of self.

Counselor task: Assist client in continuing decisions about self-disclosure. Help client express thoughts and feelings and understand actions in addressing the conflicts and joys in life. Find ways to support client in maintaining a positive self-image in spite of some continuing societal rejection.

IDENTITY INTEGRATION (Integration [Coleman, Lewis], Identity synthesis [Cass]).

Client experience: Integrates internal and external experiences into a healthy self-view. Being gay or lesbian takes much less energy and attention. Public and private identities merge into one unified and integrated self-image. Relationships are more successful and are characterized by honesty, mutual trust, and intimacy. Client proceeds on with age-appropriate issues and developmental tasks.

Counselor task: Affirm view that being gay is only one aspect of total self. Help client continue to adapt to new identity. Assist with continuing self-disclosure and self-labeling. Help client with ongoing development of personal relationships.

---

ual orientation may benefit from practicing the disclosure through role-playing. Use of the empty chair technique, allowing the client to play different parts, will help the client experience expected reactions such as fear, abuse, and abandonment.

Deciding Whether to Come Out

Each person must decide whether to identify oneself as gay. Not identifying oneself as gay and living a secret life is termed living in the "closet." To keep secret feelings and perceptions about oneself supports internalized homophobia and reinforces the feeling that this aspect of personhood is too shameful to disclose to anyone. Closeted gays blanket their entire lives with self-constriction, constantly monitoring their thoughts, emotions, and responses. Such hiding does irreparable harm to their sense of integrity and leaves them in a stressful and dissonant position, detracting from their mental health and well-being. Stress, depression, and substance abuse are all related clinically to maintaining a secret existence (Garrison, 1989).

Coming out is a never-ending process and decisions about whether to come out occur on a daily basis. The stresses of addressing the issue of sexual orientation will affect the function and quality of life no matter how far out of the closet gays are, or how carefully cloistered and defended they are about their lifestyle (Riddle & Sang, 1978). Gay individuals experience constant pressure both to stay in and to come out of the closet. For example, after a weekend when coworkers are discussing what they did, does the gay person share with whom he or she spent time, or make up an appropriate other-gender partner? At holiday times does the gay person bring his or her partner to the family dinner, or go alone and feign being unattached?

As counselors work with clients who are addressing coming out issues, they need to remember that self-disclosure is generally seen as necessary for self-acceptance and self-regard. Disclosing sexual feelings and perceived identity to at least some of the people who are important is necessary for affirmation of self-worth. Thus, choosing to stay in the closet and not identifying oneself as gay frequently supports shame and guilt and perpetuates a negative self-image. However, it is important that each person decide whether to identify as gay and how far to come out of the closet. Counselors need to counsel about, rather than give answers to, this question (Norton, 1988). Circumstances vary and counselors need to assist clients in this difficult decision-making process by assessing the issues involved in coming out. Joe, the college freshman identified earlier in the chapter, faces some difficult choices. What will be the effect on his family and friends? If he comes out, will his parents continue financial support for college? It may be the best choice to not come out until after college. If the decision is to stay in the closet, how will this affect Joe? Questions listed in Table 16–4 can help clients determine the consequences of coming out.

Identity Dysfunctions

Individuals who do not develop a positive self-view in the coming out process frequently develop an identity dysfunction. Identity dysfunctions lead the person to initiate friendships or work relationships that support the continuation of a negative self-value. The resulting behaviors mani-

TABLE 16–4 The Consequences of Coming Out—Questions to Consider.

1. What kind of reactions do you expect when you tell family members, friends, coworkers, etc.?
2. How can you determine what the reactions might be?
3. What would be the worst possible reaction?
4. What can you do to prepare yourself against this reaction?
5. What happens when or if you tell your parents?
6. Should you tell your parents together or individually?
7. Should you tell both of your parents?
8. What happens if you do not tell certain people?
9. Is it necessary to tell everyone?
10. What are the best ways to tell people?
11. Can you think of alternative ways to tell people?
12. Are you aware that responses may change over time?

fest themselves in difficulties with intimacy. Dysfunctions of identity are confusion, conflict, and denial.

Identity Confusion
Gay individuals often engage in behaviors that are not accepted by the culture and therefore experience rejection. This may be especially obvious to teenagers who do not fit the typical gender role expectations of society. For example, teenagers are expected to attend high school dances with members of the opposite sex. If gay teenagers want to take someone of the same gender to a senior prom they do not conform to the expectations of parents and peers. It is common for others to reject these nonconforming behaviors as inappropriate. This rejection may be perceived as rejection of the self or emotional abandonment, and may thus disaffirm an individual's sense of worth (Colgan, 1987). The rejection and resulting low self-worth creates identity confusion for the individual. Frequently, individuals withdraw from situations where rejection is perceived as possible and experience self-rejection and self-hatred. The following questions are often asked by gay individuals who are confused about identity issues: Who am I in this society? Why don't I fit into the roles defined by society? What can I do to be accepted in society? Counselors need to assist clients in responding to these and other questions about how to fit into a society that is nonaccepting. Answering questions like these will help clients address the confusion that they are experiencing.

Identity Conflict

Clients with identity conflicts have low self-worth and place the needs of others above their own. Identity conflict frequently involves overattachment or overidentification with another person. An individual may become lost in the self of others. This response stems from previous rejection and emotional isolation. An individual may become obsessed with another person and do whatever the partner wants to avoid the pain of rejection. As a result, the individual may become victimized and possibly sexually dysfunctional (Colgan, 1987). Individuals in identity conflict may experience feelings of unworthiness and blame themselves each time a relationship is terminated. Another common feature of overidentification is for a person to immerse himself or herself in community organizations, thus placing the needs of the community above self needs. Counselors need to address the low self-esteem issues of such clients, and help them learn to value themselves.

Identity Denial

To adopt a gay lifestyle means to seek acceptance and understanding in a hostile society and to adopt roles that do not conform to societal expectations. In this struggle of the self versus society it is common to negate the identity of oneself as gay. This denial of the self as a gay person may result in detachment from emotional expression, development of sexual performance skills while disconnecting affectively, insulation from feelings by drug and alcohol abuse, use of drugs and alcohol in conjunction with sexual encounters, and adoption of the role of "rejector" or "suitor" in relationships. The rejector acts from a sense of anger and hostility while the suitor is constantly in search of the right man or woman who will bring immediate fulfillment (Silverstein, 1981). All of these behaviors are forms of self-denial and deaden the pain the individual is feeling from the loss of the self. The counselor needs to understand and identify the dysfunctional roles taken on by the client and explore with the client alternative ways of enhancing the self rather than denying the self.

Community Identity

In the struggle against the second-class citizenship status created by homophobia, individuals often need to move beyond the establishment of a personal identity to a community identity. Gays and lesbians have established community-based organizations that are organized and managed by gays. Both social and professional groups have been established in most urban areas. Social organizations are formed around common interests such as hiking, bowling, bridge, and square dancing. Other local and national organizations have been established to serve political and advocacy functions for gays. Groups exist that address a wide range of issues, such as health, legal concerns, aging, youth, and religious and political needs. Bookstores with gay periodicals, books, and newspapers exist in most large cities.

Counselors need to be aware of the gay community resources and make this information available to their clients. Counselors located in rural communities need to be aware of national resources and the resources in the nearest large city. A sample of community and national resources is listed in the Appendix at the end of the chapter.

SPECIAL SITUATIONS IN COUNSELING

In addition to the knowledge and awareness of homophobia and coming out issues, counselors also need to be aware of a number of special situations that are likely to be prominent counseling issues with gays. These situations are not unique to gays but the lack of societal support systems often exacerbates the problem among this population.

Relationships

Most often, gay and lesbian couples will bring concerns to counseling that are no different than the issues in heterosexual relationships. These may include differences in socioeconomic and family backgrounds, level of education, religious and value differences, communication problems, previous relationships, illness, financial issues, individual emotional problems, sexual dysfunction, and jealousy. Even though gay and lesbian couples confront the very same day-to-day concerns as any two people living together, "they do not have the social, legal or moral sanctions that sustain opposite-sex couples. Thus the development and maintenance of same-sex couples involves a commitment to a difficult process with many destructive internal and external forces in its path" (Forstein, 1986, p. 105).

Contrary to popular perception, the majority of gays and lesbians live with a partner. Weinberg and Williams (1974) found that 71 percent of the men in their sample were living together as partners, and Bell and Weinberg (1978) reported that 82 percent of the lesbians they studied were living with a partner. With the advent of AIDS in the 1980s it is likely that even more gay men will choose to live with partners in a monogamous fashion.

Lesbian couples and gay male couples who live together as same-gender partners may experience relationship problems unique to sexual orientation.

Lesbians are socialized as women first, and gay men are socialized as men first. Men are taught to be assertive, competitive, and aggressive and to initiate sexual activity. Women are taught to be compliant, passive, and sexually exclusive and not to initiate sexual activity. Given this conditioning, it is not uncommon for gay male couples to experience competition as a difficulty in relationships or for lesbian couples to have trouble with fusion and difficulty in separating. (Silberman & Hawkins, 1988, p. 106)

As products of a heterosexist society, gay men and women share the expectations and rules of opposite-sex couples. Gay couples frequently base their expectations on heterosexual modeling that may include one partner taking care of the other, or one partner being more feminine or masculine (McWhirter & Mattison, 1984). There are no visible role models on which gay couples can base their relationship. Gay couples frequently express curiosity about how other gay couples deal with their everyday lives and address issues such as finances, outside relationships, family, and sex. While the lack of modeling for gay couples creates uncertainty about how to behave as a couple, the lack of societal guidelines for same-sex couples allows for creativity in establishing the ground rules for the relationship.

McWhirter and Mattison (1984) identify ignorance, prejudice, oppression, and homophobia as issues that every gay couple must address. To fight these, counselors must assess the depth of these issues and the effect on the self-concept of the individuals involved. It may be helpful to suggest to clients that they gain accurate information about homosexuality through reading, video tapes, attendance at lectures, and other sources to help them fight these issues in society. As a corollary to these concerns, couples frequently disagree about how open to be about their sexual orientation. If one member of the couple is more out of the closet than the other it will present problems for the relationship that need to be addressed in counseling.

Counselors must remember that relationship issues are frequently the same for homosexual couples as heterosexual couples, but amplified by the lack of acceptance in society. Heterosexual therapists who downplay the importance of societal homophobia may fail to maintain empathy with gay and lesbian couples (McCandlish, 1985).

Gay Male Couples
McWhirter and Mattison (1984), in a pioneering effort, developed a descriptive and developmental model of gay male relationships in which they identify six stages that describe the tasks a male couple encounters as the relationship develops.

1. Stage One—Blending (year one)
2. Stage Two—Nesting (years two and three)

3. Stage Three—Maintaining (years four and five)
4. Stage Four—Building (years six through ten)
5. Stage Five—Releasing (years eleven through twenty)
6. Stage Six—Renewing (beyond twenty years)

This model provides a basis for understanding that although each relationship has a life of its own, there are predictable developmental stages that a gay male relationship passes through. Counselors might use this model in counseling with gay couples to assess whether the couple is "on task" or whether one member of the couple has moved at a faster pace than the other. The accumulation of data and development of concepts pertinent to working with gay male couples is a recent phenomenon, and counselors would benefit from a careful perusal of the data as it develops.

Lesbian Couples

Usually both partners in a lesbian relationship value relating, communicating, and creating a climate of emotional closeness, perhaps because in many heterosexual relationships the woman usually expresses the need for openness and communication. The dynamics of lesbian relationships differ from those of heterosexual and gay male relationships because of the strong emotional bond that leads women to relate to women (McCandlish, 1985). Whereas the emphasis on closeness may be a strength of lesbian relationships, this emphasis often creates difficulties in separating.

The sexist nature of society frequently presents difficulties for women in heterosexual relationships. Lesbian relationships allow an opportunity for equality and lesbians frequently express relief about not having to follow identified sex roles. Lesbian relationships also allow for creativity in development of mutually agreed upon relationship goals.

A recent development in working with lesbian relationships is the recognition of the serious and widespread problem of violence and battering among lesbian couples (Hammond, 1989; NiCarthy, 1986). Though this development seems contradictory to the communicative and close nature of lesbian relationships depicted earlier, it is related to the difficulty that lesbians have in letting go of relationships. Rather than leave relationships they will frequently fight and vent anger toward their partner. Lesbians also batter because they want to exercise power over their partners. Individuals who batter have learned that violence is effective in getting their partners to comply with their wishes (Hart, 1989). The impact of battering on the lesbian victim can be profound as a sense of fear, mistrust, and disillusionment takes over and closeness and equality in the relationship disappears. The sensitivity of the counselor to issues of domestic violence is critical in helping to restore the integrity and self-worth of the victim. As in any issues of violence, the safety of the victim takes precedence over supporting the relationship or taking care of the batterer's current emotional needs (Hammond, 1989). Though there is an assumption that there is some battering among gay male couples there is no research to support this premise. This may be because gay males leave relationships rather than stay "in the fight."

Parenting

Gays and lesbians are coupling, creating new families, having and rearing children, and challenging society's definition of what "family" means. Sally and Jennifer, identified at the beginning of this chapter, are examples of a growing phenomenon in the United States. Of the 20 to 25 million gay persons in this country at least 33 percent of the lesbians and 10 percent of the men have children (Moses & Hawkins, 1982). Lesbians in particular are choosing to have children and to raise them in redefined families. Many of the difficulties of gay and lesbian parenting are exactly like the stresses felt in a heterosexual marriage and may include such issues as jealousy, time spent with children, privacy, and communication. However, gay parents often confront added, particular stresses.

Co-parenting another's child is frequently exacerbated by the gay couple's inability to become legal step-parents. Gay couples who wish to adopt children will find it difficult; currently only 11 recognized gay or lesbian couples in the United States have been granted legal adoptions of children. In some divorce situations, concerns arise about custody and visitation rights of the gay parent to his or her child. Many states discriminate against gay individuals in awarding child custody. In some states being gay is reason enough to be considered an unfit parent. Alaska, Oregon, Washington, California, Michigan, Indiana, South Carolina, New York, Connecticut, New Jersey, and Massachusetts laws state that sexual orientation is not relevant in custody disputes. Counselors need to be aware of the statutes in their states and help clients find supportive legal assistance.

Other issues that arise for gay parents include concerns about coming out to the wife or husband, to children, and to other family members. Issues of coming out are also pertinent to the children of gay and lesbian parents. Some children may choose to hide their parent's sexuality from friends. These issues of coming out are very delicate and intricate, as described in the earlier section, and must be considered in the framework of the developmental history of the individual. Counselors need to be cognizant of the unique concerns of being gay parents while responding to the relationship issues as they would with any couple.

Religious Issues

Gays and lesbians who are raised in families affiliated with a religious denomination are often confronted with conflicting values between their sexual orientation and their religion. Throughout history most religions have discriminated against homosexuality and viewed it as morally deviant. Frequently religions believe that sex between people of the same gender runs counter to God's plan. Such religious doctrine makes it difficult for the gay person to live authentically in the religious world. If a gay person is unable to participate actively in the spiritual and religious dimensions of life without oppression and confusion, then this issue needs to be addressed in counseling (Fortunato, 1983).

Gay clients frequently come to counseling with the belief that there is no place for them in their religion and that they are "sinners," "black sheep," or "unwanted." Some have been excommunicated from the church; others have not been allowed to be married; some have been denied ordination. Client distress manifests itself in anger toward the church and feelings of personal shame and guilt. Clients will need an opportunity to discuss the options available to them and decide whether to remain affiliated with the religion of their family, seek a new religious affiliation, or pursue other avenues to meet their spiritual needs. Gays who remain in a nonaccepting church need to learn how to balance the negative views of the church and their sexual orientation.

As therapists work with clients about religious beliefs and sexual orientation, they must be aware of their own religious value system and beliefs. Counselors who have been raised in a denomination that discriminates against gays will have to either move beyond these homophobic beliefs or refer to counselors who are gay-supportive to help clients address these difficult issues.

Most major denominations now have gay church groups affiliated with them. These groups include Dignity (Catholic), Integrity (Episcopal), Affirmation (United Methodist), Affirmation (Mormon), Evangelicals Concerned, Friends for Lesbian and Gay Concerns (Quakers), Kinship (Adventist), Lutherans Concerned (Lutheran), Seventh Day Adventist Kinship International, Gay Synagogue (Jewish), and Unitarian Universalists for Lesbian/Gay Concerns. The Metropolitan Community Church is a nondenominational gay church that has services nationwide.

Drug and Alcohol Abuse

There is a widely held assumption by mental health professionals that drug and alcohol abuse is quite high in the gay and lesbian community.

Some have stated that alcoholism is the number one health problem among both male and female homosexuals (Kus, 1987). The research in this area is sparse. However, the available research does suggest that approximately 30 to 35 percent of the gay population are chemically dependent on alcohol or drugs (Fifeld, 1975; Lohrenz et al.,1978; Saghir et al., 1970; Weinberg & Williams, 1974).

Research has shown that internalized homophobia may explain the etiology and the high incidence of alcoholism in gay American men (Kus, 1987). Gays and lesbians tend to misuse alcohol or drugs to numb their feelings of depression and anxiety, which arise from a combination of internal and external homophobia. Although the substance abuse may result from the homophobia, counselors cannot assist with resolution of the underlying problem until the substance abuse has stopped. This approach is consistent with that used with other substance-abusing populations. Acceptance of oneself as gay does not typically happen during periods of abuse. Chet, the lawyer who entered a treatment program for cocaine abuse, must be clean and sober in order to address the issues that surround leading a double life. Counselors can work with clients on the causative factors only after successful treatment of the substance abuse problem.

With such a high incidence of chemical abuse among gay clients, treatment centers need to address sexual orientation issues with clients. One suggested method is to ask clients in a nonjudgmental manner during the treatment intake session about their sexual preferences. Asking the question also allows clients to be less worried about when they will be "found out," because it sends a message that sexual orientation is a legitimate issue (Finnegan & McNally, 1987). Gay clients who come to treatment may be experiencing heightened shame and guilt. Therefore, it is important to approach questions about sexuality in routine ways that indicate to clients that any answers are acceptable. "If the question is not posed, the gay or lesbian client may feel heterosexuality is assumed and homosexuality is possibly unacceptable in this setting" (Finnegan & McNally, 1987, p. 61). Not asking about sexual orientation may indicate that the agency is not sensitive to gay issues and the underlying feelings of gay clients.

Counselors need to be aware of the relatively large percentage of gays who are chemical abusers. Assessment procedures with all gay clients should include questions about drinking and using. Self-help groups, a necessary adjunct to counseling chemically dependent individuals, are available for gays and lesbians in most cities. These include Alcoholics Anonymous, Narcotics Anonymous, Valium Anonymous, and Cocaine Anonymous. Counselors need to know about local self-help groups and make appropriate referrals.

AIDS

Acquired immunodeficiency syndrome (AIDS), first identified in 1981, is a usually fatal disease for which there is no known cure or immunization. Due to specific sexual behaviors with multiple partners, gay men were initially the hardest hit group in the United States. Thus, homophobia became intertwined with the first responses to AIDS. The subsequent societal response has been colored with moral indictment, including the frequent assertion that AIDS is a retribution for violations of a prescribed moral order (Brandt, 1988). Initially, AIDS was popularly referred to as the "gay disease" and as the Wrath of God (WOG) (McLaughlin, 1989). One writer has observed that "in some quarters the misapprehension exists that AIDS is caused by homosexuality, not a retrovirus" (Brandt, 1988, p. 165). This prejudice has also been evident in some AIDS policies that require mandatory HIV testing of those perceived to be gay.

Thus, the AIDS pandemic has had a severe impact on gay men, both personally and societaly. There are very few gay men who have not had a friend die from AIDS. All gay men are worried about their own health due to the lethal nature of AIDS. Persons with AIDS (PWAs), friends of PWAs, and people at risk for AIDS must make difficult choices as they face issues of limited sexual options, loss, and discrimination.

Like most Americans, counselors are unprepared, unskilled, and uncomfortable addressing the core issues raised by AIDS: sexual conduct, homophobia, serious illness, death, and living with the dying and grieving. However, counselors are in a pivotal position to improve the care available to those who have AIDS by acting as agents of change in schools, churches, community agencies, government programs, treatment centers, and private practice. Counselors must be able to assess and assist with the "enormous emotional needs" of the friends and family of the PWA (Greif & Porembski, 1989, p. 79). The AIDS diagnosis may force family and friends to face previously avoided issues such as sexual orientation and/or drug use. There are often efforts to keep the AIDS diagnosis a secret from particular family members or from people outside the family due to fears of rejection. Financial worries, fears of rejection, and the exhausting effort of providing intimate care to someone seriously ill can be stressful to family and friends who wish to be supportive (Greif & Porembski, 1989).

Counselors must also provide accurate information about AIDS to clients and family members, professional colleagues, and the communities where they live and work. The counselor must present the message that it is an individual's behavior, not belonging to a particular group, that puts a person at risk. It is also important for therapists to point out, in nonjudgmental ways, beliefs based on ignorance and behavior grounded in prejudice and bigotry. Counselors must learn to challenge misstatements whenever they occur, provide factual information, and encourage the reconsideration of uninformed opinions. The counselor needs to educate clients by discussing safer sex practices and the dangers of intravenous drug use.

AIDS has caused people to talk about sex and death, two subjects that people in our society avoid. It has helped bring gays, sex, and death out of the closet. Counselors must be prepared to take risks as an advocate for PWAs and their families in order to guarantee competent and compassionate treatment. Counselors must also be prepared to be leaders in AIDS education prevention strategies.

Loneliness, Guilt, and Depression

Many gays experience loneliness, depression, anxiety, guilt, anger, and suicidal thoughts owing to the conflicts that they confront in their childhood and throughout their lives. These conflicts are much the same as those experienced by all members of society, but the differences lie in the depth of feeling and the absence of hope of resolving the conflicts (Fortunato, 1983). Great anxiety and loneliness come from realizing that there may never be support from parents, siblings, family members, or loved ones. Life can be extremely painful to gays who have lost friends or a job or their church membership because of their sexual orientation. These feelings of loss must either be avoided, fought, or suffered through. Fortunato recommends that in order to address these losses gays must "grieve gay." Counselors need to assist gay clients in working through the grief associated with the losses that are inherent in being gay.

DENIAL/BARGAINING Gay clients in this stage remain closeted and secretive. Frequently, they have feelings of paranoia, are depressed, have phobic reactions, and are alcohol or drug abusers. They may recognize societal oppression, but refuse to deal with it. They will bargain with themselves about being gay, make excuses for their behavior, and deny their sexual orientation even though they may be engaging in homoerotic sexual behavior. They are caught in a codependent phase, making excuses for their behavior and defending the people who are oppressing and rejecting them. Counselors need to confront the denial and direct the focus to the source of the oppression.

ANGER Clients who are in the anger stage of grieving frequently address their anger outwardly in the form of protests, marches, letter writing, or circulating petitions. This may a very positive use of anger. However, if they direct their anger in this manner without addressing the source of the feeling, these expressions can contribute to the individual becoming rigid, defensive, and closed. The outward expression of anger can also be silent, with the individual directing inward anger and blame for being gay. This inward expression of anger is often associated with loneliness and suicidal ideation. Counselors need to work carefully with clients in this stage to express their anger in appropriate ways and to eventually work through the anger.

DEPRESSION Individuals who are in extreme denial and live totally in the closet isolate themselves from other gays and have minimal social and sexual contacts. These individuals have ingested the fear of being gay and internalized the oppression of society. Gays who are depressed may be suicidal, drink and use too much, and engage in self-pity. They see society as "right" and themselves as "wrong." Counselors need to address the feelings of guilt and encourage clients to take responsibility rather than blaming society and the people in their life for the awful state of "their world."

ACCEPTANCE Since people do not have a choice about their sexual orientation, gays need to stop asking the question "Why me?" and begin to affirm their sexual orientation. Gays need to look beyond the expectations that other people will affirm them, and look for affirmation elsewhere. This affirmation might come from within, based on a positive view of the self, or from a more mystical or transcendent source. Counselors can encourage clients to embrace the exiled state of being gay and to look for internal, cosmic, or spiritual sources of strength.

Use of a grief model allows gay clients to work through the loneliness, guilt, and depression that they experience. As in all loss models, clients may begin at any stage. Clients may also regress to an earlier stage depending upon the current experiences in their lives. The circular concept of the model provides the basis for hope that is often needed for gay clients.

PROFESSIONAL DIRECTIONS

The attitudes of counseling professionals toward gay men and lesbians have changed dramatically over the past years. In 1973, the American Psychiatric Association stopped labeling homosexuality as a form of mental illness. The American Psychological Association did the same in 1975. The assumption associated with this change was that counseling practices would be modified to reflect a view of homosexuality as an acceptable lifestyle (Corey, Corey, & Callanan, 1988). This acceptance of gays and lesbians by professional organizations has led to the development of a gay-affirmative approach for counselors. To be gay-affirmative is to value homosexuality and heterosexuality equally as natural or normal attributes (Krajeski, 1986). This gay-positive stance of mental health professionals is at odds with the prevalent view in American society that condemns homosexuality as a perversion or morally wrong.

Many professional organizations have developed a gay and lesbian task force, committee, or division to provide support for counseling professionals and a positive direction for counseling with gays and lesbians. Division 44, the Society of the Psychological Study of Lesbian and Gay Issues of the American Psychological Association (APA), and the Association of Gay, Lesbian and Bisexual Concerns of the American Association for Counseling and Development (AACD) are examples of such efforts to support gay and lesbian concerns.

The Gay Professional

Until recently it was assumed that heterosexuality was the only suitable orientation for therapists (Rochlin, 1985). However, publicly identified gay male and lesbian mental health professionals are growing in number. The gay professional who comes out serves as an important resource for the gay community, serves as a role model for gays, provides security for those who want to see a gay counselor, and acts as a resource consultant for other counselors (Woodman & Lenna, 1980). Since identification with the therapist is one of the key elements that produces change in clients, it seems important that gay and lesbian counselors continue to identify themselves publicly and serve as role models for the gay community. While some gays may prefer counseling with a publicly identified gay person, others may prefer working with an accepting nongay.

Counselor Role and Responsibility

Before counselors can work effectively with gay clients they must be comfortable talking about sexual issues in counseling. Many people either disapprove of discussing sex, are uncomfortable talking about sex, or view sexual conduct as unacceptable or immoral. Most individuals receive messages from their family of origin and society such as "Don't be sexual," "Don't ask about sex," and "Don't talk about sex" (Gray & House, 1989). Such messages create discomfort in discussing sexual issues. Unless counselors overcome this discomfort they will not be effective working with any clients who are addressing sexual concerns.

Also, counselors must overcome the homophobic societal messages about same-sex activity. Many counselors have absorbed misinformation and myths about homosexuality. For example, many counselors function under the myth that all clients are heterosexual, when at least 10 percent of the population have a same-sex preference. Questions such as "When did you first know that you were gay?" have a heterosexual bias. It could just as easily be asked "When did you first know that you were straight?" When counselors believe and act on myths about gays, they provide a disservice to gay clients.

The lack of practical knowledge about gays and the gay lifestyle is a major obstacle to satisfactory counseling. Therefore, the first responsibility for counselors is to reeducate themselves about homosexuality (Norton, 1988). Counselors can do this most easily by meeting and talking with gay people. Such face-to-face meetings will likely dispel the myths and preconceived ideas about gays. It is also important for counselors to read gay-affirmative books and periodicals and know about available resources for gays. The reference list at the end of this chapter and the resource list in the Appendix offer current sources of information.

It is crucial that therapists recognize that they may be seen as the representative of a hostile society, or as an authority figure with a heavily weighted opinion. Many gays do not go to counseling because they fear rejection if they reveal their sexual orientation. Each therapist must counter these expectations with an expressed awareness of the issues facing the gay or lesbian client and an openness to the concerns expressed. Counselors have the responsibility to let clients know that they will listen to gays. They can have gay books visibly placed on bookshelves, post supportive articles about gay issues on bulletin boards, see that gay articles get placed in the school newspaper, and reject and challenge antigay language and jokes.

It is also necessary to help change societal views to an acceptance and understanding of gays and lesbians (Loulan, 1984). Counselors, as change agents in the communities in which they live, can support public and institutional policy decisions regarding homosexuality. They can encourage tolerance in educational and religious settings, and advocate for nondiscriminatory measures. Counselors must not ignore the cultural and societal context in which their clients live. It is the counselor's responsibility to advocate for tolerance and understanding of gays and lesbians at a societal level.

Professional counselors are in a powerful position to help gays recognize and accept their sexual identity, improve their interpersonal and social functioning, and value themselves while living in a predominantly heterosexual society (Coleman, 1985). Counselors who are sensitive to sexual orientation issues, who have examined and challenged the heterosexist and homophobic assumptions of our culture, and who have confronted their own values, can assist all clients, whatever their sexual orientation.

REFERENCES

Bell, A. P., & Weinberg, M. S. (1978). *Homosexualities: A study of diversities among men and women.* New York: Simon & Schuster.

Blumenfeld, W. J. & Raymond, D. (1988). *Looking at gay and lesbian life.* Boston: Beacon.

Blumstein, P., & Schwartz, P. (1983). *American couples.* New York: William Morrow.

Brandt, A. M. (1988). AIDS: From social history to social policy. In E. Fee & D. M. Fox (Eds.), *AIDS: The burdens of history* (pp. 147–171). Berkeley: University of California

Cass, V. C. (1984). Homosexual identity formation: A concept in need of definition. *Journal of Homosexuality, 10,* 105–126.

Coleman, E. (1985). Developmental stages of the coming out process. In J. C. Gonsirek (Ed.), A guide to psychotherapy with gay and lesbian clients (pp. 31–43). New York: Harrington Park.

Coles, R., & Stokes, J. (1985). *Sex and the American teenager.* New York: Rolling Stone.

Colgan, P. (1987). Treatment of identity and intimacy issues in gay males. *Journal of Homosexuality, 14,* 101–123.

Corey, G., Corey, M. S., & Callanan, P. (1988). *Issues and ethics in the helping profession* (3rd ed.). Monterey, CA: Brooks/Cole.

Dworkin, S. H., & Gutierrez, F. (1989). Introduction to special issue. Counselors be aware: Clients come in every size, shape, color, and sexual orientation. *Journal of Counseling and Development, 68,* 6–8.

Falco, K. (1987). *Psychotherapy with lesbian clients: A manual for the psychotherapist.* Unpublished doctoral dissertation. Oregon Graduate School of Professional Psychology, Pacific University, Forest Grove.

Fifeld, L. (1975). On my way to nowhere: Alienated, isolated, drunk. Unpublished project paper. Los Angeles Office on Alcohol Abuse and Alcoholism, Los Angeles, CA.

Finnegan, D. G., & McNally, E. B. (1987). *Dual identities: Counseling chemically dependent gay men and lesbians.* Center City, MN: Hazelden Educational Materials.

Forstein, M. (1986). Psychodynamic psychotherapy with gay male couples. In T. S. Stein & C. J. Cohen (Eds.), *Contemporary perspectives on psychotherapy with lesbians and gay men* (pp. 103–137). New York: Plenum.

Fortunato, J. E. (1983). *Embracing the exile: Healing journey of gay Christians.* New York: Seabury.

Garrison, J. (1989, June 12). Creating new families. *San Francisco Examiner,* p. A17.

Gray, L. A., & House, R. M. (1989). No guarantee of immunity: AIDS and adolescents. In D. Capuzzi & D. R. Gross (Eds.), *Youth at risk: A resource for counselors, teachers and parents.* Alexandria, VA: American Association for Counseling and Development.

Greif, G. L., & Porembski, E. (1989). Implications for therapy with significant others of persons with AIDS. *Journal of Gay and Lesbian Psychotherapy, 1,* 79–86.

Hammond, N. (1989). Lesbian victims of relationship violence. In E. D. Roth-blum & E. Cole (Eds.), *Lesbianism: Affirming nontraditional roles.* New York: Haworth.

Hart, B. (1989). Lesbian battering: An examination. In K. Lobel (Ed.), *Naming the violence: Speaking out about lesbian battering.* Seattle: Seal Press.

Kinsey, A., Pomeroy, W. B., Martin, C. E., & Gebhard, R. H. (1953). *Sexual behavior in the human female.* Philadelphia: W. B. Saunders.

Kinsey, A., Pomeroy, W. B., & Martin, C. E. (1948). *Sexual behavior in the human male.* Philadelphia: W. B. Saunders.

Krajeski, J. P. (1986). Psychotherapy with gay men and lesbians: A history of controversy. In T. S. Stein & C. J. Cohen (Eds.), *Contemporary perspectives on psychotherapy with lesbians and gay men* (pp. 9–25). New York: Plenum.

Kus, R. J. (1987). Alcoholics Anonymous and gay American men. *Journal of Homosexuality, 14,* 253–276.

Lewis, L. A. (1984). The coming out process for lesbians: Integrating a stable identity. *Journal of the National Association of Social Workers, 29,* 464–469.

Lohrenz, L. J., Connely, J. C., Coyne, L., & Spare, K. E. (1978). Alcohol problems in several midwestern homosexual communities. *Journal of Studies on Alcohol, 39,* 1959–1963.

Loulan, J. (1986). Psychotherapy with lesbian mothers. In T. S. Stein & C. J. Cohen (Eds.), *Contemporary perspectives on psychotherapy with lesbians and gay men.* (pp. 103–137). New York: Plenum.

McCandlish, B. M. (1985). Therapeutic issues with lesbian couples. In J. C. Gonsiorek (Ed.), *A guide to psychotherapy with gay and lesbian clients* (pp. 71–78). New York: Harrington Park.

McLaughlin, L. (1989). AIDS: An overview. In P. O'Malley (Ed.), *The AIDS epidemic: Private rights and the public interest* (pp. 15–35). Boston: Beacon.

McWhirter, D. P., & Mattison, A. M. (1984). *The male couple: How relationships develop.* Englewood Cliffs, NJ: Prentice-Hall.

Mollenkott, V. R. (1985). *Breaking the silence, overcoming the fear: Homophobia education.* (Available from the Program Agency, United Presbyterian Church, U.S.A., 475 Riverside Drive, Room 1101, New York, NY 10015.)

Money, J. (1987). Sin, sickness, or status? Homosexual gender identity and psychoneuroendocrinology. *American Psychologist, 42,* 384–399.

Money, J. (1988). *Gay, straight, and in-between.* New York: Oxford University.

Moses, A. E., & Hawkins, R. O. (1982). *Counseling lesbian women and gay men: A life-issues approach.* Columbus, OH: Charles E. Merrill.

Moses, A. E., & Hawkins, R. O. (1985). Two-hour in-service training session in homophobia. In H. Hidalgo, T. Peterson, & N. J. Woodman (Eds.), *Lesbian and gay issues: A resource manual for social workers* (pp. 152–157). Silver Springs, MD: National Association of Social Workers.

NiCarthy, G. (1986). *Getting free: A handbook for women in abusive relationships.* Seattle: Seal Press.

National Association of Social Workers. (1985). *Lesbian and gay issues: A resource manual for social workers.* Washington, DC: NASW.

Norton, J. (1988). Gay and lesbian populations. In N. A. Vacc, J. Wittmer, & S. Devaney (Eds.), *Experiencing and counseling multicultural and diverse populations* (pp. 61–88). Muncie, IN: Accelerated Development.

Riddle, D. I., & Sang, B. (1978). Psychotherapy with lesbians. *Journal of Social Issues, 34*(3), 84–100.

Rizzi, D. (1989, June). It's repugnant. [Letter to the editor]. *San Francisco Examiner,* p. 15.

Rochlin, M. (1985). Sexual orientation of the therapist and therapeutic effectiveness with gay clients. In J. C. Gonsiorek (Ed.), *A guide to psychotherapy with gay and lesbian clients* (pp. 21–29). New York: Harrington Park.

Saghir, M. T., Robins, E., Walbran, B., & Gentry, K. E. (1970). Homosexuality: Psychiatric disorders and disability in the male homosexual. *American Journal of Psychiatry, 126,* 1079–1086.

Silberman, B. O., & Hawkins, R. O., Jr. (1988). Lesbian women and gay men: Issues for counseling. In E. Weinstein & E. Rosen (Eds.), *Sexuality counseling: Issues and implications* (pp. 101–113). Monterey, CA: Brooks/Cole.

Silverstein, C. (1981). *Man to man: Gay couples in America.* New York: William Morrow.

Sophie, J. (1987). Internalized homophobia and lesbian identity. *Journal of Homosexuality, 14,* 53–65.

A special report: Gays in America. (1989, June). *San Francisco Examiner,* pp. 1–78.

Stein, T. S., & Cohen, C. J. (1986). *Contemporary perspectives on psychotherapy with lesbians and gay men.* New York: Plenum.

Warren, S. (1989, June). Shame—Shame! [Letter to the editor]. *San Francisco Examiner,* p. 15.

Weinberg, G. (1973). *Society and the healthy homosexual.* Garden City, NY: Anchor.

Weinberg, M. S., & Williams, C. S. (1974). *Male homosexuals: Their problems and adaptations.* New York: Oxford.

Wett, A. (1989, June). Long live bashers! [Letter to the editor]. *San Francisco Examiner,* p. 15.

Woodman, N., & Lenna, H. (1980). *Counseling with gay men and women.* San Francisco: Jossey-Bass.

APPENDIX
GAY AND LESBIAN RESOURCES

ORGANIZATIONS

Affirmation (Gay and Lesbian Mormons)
Box 26302
San Francisco, CA 94126
415/641-4554

Affirmation (United Methodists for Gay and Lesbian Concerns)
Box 1021
Evanston, IL 60204
312/475-0499

American Association of Physicians for Human Rights
Box 14366
San Francisco, CA 94144

Association for Gay, Lesbian, and Bisexual Issues in Counseling (AGLBIC)
P.O. Box 216
Jenkintown, PA 19046

Association of Lesbian and Gay Psychologists
2336 Market Street, #8
San Francisco, CA 94114

The Committee on Lesbian and Gay Concerns
c/o American Psychological Association
1200 Seventeenth Street, NW
Washington, DC 22036
(Publishes a "Research Roster")

Dignity
1500 Massachusetts Avenue, N.W.
Suite 11
Washington, DC 20005
202/861-0017
     or
Dignity—Bay Area
Box 5127
San Francisco, CA 94114
415/584-1714

East End Gay Organization for Human Rights
P.O. Box 708
Bridgehampton, NY 11932
516/537-2480

Education in a Disabled Gay Environment (EDGE)
P.O. Box 305, Village Station
New York, NY 10014
212/246-3811, ext. 292

Evangelicals Concerned
c/o Dr. Ralph Blair
311 East 72nd Street
New York, NY 10021
212/517-3171

Federation of Parents and Friends of Lesbians and Gays, Inc.
Box 24565
Los Angeles, CA 90024

Friends for Lesbian and Gay Concerns (Quakers)
Box 222
Sumneytown, PA 18084
215/234-8424

Gay and Lesbian Outreach to Elders
1853 Market Street
San Francisco, CA 94103
415/552-1997

Gay Men's Health Collective
2339 Durant
Berkeley, CA 94704
415/548-2570

Gay Men's Health Crisis
Box 274
132 West 24th Street
New York, NY 10011
212/807-7660

Gay Rights National Lobby
P.O. Box 1892
Washington, DC 20013

Gay Youth Community Switchboard
Box 846
San Francisco, CA 94101
415/552-6025

Human Rights Campaign Fund
1012 14th Street, NW
Suite 600
Washington, DC 20004
202/628-4160

Institute for the Protection of Gay and Lesbian Youth
112 East 23rd Street
New York, NY 10011

International Gay Information Center
P.O. Box 2, Village Station
New York, NY 10014

Metropolitan Community Church
Usually listed in the white pages of the local telephone directory
     or
Universal Fellowship of Metropolitan Community Churches
5300 Santa Monica Boulevard #304
Los Angeles, CA 90029
213/464-5100

Lambda Legal Defense and Education Fund
132 West 43rd Street
New York, NY 10036

National Association of Lesbian and Gay Alcoholism Professionals (NAL-GAP)
204 West 20th Street
New York, NY 10011

National Gay and Lesbian Task Force
80 Fifth Avenue
Suite 1601
New York, NY 10011
     or
National Gay and Lesbian Task Force
Gay Organizations Mailing List
1517 U Street NW
Washington, DC 20009
202/332-6483

National Lesbian and Gay Health Foundation (NLGHF)
P.O. Box 65472
Washington, DC 20035
202/797-3708

Senior Action in a Gay Environment (SAGE)
208 West 13th Street
New York, NY 10011

Seventh Day Adventists-Kinship International, Inc.
Box 3840
Los Angeles, CA 90078
213/876-2076

Unitarian Universalists for Lesbian / Gay Concerns
25 Beacon Street
Boston, MA 02108
617/742-2100

World Congress of Gay and Lesbian Jewish Organizations
P.O. Box 18961
Washington, DC 20036
202/483-4801

BOOKSTORES

Chosen Books
940 West McNichols
Detroit, MI 48203
313/864-0458 or 800/225-5300

Giovanni's Room
345 South 12th Street
Philadelphia, PA 19107
800/222-6996

Glad Day Bookshop
673 Boylston Street
Boston, MA 02116
617/267-3010
    or
598A Yonge Street
Toronto, ON M4Y 1Z3
416/961-4161

Lambda Rising
1625 Connecticut Avenue
Washington, DC 20009

Oscar Wilde Memorial Bookstore
15 Christopher Street
New York, NY 10014
212/255-8097

PUBLICATIONS

The Advocate
6922 Hollywood Boulevard, 10th Floor
Los Angeles, CA 90028
213/821-1225

Gay Community News
167 Tremont Street, Fifth Floor
Boston, MA 02111
617/426-4469

Gayellow Pages
Renaissance House
Box 292, Village Station
New York, NY 10014
212/674-0120

National Gay Health Directory
National Gay Health Education Foundation
Box 784
New York, NY 10036
212/563-6313

HOT LINES

Gay Men's Health Crisis, Inc. (New York)
212/685-4952

Herpes Resource Center (Palo Alto, CA)
415/328-7710

National Center for Missing and Exploited Children
800/843-5678

National Gay Task Force AIDS Information Hotline
800/221-7044

National STD Hotline
800/227-8922

U.S. Public Health Service AIDS Hotline
800/342-AIDS

17▪

Counseling Visible Racial/Ethnic Group (VREG)* Men and Women

CHALMER E. THOMPSON, PH.D.
DONALD R. ATKINSON, PH.D.
University of California, Santa Barbara
Santa Barbara, California

THERE HAS BEEN A growing interest in the influence of race and ethnicity on counseling process and outcome over the past 20 years. This interest is exemplified in the counseling literature by a proliferation of research articles, theoretical papers, and books that serve to assist prac-

*The term "visible racial/ethnic group," or "VREG," was originally used in an article by Cook and Helms (1988) and is borrowed in this chapter to replace the more popularly used term "minority." In agreement with Cook and Helms, we believe that references to Black, Latino, Asian, and Native American people should be made without the implicit comparison to members of the dominant culture.

titioners in learning to work capably with visible racial/ethnic group (VREG) populations—that is, Asian, Black/African, Latino/Hispanic, and Native American men and women. These extensive works cover a range of content areas including, but not limited to, descriptions of the cultural characteristics of specific VREG populations, insights on how to train counselors to develop effective competency in multicultural counseling, and discussion of culture-specific theory regarding the identity development of VREG members. This chapter attempts to highlight and organize this extensive literature in order to present the reader with an overview of multicultural counseling, including its history, the current status of VREG counseling research and training, and guidelines for counseling practice.

We use the term *VREG counseling* interchangeably with *multicultural counseling* to refer to those therapeutic situations in which the client (or clients in the case of family and couples counseling) is a member of a VREG. This is in contrast to *cross-cultural counseling,* which is used to describe the counseling dyad where the counselor and client are ethnically/racially different (but most frequently used to refer to a white American counselor and an African, Latino, Native, or Asian American client). In this chapter we focus on VREG clients but recognize that the counselor may be either a white American or a member of a VREG. Thus at one level, this chapter will cover the problems and issues relevant to the white counselor–VREG client dyad. This focus is important because, in terms of sheer numbers, white Americans predominate in the counseling profession, particularly at levels of national influence such as administration and governance. Relatedly, the counseling profession, similar to other American institutions, is dominated by the attitudes and values of white, middle-class people. As members of the dominant culture, certain white American counselors may be ethnocentric or racist, which may affect their attitudes toward VREG clients and, ultimately, their practices in the counseling setting.

Compared to white counselors, many VREG counselors may share similar experiences, communication/cultural styles, and beliefs with their VREG clients and, therefore, may be more culturally sensitive. On the other hand, we do not make the assumption that VREG counselors necessarily have all the beliefs, knowledge, and skills needed to be successful with all VREG clients. The lack of studies examining the VREG counselor–VREG client limits our knowledge of the characteristics or skills that either facilitate or impede counseling effectiveness within these dyads. Moreover, the limited number of coherent theories to guide the practice of VREG counseling currently make it difficult for any counselor to be effective with a culturally diverse client. Consequently, while the dynamics related to the VREG client being paired with a white or a VREG counselor remain critical to our discussion of research and training, we emphasize that efforts to acquire the beliefs, knowledge, and skills necessary to work with culturally diverse populations should stand as a primary goal for *all* counselors.

THE VREG POPULATIONS

Similar to other American subcultures, individuals within each of the VREG populations tend to share cultural characteristics, i.e., languages/dialects, communications styles, values, belief systems, etc., that are based on their racial/ethnic group heritages. Articles and books in cultural anthropology and in counseling have documented how these characteristics have distinct meaning for members of a cultural group in terms of how they generally perceive the world, raise children, establish group norms and rituals, and assume familial roles. For example, some Native American nations believe that humans and nature are inseparable entities and represent a whole. Members of these nations, therefore, may show their respect for nature by never reaping from the land more than is needed for one day (Richardson, 1981).

Yet another perspective on VREG populations is the common element that distinguishes them from other American subcultures. VREG men and women share a history of physical, economic, and sociopolitical oppression in the United States. For example, history reveals that Blacks have endured racial injustices since their presence in America. These injustices have ranged from chattel slavery and Jim-Crowism to the more subtle and institutionalized acts of racism prevalent today, such as the limited inclusion of culture-relevant content in school curricula and the limited opportunity for the advancement of Blacks into high-level career positions. Native Americans, who have been denied rights of self-determination continually since the arrival of whites in the Western hemisphere, have likewise suffered from massacres, incarcerations, and legalized exploitations that have greatly contributed to many contemporary problems, including prevalent rates of alcoholism and low life expectancy (Richardson, 1981). Asian Americans also have been the victims of exploitation and discrimination. Chinese Americans were used for cheap labor in the past, assaulted and killed by white mobs during the "yellow peril" mania; Japanese Americans were relegated to concentration camps during World War II. Despite achieving higher educational gains than whites, both Chinese and Japanese Americans still lag behind white Americans in economic prosperity (Sue, 1973). Many first-generation Mexicans and Puerto Ricans migrated to the United States with little or no English-speaking proficiency and with limited skills to enter a competitive and technologically oriented American workforce. Due to differences in the language and restrictive work skills, these immigrants were and continue to be relegated to low-paying, low-status jobs, which often leave them vulnerable to further exploitation. While it is difficult to find agreement concerning the reasons these groups have been victims of oppression, some critics conclude that these experiences may be due to differences between the cultural patterns, languages, and skin color of VREGs with white American populations.

Both the cultural characteristics of VREGs and the common experience of oppression in America have implications for counseling practice (referred to as the cultural deterministic and ethnic minority status perspectives, respectively; Sue, Akutsu, & Higashi, 1985). From a cultural deterministic perspective, Sue and Sue (1977) describe how counseling practices tend to be characterized by the values, attitudes, and behaviors of white, middle-class society, which may conflict with the cultural characteristics of VREG clients. For example, traditional counseling practices tend to focus on individualistic goal-setting and expressiveness of personal issues by the client. Many Asian Americans (specifically Chinese and Japanese Americans) tend to value the interdependence of the family structure rather than the attainment of individual goals. Moreover, restraint of feelings and emotions is more likely to be preferred among some Asian Americans than open expression of emotions. Time orientation is another area in which white values conflict with some VREG values. White culture generally has a future orientation, whereby people place an inordinate amount of time on preparing for what will hopefully occur later in life, while others, like Black and Native Americans, generally possess a present-orientation, with emphasis on what occurs in the present. As a result, counseling goals that are future oriented may not be meeting the needs of VREG clients.

From an ethnic minority status perspective, VREG clients may perceive the counseling as an experience to approach with mistrust and suspicion, particularly with white counselors (Vontress, 1981). Some authors argue that these approaches may be considered healthy to some degree, as mistrust and suspicion have served to protect VREG members (specifically African Americans) from psychological and physical harm (Grier & Cobbs, 1968; Thomas & Sillen, 1972; Ridley, 1984). Depending on the extent of mistrust, however, the interaction between a white counselor and a VREG client may negatively influence rapport-building, presumed to be a necessary precondition to counseling effectiveness (Jourard, 1964).

Another experience common to some VREGs as a function of the ethnic minority status is the stress related to cultural conflict. Cultural conflict occurs when immigrant VREGs and their descendants attempt to maintain some of their indigenous cultural practices and values in the face of internally and/or externally imposed pressures to acculturate into mainstream society. Although cultural conflict may be most evident among second- and third-generation VREGs, it can be a problem for individuals whose ancestors have been in the United States for many generations.

A number of authors have discussed the stress associated with cultural conflict. For example, D. W. Sue (1981) discusses the psychological implications of being a "marginal" person, someone caught between two cultures. Although some individuals eventually reconceptualize the position in the more positive framework of biculturalism, many others experience it as a source of stress throughout their lifetime. The problem is exacerbated by the fact that even those individuals who choose to acculturate fully often find that they are never completely accepted by the dominant society as an assimilated person.

DIVERSITY BETWEEN AND WITHIN VREG POPULATIONS

While VREG populations do have some common experiences, it would be a serious mistake to not recognize the numerous cultural differences that exist between and within these populations. Most of us have enough familiarity with African, Asian, Latino, and Native American cultures to recognize the cultural differences between these groups; it is also important to acknowledge that by so categorizing a variety of cultural groups we are glossing over some very important subgroup differences. For example, among American Indians there is evidence that over 500 different tribes, each with its own unique cultural patterns, existed at the time that Columbus arrived in the Western hemisphere. Some of these distinct cultural patterns have survived to the present day (in spite of earlier efforts to eliminate them) and account for differences within the American Indian population. For example, the religious beliefs and practices of Hopis and Navajos are quite different, despite the fact that they frequently share some of the same geographic area. Similar cultural distinctions exist among African Americans, Asian Americans, and Latino Americans, all of whom can trace their cultural backgrounds to the many ethnic/cultural groups in, respectively, Africa, Asia, and Latin America.

Nor are cultural differences between individuals limited to differences between ethnic/cultural groups within these larger categories that we use for the sake of convenience. Within each VREG group are differences that are a function of such factors as geographic area, economic background, gender, acculturation, and ethnic identity development.

CRITICISMS OF THE PROFESSION: A HISTORICAL PERSPECTIVE

Until the mid-1960s, little attention was given to the unique experiences of VREGs and their special counseling needs. G. Wrenn's 1962 article on the culturally encapsulated counselor is generally recognized as the first to suggest that practitioners were providing counseling from their own narrow cultural perspective. He urged counselors to broaden their mono-cultural perspectives in order to be more responsive to the needs of clients from culturally different backgrounds. Only in this manner, Wrenn argued, would counselors be effective with all their clients, regardless of client background.

Although the counseling profession was slow in responding to Wrenn's charge of cultural encapsulation, by the late 1960s a ground-swell of professional criticism was beginning to emerge. Influenced by the civil rights era of the 1950s and 1960s, critics began to accuse the predominantly white mental health profession of being ethnocentric and racist in all phases of service delivery, including diagnoses, treatment decisions, counseling process, and outcome. Initially these charges were based on the observations and inferences of counselors and observers with little hard data to back them up. It was not until the mid-1970s that researchers began to collect the kind of data that could support or refute some of the criticisms being levied against the profession. In this section we discuss these criticisms and present some of the research data that bear upon them.

One of the common themes in the criticism of the counseling profession is that the services provided by the profession are biased against VREG clients. The possibility of bias seems very real given that the majority of counselors are whites who were raised in a basically racist social structure. The fact that prior to Wrenn's 1962 article so little attention was given to the special needs of VREG clients offers some support for the hypothesis of counselor bias. By the mid-1970s, however, more direct evidence relevant to the issue of counselor bias began to appear in the form of research on differential diagnosis, differential treatment, and counselor prejudice. Harrison (1975) and later Atkinson (1983) reviewed the limited number of studies that have attempted to assess counselor prejudice and stereotyping and suggested that earlier attempts to document these effects may have failed due to the limitations inherent in survey research. However, counselor prejudice can be inferred from studies that suggest that minorities receive differential diagnoses and treatment. Reviews by Sattler (1977), Abramowitz and Murray (1983), and Atkinson (1985) of archival studies concluded that there is evidence of both differential diagnoses and differential treatment being applied to VREG clients.

Another criticism of counseling and mental health services is that they simply are not addressing the needs of VREG clients. Because counseling theories and services were developed by and for middle-class white clients, these critics argued, they simply do not address the type of concerns that VREG clients are likely to have. Smith (1977) noted that the intrapsychic nature of some counseling theories and the concomitant practice of insight-oriented therapy may overlook significant factors related to a "sick" society. For instance, a VREG client's problem related to personal adjustment may relate to and be compounded by his or her difficulty in dealing with racial discrimination at work. Or an unemployed VREG client may experience difficulty solely with securing adequate employment to support his or her family. Traditionally, counselors and psychotherapists do not become involved in the day-to-day survival needs of their clients, yet the resolution of these concerns may be equally or perhaps more relevant to the client than an attainment of insight into inner conflicts.

Although no one has yet empirically demonstrated that contemporary counseling theories fail to address VREG needs, some studies provide data that support such an inference. If VREG clients see counseling services as irrelevant to their needs, then one would assume that they would not utilize these services. Reviews of research on the utilization of mental health services offer fairly consistent evidence of minority underutilization. Sattler (1977) concluded after reviewing archival studies that Blacks are underrepresented in mental health facilities and that they have a higher dropout rate than whites. Leong's (1986) review of research on Asian Americans resulted in similar conclusions for this group. Abramowitz and Murray (1983) found evidence of underutilization by minorities but concluded that recent research does not support the hypothesis that Blacks terminate therapy sooner than whites. Analysis of these reviews is also complicated because some of them include allocation (generally under the therapist's control) of mental health services with utilization (generally under the client's control) of mental health services. Analysis is further complicated by the fact that some reviews have focused on archival studies while others have relied on surveys of expectations about utilization of services. These limitations notwithstanding, the data do suggest that minorities are less likely to self-refer for counseling and more likely to drop out prematurely from counseling than are whites.

The underrepresentation of VREG members among counselors is seen as another explanation of the underutilization of counseling services and another criticism of the counseling profession. Numerous studies have documented that VREGs are underrepresented among both professional counselors and among counselor trainees (see review by Atkinson, 1985), the latter finding suggesting that underrepresentation is likely to continue to be a problem in the future. Supporting the hypothesis that the lack of VREG counselors may be a reason for under-utilization is the research on preference for counselor ethnicity. Preference for counselor race/ethnicity has been the most commonly used dependent variable in cross-cultural counseling research. Typically, minority subjects are asked to express a preference between an ethnically similar counselor and an ethnically dissimilar counselor. Harrison (1975), Sattler (1977), and Atkinson (1983) all concluded from their reviews of research that Black subjects rather consistently preferred Black counselors. Atkinson (1985) found further evidence to confirm this effect but found no evidence that it is true for other racial/ethnic groups. While not all VREG clients prefer a racially, ethnically similar counselor, it seems clear that the unavailability of such counselors is a factor that deters many VREG clients from seeking counseling services.

In the absence of culturally similar counselors, the counseling relationship may be fraught with barriers that result from cultural differences. In a landmark article, D. W. Sue (1981) elaborated on the misunderstandings that may occur from cultural variations in verbal and nonverbal communication. These misunderstandings, in turn, may impede the formation of an effective counseling relationship. Three major impediments were identified: (1) language barriers between the counselor and client; (2) class-bound values that tend to characterize treatment approaches; and (3) culture-bound values that are used to judge normality and abnormality in clients (p. 420). For each of the three types of impediments, Sue and Sue (1977) describe how generic characteristics of counseling reflected white, middle-class values and characteristics, while the values and characteristics of VREG clients may be notably different. For example, language barriers are reflective of counseling situations characterized by a monolingual orientation, while VREG clients may tend to have bilingual orientations. Class-bound characteristics inherent in generic counseling include an emphasis on verbal communication as well as emotional and behavioral expressiveness, the attainment of insight, and the willingness to disclose intimate details of one's personal life. These characteristics and others (e.g., adherence to time schedules and the valuation of long-range goals) represent aspects of middle-class values that may differ from the values of VREG clients. Lastly, the authors explain that culture-bound factors include an emphasis on an individual (vs. a family) approach to treatment and an emphasis on cause-and-effect relationships. Again, these factors may contribute to barriers to facilitating an effective counseling relationship.

CURRENT STATUS OF MULTICULTURAL COUNSELING

The counseling profession has begun to respond to the criticisms that it does not address the needs of VREG clients, although many would argue that the response has been both slow in pace and inadequate in scope. Clearly, VREG clients are recognized by the profession as a growing and important population that counselors, regardless of their own racial/ethnic background, must be prepared to serve. In this section, we examine recent developments in training culturally sensitive counselors, conducting multicultural counseling research, and building VREG-related psychological theories.

Training

In response to criticisms regarding the lack of training in multicultural counseling, professional organizations have begun to develop policies that address this concern. In fact, the Vail conference, sponsored by the American Psychological Association (APA) and held in 1973, set forth the recommendation that conducting therapy or counseling without cultural sensitivity should be declared unethical. This conference and subsequent national conferences (the Austin conference in 1975 and the Dulles conference in 1978) also yielded recommendations that spurred the creation of several policies and boards to resolve such important issues as increasing the representation of VREG populations in psychology graduate programs and establishing standards and guidelines for graduate training programs to prepare students for working with culturally diverse populations. It was further suggested that all professional psychologists obtain training and continuing education in the special issues of different religious, ethnic, sexual, and economic groups. Moreover, in order for programs to become accredited by the APA, programs have to adhere to criteria that include the need for cultural diversity among faculty and students (Casas, 1984).

A number of workshops and conferences have been organized at the national level to address the issue of multicultural counseling training, including the annual Winter Roundtable at Teachers' College, Columbia University, New York, and an NIMH-funded project at Howard University (Chunn & Dunston, 1980, cited in Casas, 1985). These efforts have led to a number of proposed training models and course curricula geared toward increasing culture sensitivity, stimulating self-awareness of racial/ethnic issues and stereotypes, and providing the necessary tools for effective counseling with people of different racial/ethnic origins. The literature continues to offer a variegated selection of training models that can be implemented within existing programs (in curricula) and as workshops and specialized training programs. The following are examples of some of these models.

Corvin and Wiggins (1989) proposed an antiracism training model for white professionals to engage in self-exploration and to examine their own racism. The authors use Standard 2 of the proposed ethical standards for counselor practice by Ibrahim and Arrendondo (1986) as the basis of their model. This model assumes that in order for a person to be able to develop cross-cultural expertise or competence, one must (1) recognize, assess, and understand oneself as a member of a particular racial group; (2) become aware of one's own racism, and (3) take active steps to effect change (p. 107).

Sue, Akutsu, and Higashi (1985) offered training suggestions for nonminorities to work with ethnic minority groups. Their training model proposed three important elements to training therapists in providing culturally consistent forms of treatment. The first of these elements is a knowledge of culture and status, whereby the trainee becomes aware not only of the client's culture (or the cultural-deterministic perspective) but also of the perceptions and behaviors of ethnic minority groups as a function of the interaction of cultural patterns and institutions in the U.S., which they refer to as the ethnic-minority group perspective. According to the authors, "In addition to acquiring knowledge of culture, one must also develop awareness of inter-ethnic relationships, racism, and the historical-political-social and psychological context in which these groups have functioned" (p. 277). The authors propose that this knowledge can be obtained through courses and curricula focusing on ethnic minority groups and issues, workshops, guest lectures, and relevant readings and media. A second element proposed by the authors is experiential in nature, requiring that students work with clients from ethnic communities to complement the intellectualization and abstraction in discussing such issues in the classroom. This opportunity will also allow students to explore beyond the generalities often focused on in the literature and to gain an appreciation of within-group heterogeneity. Lastly, these authors propose the use of innovative strategies in working with racial/ethnic group clients. They argue that because of cultural deterministic and minority status issues, traditional forms of treatment may not be effective.

Carney and Kahn (1984) proposed a developmental model for trainees in multicultural counseling. This model conceptualizes five stages through which trainees pass in expanding their ability to work with culturally diverse clients. Each stage evaluates trainees' knowledge of cultural groups, attitudinal awareness, cross-cultural sensitivity, and specific cross-cultural counseling skills. Next, the authors propose that a paradigm for training should include essential *challenges* and *supports* that will successfully move trainees on to increasing their competency in multicultural counseling. Challenges are defined as gains in knowledge, attitudes, and counseling skills that are new to trainees, and supports include a training atmosphere that promotes personal sharing and reduces threat in the learning environment, both of which are essential to growth from one stage to the next.

Johnson (1987) has criticized current multicultural training models for teaching trainees only to "know that" cultural differences exist. What these models lack is a component that teaches students to "know how" to conduct their work with individuals from culturally diverse backgrounds. According to Johnson (1987), "knowing how" constitutes the skills necessary for becoming expert in working with diverse groups; "knowing that" only addresses an awareness that cultural differences exist. Based on the conceptualizations of Ivey (1977), who defines the culturally effective individual as an effective communicator in more than one cultural content, and Pederson's (1978) triad model for multicultural counseling, Johnson developed the Minnesota Multiethnic Counselor Education Curriculum (MMCEC; Johnson, 1982). The MMCEC represents an effort to infuse content from two categories of cultural experts (ethnic minority psychologists and experienced ethnic minority clients) into the training of counselors.

Despite the impressive body of literature that offers training devices in multicultural counseling, there is evidence that only a few counselor education programs provide the training necessary for this preparation. McFadden and Wilson (1982) found that fewer than 1 percent of counselor education programs require that their students study nonwhite cultures. Bernal and Padilla (1982) reported that only 41 percent of the clinical psychology programs responding to their survey offered one or more courses "that might contribute to the students' understanding of minority or other cultures" (p. 782). This study also found that while clinical program directors tended to agree that multicultural training is "somewhat important," relatively few have implemented efforts to address the multicultural training in their graduate programs. Findings from a more recent study revealed that only one third of the counselor education programs surveyed require practicum experiences in cross-cultural counseling (Ibrahim et al., 1986). With respect to course content, Arrendondo (1985) speculated that while many programs may provide the theoretical knowledge on cultural differences, the necessary skills development is desperately lacking. She proposes that this may be a result of the lack of institutional support beyond the theoretical level. Given the evidence that counseling graduate programs may not adequately train students in multicultural counseling, there appears to be some justification to Casas, Ponterotto, and Gutierrez' (1986) vehement criticisms toward the profession. According to these authors, "continued apathy by the counseling profession toward racial and ethnic minorities will result in a significant number of counselors working from what should be regarded as an unethical position, one that could eventually result in the ethical indictment of the profession" (p. 348).

Research

The call for additional research on issues related to multicultural counseling resulted in a steady increase in empirical investigations. In 1970, Sattler published a review of research on racial "experimenter effects" in experimentation, testing, interviewing, and psychotherapy and reported that he found only three studies that included counselor or client race as an independent variable. By 1980 multicultural counseling research was beginning to appear regularly in some professional journals. In a survey of research published in the *Journal of Counseling Psychology,* Ponterotto (1988b) found that while racial/ethnic research accounted for an average of only 4.1 percent of the articles published between 1976 and 1980 (inclusive), for the six-year period from 1981 to 1986 this figure had increased to an average of 7.3 percent.

In our earlier discussion of the criticisms directed at the counseling profession, we examined some of the research reviews on multicultural counseling. Our examination of these research reviews suggests that (1) VREGs tend to underutilize counseling services (based on survey and archival data); (2) VREGs receive different diagnoses than whites (based on archival data); (3) VREGs receive differential and often less preferred types of treatment (based on archival data); (4) Black Americans prefer an ethnically similar counselor (based on survey and analogue research); and (5) VREGs are underrepresented in the counseling profession. An interesting feature of all of the multicounseling research published prior to 1980 (and the majority of research published since then) is that one client variable—client race/ethnicity—has served as the sole or primary independent variable. A general criticism of this substantial body of research on client race/ethnicity is that while it may have important implications for mental health service and training policy (documenting, for example, the need to select unbiased counselor trainees), it offers little to guide the practicing counselor when working with an ethnic minority client.

The practice of comparing various racial/ethnic groups on a variety of counseling-related dependent variables also is subject to the following criticisms. First, by lumping all individuals of a particular racial/ethnic group together for statistical purposes we fail to recognize those intragroup differences that could, in effect, mask any between-group differences that may exist. Second, this method confuses race/ethnicity with culture (Sue & Zane, 1987). Unless we group people on the basis of culture rather than race/ethnicity, we are left with the generally unacceptable finding that differences between the groups sampled are somehow a function of skin color and physical characteristics. Third, by examining mean differences between racial/ethnic groups on some criterion measure without recognizing intragroup differences, we risk the possibility of perpetuating stereotypes for an entire racial/ethnic group that may be true only for a minority of individuals in the group. Fourth, the very process of comparing various racial/ethnic groups to the majority group (variously identified as white, Anglo, Caucasian) reinforces the view that the latter group is the standard of measure on the criterion involved.

Recently, research has begun examining the effects of culture-specific variables on counseling preferences, expectations for counseling, counseling outcome, and premature termination. Three variables—acculturation, cultural mistrust, and ethnic identity development—appear to be particularly fruitful within-group variables for further study. The variable *acculturation* has been included as an independent variable in several studies involving Asian American or Mexican American samples. In a study of Mexican American college students, Sanchez and Atkinson (1983) found that subjects with a strong commitment to the Mexican American culture had less favorable attitudes toward using professional counseling services than did subjects with a weak commitment to Mexican American culture. Acculturation also was found to be related to preference for counselor ethnicity. Subjects with a strong commitment to the Mexican American culture expressed the greatest preference for a Mexican American (as opposed to an Anglo American) counselor. More recently, Ponce and Atkinson (1989) studied the effects of counselor ethnicity, subject acculturation, and counseling style on the perceptions of counselor credibility and influence that Mexican American subjects hold. It was hypothesized that subject acculturation would interact with both counselor ethnicity and counseling style in such a way that unacculturated subjects would prefer a Mexican American counselor who used a directive counseling style, while acculturated clients would have no preference for either counselor ethnicity or counseling style. The two main effects for both counselor ethnicity and counselor style were found to be significant as well as the interaction effect for these two variables. For the dimensions of expertness, attractiveness, utility, and trustworthiness, the counselor received higher ratings when identified as a Mexican American than when identified as an Anglo American. Acculturation related neither to ethnic preference for counselor or to preference for counseling styles. Atkinson and Gim (1989) hypothesized that Asian Americans (specifically, 263 Chinese, 187 Japanese, and 109 Korean American students) who strongly identify with their ethnic culture would have relatively negative attitudes toward mental health services, whereas those who are more acculturated would have relatively positive attitudes toward mental health services. Regardless of ethnicity and gender, the most acculturated students were (1) most likely to recognize personal need for professional psychological help; (2) most tolerant of the stigma associated with psychological help, and (3) most open to discussing their problems with a psychologist.

The construct of *cultural mistrust* was first introduced in Terrell and Terrell's (1981) article, and later tested to determine differences in premature termination among African American clients (Terrell & Terrell, 1984). Involving a sample of 135 Black clients visiting a community mental health setting assigned to either Black or white counselors, their study examined the relationship between counselor race, clients' cultural mistrust levels, and premature termination. As predicted, they found that Black clients with a high level of mistrust who were seen by a white counselor had a significantly higher rate of premature termination (i.e., the failure to show for a second, scheduled appointment and to contact facility within three months after the initial interview) from counseling than did highly mistrustful Black clients seen by a Black counselor. Findings from this study also revealed a main effect for trust level, with highly mistrustful clients having significantly higher rates of premature termination, regardless of the race of counselor. The authors speculated that this latter finding may be a result of the measure (Cultural Mistrust Inventory; CMI; Terrell & Terrell, 1981) reflecting a generalized mistrust toward people or that the white-oriented counseling setting may have been perceived with suspiciousness, regardless of counselor race. In a subsequent study using cultural mistrust, Watkins and Terrell (1988) found that highly mistrustful Blacks who were assigned to white rather than Black counselors tended to have diminished expectations for counseling. A recent extension of this study (Watkins et al., 1989) examined the effects of more specific expectational variables in Black–white counseling relationships. Findings revealed that in comparison to Blacks low on mistrust, highly mistrustful Blacks regarded the white counselor as less credible and less able to help them with four problem areas: general anxiety, shyness, inferiority feelings, and dating difficulties.

Black *identity development* is another intragroup variable that is beginning to be the subject of a number of studies. This research will be covered briefly in the next section, in which we discuss Cross' (1972, 1978) model of nigrescence.

Emerging Theoretical Frameworks

Although existing counseling theories have been criticized for being oriented toward white, middle-class clients, no new counseling theories specially designed for VREG clients have emerged to date. And although some writers have suggested that some of the existing counseling theories are particularly well suited for VREG clients, there is no empirical data that seriously support this contention. What has emerged, however, are a number of theories of psychological development specific to individual VREG populations that have important implications for counseling practice. In the past 20 years, a number of theoretical models designed to understand VREG clients better in terms of cultural life experiences, societal forces, and individual psychodynamics have appeared in the literature (Arrendondo, 1985). These include, but are not limited to, Cross' (1972) model of psychological nigrescence (e.g., the process of achieving Black racial consciousness), Jackson's (1975) Black Identity Development (BID), Atkinson, Morten, and Sue's (1989) Minority Identity Development model (MID), and Sue's Cultural Identity Model (1977).

Unfortunately, empirical investigations that either substantiate or extend these theories to counseling process and outcomes have not been forthcoming, with one notable exception. Cross' theory of nigrescence has been subjected to a systematic program of research by J. Helms and T. Parham. While we recognize that theories on aspects of psychological development are not always expected to undergo empirical validation and testing, we also acknowledge that one important way to advance knowledge of multicultural counseling is to study and manipulate variables consistent within organized, conceptual frameworks. Because it is the only theory of VREG psychological development that has been subjected to a systematic program of research, we have elected to discuss Cross' (1972) model of psychological nigrescence in some detail in this section. The selection of this model also was based on (1) its similarity to the other models and hence, its representative nature, and (2) the promise that subsequent elaborations to the original model appears to have.

Cross' (1972) theory of psychological nigrescence describes the stages through which Black people proceed in coming to terms with their Blackness. Influenced by the oppressive forces experienced by the generations of Black people in America, this theory espouses that Black people differ in their worldviews; these differences essentially reflect how white people and Black people are perceived. In an extension of this model, Parham (1989) notes that Black racial identity is not only influenced by these oppressive forces:

> The development of an individual's racial identity is not simply a reaction to oppressive elements within a society, although certainly those elements are very influential. This extended model assumes that Black/African self-identity is an entity independent of socially oppressive phenomena: Black/African identity is actualized through personal thoughts, feelings, and behaviors that are rooted in the values and fabric of Black/African culture itself. Identity *development* is, however, influenced by an interaction between internal (individual) and external (environmental) influences. (p. 195)

Progression through the stages of racial identity development is a lifelong process; individuals may go from one stage to the next or may experience a *recycling*, whereby former stages may be revisited any number of times (Helms, 1985; Parham, 1989). Transcendence from one stage to the next involves a combination of factors, including personal readiness, prior cultural-socialization experiences, and educational experiences (Helms, 1985).

In the first stage of Black racial identity development, the *preencounter stage*, the Black person thinks, acts, and behaves in ways that are pro-white and anti-Black. He or she reifies aspects of white people or of Anglo culture, while spurning that which is related to Black people or to Black culture. The transition from the preencounter stage to the *encounter stage* is stimulated by some significant event or events that shake the individual's worldview. According to Helms (1985), this transition is characterized either by a strongly negative experience with white people or a strongly positive experience with Black people. The *immersion-emersion stage* is characterized by a reactive psychological withdrawal into Blackness and a proactive positive acceptance of Blackness (Helms, 1989, p. 237). First, the individual immerses himself or herself into all that is related to Blackness in an attempt to rid the self and all traces of the previous identity. Finally, the *internalization stage* is characterized by a resolution of conflict whereby the individual achieves inner security and self-confidence about his or her Blackness (Parham, 1989). He or she internalizes positive acceptance of Blackness and considers the oppression of all people as significant. The original theory (Cross, 1972) also postulated a fifth stage, the *internalization-commitment stage*, where the individual contributes actively to combat oppression across the diversity of "isms" in American society.

Significantly, the theory of psychological nigrescence suggests that the development of racial identity may positively impact mental health. What follows is that therapists need to recognize the need to address issues in racial identity development with their Black clients in order to facilitate healthy psychological adjustment. According to theoretical formulations on counselor–client pairings, the movement through the stages of racial identity may be best accomplished with counselors in higher stages of identity development than their clients, hence a progressive relationship (Helms, 1984). These formulations apply not only to white counselors (using a model of white racial identity development), but also to Black counselors.

The first published study investigating Cross' theory examined Black students' preferences for counselor by race (Black versus white; Parham & Helms, 1981). Their findings revealed that among Black student participants, prowhite-antiBlack (preencounter) attitudes significantly, positively related to preferences for a white counselor, whereas encounter and internalization attitudes significantly, positively related to preference for a Black counselor. Subsequent studies (Parham & Helms, 1985a, 1985b) have generally tested and partly substantiated the original theoretical model (i.e., Cross' model of psychological nigrescence); one other study (Pomales, Claiborne, & LaFromboise, 1986) failed to employ the RIAS in a manner consistent with Cross' (1972) theory (see Helms, 1986).

In Parham and Helms' (1985a) study, the relationship between racial identity attitudes and self-actualization was examined among 65 male and 101 female, Black college students. Results from the study indicated that both prowhite-proBlack (preencounter) and proBlack-antiwhite (immersion) attitudes were significantly, negatively associated with mentally healthy self-actualizing tendencies. Encounter attitudes were positively related to self-actualization tendencies and negatively related to feelings of inferiority and anxiety. In a later study, Parham and Helms (1985b) found that racial identity attitudes also related to self-esteem. While preencounter and immersion attitudes were significantly related to low self-regard among 166 Black college students, awakening racial identity (encounter attitudes) was positively associated with self-esteem. As noted by the authors, these findings appear to provide partial support to Cross' model. For example, it was postulated that increasing Black self-consciousness (a progression from preencounter to internalization stages) would parallel the development of increasingly positive self-actualizing tendencies and positive self-image. However, these studies suggest that attitudes toward oneself and toward other people may vary from stage to stage. These investigations not only provide new developments to the previous theory, but also stimulate intriguing implications to counseling among Blacks, and, possibly, among other racial/ethnic group populations.

Two recent studies have tested variables of the psychological nigrescence model on counseling-related phenomena, one on counselor preference (Ponterotto, Alexander, and Hinkston, 1988) and students' perceptions of culturally sensitive versus culture-blind counselors (Pomales, Claiborne, & LaFromboise, 1986). Ponterotto, Alexander, & Hinkston (1988) replicated and extended an earlier investigation by (1) testing similar hypotheses on a markedly different population (Black students attending a predominantly white, midwestern university versus Black students attending a predominantly Black community college) and (2) exploring within-group differences using the RIAS (the previous study used an alternative within-group differences variable). Using a paired-comparison technique, this study found that preferences based on the racial identity stages were inconsistent with hypotheses, but "these differential rankings and percentages, however, are too slight to warrant extended discussion" (p. 180). The authors also acknowledged that their reliance on the racial identity categories based on the peak scores of respondents was not methodologically consistent with the developmental nature of the construct or with instructions of the developers of the RIAS.

Perhaps as a result of the recency of the model, there have been too few studies conducted using the psychological nigrescence model. Moreover, there have been no studies reflecting the racial identity development of non-Black racial/ethnic group populations, although Leong's (1986) review concludes pointedly that this process of development may be a critical research variable in the study of Asian Americans. Thus far, the legitimate offerings on racial identity development research have been to substantiate and reconstruct the theory. This body of research has been promising in launching pioneering efforts towards culture-specific theory building and, thereby, presenting the inherent complexity of one racial/ethnic group population. Relatedly, this growing research has stimulated thinking regarding mental health issues and implications for counseling with African American clients.

Research that directly investigates the contribution of racial identity development theory to counseling-related outcomes needs to be deliberated. Unfortunately, the few existing studies related to counseling have not followed reflected methodologically soundness in reflecting the developmental nature of the theory and the intent of the constructed measure. Other assessments of racial identity development are needed to capture this development beyond attitudes. These assessments would be particularly important if researchers are to attempt investigations of the differing types of interactions of counselors and clients based on racial identity attitudes (i.e., Helms, 1985).

GUIDELINES FOR MULTICULTURAL COUNSELING PRACTICE

Sue et al. (1982) developed a list of cross-cultural counseling competencies that we believe still serve as the best guidelines for multicultural counseling practice available today. Basically, they identified three types of minimal competencies that should be incorporated into all counselor training programs. These three areas of competence are beliefs/attitudes, knowledges, and counseling skills. We provide our own discussion of these competence areas but refer the reader to the original authors for further elaboration of the specific competencies.

Beliefs/Attitudes

To begin with, counselors who plan to work with VREG clients need to examine and evaluate their negative attitudes toward members of the VREG populations. Counselors should question whether they experience feelings of discomfort, anxiety, anger, or guilt toward VREG individuals, in general, and evaluate how these feelings may influence their effectiveness as culturally competent counselors. Further exploration may lead the counselor to uncover some of the sources of his or her attitudes. For example, one's attitudes about VREG members may stem from negative personal experiences and/or from one's ethnocentric views toward the dominant culture. This is a particularly challenging task for white counselors since the larger society constantly reinforces white ethnocentrism. When counselors find that they are unable to give up on their ethnocentric criteria for evaluating culture-specific aspects of a client's behavior, they should refer the client to a counselor who can be accepting of the client's values.

Evaluations of one's stereotypic and prejudicial attitudes may also lead counselors to training opportunities that will involve systematic efforts toward attitude change. For white counselors, these efforts may entail a process of developing their levels of white racial identity development, defined as the process through which a white person proceeds in coming to an understanding of his or her status in the dominant cultural group (Helms, 1984). This process involves an intellectual, affective, and cognitive transcendence culminating with an acceptance of VREG individuals as equals. The development of white racial identity development and other levels of awareness are critical features of such training models proposed by Corvin and Wiggins (1989), Katz and Ivey (1977), and Ponterotto (1988a).

Some VREG counselors may be motivated to work with VREG clients because they feel committed to ensuring that VREG clients receive culturally responsive services. These counselors may also feel that they are capable of providing these services because they have formulated counseling theories and practices for VREG clients either on their own or through training programs they have sought out. Nevertheless, some VREG counselors may need to evaluate their stage of racial/ethnic identity development or acculturation levels to determine how these stages or levels may influence their efficacy as counselors for VREG clients. Similar to some white counselors, some VREG counselors may harbor negative or stereotypic attitudes toward certain or all VREG clients. Naturally, these attitudes can influence the counseling relationship, process, and/or outcome. Again, we point out that these factors have quite different implications to the training of VREG versus white counselors and to their impact on treatment issues. Currently, there are no training models in the literature that specifically elaborate how VREG counselors can be most effective with VREG clients.

Knowledges

In addition to an ongoing examination of beliefs and attitudes about cultural issues, culturally sensitive counselors continually seek to ex-

their knowledge relevant to multicultural counseling. Sue et al. (1982) have identified four types of knowledge that counselors should have. The first type is knowledge of how the sociopolitical system in the United States treats VREG groups. An examination of the history of oppression of VREG groups is helpful in gaining this knowledge. This knowledge is perhaps best gained in a group where discussions focus on such topics as past and present patterns of oppression, personal experiences of oppression, and the effects of past and present discrimination on client attitudes and behaviors.

Knowledge of specific cultures is a second type of knowledge that the culturally sensitive counselor needs to have. While it is probably not possible to know all aspects of all VREG cultures, the counselor should attempt to learn all that he or she can about the culture of any client with whom the counselor is working. This includes learning about the beliefs, values, behaviors, and history of the culture.

The third type of knowledge involves an understanding of which counseling theories and techniques are based on ethnocentric principles and which are generic enough to be applied to all cultural groups. Some aspects of counseling may be incongruent with the values of a particular culture and should be avoided. For example, client self-disclosure is considered to be an essential ingredient for a number of approaches to counseling. Yet self-disclosure of intimate feelings may be an anathema in some cultures. Reading books and articles on cross-cultural and multicultural counseling can facilitate knowledge about these incongruencies.

The final type of knowledge is an awareness of the institutional barriers that contribute to VREG underutilization of mental health services. This includes an awareness of how such factors as location, language, structured appointments, etc., can contribute to underutilization. This awareness probably is best developed by discussing institutional barriers with representatives of the various VREG populations.

Counseling Skills

As with the critique of any professional behavior, we know much more about what is wrong with the counseling services provided VREG clients than we do about what are appropriate counseling skills. Much has been written about the need for culturally sensitive counselors, but beyond defining the attitude of tolerance for diversity and the knowledge of various cultures as prerequisites for effective multicultural counseling, little has been written about the specific, unique skills needed to work with VREG clients. A number of authors have discussed the need for counselors to use healing techniques from the client's indigenous culture, but these recommendations seem only appropriate for those situations where the client is completely (or almost completely) monocultural and his or her problem requires remediation rather than facilitation from a psychotherapist/healer. To the extent that counseling by definition is a facilitative, educational, preventive process that focuses on *client* decision-making, the use of indigenous healing techniques appears to have limited application.

It can reasonably be argued that any counseling procedure that is helpful in multicultural counseling also can be applied effectively with white clients. This argument should not deter us, however, from attempting to identify specific skills that may need to be employed with greater regularity and more intensely when the client is a member of a VREG population than when the client is white. With this caveat in mind, we identify three types of counseling skills that are needed when working with VREG clients: (1) assessment of cultural influences; (2) credibility building; and (3) culturally relevant strategies. It should also be noted prior to the following discussion that the ongoing examination of beliefs/attitudes and the acquisition of knowledge about cultures are essential prerequisites to developing and using these three types of skills.

Assessment of Cultural Influences

When working with a VREG client it is imperative that the counselor assess the influence of the indigenous and dominant cultures on the client's life. In order to conduct this assessment, the counselor must be knowledgeable about the relevant indigenous culture, the process of acculturation and/or ethnic identity development, and the potential for conflict between the indigenous and dominant cultures. The goals of the assessment are to (1) determine where the client is on the acculturation and/or ethnic identity development continuum; and (2) determine whether cultural conflict is playing a role in either the client's presenting or underlying problem.

The assessment of where the client is on the acculturation and/or ethnic identity development continuum must be done without an acculturation or development bias. If the counselor has a preconceived notion about acculturation and identification, it is a good indication that the counselor is still operating from an ethnocentric value structure and that further self-examination is needed in the area of beliefs/attitudes. The purpose of this assessment is to understand the client better, build credibility with the client, and determine what counseling strategies might be most effective. Although the concepts of cultural identification and acculturation apply to all racial/ethnic groups, they are most readily applied to American Indians, Asian Americans, and Latino Americans because a body of literature exists about acculturation among these groups. Similarly, although the concept of racial/ethnic identity development applies to all racial/ethnic groups, it applies most readily to African

Americans due to the earlier work on Black identity development.

The assessment of client acculturation or identity development can be done either reactively or proactively, whichever is more consistent with the counselor's own approach to counseling. A reactive assessment involves careful listening for client-initiated information about their cultural values and ethnic identification. A proactive assessment involves sensitive queries about the client's cultural/ethnic identification. Overly aggressive questions about the client's cultural/ethnic identification may be perceived by the client as intrusive and unnecessary, particularly if the client feels his or her identification is unrelated to the problem.

Assessment of the role that cultural conflict plays in the client's presenting or underlying problem also can be reactive (careful listening) or proactive (sensitive queries). In our opinion, however, the counselor should remain in a reactive mode initially, at least until the client has provided some information that suggests cultural conflict as a factor. The possibility of cultural conflict playing a role in the problem may not be apparent to the client immediately and the counselor may have to make this connection for the client after sufficient data have been collected in the interview. For example, a VREG client may present homework procrastination and poor grades in college as a major concern but in the course of the counseling session reveals that expectations of his or her ethnic community determined enrollment in a major that the client finds uninteresting. A culturally sensitive counselor does not attempt to solve the conflict but rather helps the client identify it as a possible issue and then facilitates the client's resolution of the conflict.

Credibility Building

Sue and Zane (1987) assert that counselor credibility is a particularly relevant consideration in working with culturally diverse groups. A counselor is viewed as a credible source of help when the client perceives the counselor to be an expert and trustworthy helper. According to Sue and Zane, counselor credibility is enhanced through ascribed status (the position one is assigned by others) and achieved status (status one earns as a result of one's skills). These authors go on to suggest that VREG utilization of counseling services primarily may be a function of ascribed credibility and premature termination by VREGs primarily may be a function of achieved credibility.

The obvious implication of this discussion is that counselors should attempt to optimize their ascribed and achieved credibility with VREG clients in order to increase the chances that they will enter and remain in counseling. While ascribed status may be a function of rather inflexible characteristics such as age, sex, and professional degree and how these characteristics are viewed by the client's culture, counselors can do something about their achieved status. Sue and Zane (1987) hypothesize that by conceptualizing client problems in a way that is consistent with the client's belief system, interacting with the client in ways that are consistent with the client's cultural values, and defining goals for counseling that are consistent with the client's perception of the problem, the counselor can enhance his or her credibility. On the other hand, by adhering strictly to a conceptualization of client problems based on a particular theory, placing demands on clients to interact in ways that they find repugnant or irrelevant, and devaluing the client's stated goal by focusing on a hypothesized underlying goal, the counselor may lose credibility. This discussion once again points up the importance of tolerance for diversity and knowledge about the client's culture.

Culturally Relevant Strategies
Basically, two approaches to providing culturally relevant strategies for VREG clients have been espoused. One approach, frequently cited for Asian, Latino, and Native Americans, is to adopt the healing techniques that are part of the client's indigenous culture. As suggested earlier, however, the blanket recommendation that healing techniques from the client's indigenous culture should be used with a VREG client seems unjustified given that some fully acculturated clients may prefer mainstream counseling techniques. A second approach is to adapt current counseling strategies to the client's culture. The counseling strategies that frequently are cited as culturally appropriate for VREG clients are directive counseling strategies. For example, it is recommended that for low-income Black clients, counseling that is characterized by a directive approach is more effective than an approach that is introspective and insight-oriented (MacKinnon & Michels, 1971). Similar prescriptions have been advised for Native, Latino, and Asian American clients. However, these recommendations appear to be based more on class-bound issues than on issues that are relevant to culture. For example, Vontress (1981) notes that a directive approach to counseling may be as appropriate for poor Appalachian white clients as it is for poor VREG clients. In addition to the concern that preferences for directive counseling approaches are related to class issues, some directive strategies may actually hinder the counseling relationship. Richardson (1981) noted that advice-giving should be avoided in counseling with Native Americans. He argued that advice-giving by non-Indians may be perceived as authoritarian and demeaning to the client. In fact, some counselors may believe that by giving advice they are providing a culturally appropriate form of counseling. However, clients may perceive that these counselors are viewing them as childlike or unequipped to make decisions for themselves. As one might imagine, there are many dangers to overgeneralizing approaches with certain groups that depend on a number of significant factors.

In our opinion, the counselor must have a thorough knowledge of the client's culture before attempting to either adopt indigenous healing techniques or adapt directive (or any other) counseling strategies to meet the needs of the client. We also believe that the need for culturally relevant strategies can be conceptualized as a continuum ranging from no need for the fully acculturated VREG client to considerable need for the fully traditional VREG client. Another factor that will influence the need for culturally relevant strategies is the purpose of counseling. If the purpose is to facilitate client decision making, healing techniques based on the indigenous belief system may be of little value. On the other hand, if the purpose is to remediate a psychological disorder, use of a healing technique consistent with the client's belief system may be imperative.

In our judgment, a counselor should apply prescriptive strategies only if he or she first has acquired the appropriate beliefs/attitudes and knowledge. Rather than indiscriminately applying a prescriptive approach to counseling all VREG clients, the culturally competent counselor first assesses (1) the client's level of acculturation (or stage of identity development); (2) the extent to which barriers to establishing rapport are present within the relationship; (3) the extent to which culture-specific issues may influence the problem or facilitate the treatment process; and (4) whether the goal is remediation or prevention. Given this information, the counselor can then determine if it is most appropriate to adopt a healing technique from the client's culture or adapt counseling approaches to the client's level of acculturation/identity development.

CONCLUSION

This chapter has presented an overview of the issues relevant to VREG counseling. We defined the VREG populations by describing experiences that VREG individuals share in common—discrimination and cultural conflict. We pointed out that while African, Asian, Latino, and Native Americans share some common experiences it is important to recognize the differences between and within the four groups. Before identifying the current status of multicultural or VREG counseling, we explored the criticisms that have been leveled against the profession. Although the profession has initiated some measurable changes in the areas of training and research, there is considerable room for improvement.

With respect to guidelines for practice, we recommended that counselors begin by examining and evaluating their attitudes and beliefs toward VREG individuals through identity development and suggested that this process is different for white and VREG counselors. Also critical to becoming culturally competent is the need to possess knowledge related to the sociopolitical conditions affecting VREGs, specific cultures, counseling theories and techniques based on ethnocentric principles, and the barriers to VREG underutilization. Finally, we suggested that culturally appropriate counseling skills include skills in assessing cultural influences, building credibility, and providing culturally relevant strategies.

REFERENCES

Abramowitz, S. I., & Murray, J. (1983). Race effects in psychotherapy. In J. Murray and P. R. Abramsom (Eds.), *Bias in psychotherapy* (pp. 215–255). New York: Praeger.

Arrendondo, P. (1985). Cross-cultural counselor education and training. In P. Pederson (Ed.), *Handbook of cross-cultural counseling and therapy* (pp. 281–290). Westport, CT: Greenwood Press.

Atkinson, D. R. (1983). Ethnic similarity in counseling psychology: A review of the research. *The Counseling Psychologist, 11*(3), 79–92.

Atkinson, D. R. (1985). A meta-review of research in cross-cultural counseling and psychotherapy. *Journal of Multicultural Counseling and Development, 13,* 138–153.

Atkinson, D. R., & Gim, R. H. (1989). Asian-American cultural identity and attitudes toward mental health services. *Journal of Counseling Psychology, 36,* 209–212.

Atkinson, D. R., Morten, G., & Sue, D. W. (1989). *Counseling American minorities.* Dubuque, IA: Wm. C. Brown.

Bernal, M. E., & Padilla, A. M. (1982). Status of minority curricula and training in clinical psychology. *American Psychologist, 37,* 780–787.

Carney, C. G., & Kahn, K. B. (1984). Building competencies for effective cross-cultural counseling: A developmental view. *The Counseling Psychologist, 12,* 111–119.

Casas, J. M. (1984). Policy, training, and research in counseling psychology: The racial/ethnic minority perspective. In S. D. Brown & R. W. Lent (Eds.), *Handbook of counseling psychology* (pp. 785–831). New York: John Wiley.

Casas, J. M. (1985). A reflection on the status of racial/ethnic minority research. *The Counseling Psychologist, 13,* 581–598.

Casas, J. M., Ponterotto, J. G., & Gutierrez, J. M. (1986). An ethical indictment of counseling research and training: The cross-cultural perspective. *Journal of Counseling and Development, 64,* 347–349.

Chunn, J., & Dunston, P. (1980). *Ethnic-minority curriculum development. Final report for phase I.* Submitted to the National Institute of Mental Health.

Cook, D. A., & Helms, J. E. (1988). Visible racial/ethnic group supervisees' satisfaction with cross-cultural supervision as predicted by relationship characteristics. *Journal of Counseling Psychology, 35*, 268–274.

Corvin, S. A., & Wiggins, F. (1989). An antiracism training model for white professionals. *Journal of Multicultural Counseling and Development, 17*, 105–114.

Cross, W. E., Jr. (1972). The Negro-to-black conversion experience: Toward a psychology of black liberation. *Black World, 20*(9), 12–37.

Cross, W. E., Jr. (1978). The Cross and Thomas models of psychological nigrescence. *Journal of Black Psychology, 5*, 13–19.

Grier, W. H., & Cobbs, P. M. (1968). *Black rage.* New York: Bantam Books.

Harrison, D. K. (1975). Race as a counselor-client variable in counseling and psychotherapy: A review of the research. *The Counseling Psychologist, 5*, 124–133.

Helms, J. E. (1984). Toward a theoretical explanation of the effects of race on counseling: A black and white model. *The Counseling Psychologist, 12*, 153–165.

Helms, J. E. (1985). Cultural identity in the treatment process. In P. Pederson (Ed.), *Handbook of cross-cultural counseling and therapy* (pp. 239–245). Westport, CT: Greenwood Press.

Helms, J. E. (1986). Expanding racial identity theory to cover counseling process. *Journal of Counseling Psychology, 33*, 62–64.

Helms, J. E. (1989). Considering some methodological issues in racial identity counseling research. *The Counseling Psychologist, 12*, 227–252.

Ibrahim, F. A., & Arrendondo, P. M. (1986). Ethical standards for cross-cultural counseling. Counselor preparation, practice, assessment, and research. *Journal of Counseling and Development, 64*, 349–351.

Ibrahim, F. A., Stadler, H. A., Arrendondo, P. M., & McFadden, J. (1986). Status of human rights issues in counselor education: A national survey. Paper presented at the meeting of the American Association for Counseling and Development, Los Angeles.

Ivey, A. (1977). Cultural expertise: Toward systematic outcome criteria in counseling and psychological education. *Personnel and Guidance Journal, 55*, 296–302.

Jackson, B. (1975). Black identity development. *Journal of Educational Diversity, 2*, 19–25.

Johnson, S. D., Jr. (1982). *The Minnesota Counselor Education Curriculum: The design and evaluation of an intervention for cross-cultural counselor education.* Unpublished doctoral dissertation, University of Minnesota, Minneapolis.

Johnson, S. D., Jr. (1987). Knowing that versus knowing how: Toward achieving expertise through multicultural training for counseling. *The Counseling Psychologist, 15*, 320–331.

Jourard, S. M. (1964). *The transparent self.* Princeton, NJ: D. Van Nostrand.

Katz, J. H., & Ivey, A. G. (1977). White awareness: The frontier of racism awareness training. *Personnel and Guidance Journal, 55*, 485–489.

Leong, F. T. L. (1986). Counseling and psychotherapy with Asian-Americans: A review of the literature. *Journal of Counseling Psychology, 33*(2), 196–206.

MacKinnon, R. A., Michels, R. (1971). *The psychiatric interview in clinical practice.* Philadelphia: W. B. Saunders.

McFadden, J., & Wilson, T. (1982). *Non-white academic training within counselor education, rehabilitation counseling, and student personnel programs.* Unpublished manuscript.

Parham, T. A. (1989). Cycles of psychological nigrescence. *The Counseling Psychologist, 17,* 187–226.

Parham, T. A., & Helms, J. E. (1981). The influence of Black students' racial identity attitudes on preference for counseling race. *Journal of Counseling Psychology, 28,* 250–257.

Parham, T. A., & Helms, J. E. (1985a). Relation of racial identity attitudes to self-actualization and affective states of Black students. *Journal of Counseling Psychology, 32,* 431–440.

Parham, T. A., & Helms, J. E. (1985b). Attitudes of racial identity and self-esteem of Black students: An exploratory investigation. *Journal of College Student Personnel, 26,* 143–146.

Pederson, P. B. (1978). Four dimensions of cross-cultural skill in counseling training. *Personnel and Guidance Journal, 56,* 480–484.

Pomales, J., Claiborn, C. D., & LaFromboise, T. D. (1986). Effects of Black students' racial identity on perceptions of white counselors varying in cultural sensitivity. *Journal of Counseling Psychology, 33,* 57–61.

Ponce, F. Q., & Atkinson, D. R. (1989). Mexican-American acculturation, counselor ethnicity, counseling style, and perceived counselor credibility. *Journal of Counseling Psychology, 36,* 203–208.

Ponterotto, J. G. (1988a). Racial consciousness development among white counselor trainees: A stage model. *Journal of Counseling and Development, 16,* 146–156.

Ponterotto, J. G. (1988b). Racial/ethnic minority research in the *Journal of Counseling Psychology:* A content analysis and methodological critique. *Journal of Counseling Psychology, 35,* 410–418.

Ponterotto, J. G., Alexander, C. M., & Hinkston, J. A. (1988). Afro-American preferences for counselor characteristics: A replication and extension. *Journal of Counseling Psychology, 35,* 175–182.

Richardson, E. (1981). Cultural and historical perspectives in counseling American Indians. In D. W. Sue (Ed.), *Counseling the culturally different: Theory and practice.* New York: John Wiley.

Ridley, C. (1984). Clinical treatment of the nondisclosing Black client: A therapeutic paradox. *American Psychologist, 39,* 1234–1244.

Ruiz, R. A., & Padilla, A. M. (1977). Counseling Latinos. *Personnel and Guidance Journal, 55,* 401–408.

Sanchez, A. R., & Atkinson, D. R. (1983). Mexican-American cultural commitment, preference for counselor ethnicity, and willingness to seek counseling. *Journal of Counseling Psychology, 30,* 215–220.

Sattler, J. M. (1970). Racial "experimenter effect" in experimentation, testing, and interviewing, and psychotherapy. *Psychological Bulletin, 73,* 137–160.

Sattler, J. M. (1977). The effects of therapist-client racial similarity. In A. S. Gurman & A. M. Razin (Eds.), *Effective psychotherapy: A handbook of research* (pp. 252–290). New York: Pergamon Press.

Smith, E. J. (1977). Counseling Black individuals: Some stereotypes. *Personnel and Guidance Journal, 55*(7), 390–396.

Sue, D. W. (1973). Ethnic identity: The impact of two cultures on the psychological development of Asian-in-Americans. In S. Sue & N. Wagner (Eds.), *Asian-Americans: Psychological perspectives* (pp. 140–149). Palo Alto, CA: Science and Behavior Books.

Sue, D. W. (1981). *Counseling and culturally different: Theory and practice.* New York: John Wiley.

Sue, D. W., Bernier, J. E., Duran, A., Feinberg, L., Pederson, P., Smith, E. J., & Vasquez-Nuttal, E. (1982). Position paper: Cross-cultural counseling competencies. *The Counseling Psychologist, 10*(2), 45–52.

Sue, S. (1977). Psychological theory and implications for Asian Americans. *Personnel and Guidance Journal, 55,* 381–389.

Sue, S., Akutsu, P. O., & Higashi, C. (1985). Training issues in conducting therapy with ethnic minority group clients. In P. Pederson (Ed.), *Handbook of cross-cultural counseling and therapy* (pp. 275–281). Westport, CT: Greenwood Press.

Sue, S., & Sue, D. W. (1977). Chinese-American personality and mental health. *Amerasia Journal, 1,* 36–49.

Sue, S., & Zane, N. (1987). The role of culture and cultural techniques in psychotherapy: A critique and reformulation. *American Psychologist, 42,* 37–45.

Terrell, F., & Terrell, S. (1981). An inventory to measure cultural mistrust among Blacks. *Western Journal of Black Studies, 5,* 180–184.

Terrell, F., & Terrell, S. (1984). Race of counselor, client sex, cultural mistrust level, and premature termination from counseling among Black clients. *Journal of Counseling Psychology, 31,* 371–375.

Thomas, A., & Sillen, S. (1972). *Racism and psychiatry.* New York: Brunner-Mazel.

Vontress, C. E. (1981). Racial and ethnic barriers in counseling. In P. B. Pederson, J. G. Draguns, W. J. Lonner, & J. E. Trimble (Eds.), *Counseling across cultures,* 2nd ed. (pp. 87–107). Honolulu: University of Hawaii Press.

Watkins, C. E., Jr., & Terrell, F. (1988). Mistrust level and its effects on counseling expectations in Black client-white counselor relationships: An analogue study. *Journal of Counseling Psychology, 35,* 194–197.

Watkins, C. E., Jr., Terrell, F., Miller, F., & Terrell, S. (1989). Cultural mistrust and its effects on expectational variables in Black client-white counselor relationships. *Journal of Counseling Psychology, 36,* 447–450.

Wrenn, C. G. (1962). The culturally encapsulated counselor. *Harvard Educational Review, 32,* 444–449.

18.

Counseling Clients with Disabilities

HANOCH LIVNEH
Portland State University
Portland, Oregon

COUNSELING PEOPLE WITH DISABILITIES can be construed as being quantitatively rather than qualitatively different from counseling able-bodied clients. Indeed, the prime difference lies in the prominence with which certain themes (e.g., independence vs. dependence, personal loss, coping with crisis situations) emerge during the counseling process. The present chapter focuses on the application of various concepts and counseling interventions to working with clients who have sustained a disability. Due to space limitations, the discussion will be geared toward persons who acquired physical (rather than psychiatric or mental) disabilities.

The chapter is organized into three main sections. First, a general overview of the principal goals and interventions for clients with disabilities is provided. Next, the reader is familiarized with particular concerns facing clients with specific disabilities, and with appropriate strategies to counsel them. Finally, a brief description of recommended academic education for counselors who intend to work with clients with disabilities, followed by a presentation of program accreditation and professional certification and membership issues are offered.

416

OVERVIEW OF GOALS AND INTERVENTIONS APPLIED TO CLIENTS WITH DISABILITIES

It has been suggested (Cowen, 1973; Leventhal & Hirschman, 1982) that the provision of human services may be conveniently categorized into three, temporally ordered phases—prevention, intervention, and postvention. In prevention, often termed primary intervention, the focus is on education or the creation of public awareness of the likelihood that certain activities or situations (e.g., smoking, job stress) can cause physical (e.g., lung cancer) or psychological (e.g., burnout) problems. In other words, the emphasis is upon preventing diseases and stressful situations before they are likely to occur. Intervention, the second phase, emphasizes direct and time-limited strategies, adopted by practitioners, when dealing with crisis-like situations, such as myocardial infarction or spinal cord injury (in the medical field) or suicidal threats, panic attacks, and family crisis (in the psychotherapeutic field). Emphasis, here is placed upon early detection of signs of disease or crisis situation, followed by an immediate intervention. Finally, the postvention or tertiary intervention phase is geared toward assisting people with permanent or longlasting physical, psychiatric, and mental disabilities to cope successfully and adjust to life with the functional limitations imposed by the particular disabling condition. The focus is upon restoring the client to optimal functioning. This latter phase is also known as rehabilitation.

The ultimate rehabilitation goal is improving quality of life (Crewe, 1980; Livneh, 1988), or adaptation to life with a disability. Life, however, does not proceed in a vacuum. Therefore, the abstract goal of quality of life improvement may be concretized by anchoring it in two environmental contexts, namely, community and labor force memberships. The goal of community membership, or reintegration of people with disabilities, encompasses improving life quality via independent living, self-support, or self-sufficiency in both the home and the community at large. The goal of labor force reintegration, on the other hand, pertains to the improvement of life through economic independence as typically manifested in successful gainful employment or related productive endeavors.

Rehabilitation goals may be further subdivided as to their adjustment domains—physical and psychosocial. The domain of physical adjustment refers to the body's capability to function successfully within its surroundings. It is assessed through the performance of activities of daily living (ADL), mobility, and the negotiation of the physical environment. Psychosocial adjustment, alternatively, refers to the capacity to function appropriately in the personal and interpersonal spheres. It often includes coping with the adverse effects of the disabling condition and maintaining social competency in the face of negative attitudes and restrictions imposed by others.

Similarly, rehabilitation intervention strategies may also be conceived to be associated with community and labor force contexts and to focus on the physical and psychosocial domain. Moreover, rehabilitation interventions can be further classified into person-aimed (internal focus) and environment-aimed (external focus) strategies (Livneh, 1989; Scofield et al., 1980). Person-aimed interventions are those that envision the client as their prime target and seek to modify his or her emotions, perceptions, cognitions, behaviors, and/or skills. Examples of these types of interventions include personal adjustment counseling, behavioral modification, vocational counseling, and ADL skill development.

Environment-aimed interventions, on the other hand, are those that consider the external environment as the target of interest and, hence, strive to modify it in order to meet client needs and goals. Among the latter interventions are removal of architectural barriers, use of assistive aids (e.g., hearing aids and prostheses) to restore lost perceptual and motor functions, placement of a client in a group home, job tasks modification, etc.

As is evident from the above cursory classification of rehabilitation goals and interventions, counseling is just one modality adopted by practitioners who work with clients with disabilities. Indeed, personal adjustment counseling strategies occupy a single rehabilitation intervention component belonging in the community context, focusing on the psychosocial adjustment domain and emphasizing client-aimed interventions. This chapter is primarily concerned with the application of counseling theories to personal (psychosocial) adjustment to life with a disability. The interested reader may refer to Anthony (1979), Coulton (1981), Livneh (1989), and Scofield et al. (1980) for further discussion of environment-aimed interventions and the various work-related rehabilitation modalities.

APPLICATION OF COUNSELING INTERVENTIONS TO SPECIFIC GROUPS OF CLIENTS WITH DISABILITIES

People with disabilities share several common problems. The problems that affect the personal domain include (1) lack of motivation, frequently associated with secondary gain; (2) reluctance to participate in rehabilitation tasks; (3) depression; (4) damaged body image; (5) lowered self-concept; (6) loss of control; (7) loss of reward and pleasure sources; (8) loss of physical and economic independence; (9) difficulty in accepting and adjusting to disability; and (10) inability to access the environment.

Problems having an impact on the interpersonal domain include (1) dependence (medical, psychosocial, and/or financial); (2) impaired social and vocational roles; (3) changing family dynamics and relationships; (4) disruption of social life; (5) negative attitudes toward disability; (6) societal rejection; and (7) disuse or lack of appropriate social skills (Auvenshine & Noffsinger, 1984; Backman, 1989; Medis, 1982; Thomas, Butler, & Parker, 1987; Vash, 1981; Wright, 1980).

In order to cope successfully with these issues, most authors recommend intervention strategies that emphasize the mastery of independent living and coping skills. Training modules aimed at achieving these goals typically stress that the client acquire the physical, social, emotional, and cognitive skills necessary to adapt successfully to the disability. Moos and Tsu (1977) recommend the following adaptive tasks as part of coping with disability: (1) dealing with pain and incapacitation, (2) dealing with the management of stress in both institutional and community environments, (3) managing negative feelings elicited by the disability, (4) managing a positive self-image, (5) developing a sense of competence and mastery, (6) changing personal values and life style, (7) fostering independence, (8) managing relationships with family and friends, and (9) preparing client for an uncertain future when additional losses are anticipated. Other adaptive tasks may include the provision of information on available opportunities for regaining personal and economic independence, development of assertiveness skills, and the acquisition of decision-making, problem-solving, and goal-setting skills (Vash, 1981).

Since clients' personal needs and counseling goals invariably spring directly from the nature, duration, and severity of the disability, the present section attempts to acquaint the reader with the most paramount disability-associated issues and psychosocial interventions applicable to counseling clients with disabilities. Given the large number of disabling conditions with which counselors work, only the most common conditions are dealt with in this chapter. The seven physical disabilities are blindness, deafness, spinal cord injury, cardiac impairment, epilepsy, traumatic head injury, and cancer. Each condition is first considered as related to its impact on the person's life (functional limitations, psychological implications) and then recommendations for counseling and related interventions are provided.

Counseling Clients Who Are Blind

Impact of Blindness
It is estimated that almost two million Americans are blind. Approximately two thirds are 65 years of age or older, and fewer than 10

are below the age of 45 (Kirchner & Lowman, 1978). The following represent the major functional limitations associated with blindness.

PHYSICAL IMPACT Obviously, the chief problem a blind person faces is associated with mobility limitations. Lack of freedom of movement creates considerable obstacles for persons who are blind. These obstacles compromise the capacity to live independently in the community and have direct implications for social and vocational functioning.

PSYCHOSOCIAL IMPACT The blind individual frequently faces a dependence–independence conflict (Lindemann, 1981). Socially, such a client is almost completely dependent on the environment, yet emotionally may not be prepared to accept this dependence. Hence, interpersonal relations are marked by self-restraint and cautiousness (Gloor & Bruckner, 1980). Future goals and aspirations are strongly affected, as are relationships with the physical and social worlds. Related psychosocial difficulties may include underdeveloped socialization skills, lack of assertiveness, and an increased anxiety level (Vander Kolk, 1983). Finally, a blind person often faces negative societal attitudes (rejection, pity, fear, patronization) that further impede his or her integration into the community.

Recommendations for Intervention

The initial and undoubtedly foremost intervention modality with blind and visually impaired clients include sight substitutes. Sight substitution methods include mobility training (cane travel and use of a guide dog) and compensatory communication training (e.g., large-type printer, special magnifying lenses, Braille use, Braille typewriters, Kurzweil reading machine use). The acquisition of such knowledge and skills bring about renewed positive self-esteem, a sense of independence, and control of the environment.

The following recommendations are noted in the literature concerning the psychosocial adjustment to blindness (Cull, 1973; Vander Kolk, 1983).

1. Assist the client to view disability functionally (emphasize remaining abilities) rather than anatomically (merely in terms of loss of sight).
2. Help the client to understand the emotional responses that follow adventitious blindness and accept this condition.
   Carroll (1961) argues that blind people need to reach a phase of acceptance of dying as a sighted person and rebirth as a blind person.

3. Explore feelings with regard to attitudes held by family and peers.
4. Help the client to understand feelings of family and peers that result from changes associated with the condition.
5. Be understanding and accepting of the client's emotional responses and psychological defenses and offer supportive counseling accordingly.
6. Avoid fostering unnecessary dependence in the client.
7. Teach the client socialization, assertiveness and independent living skills.

Two counseling approaches that appear to be particularly suited for clients who are blind (see, for example, Vander Kolk, 1983) are behavioral therapy and Gestalt therapy. The former techniques emphasize modeling of adaptive behaviors via the senses of touch and hearing, reinforcement of appropriate behaviors, and rehearsal of newly acquired behaviors. The latter stresses acting out feelings and attitudes, and role playing various inner conflicts associated with loss of sight. Finally, counselors must be aware that clients who are blind rely almost exclusively on auditory cues. The customary eye contact with the client is thus rendered ineffective. Similarly, long periods of silence that traditionally are judged to be constructive in allowing for reflective thinking may be interpreted by the client as signs of disinterest, distress, or rejection on the part of the counselor.

Counseling Clients Who Are Deaf

Impact of Deafness
More Americans have a hearing impairment than any other chronic physical or sensory disability. However, although approximately 15 to 16 million Americans have some form of unilateral or bilateral hearing impairment, less than 2 million are classified as totally deaf (Schein, 1981). The principal functional limitations associated with deafness are discussed below.

PHYSICAL IMPACT Since deaf people are restricted in their information intake to primarily visual channels, the paramount problem they encounter is communicative. Although fundamentally a social problem, loss of or impaired hearing poses numerous environmental obstacles that might have a direct effect upon the person's safety and security. For example, the inability to respond readily to honking horns, police or ambulance sirens, children crying, a yell for help, a phone ringing, or a tree falling could create decidedly life-threatening situations in the life of a deaf person.

PSYCHOSOCIAL IMPACT As mentioned, deafness creates a cardinal communicative handicap. The impact of deafness extends to include sociocultural deprivation, experiential deprivation, and isolation from family and friends. The entire processes of enculturation and environmental adaptation are negatively affected (Ostby & Thomas, 1984). Several authors (Costello, 1973; Eleventh Institute on Rehabilitation Services, 1974; Lindemann, 1981) suggest that the following restrictions are often noted among deaf people.

1. A tendency to deny that there is anything wrong with one's hearing.
2. Suspiciousness that often borders on paranoid thinking concerning other people's motivations and intentions.
3. Conceptual and language limitations owing to misunderstanding of many idiomatic phrases.
4. Maladaptive behavioral patterns (e.g., withdrawal, passive-aggressiveness) that prevent effective relationships with hearing peers.
5. Social and emotional immaturity.
6. Difficulties in understanding and appreciating humor.
7. Frustrations owing to inadequate communication and isolation from the hearing population.
8. Overprotective, dependency-fostering parents and significant others.

Recommendations for Intervention

When surgical or sound amplification methods (use of a hearing aid) fail to improve auditory functioning, treatment of the deaf person must resort to compensatory communication skills training. Among the most commonly used training methods are speech (lip) reading, speech therapy (especially for prelingual hearing loss), finger spelling, sign language, and the use of adaptive equipment (teletypewriters, television decoders). Counselors who work with clients who are deaf should become proficient, yet remain flexible, in the use of these communication methods (Levine, 1977), and be able to use body language and other nonverbal modes of communication (Eleventh Institute on Rehabilitation Services, 1974; Ostby & Thomas, 1984). In addition, the counselor should acquire sufficient knowledge about people who are deaf, their subculture and the psychosocial, educational, and vocational ramifications of deafness.

The following counseling guidelines (adapted from Bolton, 1976) would enable the practitioner better to serve clients who are deaf.

1. Involve parents and family members in the counseling process, paying special attention to their attitudes toward the person who is deaf.

2. Adopt a situation-specific and practical counseling approach (emphasize the here-and-now). Avoid highly verbal and abstract levels of communication, especially when clients are prelingually deaf.
3. Allow time and be patient since clients who are deaf will generally require longer periods of time for services.
4. Realize that deaf clients often require various supportive services (interpreting, letter writing, explanation of an agency's rules and regulations).
5. Prepare clients for an acceptable level of overall functioning in the community (socialization skills, sex education, parenting skills, work-related issues).
6. Become more aware of possible fatigue associated with lengthy communication periods.
7. Be direct and repeat whenever necessary.
8. Use paper and pencil to stress verbal messages.

Two counseling approaches that are of particular importance to the counselor who works with clients who are deaf are cognitive-behavioral and group counseling. In the former, the focus is on exposure to reality, learning the consequences of one's actions and choices, and the acquisition of socialization skills. Structured group counseling, on the other hand, emphasizes realization of common problems shared by participants, goal setting, and the acquisition of vocational skills (Danek, 1983).

Counseling Clients Who Are Spinal-Cord Injured

Impact of Spinal Cord Injury

The National Spinal Cord Injury Data Research Center (Young et al., 1987) estimates that there are 150,000 individuals (paraplegics and quadriplegics) in the United States who suffered spinal cord injury. Of these injuries, 70 percent were as a result of trauma and the remaining 30 percent were associated with various diseases. Most people with spinal cord injury, at the time of the accident, are young (mean age = 28) males. The incidence of spinal cord injury in the United States is approximately 6,000 to 10,000 new injuries per year (Donovan, 1981). The functional limitations attributed to spinal cord injury are summarized below.

PHYSICAL IMPACT Impaired mobility is obviously the cardinal limitation associated with spinal cord injury. However, in addition to restricted ambulation, individuals with spinal cord injury, depending on the degree and severity of their injury, might also be functionally impaired in personal hygiene (e.g., grooming and bathing activities), eating and drinking, dressing, toileting, writing, driving an automobile, and, in men, performing sexually. Further complications may arise from muscle spasticity, pressure sores, pain, cardiopulmonary and urinary system infections, and body temperature regulations (Donovan, 1981).

PSYCHOSOCIAL IMPACT Two emotional responses often associated with spinal cord injury include denial of the injury's permanency or its degree of severity, and depression and its predecessor learned helplessness (the belief that one is powerless in controlling rewards and punishments) (Crewe & Krause, 1987; Seligman, 1975).

Changes in body image invoke perceptual distortions that may result in diminished ability to acquire new physical skills and adapt to environmental requirements. Since social, occupational, and financial problems are rather common, disruption of family life and social roles may occur. Possible long-term psychological reactions to the traumatization are passivity, dependency (including secondary gain), passive-aggressiveness, frustration, and feelings of social inadequacy and embarrassment (Cull & Hardy, 1975). Finally, attitudinal barriers and public misunderstanding may create additional obstacles, impeding the person with spinal cord injury from reintegrating into the physical, social, and vocational environments.

Recommendations for Intervention

For the most part, medical interventions for spinal cord injury include (1) surgery (to relieve pressure on the cord); (2) stabilization of the vertebral column; (3) medication (to relieve autonomic disturbances); (4) skin care; (5) bladder and bowel function training; (6) proper dietary control; and (7) physical and occupational therapy to improve ambulation, mobility, and proper use of extremities.

Counseling with people who have a spinal cord injury should address problems created by the injury in any area of life, including self-concept, acceptance of disability, independent living issues, sexual and marital adjustment, social relationships, and vocational concerns (Brucker, 1983; Crewe & Krause, 1987; Cull & Hardy, 1975). Two important concerns to clients with spinal cord injury are sexual functioning and socialization. Since the fertility rate for men is low and orgasmic capability is often lost in women (Crewe & Krause, 1987), these problems are of major concern to the client. Counselors should, therefore, be ready to deal with these and related sexual and marital concerns at any time during the counseling process. Clients may also need to be taught new interpersonal skills (knowing when to refuse unnecessary help or request assistance without feeling inadequate, embarrassed, or guilty).

Several authors view the goal of spinal cord injury rehabilitation as a behavioral change of the client. Hence, they recommend appropriate counseling methods to achieve this goal. Crewe and Krause (1987), for instance, suggest a cognitive-behavioral approach to identify client belief systems and then help them to understand better how their emotions and behaviors are shaped by their self-verbalization. They further recommend teaching clients to alter their beliefs in the direction of increased internal locus of control over life events. Romano (1976) reports on social skills and assertiveness training programs successfully employing behavioral rehearsal, modeling, and feedback to clients with spinal cord injuries.

Group and peer counseling modalities are particularly suited for counseling clients with spinal cord injury (Treischmann, 1988). In these settings, emphasis has been placed on issues such as problem solving, increased self-understanding, gaining insight into the process of coping with disability, and improved feelings of self-regard (Manley, 1973; Miller, Wolfe, & Spiegel, 1975).

Counseling Clients with Cardiac Impairment

Impact of Heart Impairment

Cardiovascular diseases are the leading cause of death in the United States. A total of 30 million Americans have some form of heart and blood vessel disease. Approximately a million and a half heart attacks occur annually, 50 percent of which result in death (Houd, 1978). The major cardiovascular diseases include (1) high blood pressure (hypertension); (2) congestive heart failure (the heart's inability to pump sufficient blood to meet the body's requirements); (3) arteriosclerotic heart disease (build up of lipid deposits on the inner walls of the arteries, leading to narrowing or blocking of the passages and resulting in a heart attack or coronary thrombosis); (4) heart attack or myocardial infarction (complete occlusion of the coronary artery resulting in a portion of the heart muscle being deprived of blood supply); (5) rheumatic heart disease (a childhood disease resulting from rheumatic fever, which damages the heart muscle and valves); and (6) various congenital heart defects (Brammell, 1981).

PHYSICAL IMPACT The functional limitations associated with heart impairment are various. Chief among them are angina pectoris (chest pain), shortness of breath upon exertion, diet restriction, and limitations of vocational and avocational pursuits. The nature and degree of these limitations are linked directly to the severity and duration of the particular impairment involved.

PSYCHOSOCIAL IMPACT Individuals affected by cardiac impairments are likely to exhibit reactions of fear and anxiety during the acute illness phase (following a heart attack) and long-term depressive reactions. Anxiety and depression are often magnified owing to fears of recurrent attacks, forced dependency, other life stresses, sexual dysfunction, marital conflicts, financial worries, returning-to-work issues, and the reduction in preimpairment activities (Thoreson & Ackerman, 1981).

In addition, denial of impairment may be present. It may take one of the following forms: (1) total denial of being ill or disabled; (2) denial of major incapacitations; (3) minimization of effects of disability; or (4) admittance of illness in the past but denial of its present incapacitation (Brammell, 1981). Further psychological reactions are those of helplessness, dependency, anger, and frustration (Thoreson & Ackerman, 1981).

Family reactions to the stress generated by the life-threatening impairment are of utmost importance. Because the majority of adult-onset heart disorders, especially heart attacks, occur among employed males, the spouse's attitudes and support bear significantly on the success of the rehabilitation program. Frequently encountered spouse affective and behavioral responses, such as anxiety concerning the husband's survival, anxiety about the future (children's education, health insurance), added household and occupational responsibilities, and the like may strongly affect the husband's psychological adaptation (Thoreson & Ackerman, 1981).

Recommendations for Intervention

The goals of cardiac rehabilitation are prolongation of the patient's life and improvement of life quality, both psychosocially and vocationally. These goals are accomplished via educating the client on the nature of the impairment and its risk factors, maintaining psychosocial integrity, and sustaining vocational abilities (Brammell et al., 1979). Medical methods geared toward life extension include surgical procedures (coronary artery bypass, electronic pacemaker implantation), restrictions on existing diet practices (reduction of fat intake, salt restriction), building exercise tolerance, avoidance of tobacco use, and drug therapy to manage vessel dilation, chest pain, high blood pressure, etc.

Psychosocial management to improve quality of life can be affected by numerous physical, psychological, social, vocational, and financial factors. It is incumbent upon the counselor who works with heart patients to construct a comprehensive psychosocial rehabilitation program that incorporates the following elements (Backman, 1989; Nunes, Frank, & Kornfeld, 1987; Whitehouse, 1962):

1. Provide the client with information on the nature of and functional limitations linked to heart disease.

2. Train the client in progressive muscle relaxation procedures.
3. Encourage the client to ventilate his or her pent-up anxieties, concerns, and other negative emotions in a supportive, therapeutic environment.
4. Assist the client in cognitive restructuring, with the goal of modifying irrational emotional reactions and thoughts.
5. Apply behavioral modification procedures to enable the client to acquire appropriate behaviors necessitated by present physical conditions. Clients may be taught new adaptive behaviors through (a) thought stopping of stress-inducing themes, (b) behavioral prescriptions, (c) role playing exercises, and (d) behavioral rehearsals. These methods may be of particular importance when counseling type A pattern individuals who possess hard driving, competitive, and deadline-oriented personalities (Brammell et al., 1979; Gentry, 1978).
6. Pay attention to sexual concerns and misperceptions such as fear about coital death and impotence (Lindemann, 1981).
7. Discuss with the client issues related to returning to work. Exploration and analysis of vocational interests, assets, and limitations should be undertaken, with the goal of achieving successful and functionally appropriate vocational placement.
8. Be cognizant of the symbolic significance of the human heart. Of all organs, it is arguably the one most closely associated with life itself. In their role as providers of health and quality of life improvement services, counselors should pay particular attention to the psychological importance of the heart, and the dynamics, conscious or otherwise, associated with the process of adaptation to a chronic and life-threatening disability.

Counseling Clients with Epilepsy

Impact of Epilepsy
It is estimated that there are between $1^{1}/4$ and 5 million persons (0.5 to 2 percent of the population) in the United States who have epilepsy or recurring seizures (Howell, 1978). The reasons for these widely spread figures include different definitions and case finding techniques (Hermann, Desai, & Whitman, 1988) and unwillingness, among persons affected and their families, to disclose this often misunderstood problem. Epileptic seizures, traditionally classified as petit mal, grand mal, focal or Jacksonian, and psychomotor (currently termed partial or generalized seizures) equally affect both genders and people of all ages and ethnic groups. Approximately 75 percent of all people with epilepsy have developed seizures prior to the age of 21. With appropriate medication, 50 per-

cent of those who have epilepsy become seizure-free, and an additional 25 to 30 percent experience a reduction in their seizure frequency (Hylbert & Hylbert, 1979).

PHYSICAL IMPACT Epilepsy is a brain disorder. Its most prominent functional limitations, depending on the nature and type of seizure, is a temporary loss of consciousness (Wright, 1980). During the seizure-free periods, people with epilepsy are fully functioning members of society. Although ability to drive an automobile is usually not affected, most states' laws require of them certain seizure-free periods (that may range from 6 to 24 months) before a driving license is issued. A second cluster of functional limitations often arises from the adverse side effects of anticonvulsant medication. These medications can cause the user to have a wide array of symptoms, ranging from skin rash, gum bleeding, hand tremor, coordination difficulties, and vision problems to nausea, vertigo, fatigue, and drowsiness.

PSYCHOSOCIAL IMPACT The individual with epilepsy is confronted with numerous unresolved problems. He or she feels healthy at times and as a person with epilepsy at other times. The person with epilepsy continually has to face questions such as "Since epilepsy is a brain disorder, am I physically or mentally ill?"; "Since epilepsy has no cure or real end to it, what is the prognosis of my becoming seizure-free? in remission? and for how long?"; "Is epilepsy inherited and would the low threshold for the brain's abnormal electrical discharge be genetically transmitted to my offspring?"; and "Would the seizure occur in social or work situations? And, if it does, how would people react to the seizure?"

Obviously, the anxiety and stress associated with the anticipation of seizures, the lack of a cognitively structured environment for the person with epilepsy, and the perceived discrediting attribute of epilepsy result in an immensely taxing psychosocial world. Attempts at concealment of the condition lead to further stress and anxiety. These, in turn, are associated with increased seizures, resultant feelings of embarrassment, shame, and guilt, and, finally, social isolation.

Ososkie (1984) and DeLoach and Greer (1981) underscore the negative impact that stigmatizing public attitudes have on the life of the person with epilepsy. The way family members and society at large react to the person with epilepsy has a decidedly large effect on the person's self-concept and adjustment. Parental overprotection and the imposition of many unnecessary restrictions foster dependency and isolation. Coupled with the frequently attached stigma by employers, ignorant of the factual basis of the disorder, many persons with epilepsy find the world of work alien and frightening.

Lastly, as previously described, owing to the side effects of high toxic levels of anticonvulsant medications, many persons with epilepsy also demonstrate periodic signs of impairment in various mental processes, including memory, attention, and judgment (Ward, Fraser, & Troupin, 1981).

Recommendations for Intervention

Medical treatment of epilepsy consists of drug therapy and, in a small number of cases, brain surgery. Commonly used anticonvulsant medication, such as Tegretol, Dilantin, Phenobarbital, and Depakene, prevent either hypersynchronic neuron discharge or spread of discharge. Surgical intervention generally consists of removal of a portion of the temporal lobe, when seizures are still uncontrollable after medication use (Hermann, Desai, & Whitman, 1988). In addition, clients are advised to avoid excessive fatigue-creating activities and emotional turmoil, and assure themselves of adequate rest and a balanced diet.

General counseling goals include (1) examining the nature of the epileptic seizures and their effect on the client; (2) dispelling the misperceptions held by the client and family regarding epilepsy and its functional implications; (3) discussing with the client and family ways of coping with the adverse effects of epilepsy; and (4) minimizing the number of areas affected by the existence of epilepsy and assuming responsibility for, and independence of, one's own life. The counselor should seek to assist the client in reaching a state of acceptance of the seizure condition, its unpredictability, and the feelings associated with it (Fraser & Clemmons, 1983). Denial of epilepsy is not an infrequent occurrence. Because denial is manifested in failure to comply with medication schedules, ignoring requests to avoid alcohol intake, and/or pursuit of vocational and avocational hazardous activities, this repudiation of reality must be dealt with by a counselor.

Awareness-raising Gestalt therapy techniques and supportive confrontational procedures are appropriate to combat unyielding denial. On the other hand, clients who exhibit anxious or depressive reactions, who experience self-defeating thoughts, or who shun social interactions can benefit from cognitive and rational emotive therapy methods. Here, clients are assisted in identifying the specific situation, the activities and beliefs that led to the irrational, negative, and self-defeating cognitions, and their resultant painful emotions (anxiety, depression) (Fraser & Clemmons, 1983).

Behavioral modification (e.g., positive and negative reinforcement, timeout) and self-management (e.g., relaxation exercises) procedures have also been shown to be effective interventions with seizure-prone clients. Furthermore, their applications along with EEG biofeedback training were found to be positively associated with decreased seizure frequency (Kaplan & Wyler, 1983).

Group counseling approaches are recommended to enable clients to combat social isolation, deal with concealment or denial of impairment, and reach a state of disability acceptance (Ososkie, 1984). Similarly, group-based skill training classes are highly valuable in assisting participants to understand and accept their condition better as well as to share in the group's joint endeavors (Fraser & Clemmons, 1983). Finally, family counseling may help participants to deal with issues such as overprotection, covert or overt rejections, and guilt associated with perceived causation of impairment.

Counseling Clients with Head Injury

Impact of Head Injury

Each year, approximately 500,000 persons in the United States incur traumatic head injury (THI) requiring hospitalization. Eighty percent of these individuals survive the head injury. However, 40,000 to 50,000 of these survivors sustain severe enough impairments to render normal life virtually impossible (U.S. Department of Education, 1981). THI affects primarily young adults in their late teens and early twenties. Males outnumber females by a ratio of more than 2:1 (Twelfth Institute on Rehabilitation Issues, 1985). THI is defined as "brain damage from a blow or other externally inflicted trauma to the head that results in significant impairment to the individual's physical, psychosocial and/or cognitive functional abilities" (Twelfth Institute on Rehabilitation Issues, 1985, p. 3). Hence, THI differs from conditions emanating from internal brain traumas such as stroke or brain tumors.

PHYSICAL IMPACT Since THI results from either direct and localized damage to the brain, or from more diffuse insult (concussion, brain swelling, intracranial fluid pressure), its physical manifestations are widely varied (U.S. Department of Education, 1981). Physical correlates of THI typically include various perceptual-spatial deficits such as visual-motor incoordination, visual dysfunction, muscle spasticity, seizures, and aphasia, and might also be associated with headaches, dizziness, lack of energy, and fatigue (Novack, Roth, & Boll, 1988; Torkelson-Lynch, 1983). Almost all clients will initially be affected in their ability to read, write, eat, dress, ambulate, drive, and attend to personal hygiene (Anderson, 1981).

PSYCHOSOCIAL IMPACT The effects of THI on personality may be conveniently classified into three general categories—cognitive, affective, and behavioral. The cognitive consequences of head trauma encompass all intellectual deficits resulting from the injury. These include impairments of verbal processes, learning, memory, abstract reasoning, judgment, attention, and concentration. Affected are speech and language abilities (symbolic processing), insight, problem-solving and decision-making skills, and processing of information (Novack, Roth, & Boll, 1988; Rosenthal, 1987; Torkelson-Lynch, 1983).

The affective consequences of THI relate to the emotional reactions directly associated with the onset of injury. The most common emotional reactions include anxiety, denial, depression, and agitation. Anxiety is manifested through panic-like and catastrophic reactions to the impairment and persistent irritability (Prigatano, 1989). Denial of the disorder is a rather common reaction among head-injured persons. It may range from minimizing the consequences of the injury and its permanence to failure to acknowledge the injury itself (Rosenthal, 1987). Depression, which usually sets in following initial acknowledgment of the injury and its consequences, is manifested by low self-regard, social withdrawal, and generally diminished or blunted affect. Finally, agitation (usually considered a byproduct of lower tolerance for frustration) is typified by emotional lability (frequent and easily triggered changes in temperament), loss of control over emotions, self-centeredness, lack of concern for others' welfare, suspiciousness, and impatience (Greif & Matarazzo, 1982).

The behavioral components of THI include impulsivity, behavioral restlessness, social disinhibition, decreased initiative, and diminished goal-directed behaviors. These correlates of psychomotor agitation are often traced to temporal lobe damage (Greif & Matarazzo, 1982).

Recommendations for Interventions

A wide range of interventions is available for helping clients with THI. Since a substantial number of the THI survivors manifest behavioral disorders, the goals of most rehabilitation programs have been geared toward decreasing these behavioral disturbances, increasing socially appropriate behaviors, and preparing the individual to enter the community after the acquisition of independent living and, when feasible, educational and vocational skills. Prigatano and others (1986) further describe the goals of therapy with THI clients as (1) providing a model that helps clients understand what has happened to them, (2) helping clients deal with the meaning of the brain injury in their life, (3) helping clients achieve a sense of self-acceptance and forgiveness for themselves and others who have caused the accident, (4) helping clients make realistic commitments to interpersonal relations and work, (5) teaching clients how to behave in different social situations, (6) providing specific behavioral strategies for compensating for neuropsychological deficits, and (7) fostering a sense of realistic hope.

Bahaviorally oriented treatment approaches appear to be particularly useful when counseling clients who have sustained head injury. Behavioral management, based on operant conditioning principles such as negative reinforcement (to modify or extinguish maladaptive behaviors), positive reinforcement in the form of social praise and tangible rewards (to increase appropriate social behaviors), behavioral shaping (reinforcing approximations of desired responses), and token economies are often used with THI clients (Greif & Matarazzo, 1982; McMahon & Fraser, 1988; Wood, 1984).

Another treatment approach frequently used is based on cognitive remediation principles. Using intensive teaching, cognitive retraining, and extensive rehearsal, clients are taught to improve their mental functions and gradually ameliorate their perceptual, verbal, thought-processing, and problem-solving deficits (Ben-Yishay & Diller, 1983; Harris, 1984). In order to achieve these targets, counselors adopt a variety of highly structured activities to facilitate learning. These include the use of memory aids such as written or tape-recorded reminders and diaries, repeated explanations, and multiple examples, to gradually instill confidence in the client in the ability to cope with the cognitive challenges of everyday life activities (problem-solving, money- and time-management) (Greif & Matarazzo, 1982; Novack, Roth, & Boll, 1988).

A rather unique approach is provided by Torkelson-Lynch (1983), who uses a modified three-phase Carkhuffian model to counsel clients with THI. In her approach, Torkelson-Lynch first explores with the client his or her perceptions of each established goal (improved grooming, job exploration). Second, during the understanding-knowledge gaining phase, instructions and explanations are related to the client as clearly and explicitly as possible. Finally, in the action-skill building phase, the counselor facilitates cognitive retraining using structural skill modules, memory retraining, language and communication exercises, and social skill exercises.

Cicerone (1989) identifies one of the goals of THI rehabilitation as increasing the client's capacity for self-observation. Accordingly, he recommends the use of informative and educational counseling approaches to help clients who are unaware of their deficits. The use of videotape to provide clients with the necessary feedback on their present communication and interpersonal skills, repeated observations to assess their performance in a nonthreatening setting, and the use of real-life community based activities to avoid the artificial treatment settings, are all marshalled to increase the client's level of awareness and attentiveness.

Two final approaches, to be briefly mentioned, are family and group counseling. Personal adjustment counseling of family members (McMahon & Fraser, 1988) serves to educate the family about the implications of THI and to secure their participation throughout the treatment program. Family members learn how to provide realistic hope, structure, and protection to the client without fostering false hope or unnecessary dependence. Concomitantly, family members are also provided with the opportunity to explore their own feelings toward the injury and the injured party (guilt, rejection) and resolve those "unfinished business" issues that have surfaced following the onset of disability. Group counseling is another beneficial treatment approach for clients with THI. It offers participants several advantages. Notable among them are socialization with persons facing similar problems, expanding one's repertoire of interpersonal behaviors, alleviating isolation and demoralization, seeing how others have progressed in overcoming their difficulties, and engaging in supportive, goal-oriented group activities (Cicerone, 1989; Novack, Roth, & Boll, 1988).

Counseling Clients with Cancer

Impact of Cancer

It is estimated that one in four individuals, or approximately 60 million Americans now living, will at one point contract cancer (Dunham, 1978). Almost 1 million new cancer cases are detected each year in the United States and there are, at present, over $2^{1}/_{2}$ million persons who have survived cancer for five or more years. Cancer is not a single disease entity. There are more than 120 different types of diseases termed cancer (often referred to as malignancy or neoplastic disease). Skin cancer is the most frequent type of cancer. Among females, breast and uterine cancers are the chief causes of fatality, while lung cancer is the most common cause of death among males. Although cancer can strike at any age group, it is more common in older individuals (Healey & Zislis, 1981).

PHYSICAL IMPACT Because of the variety of cancer types, it is virtually impossible to discuss cogently all the functional limitations associated with the disorder. Hence, only the most prominent physical limitations resulting from the onset of cancer will be delineated. (The interested reader may refer to Healey and Zislis, 1981, for a more detailed treatment of the topic.) Limitations on activities of daily living (grooming, bathing, dressing, feeding, toiletry) are more commonly associated with cancers affecting the brain, head and neck, breast, lung, and upper extremities. Ambulation difficulties result more often from cancers of the lower extremities and the brain. Speech and communication are affected by cancers of the brain and the head and neck. Most cancers, with the possible exception of leukemia, lymphoma, and cancers of the lung and spinal cord, have an adverse effect on the person's sexual functioning and cosmesis (Dunham, 1978; Healey & Zislis, 1981). Finally, most forms of cancer are, at one point or another, associated with organic pain.

PSYCHOSOCIAL IMPACT The diagnosis of cancer exerts an immense impact on the client and his or her family. Anxiety is one of the initially experienced reactions to the diagnosis of cancer. Several types of fear and anxiety have been mentioned in this regard. More commonly divulged fears include fear of loss of one's future, fear of pain and mutilation associated with the cancerous growth, fear of being separated from loved ones, fear of creating a burden on family members, concern about how the family will care for itself, fear of loss of self-control, and fear of loss of identity (self-image) (Allen & Sawyer, 1984; Carey, 1976; Pattison, 1977).

A second reaction to cancer onset is denial. Denial of the condition, or its implications, may delay necessary treatment and have an adverse affect on the client and his or her family. Depression, yet another common reaction to life-threatening disorders, is a natural concomitant of cancer and is manifested by feelings of helplessness, hopelessness, vulnerability, and the like. Depressive themes may range from mourning of the anticipated loss of one's life to struggling with guilt feelings triggered by the belief that cancer may have been a punishment for past wrongdoings. Lastly, feelings of anger and bitterness are also prevalent and may be an indication of (1) inability to tolerate daily routine (medical regime, family reactions), (2) jealousy directed at others, or (3) blame projected onto others for the perceived onset of the condition of its lack of improvement.

Recommendations for Intervention

Medical treatment of cancer is accomplished through surgery, radiation therapy, and/or chemotherapy. Whereas surgery and radiation therapy are relatively straightforward procedures, chemotherapy, owing to its generalized effects on many of the body systems, carries with it a host of related side effects (nausea, hair loss, fatigue, weakness). Counselors who work with cancer clients should thoroughly familiarize themselves with these added problems and their psychosocial and social-familial implications.

Immediately following the diagnosis of cancer, the counselor's main role is to assist the client with cancer to cope effectively with the ensuing anxiety and stress. The counselor should provide the client with accurate and useful information about the disease, its course and prognosis, so that irrational fears and misperceptions may be alleviated and realistic hope instilled. Hope frequently increases the client's motivation, sense of meaning and productivity, and his or her adherence to the medical regime and successfully contributes to coping with the psychological impact of the disease (McAleer & Kluge, 1978; McCollum, 1978). Counselors, however, should be cautious in drawing a fine balance between optimism and realism. Issues of disease recurrence following treatment, the ambiguity surrounding the cause and prognosis of the disease, the effects of treatment and its associated side effects, and the financial burdens of hospital and treatment cost should all be dealt with early in the counseling process (McAleer & Kluge, 1978).

The overriding goal of rehabilitation is restoring the client to the highest possible level of physical, psychological, social, and vocational functioning. Nowhere is this goal more important than in cancer rehabilitation. Similarly, enhancing the quality of life (even if time limited) becomes a primary concern of the counselor (Allen & Sawyer, 1984). Perhaps one of the first issues to be jointly explored by client and counselor should be that of *meaning* of the involved organ (loss of breast or leg, facial disfigurement) and the resulting pain and suffering to the client (Cobb, 1973). Uncovering the client's feelings regarding these issues may, then, serve as a predecessor toward finding a sense of meaning in one's life and the inevitability of death.

Obviously, one of the most painful tasks facing the counselor and client is dealing with the issue of death, dying, and the grieving process. As the disease progresses, and if no cure is found, and the certainty of impending death looms larger, most counseling sessions should focus on the acceptance of death. Counseling for the acceptance of death (Cobb, 1973; McAleer & Kluge, 1978) should focus on issues such as facing the agony of separation from loved ones, preparation of the family for the separation, taking pride in one's past accomplishments ("Leaving a mark" on this world), and the like. In order to cope successfully with these painful topics, the counselor should provide the client with emotional support and a sense of personal security, increase the client's feelings of personal worth and dignity, create an atmosphere in which the client and family can openly and honestly express emotions, and ultimately serve as a "silent companion" to all involved persons (Allen & Sawyer, 1984; Cobb, 1973; Kubler-Ross, 1969).

Insofar as an increasingly larger number of clients with cancer survive the disease, they should be allowed to assume gradual control over their lives and be given a greater role in participating and contributing to their own treatment program. They should be routinely consulted about setting goals and making decisions concerning situations affecting personal and family welfare. In this context, family counseling assumes particular importance. Decisions concerning family role redefinitions and role modifications must be faced. McAleer and Kluge (1978) recommend teaching the family problem-solving and family management skills geared toward acceptance of disability-linked residual functional limitations (amputation, medication side effects), sexual activities, financial management, vocational readjustment, and recreational activities.

Of the various counseling approaches, two that seem to address many of the aforementioned issues are Gestalt and cognitive-behavioral therapy. Gestalt therapy may benefit clients in resolving unfinished life issues that, due to the impending death, may never be resolved (saying farewell to loved ones, and in general, gaining awareness of personal feelings toward death and dying, pain and suffering). Behavioral interventions, on the other hand, through the application of muscle relaxation techniques, systematic desensitization, thought stopping, and guided imagery can reduce muscle tension associated with anxiety, stress, and pain and allow clients to focus their thoughts on nonthreatening and pleasant scenes (Dolan, Allen, & Bell, 1988; Fleming, 1985; Lyles et al., 1982).

TRAINING AND QUALIFICATIONS OF COUNSELORS WHO WORK WITH CLIENTS WITH DISABILITIES

Academic Training and Program Accreditation

Academic training of counselors whose interest lies in working with clients with disabilities is accomplished almost invariably through Rehabilitation Counselor Education (RCE) programs. These training programs are typically graduate (master's level) programs and are offered by Counselor Education or Counseling Psychology departments. The programs normally require two years of academic and clinical training when completed on a full-time basis.

The curriculum content pursued in most of these training programs has been developed and verified by the Council on Rehabilitation Education (CORE). CORE was established in 1971 as an accreditation body to oversee the academic and clinical training of rehabilitation counselors and to promote effective delivery of rehabilitation services to people with disabilities. Of the approximately 100 RCE programs in the United States, 75 are currently CORE-accredited. These programs must show evidence of a graduate-level curriculum that provides its trainee with a course of study that includes, but is not limited to, the following knowledge and/or skill areas: (1) history and philosophy of rehabilitation; (2) rehabilitation legislation; (3) organizational structure of the rehabilitation system (public and private, nonprofit and for-profit service delivery); (4) counseling theories, approaches, and techniques; (5) case management; (6) career development and career counseling theories and practices; (7) vocational evaluation, occupational analysis, and work adjustment techniques; (8) medical aspects of disability; (9) psychosocial aspects of disability; (10) knowledge of community resources and services; (11) rehabilitation research; and (12) legal and ethical issues in rehabilitation counseling.

In addition, rehabilitation counseling trainees are required to participate in supervised practicum and internship experiences totaling a minimum of 600 clock hours in approved rehabilitation sites.

Certification and Licensure

The Commission on Rehabilitation Counseling Certification (CRCC), a division of the Board of Rehabilitation Certification (BRC), is the primary certifying body of rehabilitation counselors in the United States. (The other division overseen by BRC is the Commission on Certification of Insurance Rehabilitation Specialists). There are, at present, nearly 10,000 counselors who are rehabilitation certified.

The main purpose of CRCC is to ensure that professionals who practice counseling with clients with disabilities (rehabilitation counselors) meet acceptable standards of professional expertise. CRCC, founded in 1973, was the first national certification organization to be sponsored by an American Association for Counseling and Development (AACD) division, namely the American Rehabilitation Counseling Association (Emener & Cottone, 1989). In accordance with the knowledge and skill areas required by CORE for program accreditation purposes, CRCC tests rehabilitation applicants on the following content subjects: (1) rehabilitation philosophy, history, structure, and legislation; (2) medical and psychosocial aspects of disability; (3) counseling theories and techniques; (4) occupational information; (5) job development and placement; (6) evaluation and assessment; (7) vocational adjustment; (8) research utilization; and (9) ethical issues.

The duration of the certification is 5 years. At the end of the 5-year period, the Certified Rehabilitation Counselor (CRC) who has not accumulated a total of 150 approved contact (clock) hours of continuing education must retake and successfully pass the CRC exam to maintain his or her certification.

State-regulated licensure of counselors who work with clients with disabilities is usually accomplished through the enactment of omnibus state legislation that governs the practice of various professional counselor groups (mental health, marriage and family, community, rehabilitation). These state laws regulate individuals in the use of the title ("professional counselor"), as well as the practice of the profession.

Professional Associations

At present, the following national professional organizations offer membership to counselors who seek to specialize in working with clients disabilities: the American Rehabilitation Counseling Association (ARCA) Division of AACD; the National Rehabilitation Counseling Association (NRCA) Division of the National Rehabilitation Association (NRA); the Rehabilitation Psychology Division (Division 22) of the American Psychological Association (APA); and the National Association of Rehabilitation Professionals in the Private Sector (NARPPS).

ARCA and NRCA are organizations representing professional rehabilitation counselors and others concerned with improving the lives of persons with disabilities (educators, researchers, administrators). These two organizations, established at about the same time (1956–1957), have as their mission the provision of leadership to promote excellence in rehabilitation counseling practice, training, research, consultation, and professional growth. They further emphasize the importance of modifying environmental and attitudinal conditions and barriers so that more opportunities become available to persons with disabilities in employment, education, and community activities. The membership of ARCA and NRCA is composed of rehabilitation counselors and other practitioners employed in both the public and private sectors (Divisions of Vocational Rehabilitation, Commissions for the Blind and Visually Impaired, hospitals and rehabilitation units, mental health centers, rehabilitation workshops, self-help organizations, and private rehabilitation organizations).

The Rehabilitation Psychology Division of the APA represents members (mainly psychologists) who are interested in the psychosocial consequences of disability and rehabilitation (personal adjustment and growth, coping strategies, social and attitudinal barriers) in order to better serve persons with disabilities. This division is equally interested in the development of high standards and practices for professional psychologists who serve clients with disabilities. Most of the division members are educators, researchers, and practicing psychologists whose clientele is comprised mainly of persons with physical and cognitive impairments.

Finally, NARPPS is an organization whose members are invariably committed to the advancement of rehabilitation practices in the private for-profit rehabilitation sector. Although traditional counseling activities make up only a minor portion of the job tasks performed by private rehabilitation professionals, they nonetheless offer individual and group counseling services to clients as may be required for achievement of sound vocational choice and successful job placement. Members of NARPPS typically include rehabilitation counselors, rehabilitation nurses, vocational evaluators, and job placement specialists.

CONCLUSION

The purpose of this chapter was to acquaint the beginning counseling student with (1) the impact of various disabling conditions on the client; (2) the intervention strategies most commonly adopted by counselors who work with clients with disabilities; and (3) the academic programs, their accreditation procedures, certification and licensure considerations, and the professional organizations of counselors who serve clients with disabilities. Counselors who intend to pursue the career of rehabilitation counseling and specialize in working with clients with disabilities may find it advantageous to contact directly the following organizations: (1) ARCA/AACD, 5999 Stevenson Avenue, Alexandria, VA 22304; (2) NRCA/NRA, 633 S. Washington St., Alexandria VA 22314; and/or CORE, Room 1617, 185 N. Wabash, Chicago IL 60601.

REFERENCES

Allen, H. A., & Sawyer, H. W. (1984). Individuals with life-threatening disabilities: A rehabilitation counseling approach. *Journal of Applied Rehabilitation Counseling, 15*(2), 26–29.

Anderson, T. P. (1981). Stroke and cerebral trauma: Medical aspects. In W. C. Stolov & M. R. Clowers (Eds.), *Handbook of severe disability* (pp. 119–126). Washington, DC: U.S. Department of Education.

Anthony, W. A. (1979). *Principles of psychiatric rehabilitation.* Baltimore, MD: University Park Press.

Auvenshine, C. D., & Noffsinger, A. L. (1984). *Counseling: An introduction for the health and human services.* Baltimore, MD: University Park Press.

Backman, M. E. (1989). *The psychology of the physically ill patient: A clinician's guide.* New York: Plenum.

Ben-Yishay, Y., & Diller, L. (1983). Cognitive deficits. In M. Rosenthal, E. Griffith, M. Bond, & J. Miller (Eds.), *Rehabilitation of the head injured adult* (pp. 167–182). Philadelphia, PA: Davis.

Bolton, B. (Ed.). (1976). *Psychology of deafness for rehabilitation counselors.* Baltimore, MD: University Park Press.

Brammell, H. L. (1981). Cardiovascular diseases. In W. C. Stolov & M. R. Clowers (Eds.), *Handbook of severe disability* (pp. 289–308). Washington, DC: U.S. Department of Education.

Brammell, H. L., McDaniel, J., Niccoli, S. A., Darnell, R., & Roberson, D. R. (1979). *Cardiac rehabilitation.* Denver, CO: Webb-Warring Lung.

Brucker, B. S. (1983). Spinal cord injuries. In T. G. Burish & L. A. Bradley (Eds.), *Coping with chronic disease* (pp. 285–311). New York: Academic Press.

Carey, R. G. (1976). Counseling the terminally ill. *Personnel and Guidance Journal, 55,* 124–126.

Carroll, T. J. (1961). *Blindness.* Boston: Little, Brown.

Cicerone, K. D. (1989). Psychotherapeutic interventions with traumatically brain-injured patients. *Rehabilitation Psychology, 34,* 105–114.

Cobb, A. B. (Ed.) (1973). *Medical and psychological aspects of disability.* Springfield, IL: Charles C Thomas.

Costello, P. M. (1973). Educational and social factors in the rehabilitation of hearing disabilities. In A. B. Cobb (Ed.), *Medical and psychological aspects of disability* (pp. 303–328). Springfield, IL: Charles C Thomas.

Coulton, C. J. (1981). Person-environment fit as the focus in health care. *Social Work, 62,* 26–35.

Cowen, E. L. (1973). Social and community interventions. *Annual Review of Psychology, 24,* 423–472.

Crewe, N. M. (1980). Quality of life: The ultimate goal in rehabilitation. *Minnesota Medicine, 63,* 586–589.

Crewe, N. M., & Krause, J. S. (1987). Spinal cord injury: Psychological aspects. In B. Caplan (Ed.), *Rehabilitation psychology desk reference* (pp. 3–35). Rockville, MD: Aspen.

Cull, J. G. (1973). Psychological adjustment to blindness. In A. B. Cobb (Ed.), *Medical and psychological aspects of disability* (pp. 336–348). Springfield, IL: Charles C Thomas.

Cull, J. G., & Hardy, R. E. (1975). *Counseling strategies with special populations.* Springfield, IL: Charles C Thomas.

Danek, M. (1983). Rehabilitation counseling with deaf clients. *Journal of Applied Rehabilitation Counseling, 14*(3), 20–25.

DeLoach, C., & Greer, B. G. (1981). *Adjustment to severe physical disability: A metamorphosis.* New York: McGraw-Hill.

Dolan, J. D., Allen, H. A., & Bell, T. T. (1988). Neoplastic disease: Considerations for the rehabilitation profession. In S. E. Rubin & N. M. Rubin (Eds.), *Contemporary challenges to the rehabilitation counseling profession* (pp. 183–196). Baltimore, MD: Paul H. Brookes.

Donovan, W. H. (1981). Spinal cord injury. In W. C. Stolov & M. R. Clowers (Eds.), *Handbook of severe disability* (pp. 65–82). Washington, DC: U.S. Department of Education.

Dunham, C. S. (1978). Cancer. In R. M. Goldenson (Ed.), *Disability and rehabilitation handbook* (pp. 305–317). New York: McGraw-Hill.

Eleventh Institute on Rehabilitation Services (1974). *The Rehabilitation of the deaf.* Fayetteville, AR: University of Arkansas, Arkansas Rehabilitation Research & Training Center.

Emener, W. G., & Cottone, R. R. (1989). Professionalization, deprofessionalization, and reprofessionalization of rehabilitation counseling according to criteria of professions. *Journal of Counseling and Development, 67,* 576–581.

Fleming, V. (1985). Relaxation therapy for far-advanced cancer. *American Journal of Nursing, 77,* 1585–1588.

Fraser, R. T., & Clemmons, D. (1983). Epilepsy rehabilitation: Assessment and counseling concerns. *Journal of Applied Rehabilitation Counseling, 14*(3), 26–31.

Gentry, W. D. (1978). Behavior modification of the coronary-prone behavior pattern. In T. M. Dembroski, S. M. Weiss, J. L. Shields, S. G. Haynes, & M. Feinleib (Eds.), *Coronary-prone behavior.* New York: Springer-Verlag.

Gloor, B., & Bruckner, R. (Eds.). (1980). *Rehabilitation of the visually disabled and the blind at different ages.* Baltimore, MD: University Park Press.

Greif, E., & Matarazzo, R. G. (1982). *Behavioral approaches to rehabilitation.* New York: Springer.

Harris, J. (1984). Methods of improving memory. In B. A. Wilson & N. Moffatt (Eds.), *Clinical management of memory problems* (pp. 46–62). Rockville, MD: Aspen.

Healey, J. E., & Zislis, J. M. (1981). Cancers. In W. C. Stolov & M. R. Clowers (Eds.), *Handbook of severe disability* (pp. 363–376). Washington, DC: U.S. Department of Education.

Hermann, B. P., Desai, B. T., & Whitman, S. (1988). Epilepsy. In V. B. Van Hasselt, P. S. Strain, & M. Hersen (Eds.), *Handbook of developmental and physical disabilities* (pp. 247–270). New York: Pergamon.

Houd, H. (1978). Cardiac disorders. In R. M. Goldenson (Ed.), *Disability and rehabilitation handbook* (pp. 318–330). New York: McGraw-Hill.

Howell, L. (1978). Epilepsy. In R. M. Goldenson (Ed.), *Disability and rehabilitation handbook* (pp. 381–388). New York: McGraw-Hill.

Hylbert, K. W., & Hylbert, K. W. (1979). *Medical information for human service workers.* State College, PA: Counselor Education Press.

Kaplan, B. J., & Wyler, A. R. (1983). Coping with epilepsy. In T. G. Burish & L. A. Bradley (Eds.), *Coping with chronic disease* (pp. 259–284). New York: Academic Press.

Kirchner, C. & Lowman, C. (1978). Sources of variation in the estimated prevalence of visual loss. *Journal of Visual Impairment and Blindness, 72,* 329–333.

Kubler-Ross, E. (1969). *On death and dying.* New York: Macmillan.

Leventhal, H., & Hirschmann, R. S. (1982). Social psychology and prevention. In G. S. Sanders & J. Suls (Eds.), *Social psychology of health and illness.* (pp. 183–226). Hillsdale, NJ: Erlbaum.

Levine, E. (1977). *The preparation of psychological service providers to the deaf.* Silver Spring, MD: Professional Rehabilitation Workers with the Adult Deaf, Inc., Monograph No. 4.

Lindemann, J. E. (1981). *Psychological and behavioral aspects of physical disability.* New York: Plenum.

Livneh, H. (1988). Rehabilitation goals: Their hierarchical and multifaceted nature. *Journal of Applied Rehabilitation Counseling, 19*(3), 12–18.

Livneh, H. (1989). Rehabilitation intervention strategies: Their integration and classification. *Journal of Rehabilitation, 55,* 21–30.

Lyles, J. N., Burish, T. G., Krozely, M. G., & Oldham, R. K. (1982). Efficacy of relaxation training and guided imagery in reducing the aversiveness of cancer chemotherapy. *Journal of Consulting and Clinical Psychology, 50,* 509–524.

Manley, S. (1973). A definitive approach to group counseling. *Journal of Rehabilitation, 39,* 38–40.

McAleer, C. A., & Kluge, C. A. (1978). Counseling needs and approaches for working with a cancer patient. *Rehabilitation Counseling Bulletin, 21,* 238–245.

McCollum, P. S. (1978). Adjustment to cancer: A psychosocial and rehabilitative perspective. *Rehabilitation Counseling Bulletin, 21,* 216–223.

McMahon, B. T., & Fraser, R. T. (1988). Basic issues and trends in head injury rehabilitation. In S. E. Rubin & N. M. Rubin (Eds.), *Contemporary challenges to the rehabilitation counseling profession* (pp. 197–215). Baltimore, MD: Paul H. Brookes.

Medis, N. (1982). Counseling strategies with handicapped students. In C. W. Humes (Ed.), *Counseling the handicapped client: A series of training modules* (pp. 33–48). Falls Church, VA: American Personnel and Guidance Association.

Miller, D., Wolfe, M., & Spiegel, M. (1975). Therapeutic groups for patients with spinal cord injuries. *Archives of Physical Medicine and Rehabilitation, 56,* 130–135.

Moos, R. H., & Tsu, V. D. (1977). The crisis of physical illness: An overview. In R. H. Moos (Ed.), *Coping with physical illness* (pp. 3–21). New York: Plenum.

Novack, T. A., Roth, D. L., & Boll, T. J. (1988). Treatment alternatives following mild head injury. *Rehabilitation Counseling Bulletin, 31,* 313–324.

Nunes, E. V., Frank, K. A., & Kornfeld, D. (1987). Psychologic treatment for the type A behavior pattern and for coronary heart disease: A meta-analysis of the literature. *Psychosomatic Medicine, 48,* 159–171.

Ososkie, J. N. (1984). Epilepsy: Implications for rehabilitation. *Journal of Applied Rehabilitation Counseling, 15*(2), 12–15.

Ostby, S., & Thomas, K. R. (1984). Deafness and hearing impairment: A review and proposal. *Journal of Applied Rehabilitation Counseling, 15*(2), 7–11.

Pattison, E. M. (1977). *The experience of dying.* Englewood Cliffs, NJ: Prentice-Hall.

Prigatano, G. P. (1989). Bring it up in milieu: Toward effective traumatic brain injury rehabilitation interventions. *Rehabilitation Psychology, 34,* 135–144.

Prigatano, G. P., and others (1986). *Neuropsychological rehabilitation after brain injury.* Baltimore, MD: Johns Hopkins University Press.

Romano, M. (1976). Social skills training with the new handicapped. *Archives of Physical Medicine and Rehabilitation, 57,* 302–303.

Rosenthal, M. (1987). Traumatic head injury: Neurobehavioral consequences. In B. Caplan (Ed.), *Rehabilitation psychology desk reference* (pp. 37–63). Rockville, MD: Aspen.

Schein, J. D. (1981). Hearing impairments and deafness. In W. C. Stolov & M. R. Clowers (Eds.), *Handbook of severe disability* (pp. 395–407). Washington, DC: U.S. Department of Education.

Scofield, M., Pape, D., McCracken, N., & Maki, D. (1980). An ecological model for promoting acceptance of disability. *Journal of Applied Rehabilitation Counseling, 11*(4), 183–187.

Seligman, M. (1975). *Helplessness: On depression, development, and death.* San Francisco: W. H. Freeman.

Thomas, K., Butler, A., & Parker, R. M. (1987). Psychosocial counseling. In R. M. Parker (Ed.), *Rehabilitation counseling: Basics and beyond* (pp. 65–95). Austin, TX: Pro Ed.

Thoreson, R. W., & Ackerman, M. (1981). Cardiac rehabilitation: Basic principles and psychosocial factors. *Rehabilitation Counseling Bulletin, 24,* 223–255.

Torkelson-Lynch, R. (1983). Traumatic head injury: Implications for rehabilitation counseling. *Journal of Applied Rehabilitation Counseling, 14*(3), 32–35.

Treischmann, R. B. (1988). *Spinal cord injuries: Psychological, social, and vocational rehabilitation* (2nd ed.). New York: Demos.

Twelfth Institute on Rehabilitation Issues (1985). *Rehabilitation of the traumatic brain injured.* Menomonie, WI: University of Wisconsin-Stout, Vocational Rehabilitation Institute, Research and Training Center.

U.S. Department of Education, Office of Special Education and Rehabilitation Services (1981). Head injury: The problem, the need. *Programs for the Handicapped, 6,* 1–3.

Vander Kolk, C. J. (1983). Rehabilitation counseling with the visually impaired. *Journal of Applied Rehabilitation Counseling, 14*(3), 13–19.

Vash, C. L. (1981). *The psychology of disability.* New York: Springer-Verlag.

Ward, A. A., Fraser, R. T., & Troupin, A. S. (1981). Epilepsy. In W. C. Stolov & M. R. Clowers (Eds.), *Handbook of severe disability* (pp. 155–168). Washington, DC: U.S. Department of Education.

Whitehouse, F. A. (1962). Cardiovascular disability. In J. F. Garrett & E. S. Levine (Eds.), *Psychological practices with the physically disabled* (pp. 85–124). New York: Columbia University Press.

Wood, R. L. (1984). Behavior disorders following severe brain injury: Their presentation and psychological management. In N. Brooks (Ed.), *Closed head injury: Psychological, social and family consequences* (pp. 195–219). London: Oxford University Press.

Wright, G. N. (1980). *Total rehabilitation.* Boston: Little, Brown.

Young, J. S., Burns, P. E., Bowen, A. M., & McCutchen, R. (1987). *Spinal cord injury statistics: Experience of the regional spinal cord injury systems.* Phoenix, AZ: Good Samaritan Medical Center.

PART FOUR■

Counseling Perspectives

The relationship between the client and the counselor does not exist in a vacuum; rather, it is interlineated into the personal, legal, and ethical context of our society. Counselors are often called upon to make decisions regarding clients in which the "correct" mode of action may not be immediately clear. There may be two contradictory obligations—for example, the obligation to respect the confidentiality of a client and the obligation to protect that client from self harm or the harming of others. When faced with situations such as this, the counselor cannot rely simply on personal judgment but, instead, needs to act from the basis of the professional guidelines and codes of ethics of the counseling and human development professions.

Chapter Nineteen, "Ethical and Legal Issues Related to Counseling," provides an overview of the ethical and legal guidelines on which counselors must base their decisions. It discusses the role of personal values versus professional ethics; the question of counselor competence, clients' rights, confidentiality, and informed consent; and the practicalities of dealing with legal issues and client-related litigation. Such concepts are essential for the beginning counselor to understand and incorporate in gaining a sense of the professional status of the counselor.

Counseling as a profession has changed significantly in its scope and focus since its early beginnings at the start of this century. It is probable that the role of the counselor will continue to grow and expand in response to the even greater rate of technologic, social, and economic changes that will inevitably occur in the near future. Chapter Twenty, "Counseling in the Twenty-first Century," presents an overview of the social and political conditions that may have an impact on the issues that counselors will need to deal with in the future, such as poverty, racism, diminishing natural resources, and the threat of nuclear war. Within that context, the professional identity of the counselor is discussed. The implications for current trends in the counseling profession, such as licensure and the legal and ethical issues discussed in Chapter Nineteen, are reviewed. In essence, the author states, the counselor of the future will need to be both technologically and culturally sophisticated to meet the needs of clients in such a society.

19.

Ethical and Legal Issues Related to Counseling: or It's Not As Easy As It Looks

SHARON E. ROBINSON, PH.D., N.C.C.
Arizona State University
Tempe, Arizona

HERE YOU ARE IN one of your first courses in counseling, and, if you are like me when I was a beginning master's student, you are feeling overwhelmed with everything you are expected to learn. Not the least of these is how to make professional decisions that are both ethical and legal while still being helpful to your clients. The purpose of this chapter is to introduce you to the basic ethical concepts and legal guidelines that will influence your behavior as counselors. With that goal in mind, I hope to challenge your preconceived notions regarding right and wrong, moral and immoral, ethical and unethical, and legal and illegal.

447

First, let's discuss what the word "ethical" means. According to the *Webster's New World Dictionary* (1979), it is defined as "1. having to do with ethics; of or conforming to moral standards, 2. conforming to professional standards of conduct" (p. 210). Notice that these two definitions are distinctly different. The first is a personal phenomenon—that is, what is moral is decided most often by individuals. In contrast, the second definition encompasses behaviors that are considered ethical by some professional group. In the mental health profession, that group could be the American Psychological Association (APA), the National Academy of Certified Clinical Mental Health Counselors (NACCMHC), or the National Board of Certified Counselors (NBCC), just to name a few. For the purposes of this chapter, I will emphasize the definition that includes meeting the standards of the mental health profession and focus primarily on the Ethical Standards of AACD (1988a) and the Ethical Principles of Psychologists (APA, 1981).

This chapter will be organized into four sections, starting with an exploration of why individuals decide to enter the counseling profession. The discussion will then shift to counselor competence, client rights, and, finally, the real world.

CHOOSING TO BE A COUNSELOR: AN ETHICAL BEGINNING

If someone asked you, "Why do you want to become a counselor?," what would you say? In my experience as an instructor of students in introductory counseling courses, I have found that students enter this field for three reasons. One, they say that the only reason they are entering this profession is because they want to help others to grow as individuals and to become "healthier" without any concern or benefit for themselves. These people see themselves as very altruistic. Two, some need counseling themselves and think that this is a safe and easy way to get help. Of course they do not realize that students of counseling are required to do a significant amount of self-examination and introspection regarding who they are and what they can offer clients. This process often causes them stress and discomfort, which may be a manifestation of their denial of their real need to seek personal counseling. The third reason is just to explore a possible professional area. People who fit this last category are usually very social, outgoing, and would like to work with people in a way that is beneficial while still earning a living themselves. This third group causes me little concern; however, I often find cause for worry about individuals who fit the first two categories.

Throughout your counseling coursework, you will hear and read about the personhood of the counselor and how this is integral to the effectiveness of the counseling process. In 1972, Max Hammer wrote a classic chapter entitled "To Students Interested in Becoming Psychotherapists." Although his writing tends to be slanted toward a psychoanalytic perspective and the language is sexist, he presents a compelling discussion of the essence of psychotherapy and motivations for becoming a psychotherapist.

According to Hammer (1972), "the kind of person that the therapist is will be the primary determinant of whether or not there will be therapeutic results" (p. 3). He goes on to discuss the most important quality that a prospective counselor should have, that is,

> the capacity to be sensitive enough to clearly and deeply hear and understand in the patient those rejected truths that have become disassociated from himself and have caused his disintegration and which, when heard and understood by the patient, lead to his reintegration, growth and liberation from his conflicts, fears and tensions. (p. 4)

In order to hear and understand the patient/client, the counselor must be psychologically healthy, which Hammer defines as being nondefensive and totally open to the moment-to-moment reality of himself.

To be fully attuned with the deepest levels of empathy for the client, the counselor must be in the state of "quiet mind" (p. 7). A quiet mind for the counselor exists when there is no deliberate thought or mental activity that is attempting to control or evaluate what is occurring in the counseling session, but rather "one just permits thought to come to awareness and watches it without any kind of interference" (p. 7). Hammer refers to this process as a state of creative understanding during which the "soft whisperings of unconscious thoughts, feelings or impulses" (p. 7) are able to be heard. According to Hammer, the goal of counseling is for the client to come to his or her own creative understanding, which will result in self-healing.

What prevents a counselor from being able to bring a quiet mind to the counseling session? I agree with Hammer when he stresses that it is the counselor who gets in his or her own way and that the client "probably cannot grow beyond the level of emotional health and maturity achieved by his therapist" (p. 21). This may be a hard pill for many beginning counselors to swallow. Even more difficult to accept would be Hammer's statement that

> to be really effective, the therapist needs to know from *personal experience* what the "path" is that leads from internal conflict and contradiction to liberation. If you do not know how to liberate yourself from an internal con-

flict, fear or pain, then you are not in a position to help others do it either. . . . What right does the therapist have to ask the patient to face his rejected truths and anxiety and to take risks in terms of exposing himself and making himself vulnerable, if the therapist is not willing or able to do so? (p. 12)

These are central personal, professional, and ethical issues that all beginning counselors must ponder and answer for themselves. This message is echoed by Corey, Corey, and Callanan (1988), who state that a willingness to serve as models for clients by *not* asking them to do what you are not willing to do is one of the essential characteristics of effective counselors.

Both Hammer (1972) and Corey et al. (1988) discuss motivations for entering the helping profession. Hammer believed that persons often had the wrong reasons, such as the need to be dominant, to be needed and loved, to be a voyeur on other's lives, to be an omnipotent healer, to escape one's own life, and to cure themselves by curing others. Corey et al. indicate that the therapeutic process can be blocked when therapists use the client to fulfill their own needs, to nurture others, to feel powerful or important, or to win acceptance, admiration, respect, or awe. Acknowledging that therapists do have their own needs, Corey et al. caution that "therapists should be clearly aware of the danger of working primarily to be appreciated by others instead of working toward the best interests of their clients" (p. 31).

In each of these instances, the counselor is primarily meeting his or her own needs, and this is unethical. APA's (1981) Ethical Principles address this specifically in Principle 6: Welfare of the Consumer: "a. Psychologists are continually cognizant of their own needs and of their potentially influential position vis-a-vis persons such as clients, students, and subordinates. They avoid exploiting the trust and dependency of such persons" (p. 636). The AACD (1988a) Standards caution us to determine our abilities to be of professional assistance to the client and to avoid engaging in activities that seek to meet our personal needs at the expense of the client. An excellent example of the counselor meeting his or her needs at the expense of the client is the counselor who becomes sexually involved with the client. Perhaps his or her own need to be loved and appreciated prevents the realization of the tremendous damage being done to the client.

Some of the most explicit statements regarding counselor emotional health are made in the Code of Ethics for Certified Clinical Mental Health Counselors (1985). This code states:

Clinical mental health counselors/practitioners recognize that their effectiveness depends in part upon their ability to maintain sound interpersonal relations, that temporary or more enduring aberrations on their part may interfere with their abilities or distort their appraisals of others. Therefore, they refrain from undertaking any activity in which their personal problems are likely to lead to inadequate professional services or harm to a client, or, if they are already engaged in such activity when they become aware of their personal problems, they would seek competent professional assistance to determine whether they should suspend or terminate services to one or all of the clients. (Principle 2. No. e)

Based on the writings of Corey et al. (1988), Hammer (1972), and the various ethical guidelines, I would say to all beginning counselor trainees (and to all of us who are already active in the profession), your first ethical responsibility is to be as emotionally healthy as possible, to be continually aware of how your own "unfinished business" could potentially influence your attempts to be helpful to others, and to seek professional help as soon as you are aware that some aspect of your own life may be infringing on your work as a counselor. Your competence is limited by your own self-awareness and psychological health and maturity (Robinson, 1988).

COUNSELOR COMPETENCE

This naturally brings us to a discussion of counselor competence. Gross and Robinson (1987) have outlined four global areas of professional competence: (1) providing only services for which one is qualified; (2) professional growth through continuing education; (3) maintaining accurate knowledge and expertise in specialized areas; and (4) accurate representation of professional qualifications. To these I would add your responsibilities as counselors-in-training to learn basic skills, to integrate academic study with supervised practice, to develop self-understanding, to seek continual evaluation and appraisal, and to become intimately familiar with ethical guidelines (AACD, 1988a, Section H). It is your professors' responsibility not only to foster your learning of the above but also to "be aware of the personal limitations of the learner that might impede future performance. The instructor must not only assist the learner in securing remedial assistance but also screen from the program those individuals who are unable to provide competent services" (AACD, 1988a, Section H, No. 5). While you are a student, your competence is a shared responsibility between you and your professors. When you graduate and enter the professional world, it is your responsibility to remain competent.

One of your primary responsibilities is to recognize your strengths and limitations and to offer services only in those areas in which you are strong (Robinson & Gross, 1986). Defining your areas of competence occurs through both subjective and external processes. The subjective component usually involves critical and honest self-examination. The objective component typically includes completing the appropriate graduate training and taking professional and state credentialing exams in order to solidify your identification with the profession and to verify that you have achieved some level of competence as demonstrated by passing an exam. Some of the exams you might choose to take are the National Board of Certified Counselors (NBCC) exam or the National Academy of Certified Clinical Mental Health Counselors (NACCMHC) exam. The NBCC exam tests eight content areas: human growth and development; social and cultural foundations; group dynamics, process, and counseling; life span and career development; appraisal of individuals; research and evaluation; and professional orientation and ethics. The NACCMHC exam, in addition to testing similar content, has an experiential component where the examinee must submit a tape recording of his or her clinical work and a case analysis and treatment plan for that client.

Taking an exam to prove that you have a certain knowledge base is not enough, however. The Ethical Standards (AACD, 1988a) are quite explicit about professional qualifications. Section A, No. 7 states that "Members recognize their boundaries of competence and provide only those services and use only those techniques for which they are qualified by training or experience. Members should accept only those positions for which they are professionally qualified." The preamble of APA (1981) Principle 2, which is devoted entirely to the topic of counselor competence, indicates that

> The maintenance of high standards of competence is a responsibility shared by all psychologists in the interest of the public and the profession as a whole. Psychologists recognize the boundaries of their competence and the limitations of their techniques. They only provide services and use only techniques for which they are qualified by training and experience.

Notice that APA requires both training and experience and AACD indicates that either training or experience is adequate. I would prefer to err on the conservative side and stress that both training and experience are essential for you to claim competence.

If you are not qualified to treat a certain client problem, what should you do ethically? Your first choice is to refer the client to someone who is more qualified to help him or her. If there is no one available (which would be the exception rather than the rule), then it is incumbent on you to get continuing education, to devour library books and articles on the presenting problem, and to seek supervision. You do not just proceed as if what you already know can generalize to every client problem. You are responsible for the welfare of that client, and it is your professional and ethical responsibility to find for that client the best services possible—be it from you or from someone else. Clients are not subjects for your trial-and-error learning but deserve the best professional care possible (Robinson, 1988).

Just as you continually have to assess your existing strengths, you also need to pursue continuing education not only to stay current with the developments in the profession but also to grow professionally. Continuing education can be formal graduate coursework, advanced seminars and workshops, training institutes, and papers and other presentations at professional conferences, just to name a few. As one of my previous doctoral students recently told me, "When I decided that I was really going to be a psychologist and do therapy, I attended every training seminar, conference, and workshop I could so that I could be really good at what I do." Unlike so many graduates, be it from a master's or a doctoral program, he realized that he was not a finished product upon receipt of the degree. In order to become truly proficient at what he had chosen to do, he had to seek all the advanced didactic and experiential input he could. Only by continually growing himself is he comfortable offering his services to those who need help.

One area of professional competence in which many students are not adequately trained is diagnosis, although many of the states that certify mental health professionals have certification laws that indicate that diagnosis is an area of professional expertise. Typically, diagnosis involves evaluating the client and classifying the problem according to the DSM-III-R criteria. A recent court case in Arizona focused on whether a mental health professional is liable to someone other than a client for a misdiagnosis (Cook v. Berlin, 1987). In this case a master's level social worker diagnosed a client as paranoid, and this diagnosis was confirmed by a psychiatrist who prescribed antipsychotic drugs for the patient. The patient soon terminated therapy and moved to another city. She later returned and killed the man she believed was watching her. Under court examination it was discovered that the patient was atypical psychosis, not paranoid, and she was found not guilty due to insanity. The widow of the murdered man sued the social worker and the psychiatrist, but the case was settled before the Arizona Supreme Court could hear it.

The out-of-court settlement of this case left several important questions unanswered: What is the appropriate scope of practice of the various mental health professionals? Had there been a competent diagnosis, would there have been an assessment of dangerousness resulting in a duty to warn? When can one professional, especially an unlicensed one, provide information to another without risk of malpractice? These questions all center on knowing the limits of one's competence and behaving within the boundaries of professional training and experience.

Another area of competence is recognizing when you have a dual relationship with a client. Since your "primary obligation is to respect the integrity and promote the welfare of the client(s)" (AACD, 1988a, Section B, No. 1), ". . . dual relationships with clients that might impair the member's objectivity and professional judgment (e.g., as with close friends or relatives) must be avoided and/or the counseling relationship terminated through referral to another competent professional" (AACD, 1988a, Section B, No. 13). Dual relationships can occur in a variety of helping relationships. For example, it is considered unethical to have a relationship with your client outside of the therapy session, such as being their friend or relative or lover. It is also taboo for you to have a dual relationship with your clinical supervisors in that the relationship might influence their objective evaluation of your skills as a clinician. Even taking classes from someone with whom you have another relationship must be avoided.

A final area of professional competence I would like to discuss is ethically presenting your services and qualifications to the public. Most codes of ethics warn professionals against making false claims regarding expertise and qualifications, with the AACD (1988a) Standards holding members responsible for correcting misrepresentations of their qualifications by others (Section A, No. 4). For example, if you are called "doctor" by someone and you do not hold a doctoral degree, it is your responsibility to correct that misperception immediately. In addition, when advertising your services as practitioners, only the ". . . highest relevant degree, type, and level of certification and/or license, address, telephone number, office hours, type and/or description of services, and other relevant information" may be listed (AACD, 1988a, Section F, No. 3). It is also unethical to imply a higher level of credentialing than one actually has. For example, to indicate that one is a "candidate for the doctorate" instead of listing the highest degree actually obtained or to indicate or imply that one has a degree from a department or program with a different title than the actual title (counseling psychology vs. counselor education vs. guidance and counseling) would be unethical. When trying to build a business, client testimonials must be avoided, as well as "implying unusual, unique, or one-of-a-kind abilities" (APA, 1981, Principle 4b).

There is more latitude for advertising as a result of the Goldfarb v. Virginia State Bar (1975) ruling, which indicated that state law bars could not dictate attorney fee structures but said that consumers have the right to choose attorneys with fees being one of the selection criteria. Because of this decision, the Federal Trade Commission has granted considerable freedom for advertising—often more than the professional associations believe is appropriate and ethical. This is only one of the many times when you will have to weigh what is permitted legally (what the courts have ruled) with what is acceptable ethically (what your professional group considers to be appropriate behavior).

CLIENT RIGHTS

When clients enter a counseling relationship, they have a right to assume that you are competent. In addition, they have certain rights, known as client rights, and responsibilities. These rights have their foundation in the Bill of Rights, particularly the first and fourth Amendments to the Constitution of the United States, which are freedom of religion, speech, of the press; and right of petition and freedom from unreasonable searches and seizures, respectively. The concepts of confidentiality, privileged communication, and informed consent are based on the Fourth Amendment, which guarantees privacy. Privacy has been defined as the freedom of individuals to choose for themselves the time and the circumstances under which and the extent to which their beliefs, behaviors, and opinions are to be shared or withheld from others.

Confidentiality and Privileged Communications

Confidentiality is a professional concept that protects the client from unauthorized disclosures of information given in confidence without the expressed consent of that client (Schwitzgebel & Schwitzgebel, 1980). In contrast, privileged communication is a legal term that indicates that the client's communications cannot be disclosed in a court of law without that client's consent. The privilege belongs to the client, not the counselor, and under most circumstances only the client can waive the privilege. Breaching confidentiality is considered an invasion of the client's privacy (Everstine et al., 1980).

Most states grant privileged communication to clients of legally certified mental health professionals, for example, psychologists, certified professional counselors, or certified marriage and family counselors. A client's communications are not privileged if the professional is not legally certified by the state in which he or she practices; therefore, it is very important to ensure that your state has formally recognized master's level practitioners through passage of a credentialing bill. The courts will not typically recognize certification awarded by a professional association as grounds for granting clients privileged communication rights.

Schwitzgebel and Schwitzgebel (1980) outlined the four steps essential to establishing communications as privileged. These are:

1. The communication must have originated in confidence that the communication would not be disclosed.
2. Confidentiality must be essential to the full and satisfactory maintenance of the relationship.
3. The relationship must be one that in the opinion of the community ought to be sedulously fostered.
4. The injury to the relationship by the disclosure of the communication must be greater than the benefit gained by correct disposal of the litigation.

If as a counselor you can claim these four, your clients' communications are not only confidential, but also they are privileged and, therefore, are protected from being disclosed in a court of law. One must remember, however, that there is always a balance between a clients' right to privacy (privileged communication) and society's need to know.

There are circumstances in which privileged communication does not apply. Every state has passed a law mandating the reporting of child abuse. Regardless of the counselor's personal feelings about helping the client to overcome his or her abusive behavior, the counselor must report child abuse. In this instance, society has ruled that its need to know in order to protect the child from further harm is greater than the client's right of privacy. Another instance in which privilege is automatically waived and confidentiality is broken is when the client is a clear and imminent danger to self or others. "When the client's condition indicates that there is clear and imminent danger to the client or others, the member must take reasonable personal action or inform responsible authorities" (AACD, 1988a, Section B, No. 4).

A well-known court case establishing mandatory disclosure by a therapist is Tarasoff *v.* Regents of the University of California (1976). A young graduate student from India had been working with a University psychologist regarding his depression and anger resulting from being rejected by a girl and had told his psychologist of his intent to buy a gun. The psychologist notified campus police, both verbally and in writing, that Poddar (the young man) was dangerous and should be taken to the community mental health facility. The police interviewed Poddar, decided that he was not dangerous, and released him from custody. The psychologist's supervising psychiatrist decided that the letter to the police and certain case notes should be destroyed. Shortly thereafter, Poddar shot and stabbed the girl to death. The state supreme court hearing the case held that "Once a therapist does in fact determine, or under applicable professional standards reasonably should have determined, that a patient poses a serious danger of violence to others, he bears a duty to exercise reasonable care to protect the foreseeable victims of that danger" (Tarasoff, 1976). This has since been interpreted as the duty to protect the foreseeable potential victim. In these instances, the client loses the privilege automatically since the counselor's overriding responsibility is to protect others from harm that could result from the client's actions.

Other instances when the privilege is automatically lost include when the client introduces his or her mental condition as an element in a court case, when the mental stability of either spouse is introduced in a child custody case, when the counselor is working for the court such as in conducting a court-ordered examination, when the client is suing the counselor, and when the counselor believes that the client is in need of immediate hospitalization for a mental disorder.

Most writers on this topic advise counselors to inform their clients through use of an informed consent form that confidentiality does not exist under certain specified conditions before clients actually begin therapy. Clients can then make informed decisions about what they will reveal to you. In addition, when it becomes necessary to break confidentiality, Corey et al. (1988) recommend telling the client of your intention prior to actually revealing the information and involving the client as much as possible in this process. A good example here might be informing significant others if a client is suicidal. It is far better to get the client to take responsibility for seeking the help of others than for the counselor to assume total responsibility for the client's behaviors. If the client is not willing to seek help, the counselor should not hesitate to intervene, however. As Biggs and Blocher (1987) have pointed out, ethical obligations are always relative, not absolute, and the sanctity of life outweighs confidence.

The discussion thus far has focused on confidentiality regarding the verbal communications in therapy. Counselors must also be concerned with confidentiality of client records. In addition to describing the characteristics of adequate client records, Snider (1987) makes some very practical and useful suggestions for protecting written material such as case notes and test data. According to Snider, the absolute minimal storage system is a locked file cabinet—it is not enough to just lock your office door. While Beis (1984) recommended that records be kept for 10 years, Snider points out that they should be kept for the period reflecting the statute of limitations in your state. Interestingly, a client's records cannot be sold to another therapist should the counselor decide to retire or leave his or her practice. "The record has been developed during the counselor-client relationship; thus, to sell it would tend to make the client subject to barter to the highest bidder" (Snider, 1987, p. 140).

It would be remiss not to discuss subpoenas and how counselors should respond to them in an attempt to protect the client's confidentiality. There are two basic types of subpoenas—the typical subpoena, which just requires your attendance at court or at a deposition, and a subpoena duces tecum, which requires you to bring your records with you to court or to the deposition. Schwitzgebel and Schwitzgebel (1980) have recommended that you should initially claim the privilege for your client whether or not you believe that your client is granted privileged communication under your state's laws. This forces either the court or the client's attorney, who is acting on behalf of the client legally and thus speaks for the client, to require you to breach confidentiality. Because you have tried to protect the client's communications and records, you are protected from malpractice since you were acting under court order. You also have the option of refusing to testify or to produce your records, in which case you may be ruled in contempt and have to go to jail. In these instances, as a counselor you need to find a personally acceptable balance among what the law requires, what is ethically appropriate, and what you find to be morally correct. Again, this is a personal decision that only you can make, since you will be the one experiencing the consequences.

It should be noted that Biggs and Blocher (1987) recommend that the counselor have formal records and private "memo to myself" notes. While formal records can be subpoenaed, according to Biggs and Blocher, the latter cannot *if they are used exclusively by the counselor*. If this is the case, they are not viewed as formal records. While this may sound like the perfect solution to avoid having to reveal your records, there is a Catch 22 here. If these are private memos to yourself, they can never be used to defend yourself from client charges of negligence or malpractice.

Informed Consent

This brings us to a discussion of informed consent. Three elements must be present for informed consent to be legal (Everstine et al., 1980). Competence, the first element, requires that the person granting the consent is able to engage in rational thought to a sufficient degree to make competent decisions about his or her life. If the person is under the age of 18, the consent must be obtained from the parent or legal guardian. The second element, informed, requires that the individual is given the relevant information about the procedures to be performed in a language that he or she can understand. And the last element, voluntariness, requires that the consent is given freely by the client. Informed consent exists when these three conditions are met. I suggest that you get informed consent from every client that you see as a means of ensuring that the client is fully informed about the process of therapy, your responsibilities as the counselor, and his or her rights as the client. If you are interacting with a minor, you need not only the parent or guardian consent, but also it is wise to get assent from the minor if he or she is over seven years old.

If you are asked by the client to disclose to a third party information revealed in therapy, have the client sign an informed consent form for disclosure. On this form the exact information to be disclosed, to whom, for what purpose, the name of the client, the name of the person permitted to make the disclosure, the date of the request for disclosure, and the date, event, or condition that will revoke the consent for disclosure should be clearly specified. It may be surprising to you to learn that counselors are not even permitted to respond to inquiries about whether a person is in therapy—even the client's name and status in counseling are confidential unless the client has granted permission for this information to be released.

One exception is when the client is paying for your services with insurance. This automatically grants the insurance company limited access to information regarding the client. However, the client should have been made aware of the parameters of the information that will be shared with the insurance company prior to beginning therapy. Again, it is evident how important it is to have potential clients sign an informed consent form before they become clients.

Right to Treatment

Another essential right implied by the informed consent procedure is the client's right to receive and to refuse treatment. Many court cases have been based on the right-to-treatment issue. In the early 1970s, Wyatt *v.* Stickney (1974) was the first case in which the right to treatment was ruled a constitutionally protected right. The case was filed against the state of Alabama on behalf of mentally retarded institutionalized patients who were being kept confined under conditions of psychological and physical deprivation. There was one physician for 2000 patients, making adequate medical care impossible. The court ruled that involuntarily committed patients have a constitutional right to receive "such individual treatment as will give each of them a realistic opportunity to be cured or to improve." In addition, the court required the institution to have an individualized treatment plan developed by qualified mental health professionals for each patient. Other rights committed patients have are the right to their own clothing, to receive minimal pay for labor performed, to receive mail, to exercise several times per week, and to have an appropriate physical environment in which to live.

Institutionalized patients' rights to refuse treatment has been addressed in Rogers *v.* Orkin (1980) and in Rennie *v.* Klein (1981). In Rogers, the court ruled the "power to produce ideas as fundamental to our cherished right to communicate." The court indicated that the right to refuse medication and seclusion was a Fourth Amendment right but cited several state interests that can overrule a persons' right to this privacy: police power—the right of the state to protect others from harm; parens patriae—the duty of the state to prevent the patient's condition from deteriorating; and consideration of the financial costs of operating facilities that may result from extended hospitalization (Levenson, 1989). Rennie held that the right to refuse medication could only be overruled under due process, except in an emergency.

To leave the right-to-treatment issue without discussing my state of residence, Arizona, would leave an unnecessary gap in your understanding of the real world. While cases such as those just cited hopefully are making life better for both institutionalized and noninstitutionalized patients, many states are still doing little for their mentally ill. Indeed, Arizona is ranked fiftieth in the nation for its services for the mentally ill. In 1981, the Arizona Department of Health Services, Arizona State Hospital, and Maricopa County Board of Supervisors were sued by a Mr. Arnold on behalf of the chronically mentally ill in the county (Arnold *v.* Department of Health Services, 1989). On March 13, 1989, the Arizona State Supreme Court upheld a lower-court ruling that the state must provide a continuum of care that includes housing, vocational training, recreational facilities, and case management services. From this ruling, it sounds as if the original ruling in Wyatt *v.* Stickney had never been read by those charged with administering care for the chronically mentally ill in Arizona.

Client Welfare

All of the above discussions rest on the premise that the counselor's primary obligation is to protect the welfare of the client. According to the AACD (1988a) Ethical Standards, Section B, No. 1, "The member's primary obligation is to respect the integrity and promote the welfare of the client(s), whether the client(s) is (are) assisted individually or in a group relationship." The APA Ethical Principles have an entire principle (No. 6) devoted to welfare of the consumer. Dual relationships, counselor's personal needs, and conflicts between the demands of an employing institution and client needs all influence client welfare and need to be addressed. Dual relationships and counselor's personal needs have been extensively addressed, but the third example presents unique ethical concerns that are not atypical of life in the real world.

Employer conflict and client needs may vary drastically, especially in an institutional setting where the counselor is trying to work with committed clients. For example, suppose you work in a prison setting and an inmate tells you that he or she is using drugs, which is against all prison rules. What are you going to do? Or imagine that you are a school counselor and during a counseling session a 15-year-old student tells you that he or she is using drugs. What actually is in the best interests of the client in each of these two cases? How will your behavior affect your relationship with your client, your future clients, and your position within the institution? Similar conflicts may arise when you are employed by a business or industry and the needs of the employee/client may not be in agreement with the goals of the business. To whom do you owe loyalty? To the employer who signs your paycheck or to the employee/client? These questions are not always easy to answer, nor is there always one correct answer. In cases such as these, you must decide what is ethical or unethical based on the current ethical standards and what is right or wrong for you personally.

Thus far the discussion has focused on work with individual clients. The ethical standards also apply in situations involving more than one client, such as in group counseling. Some of the special client rights when the therapeutic setting is a group include having a qualified group leader, signing an informed consent form, knowing the limits of confidentiality when there is more than one client, and understanding how individuals will be protected and growth nurtured in the group setting.

Unlike individual counseling, clients who want to be involved in a group experience need to be screened before being allowed to join a group. The AACD Standards, Section B, No. 10 (1988a) specifically refer to this ethical requirement: "The member must screen prospective group participants, especially when the emphasis is on self-understanding and growth through self-disclosure. The member must maintain an awareness of the group participants' compatibility throughout the life of the group." This screening not only ensures that the client is appropriate for the group, but also it helps to protect other group members from a potentially dysfunctional group member.

Confidentiality is not guaranteed in a group setting since there are more than two individuals privy to the communications. Rules about confidentiality need to be established by the group members and then respected by all. It is the counselor's responsibility to ". . . set a norm of confidentiality regarding all group participant disclosures" (AACD, 1988a, Section B, No. 2). If confidentiality is broken, this will destroy group productivity and cohesiveness, which are dependent on members' trust and willingness to disclose further (Davis & Meara, 1982). Eventually, the vitality of the group will be at risk.

As can be seen from the above, client welfare rests squarely on the shoulders of the counselor. The counselor must be cognizant of the various aspects of the counseling relationship that jeopardize the client's welfare and take the steps necessary to alleviate the situation. Gross and Robinson (1987) offer several suggestions for safeguarding the welfare of each client:

1. Check to be sure your clients are not currently involved in other counseling relationships.
2. Develop clear written descriptions of what clients may expect in the way of tests, reports, billing, counseling regime, and schedules.
3. Know your own limitations and do not hesitate to utilize appropriate referral sources.
4. Be sure that the approaches and techniques utilized are appropriate for the clients and that you have the skills to implement them.
5. Do not establish a counseling relationship with a supervisee, friend, relative, or employee unless all other referral possibilities have been exhausted (p. 10).

I would be remiss if I ended the discussion of client welfare without mentioning the problems that can arise from our technologic society. In this age of computers, client confidentiality is continually at risk since anyone sophisticated in computer programming can tap into insurance records, university records, etc. Also, testing by computers has become popular due to the ease of administration and computer scoring. We must ask ourselves whether this is what is best for the client. What happens to the all-important human element if the client just interacts with a computer? Indeed, recent research challenges the effectiveness of microcomputer programs to influence client growth and understanding in areas such as career development, decision making, and knowledge of chemical substances.

With respect to using a computer for testing or for providing test interpretations, the AACD Standards, Section C, offer us concrete guidelines. "In situations where a computer is used for test administrations and scoring, the member is responsible for ensuring that administration and scoring programs function properly to provide clients with accurate test results" (No. 5), and "When computer-based test interpretations are developed by the member to support the assessment process, the member must ensure that the validity of such interpretations is established prior to the commercial distribution of such a computer application" (No. 13).

Client Rights—Summary

The rights of your clients are many and varied. Perhaps the best statement regarding client rights has been prepared by the NBCC (1987), which lists both consumer rights and consumer responsibilities. I would like to list both as a reminder to you of how very important and necessary they are:

Consumer Rights

- Be informed of the qualifications of your counselor: education, experience, and professional counseling certification(s) and state licensure(s).
- Receive an explanation of services offered, your time commitments, and fee scales and billing policies prior to receipt of services.
- Be informed of limitations of the counselor's practice to special areas of expertise (e.g., career development, ethnic groups, etc.) or age group (e.g., adolescents, older adults, etc.).
- Have all that you say treated confidentially and be informed of any state laws placing limitations on confidentiality in the counseling relationship.
- Ask questions about the counseling techniques and strategies and be informed of your progress.
- Participate in setting goals and evaluating progress toward meeting them.
- Be informed of how to contact the counselor in an emergency situation.
- Request referral for a second opinion at any time.
- Request copies of records and reports to be used by other counseling professionals.
- Receive a copy of the code of ethics to which your counselor adheres.
- Contact the appropriate professional organization if you have doubts or complaints relative to the counselor's conduct.
- Terminate the counseling relationship at any time.

Consumer Responsibilities

- Set and keep appointments with your counselor. Let him or her know as soon as possible if you cannot keep an appointment.
- Pay your fees in accordance with the schedule you preestablished with the counselor.
- Help plan your goals

- Follow through with agreed-upon goals.
- Keep your counselor informed of your progress toward meeting your goals.
- Terminate your counseling relationship before entering into arrangements with another counselor.

Notice that the consumer responsibilities require the counselor to have provided the client with essential information initially. Also note that the client cannot behave unethically in terms of our professional ethics; that mistake can only be made by the counselor.

THE REAL WORLD

When you graduate and enter the so-called real world, you will find yourself frequently involved in situations in which you are uncertain exactly what is ethical and what is not. Research has shown that this uncertainty is not unusual among practitioners. A recent article by Pope, Tabachnick, and Keith-Spiegel (1987) examined the beliefs and practices of psychologists regarding ethical behaviors. They found that while psychologists act in accordance with their ethical beliefs, often they were unsure as to what was ethical. Specific behaviors that posed difficulty were "performing forensic work for a contingency fee," "accepting goods (rather than money) as payment," "using sexual surrogates with clients," "earning a salary which is a percentage of client fees," "avoiding certain clients for fear of being sued," "sending holiday greeting cards to your clients," "giving personal advice on radio, t.v., etc.," "engaging in sexual fantasy about a client," "limiting treatment notes to name, date, and fee," "inviting clients to an office open house," and "allowing a client to run up a large unpaid bill" (p. 999). From the information and advice I have offered earlier in this chapter, what are your opinions about whether each of these is ethical? The answer in many cases is not instantly clear, which demonstrates that ethics are not always just black and white and sometimes the surrounding circumstances have to be considered.

Robinson and Gross (1989) sent a series of vignettes to 500 members of the American Mental Counselors Association to examine applied ethical behaviors. They found that mental health counselors who had not had a course in ethics had particular difficulty recommending appropriate ethical behavior in the various situations. The behavior that was recommended even by those who had a course in ethics was less than totally appropriate and ethical. Based on their findings, Robinson and Gross suggest that training programs increase their emphasis on ethics education. It is not enough for students just to be familiar with the various ethical codes, they need to practice translating them into practice.

Perhaps if our training programs did a better job of teaching ethics, there would not be the current increase in malpractice suits in our profession. Wright (1981) pointed out that approximately 34 percent of malpractice suits are for improper or incorrect diagnosis and negligence, which calls into question whether practitioners are practicing within their levels of competence and whether they are making accurate judgments about these levels.

Because the relationship between a counselor and a client is a fiduciary relationship, one which fosters great trust and confidence, the legal systems become involved when this trust is violated and the client does not receive what he or she believes is a reasonable standard of care. To prove malpractice against a counselor, the client/plaintiff must allege and demonstrate four legal elements (Thompson, 1983):

1. The defendant (counselor) owed a legal duty to the client.
2. The defendant's (counselor's) conduct violated that duty by failing to conform to a legal standard established to prevent unreasonable risk or harm (psychological or physical).
3. There is a sufficient causal connection between the conduct of the defendant (counselor) and the harm suffered by the plaintiff (client).
4. The harm to the plaintiff (client) is an actual personal injury that can be measured in economic terms.

Although these may seem difficult to prove, more and more clients are winning their cause against mental health professionals. This in turn results not only in a decrease in public confidence regarding our profession but also in an increase in insurance rates. Indeed, as a result of the growing prevalence of lawsuits against psychologists, the AACD insurance carrier dropped clinical psychologists from the list of professionals it was willing to cover. While insurance rates are high, varying between a couple of hundred to a thousand dollars, "going bare" (not carrying insurance) is dangerous in that it puts the professional at risk for being personally responsible for all costs and damages in a malpractice lawsuit.

In addition to an increase in lawsuits, there is a corresponding increase in ethical complaints being filed against mental health professionals. When this occurs, a formal investigation and hearing are con-

ducted by a board or committee representing the professional association and/or state, if the defendant is licensed/certified. The AACD
Ethics Committee, after reviewing a case, can dismiss the charges as
being unfounded, find the practice to be unethical and request the member to stop the practice, or find the practice to be unethical and impose
sanctions on the practitioner. These sanctions might be a formal repri-
mand with recommendations for corrective action, withdrawal of eligibility for membership in AACD for a specified time period, placing the
member on probation, or expelling the member from AACD permanent-
ly (AACD, 1988b). The APA has similar procedures but is more specific
about the sanctions it will impose. In addition, once a year, APA sends
to all of its members a list of the names of psychologists who have been
dropped from membership due to either legal or ethical convictions.
This list also includes the ethical principle violated or the crime for
which the member was convicted.

I do not want to end this chapter on such a negative note. You each
have decided to enter this profession believing that you can help others
while earning a living for yourself. For me, counseling is a noble profession, especially if you give your best to each of your clients by being
aware of when you are burned out, stressed, or just plain tired and
when your personal problems could interfere with the quality of your
help and limiting your client contact during these periods. If you keep
the ethical codes in mind at all times; strive to be mentally, psychologically, physically, and spiritually healthy; obtain a thorough graduate
education that emphasizes both knowledge and practice; and seek
advanced training and supervision when you are in the field, then you
should be a benefit to your clients and to the profession. With those
last tidbits of advice, I welcome you to your journey and evolution as a
counselor.

REFERENCES

American Association for Counseling and Development. (1988a). *Ethical
standards*. Alexandria, VA: AACD.
American Association for Counseling and Development. (1988b). *Policies and
procedures for processing complaints of ethical violations*. Alexandria, VA:
AACD.
American Psychological Association. (1981). Ethical principles of psychologists.
American Psychologist, 36, 633–638.
Arnold v. Department of Health Services. 30 Ariz. Adv. Rep. 3 (March 13, 1989).

Beis, E. (1984). *Mental health and the law*. Rockville, MD: Aspen.

Biggs, D., & Blocher, D. (1987). *Foundations of ethical counseling*. New York: Springer.

Cooke v. Berlin, ___ Ariz. ___, 735P.2d 830 (App. 1987).

Corey, G., Corey, M. S., & Callanan, P. (1988). *Issues and ethics in the helping professions*. Monterey, CA: Brooks/Cole.

Davis, K. L., & Meara, N. M. (1982). So you think it is a secret. *The Journal for Specialists in Group Work, 7*(3), 149–153.

Everstine, L., Everstine, D. S., Geymann, G. M., True, R. H., Frey, D. H., Johnson, H. G., & Seiden, R. H. (1980). Privacy and confidentiality in psychotherapy. *American Psychologist, 35*(9), 828–840.

Goldfarb v. Virginia State Bar (1975), 421 U.S. 773.

Gross, D. R., & Robinson, S. E. (1987). Ethics in counseling: A multiple role perspective. *TACD Journal, 15*(1), 5–16.

Hammer, M. (1972). To students interested in becoming psychotherapists. In M. Hammer (Ed.), *The theory and practice of psychotherapy with specific disorders*. Springfield, IL: Charles C Thomas.

Levenson, M. (1989). *Right to accept or refuse treatment: Implications for the mental health professional*. Unpublished manuscript.

National Board of Certified Counselors (1987). *Counseling services: Consumer rights and responsibilities*. Alexandria, VA: NBCC.

National Academy of Certified Clinical Mental Health Counselors (1985). *Code of ethics for certified clinical mental health counselors*. Alexandria, VA: NACCMHC.

Pope, K. S., Tabachnick, B. G., & Keith-Spiegel, P. (1987). Ethics of practice: The beliefs and behaviors of psychologists as therapists. *American Psychologist, 42*(11), 993–1006.

Rennie v. Klein, 476 F. supp. 1294 (D.N.J., 1979, modified, Nos. 79-2576 and 70-2577 (3rd Cir., July 9, 1981).

Robinson, S. E. (1988). Counselor competency and malpractice suits: Opposite sides of the same coin. *Counseling and Human Development, 20*(9), 1–8.

Robinson, S. E. & Gross, D. R. (1986). Ethics in mental health counseling. In A. J. Palmo & W. J. Weikel (Eds.), *Foundations of mental health counseling*, (pp. 309–327). Springfield, IL: Charles C Thomas.

Robinson, S. E. & Gross, D. R. (1989). Applied ethics and the mental health counselor. *Journal of Mental Health Counseling, 11*(3), 289–299.

Rogers v. Orkin, 634 F. 2nd 650 (1st Cir., 1980).

Schwitzgebel, R. L., & Schwitzgebel, R. K. (1980). *Law and psychological practice*. New York: John Wiley.

Snider, P. D. (1987). Client records: Inexpensive liability protection for mental health counselors. *Journal of Mental Health Counseling, 9*(3), 134–141.

Tarasoff v. Regents of the University of California, 131 Cal. Pptr. 14, 551 P.2d 334 (1976).

Thompson, A. (1983). *Ethical concerns in psychotherapy and their legal ramifications*. New York: University of America Press.

Webster's New World Dictionary. (1979). New York: William Collins.

Wright, R. H. (1981). Psychologists and professional liability (malpractice) insurance: A retrospective review. *American Psychologist, 36,* 1485–1493.

Wyatt v. Stickney, 325 F. Supp. 781 (M.D. Ala. 1971), sub nom Wyatt v. Aderholt, 503 F. 2nd 1305 (5th Cir. 1974).

20

Counseling in the Twenty-first Century

BROOKE B. COLLISON, PH.D.
Oregon State University
Corvallis, Oregon

TO THINK ABOUT COUNSELING in the next century is a difficult exercise in prophesy. The next century will be upon us soon, but it is far enough away that most people can only think about it or plan for it if they devote special time and energy to the task of anticipation. People who think about the future and put their thoughts into words risk ridicule through their public errors, for it is always easier to describe what has been or is than to describe what will be. However, this chapter will put forward some thoughts about what *will be* to encourage readers to think about the world they will live in and work in as counselors. To do less is to be poorly prepared for one's work.

Forecasters have been warned by many people: Epicurus said, "No means of predicting the future really exists . . .," Einstein described his own view by saying, "I never think of the future. It comes soon enough" (Flesch, 1957). These views about the difficulty of knowing the future are easily understood, for they describe the uncertainty of an individual who contemplates what is ahead. The irony, of course, is that much that in counseling is contemplation of the future—career planning, personal decision making, and problem resolution all require a degree of speculation about one's own future.

469

To extend prediction beyond the personal to the system—whether that be for a family, an institution, a community, a state, a nation, or the world—requires the same kind of thinking that is demanded of the individual, although the thinking must be applied on a more expansive scale with much more information required as input data for the predictive decision process. Prediction of the future has taken many forms over the years, from careful scientific models to sweeping fantasies presented through novels or other media. In effect, all prediction is extrapolation from what we know to what might be.

Our current fascination with "the twenty-first century" is interesting to consider in itself. The year "2000" will see all manner of celebrations, social and political events, scientific displays, historical reviews, and future predictions. Why? What is the intrigue that surrounds the date marker, *2000*?

Part of the fascination stems from a Christian cultural heritage and the implication of "the second millennium" events that religious scholars have described. In that regard, it is interesting to speculate on the thoughts of an early Scythian monk, Dionysius Exiguus, who was most significant in setting the calendar in place that marks the year 2000. Did he understand what the world of 2000 would be like, or what kind of activity would be generated just by the occurrence of that particular numbered year?

From a broader perspective, emphasis on the twenty-first century reflects a somewhat ethnocentric cultural view, for there are several calendars in place that predate the one that Dionysius Exiguus created. The Moslem, Chinese, Hebrew, and other calendars all mark the years in some fashion; therefore, twenty-first century celebrants need to begin by realizing that they are one group among many. The future may be a place where those differences are narrowed—or at least better understood.

O'Neill (1981) has analyzed many examples of "prophecy" or prediction, both scientific forecasts and creative works of novelists and artists. His conclusion is that most prophets have overestimated how much the world would be changed by social and political change and have underestimated the forces of technologic change. In order to look at counseling in the twenty-first century, social and political as well as technologic change must be considered. One starting point can be a personal review and examination of the changes that have had an effect on your own life.

A REVIEW OF THE PAST

Select a time period that represents the last one quarter to one half of your life (e.g., if you are 30 years old, think of the period between the last seven and 15 years of your life). Prepare two lists, representing events in that recent part of your life:

- what *social or political changes* can you identify in the time period you have selected that have had some effect on you, the people you know or work with, and/or the institution you identify with most closely?
- what *technologic changes* can you identify in the time period you have selected that have had some effect on you, the people you know or work with, and/or the institution you identify with most closely?

A sample of a person's partial list might look like this:

Social / Political	*Technologic*
Specific Supreme Court decisions	Plastic money
Increase in drug traffic	Cellular phones and call-forwarding
AIDS	Personal computers
Increase of Asian population	High-tech industries
.	.
.	.
.	.
etc.	etc.

Once you have developed your lists, think about these three questions:

1. at the start of the time period you selected, how well could you have predicted what the events would have been?
2. how have the events on your list affected you? and
3. in an equal time period in the future, what do you think will be on your list and what will be the effect on you?

PREDICTING FOR COUNSELING

In preparation for predicting the future for counseling, the reader should first examine how events and phenomena in several categories have an effect on current counseling practice. Extrapolating to the future in each category then enables the reader to describe implications for counseling. The information categories are as follows:

1. Population characteristics and changes that can be projected by demographers.
2. Cultural characteristics and values that would have an impact on the counselor and the persons the counselor would serve.
3. Social and political conditions that have an impact on the persons counselors serve as well as on the counselor.
4. Technologic advances that will continue to have a specific impact on counseling procedures.
5. Professional issues—both knowledge and skill issues as well as professional organization issues—that influence how and where counselors will work.

At this point, the reader is asked to pause and reflect on the list above: What does the reader know about the five categories based on personal knowledge? What would the future bring for each of the five categories in terms of changes that may occur and the impact that those changes would have on counseling in the next century?

POPULATION CHARACTERISTICS

Population characteristics are important, for they describe the client groups with whom we work and will work in the future. Some changes are obvious to even a casual observer; other changes are subtle but significant and are known only to the statistician who studies world population figures. Local, state, national, and global population trends are important to examine, for one certainty that the world faces is an increasing global interdependence (Naisbitt, 1982). An event in another country does and will have an effect on even the smallest communities around the world: witness the immigration changes that followed the Vietnam conflict or the number of Spanish-speaking persons in various communities who come from Mexico or Central America as a result of economic hardship or political adversity.

Demographers and futurists have identified the following trends, which will alter the look of the United States in the future:

- by 2010, the U.S. population will have increased by nearly 30 million.
- the world population, which reached 5 billion in the later

1980s, will reach 6 billion before the year 2000. The U.S. population will represent about 8 percent of that total.

- the labor force in 2000 will have more minority and female workers and fewer young workers than it has today.
- Black and Asian populations will represent larger proportions of the U.S. population.
- persons with less than a high school education will have more difficulty finding a job with good pay and chances for advancement.
- the service sector will be the fastest growing occupation, (estimated at 88 percent in 2000 from 72 percent in 1984), with eating places representing half the growth in retail trade occupations.
- there will be an older work force than in the 1980s.
- three fifths of all women over age 16 will be at work in the year 2000.
- occupational mobility will increase.
- the labor force will be much more specialized.
- retirement age will be raised as life expectancy (and work life expectancy) increases.

[The list above was extracted from Abramson (1987), Bureau of the Census (1989), Cetron, Rocha, & Luckins (1988), Hoffman (1989), Johnston (1987), and Kutscher (1988).]

CULTURAL ISSUES

Much of what we believe, value, do, say, and expect of ourselves and others is culturally determined. In a world in which cultural diversity is valued and in which cultural isolation is less possible as improved transportation and communication methods increase the probability of cultural interaction, it is incumbent on counselors to increase their cultural awareness. Counselors must know cultural values, as they have significant bearing on what is appropriate in cross-cultural counseling (Atkinson, Morten, & Sue, 1979; Sue, 1978).

Many of the issues that are related to individual or family stress—and subsequently become counseling matters—are culturally related. Attitudes toward human sexuality and sexual behavior is an example of a culturally embedded value system counselors deal with frequently. In recent years, the increase in the number of single parents or the tendency for couples to delay pregnancy in deference to careers are both illustrations of events that will have effects far into the next century. Single parenting will result in increased numbers of twenty-first century adults who will have less of a traditional family history to relate to during their own adulthood. Delayed pregnancies—a tendency among the young, upwardly mobile adults of the 1980s—will result in a phenomenon in the next century that will have older parents moving into their declining years more dependent on younger children to care for them. An equal concern will be children moving through adolescence and young adulthood with older parents who may have different relationships with them than many of their peers. Cultural expectations surround both situations—single parenting and older adult pregnancy. Counselors who will respond to these situations need proper education and preparation in advance of the time they will encounter the situations in their practice.

Either situation can be viewed as merely a change in population demographics—the changing numbers of births that will occur among different age and income groups. The issue may or may not be a concern brought to counselors as client populations change; however, cultural values will determine how persons view their own experience and the experience of others in such situations.

Another example could be cited from the work of Gallup and Proctor (1984), who point out that future society is expected to be more impersonal and regimented. Individuals are expected to become more self-reliant while improving their grasp of global issues. Gallup and Proctor state that people planning for the year 2000 should concentrate on gaining more vocational skills and should assume more personal responsibility. Both of these trends have implications for counselors—in both developmental work and approach to counseling process.

What kind of list could you make to describe some of the cultural issues that might have an impact of counseling in the next century?

SOCIAL AND POLITICAL CONDITIONS

We live in a politically interdependent world. When a U.S. purchaser buys a product manufactured in Japan from raw materials imported from South America, the impact may be felt in several continents and communities. The political response may be for one country to restrict imports from another so as to gain or maintain some economic advantage. The social effect may be to create buying power for one person and take employment from another. U.S. manufacturing processes create acid rain, which alters Canada's environment. Nutritional patterns and economic factors contribute to a continued depletion of the

South American rain forest, which is cut or burned to provide less efficient but higher demand consumer products. In turn, rain forest depletion will have a long-term effect on local economies, as well as on national and global environmental conditions. The solutions require concerted political responses from more than one nation.

Counselors in the next century, as now, will work with clients whose lives are affected by political decisions made in different parts of the world. Counselors may feel powerless to control the events that occur in a global social or political system, but they will see the effect.

The social issues of the last half of the twentieth century—poverty, racism, sexism, changing family structures, the new morality, new sexual norms, affluence vs. poverty, gangs, nuclear threat—all remain during the last part of the twentieth century and will most likely prevail during the twenty-first. The effect of those issues and conditions on people creates needs counselors must respond to on the personal, community, and national levels. For example, children in poverty often experience lowered self-esteem, they frequently lack access to adequate education systems, they have poorer chances for employment, and they experience strained family relations. Using only these four effects of poverty, what could counselors do in response?

Condition/Issue	Effect	Response
1.0 Poverty	1.1 Lowered self-esteem	1.1.1 Group and individual counseling
	1.2 Inadequate education systems	1.2.1 Enhance classroom instruction
	1.3 Under- and unemployment	1.3.1 Employment training and development of opportunities
	1.4 Strained family relations	1.4.1 Provide family education, intervention, and counseling
2.0 Racism	(What effects can you list?)	(What counselor responses can you list? Which responses would be individual and which ones would be institutional, or global?)

What other social and political conditions can you list that will have an impact on counselors and the persons they will work with in the next century? What could you list as possible counselor responses that could assist persons affected by the conditions you have listed? Would it be possible for you to develop preventive responses as well as therapeutic responses to effects that people already experience?

As you think about the next century, what do you believe will be the emerging social and political conditions that will have an effect on persons and will require a response from counselors? What new strategies and techniques will counselors need to be most effective?

TECHNOLOGIC ADVANCES

Technology has had an impact on all persons throughout the years. The last half of the twentieth century has seen numerous advances that have had a particular impact on counselors and the people with whom they work. Naisbitt (1982) has described how our world has moved from an agrarian to an industrial economy and then to an information age. That change has been influenced by technologic advance.

Counselors have seen technology change the way they now work with clients. Computer technology has enabled counselors to maintain records easily; send communications quickly and with a minimum of effort; manipulate data about individuals and groups of clients; analyze data in research studies; provide immediate results on interest, personality, and other individual assessments; and many other applications.

In the future, the kinds of technologic advances that have been experienced will most likely accelerate. The immediate effect will be to make records and information-processing easier as computers become smaller, faster, more economical, and more common for all persons. The future fantasies of personal record-keeping and medical treatment envisioned on *Star Trek* or other science fiction movies are entirely probable. As a result, counselors will be able to work with much more information available to them and their clients than ever before. Time now spent in data manipulation will be reduced, resulting in increased time for person-to-person contact.

As you consider the technologic advances known to you, what additional examples can you list? What can you envision for the future? What kind of personal and ethical dilemmas would be produced for counselors as a result of the technologic advances you identify?

PROFESSIONAL ISSUES

Counseling is a profession. That means that there is a specific body of knowledge one must acquire in order to be a professional counselor. In addition, a code of ethics exists that guides appropriate behavior for counseling professionals and outlines the consequences of unethical behavior. A professional association exists to which counselors belong. And there are licensing and certification standards that cover the scope of practice of professional counselors.

The growth of the profession of counseling has been steady but not always smooth. The future of the profession looks bright—and with potential controversy attached to the changes that will take place between the present and the start of the next century. How those professional controversies will be resolved in the next century is difficult to describe.

Recent professional issues are likely to remain active into and through the next decade. They can be described as issues surrounding
- professional identity,
- professional knowledge and practice,
- licensing and certification,
- legal implications of practice activities,
- access to counseling, and
- the nature of professional counselor associations.

PROFESSIONAL IDENTITY Who is a counselor? And what do counselors do? The identity of professional counselors has been clouded by the number of separate groups that have taken on the word "counselor" as part of their own identity. How many occupational titles can you list that use the word "counselor" as part of their designation?

- Mental health counselor
- School counselor
- Rehabilitation counselor
- Financial counselor
- Retirement counselor

etc.

A second test to apply to your identity list would be to mark those occupational titles that have emerged in the past 10 years. A more futuristic exercise would be to extend your list to include the occupational titles that include the word "counselor" that you would expect to find at the start of the next century. The term "mental health counselor" has been used for several years, but those professionals created a professional association to serve their needs only in 1978. If you included "AIDS Counselor" on your list of occupational titles, it certainly is one that has been added in recent years. Both professional movements and specific human conditions may work to create new occupational titles that include the word "counselor."

PROFESSIONAL KNOWLEDGE AND PRACTICE Although practitioners and theoreticians alike have studied and written about counseling over the
decades, it remains much as it began—a "talking" therapy that takes
place between a counselor and a client. There has been an increase over
the years in the number of situations in which a counselor works with a
small group of persons at one time—such as in family or marriage counseling—and in the increase of material written about that counseling
modality; however, the pervasive principles of the counselor's work have
changed very little since the late 1940s and early 1950s.

The greatest change in professional knowledge and practice observed in recent years, and expected to change in the future, would be
with respect to the use of technologic applications to counseling practice. Computer use should eliminate time delays between the need for
and availability of information; personal data should be accurate and
thorough and collected economically, with redundant information collection eliminated; the ease of tracking persons across time should enable
better outcome studies to be done by counseling researchers which, in
turn, would provide answers to questions about relative effectiveness of
counseling methods.

The challenge to counseling theorists is to develop counseling models that will reflect advances in practice commensurate with the advances in technologic application. A second challenge is to develop the
needed ethical principles that will be demanded by such a highly technical system. What else could you envision in a next-century counseling
system that would combine technologic advance with professional practice improvement?

LICENSING AND CERTIFICATION The decade of the 1980s marked many
changes in licensing laws that govern counselors in the various states.
The decade could be described as a licensing decade, in which about two
thirds of the states passed counselor licensing legislation. Accompanying
that thrust in licensing was an equal emphasis on refined certification
methods, for it is obvious that it is easier to license a person who is certified to be something than it is to license a person who merely says that
they are that same thing.

Standards can be applied to professional counselor preparation
programs through an accreditation process. Graduates of accredited
programs are usually in an advantageous position to be certified or licensed in the various states or categories of practice. A discussion of accreditation, including a list of several accrediting bodies, can be found
in Hollis and Wantz (1986), a counselor-preparation directory produced
periodically that lists much valuable information for persons interested
in counselor-preparation programs. An extended discussion of certification and accreditation can be found in Wittmer and Loesch (1986).

The effect of licensing, a function controlled by the states, has been to add an additional dimension of credibility to professional counselor identity. That credibility has enabled clients in many states to have access to counselors that had previously been denied. In addition, agencies that fund counseling services are more likely to extend funds for services to licensed persons. The economic impact, both on counselors and on clients, has been significant.

The professional implication of licensing has also had its impact on the identity of counselors. As licensing has refined the parameters of professional practice, it has also differentiated among counseling groups—mental health counselors, rehabilitation counselors, and the like. Defining boundaries and differentiating can lead to conflict among groups if the newly sharpened definitions either include or exclude responsibilities thought to be the province of another group.

LEGAL IMPLICATIONS OF COUNSELING PRACTICE. Counselors have witnessed an increase in the amount of legal activity in their profession in the last half of the twentieth century. Legislation in the 1960s (Family Rights and Privacy Act) increased the number of procedures counselors had to be concerned with to protect the rights of clients through proper collection, maintenance, and dissemination of records. A concurrent increased emphasis on consumer rights brought attention to the counselor's duty to warn clients about treatment procedures, limits of confidentiality, and client rights. As a result, the classic Tarasoff case (Tarasoff v. Regents of the University of California et al., 1976) has probably been discussed in every counselor education program since it was first published.

Counselors have moved from an early posture where few who practiced their profession did so under the coverage of professional liability insurance to a position in the late 1980s where professional liability insurance coverage has become common. In addition, professional liability insurance frequently includes free or inexpensive access to attorneys who are "on call" to answer questions raised by any insured (B. Bertram, personal communication, August, 1989). Through the 1980s, the most common reason for a counselor to be sued for malpractice continued to be "undue familiarity"—some kind of sexually inappropriate behavior on the counselor's part.

Counselor education institutions also have felt the increased pressure of potential lawsuits, which are commonplace in a litigious society. Many counselor education programs require students to have their own professional liability coverage before they can enroll in counseling practice or internships (L. Eacho, personal communication, August 1989).

As the century comes to a close and the new century begins, it is difficult to define the legal issues that will emerge to be as compelling as the ones that have characterized the 1970s and 1980s. Certainly the trends that have been established are likely to continue to increase in number and intensity. There will likely be additional emphasis on issues such as privacy and personal rights (motivated by issues surrounding AIDS counseling and testing), delivery of services to minors (motivated by court decisions concerning parental right to know about access to sexuality counseling and birth control), and counselor accountability (motivated by suits directed against counselors by persons who believe that counselor statements have restricted their access to job or school placements). Other issues are as likely to dominate the counselor–legal scene in the next several years. What would you identify on the legal horizon for counselors?

A second major area of legal emphasis is in the realm of action taken by counselors to redress grievances they have experienced either as individuals or as members of a professional group. For example, members of the American Mental Health Counselors Association (AMHCA) have suggested that legal action should be initiated on behalf of counselors against associations and other groups who have, by their corporate actions, inhibited client access to counselors, worked against counselor licensure, reduced the probability of counselors receiving third- party reimbursement, or in other ways restrained ability to practice.

ACCESS TO COUNSELING   A critical question for counselors and clients alike is, "Who has access to counseling?" A corollary question is, "Who is denied (or restricted) access to counseling?" At the root of the question is the issue of how counseling services are funded. In general, services are supported by personal payment; by public or private agency funding—either through tax base monies or grant support; by third-party payments—insurance programs or the like; or by voluntary contribution of the counselor's time.

If a counselor is not eligible to receive either public or private agency payment for services or for reimbursement by third-party payers, then the client who might be served through those routes is denied access to counseling unless they are willing to pay for services themselves—or unless the counselor is willing to contribute services at reduced or no cost. The decision, made by the agencies and third-party payers, is most critical in limiting or enabling access.

In the 1980s several decisions by large funding groups enabled increased numbers of counselors to receive payment for counseling services. Governmental service insurers, such as the Civilian Health and Medical Program for the Uniformed Services (CHAMPUS), changed their regulations to include mental health counselors as approved providers of mental health services. This action increased access to counseling for thousands of military personnel. Similar decisions have been made or are pending for other large groups of federal and corporate employees. The implication for counselors will be profound.

An additional mechanism observed in the late 1980s was the formation of preferred provider organizations (PPOs) and health maintenance organizations (HMOs) that included provision of mental health services. Counselors were included in some of those organizations and excluded from others. The potential client who wished to see a mental health counselor, but whose PPO or HMO did not include counselors as providers, was denied access to services.

Economics drives many of the decisions described above. Insurers and agencies wish to provide as much service as they can for the lowest dollar expenditure possible. Providers, such as psychologists or counselors, have a right to be compensated for their services and wish to have as broad a potential client group available to them as possible. The interaction of economic and professional definition issues may result in limited access by potential clients and restrained practice on the part of counselors or other professionals.

As we move into the next century, the forces described above are likely to escalate in intensity. Each professional group will want its share of the mental health market, insurers and other health care organizations will want to keep their costs as low as possible, potential clients will want as broad a range of services available to them as they can have, and the government will continue to struggle with decisions about the degree to which they provide coverage without excessive regulation for the gaps that exist.

PROFESSIONAL COUNSELOR ASSOCIATIONS One characteristic of a profession is that there is an association of professionals who gather together for a variety of common purposes—both those that serve the professional members and those that serve the goals of the clients served by those professional members. A variety of professional associations is available for counselors. The nature of those associations has been changing through the decades of the 1970s and 1980s. They are likely to continue to change through the rest of this century and into the next.

Four major associations are designed for counselors and others in the mental health professions: the American Association for Counseling and Development (AACD), the American Psychological Association (APA), the American Association for Marriage and Family Therapy (AAMFT), and the National Association of Clinical Social Work (NACSW).

AACD was formed in 1952, as a loose confederation of four existing organizations that had counseling and guidance as a common element. Over the next 35 years, AACD grew to include 16 different identified groups of professionals interested in counseling and development. If the history of the first 35 years is indicative of the next several years, the AACD will no doubt continue to grow in membership numbers—in part because it will take in additional groups of professionals who seek enhancement of their defined identity and wish to have a place for their particular interests to be promoted.

The historical growth of AACD can be reflected in the year that each of the groups gained status with the association through divisional membership. That chronology is presented in Table 20-1 in order to trace the historical growth and to make projections on future possibilities.

Table 20-1   Growth of the AACD.

Year	Division Name	1990 Membership
1953	American College Personnel Association (ACPA)	7,676
1953	Association for Counselor Education and Supervision (ACES)	2,987
1953	National Career Development Association (NCDA)	5,756
1952	Association for Humanistic Education and Development (AHEAD)	2,784
1953	American School Counselor Association (ASCA)	12,628
1958	American Rehabilitation Counseling Association (ARCA)	2,673
1965	Association for Measurement and Evaluation in Counseling and Development (AMECD)	1,650
1966	National Employment Counselors Association (NECA)	1,685
1972	Association for Multicultural Counseling and Development (AMCD)	2,938
1974	Association for Religious and Value Issues in Counseling (ARVIC)	4,037
1974	Association for Specialists in Group Work (ASGW)	5,444
1974	International Association for Addictions and Offender Counselors, (IAAOC), (an organizational affiliate)	931
1978	American Mental Health Counselors Association (AMHCA)	11,973
1984	Military Educators and Counselors Association (MECA) (an organizational affiliate)	634
1986	Association for Adult Development and Aging (AADA)	1,981
1989	International Association of Marriage and Family Counselors (IAMFC)	3,537

If future patterns emulate previous events, AACD, and other counseling associations, will continue to reflect expansion of the field of counseling and human development. The expansion will represent increases in the number of persons who work in the counseling field and it will also represent more specific emphasis on specialization within the profession (Cetron, Rocha, & Luckins, 1988). From the original four groups that represented most of the people working in the counseling field, the change is obvious. In the same way that Naisbitt (1982) has described the emerging world as one in which there are many options and specialties available to consumers, the future for counseling may also be one of a plethora of specialties and options available. The challenge for professional associations in a world of multiple options among the professions under one general rubric—counseling—will be to develop activities and services that are equally attractive to professionals regardless of their specialty designation.

Can you think of the world of the future and identify some of the counseling specialties that might exist that do not exist now?

- Telecommunications counseling specialist
- Intercultural mediator
-
-
- etc.

FUTURE SCENARIO—PROBABLE AND POSSIBLE

Futurists and prophets always struggle to decide whether to describe the world they believe will come about or to describe the world they would like to see come about. The next several paragraphs will mix the two to discuss both the probable future and the possible future. Time will be required to determine whether either description approximates accuracy.

It will be necessary for the counselor of the future to be multiculturally aware. The increase in cultural diversity that the future will present as a result of increased personal mobility—both nationally and internationally—will force counselors to be ready to work with much more heterogeneous groups than ever before. The question of who is responsible for multicultural awareness, education, and change cannot be left for a single group to own—it must be universally owned by persons in the counseling profession. In addition, the increase in multicultural diversity, age and family diversity, and economic diversity must be examples of how diversity enriches. Counselors must be in the forefront of human activities designed to develop appreciation for the diversities all people will experience.

Counselors of the future must be technologically sophisticated. Their use of computers and other electronic equipment must be examples of the best applications of those technologies to enhance human potential. In addition, the unimagined technologies that will be present in the next century must be tools that will increase the kind of personal interaction that will remain the special domain of human counselors. Rather than struggle against the increase of technologic advance, counselors must encourage new applications and, in doing so, ensure that those new applications are made with ethical and humane criteria at their core.

Some of the negative social conditions counselors face through the clients they work with will no doubt persist into the next century. Conditions such as racism, sexism, and ageism have been in place for years and years; their effects are not eliminated in a brief span of time. Economic disadvantage is an insidious agent; it will be present in future generations. Counselors of the future must be ready to make decisions about their own professional priorities—if there are limits on the amount of time they have to spend, will they commit significant proportions of their time to socially relevant activities (frequently poorly compensated) or will they yield to the seductive persuasion of income and serve only those who can afford to pay? Mental health and counseling services must be available to all segments of the population. In the next century, support systems must be in place that equalize opportunity and access to counseling for all.

The counselor in the next century will have immediate access to a full range of information about any client and to the situations in which the client lives, works, and interacts. Those technologic advances will enable clients to make fully informed decisions about careers because they will have thorough information matrices instantaneously available at any time. Job banks will be complete and available on any geographic scale desired, making international work opportunities truly functional. The result will be to equalize opportunity in ways unknown at present. The same electronic communication systems will enable counselors and clients to maintain contact across distances as counseling methods are adapted to new technologies. The prospect of full-size holographic imaging might enable counselors and clients to interact across distances and still be able to respond to subtle nonverbal cues and body movement as well as changes in voice inflection. Imagine the changes required in counseling techniques, counseling ethics, and counseling practice demanded by such a highly developed system.

The counselor in the next century must be ready to adapt to new situations and conditions that will emerge among client groups as a result of social, economic, or political change. Equally a concern will be the conditions counselors can respond to resulting from technologic changes that have occupational impact for persons. Key for the counselors will be the kind of environmental scanning that will permit anticipation of changes and trends and the ability to develop appropriate responses.

The kinds of changes described by futurists already referred to in this chapter will demand quick adaptation of counseling methodology, delivery of intense but short-term assistance, and a focus on specific needs associated with sharply differentiated conditions. In addition, the counselor of the future will need to be a more visible, stable referent in a world that will be characterized by speed of change.

The speed of change envisioned for the next century will also demand new forms of professional development available for experienced counselors. New technologies will need to be applied to in-service and reeducation processes in order for counselors trained in the current century to be fully effective in the next.

The next century will be an exciting place for counselors to work if they are ready to create and adapt.

REFERENCES

Abramson, E. (1987). Projections 2000. *Occupational Outlook Quarterly, 31*(3), 2–36.

Atkinson, D. W., Morten, G., & Sue, D. W. (1979). *Counseling American minorities.* Dubuque, IA: Wm. C. Brown.

Bureau of the Census. (1989). *Statistical abstract of the United States* (109th ed.). Washington, DC: Bureau of the Census.

Cetron, M. J., Rocha, W., & Luckins, R. (1988). Into the 21st century: Long-term trends affecting the United States. *The Futurist, 22*(4), 29–39.

Flesch, R. (Ed.). (1957). *The book of unusual quotations.* New York: Harper & Row.

Gallup, G., Jr., & Proctor, W. (1984). Forecast 2000. *Omni, 6*(10), 84–89.

Hoffman, M. S. (Ed.). (1989). *The world almanac and book of facts.* New York: Pharos Books.

Hollis, J. W., & Wantz, R. A. (1986). *Counselor preparation 1986–1989: Programs, personnel, trends* (6th ed.). Muncie, IN: Accelerated Development, Inc.

Johnston, W. B. (1987). *Workforce 2000: Work and workers for the 21st century.* Indianapolis, IN: Hudson Institute.

Kutscher, R. E. (1988). An overview of the year 2000. *Occupational Outlook Quarterly, 32*(1), 2–9.

Naisbitt, J. (1982). *Megatrends: Ten new directions transforming our lives.* New York: Warner.

O'Neill, G. K. (1981). *2081: A hopeful view of the human future.* New York: Simon and Schuster.

Sue, D. (1978). Eliminating cultural oppression in counseling: Toward a general theory. *The Counseling Psychologist, 25,* 419–428.

Tarasoff v. Regents of the University of California et al., 17 Cal.3d 425,551 P.2d 334 (1976).

Wittmer, J. P., & Loesch, L. C. (1986). Professional orientation. In M. Lewis, R. Hayes, & J. Lewis (Eds.), *An introduction to the counseling profession* (pp. 301–330). Itasca, IL: Peacock.

Index